THE

LITURGICAL YEAR.

BY THE

VERY REV. DOM PROSPER GUÉRANGER,

ABBOT OF SOLESMES.

Translated from the French,
BY THE
REV. DOM LAURENCE SHEPHERD,
MONK OF THE ENGLISH-BENEDICTINE CONGREGATION.

PASSIONTIDE

AND

HOLY WEEK.

PASSIONTIDE

AND

HOLY WEEK.

PREFACE.

This Volume completes our explanation of the Lenten Liturgy; but it has its own special character, because of the subject it treats of. The Church devotes the last two weeks of Lent to the Sufferings and Death of Jesus: the Passion, therefore, is the great subject of this portion of our *Liturgical Year*.

Though the Volume be so bulky, yet we are far from having exhausted our subject. We have been obliged to limit ourselves to a *choice* from the riches offered to us in the magnificent Offices of these fourteen days; and such a choice was no easy matter, when it had to be made from such abundant Mysteries, teeming with sublime and pathetic teachings. We are far from flattering ourselves that we have said all that can be said of Holy Week. We have

PREFACE.

but given a short compendium of its wonderful beauties; and we shall have gained the object we proposed to ourselves, if these pages assist the Faithful to relish the Divine Mystery of the Passion, and to follow the Church in her celebration of it.

We have not inserted in this Volume the Saints' Feasts, which may be kept during Passion Week. The number of such Feasts is very great, owing to the variation of Easter-Tide; and their insertion would have made our Volume inconveniently large. Our readers, therefore, must refer to our "Lent" for the Feasts of that Week.

CONTENTS.

	PAGE
PREFACE,	iii

PASSIONTIDE AND HOLY WEEK.

CHAPTER I.—The History of Passiontide and Holy Week, ... 1
CHAP. II.—The Mystery of Passiontide and Holy Week, ... 11
CHAP. III.—Practice during Passiontide and Holy Week, ... 15
CHAP. IV.—Morning and Night Prayers for Passiontide and Holy Week, . . . 25
CHAP. V.—On hearing Mass, during Passiontide and Holy Week, ... 38
CHAP. VI.—On Holy Communion, during Passiontide and Holy Week, . . . 73
CHAP. VII.—Of the Office of Vespers for Sundays and Feasts, during Passiontide and Holy Week, ... 80
CHAP. VIII.—On the Office of Compline, during Passiontide and Holy Week, . . 91

PROPER OF THE TIME.

PASSION SUNDAY, ... 103
    Mass, ... 107
    Vespers, ... 118
Monday in Passion Week, ... 121
Tuesday, ... 132

CONTENTS.

	PAGE
Wednesday,	141
Thursday,	150
Friday in Passion Week.—The Seven Dolours of the Blessed Virgin.—.	161
Saturday,	182
PALM SUNDAY,	194
The Blessing of the Palms,	203
The Procession,	214
Mass,	219
Vespers,	238
Monday in Holy Week,	244
Tuesday in Holy Week,	258
Wednesday in Holy Week,	277
Office of Tenebræ,	300
MAUNDY THURSDAY,	304
The Night Office,	ibid.
The Morning,	352
The Reconciliation of Penitents,	354
The Blessing of the Holy Oils,	360
The Mass,	368
Vespers,	386
The Stripping of the Altars,	392
The Washing of the Feet,	396
The Office of Tenebræ,	402
The Evening,	ibid.
GOOD FRIDAY,	414
The Night Office,	ibid.
The Morning,	450
The Morning Service,	464
The Lessons,	465
The Prayers,	479
The Veneration of the Cross,	485
The "Improperia" or "Reproaches,"	490

CONTENTS.

	PAGE
Mass of the Presanctified,	495
Vespers,	500
Afternoon,	501
The Office of Tenebræ,	510
The Evening,	ibid.

HOLY SATURDAY,	519
The Night Office,	ibid.
The Morning,	546
The Morning Service,	550
The blessing of the new Fire and Incense,	552
The Paschal Candle,	560
The Prophecies,	566
The blessing of the Font,	603
Baptism,	614
Confirmation,	616
The Litany,	619
Mass,	622
Vespers,	630
The Evening,	632

PASSIONTIDE

AND

HOLY WEEK.

CHAPTER THE FIRST.

THE ̄ ̄TORY OF PASSIONTIDE AND HOLY WEEK.

AFTER having proposed the forty-days' Fast of Jesus in the Desert to the meditation of the Faithful, during the first four weeks of Lent, the Holy Church gives the two weeks, which still remain before Easter, to the commemoration of the Passion. She would not have her children come to the great Day of the immolation of the Lamb, without their having prepared for it by compassionating with him in the Sufferings he endured in their stead.

The most ancient Sacramentaries and Antiphonaries of the several Churches attest, by the Prayers, the Lessons, and the whole Liturgy of these two weeks, that the Passion of our Lord is now the one sole thought of the Christian world. During Passion Week, a Saint's Feast, if it occur, will be kept; but Passion Sunday admits no Feast, however solemn it may be; and even on those which are kept during the days intervening between Passion and Palm Sundays, there is always made a commemoration of the Passion, and the holy Images are not allowed to be uncovered.

We cannot give any historical details upon the

first of these two Weeks; its ceremonies and rites have always been the same as those of the four preceding ones.[1] We, therefore, refer the reader to the following Chapter, in which we treat of the mysteries peculiar to Passiontide. The second week, on the contrary, furnishes us with abundant historical details; for there is no portion of the Liturgical Year, which has interested the Christian world so much as this, or which has given rise to such fervent manifestations of piety.

This week was held in great veneration even as early as the 3rd century, as we learn from St. Denis, Bishop of Alexandria, who lived at that time.[2] In the following century, we find St. John Chrysostom calling it the *Great Week*:[3] "not," says the holy Doctor, " that it has more days in it than other weeks, " or that its days are made up of more hours than " other days; but we call it *Great*, because of the " great Mysteries which are then celebrated." We find it called also by other names: the *Painful Week (Hebdomada Pœnosa),* on account of the Sufferings of our Lord Jesus Christ, and of the fatigue required from us in celebrating them; the *Week of Indulgence,* because sinners are then received to penance; and, lastly, *Holy Week,* in allusion to the holiness of the Mysteries which are commemorated during these seven days. This last name is the one, under which it most generally goes with us; and the very days themselves are, in many countries, called by the same name, *Holy Monday, Holy Tuesday, Good Friday, Holy Saturday.*

The severity of the Lenten Fast is increased during these its last days; the whole energy of the spirit of penance is now brought out. Even with us, the

---

[1] It would be out of place to enter here on a discussion with regard to the name *Mediana*, under which title we find Passion Sunday mentioned both in ancient Liturgies and in Canon Law.
[2] *Epist. ad Basilidem.* Canon I.   [3] *Hom.* xxx. *in Genes.*

dispensation which allows the use of eggs ceases towards the middle of this Week. The Eastern Churches have kept up far more of the ancient traditions; and their observance of abstinence, during these days, is far more severe than ours. The Greeks call this week *Xérophagia*, that is, the week when no other food is allowed but that which is dry, such as bread, water, salt, dried fruits, raw vegetables: every kind of seasoning is forbidden. In the early ages, Fasting, during Holy Week, was carried to the utmost limits that human nature could endure. We learn from St. Epiphanius,[1] that there were some of the Christians who observed a strict fast from Monday morning to cock-crow of Easter Sunday. Of course, it must have been very few of the Faithful who could go so far as this. Many passed two, three, and even four consecutive days, without tasting any food; but the general practice was to fast from Maundy Thursday evening to Easter morning. Many Christians in the East, and in Russia, observe this fast, even in these times:—would that such severe penance were always accompanied by a firm faith and union with the Church, out of which, the merit of such penitential works is of no avail for salvation!

Another of the ancient practices of Holy Week were the long hours spent, during the night, in the Churches. On Maundy Thursday, after having celebrated the divine mysteries in remembrance of the Last Supper, the faithful continued a long time in prayer.[2] The night between Friday and Saturday was spent in one uninterrupted vigil, in honour of our Lord's Burial.[3] But the longest of all these vigils was that of Saturday, which was kept up till Easter Sunday morning: it was one in which the whole of the people

---

[1] *Expositio fidei*. ix. *Hæres*. xxii.
[2] St. John Chrysostom, *Hom.* xxx. *in Genes*.
[3] St. Cyril of Jerusalem, *Catech.* xviii.

joined: they assisted at the final preparation of the Catechumens, as also at the administration of Baptism, nor did they leave the Church until after the celebration of the Holy Sacrifice, which was not over till sunrise.[1]

Cessation from servile work was, for a long time, an obligation during Holy Week. The civil law united with that of the Church in order to bring about this solemn rest from toil and business, which so eloquently expresses the state of mourning of the christian world. The thought of the sufferings and death of Jesus was the one pervading thought: the divine Offices and Prayer were the sole occupation of the people: and, indeed, all the strength of the body was needed for the support of the austerities of fasting and abstinence. We can readily understand what an impression was made upon men's minds, during the whole of the rest of the year, by this universal suspension of the ordinary routine of life. Moreover, when we call to mind how, for five full weeks, the severity of Lent had waged war on the sensual appetites, we can imagine the simple and honest joy, wherewith was welcomed the feast of Easter, which brought both the regeneration of the soul, and respite to the body.

In the preceding volume, we mentioned the laws of the Theodosian Code, which forbade all law business during the forty days preceding Easter. This law of Gratian and Theodosius, which was published in 380, was extended by Theodosius, in 389; this new decree forbade all pleadings during the seven days before, and the seven days after, Easter. We meet with several allusions to this then recent law, in the Homilies of St. John Chrysostom, and in the Sermons of St. Augustine. In virtue of this decree, each of these fifteen days was considered, as far as the courts of law were concerned, as a Sunday.

[1] Const. Apost. *lib.* i. *cap.* xviii.

But christian Princes were not satisfied with the mere suspension of human justice during these days, which are so emphatically days of mercy; they would, moreover, pay homage, by an external act, to the fatherly goodness of God, who has deigned to pardon a guilty world, through the merits of the death of his Son. The Church was on the point of giving *Reconciliation* to repentant sinners, who had broken the chains of sin, whereby they were held captives: christian Princes were ambitious to imitate this their Mother, and they ordered that prisoners should be loosened from their chains, that the prisons should be thrown open, and that freedom should be restored to those who had fallen under the sentence of human tribunals. The only exception made was that of criminals, whose freedom would have exposed their families or society to great danger. The name of Theodosius stands prominent in these acts of mercy. We are told by St. John Chrysostom,[1] that this Emperor sent letters of pardon to the several cities, ordering the release of prisoners, and granting life to those that had been condemned to death, and all this in order to sanctify the days preceding the Easter Feast. The last Emperors made a law of this custom, as we find in one of St. Leo's Sermons, where he thus speaks of their clemency: "The Roman Emperors "have long observed this holy practice. In honour of "our Lord's Passion and Resurrection, they humbly "withold the exercise of their sovereign justice, and, "laying aside the severity of their laws, they grant "pardon to a great number of criminals. Their in- "tention in this is to imitate the divine goodness by "their own exercise of clemency during these days, "when the world owes its salvation to the divine "mercy. Let, then, the christian people imitate their

---

[1] *Homil. in magn. Hebdom. Homil.* xxx. *in Genes. Homil.* vi. *ad popul. Antioch.*

"Princes, and let the example of kings induce subjects
"to forgive each other their private wrongs, for, surely,
"it is absurd that private laws should be less un-
"relenting than those which are public. Let tres-
"passes be forgiven, let bonds be taken off, let
"offences be forgotten, let revenge be stifled; that
"thus the sacred Feast may, by both divine and human
"favours, find us all happy and innocent."[1]

This christian amnesty was not confined to the Theodosian Code; we find traces of it in the laws of several of our western countries. We may mention France as an example. Under the first race of its kings, St. Eligius, Bishop of Noyon, in a sermon for Maundy Thursday, thus expresses himself: "On "this day, when the Church grants indulgence to "Penitents and absolution to sinners,—Magistrates, "also, relent in their severity, and grant pardon to "the guilty. Throughout the whole world, prisons "are thrown open; Princes show clemency to crimi- "nals; Masters forgive their slaves."[2] Under the second Race, we learn, from the *Capitularia* of Charlemagne, that Bishops had a right to exact from the Judges, for the love of Jesus Christ, (as it is expressed,) that prisoners should be set free on the days preceding Easter,[3] and, should the Magistrates refuse to obey, the Bishops could refuse them admission into the Church.[4] And, lastly, under the third Race, we find Charles the 6th, after quelling the rebellion at Rouen, giving orders, later on, that the prisoners should be set at liberty, because it was *Painful* Week, and very near to the Easter Feast.[5]

A last vestige of this merciful legislation was a custom observed by the Parliament of Paris. The ancient christian practice of suspending its sessions

---

[1] *Serm.* xl. *de Quadragesima,* ii.   [2] *Serm.* x.
[3] We learn from the same *Capitularia,* that this privilege was also extended to Christmas and Pentecost.
[4] *Capitular.* lib. vi.   [5] Jean Juvénal des Ursins, year 1382.

during the whole of Lent, had long been abolished: it was not till the Wednesday of Holy Week that the House was closed, which it continued to be from that day until after Low Sunday. On the Tuesday of Holy Week, which was the last day granted for audiences, the Parliament repaired to the Palace prisons, and there, one of the Grand Presidents, generally the last installed, held a session of the House. The prisoners were questioned; but, without any formal judgment, all those whose case seemed favourable, or who were not guilty of some capital offence, were set at liberty.

The revolutions of the last eighty years have produced in every country in Europe, the *secularisation* of society, that is to say, the effacing from our national customs and legislation everything which had been introduced by the supernatural element of Christianity. The favourite theory of the last half century or more, has been that all men are equal. The people of the Ages of Faith had something far more convincing than theory, of the sacredness of their rights. At the approach of those solemn anniversaries which so forcibly remind us of the Justice and Mercy of God, they beheld Princes abdicating, as it were, their sceptre, leaving in God's hands the punishment of the guilty, and assisting at the holy Table of Paschal Communion, side by side with those very men, whom, a few days before, they had been keeping chained in prison, for the good of society. There was one thought, which, during these days, was strongly brought before all nations: it was the thought of God, in whose eyes all men are sinners, of God, from whom alone proceed justice and pardon. It was in consequence of this deep christian feeling, that we find so many diplomas and charts of the Ages of Faith speaking of the days of Holy Week as being the *Reign of Christ:* such an event, they say, happened on such a day, " Under the Reign of our Lord Jesus Christ:" *Regnante Domino nostro Jesu Christo.*

When these days of holy and christian *equality* were over, did subjects refuse submission to their Sovereigns? Did they abuse the humility of their Princes, and take occasion for drawing up what modern times call the *Rights of Man?* No: that same thought which had inspired human justice to humble itself before the Cross of Jesus, taught the people their duty of obeying the powers established by God. The exercise of power, and submission to that power, both had God for their motive. They who wielded the sceptre might be of various dynasties; the respect for authority was ever the same. Now-a-days, the Liturgy has none of her ancient influence on society; Religion has been driven from the world at large, and her only life and power is now with the consciences of individuals; and as to political institutions, they are but the expression of human pride, seeking to command, or refusing to obey.

And yet, the 4th century, which, in virtue of the christian spirit, produced the laws we have been alluding to, was still rife with the pagan element. How comes it, that we, who live in the full light of Christianity, can give the name of *Progress* to a system, which tends to separate society from everything that is supernatural? Men may talk as they please,—there is but one way to secure order, peace, morality, and security to the world; and that is God's way, the way of Faith, the living in accordance with the teachings and spirit of Faith. All other systems can, at best, but flatter those human passions, which are so strongly at variance with the mysteries of our Lord Jesus Christ, which we are now celebrating.

We must mention another law made by the Christian Emperors in reference to Holy Week. If the spirit of charity, and a desire to imitate Divine Mercy, led them to decree the liberation of prisoners; it was but acting consistently with these principles, that, during these days, when our Saviour shed his blood for the emancipation of the human race, they should interest themselves in what regards Slaves. Slavery, a consequence of sin, and the fundamental institution of the pagan world, had received its death-blow, by the preaching of the Gospel; but its gradual abolition was left to individuals, and to their practical exercise of the principle of Christian Fraternity. As our Lord and his Apostles had not exacted the immediate abolition of Slavery, so, in like manner, the Christian Emperors limited themselves to passing such laws as would give encouragement to its gradual abolition. We have an example of this in the Justinian Code, where this Prince, after having forbidden all law-proceedings during Holy Week and the week following, lays down the following exception: " It " shall, nevertheless, be permitted to give Slaves their " liberty; in such manner, that the legal acts neces- " sary for their emancipation shall not be counted " as contravening this present enactment."[1] This charitable law of Justinian was but the applying to the fifteen days of Easter the decree passed by Constantine, which forbade all legal proceedings on the Sundays throughout the year, excepting only such acts as had for their object the emancipation of Slaves.

But long before the peace given her by Constantine, the Church had made provision for Slaves, during these days when the mysteries of the world's redemption were accomplished. Christian Masters were obliged to grant them total rest from labour during this holy fortnight. Such is the law laid down in the *Apostolic Constitutions*, which were compiled

---

[1] *Cod.* lib. iii. tit. xii. de feriis. Leg. 8.

previously to the 4th century. "During the Great "Week preceding the Day of Easter, and during the "week that follows, Slaves rest from labour, inasmuch "as the first is the Week of our Lord's Passion, and "the second is that of his Resurrection, and the "Slaves require to be instructed upon these mys- "teries."[1]

Another characteristic of the two Weeks, upon which we are now entering, is that of giving more abundant alms, and of greater fervour in the exercise of works of mercy. St. John Chrysostom assures us that such was the practice of his times; he passes an encomium on the Faithful, many of whom redoubled, at this period, their charities to the poor, which they did out of this motive,—that they might, in some slight measure, imitate the Divine generosity, which is now so unreservedly pouring out his graces on sinners.

[1] *Constit. Apost.* Lib. vii. cap. xxxiii.

CHAPTER THE SECOND.

THE MYSTERY OF PASSIONTIDE AND HOLY WEEK.

THE holy Liturgy is rich in mystery, during these days of the Church's celebrating the anniversaries of so many wonderful events; but as the principal part of these mysteries is embodied in the rites and ceremonies of the respective days, we shall give our explanations according as the occasion presents itself. Our object, in the present Chapter, is to say a few words respecting the general character of the Mysteries of these two Weeks.

We have nothing to add to the explanation, already given in our "Lent," on the mystery of *Forty*. The holy season of expiation continues its course, until the fast of sinful man has imitated, in its duration, that observed by the Man-God in the desert. The army of Christ's faithful children is still fighting against the invisible enemies of man's salvation; they are still vested in their spiritual armour, and, aided by the Angels of light, they are struggling hand to hand with the spirits of darkness, by compunction of heart and by mortification of the flesh.

As we have already observed, there are three objects which principally engage the thoughts of the Church during Lent. The Passion of our Redeemer, which we have felt to be coming nearer to us each week; the preparation of the Catechumens for Baptism, which is to be administered to them on the Easter eve; the Reconciliation of the public Penitents, who are to be re-admitted into the Church, on the Thursday, the day of the Last Supper.

Each of these three objects engages more and more the attention of the Church, the nearer she approaches the time of their celebration.

The miracle performed by our Saviour, almost at the very gates of Jerusalem, and by which he restored Lazarus to life, has roused the fury of his enemies to the highest pitch of phrensy. The people's enthusiasm has been excited at seeing *him*, who had been four days in the grave, walking in the streets of their City. They ask each other, if the Messias, when he comes, can work greater wonders than these done by Jesus, and whether they ought not at once to receive this Jesus as the Messias, and sing their Hosanna to him, for he is the Son of David? They cannot contain their feelings:—Jesus enters Jerusalem, and they welcome him as their King. The High Priests and Princes of the people are alarmed at this demonstration of feeling; they have no time to lose; they are resolved to destroy Jesus. We are going to assist at their impious conspiracy: the Blood of the Just Man is to be sold, and the price put on it is thirty silver pieces. The Divine Victim, betrayed by one of his Disciples, is to be judged, condemned, and crucified. Every circumstance of this awful tragedy is to be put before us by the Liturgy, not merely in words, but with all the expressiveness of a sublime ceremonial.

The Catechumens have but a few more days to wait for the Fount that is to give them Life. Each day, their instruction becomes fuller; the figures of the Old Law are being explained to them; and very little now remains for them to learn with regard to the mysteries of salvation. The Symbol of Faith is soon to be delivered to them. Initiated into the glories and the humiliations of the Redeemer, they will await, with the Faithful, the moment of his glorious Resurrection; and we shall accompany them, with our prayers and hymns, at that solemn hour, when, leaving the defilements of sin in the life-giving waters of the Font, they shall come forth pure and radiant with innocence, be enriched with the gifts of the Holy Spirit, and be fed with the divine Flesh of the Lamb that liveth for ever.

The Reconciliation of the Penitents, too, is close at hand. Clothed in sackcloth and ashes, they are continuing their work of expiation. The Church has still several passages from the Sacred Scriptures to read to them, which, like those we have already heard during the last few weeks, will breathe consolation and refreshment to their souls. The near approach of the day, when the Lamb is to be slain, increases their hope, for they know that the Blood of this Lamb is of infinite worth, and can take away the sins of the whole world. Before the day of Jesus' Resurrection, they will have recovered their lost innocence; their pardon will come in time to enable them, like the penitent Prodigal, to join in the great Banquet of that Thursday, when Jesus will say to his guests: *With desire I have desired to eat this Pasch with you, before I suffer.*[1]

Such are the sublime subjects which are about to be brought before us: but, at the same time, we shall see our holy Mother the Church mourning, like a disconsolate widow, and sad beyond all human grief. Hitherto she has been weeping over the sins of her children; now she bewails the death of her Divine Spouse. The joyous *Alleluia* has long since been hushed in her canticles; she is now going to suppress another expression, which seems too glad for a time like the present. Partially, at first,[2] but entirely during the last three days, she is about to deny herself the use of that formula, which is so

[1] St. Luke, xxii. 15.
[2] Unless it be the Feast of a Saint, as frequently happens during the first of these two Weeks. The same exception is to be made in what follows.

dear to her: *Glory be to the Father, and to the Son, and to the Holy Ghost.* There is an accent of jubilation in these words, which would ill suit her grief and the mournfulness of the rest of her chants.

Her Lessons, for the Night Office, are taken from Jeremias, the Prophet of lamentation above all others. The colour of her Vestments is the one she had on when she assembled us at the commencement of Lent to sprinkle us with ashes; but when the dreaded day of Good Friday comes, purple would not sufficiently express the depth of her grief; she will clothe herself in black, as men do when mourning the death of a fellow-mortal, for Jesus, her Spouse, is to be put to death on that day: the sins of mankind and the rigors of the Divine Justice are then to weigh him down, and, in all the realities of a last agony, he is to yield up his soul to his Father.

The presentiment of that awful hour leads the afflicted Mother to veil the image of her Jesus: the Cross is hid from the eyes of the Faithful. The statues of the Saints, too, are covered; for it is but just, that if the glory of the Master be eclipsed, the Servant should not appear. The interpreters of the Liturgy tell us, that this ceremony of veiling the Crucifix, during Passiontide, expresses the humiliation, to which our Saviour subjected himself, of hiding himself when the Jews threatened to stone him, as is related in the Gospel of Passion Sunday. The Church begins this solemn rite with the Vespers of the Saturday before Passion Sunday. Thus it is, that in those years, when the Feast of our Lady's Annunciation falls in Passion Week, the statue of Mary, the Mother of God, remains veiled, even on that very day when the Archangel greets her as being *full of grace, and Blessed among women.*

CHAPTER THE THIRD.

PRACTICE DURING PASSIONTIDE AND HOLY WEEK.

THE past four weeks seem to have been but a preparation for the intense grief of the Church during these two. She knows that men are in search of her Jesus, and that they are bent on his Death. Before twelve days are over, she will see them lay their sacrilegious hands upon him. She will have to follow him up the hill of Calvary; she will have to receive his last breath; she must witness the stone placed against the Sepulchre where his lifeless body is laid. We cannot, therefore, be suprised at her inviting all her children to contemplate, during these weeks, Him who is the object of all her love and all her sadness.

But our Mother asks something more of us than compassion and tears; she would have us profit by the lessons we are to be taught by the Passion and Death of our Redeemer. He himself, when going up to Calvary, said to the holy women, who had the courage to show their compassion even before his very executioners: *Weep not over me; but weep for yourselves and for your children.*[1] It was not that he refused the tribute of their tears, for he was pleased with this proof of their affection; but it was his love for them that made him speak thus. He desired, above all, to see them appreciate the importance of what they were witnessing, and learn from it how inexorable is God's justice against sin.

During the four weeks that have preceded, the Church has been leading the Sinner to his conversion; so far, however, this conversion has been but begun;

---

[1] St. Luke, xxiii. 28.

now, she would perfect it. It is no longer our Jesus fasting and praying in the Desert, that she offers to our consideration; it is this same Jesus, as the great Victim immolated for the world's salvation. The fatal hour is at hand; the power of darkness is preparing to make use of the time that is still left; the greatest of crimes is about to be perpetrated. A few days hence, and the Son of God is to be in the hands of sinners, and they will put him to death. The Church no longer needs to urge her children to repentance; they know too well, now, what sin must be, when it could require such expiation as this. She is all absorbed in the thought of the terrible event, which is to close the life of the God-Man on earth; and by expressing her thoughts through the holy Liturgy, she teaches us what our own sentiments should be.

The pervading character of the prayers and rites of these two weeks, is a profound grief at seeing the Just One persecuted by his enemies even to death, and an energetic indignation against the deicides. The formulas, expressive of these two feelings, are, for the most part, taken from David and the Prophets. Here, it is our Saviour himself, disclosing to us the anguish of his soul; there, it is the Church, pronouncing the most terrible anathemas upon the executioners of Jesus. The chastisement, that is to befal the Jewish nation, is prophesied in all its frightful details; and on the last three days, we shall hear the Prophet Jeremias uttering his Lamentations over the faithless City. The Church does not aim at exciting idle sentiment; what she principally seeks, is to impress the hearts of her children with a salutary fear. If Jerusalem's crime strike them with horror, and if they feel that they have partaken of her sin, their tears will flow in abundance.

Let us, therefore, do our utmost to receive these strong impressions, too little known, alas! by the superficial piety of these times. Let us reflect upon the love and affection of the Son of God, who has treated his creatures with such unlimited confidence, lived their own life, spent his three and thirty years amidst them, not only humbly and peaceably, but in *going about, doing good.*[1] And now, this life of kindness, condescension and humility, is to be cut short by the disgraceful death, which none but slaves endured—the death of the Cross. Let us consider, on the one side, this sinful people, who, having no crimes to lay to Jesus' charge, accuse him of his benefits, and carry their detestable ingratitude to such a pitch, as to shed the Blood of this innocent and Divine Lamb; and then, let us turn to this Jesus, the Just by excellence, and see him become a prey to every bitterest suffering,—his Soul *sorrowful even unto death,*[2]—weighed down by the malediction of our sins,—drinking, even to the very dregs, the Chalice he so humbly asks his Father to take from him;— and, lastly, let us listen to his dying words: *My God, my God, why hast thou forsaken me?*[3] This it is that fills the Church with her immense grief; this it is that she proposes to our consideration: for she knows, that if we once rightly understood the Sufferings of her Jesus, our attachments to sin must needs be broken, for, by sin, we make ourselves guilty of the crime we detest in these Jews.

But the Church knows, too, how hard is the heart of man, and how, to make him resolve on a thorough conversion, he must be made to fear. For this reason, she puts before us those awful imprecations, which the Prophets, speaking in Jesus' person, pronounced against them that put our Lord to death. These prophetic anathemas were literally fulfilled against the obdurate Jews. They teach us what the Christian, also, must expect, if, as the Apostle so

---

[1] Acts, x. 38.   [2] St. Matth. xxvi. 38.   [3] *Ibid.* xxvii. 46.

forcibly expresses it, *we again crucify the Son of God.*[1] In listening to what the Church now speaks to us, we cannot but tremble as we recal to mind those other words of the same Apostle: *How much more, think ye, doth he deserve worse punishments, who hath trodden under foot the Son of God, and hath esteemed the Blood of the testament unclean,* (as though it were some vile thing,) *by which he was sanctified, and hath offered an affront to the Spirit of grace? For we know Him that hath said: Vengeance belongeth to me, and I will repay. And again: The Lord shall judge his people. It is a fearful thing to fall into the hands of the living God.*[2]

Fearful indeed it is! Oh! what a lesson God gives us of his inexorable Justice, during these days of the Passion! *He that spared not even his own Son,*[3]—his *beloved Son, in whom he is well pleased,*[4]—will he spare *us,* if, after all the graces he has bestowed upon us, he should find us in sin, which he so unpitifully chastised even in Jesus, when he took it upon himself, that he might atone for it? Considerations such as these,—the Justice of God towards the most innocent and august of Victims, and the punishments that befel the impenitent Jews,—must surely destroy within us every affection to sin, for they will create within us that salutary fear, which is the solid foundation of firm hope and tender love.

For, if, by our sins, we have made ourselves guilty of the death of the Son of God, it is equally true, that the Blood, which flows from his sacred Wounds, has the power to cleanse us from the guilt of our crime. The Justice of our heavenly Father cannot be appeased, save by the shedding of this precious Blood; and the Mercy of this same Father of ours wills that

---

[1] Heb. vi. 6.
[2] *Ibid.* x. 29, 30, 31.
[3] Rom. viii. 32.
[4] St. Matth. iii. 17.

it be spent for our ransom. The cruelty of Jesus' executioners have made Five Wounds in his sacred Body; and from these, there flow Five sources of salvation, which purify the world, and restore within each one of us that image of God, which sin had destroyed. Let us, then, approach with confidence to this redeeming Blood, which throws open to the sinner the gates of heaven, and whose worth is such that it could redeem a million worlds, were they even more guilty than this of ours. We are close upon the anniversary of the day when it was shed; long ages have passed away since it flowed down the wounded body of our Jesus, and fell in streams, from the cross, upon this ungrateful earth; and yet, its power is as great as ever.

Let us go, then; and *draw from the Saviour's fountains*;[1] our souls will come forth full of life, all pure, and dazzling with heavenly beauty; not one spot of their old defilements will be left; and the Father will love us with the love wherewith he loves his own Son. Why did he deliver up unto death this his tenderly beloved Son? Was it not that he might regain *us*, the children whom he had lost? We had become, by our sins, the possession of Satan; hell had undoubted claims upon us; and lo! we have been suddenly snatched from both, and all our primitive rights have been restored to us. Yet, God used no violence in order to deliver us from our enemy; how comes it, then, that we are now free? Listen to the Apostle: *Ye are bought at a great price.*[2] And what is this *price?* The Prince of the Apostles explains it: *Know ye,* says he, *that ye were not redeemed with corruptible things, as gold or silver,—but with the precious Blood of Christ, as of a Lamb unspotted and undefiled.*[3] This divine

---

[1] Is. xii. 3.
[2] I. Cor. vi. 20.
[3] I. St. Pet. i. 18, 19.

Blood was placed in the scales of God's Justice, and so far did it outweigh the weight of our iniquities, as to make the bias in our favour. The power of this Blood has broken the very gates of hell, severed our chains, and *made peace both as to the things on earth, and the things that are in heaven.*[1] Let us receive upon us, therefore, this precious Blood, wash our wounds in it, and sign our foreheads with it as with an indelible mark, which may protect us on the day of wrath, from the sword of vengeance.

There is another object most dear to the Church, and which she, during these two weeks, recommends to our deepest veneration; it is the Cross, which is, as it were, the altar upon which our incomparable Victim is immolated. Twice, during the course of the year, that is, on the Feasts of its Invention and Exaltation, this sacred Wood will be offered to us that we may honour it as the trophy of our Jesus' victory; but now, it speaks to us but of his Sufferings, it brings with it no other idea than that of his humiliation. God had said in the ancient Covenant: *Accursed is he that hangeth on a tree.*[2] The Lamb, that saved us, disdained not to suffer this *curse;* but, for that very cause, this *tree,* this wood, of infamy, has become dear to us beyond measure. It is the instrument of our salvation, it is the sublime pledge of Jesus' love for us. On this account, the Church is about to lavish her veneration and love upon it; and we intend to imitate her, and join her, in this as in all else she does. An adoring gratitude towards the Blood that has redeemed us, and a loving veneration of the holy Cross,—these are the two sentiments which are to be uppermost in our hearts, during these two weeks.

But for the Lamb himself,—for him that gave us this Blood, and so generously embraced the Cross

---

[1] Coloss. i. 20. [2] Deut. xxi. 23.

that saved us,—what shall we do? Is it not just, that we should keep close to him, and that, more faithful than the Apostles who abandoned him during his Passion, we should follow him, day by day, nay hour by hour, in the way of the Cross that he treads for us? Yes,—we will be his faithful companions, during these last days of his mortal life, when he submits to the humiliation of having to hide himself from his enemies. We will envy the lot of those devoted few, who shelter him in their houses, and expose themselves, by this courageous hospitality, to the rage of his enemies. We will compassionate his Mother, who suffered an anguish that no other heart could feel, because no other creature could love him as She did. We will go, in spirit, into that most hated Sanhedrim, where they are laying the impious plot against the life of the Just One. Suddenly, we shall see a bright speck gleaming on the dark horizon; the streets and squares of Jerusalem will re-echo with the cry of Hosanna to the Son of David. That unexpected homage paid to our Jesus, those palm branches, those shrill voices of admiring Hebrew children, will give a momentary truce to our sad forebodings. Our love shall make us take part in the loyal tribute thus paid to the King of Israel, who comes so meekly to visit the daughter of Sion, as the Prophet had foretold he would: but, alas! this joy will be short-lived, and we must speedily relapse into our deep sorrow of soul!

The traitorous disciple will soon strike his bargain with the High Priests; the last Pasch will be kept, and we shall see the figurative lamb give place to the true One, whose Flesh will become our food, and his Blood our drink. It will be *our Lord's Supper*. Clad in the nuptial robe, we will take our place there, together with the Disciples; for that day is the day of Reconciliation, which brings together, to the same Holy Table, both the penitent sinner, and the just that has been ever faithful. Then, we shall have to turn our steps towards the fatal Garden, where we shall learn what sin is, for we shall behold our Jesus agonising beneath its weight, and asking some respite from his Eternal Father. Then, in the dark hour of mid-night, the servants of the High Priests and the soldiers, led on by the vile Iscariot, will lay their impious hands on the Son of God; and yet, the legions of Angels who adore him, will be withheld from punishing the awful sacrilege! After this, we shall have to repair to the various tribunals, whither Jesus is led, and witness the triumph of injustice. The time that elapses between his being seized in the Garden and his having to carry his Cross up the hill of Calvary, will be filled up with the incidents of his mock trial,—lies, calumnies, the wretched cowardice of the Roman Governor, the insults of the by-standers, and the cries of the ungrateful populace thirsting for innocent Blood! We shall be present at all these things; our love will not permit us to separate ourselves from that dear Redeemer, who is to suffer them for our sakes, for our salvation.

Finally, after seeing him struck and spit upon, and after the cruel scourging and the frightful insult of the crown of thorns, we will follow our Jesus up Mount Calvary; we shall know where his sacred feet have trod by the Blood that marks the road. We shall have to make our way through the crowd, and, as we pass, we shall hear terrible imprecations uttered against our Divine Master. Having reached the place of execution, we shall behold this august Victim stripped of his garment, nailed to the cross, hoisted into the air, as if the better to expose him to insult! We will draw near to the Tree of Life, that we may lose neither one drop of that Blood which flows for the cleansing of the world, nor one single Word spoken, for its instruction, by our dying Jesus. We will compassionate his Mother, whose Heart is pierced through with a sword of sorrow ; we will stand close to her, when her Son, a few moments before his Death, shall consign us to her fond care. After his three hours' agony, we will reverently watch his sacred Head bow down, and receive, with adoring love, his last breath.

A bruised and mangled corpse, stiffened by the cold of death,—this is all that remains to us of that Son of Man, whose first coming into the world caused us such joy! This Son of the Eternal Father was not satisfied with *emptying himself, and taking the form of a servant ;*[1] this his being born in the flesh was but the beginning of his sacrifice ; his love was to lead him even unto death, even to the death of the cross. He foresaw that he would not win *our* love save at the price of such a generous immolation, and his heart hesitated not to make it. *Let us, therefore, love God,* says St. John, *because God first loved* us.[2] This is the end the Church proposes to herself by the celebration of these solemn anniversaries. After humbling our pride and our resistance to grace, by showing us how Divine Justice treats sin, —she leads our hearts to love that Jesus, who delivered himself up, in our stead, to the rigors of that Justice. Wo to us, if this great Week fail to produce in our souls a just return towards Him, who loved us more than himself, though we were, and had made ourselves, his enemies. Let us say with the Apostle: *The charity of Christ presseth us ; that they who live, may not now live to themselves, but unto Him who died for them.*[3] We owe this return to Him who made himself a Victim for our sakes, and who, up to the very last moment, instead of pronouncing against us the curse we so justly

---

[1] Philipp. ii. 7.
[2] I. St. John, iv. 19.
[3] 2. Cor. v. 14, 15.

deserved, prayed and obtained for us mercy and grace. He is, one day, to re-appear on the clouds of heaven, and, as the Prophet says, *men shall look upon Him, whom they have pierced.*[1] God grant that we may be of the number of those who, having made amends, by their love, for the crimes they had committed against the Divine Lamb, will then find confidence at the sight of those Wounds!

Let us hope that, by God's mercy, the holy time we are now entering upon will work such a happy change in us, that, on the Day of Judgment, we may confidently fix our eyes on Him we are now about to contemplate crucified by the hands of sinners. The Death of Jesus puts the whole of nature in commotion; the mid-day sun is darkened, the earth is shaken to its very foundations, the rocks are split;—may it be, that our hearts, too, be moved, and pass from indifference to fear, from fear to hope, and, at length, from hope to love; so that, having gone down, with our Crucified, to the very depths of sorrow, we may deserve to rise again with him unto light and joy, beaming with the brightness of his Resurrection upon us, and having within ourselves the pledge of a new life, which shall then die no more!

[1] Zach. xii. 10.

CHAPTER THE FOURTH.

MORNING AND NIGHT PRAYERS,

FOR PASSIONTIDE AND HOLY WEEK.

DURING these two weeks, the Christian, on waking in the morning, should unite himself with the Church, who repeats these words of St. Paul at every Hour of the Divine Office during the last three days of Holy Week:

Christ became, for our sakes, obedient unto death, even to the death of the Cross.	Christus factus est pro nobis obediens usque ad mortem, mortem autem crucis.

He should, after this, profoundly adore that great God, who was not to be appeased but by the Blood of Jesus; he should, also, adore the infinite goodness of this Jesus, who made himself a Victim, that he might save us sinners. It is with these two sentiments, that he must perform the first acts of religion, both interior and exterior, wherewith he begins each day of this present Season. The time for Morning Prayer being come, he may use the following method, which is formed upon the very prayers of the Church :—

MORNING PRAYER.

First, praise and adoration of the Most Holy Trinity :—

℣. Let us bless the Father and the Son, and the Holy Ghost.
℟. Let us praise him and extol him above all, for ever.

℣. Benedicamus Patrem et Filium, cum Sancto Spiritu :
℟. Laudemus et superexaltemus eum in sæcula.

℣. Gloria Patri et Filio, et Spiritui Sancto ;

℟. Sicut erat in principio, et nunc et semper, et in sæcula sæculorum. Amen.

℣. Glory be to the Father, and to the Son, and to the Holy Ghost.

℟. As it was in the beginning, is now, and ever shall be, world without end. Amen.

Then, praise to our Lord and Saviour, Jesus Christ:

℣. Adoramus te, Christe, et benedicimus tibi.

℟. Quia per Crucem tuam redemisti mundum.

℣. We adore thee, O Christ, and we bless thee.

℟. Because by thy Cross thou hast redeemed the world.

Thirdly, invocation of the Holy Ghost:

Veni, Sancte Spiritus, reple tuorum corda fidelium, et tui amoris in eis ignem accende.

Come, O Holy Spirit, fill the hearts of thy faithful, and enkindle within them the fire of thy love.

After these fundamental acts of Religion, recite the Lord's Prayer, begging your Heavenly Father to be mindful of his infinite mercy and goodness,—to *forgive* you your *trespasses*, through the merits of the Blood of Jesus,—to come to your assistance in the *temptations* and dangers which so thickly beset the path of this life,—and finally, to *deliver* you *from evil*, by removing from you every remnant of sin, which is the great *evil*, the *evil* that offends God, and entails the sovereign *evil* of man himself.

THE LORD'S PRAYER.

Pater noster, qui es in cœlis, sanctificetur nomen tuum : adveniat regnum tuum : fiat voluntas tua sicut in cœlo, et in terra. Panem nostrum quotidianum da nobis hodie: et dimitte nobis debita nostra, sicut et nos dimittimus debitoribus nostris : et ne nos inducas in tentationem : sed libera nos a malo. Amen.

Our Father, who art in heaven, hallowed be thy name: thy kingdom come : thy will be done on earth as it is in heaven. Give us this day our daily bread ; and *forgive us our trespasses*, as we forgive them that trespass against us: and lead us not into temptation : but deliver us from evil. Amen.

Then, address our Blessed Lady, using the words of the Angelical Salutation. Pray to her with confidence and love, for she is the *Refuge of Sinners*.

THE ANGELICAL SALUTATION.

Hail Mary, full of grace; the Lord is with thee; blessed art thou among women, and blessed is the fruit of thy womb, Jesus.

Holy Mary, Mother of God, *pray for us sinners*, now and at the hour of our death. Amen.

Ave Maria, gratia plena, Dominus tecum; benedicta tu in mulieribus, et benedictus fructus ventris tui, Jesus.

Sancta Maria, Mater Dei, ora pro nobis peccatoribus, nunc et in hora mortis nostræ. Amen.

After this, you should recite the *Creed*, that is, the Symbol of Faith. It contains the dogmas we are to believe; and during this season, you should dwell with loving attention on that Article, of our having been redeemed by the *Sufferings* and *Death* of Jesus. Let us lovingly confess this mystery of a God suffering and dying for us. Let us, by our repentance and amendment, merit that this Precious Blood may perfect the *conversion*, that has been begun in us.

THE APOSTLES' CREED.

I believe in God the Father Almighty, Creator of heaven and earth. And in Jesus Christ, his only Son our Lord, who was conceived by the Holy Ghost, born of the Virgin Mary; suffered under Pontius Pilate, was crucified, dead, and buried; he descended into hell, the third day he arose again from the dead; he ascended into heaven, sitteth at the right hand of God the

Credo in Deum Patrem omnipotentem, creatorem cœli et terræ. Et in Jesum Christum Filium ejus unicum, Dominum nostrum: qui conceptus est de Spiritu Sancto, natus ex Maria Virgine, passus sub Pontio Pilato, crucifixus, mortuus, et sepultus: descendit ad inferos, tertia die resurrexit a mortuis: ascendit ad cœlos, sedet ad dexteram Dei Patris omnipotentis: inde venturus est judicare vivos et mortuos.

Credo in Spiritum Sanctum, sanctam Ecclesiam Catholicam, Sanctorum communionem, remissionem peccatorum, carnis resurrectionem, vitam æternam. Amen.

Father Almighty; from thence he shall come to judge the living and the dead.

I believe in the Holy Ghost; the Holy Catholic Church ; the communion of Saints, the *forgiveness of sins*, the resurrection of the body, and life everlasting. Amen.

After having thus made the Profession of your Faith, endeavour to excite yourself to sorrow for the sins you have committed. Ask our Lord to give you the graces appropriate to this holy Season ; and, for this end, recite the following Hymn, which the Church uses in her Lauds for Lent:

HYMN.

O sol salutis, intimis,
Jesu, refulge mentibus,
Dum nocte pulsa gratior
Orbi dies renascitur.

Dans tempus acceptabile,
Da lacrymarum rivulis
Lavare cordis victimam,
Quam læta adurat charitas.

Quo fonte manavit nefas,
Fluent perennes lacrymæ,
Si virga pœnitentiæ
Cordis rigorem conterat.

Dies venit, dies tua,
In qua reflorent omnia :
Lætemur et nos, in viam
Tua reducti dextera.

O Jesus ! thou Sun of the world's salvation ! shine in the depths of our souls ; for now is the hour of night's departure, and sweeter day-break dawns upon the earth.

O thou that givest us this *acceptable time !* give us to wash, with our tears, the victim we offer thee,—which is our heart ; and grant that it may burn with joyous love.

If the rod of penance but strike these hearts of stone, a flood of ceaseless tears will flow from that same fount, whence came our many sins.

The day, thine own day, is at hand, when all things bloom afresh ; oh ! grant, that we, too, may rejoice, being brought once more to the path, by thy right hand.

O merciful Trinity! may the world prostrate itself before thee, and adore; and we, made new by grace, sing a new canticle of praise. Amen.

Te prona mundi machina, Clemens, adoret, Trinitas, Et nos novi per gratiam Novum canamus canticum. Amen.

Then, make an humble confession of your sins, reciting the general formula made use of by the Church.

THE CONFESSION OF SINS.

I confess to Almighty God, to blessed Mary ever Virgin, to blessed Michael the Archangel, to blessed John Baptist, to the holy Apostles Peter and Paul, and to all the saints, that I have sinned exceedingly in thought, word, and deed; through my fault, through my fault, through my most grievous fault. Therefore I beseech the blessed Mary ever Virgin, blessed Michael the Archangel, blessed John Baptist, the holy Apostles Peter and Paul, and all the saints, to pray to our Lord God for me.

Confiteor Deo Omnipotenti, beatæ Mariæ semper Virgini, beato Michaeli Archangelo, beato Joanni Baptistæ, sanctis Apostolis Petro et Paulo, et omnibus sanctis, quia peccavi nimis cogitatione, verbo, et opere: mea culpa, mea culpa, mea maxima culpa. Ideo precor beatam Mariam semper Virginem, beatum Michaelem Archangelum, beatum Joannem Baptistam, sanctos Apostolos Petrum et Paulum, et omnes sanctos, orare pro me ad Dominum Deum nostrum.

May Almighty God have mercy on us, and, our sins being forgiven, bring us to life everlasting. Amen.

Misereatur nostri omnipotens Deus, et dimissis peccatis nostris, perducat nos ad vitam æternam. Amen.

May the Almighty and merciful Lord grant us pardon, absolution, and remission of our sins. Amen.

Indulgentiam, absolutionem, et remissionem peccatorum nostrorum tribuat nobis omnipotens et misericors Dominus. Amen.

This is the proper time for making your Meditation, as no doubt you practice this holy exercise. During these two weeks, the following should be the leading subjects of our Meditations:—The severity of

God's Justice towards his Divine Son, who had taken upon himself *our* sins; the ingratitude of the Jews, who, though laden by Jesus with favours, clamour for his Death; the share we have taken, by our sins, in the Crucifixion; the Sufferings, both of body and soul, endured by our Redeemer; his patience and meekness under every injury; and finally, the infinite love he shows he has for us, by saving us at the cost of his Blood, yea, of his very Life.

The next part of your Morning Prayer must be to ask of God, by the following prayers, grace to avoid every kind of sin during the day you are just beginning. Say, then, with the Church, whose prayers must always be preferred to all others:

℣. Domine, exaudi orationem meam.

℟. Et clamor meus ad te veniat.

℣. O Lord, hear my prayer.

℟. And let my cry come unto thee.

OREMUS.

Domine, Deus omnipotens, qui ad principium hujus diei nos pervenire fecisti, tua nos hodie salva virtute, ut in hac die ad nullum declinemus peccatum, sed semper ad tuam justitiam faciendam nostra procedant eloquia, dirigantur cogitationes et opera. Per Dominum nostrum Jesum Christum Filium tuum, qui tecum vivit et regnat in unitate Spiritus Sancti Deus, per omnia sæcula sæculorum. Amen.

LET US PRAY.

Almighty Lord and God, who hast brought us to the beginning of this day, let thy powerful grace so conduct us through it, that we may not fall into any sin, but that all our thoughts, words, and actions may be regulated according to the rules of thy heavenly justice, and tend to the observance of thy holy law. Through Jesus Christ our Lord. Amen.

Then, beg the divine assistance for the actions of the day, that you may do them well; and say thrice:

℣. Deus, in adjutorium meum intende.

℟. Domine, ad adjuvandum me festina.

℣. Incline unto my aid, O God.

℟. O Lord, make haste to help me.

℣. Incline unto my aid, O God.
℟. O Lord, make haste to help me.
℣. Incline unto my aid, O God.
℟. O Lord, make haste to help me.

℣. Deus, in adjutorium meum intende.
℟. Domine, ad adjuvandum me festina.
℣. Deus, in adjutorium meum intende.
℟. Domine, ad adjuvandum me festina.

LET US PRAY.

Lord God, and King of heaven and earth, vouchsafe this day to rule and sanctify, to direct and govern our souls and bodies, our senses, words, and actions in conformity to thy law, and strict obedience to thy commands; that by the help of thy grace, O Saviour of the world! we may be fenced and freed from all evils. Who livest and reignest for ever and ever. Amen.

OREMUS.

Dirigere et sanctificare, regere et gubernare dignare, Domine Deus, Rex cœli et terræ, hodie corda et corpora nostra, sensus, sermones, et actus nostros in lege tua, et in operibus mandatorum tuorum, ut hic et in æternum, te auxiliante, salvi et liberi esse mereamur, Salvator mundi. Qui vivis et regnas in sæcula sæculorum. Amen.

During the day, you will do well to use the instructions and prayers which you will find in this volume, for each day of the Season. In the Evening, you may use the following Prayers.

NIGHT PRAYERS.

After having made the sign of the Cross, let us adore that Sovereign Lord, who has so mercifully preserved us during this day, and blessed us, every hour, with his grace and protection. For this end, let us recite the following Hymn, which the Church sings in her Vespers of Passiontide:

HYMN.

The Standard of our King comes forth: the mystery of

Vexilla Regis prodeunt;
Fulget Crucis mysterium,

Qua Vita mortem pertulit,
Et morte vitam protulit.

Quæ vulnerata lanceæ
Mucrone diro, criminum
Ut nos lavaret sordibus,
Manavit unda et sanguine.

Impletasunt quæ concinit
David fideli carmine,
Dicendo nationibus :
Regnavit a ligno Deus.

Arbor decora et fulgida,
Ornata regis purpura,
Electa digno stipite
Tam sancta membra tangere.

Beata cujus brachiis
Pretium pependit sæculi,
Statera facta corporis,
Tulitque prædam tartari.

O Crux, ave, spes unica,
Hoc Passionis tempore,
Piis adauge gratiam,
Reisque dele crimina.

Te, fons salutis, Trinitas,
Collaudet omnis spiritus :
Quibus Crucis victoriam
Largiris, adde præmium.
    Amen.

the Cross shines upon us,—that Cross on which Life suffered death, and by his Death gave life.

He was pierced with the cruel Spear, that, by the Water and the Blood, which flowed from the wound, he might cleanse us from sin.

Here, on the Cross was fulfilled the prophecy foretold in David's truthful words : "God hath reigned from the Tree."

O fair and shining Tree! beautified by the scarlet of the King, and chosen as the noble trunk that was to touch such sacred limbs!

O blessed Tree! on whose arms hung the ransom of the world! It was the balance, wherein was placed the Body of Jesus, and thereby hell lost its prey.

Hail, O Cross! our only hope! During these days of the Passion, increase to the good their grace, and cleanse sinners from their guilt.

May every spirit praise thee, O Holy Trinity, thou Fount of Salvation! and by the Cross, whereby thou gavest us victory, give us, too, our recompense. Amen.

After this Hymn, say the *Our Father, Hail Mary*, and the *Apostles' Creed*, as in the Morning.

Then, make the Examination of Conscience, going over in your mind all the faults you have committed during the day. Think, how great is the obstacle put by sin to the merciful designs your God would work in you; and make a firm resolution to avoid it for the time to come, to do penance for it, and to shun the occasions which might again lead you into it.

The Examination of Conscience concluded, recite the *Confiteor* (or *I confess*) with heartfelt contrition, and then give expression to your sorrow by the following Act, which we have taken from the Venerable Cardinal Bellarmine's Catechism :

ACT OF CONTRITION.

O my God, I am exceedingly grieved for having offended thee, and with my whole heart I repent for the sins I have committed : I hate and abhor them above every other evil, not only because, by so sinning, I have lost Heaven and deserve Hell, but still more because I have offended thee, O infinite Goodness, who art worthy to be loved above all things. I most firmly resolve, by the assistance of thy grace, never more to offend thee for the time to come, and to avoid those occasions which might lead me into sin.

You may then add the Acts of Faith, Hope, and Charity, to the recitation of which Pope Benedict the Fourteenth has granted an indulgence of seven years and seven quarantines for each time.

ACT OF FAITH.

O my God, I firmly believe whatsoever the Holy Catholic Apostolic Roman Church requires me to believe : I believe it, because thou hast revealed it to her, thou who art the very Truth.

ACT OF HOPE.

O my God, knowing thy almighty power, and thy infinite goodness and mercy, I hope in thee that, by the merits of the Passion and Death of our Saviour Jesus Christ, thou wilt grant me eternal life, which thou hast promised to all such as shall do the works of a good Christian ; and these I resolve to do, with the help of thy grace.

ACT OF CHARITY.

O my God, I love thee with my whole heart and above all things, because thou art the sovereign Good : I would rather lose all things than offend thee. For thy love also, I love and desire to love my neighbour as myself.

Then say to our Blessed Lady the following Anthem, which the Church uses from the Feast of the Purification to Easter:

ANTHEM TO THE BLESSED VIRGIN.

Ave Regina cœlorum, Ave Domina Angelorum: Salve radix, salve porta, Ex qua mundo lux est orta; Gaude, Virgo gloriosa, Super omnes speciosa: Vale, O valde decora, Et pro nobis Christum exora.	Hail Queen of Heaven! Hail Queen of Angels! Hail blest Root and Gate, from which came Light upon the world! Rejoice, O glorious Virgin, that surpassest all in beauty! Hail, most lovely Queen! and pray to Christ for us.
℣. Dignare me laudare te, Virgo sacrata. ℟. Da mihi virtutem contra hostes tuos.	℣. Vouchsafe, O Holy Virgin, that I may praise thee. ℟. Give me power against thine enemies.

OREMUS.	LET US PRAY.
Concede, misericors Deus, fragilitati nostræ præsidium: ut, qui sanctæ Dei Genitricis memoriam agimus, intercessionis ejus auxilio, a nostris iniquitatibus resurgamus. Per eumdem Christum Dominum nostrum. Amen.	Grant, O merciful God, thy protection to us in our weakness; that we who celebrate the memory of the Holy Mother of God, may, through the aid of her intercession, rise again from our sins. Through the same Christ our Lord. Amen.

You would do well to add the *Stabat Mater*, which is given further on, for Friday in Passion Week.

Here invoke the Holy Angels, whose protection is, indeed, always so much needed by us, but never so much as during the hours of night. Say with the Church:

Sancti Angeli, custodes nostri, defendite nos in prælio, ut non pereamus in tremendo judicio.	Holy Angels, our loving Guardians, defend us in the hour of battle, that we may not be lost at the dreadful judgment.

℣. God hath given his Angels charge of thee.
℟. That they may guard thee in all thy ways.

℣. Angelis suis Deus mandavit de te.
℟. Ut custodiant te in omnibus viis tuis.

LET US PRAY.

O God, who in thy wonderful providence hast been pleased to appoint thy holy Angels for our guardians: mercifully hear our prayers, and grant we may rest secure under their protection, and enjoy their fellowship in heaven for ever. Through Christ our Lord. Amen.

OREMUS.

Deus, qui ineffabili providentia sanctos Angelos tuos ad nostram custodiam mittere dignaris: largire supplicibus tuis, et eorum semper protectione defendi, et æterna societate gaudere. Per Christum Dominum nostrum. Amen.

Then beg the assistance of the Saints by the following antiphon:

ANT. All ye saints of God, vouchsafe to intercede for us and for all men, that we may be saved.

ANT. Sancti Dei omnes, intercedere dignemini pro nostra omniumque salute.

And here you may add a special mention of the Saints to whom you bear a particular devotion, either as your Patrons or otherwise; as also of those whose feast is kept in the Church that day, or at least who have been commemorated in the Divine Office.

This done, remember the necessities of the Church Suffering, and beg of God that he will give to the souls in Purgatory a place of refreshment, light, and peace. For this intention recite the usual prayers.

PSALM 129.

From the depths I have cried to thee, O Lord; Lord, hear my voice.

Let thine ears be attentive to the voice of my supplication.

If thou wilt observe iniqui-

De profundis clamavi ad te, Domine: Domine, exaudi vocem meam.

Fiant aures tuæ intendentes: in vocem deprecationis meæ.

Si iniquitates observaveris, Domine: Domine, quis sustinebit?

Quia apud te propitiatio est: et propter legem tuam sustinui te, Domine.

Sustinuit anima mea in verbo ejus: speravit anima mea in Domino.

A custodia matutina usque ad noctem: speret Israel in Domino.

Quia apud Dominum misericordia: et copiosa apud eum redemptio.

Et ipse redimet Israel; ex omnibus iniquitatibus ejus.

Requiem æternam dona eis, Domine.

Et lux perpetua luceat eis.

℣. A porta inferi.
℟. Erue, Domine, animas eorum.
℣. Requiescant in pace.
℟. Amen.
℣. Domine, exaudi orationem meam.
℟. Et clamor meus ad te veniat.

ties, O Lord, Lord, who shall endure it?

For with thee there is merciful forgiveness; and by reason of thy law I have waited for thee, O Lord.

My soul hath relied on his word; my soul hath hoped in the Lord.

From the morning watch even until night, let Israel hope in the Lord.

Because with the Lord there is mercy, and with him plentiful redemption.

And he shall redeem Israel from all his iniquities.

Eternal rest give to them, O Lord.

And let perpetual light shine upon them.

℣. From the gate of hell.
℟. Deliver their souls, O Lord.
℣. May they rest in peace.
℟. Amen.
℣. O Lord, hear my prayer
℟. And let my cry come unto thee.

OREMUS.

Fidelium Deus omnium Conditor et Redemptor, animabus famulorum famularumque tuarum, remissionem cunctorum tribue peccatorum: ut indulgentiam, quam semper optaverunt, piis supplicationibus consequantur. Qui vivis et regnas in sæcula sæculorum. Amen.

LET US PRAY.

O God, the Creator and Redeemer of all the faithful, give to the souls of thy servants departed the remission of their sins: that through the help of pious supplications, they may obtain the pardon they have always desired. Who livest and reignest for ever and ever. Amen.

Here make a special memento of such of the Faithful departed as have a particular claim upon your charity; after which, ask of God to give you his assistance, whereby you may pass the night free from danger. Say then, still keeping to the words of the Church:

ANT. Save us, O Lord, whilst awake, and watch us as we sleep; that we may watch with Christ, and rest in peace.
℣. Vouchsafe, O Lord, this night.
℟. To keep us without sin.

℣. Have mercy on us, O Lord.
℟. Have mercy on us.
℣. Let thy mercy, O Lord, be upon us.
℟. As we have hoped in thee.
℣. O Lord, hear my prayer.
℟. And let my cry come unto thee.

ANT. Salva nos, Domine, vigilantes, custodi nos dormientes: ut vigilemus cum Christo, et requiescamus in pace.
℣. Dignare, Domine, nocte ista.
℟. Sine peccato nos custodire.

℣. Miserere nostri, Domine.
℟. Miserere nostri.
℣. Fiat misericordia tua, Domine, super nos.
℟. Quemadmodum speravimus in te.
℣. Domine, exaudi orationem meam.
℟. Et clamor meus ad te veniat.

LET US PRAY.

Visit, we beseech thee, O Lord, this house and family, and drive from it all snares of the enemy: let thy holy Angels dwell herein, who may keep us in peace, and may thy blessing be always upon us. Through Jesus Christ our Lord, thy Son, who liveth and reigneth with thee, in the unity of the Holy Ghost, God, world without end. Amen.

OREMUS.

Visita, quæsumus, Domine, habitationem istam, et omnes insidias inimici ab ea longe repelle: Angeli tui sancti habitent in ea, qui nos in pace custodiant, et benedictio tua sit super nos semper. Per Dominum nostrum Jesum Christum, Filium tuum, qui tecum vivit et regnat in unitate Spiritus Sancti Deus, per omnia sæcula sæculorum. Amen.

And that you may end the day in the same sentiments wherewith you began it, say once more these words of the Apostle:

Christ became, for our sakes, obedient unto death, even to the death of the Cross.

Christus factus est pro nobis obediens usque ad mortem, mortem autem crucis.

CHAPTER THE FIFTH.

ON HEARING MASS, DURING PASSIONTIDE AND HOLY WEEK.

IF there be any time in the Year, when the Holy Sacrifice of the Mass should excite the heart of the Christian to devotion, it is Passiontide. During these days, set apart for the celebration of the Death of our Redeemer, the faithful soul can scarcely turn her thoughts from her Jesus expiring on the Cross: she envies those who were witnesses of the sublime mystery on Calvary: she wishes that she could have stood at the foot of the Cross, have compassionated the Sufferings of her Saviour, have heard his last Words, and reverently have taken up each drop of the precious Blood and applied it to her own wounds.

These holy desires have not been given to the Christian that they might be nothing but desires: God has given him the means of carrying them into effect, for the Sacrifice of the Mass is no other than the Sacrifice of Calvary. Jesus offered himself but once on the Cross for our sins; but he renews the offering, by an unbloody, yet by a real and complete, immolation on our Altars. He comes down on the Altar as soon as the sacred words of Consecration are pronounced by the Priest, and he comes as the Victim of the world's salvation. His Body is really present there, under the appearance of bread; the chalice contains his Blood under the species of wine; and why this mystic separation of the Body and Blood of the Man-God, who can die now no more, if it be not to represent before the Divine Majesty the real Death which was once suffered in a bloody manner on Calvary, and to renew, in man's favour, the merits and fruits of that Death?

This is the Sacrifice of the New Law, as far above all the sacrifices of the Old, both in holiness and efficacy, as the Creator is above all his creatures. The omnipotence of our Jesus' love has invented a means for uniting his dignity, as Immortal King of ages, with his office of our Victim. He can die now no more; but his Death is truly represented on the Altar: it is the self-same Body, bearing on it its five precious Wounds; it is the self-same Blood, the Blood which redeemed us. If it were possible for him to die again, the power of the mysterious words, which produce the presence of his Blood in the chalice, would be the sword of his immolation.

Let, then, the Christian approach with confidence; on the holy Altar, he will find his Saviour dying for him, and offering himself as the great High Priest. Yes, he is there, with the same love he had for us on Calvary; he is there, making intercession for all men, but, in a special manner, for those who are present at the Mass, and unite themselves with him. Let us see, in the action of the Holy Sacrifice, that same Immolation of which we have read the history in the Gospel. Let us hope for everything from that adorable goodness, which thus makes use of omnipotence in order to facilitate, by such stupendous means, the salvation and santification of man.

We will now endeavour to embody these sentiments in our explanation of the Mysteries of the Holy Mass, and initiate the Faithful into these divine secrets; not, indeed, by indiscreetly presuming to translate the sacred formulæ, but by suggesting such Acts, as will enable those who hear Mass, to enter into the ceremonies and spirit of the Church and the Priest.

The purple vestments, and the other rites of which we have already treated, give to the Holy Sacrifice an appearance of mournfulness, so well suited to the

Season. Nevertheless, if there occur the Feast of a Saint, between Passion and Palm Sunday, the Church lays aside her purple, and celebrates the Mass in honour of the Saint. The Crucifix and the holy Images, however, continue to be veiled, beginning from the first Vespers of Passion Sunday.

On the Sundays, if the Mass, at which the Faithful assist, be the *Parochial*, or, as it is often called, the Public Mass, two solemn rites precede it, and they are full of instruction and blessing;—the *Asperges*, or sprinkling of the Holy Water, and the *Procession*.

During the *Asperges*, let us ask with David, whose words are used by the Church in this ceremony, that our souls may be purified by the *hyssop* of humility and become *whiter than snow*.

ANTIPHON OF THE ASPERGES.

Asperges me, Domine, hyssopo, et mundabor; lavabis me, et super, nivem dealbabor.

Ps. Miserere mei, Deus, secundum magnam misericordiam tuam.

ANT. Asperges me, &c.
℣. Ostende nobis, Domine, misericordiam tuam.
℟. Et salutare tuum da nobis.
℣. Domine, exaudi orationem meam.
℟. Et clamor meus ad te veniat.
℣. Dominus vobiscum.
℟. Et cum spiritu tuo.

Thou shalt sprinkle me with hyssop, O Lord, and I shall be cleansed; thou shalt wash me, and I shall be made whiter than snow.

Ps. Have mercy on me, O God, according to thy great mercy.

ANT. Sprinkle me, &c.
℣. Show us, O Lord, thy mercy.
℟. And grant us thy salvation.
℣. O Lord, hear my prayer.
℟. And let my cry come unto thee.
℣. The Lord be with you.
℟. And with thy spirit.

OREMUS.

Exaudi nos, Domine sancte, Pater omnipotens, æterne Deus: et mittere digneris sanctum Angelum tuum de

LET US PRAY.

Graciously hear us, O holy Lord, Father Almighty, Eternal God: and vouchsafe to send thy holy Angel from

heaven, who may keep, cherish, protect, visit, and defend all who are assembled in this place. Through Christ our Lord.
℟. Amen.

cœlis, qui custodiat, foveat, protegat, visitet atque defendat omnes habitantes in hoc habitaculo. Per Christum Dominum nostrum.
℟. Amen.

The *Procession*, which immediately precedes the Mass, shows us the ardour wherewith the Church advances towards her God. Let us imitate her fervour, for it is written: *The Lord is good to them that hope in him, to the soul that seeketh him.*[1]

But see, Christians! the Sacrifice begins! The Priest is at the foot of the altar; God is attentive, the Angels are in adoration, the whole Church is united with the Priest, whose priesthood and action are those of the great High Priest, Jesus Christ. Let us make the sign of the cross with him.

THE ORDINARY OF THE MASS.

In the name of the Father, and of the Son, and of the Holy Ghost. Amen.

In nomine Patris, et Filii, et Spiritus Sancti. Amen.

I unite myself, O my God, with thy Church, whose heart is filled with the hope of soon seeing, and in all the splendour of his Resurrection, Jesus Christ thy Son, who is the true *Altar*.

℣. Introibo ad altare Dei.
℟. Ad Deum qui lætificat juventutem meam.

Like her, I beseech thee to defend me against the malice of the enemies of my salvation.

Judica me, Deus, et discerne causam meam de gente non sancta: ad homine iniquo et doloso erue me.

It is in thee that I have put my hope; yet do I feel sad and troubled at being in the midst of the snares which are set for me.

Quia tu es, Deus, fortitudo mea: quare me repulisti? et quare tristis incedo dum affligit me inimicus?

Send me, then, him who is

Emitte lucem tuam et ve-

---
[1] Lament. iii. 25.

ritatem tuam : ipsa me deduxerunt et adduxerunt in montem sanctum tuum, et in tabernacula tua.

Et introibo ad altare Dei : ad Deum qui lætificat juventutem meam.

Confitebor tibi in cithara Deus, Deus meus : quare tristis es anima mea? et quare conturbas me?

Spera in Deo, quoniam adhuc confitebor illi : Salutare vultus mei, et Deus meus.

Gloria Patri, et Filio, et Spiritui Sancto.

Sicut erat in principio, et nunc et semper, et in sæcula sæculorum. Amen.

℣. Introibo ad altare Dei.
℟. Ad Deum qui lætificat juventutem meam.

℣. Adjutorium nostrum in nomine Domini.
℟. Qui fecit cœlum et terram.

light and *truth:* it is he will open to us the way to thy holy mount, to thy heavenly tabernacle.

He is the Mediator, and the living Altar ; I will draw nigh to him, and be filled with joy.

When he shall have come, I will sing in my gladness. Be not sad, O my soul ! Why wouldst thou be troubled?

Hope in thy Jesus, who will soon show himself to thee as the conqueror of that Death which he will have suffered in thy stead ; and *thou* wilt rise again together with him.

Glory be to the Father, and to the Son, and to the Holy Ghost.

As it was in the beginning, is now, and ever shall be, world without end. Amen.

I am to go to the altar of God, and feel the presence of him who desires to give me a new life !

This my hope comes not to me as thinking that I have any merits, but from the all-powerful help of my Creator.

The thought of his being about to appear before his God, excites, in the soul of the Priest, a lively sentiment of compunction. He cannot go further in the holy Sacrifice without confessing, and publicly, that he is a sinner, and deserves not the grace he is about to receive. Listen, with respect, to this confession of God's Minister, and earnestly ask our Lord to show mercy to him ; for the Priest is your Father ; he is answerable for your salvation, for which he every day risks his own. When he has finished, unite with the Servers, or the Sacred Ministers, in this prayer :

THE ORDINARY OF THE MASS. 43

May Almighty God have mercy on thee, and, forgiving thy sins, bring thee to everlasting life.

Misereatur tui omnipotens Deus, et dimissis peccatis tuis, perducat te ad vitam æternam.

The Priest having answered *Amen*, make your confession, saying with a contrite spirit:

I confess to Almighty God, to blessed Mary ever Virgin, to blessed Michael the Archangel, to blessed John Baptist, to the holy Apostles Peter and Paul, to all the saints, and to thee, Father, that I have sinned exceedingly in thought, word, and deed, through my fault, through my fault, through my most grievous fault. Therefore I beseech the blessed Mary ever Virgin, blessed Michael, the Archangel, blessed John Baptist, the holy Apostles Peter and Paul, and all the saints, and thee, Father, to pray to our Lord God for me.

Confiteor Deo omnipotenti, beatæ Mariæ semper Virgini, beato Michæli Archangelo, beato Joanni Baptistæ, sanctis Apostolis Petro et Paulo, omnibus Sanctis, et tibi, Pater: quia peccavi nimis, cogitatione, verbo, et opere: mea culpa, mea culpa, mea maxima culpa. Ideo precor beatam Mariam semper Virginem, beatum Michaelem Archangelum, beatum Joannem Baptistam, sanctos Apostolos Petrum et Paulum, omnes Sanctos, et te, Pater, orare pro me ad Dominum Deum nostrum.

Receive with gratitude the paternal wish of the Priest, who says to you:

May Almighty God be merciful to you, and, forgiving your sins, bring you to everlasting life.
℟. Amen.
May the Almighty and merciful Lord grant us pardon, absolution, and remission of our sins.
℟. Amen.

Misereatur vestri omnipotens Deus, et dimissis peccatis vestris, perducat vos ad vitam æternam.
℟. Amen.
Indulgentiam, absolutionem, et remissionem peccatorum nostrorum, tribuat nobis omnipotens et misericors Dominus.
℟. Amen.

Invoke the divine assistance, that you may approach to Jesus Christ.

℣. Deus, tu conversus vivificabis nos.
℟. Et plebs tua lætabitur in te.
℣. Ostende nobis, Domine, misericordiam tuam.
℟. Et Salutare tuum da nobis.

℣. Domine, exaudi orationem meam.
℟. Et clamor meus ad te veniat.

℣. O God, it needs but one look of thine to give us life.
℟. And thy people shall rejoice in thee.
℣. Show us, O Lord, thy mercy.
℟. And give us to know and love the Saviour whom thou hast sent unto us.
℣. O Lord, hear my prayer.
℟. And let my cry come unto thee.

The Priest here leaves you to ascend to the altar; but first he salutes you:

℣. Dominus vobiscum.

℣. The Lord be with you.

Answer him with reverence:

℟. Et cum spiritu tuo.

℟. And with thy spirit.

OREMUS.

LET US PRAY.

He ascends the steps, and comes to the Holy of Holies. Ask, both for him and yourself, the deliverance from sin:

Aufer a nobis quæsumus, Domine, iniquitates nostras; ut ad Sancta sanctorum puris mereamur mentibus introire. Per Christum Dominum nostrum. Amen.

Take from our hearts, O Lord, all those sins, which make us unworthy to appear in thy presence, we ask this of thee by thy divine Son, our Lord.

When the Priest kisses the altar, out of reverence for the relics of the Martyrs which are there, say:

Oramus te, Domine, per merita sanctorum tuorum, quorum reliquiæ hic sunt, et

Generous soldiers of Jesus Christ, who have mingled your own blood with his, in-

THE ORDINARY OF THE MASS. 45

tercede for us that our sins may be forgiven: that so we may, like you, approach unto God.

omnium sanctorum: ut indulgere digneris omnia peccata mea. Amen.

If it be a High Mass at which you are assisting, the Priest incenses the Altar in a most solemn manner; and this white cloud, which you see ascending from every part of the Altar, signifies the prayer of the Church, who addresses herself to Jesus Christ; and which this Divine Mediator then causes to ascend, united with his own, to the throne of the majesty of his Father.

The Priest then says the Introit. It is a solemn opening-anthem, in which the Church, at the very commencement of the Holy Sacrifice, gives expression to the sentiments which fill her heart.

It is followed by nine exclamations, which are even more earnest,—for they ask for mercy. In addressing them to God, the Church unites herself with the nine choirs of Angels, who are standing round the altar of Heaven, one and the same as this before which you are kneeling.

To the Father:

Lord, have mercy on us!	Kyrie eleison.
Lord, have mercy on us!	Kyrie eleison.
Lord, have mercy on us!	Kyrie eleison.

To the Son:

Christ, have mercy on us!	Christe eleison.
Christ, have mercy on us!	Christe eleison.
Christ, have mercy on us!	Christe eleison.

To the Holy Ghost:

Lord, have mercy on us!	Kyrie eleison.
Lord, have mercy on us!	Kyrie eleison.
Lord, have mercy on us!	Kyrie eleison.

As we have already mentioned, the Church abstains, during this Season, from the heavenly

Hymn which the Angels sang over the Crib of the Divine Babe. But, if she be keeping the Feast of a Saint, she recites this beautiful Canticle on that day. The beginning of the *Angelic Hymn* seems more suitable for heavenly than for earthly voices; but the second part is in no ways out of keeping with the sinner's wants and fears, for we there remind the Son of the Eternal Father that he is the *Lamb,* who came down from heaven that he might *take away the sins of the world.* We beseech him to *have mercy on us,* and *receive our humble prayer.* Let us foster these sentiments within us, for they are so appropriate to the present Season.

THE ANGELIC HYMN.

Gloria in excelsis Deo, et in terra pax hominibus bonæ voluntatis.

Laudamus te: benedicimus te: adoramus te: glorificamus te: gratias agimus tibi propter magnam gloriam tuam.

Domine Deus Rex cœlestis, Deus Pater omnipotens.

Domine, Fili unigenite, Jesu Christe.

Domine Deus, Agnus Dei, Filius Patris.

Qui tollis peccata mundi, miserere nobis.

Qui tollis peccata mundi, suscipe deprecationem nostram.

Qui sedes ad dexteram Patris, miserere nobis.

Quoniam tu solus sanctus, tu solus Dominus, tu solus Altissimus, Jesu Christe, cum Sancto Spiritu, in gloria Dei Patris. Amen.

Glory be to God on high, and on earth peace to men of good will.

We praise thee: we bless thee: we adore thee: we glorify thee: we give thee thanks for thy great glory.

O Lord God, Heavenly King, God the Father Almighty.

O Lord Jesus Christ, the only begotten Son.

O Lord God, *Lamb of God*, Son of the Father.

Who takest away the sins of the world have mercy on us.

Who takest away the sins of the world, receive our humble prayer.

Who sittest at the right hand of the Father, have mercy on us.

For thou alone art holy, thou alone art Lord, thou alone, O Jesus Christ, together with the Holy Ghost, art most high, in the glory of God the Father. Amen.

The Priest then turns towards the people, and again salutes them, as it were to make sure of their pious attention to the sublime act, for which all this is but the preparation.

Then follows the *Collect* or *Prayer*, in which the Church formally expresses to the divine Majesty the special intentions she has in the Mass which is being celebrated. You may unite in this prayer, by reciting with the Priest the Collects which you will find in their proper places: but on no account omit to join with the server of the Mass in answering *Amen*.

After this, comes the *Epistle*, which is, generally, a portion of one or other of the Epistles of the Apostles, or a passage from some Book of the Old Testament. Whilst it is being read, ask of God that you may profit of the instructions it conveys.

The *Gradual* is an intermediate formula of prayer between the Epistle and Gospel. It again brings to us the sentiments already expressed in the Introit. Read it with devotion, that so you may enter more and more into the spirit of the mystery proposed to you by the Church.

During every other portion of her Year, the Church here repeats her joyous *Alleluia;* but now she denies herself this demonstration of gladness, until such time as her Divine Spouse has passed through that sea of bitterness, into which our sins have plunged him. Instead of the *Alleluia*, then, she sings in a plaintive tone some verses from the Psalms, appropriate to the rest of that day's Office. This is the *Tract*, of which we have already spoken.

If it be a *High Mass*, the Deacon, meanwhile, prepares to fulfil his noble office,—that of announcing the *Good Tidings* of salvation. He prays God to cleanse his heart and lips. Then kneeling before the Priest, he asks a blessing; and, having received it, at once goes to the place where he is to sing the Gospel.

As a preparation for hearing it worthily, you may thus pray, together with both Priest and Deacon:

Munda cor meum, ac labia mea, Omnipotens Deus, qui labia Isaiæ Prophetæ calculo mundasti ignito: ita me tua grata miseratione dignare mundare, ut sanctum Evangelium tuum digne valeam nuntiare. Per Christum Dominum nostrum. Amen.

Alas! these ears of mine are but too often defiled with the world's vain words: cleanse them, O Lord, that so I may hear the words of eternal life, and treasure them in my heart. Through our Lord Jesus Christ. Amen.

Dominus sit in corde meo, et in labiis meis: ut digne et competenter annuntiem Evangelium suum: In nomine Patris, et Filii, et Spiritus Sancti. Amen.

Grant to thy ministers thy grace, that they may faithfully explain thy law; that so all, both pastors and flock, may be united to thee for ever. Amen.

You will stand during the Gospel, as though you were waiting the orders of your Lord; and at the commencement, make the sign of the Cross on your forehead, lips, and breast; and then listen to every word of the Priest or Deacon. Let your heart be ready and obedient. *Whilst my beloved was speaking*, says the Spouse in the Canticle, *my soul melted within me.*[1] If you have not such love as this, have at least the humble submission of Samuel, and say: *Speak, Lord! thy servant heareth.*[2]

After the Gospel, if the Priest says the Symbol of Faith, the *Credo*, you will say it with him. Faith is that gift of God, without which we cannot please him. It is Faith that makes us see *the Light which shineth in darkness*, and which *the darkness* of unbelief *did not comprehend.* It is Faith alone that teaches us what we are, whence we come, and the end for which we are made. It alone can point out to us the path whereby we may return to our God, when once we have separated ourselves from him.

---

[1] Cant. v. 6. [2] 1 Kings, iii. 10.

Let us love this admirable Faith, which, if we but make it fruitful by good works, will save us. Let us, then, say with the Catholic Church, our Mother:

THE NICENE CREED.

I believe in one God, the Father Almighty, maker of heaven and earth, and of all things visible and invisible.

And in one Lord Jesus Christ, the only begotten Son of God. And born of the Father before all ages; God of God, light of light; true God of true God. Begotten, not made; consubstantial to the Father, by whom all things were made. Who for us men, and for our salvation, came down from heaven. And became incarnate by the Holy Ghost of the Virgin Mary; AND WAS MADE MAN. He was crucified also for us, under Pontius Pilate, suffered, and was buried. And the third day he rose again, according to the Scriptures. And ascended into heaven, sitteth at the right hand of the Father. And he is to come again with glory, to judge the living and the dead; of whose kingdom there shall be no end.

And in the Holy Ghost, the Lord and giver of life, who proceedeth from the Father and the Son. Who together with the Father and the Son, is adored and glorified; who spoke by the Prophets. And one holy Catholic and Apostolic Church. I

Credo in unum Deum, Patrem omnipotentem, factorem cœli et terræ, visibilium omnium et invisibilium.

Et in unum Dominum Jesum Christum, Filium Dei unigenitum. Et ex Patre natum ante omnia sæcula, Deum de Deo, lumen de lumine, Deum verum de Deo vero. Genitum non factum, consubstantialem Patri, per quem omnia facta sunt. Qui propter nos homines, et propter nostram salutem, descendit de cœlis. Et incarnatus est de Spiritu Sancto, ex Maria Virgine; ET HOMO FACTUS EST. Crucifixus etiam pro nobis sub Pontio Pilato, passus, et sepultus est. Et resurrexit tertia die, secundum Scripturas. Et ascendit in cœlum; sedet ad dexteram Patris. Et iterum venturus est cum gloria judicare vivos et mortuos; cujus regni non erit finis.

Et in Spiritum Sanctum, Dominum et vivificantem, qui ex Patre Filioque procedit. Qui cum Patre et Filio simul adoratur, et conglorificatur; qui locutus est per Prophetas. Et unam sanctam Catholicam et Apostolicam Ecclesiam. Confiteor

unum Baptisma in remissionem peccatorum. Et exspecto resurrectionem mortuorum, et vitam venturi sæculi. Amen.	confess one Baptism for the remission of sins. And I expect the resurrection of the dead, and the life of the world to come. Amen.

The Priest and the people should, by this time, have their hearts ready: it is time to prepare the offering itself. And here we come to the second part of the Holy Mass, which is called the *Oblation*, and which immediately follows that, which was called the *Mass of Catechumens*, on account of its being formerly the only part, at which the candidates for Baptism had a right to be present.

See, then, dear Christians! bread and wine are about to be offered to God, as being the noblest of inanimate creatures, since they are made for the nourishment of man; and even that is only a poor material image of what they are destined to become in our Christian Sacrifice. Their substance will soon give place to God himself, and of themselves nothing will remain but the appearances. Happy creatures, thus to yield up their own being, that God may take its place! We, too, are to undergo a like transformation, when, as the Apostle expresses it, *that which to us is mortal, shall put on immortality.*[1] Until that happy change shall be realised, let us offer ourselves to God, as often as we see the bread and wine presented to him in the Holy Sacrifice; and let us glorify Him, who, by assuming our human nature, has made us *partakers of the divine nature.*[2]

The Priest again turns to the people with the usual salutation, as though he would warn them to redouble their attention. Let us read the Offertory with him, and when he offers the Host to God, let us unite with him in saying:

Suscipe, sancte Pater, omnipotens æterne Deus,	All that we have, O Lord, comes from thee, and belongs

[1] 1 Cor. xv. 53.   [2] 2 St. Pet. i. 4.

to thee; it is just, therefore, that we return it unto thee. But how wonderful art thou in the inventions of thy immense love! This bread which we are offering to thee, is to give place, in a few moments, to the sacred Body of Jesus. We beseech thee, receive, together with this oblation, our hearts which long to live by thee, and to cease to live their own life of self.

hanc immaculatam hostiam, quam ego indignus famulus tuus offero tibi Deo meo vivo et vero, pro innumerabilibus peccatis et offensionibus et negligentiis meis, et pro omnibus circumstantibus, sed et pro omnibus fidelibus christianis vivis atque defunctis; ut mihi et illis proficiat ad salutem in vitam æternam. Amen.

When the Priest puts the wine into the chalice, and then mingles with it a drop of water, let your thoughts turn to the divine mystery of the Incarnation, which is the source of our hope and our salvation; and say:

O Lord Jesus, who art *the true Vine*, and whose Blood, like a generous wine, has been poured forth under the pressure of the Cross! thou hast deigned to unite thy divine nature to our weak humanity, which is signified by this drop of water. O come and make us partakers of thy divinity, by showing thyself to us in thy sweet and wondrous visit.

Deus qui humanæ substantiæ dignitatem mirabiliter condidisti, et mirabilius reformasti: da nobis per hujus aquæ et vini mysterium, ejus divinitatis esse consortes, qui humanitatis nostræ fieri dignatus est particeps, Jesus Christus Filius tuus Dominus noster: qui tecum vivit et regnat in unitate Spiritus Sancti Deus, per omnia sæcula sæculorum. Amen.

The Priest then offers the mixture of wine and water, beseeching God graciously to accept this oblation, which is so soon to be changed into the reality, of which it is now but the figure. Meanwhile, say, in union with the Priest:

Graciously accept these gifts, O sovereign Creator of all things. Let them be fitted

Offerimus tibi, Domine, calicem salutaris, tuam deprecantes clementiam: ut in

conspectu divinæ Majestatis tuæ, pro nostra et totius mundi salute, cum odore suavitatis ascendat. Amen.	for the divine transformation, which will make them, from being mere offerings of created things, the instrument of the world's salvation.

After having thus held up the sacred gifts towards heaven, the Priest bows down: let us, also, humble ourselves, and say:

In spiritu humilitatis, et in animo contrito suscipiamur a te, Domine: et sic fiat sacrificium nostrum in conspectu tuo hodie, ut placeat tibi, Domine Deus.	Though daring, as we do, to approach thy altar, O Lord, we cannot forget that we are sinners. Have mercy on us, and delay not to send us thy Son, who is our saving Host.

Let us next invoke the Holy Ghost, whose operation is about to produce on the altar the presence of the Son of God, as it did in the womb of the Blessed Virgin Mary, in the divine mystery of the Incarnation:

Veni, Sanctificator omnipotens æterne Deus, et benedic hoc sacrificium tuo sancto nomini præparatum.	Come, O Divine Spirit, make fruitful the offering which is upon the altar, and produce in our hearts Him whom they desire.

If it be a High Mass, the Priest, before proceeding any further with the Sacrifice, takes the thurible a second time. He first incenses the bread and wine which have been just offered, and then the altar itself; hereby inviting the faithful to make their prayer, which is signified by the incense, more and more fervent, the nearer the solemn moment approaches.

But the thought of his own unworthiness becomes more intense than ever in the heart of the Priest. The public confession, which he made at the foot of the altar, is not enough; he would now, at the altar itself, express to the people, in the language of a solemn rite, how far he knows himself to be from that spotless sanctity, wherewith he should approach to God. He washes his *hands*. Our hands signify our *works*; and the Priest, though by his priesthood he bear the office of Jesus Christ, is, by his works, but man. Seeing your Father thus humble himself, do you also make an act of humility, and say with him these verses of the Psalm.

PSALM 25.

I, too, would wash my hands, O Lord, and become like unto those who are innocent, that so I may be worthy to come near thy altar, and hear thy sacred Canticles, and then go and proclaim to the world the wonders of thy goodness. I love the beauty of thy House, which thou art about to make the dwelling-place of thy glory. Leave me not, O God, in the midst of them that are enemies both to thee and me. Thy mercy having separated me from them, I entered on the path of innocence, and was restored to thy grace; but have pity on my weakness still; redeem me yet more, thou who hast so mercifully brought me back to the right path. In the midst of these thy faithful people, I give thee thanks. Glory be to the Father and to the Son, and to the Holy Ghost; as it was in the beginning, is now, and ever shall be, world without end. Amen.

Lavabo inter innocentes manus meas: et circumdabo altare tuum, Domine.
Ut audiam vocem laudis: et enarrem universa mirabilia tua.
Domine, dilexi decorem domus tuæ, et locum habitationis gloriæ tuæ.
Ne perdas cum impiis, Deus, animam meam, et cum viris sanguinum vitam meam.
In quorum manibus iniquitates sunt: dextera eorum repleta est muneribus.
Ego autem in innocentia mea ingressus sum: redime me, et miserere mei.
Pes meus stetit in directo: in ecclesiis benedicam te, Domine.
Gloria Patri, et Filio, et Spiritui Sancto.
Sicut erat in principio, et nunc, et semper, et in sæcula sæculorum. Amen.

The Priest, taking encouragement from the act of humility he has just made, returns to the middle of the altar, and bows down full of respectful awe, begging of God to receive graciously the Sacrifice which is about to be offered to him, and expresses the intentions for which it is offered. Let us do the same.

Suscipe, sancta Trinitas, hanc oblationem, quam tibi offerimus ob memoriam Passionis, Resurrectionis, et Ascensionis Jesu Christi Domini nostri : et in honore beatæ Mariæ semper Virginis, et beati Joannis Baptistæ, et sanctorum Apostolorum Petri et Pauli, et istorum, et omnium Sanctorum : ut illis proficiat ad honorem, nobis autem ad salutem : et illi pro nobis intercedere dignentur in cœlis, quorum memoriam agimus in terris. Per eumdem Christum Dominum nostrum. Amen.	O Holy Trinity, graciously accept the Sacrifice we have begun. We offer it in remembrance of the Passion, Resurrection, and Ascension of our Lord Jesus Christ. Permit thy Church to join with this intention that of honouring the ever glorious Virgin Mary, the Blessed Baptist John, the holy Apostles Peter and Paul, the Martyrs whose relics lie here under our altar awaiting their resurrection, and the Saints whose memory we this day celebrate. Increase the glory they are enjoying, and receive the prayers they address to thee for us.

The Priest again turns to the people; it is for the last time before the sacred Mysteries are accomplished. He feels anxious to excite the fervour of the people. Neither does the thought of his own unworthiness leave him; and before entering the cloud with the Lord, he seeks support in the prayers of his brethren who are present. He says to them:

Orate, fratres : ut meum ac vestrum sacrificium acceptabile fiat apud Deum Patrem omnipotentem.	Brethren, pray that my Sacrifice, which is yours also, may be acceptable to God, our Almighty Father.

This request made, he turns again to the altar, and you will see his face no more, until our Lord himself shall have come down from heaven upon that same altar. Assure the Priest that he has your prayers, and say to him:

May our Lord accept this Sacrifice at thy hands, to the praise and glory of his name, and for our benefit and that of his holy Church throughout the world.	Suscipiat Dominus sacrificium de manibus tuis, ad laudem et gloriam nominis sui, ad utilitatem quoque nostram totiusque Ecclesiæ suæ sanctæ.

Here the Priest recites the prayers called *the Secrets*, in which he presents the petition of the whole Church for God's acceptance of the Sacrifice, and then immediately begins to fulfil that great duty of religion,—*Thanksgiving.* So far he has adored God, and has sued for mercy; he has still to give thanks for the blessings bestowed on us by the bounty of our heavenly Father, the chief of which, during this Season, is his giving us his Only Begotten Son, to be our Mediator by his Blood. The Priest, in the name of the Church, is about to give expression to the gratitude of all mankind. In order to excite the Faithful to that intensity of gratitude which is due to God for all his gifts, he interrupts his own and their silent prayer by terminating it aloud, saying:

For ever and ever!	Per omnia sæcula sæculorum!

In the same feeling, answer your *Amen!* Then he continues:

℣. The Lord be with you.	℣. Dominus vobiscum.
℟. And with thy spirit.	℟. Et cum spiritu tuo.
℣. Lift up your hearts!	℣. Sursum corda!

Let your response be sincere:

℟. We have them fixed on God.	℟. Habemus ad Dominum.

And when he adds:

℣. Let us give thanks to the Lord our God.	℣. Gratias agamus Domino Deo nostro.

Answer him with all the earnestness of your soul,

℟. Dignum et justum est.   ℟. It is meet and just.

Then the Priest:

THE PREFACE.

Vere dignum et justum est, æquum et salutare, nos tibi semper, et ubique gratias agere, Domine sancte, Pater omnipotens, æterne Deus. Qui salutem humani generis in ligno Crucis constituisti, ut unde mors oriebatur, inde vita resurgeret; et qui in ligno vincebat, in Ligno quoque vinceretur; per Christum Dominum nostrum; per quem majestatem tuam laudant Angeli, adorant Dominationes, tremunt Potestates, Cœli, cœlorumque Virtutes, ac beata Seraphim, socia exsultatione concelebrant. Cum quibus et nostras voces, ut admitti jubeas deprecamur, supplici confessione dicentes.

It is truly meet and just, right and available to salvation, that we should always and in all places give thanks to thee, O Holy Lord, Father Almighty, Eternal God. Who hast appointed, that the salvation of mankind should be wrought on the wood of the Cross; that from whence death came, thence life might arise; and that he who overcame by the tree, might also by the Tree be overcome; through Christ our Lord; by whom the Angels praise thy majesty, the Dominations adore it, the Powers tremble before it; the Heavens and the heavenly Virtues, and the blessed Seraphim, with common jubilee, glorify it. Together with whom, we beseech thee that we may be admitted to join our humble voices, saying:

Here unite with the Priest, who, on his part, unites himself with the blessed Spirits, in giving thanks to God for the unspeakable Gift: bow down and say:

Sanctus, Sanctus, Sanctus, Dominus Deus sabaoth!
Pleni sunt cœli et terræ gloria tua.
Hosanna in excelsis!

Holy, Holy, Holy, Lord God of hosts!
Heaven and earth are full of thy glory.
Hosanna in the highest!

Blessed be the Saviour who is coming to us in the name of the Lord who sends him.	Benedictus qui venit in nomine Domini.
Hosanna be to him in the highest!	Hosanna in excelsis!

After these words commences the *Canon*, that mysterious prayer, in the midst of which heaven bows down to earth, and God descends unto us. The voice of the Priest is no longer heard; yea, even at the altar, all is silence. Let a profound respect stay all distractions, and keep our senses in submission to the soul. Let us fix our eyes on what the Priest does in the Holy Place.

THE CANON OF THE MASS.

In this mysterious colloquy with the great God of heaven and earth, the first prayer of the sacrificing Priest is for the Catholic Church, his and our Mother.

O God, who manifestest thyself unto us by means of the mysteries which thou hast entrusted to thy holy Church, our Mother; we beseech thee, by the merits of this sacrifice, that thou wouldst remove all those hindrances which oppose her during her pilgrimage in this world. Give her peace and unity. Do thou thyself guide our Holy Father the Pope, thy Vicar on earth. Direct thou our Bishop, who is our sacred link of unity; and watch over all the orthodox children of the Catholic Apostolic Roman Church.	Te igitur, clementissime Pater, per Jesum Christum Filium tuum Dominum nostrum, supplices rogamus ac petimus, uti accepta habeas, et benedicas hæc dona, hæc munera, hæc sancta sacrificia illibata, in primis quæ tibi offerimus pro Ecclesia tua sancta Catholica: quam pacificare, custodire, adunare, et regere digneris toto orbe terrarum, una cum famulo tuo Papa nostro N., et Antistite nostro N., et omnibus orthodoxis, atque catholicæ et apostolicæ fidei cultoribus.

Here pray, together with the Priest, for those whose interests should be dearest to you.

Memento, Domine, famulorum famularumque tuarum N. et N., et omnium circumstantium, quorum tibi fides cognita est, et nota devotio: pro quibus tibi offerimus, vel qui tibi offerunt hoc sacrificium laudis, pro se, suisque omnibus, pro redemptione animarum suarum, pro spe salutis et incolumitatis suæ; tibique reddunt vota sua æterno Deo, vivo et vero.

Permit me, O God, to intercede with thee in more earnest prayer for those, for whom thou knowest that I have a special obligation to pray: * * * Pour down thy blessings upon them. Let them partake of the fruits of this divine Sacrifice, which is offered unto thee in the name of all mankind. Visit them by thy grace, pardon them their sins, grant them the blessings of this present life and of that which is eternal.

Here let us commemorate the Saints: they are that portion of the Body of Jesus Christ, which is called the *Church Triumphant.*

Communicantes, et memoriam venerantes, in primis gloriosæ semper Virginis Mariæ, Genitricis Dei et Domini nostri Jesu Christi: sed et beatorum Apostolorum ac Martyrum tuorum, Petri et Pauli, Andreæ, Jacobi, Joannis, Thomæ, Jacobi, Philippi, Bartholomæi, Matthæi, Simonis, et Thaddæi: Lini, Cleti, Clementis, Xysti, Cornelii, Cypriani, Laurentii, Chrysogoni, Joannis et Pauli, Cosmæ et Damiani, et omnium sanctorum tuorum, quorum meritis precibusque concedas, ut in omnibus protectionis tuæ muniamur auxilio. Per eumdem Christum Dominum nostrum. Amen.

But the offering of this Sarifice, O my God, does not unite us with those only of our brethren who are still in this transient life of trial: it brings us closer to those also, who are already in possession of heaven. Therefore it is, that we wish to honour by it the memory of the glorious and ever Virgin Mary, of whom Jesus was born to us; of the Apostles, Confessors, Virgins, and of all the Saints; that so they may assist us, by their powerful intercession, to become worthy to contemplate thee, as they now do, in the mansion of thy glory.

The priest, who, up to this time, had been praying with his hands extended, now joins them, and holds them over the bread and wine, as the High Priest of the Old Law did over the figurative victim: he thus expresses his intention of bringing these gifts more closely under the notice of the Divine Majesty, and of marking them as the material offering whereby we profess our *dependence,* and which is, in a few instants, to yield its place to the living Host, upon whom are laid all our iniquities.

Vouchsafe, O God, to accept this offering which this thy assembled family presents to thee as the homage of its most happy servitude. In return, give us peace, save us from thy wrath, and number us among thy elect, through Him who is coming to us—thy Son our Saviour.

Yea, Lord, this is the moment when this bread is to become his sacred Body, which is our food; and this wine is to be changed into his Blood, which is our drink. Ah! delay no longer, but send to us this divine Son our Saviour!

Hanc igitur oblationem servitutis nostræ, sed et cunctæ familiæ tuæ, quæsumus Domine, ut placatus accipias: diesque nostros in tua pace disponas, atque ab æterna damnatione nos eripi, et in electorum tuorum jubeas grege numerari. Per Christum Dominum nostrum. Amen.

Quam oblationem tu Deus in omnibus quæsumus, benedictam, adscriptam, ratam, rationabilem, acceptabilemque facere digneris; ut nobis Corpus et Sanguis fiat dilectissimi Filii tui Domini nostri Jesu Christi.

And here the Priest ceases to act as man; he now becomes more than a mere minister of the Church. His word becomes that of Jesus Christ, with all its power and efficacy. Prostrate yourself in profound adoration; for God himself is about to descend upon our Altar, coming down from heaven.

What, O God of heaven and earth, my Jesus, the long expected Messias, what else can I do at this solemn moment but adore thee, in silence, as my sovereign Master, and open my whole heart to thee,

Qui pridie quam pateretur, accepit panem in sanctas ac venerabiles manus suas: et elevatis oculis in cœlum, ad te Deum Patrem suum omnipotentem, tibi gratias agens, benedixit, fregit, deditque discipulis suis, dicens: Accipite, et manducate ex hoc omnes. Hoc EST ENIM CORPUS MEUM.

as to its dearest King! Come, then, Lord Jesus, come!

The Divine Lamb is now lying on our Altar! Glory and love be to him for ever! But he is come, that he may be immolated. Hence, the Priest, who is the minister of the will of the Most High, immediately pronounces over the Chalice those sacred words, which will produce the great mystical immolation, by the separation of the Victim's Body and Blood. The substances of bread and wine have ceased to exist: the species alone are left, veiling, as it were, the Body and Blood, lest fear should keep us from a mystery, which God gives us in order to give us confidence. Let us associate ourselves to the Angels, who tremblingly look upon this deepest wonder.

Simili modo postquam cœnatum est, accipiens et hunc præclarum Calicem in sanctas ac venerabiles manus suas: item tibi gratias agens, benedixit, deditque discipulis suis, dicens: Accipite et bibite ex eo omnes. HIC EST ENIM CALIX SANGUINIS MEI, NOVI ET ÆTERNI TESTAMENTI: MYSTERIUM FIDEI: QUI PRO VOBIS ET PRO MULTIS EFFUNDETUR IN REMISSIONEM PECCATORUM. Hæc quotiescumque feceritis, in mei memoriam facietis.

O Precious Blood! thou price of my salvation! I adore thee! Wash away my sins, and give me a purity above the whiteness of snow. Lamb ever slain, yet ever living, thou comest to take away the sins of the world! Come also and reign in me by thy power and by thy love.

The Priest is now face to face with God. He again raises his hands towards heaven, and tells our heavenly Father, that the oblation, now on the altar, is no longer an earthly offering, but the Body and Blood, the whole Person, of his divine Son.

THE ORDINARY OF THE MASS. 61

Father of infinite holiness, the Host so long expected is here before thee! Behold this thy eternal Son, who suffered a bitter passion, rose again with glory from the grave, and ascended triumphantly into heaven. He is thy Son; but he is also our Host, Host pure and spotless, —our Meat and Drink of everlasting life.

Heretofore thou didst accept the sacrifice of the innocent lambs offered to thee by Abel; and the sacrifice which Abraham made thee of his son Isaac, who, though immolated, yet lived; and, lastly, the sacrifice, which Melchisedech presented thee, of bread and wine. Receive our Sacrifice, which is above all those others. It is the Lamb, of whom all others could be but figures: it is the undying Victim: it is the Body of thy Son, who is the Bread of Life, and his Blood, which, whilst a Drink of immortality for us, is a tribute adequate to thy glory.

Unde et memores, Domine, nos servi tui, sed et plebs tua sancta, ejusdem Christi Filii tui Domini nostri tam beatæ Passionis, necnon et ab inferis Resurrectionis, sed et in cœlos gloriosæ Ascensionis: offerimus præclaræ majestati tuæ de tuis donis ac datis Hostiam puram, Hostiam sanctam, Hostiam immaculatam: Panem sanctum vitæ æternæ, et Calicem salutis perpetuæ.

Supra quæ propitio ac sereno vultu respicere digneris: et accepta habere, sicuti accepta habere dignatus es munera pueri tui justi Abel, et sacrificium Patriarchæ nostri Abrahæ, et quod tibi obtulit summus Sacerdos tuus Melchisedech, sanctum sacrificium, immaculatam hostiam.

The Priest bows down to the altar, and kisses it as the throne of love on which is seated the Saviour of men.

But, O God of infinite power, these sacred gifts are not only on this altar here below; they are also on that sublime Altar of heaven, which is before the throne of thy divine Majesty. These two altars are but one and the same,

Supplices te rogamus, omnipotens Deus: jube hæc perferri per manus sancti Angeli tui in sublime Altare tuum, in conspectu divinæ Majestatis tuæ: ut quotquot ex hac altaris participatione, sacrosanctum Filii tui Cor-

pus et Sanguinem sumpserimus, omni benedictione cœlesti et gratia repleamur. Per eumdem Christum Dominum nostrum. Amen.	on which is accomplished the great mystery of thy glory and our salvation. Vouchsafe to make us partakers of the Body and Blood of the august Victim, from whom flow every grace and blessing.

Nor is the moment less favourable for making supplication for the Church Suffering. Let us, therefore, ask the divine Liberator, who has come down among us, that he mercifully visit, by a ray of his consoling light, the dark abode of Purgatory, and permit his Blood to flow, as a stream of mercy's dew, from this our altar, and refresh the panting captives there. Let us pray expressly for those among them, who have a claim on our suffrages.

Memento etiam, Domine, famulorum famularumque tuarum N. et N., qui nos præcesserunt cum signo fidei, et dormiunt in somno pacis. Ipsis Domine, et omnibus in Christo quiescentibus, locum refrigerii, lucis et pacis, ut indulgeas, deprecamur. Per eumdem Christum Dominum nostrum. Amen.	Dear Jesus! let the happiness of this thy visit extend to every portion of thy Church. Thy face gladdens the elect in the holy City; even our mortal eyes can see beneath the veil of our delighted faith; ah! hide not thyself from those brethren of ours, who are imprisoned in the place of expiation. Be thou refreshment to them in their flames, light in their darkness, and peace in their agonies of torment.

This duty of charity fulfilled, let us pray for ourselves, sinners, alas! and who profit so little by the visit, which our Saviour pays us. Let us, together with the Priest, strike our breast, saying:

Nobis quoque peccatoribus famulis tuis, de multitudine miserationum tuarum sperantibus, partem aliquam et societatem do-	Alas! we are poor sinners, O God of all sanctity! yet do we hope that thy infinite mercy will grant us to share in thy kingdom, not, indeed,

by reason of our works, which deserve little more than punishment, but because of the merits of this Sacrifice, which we are offering to thee. Remember, too, the merits of thy holy Apostles, of thy holy Martyrs, of thy holy Virgins, and of all thy Saints. Grant us, by their intercession, grace in this world, and glory eternal in the next : which we ask of thee, in the name of our Lord Jesus Christ, thy Son. It is by him thou bestowest upon us thy blessings of life and sanctification ; and by him also, with him, and in him, in the unity of the Holy Ghost, may honour and glory be to thee !

nare digneris cum tuis sanctis Apostolis et Martyribus : cum Joanne, Stephano, Mathia, Barnaba, Ignatio, Alexandro, Marcellino, Petro, Felicitate, Perpetua, Agatha, Lucia, Agnete, Cæcilia, Anastasia, et omnibus Sanctis tuis ; intra quorum nos consortium, non æstimator meriti, sed veniæ, quæsumus, largitor admitte. Per Christum Dominum nostrum. Per quem hæc omnia, Domine, semper bona creas, sanctificas, vivificas, benedicis, et præstas nobis : per ipsum, et cum ipso et in ipso, est tibi Deo Patri omnipotenti, in unitate Spiritus Sancti, omnis honor et gloria.

Whilst saying these last few words, the Priest has taken up the sacred Host, which was on the altar ; he has held it over the chalice, thus re-uniting the Body and Blood of the divine Victim, in order to show that He is now immortal. Then raising up both Chalice and Host, he offers to God the most noble and perfect homage which the divine Majesty could receive.

This solemn and mysterious rite ends the Canon. The silence of the Mysteries is broken. The Priest concludes his long prayers, by saying aloud, and so giving the faithful the opportunity of expressing their desire that his supplications be granted :

For ever and ever.

Per omnia sæcula sæculorum.

Answer him with faith, and in a sentiment of union with your holy Mother the Church :

Amen ! I believe the mystery which has just been ac-

Amen.

complished. I unite myself to the offering which has been made, and to the petitions of the Church.

It is time to recite the Prayer, which our Saviour himself has taught us. Let it ascend up to heaven together with the sacrifice of the Body and Blood of Jesus Christ. How could it be otherwise than heard, when he himself who made it for us, is in our very hands now whilst we say it? As this prayer belongs in common to all God's children, the Priest recites it aloud, and begins by inviting us all to join in it.

OREMUS.

LET US PRAY.

Præceptis salutaribus moniti, et divina institutione formati, audemus dicere :

Having been taught by a saving precept, and following the form given us by a divine instruction, we thus presume to speak :

THE LORD'S PRAYER.

Pater noster, qui es in cœlis : Sanctificetur nomen tuum : Adveniat regnum tuum : Fiat voluntas tua, sicut in cœlo, et in terra : Panem nostrum quotidianum da nobis hodie : Et dimitte nobis debita nostra, sicut et nos dimittimus debitoribus nostris. Et ne nos inducas in tentationem.

Our Father, who art in heaven, hallowed be thy name ; thy kingdom come ; thy will be done on earth as it is in heaven. Give us this day our daily Bread ; *and forgive us our trespasses,* as we forgive them that trespass against us ; and lead us not into temptation.

Let us answer, with deep feeling of our misery :

Sed libera nos a malo.

But deliver us from evil.

The Priest falls once more into the silence of the holy Mysteries. His first word is an affectionate *Amen* to your last petition—*deliver us from evil*—on which he forms his own next prayer : and could

THE ORDINARY OF THE MASS. 65

he pray for anything more needed? *Evil* surrounds us everywhere, and the Lamb on our altar has been sent to expiate it and deliver us from it.

How many, O Lord, are the evils which beset us! Evils *past*, which are the wounds left on the soul by our sins, and strengthen her wicked propensities. Evils *present*, that is, the sins now at this very time upon our soul; the weakness of this poor soul; and the temptations which molest her. There are, also, *future* evils, that is the chastisement which our sins deserve from the hand of thy justice. In presence of this Host of our Salvation, we beseech thee O Lord, to deliver us from all these evils, and to accept in our favour the intercession of Mary the Mother of Jesus, of thy holy Apostles Peter and Paul and Andrew. Liberate us, break our chains, give us peace: through Jesus Christ, thy Son, who with thee liveth and reigneth God.

Libera nos, quæsumus, Domine, ab omnibus malis, præteritis, præsentibus et futuris: et, intercedente beata et gloriosa semper Virgine Dei Genitrice Maria, cum beatis Apostolis tuis Petro et Paulo, atque Andrea, et omnibus Sanctis, da propitius pacem in diebus nostris: ut ope misericordiæ tuæ adjuti, et a peccato simus semper liberi, et ab omni perturbatione securi. Per eumdem Dominum nostrum Jesum Christum Filium tuum, qui tecum vivit et regnat in unitate Spiritus Sancti Deus.

The Priest is anxious to announce the Peace, which he has asked and obtained; he therefore finishes his prayer aloud, saying:

World without end.

℟. Amen.

Per omnia sæcula sæculorum.

℟. Amen.

Then he says:

May the Peace of our Lord be ever with you.

Pax Domini sit semper vobiscum.

To this paternal wish, reply:

℟. And with thy spirit. ℟. Et cum spiritu tuo.

The Mystery is drawing to a close: God is about to be united with man, and man with God, by means of Communion. But first, an imposing and sublime rite takes place at the altar. So far the Priest has announced the Death of Jesus; it is time to proclaim his Resurrection. To this end, he reverently breaks the sacred Host; and having divided it into three parts, he puts one into the Chalice, thus reuniting the Body and Blood of the immortal Victim. Do you adore and say:

Hæc commixtio et consecratio Corporis et Sanguinis Domini nostri Jesu Christi, fiat accipientibus nobis in vitam æternam. Amen.	Glory be to thee, O Saviour of the world, who didst, in thy Passion, permit thy precious Blood to be separated from thy sacred Body, afterwards uniting them again together by thy divine power.

Offer now your prayer to the ever-living Lamb, whom St. John saw on the Altar of Heaven *standing, though slain*:[1] say to this your Lord and King, who has taken upon himself all our iniquities, in order to wash them away by his Blood:

Agnus Dei, qui tollis peccata mundi, miserere nobis.	Lamb of God, who takest away the sins of the world, have mercy on us.
Agnus Dei, qui tollis peccata mundi, miserere nobis.	Lamb of God, who takest away the sins of the world, have mercy on us.
Agnus Dei, qui tollis peccata mundi, dona nobis pacem.	Lamb of God, who takest away the sins of the world, give us *Peace*.

Peace is the grand object of our Saviour's coming into the world: he is the *Prince of Peace*. The divine Sacrament of the Eucharist ought therefore to be the Mystery of Peace, and the bond of Catholic Unity; for, as the Apostle says, *all we who partake of one Bread, are all one Bread and one Body*.[2] It

---

[1] Apoc. v. 6. [2] I. Cor. x. 17.

THE ORDINARY OF THE MASS. 67

is on this account that the Priest, now that he is on the point of receiving, in Communion, the Sacred Host, prays that fraternal Peace may be preserved in the Church, and more especially in this portion of it, which is assembled round the altar. Pray with him, and for the same blessing:

Lord Jesus Christ, who saidst to thy Apostles, "my peace I leave with you, my peace I give unto you:" regard not my sins, but the faith of thy Church, and grant her that peace and unity which is according to thy will. Who livest and reignest God for ever and ever. Amen.	Domine Jesu Christe, qui dixisti Apostolis tuis : Pacem relinquo vobis, pacem meam do vobis : ne respicias peccata mea, sed fidem Ecclesiæ tuæ : eamque secundum voluntatem tuam pacificare, et coadunare digneris. Qui vivis et regnas Deus, per omnia sæcula sæculorum. Amen.

If it be a High Mass, the Priest here gives the kiss of peace to the Deacon, who gives it to the Sub-Deacon, and he to the Choir. During this ceremony, you should excite within yourself feelings of Christian charity, and pardon your enemies, if you have any. Then continue to pray with the Priest:

Lord Jesus Christ, Son of the living God, who, according to the will of thy Father, through the co-operation of the Holy Ghost, hast by thy death given life to the world ; deliver me by this thy most sacred Body and Blood from all my iniquities, and from all evils ; and make me always adhere to thy commandments, and never suffer me to be separated from thee, who with the same God the Father and the Holy Ghost, livest and reignest God for ever and ever. Amen.	Domine Jesu Christe, Fili Dei vivi, qui ex voluntate Patris, cooperante Spiritu Sancto, per mortem tuam mundum vivificasti : libera me per hoc sacrosanctum Corpus, et Sanguinem tuum, ab omnibus iniquitatibus meis, et universis malis, et fac me tuis semper inhærere mandatis, et a te nunquam separari permittas. Qui cum eodem Deo Patre et Spiritu Sancto vivis et regnas Deus in sæcula sæculorum. Amen.

If you are going to Communion at this Mass, say the following Prayer; otherwise prepare yourself to make a Spiritual Communion:

Perceptio Corporis tui Domine Jesu Christe, quod ego indignus sumere præsumo, non mihi proveniat in judicium et condemnationem: sed pro tua pietate prosit mihi ad tutamentum mentis et corporis, et ad medelam percipiendam. Qui vivis et regnas cum Deo Patre in unitate Spiritus Sancti Deus, per omnia sæcula sæculorum. Amen.

Let not the participation of thy Body, O Lord Jesus Christ, which I, though unworthy, presume to receive, turn to my judgment and condemnation; but through thy mercy may it be a safeguard and remedy both to my soul and body. Who with God the Father, in the unity of the Holy Ghost, livest and reignest God for ever and ever. Amen.

When the Priest takes the Host into his hands, in order to his receiving it in Communion, say:

Panem cœlestem accipiam, et nomen Domini invocabo.

Come, my dear Jesus, come!

When he strikes his breast, confessing his unworthiness, say thrice with him these words, and in the same disposition as the Centurion of the Gospel, who first used them:

Domine, non sum dignus, ut intres sub tectum meum: sed tantum dic verbo, et sanabitur anima mea.

Lord, I am not worthy thou shouldst enter under my roof; say it only with one word of thine, and my soul will be healed.

Whilst the Priest receives the sacred Host, if you also are to communicate, adore profoundly your God, who is ready to take up his abode within you, and again say to him with the spouse: *Come, Lord Jesus, come!*

But should you not be going to receive sacramen-

THE ORDINARY OF THE MASS.

tally, make a Spiritual Communion. Adore Jesus Christ who thus visits your soul by his grace, and say to him:

' I give thee, O Jesus, this heart of mine, that thou mayest dwell in it, and do with me what thou wilt.	Corpus Domini nostri Jesu Christi, custodiat animam meam in vitam æternam. Amen.

Then the Priest takes the Chalice, in thanksgiving, and says:

What return shall I make to the Lord for all he hath given to me? I will take the Chalice of salvation, and will call upon the name of the Lord. Praising I will call upon the Lord, and I shall be saved from mine enemies.	Quid retribuam Domino pro omnibus, quæ retribuit mihi? Calicem salutaris accipiam, et nomen Domini invocabo. Laudans invocabo Dominum, et ab inimicis meis salvus ero.

But if you are to make a Sacramental Communion, you should, at this moment of the Priest's receiving the precious Blood, again adore the God who is coming to you, and keep to your prayer: *Come, Lord Jesus, come!*

If, on the contrary, you are going to communicate only spiritually, again adore your divine Master, and say to him:

I unite myself to thee, my beloved Jesus! do thou unite thyself to me! and never let us be separated.	Sanguis Domini nostri Jesu Christi custodiat animam meam in vitam æternam. Amen.

It is here that you must approach to the altar, if you are going to Communion. The dispositions suitable for Holy Communion, during this season of Septuagesima, are given in the next Chapter.

The Communion being finished, and whilst the Priest is purifying the Chalice the first time, say:

Quod ore sumpsimus, Domine, pura mente capiamus: et de munere temporali fiat nobis remedium sempiternum.	Thou hast visited me, O God, in these days of my pilgrimage; give me grace to treasure up the fruits of this visit for my future eternity.

Whilst the Priest is purifying the Chalice the second time, say:

Corpus tuum, Domine, quod sumpsi, et Sanguis quem potavi, adhæreat visceribus meis: et præsta ut in me non remaneat scelerum macula, quem pura et sancta refecerunt Sacramenta. Qui vivis et regnas in sæcula sæculorum. Amen.	Be thou for ever blessed, O my Saviour, for having admitted me to the sacred mystery of thy Body and Blood. May my heart and senses preserve, by thy grace, the purity which thou hast imparted to them; and I thus be rendered less unworthy of thy divine visit.

The Priest having read the Antiphon called the *Communion*, which is the first part of his Thanksgiving for the favour just received from God, whereby he has renewed his divine presence among us,—turns to the people with the usual salutation; after which he recites the Prayers, called the *Postcommunion*, which are the completion of the Thanksgiving. You will join him here also, thanking God for the unspeakable gift he has just lavished on you, and asking him, with most earnest entreaty, that he will bestow upon you a lasting spirit of compunction.

These Prayers having been recited, the Priest again turns to the people, and full of joy for the immense favour he and they have been receiving, he says:

Dominus vobiscum.	The Lord be with you.

Answer him:

Et cum spiritu tuo.	And with thy spirit.
Ite, Missa est.	Go, the Mass is finished.
℟. Deo gratias.	℟. Thanks be to God.

THE ORDINARY OF THE MASS.

The Priest makes a last Prayer, before giving you his blessing; pray with him:

Eternal thanks be to thee, O adorable Trinity, for the mercy thou hast showed to me, in permitting me to assist at this divine Sacrifice. Pardon me the negligence and coldness wherewith I have received so great a favour, and deign to confirm the Blessing, which thy Minister is about to give me in thy Name.

Placeat tibi, sancta Trinitas, obsequium servitutis meæ, quod oculis tuæ majestatis indignus obtuli, tibi sit acceptabile, mihique, et omnibus, pro quibus illud obtuli, sit, te miserante, propitiabile. Per Christum Dominum nostrum. Amen.

The Priest raises his hand, and thus blesses you:

May the Almighty God, Father, Son, and Holy Ghost, bless you!
℟. Amen.

Benedicat vos omnipotens Deus, Pater, et Filius, et Spiritus Sanctus.
℟. Amen.

He then concludes the Mass, by reading the first fourteen verses of the Gospel according to St. John, which tell us of the eternity of the Word, and of the mercy which led him to take upon himself our *flesh*, and to *dwell among us*. Pray that you may be of the number of those, who, now that he has come *unto his own, receive him*, and are made *the sons of God*.

℣. The Lord be with you.
℟. And with thy spirit.

℣. Dominus vobiscum.
℟. Et cum spiritu tuo.

THE LAST GOSPEL.

The beginning of the Holy Gospel according to John.

Initium sancti Evangelii secundum Joannem.

Ch. I.

In the beginning was the Word, and the Word was with God, and the Word was God. The same was in the beginning with God. All things were made by him, and with-

Cap. I.

In principio erat Verbum, et Verbum erat apud Deum, et Deus erat Verbum. Hoc erat in principio apud Deum. Omnia per ipsum facta sunt; et sine ipso factum est nihil. Quod factum est, in ipso vita erat, et vita erat lux hominum: et lux in tenebris lucet, et tenebræ eam non comprehenderunt. Fuit homo missus a Deo, cui nomen erat Joannes. Hic venit in testimonium, ut testimonium perhiberet de lumine, ut omnes crederent per illum. Non erat ille lux, sed ut testimonium perhiberet de lumine. Erat lux vera, quæ illuminat omnem hominem venientem in hunc mundum. In mundo erat, et mundus per ipsum factus est, et mundus eum non cognovit. In propria venit, et sui eum non receperunt. Quotquot autem receperunt eum, dedit eis potestatem filios Dei fieri, his, qui credunt in nomine ejus: qui non ex sanguinibus, neque ex voluntate carnis, neque ex voluntate viri, sed ex Deo nati sunt. ET VERBUM CARO FACTUM EST, et habitavit in nobis: et vidimus gloriam ejus, gloriam quasi Unigeniti a Patre, plenum gratiæ et veritatis.

℟. Deo gratias.

out him was made nothing that was made. In him was life, and the life was the light of men; and the light shineth in the darkness, and the darkness did not comprehend it. There was a man sent from God, whose name was John. This man came for a witness, to give testimony of the light, that all men might believe through him. He was not the light, but was to give testimony of the light. That was the true light which enlighteneth every man that cometh into this world. He was in the world, and the world was made by him, and the world knew him not. He came unto his own, and his own received him not. But as many as received him, to them he gave power to be made the sons of God; to them that believe in his name, who are born, not of blood, nor of the will of the flesh, nor of the will of man, but of God. AND THE WORD WAS MADE FLESH, and dwelt among us; and we saw his glory, as it were the glory of the Only-Begotten of the Father, full of grace and truth.

℟. Thanks be to God.

CHAPTER THE SIXTH.

ON HOLY COMMUNION

DURING PASSIONTIDE AND HOLY WEEK.

The Holy Mass is the true Sacrifice, of which the sacrifices of the Old Law were but figures. This Sacrifice was expected by mankind for four thousand years. It was during the present season that it was first offered up. It is now mysteriously renewed, each day, upon our Christian Altars.

No greater glory can be given to God than the celebration of this Sacrifice, wherein God himself is the Victim; at the same time, nothing can be more advantageous to man than the partaking of this divine Victim,—the becoming himself this Victim, the incorporating it with himself by Holy Communion, whereby is realised that wonderful promise of our Redeemer: *He that eateth my Flesh and drinketh my Blood, abideth in me, and I in him.*[1]

Now, it is by the immolation of our Redeemer on the Cross, that the Flesh of this Lamb of God has become *truly our food*,[2] and his Blood *truly our drink*.[3] By the mysteries of his Incarnation and Birth, we had him as our Brother; his Passion and Death have made him, both our Saviour, and our Food. Thus was realised that figurative sacrifice, which God prescribed to his people through Moses, and in which the victim, after being immolated, was to be eaten by the priest who offered it, and by the person in whose name it was offered.

---

[1] St. John, vi. 57.   [2] *Ibid.* 55.   [3] *Ibid.*

St. Paul, writing to the Corinthians, speaks thus: *As often as you shall eat this bread, and drink the chalice, you shall show the Death of the Lord, until he come.*[1] Therefore, there is a close relation between Holy Communion and our Saviour's Passion; and it is on this account that we are going to celebrate, during this present Season, the institution of the Holy Eucharist and the sacrifice of the Lamb, our Redeemer. The two anniversaries come close to each other. If Jesus has *desired with* so ardent a *desire to eat this* last *Pasch* with his Disciples,[2] it is because he had something infinitely grander to give them than he had given them the two preceding years: *then,* he gave them to eat of the flesh of the figurative lamb; but *now,* in this, the last Pasch, he is going to give them a pledge of pardon and immortality, by making them partake of the very substance of the true Lamb, whose Blood imparts remission of sin and opens the gate of heaven. He immolates himself on the Table of the Last Supper before men immolate him on Calvary; and this wondrous anticipation of his Sacrifice, in which he gives such a rich proof of his love and his power, is founded on the real Sacrifice of the morrow, which is to cost him every drop of his Blood.

In approaching, therefore, the Holy Table, during this Season of the Passion, the Faithful must be absorbed in the remembrance of the Lamb that was sacrificed for us: they must keep this great truth uppermost in their hearts,—that the divine Food which nourishes their souls, was prepared on Calvary; and that, although this Lamb is now living and impassable, yet it was by his Death on the Cross that he became our Food. The *Sinner,* reconciled to his offended God, must receive the Body of Jesus with sentiments of hearty contrition, and reproach

---

[1] I. Cor. xi. 26.　　[2] St. Luke, xxii. 15.

himself in all the bitterness of his soul, for having shed that precious Blood by his multiplied sins. The *Just* man must make his Communion, and humble himself with the thought, that he, too, has had too great a share in causing suffering to the innocent Lamb; and that if he now have reason to believe himself to be in the state of grace, he owes it to the Blood of the Victim who is about to be given to him for the increase of his spiritual life.

We will here give, as in our other Volumes, Acts which may serve as a preparation for Holy Communion during these two weeks. There are souls that feel the want of some such assistance as this; and, for the same reason, we will add a form of Thanksgiving for after Communion.

BEFORE COMMUNION.

ACT OF FAITH.

The signal grace which thou, O my God, hast granted to me, that I should know the wounds of my soul, has revealed to me the greatness of my misery. I have been taught how deep was the darkness that covered me, and how much I needed thy Divine Light. But, whilst the torch of Faith has thus shown me the abyss of my own poor nature, it has also taught me how wonderful are the works, which thy love of thy ungrateful creature has made thee undertake, in order that thou mightest raise him up and save him. It was for me thou didst assume my human nature, and wast born at Bethlehem; it is for me that thou fastest forty days in the Desert; it is for me that thou art soon to shed thy Blood on the Cross. Thou commandest me to believe these miracles of thy love. I do believe them, O my God, humbly and gratefully. I also believe, and with an equally lively Faith, that in a few moments, thou art to give thyself to me in this ineffable Mystery of Holy Communion. Thou sayest to me: *This is my Body—this is my Blood:*—thy word is enough; in spite of my unworthiness seeming to forbid the possibility of such Communion, I believe, I consent, I bow me down before thine infinite Truth. Oh! can there be Communion between the God of all holiness and a Sinner such as I?— And yet, thou assurest me, that thou art verily coming to me! I tremble, O Eternal Truth—but I believe. I confess that thy love of me is infinite, and that having resolved to give thyself to thy poor and sinful creature, thou wilt suffer no obstacle to stand in thy way!

ACT OF HUMILITY.

During the season just past, I have often contemplated, O my Jesus, thy coming from thy high throne into the bosom of Mary, thy uniting thy divine person to our weak mortal nature, and thy being born in the crib of a poor stable: and when I thought on these humiliations of my God, they taught me not only to love *thee* tenderly, but to know also my own nothingness, for I saw more clearly what an infinite distance there is between the Creature and his Creator; and, seeing these prodigies of thy immense love, I gladly confessed my own vileness. But now, dearest Saviour, I am led to consider something far more humiliating than the lowliness of my nature. That *Nothingness* should be but nothingness, is not a sin. No,—it is my sins that appal me. Sin has so long tyrannised over me; its consequences are still upon me; it has given me such dangerous tendencies; and I am so weak in resisting its bidding. When my first Parent sinned, he hid himself, lest he should meet thee; and thou biddest *me come* unto thee, not to sentence me to the punishment I deserve but to give me, oh! such a mark of love,—union with thyself! Can this be? Art thou not the infinitely holy God?—I must needs yield, and come, for thou art my sovereign Master; and who is there that dares resist thy will? I come, then, humbling myself, even to my very nothingness, before thee, and beseeching thee to pardon my coming, for I come because thou wilt have it so.

ACT OF CONTRITION.

And shall I, O my Jesus, confess thus the grievousness and multitude of my sins, without promising thee to sin no more? Thou wishest this sinner to be reconciled with thee, thou desirest to press him to thy Sacred Heart:—and could *he*, whilst thanking thee for this thy wonderful condescension, still love the accursed cause which made him thine enemy?—No, my infinitely merciful God, no! I will not, like my first Parent, seek to escape thy justice, but, like the Prodigal Son, I will arise and go to my Father; like Magdalene, I will take courage and enter the banquet-hall; and, though trembling at the sight of my sins, I will comply with thy loving invitation. My heart has no further attachment to sin, which I hate and detest as the enemy of thy honour and my own happiness. I am resolved to shun it from this time forward, and to spare no pains to free myself from its tyranny. There shall be no more of that easy life which chilled my love, nor of that studied indifference which dulled my conscience, nor of those dangerous habits which led me to stray from my loyalty to thee. Despise not, O God, this my humble and contrite heart.

ACT OF LOVE.

Such is thy love for us in this world, O my Jesus, that, as thyself sayest, thou art *come not to judge, but to save.* I should not satisfy thee, in this happy Communion hour, were I to offer thee but this salutary fear, which has led me to thy sacred feet, and this shame-stricken conscience, which makes me tremble in thy holy presence. The visit thou art about to pay me, is a visit of Love. The Sacrament, which is going to unite me to thee, is the Sacrament of thy Love. Thou, my Good Shepherd, hast said, that he *loves* most, who has been *forgiven* most. *My* heart then must dare to love thee; it must love thee with all its warmth ; the very recollection of its past disloyalty must make its loving thee doubly needed and doubly fervent. Ah! sweet Lord!—see this poor heart of mine ; strengthen it, console it, drive away its fears, make it feel that thou art its Jesus ! It has come back to thee, because it *feared* thee ; if it *love* thee, it will never again leave thee.

And thou, O Mary, *Refuge of Sinners,* help me to love Him, who is thy Son, and our Brother.—Holy Angels!—ye who live eternally on that love, which has never ceased to glow in your mighty spirits,—remember, I reverently pray you, that this God created me, as he did you, that I might love him.—All ye holy Saints of God ! I beseech you, by the love wherewith ye are inebriated in heaven, graciously give me a thought, and prepare now my heart to be united with him. Amen.

AFTER COMMUNION.

ACT OF ADORATION.

Thou art here within me, great God of heaven! Thou art, at this moment, residing in a sinner's heart ! I, yea, I, am thy temple, thy throne, thy resting-place !—How shall I worthily adore thee, thee that hast deigned to come down into this abyss of my lowliness and misery ? The angels veil their faces in thy presence ; thy Saints lay their crowns at thy feet ; and I, that am but a sinful mortal, how shall I sufficiently honour thee, O Infinite Power, Infinite Wisdom, Infinite Goodness?—This soul, wherein thou art now dwelling, has presumed so many times to set thee at defiance, and boldly disobey and break thy commands. And thou canst come to me after all this, and bring all thy beauty and greatness with thee!—What else can I do, but give thee the homage of a heart, that knows not how to bear the immensity of the honour thou art now lavishing on me? Yes, my own wonderful and loving God, I adore thee; I acknowledge thee to be the Sovereign Being, the Creator and preserver of all creatures, and the undisputed Master of everything that belongs to me. I delightedly confess my dependence on thee, and offer thee, with all my heart, my humble service.

ACT OF THANKSGIVING.

Thy greatness, O my God, is infinite; but thy goodness to me is incomprehensible. Thy being now, present within this breast of mine is, I know, a proof of that immense power, which shows itself where and when it wills; but it is also a mark of thy love for me. Thou art come to my soul, that thou mayest be closely united with her, comfort her, give her a new life, and bring her all good things. Oh! who will teach me how to value this grace, and thank thee for it in a becoming way? But, how shall I hope to value it as I ought, when I am not able to understand either the love, that brings thee thus within me, nor my own need of having thee? And when I think of my inability to make thee a suitable return of thanks, I feel as though I can give thee nothing but my speechless gratitude. Yet thou willest that this my heart, poor as it is, should give thee its thanks; thou takest delight in receiving its worthless homage. Take it, then, my loving Jesus! I give it thee with all possible joy, and beseech thee to reveal unto me the immensity of thy gift, and to *enrich* me more that I may *give* thee more.

ACT OF LOVE.

But nothing will satisfy thee, O my Infinite Treasure unless I give thee my *love*. Thou hast ever loved *me*, and thou art still loving me; I must love thee in return! Thou hast borne with me, thou hast forgiven me, thou art, at this moment, overpowering me with honour and riches; and all this out of love for me! The return thou askest of me, is my *love*. Gratitude will not content thee—thou wilt have my *love!*—But, Jesus, my dear Jesus!—my past life—the long years I have spent in offending thee—rise up before me, and tell me to hide myself from thee! And yet, whither could I go without carrying thee within me, for thou hast taken up thine abode in my inmost soul? No,—I will not run from thee! I will summon all the energies of my heart, to tell thee, that I love thee; that thy love for me has emboldened me; that I belong to thee; that I love thee above all else that I love; and that henceforth, all my joy and happiness shall be in pleasing thee, and doing whatsoever thou askest of me.

ACT OF OBLATION.

I know, dear Jesus, that what thou askest of me is not the passing sentiment of a heart excited by the thought of thy goodness towards it. Thou hast loved me from eternity; thou lovedst me, even when I was doing nothing for thee; thou hast given me light to know my miseries; thou hast shielded me against thine own angry justice; thou hast mercifully pardoned me a countless number of times; thou art even now embracing me with tenderest love;—and all these works of thy almighty hand have been but for one end,—to make me give myself to thee, and live, at last, for thee. It is this thou wouldst obtain of me, by granting me this precious earnest of thy love, which I have just received. Thou hast said, speaking of this ineffable gift: *As I live by the Father; so he that eateth me, the same also shall live by me.*[1] Henceforth, O *Bread, which came down from heaven!*[2] thou art the source of my life. Now, more than ever, my life belongs to thee. I give it unto thee. I dedicate unto thee my soul, my body, my faculties, my whole being. Do thou direct and govern me. I resign myself entirely into thy hands. I am blind, but thy light will guide me; I am weak, but thy power will uphold me; I am inconstant, but thy unchangeableness will give me stability. I trust unreservedly in thy mercy, which never abandon them that hope in thee.

O Mary! pray for me, that I lose not the fruit of this Visit.—Holy Angels! watch over this dwelling-place of your Lord, which he has so mercifully chosen: let nothing defile it.—Oh! all ye Saints of God! pray for the sinner, unto whom he has given this pledge of his Divine pardon.

---

[1] St. John, vi. 58. [2] *Ibid.* 51.

CHAPTER THE SEVENTH.

OF THE OFFICE OF VESPERS FOR SUNDAYS AND FEASTS,

DURING PASSIONTIDE AND HOLY WEEK.

THE Office of *Vespers*, or *Even-Song*, consists firstly of the Five following Psalms, and Antiphons. According to our custom, we preface each Psalm with a short explanation, in order to draw the attention to what is most in harmony with the spirit of this Season.

After the *Pater* and *Ave* have been said in secret, the Church commences this Hour with her favourite supplication:

℣. Deus in adjutorium meum intende.	℣. Incline unto my aid, O God.
℟. Domine, ad adjuvandum me festina.	℟. O Lord, make haste to help me.
Gloria Patri, et Filio, et Spiritui Sancto:	Glory be to the Father, and to the Son, and to the Holy Ghost.
Sicut erat in principio et nunc et semper, et in sæcula sæculorum. Amen.	As it was in the beginning, is now, and ever shall be, world without end. Amen.
Laus tibi, Domine, Rex æternæ gloriæ.	Praise be to thee, O Lord, King of eternal glory.
ANT. Dixit Dominus.	ANT. The Lord said.

The first Psalm is a prophecy of the future glory of the Messias; but it also speaks of his humiliations. It tells of the triumphs of Christ; but, before his exaltation, he is to *drink of the torrent* of sufferings.

SUNDAY'S VESPERS.

PSALM 109.

The Lord said to my Lord, *his Son:* Sit thou at my right hand, *and reign with me.*
Until, *on the day of thy last coming,* I make thy enemies thy footstool.
O Christ! the Lord thy *Father,* will send forth the sceptre of thy power out of Sion: *from thence* rule thou in the midst of thy enemies.
With thee is the principality in the day of thy strength, in the brightness of the saints: *For the Father hath said to thee:* From the womb before the day-star I begot thee.
The Lord hath sworn, and he will not repent: *he hath said, speaking of thee, the God-Man:* Thou art a Priest for ever, according to the order of Melchisedech.
Therefore, O Father, the Lord *thy Son* is at thy right hand: he· hath broken kings in the day of his wrath.
He shall *also* judge among nations: *in that terrible coming,* he shall fill the ruins *of the world:* he shall crush the heads in the land of many.
He cometh now in humility; he shall drink, in the way, of the torrent *of sufferings:* therefore, shall he lift up the head.
ANT. The Lord said to my Lord, sit thou at my right hand.
ANT. Faithful.

Dixit Dominus Domino meo: * Sede a dextris meis.
Donec ponam inimicos tuos: * scabellum pedum tuorum.
Virgam virtutis tuæ emittet Dominus ex Sion: * dominare in medio inimicorum tuorum.
Tecum principium in die virtutis tuæ in splendoribus sanctorum: * ex utero ante luciferum genui te.
Juravit Dominus, et non pœnitebit eum: * Tu es Sacerdos in æternum secundum ordinem Melchisedech.

Dominus a dextris tuis :* confregit in die iræ suæ reges.

Judicabit in nationibus, implebit ruinas: * conquassabit capita in terra multorum.

De torrente in via bibet: * propterea exaltabit caput.

ANT. Dixit Dominus Domino meo, sede a dextris meis.
ANT. Fidelia.

The following Psalm commemorates the mercies of God to his *people:* but of these, the greatest is his having given us a *Redeemer*. He has made an eternal *Covenant* with us: but this *Covenant* was signed with the Blood of his own Son.

PSALM 110.

Confitebor tibi, Domine, in toto corde meo : * in concilio justorum et congregatione.

Magna opera Domini : * exquisita in omnes voluntates ejus.

Confessio et magnificentia opus ejus : * et justitia ejus manet in sæculum sæculi.

Memoriam fecit mirabilium suorum, misericors et miserator Dominus : * escam dedit timentibus se.

Memor erit in sæculum testamenti sui : * virtutem operum suorum annuntiabit populo suo.

Ut det illis hereditatem Gentium : * opera manuum ejus veritas et judicium.

Fidelia omnia mandata ejus, confirmata in sæculum sæculi : * facta in veritate et æquitate.

Redemptionem misit populo suo : * mandavit in æternum testamentum suum.

Sanctum et terribile nomen ejus : * initium sapientiæ timor Domini.

Intellectus bonus omnibus facientibus eum : * laudatio ejus manet in sæculum sæculi.

ANT. Fidelia omnia man-

I will praise thee, O Lord, with my whole heart: in the counsel of the just, and in the congregation.

Great are the works of the Lord: sought out according to all his wills.

His work is praise and magnificence: and his justice continueth for ever and ever.

He hath made a remembrance of his wonderful works, being a merciful and gracious Lord: he hath given food to them that fear him.

He will be mindful for ever of his covenant *with men:* he will show forth to his people the power of his works.

That he may give them, *his Church,* the inheritance of the Gentiles: the works of his hand are truth and judgment.

All his commandments are faithful, confirmed for ever and ever: made in truth and equity.

He hath sent redemption to his people; he hath *thereby* commanded his covenant for ever.

Holy and terrible is his name: the fear of the Lord is the beginning of wisdom.

A good understanding to all that do it: his praise continueth for ever and ever.

ANT. Faithful are all his

commandments; confirmed for ever and ever.
ANT. In his commandments.

data ejus; confirmata in sæculum sæculi.
ANT. In mandatis.

The next Psalm sings the happiness of the *just man*, and his hopes on the day of his Lord's coming. It tells us, likewise, of the confusion and despair which will torment the *sinner*, who, during life, was insensible to his own interests, and deaf to the invitations made him by the Church.

PSALM 111.

Blessed is the man that feareth the Lord: he shall delight exceedingly in his commandments.

His seed shall be mighty upon earth: the generation of the righteous shall be blessed.

Glory and wealth shall be in his house: and his justice remaineth for ever and ever.

To the righteous a light is risen up in darkness: he is merciful, and compassionate, and just.

Acceptable is the man that showeth mercy and lendeth; he shall order his words with judgment: because he shall not be moved for ever.

The just shall be in everlasting remembrance: he shall not fear the evil hearing.

His heart is ready to hope in the Lord; his heart is strengthened: he shall not be moved until he look over his enemies.

He hath distributed, he hath given to the poor; his

Beatus vir, qui timet Dominum : * in mandatis ejus volet nimis.

Potens in terra erit semen ejus : * generatio rectorum benedicetur.

Gloria, et divitiæ in domo ejus : * et justitia ejus manet in sæculum sæculi.

Exortum est in tenebris lumen rectis : * misericors, et miserator, et justus.

Jucundus homo, qui miseretur et commodat, disponet sermones suos in judicio : * quia in æternum non commovebitur.

In memoria æterna erit justus : * ab auditione mala non timebit.

Paratum cor ejus sperare in Domino, confirmatum est cor ejus : * non commovebitur donec despiciat inimicos suos.

Dispersit, dedit pauperibus, justitia ejus manet in

sæculum sæculi : * cornu ejus exaltabitur in gloria.

Peccator videbit, et irascetur, dentibus suis fremet et tabescet : * desiderium peccatorum peribit.

ANT. In mandatis ejus cupit nimis.

ANT. Sit nomen Domini.

justice remaineth for ever and ever : his horn shall be exalted in glory.

The wicked shall see, and shall be angry ; he shall gnash with his teeth, and pine away; the desire of the wicked shall perish.

ANT. In his commandments he delighteth exceedingly.

ANT. May the name of the Lord.

The Psalm, *Laudate pueri*, is a Canticle of praise to the Lord, who, from his high heaven, has taken pity on the fallen human race, and facilitated its return to its Maker.

PSALM 112.

Laudate, pueri, Dominum : * laudate nomen Domini.

Sit nomen Domini benedictum : * ex hoc nunc et usque in sæculum.

A solis ortu usque ad occasum : * laudabile nomen Domini.

Excelsus super omnes Gentes Dominus : * et super cœlos gloria ejus.

Quis sicut Dominus Deus noster qui in altis habitat : * et humilia respicit in cœlo et in terra ?

Suscitans a terra inopem:* et de stercore erigens pauperem.

Ut collocet eum cum principibus : * cum principibus populi sui.

Qui habitare facit sterilem

Praise the Lord, ye children ; praise ye the name of the Lord.

Blessed be the name of the Lord : from henceforth now and for ever.

From the rising of the sun unto the going down of the same, the name of the Lord is worthy of praise.

The Lord is high above all nations : and his glory above the heavens.

Who is as the Lord our God, who dwelleth on high : and looketh down on the low things in heaven and in earth ?

Raising up the needy from the earth : and lifting up the poor out of the dunghill.

That he may place him with princes : with the princes of his people.

Who maketh a barren woman to dwell in a house, the joyful mother of children: * matrem filiorum lætantem.

ANT. May the name of the Lord be for ever blessed.

ANT. Sit nomen Domini benedictum in sæcula.

ANT. We that live.

ANT. Nos qui vivimus.

The fifth Psalm, *In exitu*, recounts the prodigies witnessed under the ancient Covenant: they were *figures*, whose realities are to be accomplished in us, if we will but return to the Lord our God. He will deliver *Israel* from Egypt, emancipate the *Gentiles* from their idolatry, and pour out a *blessing* on every man who will consent to fear and love the Lord.

PSALM 113.

When Israel went out of Egypt, the house of Jacob from a barbarous people.

Judea was made his sanctuary, Israel his dominion.

The sea saw and fled; Jordan was turned back.

The mountains skipped like rams: and the hills like the lambs of the flock.

What ailed thee, O thou sea, that thou didst flee: and thou, O Jordan, that thou wast turned back?

Ye mountains that ye skipped like rams: and ye hills like lambs of the flock?

At the presence of the Lord the earth was moved, at the presence of the God of Jacob.

Who turned the rock into pools of water, and the stony hills into fountains of waters.

Not to us, O Lord, not to us: but to thy name give glory.

For thy mercy, and for thy

In exitu Israel de Ægypto: * domus Jacob de populo barbaro.

Facta est Judæa sanctificatio ejus: * Israel potestas ejus.

Mare vidit, et fugit: * Jordanis conversus est retrorsum.

Montes exsultaverunt ut arietes: * et colles sicut agni ovium.

Quid est tibi, mare, quod fugisti: * et tu, Jordanis, quia conversus es retrorsum?

Montes exsultastis sicut arietes: * et colles sicut agni ovium?

A facie Domini mota est terra: a facie Dei Jacob.

Qui convertit petram in stagna aquarum: * et rupem in fontes aquarum.

Non nobis, Domine, non nobis: * sed nomini tuo da gloriam.

Super misericordia tua, et

veritate tua : * nequando dicant Gentes: Ubi est Deus eorum ?

Deus autem noster in cœlo : * omnia quæcumque voluit, fecit.

Simulacra Gentium argentum et aurum : * opera manuum hominum.

Os habent, et non loquentur : * oculos habent, et non videbunt.

Aures habent, et non audient :* nares habent et non odorabunt.

Manus habent, et non palpabunt, pedes habent et non ambulabunt : * non clamabunt in gutture suo.

Similes illis fiant qui faciunt ea: * et omnes qui confidunt in eis.

Domus Israël speravit in Domino : * adjutor eorum, et protector eorum est.

Domus Aaron speravit in Domino : * adjutor eorum, et protector eorum est.

Qui timent Dominum, speraverunt in Domino : * adjutor eorum, et protector eorum est.

Dominus memor fuit nostri : * et benedixit nobis.

Benedixit domui Israel : * benedixit domui Aaron.

Benedixit omnibus qui timent Dominum : * pusillis cum majoribus.

Adjiciat Dominus super vos : * super vos, et super filios vestros.

Benedicti vos a Domino : * qui fecit cœlum et terram.

Cœlum cœli Domino : *

truth's sake : lest the Gentiles should say : Where is their God?

But our God is in heaven : he hath done all things whatsoever he would.

The idols of the Gentiles are silver and gold : the works of the hands of men.

They have mouths, and speak not : they have eyes, and see not.

They have ears, and hear not : they have noses, and smell not.

They have hands, and feel not : they have feet, and walk not : neither shall they cry out through their throat.

Let them that make them become like unto them : and all such as trust in them.

The house of Israel hath hoped in the Lord : he is their helper and their protector.

The house of Aaron hath hoped in the Lord : he is their helper and their protector.

They that feared the Lord have hoped in the Lord : he is their helper and their protector.

The Lord hath been mindful of us, and hath blessed us.

He hath blessed the house of Israel : he hath blessed the house of Aaron.

He hath blessed all that fear the Lord, both little and great.

May the Lord add blessings upon you: upon you, and upon your children.

Blessed be you of the Lord, who made heaven and earth.

The heaven of heaven is the

Lord's: but the earth he has given to the children of men.

The dead shall not praise thee, O Lord: nor any of them that go down to hell.

But we that live bless the Lord: from this time now and for ever.

A<small>NT</small>. We that live bless the Lord.

terram autem dedit filiis hominum.

Non mortui laudabunt te, Domine: * neque omnes qui descendunt in infernum.

Sed nos qui vivimus, benedicimus Domino: * ex hoc nunc et usque in sæculum.

A<small>NT</small>. Nos qui vivimus, benedicimus Domino.

After these five Psalms, a short Lesson from the holy Scriptures is then read. It is called *Capitulum*, because it is always very short. The ones for the Sundays of Lent are given in the *Proper* of each.

After the Capitulum, follows the Hymn, *Vexilla Regis*. It is the "Hymn of the Cross," and was composed by St. Venantius Fortunatus, at the request of St. Radegund.

HYMN.*

The Standard of our King comes forth: the mystery of the Cross shines upon us,— that Cross on which Life suffered death, and by his Death gave life.

Vexilla Regis prodeunt; Fulget Crucis mysterium, Qua Vita mortem pertulit, Et morte vitam protulit.

---

* According to the Monastic Rite, it is as follows:—

R. *breve*. De ore leonis, * Libera me, Domine. De ore.
V. Et a cornibus unicornium humilitatem meam. * Libera.
Then is repeated: R. De ore.

Vexilla Regis prodeunt;
Fulget Crucis mysterium,
Quo carne carnis Conditor
Suspensus est patibulo.
Quo vulneratus insuper
Mucrone diro lanceæ,
Ut nos lavaret crimine,
Manavit unda et sanguine.
Impleta sunt quæ concinit
David fideli carmine,

Dicens: In nationibus
Regnavit a ligno Deus.
Arbor decora et fulgida,
Ornata Regis purpura,
Electa digno stipite
Tam sancta membra tangere.
O Crux, ave, spes unica,
Hoc Passionis tempore,
Auge piis justitiam,
Reisque dona veniam.
Te summa, Deus, Trinitas,
Collaudet omnis spiritus:
Quos per Crucis mysterium
Salvas, rege per sæcula. Amen.

Quæ vulnerata lanceæ
Mucrone diro, criminum
Ut nos lavaret sordibus,
Manavit unda et sanguine.

Impleta sunt quæ concinit
David fideli carmine,
Dicendo nationibus :
Regnavit a ligno Deus.

Arbor decora et fulgida,
Ornata regis purpura,
Electa digno stipite
Tam sancta membra tangere.
Beata cujus brachiis
Pretium pependit sæculi,
Statera facta corporis,
Tulitque prædam tartari.

O Crux, ave, spes unica,
Hoc Passionis tempore,
Piis adauge gratiam,
Reisque dele crimina.

Te, fons salutis, Trinitas,
Collaudet omnis spiritus :
Quibus Crucis victoriam
Largiris, adde præmium.
　　Amen.

℣. Eripe me, Domine, ab homine malo.
℟. A viro iniquo eripe me.

He was pierced with the cruel Spear, that, by the Water and the Blood, which flowed from the wound, he might cleanse us from sin.
Here, on the Cross, was fulfilled the prophecy, foretold to the nations in David's truthful words : "God hath reigned from the Tree."
O fair and shining Tree ! beautified by the scarlet of the King, and chosen as the noble trunk that was to touch such sacred limbs !
O blessed Tree ! on whose arms hung the ransom of the world ! It was the balance, wherein was placed the Body of Jesus, and thereby hell lost its prey.
Hail, O Cross ! our only hope ! During these days of the Passion, increase to the good their grace, and cleanse sinners from their guilt.
May every spirit praise thee, O Holy Trinity, thou Fount of Salvation ! and by the Cross, whereby thou gavest us victory, give us, too, our recompense. Amen.

℣. Deliver me, O Lord, from the evil man.
℟. Rescue me from the unjust man.

Then is said the *Magnificat* Antiphon, which is to be found in the *Proper*. After this, the Church sings the Canticle of Mary, the *Magnificat*, in which are celebrated the Divine Maternity and all its consequent blessings. This exquisite Canticle is an essential part of the Vespers throughout the year. Let us unite with *all generations*, and *call* her "*Blessed ;*" but let us, also, enter into those sentiments of *Humility*, which she recommends to us both by her words and her example. Her inspired lips speak to us this promise: If the great God whose triumph is to gladden us on the glorious Day of Easter, find us humble and submissive,—he will *exalt* us, yea, raise us up even to himself; if we confess our misery and *poverty* to him, he will *enrich* us, even to the *full*, with every blessing.

OUR LADY'S CANTICLE.

(St. Luke, i.)

My soul doth magnify the Lord;

And my spirit hath rejoiced in God my Saviour.

Because he hath regarded the humility of his handmaid: for, behold from henceforth all generations shall call me Blessed.

Because he that is mighty hath done great things to me: and holy is his name.

And his mercy is from generation unto generation, to them that fear him.

He hath showed might in his arm: he hath scattered the proud in the conceit of their heart.

He hath put down the mighty from their seat: and hath exalted the humble.

He hath filled the hungry with good things: and the rich he hath sent empty away.

He hath received Israel his servant, being mindful of his mercy.

As he spake to our fathers, to Abraham and to his seed for ever.

Magnificat: * anima mea Dominum:

Et exsultavit spiritus meus: * in Deo salutari meo.

Quia respexit humilitatem ancillæ suæ: * ecce enim ex hoc Beatam me dicent omnes generationes.

Quia fecit mihi magna qui potens est: * et sanctum nomen ejus.

Et misericordia ejus a progenie in progenies: * timentibus eum.

Fecit potentiam in brachio suo: * dispersit superbos mente cordis sui.

Deposuit potentes de sede: * et exaltavit humiles.

Esurientes implevit bonis: * et divites dimisit inanes.

Suscepit Israël puerum suum: * recordatus misericordiæ suæ.

Sicut locutus est ad patres nostros: * Abraham et semini ejus in sæcula.

The *Magnificat* Antiphon is then repeated. The Prayer, or Collect, will be found in the Proper of each Sunday.

The Vespers end with the following Versicles:

℣. Benedicamus Domino.
℟. Deo gratias.
℣. Fidelium animæ per misericordiam Dei requiescant in pace.

℟. Amen.

℣. Let us bless the Lord.
℟. Thanks be to God.
℣. May the souls of the Faithful departed, through the mercy of God, rest in peace.

℟. Amen.

CHAPTER THE EIGHTH.

ON THE OFFICE OF COMPLINE,

DURING PASSIONTIDE AND HOLY WEEK.

This Office, which concludes the day, commences by a warning of the dangers of the night: then immediately follows the public Confession of our sins, as a powerful means of propitiating the divine justice, and obtaining God's help, now that we are going to spend so many hours in the unconscious and therefore dangerous state of sleep, which is also such an image of death.

The Lector, addressing the Priest, says to him:

Pray, Father, give thy blessing.	℣. Jube, Domine, benedicere.

The Priest answers:

May the Almighty Lord grant us a quiet night and a perfect end. ℞. Amen.	Noctem quietam, et finem perfectum concedat nobis Dominus omnipotens. ℞. Amen.

The Lector then reads these words, from the first Epistle of St. Peter:

Brethren, be sober and watch: for your adversary the devil goes about like a roaring lion, seeking whom he may devour: resist him, being strong in faith. But thou, O Lord, have mercy on us.	Fratres: Sobrii estote, et vigilate: quia adversarius vester diabolus, tamquam leo rugiens circuit quærens quem devoret: cui resistite fortes in fide. Tu autem, Domine, miserere nobis.

The Choir answers:

℟. Deo gratias.   ℟. Thanks be to God.

Then, the Priest:

℣. Adjutorium nostrum in nomine Domine.   ℣. Our help is in the name of the Lord.

The Choir:

℟. Qui fecit cœlum et terram.   ℟. Who hath made heaven and earth.

Then the Lord's Prayer is recited in secret; after which the Priest says the *Confiteor*; and, when he has finished, the Choir says:

Misereatur tui omnipotens Deus, et dimissis peccatis tuis, perducat te ad vitam æternam.   May Almighty God be merciful to thee, and, forgiving thy sins, bring thee to everlasting life.

The Priest having answered *Amen*, the Choir repeats the *Confiteor*, thus:

Confiteor Deo Omnipotenti, beatæ Mariæ semper Virgini, beato Michaeli Archangelo, beato Joanni Baptistæ, sanctis Apostolis Petro et Paulo, omnibus sanctis, et tibi Pater: quia peccavi nimis, cogitatione, verbo, et opere: mea culpa, mea culpa, mea maxima culpa. Ideo precor beatam Mariam semper Virginem, beatum Michaelem Archangelum, beatum Joannem Baptistam, sanctos Apostolos Petrum et Paulum, omnes sanctos, et te, Pater, orare pro me ad Dominum Deum nostrum.   I confess to Almighty God, to Blessed Mary ever Virgin, to blessed Michael the Archangel, to blessed John Baptist, to the holy Apostles Peter and Paul, to all the saints, and to thee, Father, that I have sinned exceedingly in thought, word, and deed, through my fault, through my fault, through my most grievous fault. Therefore I beseech the Blessed Mary ever Virgin, blessed Michael the Archangel, blessed John Baptist, the holy Apostles Peter and Paul, and all the saints, and thee, Father, to pray to our Lord God for me.

The Priest then says:

May Almighty God be merciful to you, and, forgiving your sins, bring you to everlasting life.
℟. Amen.
May the Almighty and merciful Lord grant us pardon, absolution, and remission of our sins.

℟. Amen.
℣. Convert us, O God, our Saviour.
℟. And turn away thy anger from us.
℣. Incline unto my aid, O God.
℟. O Lord, make haste to help me.
Glory, &c.
Praise be to thee, O Lord, King of eternal glory.
ANT. Have mercy.

Misereatur vestri omnipotens Deus, et dimissis peccatis vestris, perducat vos ad vitam æternam.
℟. Amen.
Indulgentiam, absolutionem, et remissionem peccatorum nostrorum, tribuat nobis omnipotens et misericors Dominus.

℟. Amen.
℣. Converte nos, Deus, Salutaris noster.
℟. Et averte iram tuam a nobis.
℣. Deus, in adjutorium meum intende.
℟. Domine, ad adjuvandum me festina.
Gloria Patri, &c.
Laus tibi, Domine, Rex æternæ gloriæ.
ANT. Miserere.

The *first* Psalm expresses the confidence with which the just man *sleeps in peace;* but it, also, rebukes those tepid Christians, whose *dull hearts* are but too often enslaved to *vanity* and *lies,* and exhorts them to examine, at the close of the day, the thoughts of their *hearts,* and be *sorry for them* at that time of stillness and repose.

PSALM 4.

When I called upon him, the God of my justice heard me: when I was in distress, thou hast enlarged me.
Have mercy on me: and hear my prayer.
O ye sons of men, how long

Cum invocarem exaudivit me Deus justitiæ meæ: * in tribulatione dilatasti mihi.
Miserere mei: * et exaudi orationem meam.
Filii hominum, usquequo

gravi corde : * ut quid diligitis vanitatem, et quæritis mendacium ?	will you be dull of heart ? why do you love vanity, and seek after lying ?
Et scitote quoniam mirificavit Dominus sanctum suum : * Dominus exaudiet me, cum clamavero ad eum.	Know ye also that the Lord hath made his Holy One wonderful : the Lord will hear me, when I shall cry unto him.
Irascimini, et nolite peccare : * quæ dicitis in cordibus vestris, in cubilibus vestris compungimini.	Be ye angry, and sin not : the things you say in your hearts, be sorry for them upon your beds.
Sacrificate sacrificium justitiæ, et sperate in Domino: * multi dicunt : Quis ostendit nobis bona?	Offer up the sacrifice of justice, and trust in the Lord : many say, who showeth us good things ?
Signatum est super nos lumen vultus tui Domine : * dedisti lætitiam in corde meo.	The Light of thy countenance, O Lord, is signed upon us : thou hast given gladness in my heart.
A fructu frumenti, vini et olei sui : * multiplicati sunt.	By the fruit of their corn, their wine, and oil, they are multiplied.
In pace in idipsum : * dormiam et requiescam.	In peace, in the self same, I will sleep, and I will rest.
Quoniam tu, Domine, singulariter in spe : * constituisti me.	For thou, O Lord, singularly hast settled me in hope.

The Church has introduced here the first six Verses of the thirtieth Psalm, because they contain the prayer which our Saviour made when dying : *Into thy hands, O Lord, I commend my spirit!*— words so beautifully appropriate in this Office of the close of day.

PSALM 30.

In te, Domine, speravi, non confundar in æternum: * in justitia tua libera me.	In thee, O Lord, have I hoped, let me never be confounded : deliver me in thy justice.
Inclina ad me aurem tuam : * accelera ut eruas me.	Bow down thy ear to me : make haste to deliver me.

Be thou unto me a God, a protector and a house of refuge, to save me.

For thou art my strength, and my refuge : and for thy name's sake thou wilt lead me, and nourish me.
Thou wilt bring me out of this snare, which they have hidden for me : for thou art my protector.
Into thy hands I commend my spirit: thou hast redeemed me, O Lord, the God of truth.

Esto mihi in Deum protectorum, et in domum refugii : * ut salvum me facias.
Quoniam fortitudo mea, et refugium meum es tu : * et propter nomen tuum deduces me, et enutries me.
Educes me de laqueo hoc, quem absconderunt mihi: * quoniam tu es protector meus.
In manus tuas commendo spiritum meum : * redemisti me, Domine, Deus veritatis.

The *third* Psalm gives the motives of the Just man's confidence, even during the dangers of the night. The description here given of Peace of mind, should make the sinner long for a reconciliation with his God, that so he, too, may enjoy that divine protection, without which there can be no security or happiness in this life of peril and misery.

PSALM 90.

He that dwelleth in the aid of the Most High, shall abide under the protection of the God of heaven.
He shall say to the Lord: Thou art my protector, and my refuge : my God, in him will I trust.
For he hath delivered me from the snare of the hunters: and from the sharp word.
He will overshadow thee with his shoulders: and under his wings thou shalt trust.
His truth shall compass thee with a shield : thou shalt not be afraid of the terror of the night.

Qui habitat in adjutorio Altissimi : * in protectione Dei cœli commorabitur.

Dicet Domino : Susceptor meus es tu, et refugium meum : * Deus meus, sperabo in eum.
Quoniam ipse liberavit me de laqueo venantium : * et a verbo aspero.
Scapulis suis obumbrabit tibi : * et sub pennis ejus sperabis.
Scuto circumdabit te veritas ejus : * non timebis a timore nocturno.

*

A sagitta volante in die, a negotio perambulante in tenebris : * ab incursu, et dæmonio meridiano.

Cadent a latere tuo mille, et decem millia a dextris tuis : * ad te autem non appropinquabit.

Verumtamen oculis tuis considerabis : * et retributionem peccatorum videbis.

Quoniam tu es, Domine, spes mea : Altissimum posuisti refugium tuum.

Non accedet ad te malum: * et flagellum non appropinquabit tabernaculo tuo.

Quoniam Angelis suis mandavit de te: * ut custodiant te in omnibus viis tuis.

In manibus portabunt te: * ne forte offendas ad lapidem pedem tuum.

Super aspidem et basiliscum ambulabis: * et conculcabis leonem et draconem.

Quoniam in me speravit, liberabo eum : * protegam eum, quoniam cognovit nomen meum.

Clamabit ad me, et ego exaudiam eum : * cum ipso sum in tribulatione, eripiam eum, et glorificabo eum.

Longitudine dierum replebo eum : * et ostendam illi Salutare meum.

Of the arrow that flieth in the day : of the business that walketh about in the dark : of invasion, or of the noonday devil.

A thousand shall fall at thy side, and ten thousand at thy right hand : but it shall not come nigh thee.

But thou shalt consider with thy eyes : and shalt see the reward of the wicked.

Because *thou hast said*. Thou, O Lord, art my hope : thou hast made the Most High thy refuge.

There shall no evil come to thee, nor shall the scourge come near thy dwelling.

For he hath given his Angels charge over thee: to keep thee in all thy ways.

In their hands they shall bear thee up : lest thou dash thy foot against a stone.

Thou shalt walk upon the asp and basilisk : and thou shalt trample under foot the lion and the dragon.

God will say of thee: Because he hoped in me, I will deliver him : I will protect him, because he hath known my Name.

He will cry to me, and I will hear him : I am with him in tribulation, I will deliver him, and I will glorify him.

I will fill him with length of days : and I will show him my Salvation.

The *fourth* Psalm invites the *Servants* of God to persevere, with fervour, in the prayers they offer during the *Night*. The Faithful should say this Psalm in a spirit of gratitude to God, for his raising up, in the Church, adorers of his holy name, whose grand vocation is to *lift up their hands*, day and night, for the safety of Israel. On such prayers depend the happiness and destinies of the world.

PSALM 133.

Behold now bless ye the Lord, all ye servants of the Lord.	Ecce nunc benedicite Dominum : * omnes servi Domini.
Who stand in the house of the Lord, in the courts of the house of our God.	Qui statis in domo Domini : * in atriis domus Dei nostri.
In the nights lift up your hands to the holy places, and bless ye the Lord.	In noctibus extollite manus vestras in sancta : * et benedicite Dominum.
Say to Israel : May the Lord out of Sion bless thee, he that made heaven and earth.	Benedicat te Dominus ex Sion : * qui fecit cœlum et terram.
ANT. Have mercy on me, O Lord, and hear my prayer.	ANT. Miserere mei, Domine, et exaudi orationem meam.

HYMN.*

Before the closing of the light, we beseech thee, Creator of all things ! that in thy clemency, thou be our protector and our guard.	Te lucis ante terminum, Rerum Creator, poscimus, Ut pro tua clementia Sis præsul et custodia.
May the dreams and phantoms of night depart far from us ; and do thou repress our enemy, lest our bodies be profaned.	Procul recedant somnia, Et noctium phantasmata ; Hostemque nostrum comprime, Ne polluantur corpora.
Most merciful Father ! and thou, his Only Begotten Son,	Præsta, Pater piisime, Patrique compar Unice,

---

* According to the Monastic Rite, as follows :—

Te lucis ante terminum, Rerum Creator, poscimus, Ut solita clementia Sis præsul ad custodiam.	Hostemque nostrum comprime Ne polluantur corpora. Præsta Pater omnipotens, Per Jesum Christum Dominum,
Procul recedant somnia Et noctium phantasmata	Qui tecum in perpetuum Regnat cum Sancto Spiritu.

PASSIONTIDE.

CAPITULUM.

(Jeremias, xiv.)

Tu autem in nobis es, Domine, et nomen sanctum tuum invocatum est super nos ; ne derelinquas nos, Domine Deus noster.

℟. In manus tuas, Domine : * Commendo spiritum meum. In manus tuas.

℣. Redemisti nos, Domine Deus veritatis. * Commendo.

Gloria. In manus tuas.

℣. Custodi nos, Domine, ut pupillam oculi.

℟. Sub umbra alarum tuarum protege nos.

ANT. Salva nos.

But thou art in us, O Lord, and thy holy name has been invoked upon us : forsake us not, O Lord our God.

℟. Into thy hands, O Lord: * I commend my spirit. Into thy hands.

℣. Thou hast redeemed us, O Lord God of truth. * I commend.

Glory. Into thy hands.

℣. Preserve us, O Lord, as the apple of thine eye.

℟. Protect us under the shadow of thy wings.

ANT. Save us.

The Canticle of the venerable Simeon—who, whilst holding the divine Infant in his arms, proclaimed him to be the *Light of the Gentiles*, and then slept the sleep of the just,—admirably expresses the repose of heart which the soul, that is in the Grace of God, will experience in her Jesus; for as the Apostle says, *we may live together with Jesus, whether we are awake or asleep*.[1]

CANTICLE OF SIMEON.

(St. Luke, ii.)

Nunc dimittis servum tuum Domine : * secundum verbum tuum in pace.

Now dost thou dismiss thy servant, O Lord, according to thy word in peace.

---

[1] I. Thess. v. 10.

COMPLINE. 99

Because my eyes have seen thy Salvation.
Which thou hast prepared before the face of all peoples.
The light to the revelation of the Gentiles, and the glory of thy people Israel.
Glory, &c.
ANT. Save us, O Lord, whilst awake, and watch us as we sleep; that we may watch with Christ, and rest in peace.

Quia viderunt oculi mei : * salutare tuum.
Quod parasti : * ante faciem omnium populorum.
Lumen ad revelationem Gentium : * et gloriam plebis tuæ Israël.
Gloria Patri, et Filio, &c.
ANT. Salva nos, Domine, vigilantes : custodi nos dormientes, ut vigilemus cum Christo, et requiescamus in pace.

PRAYERS.

Lord have mercy on us. Christ have mercy on us. Lord have mercy on us.
Our Father.
℣. And lead us not into temptation.
℟. But deliver us from evil.
I believe in God, &c.
℣. The resurrection of the body.
℟. And life everlasting. Amen.
℣. Blessed art thou, O Lord God of our fathers.
R. And praiseworthy and glorious for ever.
℣. Let us bless the Father and the Son, with the Holy Ghost.
℟. Let us praise and magnify him for ever.
℣. Thou art blessed, O Lord, in the firmament of heaven.
℟. And praiseworthy, and glorious, and magnified for ever.
℣. May the Almighty and merciful Lord bless us and keep us. ℟. Amen.

Kyrie eleison.
Christe eleison.
Kyrie eleison.
Pater noster.
℣. Et ne nos inducas in tentationem.
℟. Sed libera nos a malo.
Credo in Deum, &c.
℣. Carnis resurrectionem.

℟. Vitam æternam. Amen.

℣. Benedictus es, Domine Deus patrum nostrorum.
℟. Et laudabilis et gloriosus in sæcula.
℣. Benedicamus Patrem et Filium cum Sancto Spiritu.
℟. Laudemus, et superexaltemus eum in sæcula.
℣. Benedictus es, Domine, in firmamento cœli.

℟. Et laudabilis, et gloriosus et superexaltatus in sæcula.
℣. Benedicat et custodiat nos omnipotens et misericors Dominus. R. Amen.

℣. Dignare, Domine, nocte ista.
℟. Sine peccato nos custodire.
℣. Miserere nostri, Domine.
℟. Miserere nostri.
℣. Fiat misericordia tua, Domine, super nos.
℟. Quemadmodum speravimus in te.
℣. Domine, exaudi orationem meam.
℟. Et clamor meus ad te veniat.

℣. Vouchsafe, O Lord, this night.
℟. To keep us without sin.
℣. Have mercy on us, O Lord.
℟. Have mercy on us.
℣. Let thy mercy be upon us, O Lord.
℟. As we have hoped in thee.
℣. O Lord, hear my prayer.
℟. And let my cry come unto thee.

After these *Prayers,* (which are omitted if the Office be of a *double* rite,) the Priest says:

℣. Dominus vobiscum.
℟. Et cum spiritu tuo.

℣. The Lord be with you.
℟. And with thy spirit.

OREMUS.

Visita, quæsumus Domine, habitationem istam, et omnes insidias inimici ab ea longe repelle: Angeli tui sancti habitent in ea, qui nos in pace custodiant: et benedictio tua sit super nos semper. Per Dominum nostrum Jesum Christum Filium tuum, qui tecum vivit et regnat in unitate Spiritus Sancti Deus, per omnia sæcula sæculorum. Amen.
℣. Dominus vobiscum.
℟. Et cum spiritu tuo.
℣. Benedicamus Domino.
℟. Deo gratias.
Benedicat et custodiat nos omnipotens et misericors Dominus, Pater, et Filius, et Spiritus Sanctus.
℟. Amen.

LET US PRAY.

Visit, we beseech thee, O Lord, this house and family, and drive from it all snares of the enemy: let thy holy Angels dwell herein, who may keep us in peace, and may thy blessing be always upon us. Through Jesus Christ our Lord, thy Son, who liveth and reigneth with thee, in the unity of the Holy Ghost, God, world without end. Amen.
℣. The Lord be with you.
℟. And with thy spirit.
℣. Let us bless the Lord.
℟. Thanks be to God.
May the Almighty and merciful Lord, Father, Son, and Holy Ghost, bless and preserve us.
℟. Amen.

ANTHEM TO THE BLESSED VIRGIN.

Hail Queen of Heaven! Hail Queen of Angels! Hail blest Root and Gate, from which came Light upon the world! Rejoice, O glorious Virgin, that surpassest all in beauty! Hail most lovely Queen! and pray to Christ for us.
℣. Vouchsafe, O Holy Virgin, that I may praise thee.
℟. Give me power against thine enemies.

Ave Regina cœlorum, Ave Domina Angelorum: Salve Radix, salve Porta, Ex qua mundo lux est orta; Gaude, Virgo gloriosa, Super omnes speciosa: Vale, o valde decora, Et pro nobis Christum exora.
℣. Dignare me laudare te, Virgo sacrata.
℟. Da mihi virtutem contra hostes tuos.

LET US PRAY.

Grant, O merciful God, thy protection to us in our weakness; that we who celebrate the memory of the Holy Mother of God, may, through the aid of her intercession, rise again from our sins. Through the same Christ our Lord.
℟. Amen.
℣. May the divine assistance remain always with us.
℟. Amen.*

OREMUS.

Concede, misericors Deus, fragilitati nostræ præsidium: ut, qui sanctæ Dei Genitricis memoriam agimus, intercessionis ejus auxilio, a nostris iniquitatibus resurgamus. Per eumdem Christum Dominum nostrum.
℟. Amen.
℣. Divinum auxilium maneat semper nobiscum.
℟. Amen.*

Then, in secret, *Pater, Ave,* and *Credo;* page 26.

---

* In the Monastic Rite, this *Response* is as follows:

℟. And with our absent Brethren. Amen.

℟. Et cum fratribus nostris absentibus. Amen.

PROPER OF THE TIME.

PASSION SUNDAY.

| To-day, if ye shall hear the voice of the Lord, harden not your hearts. | Hodie, si vocem Domini audieritis, nolite obdurare corda vestra. |

THE Holy Church begins her Night Office of this Sunday with these impressive words of the Royal Prophet. Formerly, the faithful considered it their duty to assist at the Night Office, at least on Sundays and Feasts; they would have grieved to have lost the grand teachings given by the Liturgy. Such fervour has long since died out; the assiduity at the Offices of the Church, which was the joy of our Catholic forefathers, has now become a thing of the past; and, even in countries which have not apostatised from the faith, the clergy have ceased to celebrate publicly Offices at which no one assisted. Excepting in Cathedral Churches and in Monasteries, the grand harmonious system of the Divine Praise has been abandoned, and the marvellous power of the Liturgy has no longer its full influence upon the Faithful.

This is our reason for drawing the attention of our readers to certain beauties of the Divine Office, which would otherwise be totally ignored. Thus, what can be more impressive than this solemn Invitatory of to-day's Matins, which the Church takes from one of the psalms, and which she repeats on every Feria between this and Maundy Thursday?

She says: *To-day, if ye shall hear the voice of the Lord, harden not your hearts!* The sweet voice of your suffering Jesus now speaks to you, poor sinners! be not your own enemies by indifference and hardness of heart. The Son of God is about to give you the last and greatest proof of the love that brought him down from heaven; his Death is nigh at hand: men are preparing the wood for the immolation of the new Isaac: enter into yourselves, and let not your hearts, after being touched with grace, return to their former obduracy,—for nothing could be more dangerous. The great anniversaries we are to celebrate have a renovating power for those souls that faithfully correspond with the grace which is offered them; but they increase insensibility in those who let them pass without working their conversion. *To-day*, therefore, *if you hear the voice of the Lord, harden not your hearts!*

During the preceding four weeks, we have noticed how the malice of Jesus' enemies has been gradually increasing. His very presence irritates them; and it is evident, that any little circumstance will suffice to bring the deep and long nurtured hatred to a head. The kind and gentle manners of Jesus are drawing to him all hearts that are simple and upright; at the same time, the humble life he leads, and the stern purity of his doctrines, are perpetual sources of vexation and anger, both to the proud Jew that looks forward to the Messias being a mighty conqueror, and to the Pharisee, who corrupts the Law of God, that he may make it the instrument of his own base passions. Still, Jesus goes on working miracles; his discourses are more than ever energetic; his prophecies foretell the fall of Jerusalem, and such a destruction of its famous Temple, that not a stone is to be left on stone. The doctors of the Law should, at least, reflect upon what they hear; they should examine these wonderful works, which render such strong testimony in favour of the Son of David, and they should consult those divine prophecies which, up to the present time, have been so literally fulfilled in his person. Alas! they themselves are about to carry them out to the very last iota. There is not a single outrage or suffering foretold by David and Isaias, as having to be put upon the Messias, which these blind men are not scheming to verify.

In them, therefore, was fulfilled that terrible saying: *He that shall speak against the Holy Ghost, it shall not be forgiven him, neither in this world, nor in the world to come.*[1] The Synagogue is nigh to a curse. Obstinate in her error, she refuses to see or to hear; she has deliberately perverted her judgment: she has extinguished within herself the light of the Holy Spirit; she will go deeper and deeper into evil, and at length fall into the abyss. This same lamentable conduct is but too often witnessed now-a-days, in those sinners, who, by habitual resistance to the light, end by finding their happiness in sin. Neither should it surprise us, that we find in people of our own generation a resemblance to the murderers of our Jesus: the history of his Passion will reveal to us many sad secrets of the human heart and its perverse inclinations; for what happened in Jerusalem, happens also in every sinner's heart. His heart, according to the saying of St. Paul, is a Calvary, where Jesus is crucified. There is the same ingratitude, the same blindness, the same wild madness, with this difference,—that the sinner who is enlightened by faith, knows Him whom he crucifies; whereas the Jews, as the same Apostle tells us, knew not the Lord of Glory.[2] Whilst, therefore, we listen to the Gospel, which relates the history of the Passion, let us turn the indignation we feel for the Jews against ourselves and our

[1] St. Matth. xii. 32. [2] I. Cor. ii. 8.

own sins: let us weep over the sufferings of our Victim, for *our* sins caused him to suffer and die.

Everything around us urges us to mourn. The images of the Saints, the very crucifix on our Altar, are veiled from our sight. The Church is oppressed with grief. During the first four weeks of Lent, she compassionated her Jesus fasting in the desert; his coming Sufferings and Crucifixion and Death are what now fill her with anguish. We read in to-day's Gospel, that the Jews threaten to stone the Son of God as a blasphemer: but his hour is not yet come. He is obliged to flee and hide himself. It is to express this deep humiliation, that the Church veils the Cross. A God hiding himself, that he may evade the anger of men,—what a mystery! Is it weakness? Is it, that he fears death? No,—we shall soon see him going out to meet his enemies: but, at present, he hides himself from them, because all that had been prophesied regarding him has not been fulfilled. Besides, his death is not to be by stoning; he is to die upon a Cross, the *tree* of malediction, which, from that time forward, is to be the Tree of Life. Let us humble ourselves, as we see the Creator of heaven and earth thus obliged to hide himself from men, who are bent on his destruction! Let us go back, in thought, to the sad day of the first sin, when Adam and Eve hid themselves because a guilty conscience told them they were naked. Jesus is come to assure us of our being pardoned! and lo! he hides himself, not because he is naked,—He that is to the Saints the garb of holiness and immortality, —but because he made himself weak, that he might make us strong. Our First Parents sought to hide themselves from the sight of God; Jesus hides himself from the eye of men; but it will not be thus for ever. The day will come, when sinners, from whose anger he now flees, will pray to the mountains that they fall on them to shield them from his gaze; but their prayer will not be granted, *and they shall see the Son of man coming in the clouds of heaven, with much power and majesty.*[1]

This Sunday is called *Passion Sunday,* because the Church begins, on this day, to make the Sufferings of our Redeemer her chief thought. It is called also, *Judica,* from the first word of the Introit of the Mass; and again, *Neomania,* that is, the Sunday of the *new* (or, the *Easter*) *moon,* because it always falls after the new moon which regulates the Feast of Easter Day.

In the Greek Church, this Sunday goes under the simple name of the Fifth Sunday *of the Holy Fests.*

MASS.

At Rome, the Station is in the Basilica of St. Peter. The importance of this Sunday, which never gives way to any Feast, no matter what its solemnity may be, required that the place for the assembly of the Faithful should be in one of the chief Sanctuaries of the Holy City.

The Introit is taken from the first verses of the 42nd Psalm. The Messias appeals to God's tribunal, and protests against the sentence about to be pronounced against him by men. He likewise expresses his confidence in his Father's help, who, after his Sufferings and Death, will lead him in triumph into the *Holy Mount.*

INTROIT.

Judge me, O God, and distinguish my cause from the nation that is not holy; de-	Judica me, Deus, et discerne causam meam de gente non sancta: ab ho-

[1] St. Matth. xxiv. 30.

mine iniquo et doloso eripe me: quia tu es Deus meus, et fortitudo mea.

Ps. Emitte lucem tuam et veritatem tuam: ipsa me deduxerunt et adduxerunt in montem sanctum tuum, et in tabernacula tua. Judica me.

liver me from the unjust and deceitful man; for thou art my God and my strength.

Ps. Send forth thy light and thy truth; for they have conducted me, and brought me to thy holy mount, and into thy tabernacles. Judge me, &c.

The *Gloria Patri* is not said during Passiontide and Holy Week, (unless a Saint's Feast be kept,) but the Introit is repeated immediately after the Psalm.

In the Collect, the Church prays that there may be produced, in her children, that total reformation, which the holy Season of Lent is intended to produce. This reformation is such, that it will not only subject the body to the spirit, but preserve also the spirit itself from those delusions and passions, to which it has been, hitherto, more or less, a slave.

COLLECT.

Quæsumus, omnipotens Deus, familiam tuam propitius respice: ut, te largiente, regatur in corpore, et, te servante, custodiatur in mente. Per Dominum.

Mercifully look down on thy people, we beseech thee, O Almighty God, that, by thy bounty and protection, they may be governed and guarded both in body and soul. Through, &c.

Then is added one of the following Prayers:

AGAINST THE PERSECUTORS OF THE CHURCH.

Ecclesiæ tuæ, quæsumus, Domine, preces, placatus admitte: ut, destructis adversitatibus et erroribus universis, secura tibi serviat libertate. Per Dominum.

Mercifully hear, we beseech thee, O Lord, the prayers of thy Church: that, all oppositions and errors being removed, she may serve thee with a secure liberty. Through, &c.

FOR THE POPE.

O God, the Pastor and Ruler of all the Faithful, look down, in thy mercy, on thy servant N., whom thou hast appointed Pastor over thy Church; and grant, we beseech thee, that both by word and example, he may edify all those that are under his charge : and, with the flock intrusted to him, arrive at length at eternal happiness. Through, &c.

Deus, omnium fidelium Pastor et Rector, famulum tuum N., quem Pastorem Ecclesiæ tuæ præesse voluisti, propitius respice: da ei, quæsumus, verbo et exemplo, quibus præest, proficere ; ut ad vitam, una cum grege sibi credito, perveniat sempiternam. Per Dominum.

EPISTLE.

Lesson of the Epistle of St. Paul the Apostle to the Hebrews.

Lectio Epistolæ beati Pauli Apostoli ad Hebræos.

Ch. IX.

Cap. IX.

Brethren : Christ being come, an High Priest of the good things to come, by a greater and more perfect tabernacle not made with hands, that is, not of this creation, neither by the blood of goats or of the calves, but by his own Blood, entered once into the Holies, having obtained eternal redemption. For, if the blood of goats and of oxen, and the ashes of an heifer being sprinkled, sanctify such as are defiled, to the cleansing of the flesh ; how much more shall the Blood of Christ (who by the Holy Ghost offered himself unspotted unto God), cleanse our conscience from dead works to serve the living God? And, therefore, he is

Fratres : Christus assistens Pontifex futurorum bonorum, per amplius et perfectius tabernaculum non manufactum, id est, non hujus creationis: neque per sanguinem hircorum aut vitulorum, sed per proprium Sanguinem introivit semel in Sancta, æterna redemptione inventa. Si enim sanguis hircorum et taurorum, et cinis vitulæ aspersus inquinatos sanctificat ad emundationem carnis: quanto magis Sanguis Christi, qui per Spiritum Sanctum semetipsum obtulit immaculatum Deo, emundabit conscientiam nostram ab operibus mortuis, ad serviendum Deo viventi? Et ideo

| novi Testamenti mediator est : ut morte intercedente, in redemptionem earum prævaricationum, quæ erant sub priori Testamento, repromissionem accipiant, qui vocati sunt, æternæ hæreditatis : in Christo Jesu Domino nostro. | the mediator of the New Testament ; that by means of his death, for the redemption of those transgressions which were under the former testament, they that are called may receive the promise of eternal inheritance. |

It is by Blood alone that man is to be redeemed. He has offended God. This God cannot be appeased by anything short of the extermination of his rebellious creature, who, by shedding his blood, will give an earnest of his repentance and his entire submission to the Creator, against whom he dared to rebel. Otherwise, the justice of God must be satisfied by the sinner's suffering eternal punishment. This truth was understood by all the people of the ancient world, and all confessed it by shedding the blood of victims, as in the sacrifices of Abel, at the very commencement of the world; in the hecatombs of Greece; in the countless immolations whereby Solomon dedicated the Temple. And yet, God thus speaks to his people: *Hear, O my people, and I will speak: O Israel, and I will testify to thee: I am God thy God. I will not reprove thee for thy sacrifices, and thy burnt-offerings are always in my sight. I will not take calves out of thy house, nor he-goats out of thy flocks.* I need them not: *for all the beasts of the woods are mine. If I should be hungry, I would not tell thee; for the world is mine, and the fulness thereof. Shall I eat the flesh of bullocks? or shall I drink the blood of goats?*[1] Thus, God commands the blood of victims to be offered to him, and, at the same time, declares that neither it nor they are precious in his sight. Is this a contra-

---

[1] Ps. xlix. 7-13.

diction? No: God would hereby have man understand, that it is only by Blood that he can be redeemed, but that the blood of brute animals cannot effect this redemption. Can the blood of man himself bring him his own redemption, and appease God's justice? No, not even man's blood, for it is defiled; and even were it undefiled, it is powerless to compensate for the outrage done to God by sin. For this, there was needed the Blood of a God; *that* was the Blood of Jesus, and he has come that he may shed it for our redemption.

In him is fulfilled the most sacred of the figures of the Old Law. Once each year, the High-Priest entered into the Holy of Holies, there to make intercession for the people. He went within the Veil, even to the Ark of the Covenant; but he was not allowed to enjoy this great privilege, unless he entered the holy place carrying in his hands the blood of a newly-offered victim. The Son of God, the true High-Priest, is now about to enter heaven, and we are to follow him thither; but unto this, he must have an offering of blood, and that Blood can be none other than his own. We are going to assist at this his compliance with the divine ordinance. Let us open our hearts, that this precious Blood may, as the Apostle says in to-day's Epistle, *cleanse our conscience from dead works to serve the living God.*

The Gradual is taken from the Psalms. Our Saviour here prays to be delivered from his enemies, and protected from the rage of them that have risen up against him; yet, is he ready to do the will of his Father, by whom he will be avenged.

In the Tract, which is also taken from the Psalms, the Messias, under the name of Israel, complains of the persecution he has met from the Jews, even from his youth. They are now about to scourge him in a most cruel manner. But he also foretells the punishment their deicide is to bring upon them.

GRADUAL.

Eripe me, Domine, de inimicis meis : doce me facere voluntatem tuam.

℣. Liberator meus, Domine, de gentibus iracundis : ab insurgentibus in me exaltabis me : a viro iniquo eripies me.

Deliver me, O Lord, from my enemies ; teach me to do thy will.

℣. Thou, O Lord, art my deliverer from the enraged Gentiles : thou wilt put me out of the reach of those that assault me ; and thou wilt rescue me from the unrighteous man.

TRACT.

Sæpe expugnaverunt me a juventute mea.

℣. Dicat nunc Israël : Sæpe expugnaverunt me a juventute mea.

℣. Etenim non potuerunt mihi : supra dorsum meum fabricaverunt peccatores.

℣. Prolongaverunt iniquitates suas : Dominus justus concidet cervices peccatorum.

Many a time have they fought against me from my youth.

℣. Let Israel now say : They have often attacked me from my youth.

℣. But they could not prevail over me : the wicked have wrought upon my back.

℣. They have lengthened their iniquity : the Lord, who is just, will cut the necks of sinners.

GOSPEL.

Sequentia sancti Evangelii secundum Joannem.

Cap. VIII.

In illo tempore : Dicebit Jesus turbis Judæorum : Quis ex vobis arguet me de peccato ? Si veritatem dico vobis, quare non creditis mihi ? Qui ex Deo est verba Dei audit. Propterea vos non auditis, quia ex Deo non estis. Responderunt ergo Judæi, et dixerunt ei :

Sequel of the Holy Gospel, according to John.

Ch. VIII.

At that time : Jesus said to the multitude of the Jews : Which of you shall convince me of sin ? If I say the truth to you, why do you not believe me ? He that is of God, heareth the words of God. Therefore, you hear them not, because you are not of God. The Jews, therefore, answered, and said to him: Do not we say well that thou art a Samaritan, and hast a devil? Jesus answered: I have not a devil; but I honour my Father, and you have dishonoured me. But I seek not my own glory: there is one that seeketh and judgeth. Amen, amen, I say to you: If any man keep my word, he shall not see death for ever. The Jews therefore said: Now we know that thou hast a devil. Abraham is dead, and the prophets; and thou sayest: If any man keep my word, he shall not taste death for ever. Art thou greater than our Father Abraham, who is dead? And the prophets are dead. Whom dost thou make thyself? Jesus answered: If I glorify myself, my glory is nothing. It is my Father that glorifieth me, of whom you say that he is your God; and you have not known him, but I know him. And if I should say that I know him not, I should be like to you, a liar. But I do know him, and do keep his word. Abraham your father rejoiced that he might see my day: he saw it, and was glad. The Jews then said to him: Thou art not yet fifty years old, and hast thou seen Abraham? Jesus said to them: Amen, amen, I say unto you, before Abraham was made, I am. They took up stones therefore to cast at him. But Jesus hid himself, and went out of the temple.

Nonne bene dicimus nos quia Samaritanus es tu, et dæmonium habes? Respondit Jesus: Ego dæmonium non habeo: sed honorifico Patrem meum, et vos inhonorastis me. Ego autem non quæro gloriam meam: est qui quærat et judicet. Amen, amen dico vobis: Si quis sermonem meum servaverit, mortem non videbit in æternum. Dixerunt ergo Judæi: Nunc cognovimus quia dæmonium habes. Abraham mortuus est, et Prophetæ: et tu dicis: Si quis sermonem meum servaverit, non gustabit mortem in æternum. Numquid tu major es patre nostro Abraham, qui mortuus est? et Prophetæ mortui sunt. Quem teipsum facis? Respondit Jesus: Si ego glorifico meipsum, gloria mea nihil est: est Pater meus, qui glorificat me, quem vos dicitis quia Deus vester est, et non cognovistis eum; ego autem novi eum: et si dixero quia non scio eum, ero similis vobis mendax. Sed scio eum, et sermonem ejus servo. Abraham pater vester exsultavit ut videret diem meum: vidit, et gavisus est. Dixerunt ergo Judæi ad eum: Quinquaginta annos nondum habes, et Abraham vidisti? Dixit eis Jesus: Amen, amen dico vobis, antequam Abraham fieret, ego sum. Tulerunt ergo lapides ut jacerent in eum: Jesus autem abscondit se, et exivit de templo.

The fury of the Jews is evidently at its height, and Jesus is obliged to hide himself from them. But he is to fall into their hands before many days are over; then will they triumph and put him to death. They triumph, and Jesus is their victim; but how different is to be *his* lot from *theirs!* In obedience to the decrees of his heavenly Father, and out of love for men, he will deliver himself into the hands of his enemies, and they will put him to death; but he will rise victorious from the tomb, he will ascend into heaven, he will be throned on the right hand of his Father. His enemies, on the contrary, after having vented all their rage, will live on without remorse, until the terrible day come for their chastisement. That day is not far off, for observe the severity wherewith our Lord speaks to them: *You hear not the words of God, because you are not of God.* Yet there was a time, when they were *of God*, for the Lord gives his grace to all men; but they have rendered this grace useless; they are now in darkness, and the light they have rejected will not return.

You say, that my Father is your God, and you have not known him; but I know him. Their obstinacy in refusing to acknowledge Jesus as the Messias, has led these men to ignore that very God, whom they boast of honouring; for if they knew the Father, they would not reject his Son. Moses, and the Psalms, and the Prophets, are all a dead letter to them; these sacred Books are soon to pass into the hands of the Gentiles, who will both read and understand them. *If*, continues Jesus, *I should say that I know him not, I should be like to you, a liar.* This strong language is that of the angry Judge who is to come down, at the last day, to destroy sinners. Jerusalem has not known the time of her visitation: the Son of God has visited her, he is with her, and she dares to say to him: *Thou hast a devil!* She says to the Eternal Word, who proves himself to be God by the most astounding miracles, that *Abraham and the Prophets are greater* than He! Strange blindness, that comes from pride and hardness of heart! The Feast of the Pasch is at hand: these men are going to eat, and with much parade of religion, the flesh of the figurative lamb; they know full well, that this lamb is a symbol, or a figure, which is to have its fulfilment. The true Lamb is to be sacrificed by their hands, and they will not know him. He will shed his Blood for them, and it will not save them. How this reminds us of those sinners, for whom this Easter promises to be as fruitless as those of the past years! Let us redouble our prayers for them, and beseech our Lord to soften their hearts, lest trampling the Blood of Jesus under their feet, they should have it to cry vengeance against them before the throne of the Heavenly Father.

At the Offertory, confiding in the merits of the Blood that has redeemed us, let us, in the words of the Psalm, give praise to God, and proclaim him to be the author of that New Life, of which the sacrifice of the Lamb is the never-failing source.

OFFERTORY.

I will praise thee, O Lord, with my whole heart: reward thy servant: I shall live, and keep thy commandments: save me according to thy word, O Lord.	Confitebor tibi, Domine, in toto corde meo: retribue servo tuo; vivam, et custodiam sermones tuos: vivifica me secundum verbum tuum, Domine.

The sacrifice of the spotless Lamb has produced two effects upon the sinner: it has broken his fetters, and has made him the object of God's love. The Church prays, in the Secret, that the Sacrifice she is about to offer, and which is one with that of the Cross, may work these same results in us.

SECRETS.

Hæc munera, quæsumus, Domine, et vincula nostræ pravitatis absolvant, et tuæ nobis misericordiæ dona concilient. Per Dominum.

May these offerings, O Lord, both loosen the bonds of our wickedness, and obtain for us the gifts of thy mercy. Through, &c.

AGAINST THE PERSECUTORS OF THE CHURCH.

Protege nos, Domine, tuis mysteriis servientes: ut divinis rebus inhærentes, et corpore tibi famulemur et mente. Per Dominum.

Protect us, O Lord, while we assist at thy sacred mysteries: that being employed in acts of religion, we may serve thee both in body and mind. Through, &c.

FOR THE POPE.

Oblatis, quæsumus, Domine, placare muneribus: et famulum tuum N. quem Pastorem Ecclesiæ tuæ præesse voluisti, assidua protectione guberna. Per Dominum.

Be appeased, O Lord, with the offering we have made: and cease not to protect thy servant N., whom thou hast been pleased to appoint Pastor over thy Church. Through, &c.

The Communion-Antiphon is formed out of the very words spoken by Jesus, when instituting the august Sacrifice that has just been celebrated, and of which the Priest and people have partaken, in memory of the Passion, for it renews both the remembrance and the merits of the Passion.

COMMUNION.

Hoc corpus, quod pro vobis tradetur: hic calix novi testamenti est in meo sanguine, dicit Dominus: hoc facite, quotiescumque sumitis in meam commemorationem.

This is the body which shall be delivered up for you; this is the cup of the new covenant in my blood, saith the Lord. As often as you receive them, do it in remembrance of me.

PASSION SUNDAY.

In the Postcommunion, the Church prays to God, that he would maintain in the Faithful the fruits of the visit he has so graciously paid them, for, by their participation in the Sacred Mysteries, he has entered into them.

POSTCOMMUNIONS.

Help us, O Lord our God, and for ever protect those whom thou hast refreshed with thy sacred mysteries. Through, &c.

Adesto nobis, Domine Deus noster: et, quos tuis mysteriis recreasti, perpetuis defende subsidiis. Per Dominum.

AGAINST THE PERSECUTORS OF THE CHURCH.

We beseech thee, O Lord our God, not to leave exposed to the dangers of human life, those whom thou hast permitted to partake of these divine mysteries. Through, &c.

Quæsumus, Domine Deus noster: ut quos divina tribuis participatione gaudere, humanis non sinas subjacere periculis. Per Dominum.

FOR THE POPE.

May the participation of this divine Sacrament protect us, we beseech thee, O Lord; and always procure safety and defence to thy servant N., whom thou hast appointed Pastor over thy Church, together with the flock committed to his charge. Through, &c.

Hæc nos, quæsumus, Domine, divini Sacramenti perceptio protegat: et famulum tuum N. quem Pastorem Ecclesiæ tuæ præesse voluisti, una cum commisso sibi grege salvet semper et muniat. Per Dominum.

VESPERS.

The Psalms and Antiphons are given in *page* 80.

CAPITULUM.

(*Heb. IX.*)

Fratres: Christus assistens Pontifex futurorum bonorum, per amplius et perfectius tabernaculum non manufactum, id est, non hujus creationis, neque per sanguinem hircorum, aut vitulorum, sed per proprium sanguinem, introivit semel in Sancta, æterna redemptione inventa.	Brethren: Christ being come an High Priest of the good things to come, by a greater and more perfect tabernacle not made with hands, that is, not of this creation, neither by the blood of goats or of calves, but by his own Blood, entered once into the Holies, having obtained eternal redemption.

For the Hymn and Versicle, see *page* 87.

ANTIPHON OF THE *Magnificat.*

Abraham pater vester exsultavit ut videret diem meum: vidit et gavisus est.	Abraham your father rejoiced that he might see my day: he saw it, and was glad.

OREMUS.	LET US PRAY.
Quæsumus, omnipotens Deus, familiam tuam propitius respice: ut, te largiente, regatur in corpore, et, te servante, custodiatur in mente. Per Dominum.	Mercifully look down on thy people, we beseech thee, O Almighty God, that by thy bounty and protection, they may be governed and guarded both in body and soul. Through, &c.

The following appropriate Prayer is from the Mozarabic Breviary.

PASSION SUNDAY.

CAPITULUM.

The course of the year has brought us to the time for celebrating, with devout hearts and offices, the Feast of thy Passion, O Jesus, Son of God! wherein, for our sakes, thou didst suffer the calumnies of thine enemies, and wast crucified by the wounds of them that betrayed thee. We pray and beseech thee, that thou depart not from us; and whereas tribulation is nigh at hand, and there is none to help us, do thou, by the help of thy Passion, become our sole protector. Deliver us not, therefore, into the hands of our enemies unto evil, but receive us, as thy servants, unto good; that the haughty ones who calumniate us, namely the enemies of our souls, may be repelled by the might of thy power. Thou, by the human nature thou hast assumed, art the lamp set on the stand of the Cross: we beseech thee, therefore, that thou enkindle us by thy flame, lest we become a prey to punishment. Behold us now entering, with devout hearts, upon the feast of thy Passion; oh! grant that we partake of the merits of thy Passion: that thus, being delivered from the error of our darkness, we may be fortified by the help of thy Light.

Passionis tuæ festum, Christe Dei Filius, devotis cordium officiis, recursu temporis inchoantes, quo pro nobis et linguas fuisti persequentium passus, et tradentium te vulneribus crucifixus; rogamus atque exposcimus ne te elonges a nobis: ut quia proximante tribulatione, non est qui adjuvet; tu solus Passionis tuæ nos subleves ope: ne tradas ergo nos inimicis nostris in malum, sed excipe servos tuos in bonum: ut nos calumniantes superbi, inimici scilicet animarum nostrarum, virtutis tuæ potentia propellantur; tu es enim divina lucerna per humanitatem super candelabrum crucis imposita: ideo te rogamus, ut nos accendas, ne veniamus in pœnam. Quos ergo perspicis initiatum Passionis tuæ festum devotis cordibus excepisse, facito eos Passioni tuæ communicare: ut tenebrarum nostrarum errore discusso, lucis tuæ muniamur præsidio.

That we may the better honour the holy Cross, we give, for each day of this week, an appropriate Hymn from one or other of the various ancient

Liturgies. The one we have selected for to-day is the composition of St. Venantius Fortunatus, Bishop of Poitiers.

HYMN.

Crux benedicta nitet, Dominus qua carne pependit.
Atque cruore suo vulnera nostra lavat.
Mitis amore pio pro nobis victima factus,
Traxit ab ore lupi qua sacer Agnus oves.

Transfixis palmis ubi mundum a clade redemit,
Atque suo clausit funere mortis iter.
Hic manus illa fuit clavis confixa cruentis,
Quæ eripuit Paulum crimine, morte Petrum.
Fertilitate potens, o dulce et nobile lignum,
Quando tuis ramis tam nova poma geris.
Cujus odore novo defuncta cadavera surgunt,
Et redeunt vitæ qui caruere die.
Nullum uret æstus sub frondibus arboris hujus:
Luna nec in noctem, sol neque meridie.
Tu plantata micas secus est ubi cursus aquarum:
Spargis et ornatas flore recente comas.
Appensa est vitis inter tua brachia, de qua
Dulcia sanguineo vina rubore fluunt.

Brightly shineth the blessed Cross, whereon hung the body of our Lord, when, with his Blood, he washed our wounds.

Become, out of tender love for us, a meek Victim, this divine Lamb did, by the Cross, rescue us his sheep from the jaws of the wolf.

'Twas there, with his hands nailed to the wood, that he redeemed the world from ruin, and by his own death, closed the way of death.

Here was fastened with cruel nails that hand, which delivered Paul from sin, and Peter from death.

O sweet and noble Tree! how vigorous is thy growth, when, on thy branches, hang fruits so rare as these!

Thy fresh fragrance gives resurrection to many that lay in the tomb, and restores the dead to life.

He that shelters beneath thy shade, shall not be scorched either by the moon at night or by the mid-day sun.

Planted near the running waters, thou art lovely in thy verdure, and blossoms ever fresh blow on each fair branch,

Between thine arms hangs the pendant Vine, whence wine most sweet flows in a ruddy stream.

MONDAY

IN PASSION WEEK.

The Station, at Rome, is in the Church of Saint Chrysogonus, one of the most celebrated Martyrs of the Church of Rome. His name is inserted in the Canon of the Mass.

COLLECT.

Sanctify, O Lord, we beseech thee, our fasts, and mercifully grant us the pardon of all our sins. Through Christ our Lord. Amen.

Sanctifica, quæsumus, Domine, nostra jejunia: et cunctarum nobis indulgentiam propitius largire culparum. Per Christum Dominum nostrum. Amen.

EPISTLE.

Lesson from Jonas the Prophet.

Ch. III.

Lectio Jonæ Prophetæ.

Cap. III.

In those days: The word of the Lord came to Jonas the second time, saying: Arise and go to Ninive, the great city: and preach in it the preaching that I bid thee. And Jonas arose, and went to Ninive, according to the word of the Lord. Now Ninive was a great city of three days' journey. And Jonas began to enter into the city one day's

In diebus illis: Factum est verbum Domini ad Jonam Prophetam secundo, dicens: Surge, et vade in Niniven civitatem magnam : et prædica in ea prædicationem quam ego loquor ad te. Et surrexit Jonas, et abiit in Niniven juxta verbum Domini. Et Ninive erat civitas magna itinere trium dierum. Et cœpit Jonas introire in civitatem itinere diei unius : et clamavit, et dixit : Adhuc quadraginta dies et Ninive subvertetur. Et crediderunt viri Ninivitæ in Deum : et prædicaverunt jejunium, et vestiti sunt saccis a majore usque ad minorem. Et pervenit verbum ad regem Ninive : et surrexit de solio suo, et abjecit vestimentum suum a se, et indutus est sacco, et sedit in cinere. Et clamavit, et dixit in Ninive ex ore regis, et principum ejus, dicens : Homines, et jumenta, et boves, et pecora non gustent quidquam : nec pascantur, et aquam non bibant. Et operiantur saccis homines, et jumenta, et clament ad Dominum in fortitudine, et convertatur vir a via sua mala, et ab iniquitate, quæ est in manibus eorum. Quis scit si convertatur, et ignoscat Deus : et revertatur a furore iræ suæ, et non peribimus ? Et vidit Deus opera eorum, quia conversi sunt de via sua mala : et misertus est populo suo Dominus Deus noster.

journey : and he cried and said : Yet forty days and Ninive shall be destroyed. And the men of Ninive believed in God : and they proclaimed a fast, and put on sackcloth from the greatest to the least. And the word came to the king of Ninive : and he rose up out of his throne, and cast away his robe from him, and was clothed with sackcloth, and sat in ashes. And he caused it to be proclaimed and published in Ninive, from the mouth of the king and of his princes, saying : Let neither men nor beasts, oxen nor sheep, taste any thing : let them not feed, nor drink water. And let men and beasts be covered with sackcloth, and cry to the Lord with all their strength, and let them turn every one from his evil way, and from the iniquity that is in their hands. Who can tell if God will turn and forgive : and will turn away from his fierce anger, and we shall not perish ? And God saw their works, that they were turned from their evil way : and the Lord our God had mercy on his people.

The Church's intention in this day's lesson, is to encourage us to earnestness and perseverance in our penance. Here we have an idolatrous city, a haughty and debauched capital, whose crimes have merited the anger of heaven. God threatens it with his vengeance: *yet forty days, and Ninive* and its inhabitants *shall be destroyed.* How came it, that the threat was not carried into effect ? What was it that caused Ninive to be spared? Its people returned to the God they had left; they sued for mercy; they humbled themselves, and fasted; and the Church concludes the Prophet's account by these touching words of her own: "And the Lord our God had mercy on *his people.*" They were Gentiles, but they became *his people,* because they did penance at the preaching of the Prophet. God had made a covenant with one only nation,—the Jews; but he rejected not the Gentiles, as often as they renounced their false Gods, confessed his holy name, and desired to serve him. We are here taught the efficacy of corporal mortification; when united with spiritual penance, that is, with the repentance of the heart, it has power to appease God's anger. How highly, then, should we not prize the holy exercises of penance put upon us by the Church, during this holy Season! Let us also learn to dread that false spirituality, which tells us that exterior mortification is of little value: such doctrine is the result of rationalism and cowardice.

This passage from the Prophet Jonas is also intended for the Catechumens, whose baptism is so close at hand. It teaches them to have confidence in this merciful God of the Christians, whose threats are so terrible, but who, notwithstanding, *turns* from his threats to *forgive* the repentant sinner. These Catechumens, who had hitherto lived in the Ninive of paganism, were here taught that God, even before sending his Son into the world, invited all men to become *his people.* Seeing the immense obstacles their Gentile ancestors had to surmount in order to receive and persevere in the grace offered them, they would bless God their Saviour, for having, by his Incarnation, his Sacrifice, his Sacraments, and his Church, facilitated salvation for us who live under the New Testament. True, he was the source of salvation to all preceding generations: but with what incomparable richness is he the source of *ours!* The Public Penitents, too, had their instruction in this Epistle. What an encouragement for them to hope for pardon! God had shown mercy to **Ninive**, sinful as it was, and sentenced to destruction: he would, therefore, accept their repentance and penance, he would stay his justice, and show them mercy and pardon.

GOSPEL.

Sequentia sancti Evangelii secundum Joannem.

Sequel of the holy Gospel according to John.

Cap. VII.

Ch. VII.

In illo tempore: Miserunt principes et Pharisæi, ministros, ut apprehenderent Jesum. Dixit ergo eis Jesus: Adhuc modicum tempus vobiscum sum: et vado ad eum qui me misit. Quæretis me, et non invenietis: et ubi ego sum vos non potestis venire. Dixerunt ergo Judæi ad semetipsos: Quo hic iturus est, quia non inveniemus eum? Numquid in dispersionem Gentium iturus est, et docturus Gentes? Quis est hic sermo, quem dixit: Quæretis me, et non invenietis: et ubi sum ego, vos non potestis venire? In novissimo autem die magno festivitatis stabat Jesus, et clamabat dicens: Si quis sitit, veniat ad me, et bibat. Qui credit in me, sicut dicit Scriptura, flumina de ventre ejus fluent aquæ vivæ. Hoc autem dixit de Spiritu, quem accepturi erant credentes in eum.

At that time: The rulers and Pharisees sent ministers to apprehend Jesus. **Jesus** therefore said to them: **Yet a little while I am with you:** and then I go to him that sent me. You shall seek me, and shall not find me: and where I am, thither you cannot come. The Jews, therefore, said among themselves: Whither will he go, that we shall not find him? Will he go to the dispersed among the Gentiles, and teach the Gentiles? What is this saying that he hath said: You shall seek me, and shall not find me; and where I am, you cannot come? And on the last and great day of the festival, Jesus stood and cried, saying: If any man thirst, let him come to me, and drink. He that believeth in me, as the Scripture saith, "Out of his belly shall flow rivers of living water." Now this he said of the Spirit which they should receive who believed in him.

The enemies of Jesus sought to stone him to death, as we were told in yesterday's Gospel; to-day they are bent on making him a prisoner, and send soldiers to seize him. This time, Jesus does not hide himself; but how awful are the words he speaks: *I go to Him that sent me: you shall seek me, and shall not find me!* The sinner, then, who has long abused the grace of God, may have his ingratitude and contempt punished in this just, but terrific way,—that he shall not be able to find the Jesus he has despised: *he shall seek, and shall not find.* Antiochus, when humbled under the hand of God, prayed, yet obtained not mercy.[1] After the Death and Resurrection of Jesus, whilst the Church was casting her roots in the world, the Jews, who had crucified the Just One, were *seeking* the Messias in each of the many impostors, who were then rising up in Judea, and fomenting rebellions, which led to the destruction of Jerusalem. Surrounded on all sides by the Roman legions, with their temple and palaces a prey to flames, they sent up their cries to heaven, and besought the God of their fathers to send, as he had promised, the Deliverer! It never occurred to them, that this Deliverer had shown himself to their fathers, to many even of themselves; that they had put him to death, and that the Apostles had already carried his name to the ends of the earth. They went on looking for him, even to the very day when the deicide city fell, burying beneath its ruins them that the sword had spared. Had they been asked, what it was they were awaiting, they would have replied, that they were expecting their Messias! He had come, and gone. *You shall seek me, and shall not find me!* Let them, too, think of these terrible words of Jesus, who intend to neglect the graces offered them during this Easter. Let us pray, let us make intercession for them, lest they fall into that

[1] II. Mach. ix. 13.

awful threat, of a repentance that seeks mercy when it is too late to find aught save an inexorable Justice.

But, what consoling thoughts are suggested by the concluding words of our Gospel! Faithful souls, and you that have repented! listen to what your Jesus says, for it is to you that he speaks: *If any man thirst, let him come to me and drink.* Remember the prayer of the Samaritan woman: *Give me, O Lord, to drink of this water!* This *water* is divine grace : come, and drink your fill at the *fountains of your Saviour,* as the Prophet Isaias bids you.[1] This *water* gives purity to the soul that is defiled, strength to them that are weak, and love to them that have no fervour. Nay, our Saviour assures us, that *he who believes in Him,* shall himself become as a fountain of *living water,* for the Holy Ghost will come upon him, and this soul shall pour out upon others of the fulness that she herself has received. With what joy must not the Catechumen have listened to these words, which promised him that his thirst should soon be quenched at the holy Font! Jesus has made himself everything to the world he has come to save: *Light* to guide us, *Bread* to nourish us, a *Vine* to gladden our hearts with its fruit, and, lastly, a *Fountain of Living Water* to quench our thirst.

Humiliate capita vestra Deo.

Da, quæsumus, Domine, populo tuo salutem mentis et corporis : ut bonis operibus inhærendo, tua semper mereatur protectione defendi. Per Christum Dominum nostrum. Amen.

Bow down your heads to God.

Grant, O Lord, we beseech thee, to thy people, health both of body and mind, that being constant in the practice of good works, they may always be safe under thy protection. Through Christ our Lord. Amen.

[1] Is. xii. 3.

MONDAY IN PASSION WEEK. 127

This being the day on which the Church offers to our meditations the history of the Prophet Jonas preaching to Ninive, we subjoin a new fragment from the Hymn of Prudentius on Fasting. It is the passage where he relates the life of this Prophet, and the repentance of the wicked City.

HYMN.

I fain would now, in holy Fasting's praise, tell, from the book of truth, how God our Father, with his wonted love, repressed the fire and thunder of his wrath, and spared the city doomed to be destroyed.

In ancient days, a city flourished, whose mighty power drove her into haughtiness extreme. Criminal indulgence and lewd corruption had destroyed the morals of her people, so brutalising them, that they left the worship of the God of heaven.

At length, the tired patience of God's long-suffering gave way to justice, which moves his hand to prepare his arrowed lightnings, and storm-voiced clouds, and jarring whirlwinds, and thunder-bolts that shake the vault of heaven.

Yet does he grant them time for penitence, wherein to tame and break the wickedness of their lust and wonted follies. Mercy, that waits for prayer, holds back the blow of

Referre prisci stemma nunc jejunii
Libet, fideli proditum volumine,
Ut diruendæ civitatis incolis
Fulmen benigni mansuefactum Patris,
Pie repressis ignibus, pepercerit.
Gens insolenti præpotens jactantia
Pollebat olim : quam fluentem nequiter
Corrupta vulgo solverat lascivia ;
Et inde bruto contumax fastidio
Cultum superni negligebat Numinis.
Offensa tandem jugis indulgentiæ
Censura, justis excitatur motibus,
Dextram perarmat rhomphæali incendio,
Nimbos crepantes, et fragosos turbines
Vibrans tonantum nube flammarum quatit.
Sed pœnitendi dum datur diecula,
Si forte vellent improbam libidinem
Veteresque nugas condemare, ac frangere.

Suspendit ictum terror exo-
rabilis,
Paulumque dicta substitit
sententia.
  Jonam prophetam mitis
ultor excitat,
Pœnæ imminentis iret ut
prænuncius ;
Sed nosset ille quum mina-
cem judicem
Servare malle, quam ferire
ac plectere,
Tectam latenter vertit in
Tharsos fugam.
  Celsam paratis pontibus
scandit ratem :
Udo revincta fune puppis
solvitur.
Itur per altum : fit procel-
losum mare :
Tum causa tanti quæritur
periculi :
Sors in fugacem missa va-
tem decidit.
  Jussus perire solus e cunc-
tis reus,
Cujus voluta crimen urna
expresserat,
Præceps rotatur, et pro-
fundo immergitur :
Exceptus inde belluinis fau-
cibus,
Alvi capacis vivus hauritur
specu.
  Intactus exin tertiæ noc-
tis vice
Monstri vomentis pellitur
singultibus,
Qua murmuranti fine fluc-
tus frangitur,
Salsosque candens spuma
tundit pumices,
Ructatus exit, seque ser-
vatum stupet.
  In Ninivitas se coactus
percito

anger; a brief delay puts off the day of doom.

The meek Avenger sends a herald of the coming woe : it is Jonas the Prophet. But he, well knowing that the threatening Judge is prone to save, rather than to strike and punish, stealthily to Tharsis flees.

A noble vessel was prepared for sail, whereon he takes his place. The anchor weighed, the vessel puts from shore. She ploughs the deep, when, lo! a storm. Endangered thus, the crew would know the cause, and casting lots, it falls upon the fugitive, the Prophet. Of all, the only one in fault is he. His guilt is clear, the lot has told the tale. Head-long is he cast, and buried in the deep ; and as he falls, a whale's huge jaw receives the Prophet, burying him alive in the sepulchre of his capacious womb.

There, for three nights, does Jonas lie unhurt ; which passed, the sick monster heaves him from his womb, just where the murmuring bil-lows break upon the shore, and whiten the salty rocks with foam. The Prophet comes forth,—wondering, but safe.
Compelled, to Ninive he turns his hurried steps. He

chides, he censures, he charges her with all her shameless crimes, saying: "The anger "of the great Avenger shall "fall upon you, and speedily "your City shall be made a "prey to fire. Believe the "prophecy I speak."

Then to the summit of a lofty hill he goes, from whence to see the thickened clouds of smoke rising from the ruined heap, and gaze upon the pile of unpitied dead. Suddenly there grows upon the spot an ivy-tree, whose knotted branches yield a shaded cover.

But scarce had the mournful City felt the wound of her coming grief, than deathly fear possesses her. Her people and her senate, her young and old, youths pale with panic, and women wailing loud, scamper in groups along the spacious walls.

It is decreed,—the anger of Christ shall by fasting be appeased. Henceforth, they spurn to eat. Matrons doff their trinkets, and vest in dingy garbs, and, for their wreaths of pearls and silks, sprinkle ashes on their hair.

Patricians put on robes of sombre hue; the people, weeping, take hair-shirts for their dress; disheveled maidens clad in skins of beasts, and hide their faces in veils of black. Children, too, make the dust of earth their bed.

Gressu reflectit; quos ut increpaverat,
Pudenda censor imputans opprobria.
Impendet, inquit, ira summi vindicis,
Urbemque flamma mox cremabit : credite.
Apicem deinceps ardui montis petit,
Visurus inde conglobatum turbidæ
Fumum ruinæ, cladis et diræ struem,
Tectus flagellis multinodi germinis,
Nato et repente perfruens umbraculo.

Sed mœsta postquam civitas vulnus novi
Hausit doloris, heu ! supremum palpitat.
Cursant per ampla congregatim mœnia
Plebs, et senatus, omnis ætas civium,
Pallens juventus, ejulantes feminæ.

Placet frementem publicis jejuniis
Placare Christum : mos edendi spernitur.
Glaucos amictus induit monilibus
Matrona demptis, proque gemma, et serico
Crinem fluentem sordidus spargit cinis.

Squalent recincta veste pullati patres,
Setasque plangens turba sumit textiles,
Impexa villis virgo bestialibus,
Nigrante vultum contegit velamine,
Jacens arenis et puer provolvitur.

Rex ipse Coos æstuan-
    tem murices
Lænam revulsa dissipabat
    fibula,
Gemmas virentes, et lapil-
    los sutiles,
Insigne frontis exuebat vin-
    culum
Turpi capillos impeditus
    pulvere.

The king himself from his shoulders tears the Cossian purple robe, and for the diadem that decks his brow with emeralds and gems, strews grim ashes on his head.

Nullus bibendi, nemo
    vescendi memor:
Jejuna mensas pubes omnis
    liquerat:
Quin et negato lacte vagien-
    tium
Fletu madescunt parvulo-
    rum cunulæ:
Succum papillæ parca nu-
    trix derogat.

None think of drink or meat. Among the youths, not one would touch the food prepared. Nay, babes are kept from their mothers' breasts, and in their cradles, wet with tears, these little fasters lie.

Greges et ipsos claudit
    armentalium
Solers virorum cura, ne
    vagum pecus
Contingat ore rorulenta
    gramina,
Potum strepentis neve fontis
    hauriat;
Vacuis querelæ personant
    præsepibus.

The herdsman, too, pens up his flock with care, lest, left to roam, the dewy grass or rippling fount should tempt them to transgress the universal fast; but now, pent up, their moans rebellow through their prison-cave.

Mollitus his, et talibus,
    brevem Deus
Iram refrænat, temperans
    oraculum
Prosper sinistrum: prona
    nam clementia
Haud difficulter supplicum
    mortalium
Solvit reatum, fitque fau-
    trix flentium.

Thus is God appeased, his anger brief restrained, and threatened evil yields to proffered love: for mercy leans to pardon men their sins, if they but humbly pray; and when they weep, she makes herself their friend.

Let us close the day with these stanzas in honour of the holy Cross. We have taken them from the Triodion of the Greek Church.

HYMN.

(Feria VI. mediæ Septimanæ.)

Purified by our fast, let us, to the praise and glory of the Omnipotent God, venerate that most holy Cross, whereon Christ, with his arms stretched forth, overcame the power of our enemy.

The saving Cross, that sanctifies us, is now exposed before our eyes. Let us draw nigh, having purified our body and our soul.

Cleanse me, O merciful Saviour, by the fire of thy commandments, and grant that I may contemplate thy saving Passion, and lovingly adore it, having the Cross for my protection and defence.

Having our hearts purified by the waters of our fast, let us, with faith, embrace the wood of the Cross, on which Christ was crucified, and gave us the water of immortality.

Having thy Cross as our sail, we have already winged our way half through the saving voyage of our fast. Lead us by the same, O Jesus our Saviour, into the haven of thy Passion.

Moses on the mount was a figure of thee, O holy Cross, *(when he prayed with his outstretched arms,)* unto the destruction of the Amalekites. Grant that we, who sign thee on ourselves, and lovingly gaze on and venerate thee, may, by thy power, put our spiritual enemies to flight.

Sanctissimum lignum, in quo Christus manibus extensis adversarias potestates devicit, adoremus jejunio nitidi, ad laudem et gloriam Omnipotentis.

Crux salutifera sanctificationem suppeditans proposita cernitur. Accedamus, cor et corpus emundantes.

Igne mandatorum tuorum munda me, benigne, et da, ut salutiferam Passionem tuam intuear, et cum desiderio adorem, Cruce vallatus et conservatus.

Aquis jejunii pectora purgati, lignum Crucis fideliter amplectamur, in quo Christus crucifixus aquam immortalitatis nobis emisit.

Crucis velut velo alati, salutarem jejunii navigationem jam mediam emensi sumus, Jesu Salvator, per quam deduc nos ad Passionis tuæ portum.

Præmonstrabat te Moyses in monte, o Crux, in gentium interitum. Nos vero efformantes te, et corde intuentes et adorantes, hostes carnis expertes virtute tua profligamus.

TUESDAY

IN PASSION WEEK.

THE Station, in Rome, was formerly the Church of the Martyr Saint Cyriacus, and as such it is still given in the Roman Missal; but this holy sanctuary having been destroyed, and the relics of the holy Deacon translated to the Church of Saint Mary *in Via lata*, it is here that the Station is now held.

COLLECT.

Nostra tibi, Domine, quæsumus, sint accepta jejunia: quæ nos expiando, gratia tua dignos efficiant; et ad remedia perducant æterna. Per Christum Dominum nostrum. Amen.

May our fast, O Lord, we beseech thee, be acceptable to thee, and, having purified us from sin, make us worthy of thy grace, and procure us everlasting remedies. Through Christ our Lord. Amen.

EPISTLE.

Lectio Danielis Prophetæ.

Cap. XIV.

In diebus illis: Congregati sunt Babylonii ad regem, et dixerunt ei: Trade nobis Danielem, qui Bel destruxit, et draconem interfecit; alioquin interficiemus te et domum tuam. Vidit ergo rex quod irruerent in

Lesson from Daniel the Prophet.

Ch. XIV.

In those days: The people of Babylon gathered together against the king, and said to him: Deliver up to us Daniel, who hath destroyed Bel, and killed the Dragon, otherwise we will destroy thee and thy house. And the king saw that they pressed upon him violently; and being constrained by necessity, he delivered Daniel to them. And they cast him into the den of lions, and he was there six days. And in the den there were seven lions, and they had given to them two carcases every day, and two sheep: but then they were not given unto them, to the intent that they might devour Daniel. Now there was in Judea a prophet called Habacuc, and he had boiled pottage, and had broken bread in a bowl; and was going into the field to carry it to the reapers. And the Angel of the Lord said to Habacuc: Carry the dinner which thou hast, into Babylon, to Daniel, who is in the lions' den. And Habacuc said: Lord, I never saw Babylon, nor do I know the den. And the Angel of the Lord took him by the top of his head, and carried him by the hair of his head, and set him in Babylon, over the den, in the force of his spirit. And Habacuc cried, saying: O Daniel, thou servant of God, take the dinner that God hath sent thee. And Daniel said: Thou hast remembered me, O God, and thou hast not forsaken them that love thee. And Daniel arose and ate. And the Angel of the Lord presently set Habacuc again in his own place. And upon the seventh day the king came to bewail Daniel: and he came to the den, and looked in, and behold Daniel was sitting in the midst of the

eum vehementer: et necessitate compulsus tradidit eis Danielem. Qui miserunt eum in lacum leonum, et erat ibi diebus sex. Porro in lacu erant leones septem, et dabantur eis duo corpora quotidie, et duæ oves: et tunc non data sunt eis, ut devorarent Danielem. Erat autem Habacuc propheta in Judæa, et ipse coxerat pulmentum, et intriverat panes in alveolo: et ibat in campum, ut ferret messoribus. Dixitque Angelus Domini ad Habacuc: Fer prandium quod habes, in Babylonem Danieli, qui est in lacu leonum. Et dixit Habacuc: Domine, Babylonem non vidi, et lacum nescio. Et apprehendit eum Angelus Domini in vertice ejus, et portavit eum capillo capitis sui, posuitque eum in Babylone supra lacum in impetu spiritus sui. Et clamavit Habacuc, dicens: Daniel, serve Dei, tolle prandium quod misit tibi Deus. Et ait Daniel: Recordatus es mei Deus, et non dereliquisti diligentes te. Surgensque Daniel comedit. Porro Angelus Domini restituit Habacuc confestim in loco suo. Venit ergo rex die septimo, ut lugeret Danielem: et venit ad lacum, et introspexit, et ecce Daniel sedens in medio leonum. Et exclamavit voce magna rex, dicens: Magnus es, Domine Deus Danielis. Et extraxit eum de lacu leonum. Porro illos qui perditionis ejus causa fuerant, intromisit in lacum, et devorati sunt in momento coram eo. Tunc rex ait : Paveant omnes habitantes in universa terra Deum Danielis ; quia ipse est salvator, faciens signa et mirabilia in terra : qui liberavit Danielem de lacu leonum.

lions. And the king cried out with a loud voice, saying : Great art thou, O Lord, the God of Daniel. And he drew him out of the lions' den. But those that had been the cause of his destruction, he cast into the den, and they were devoured in a moment before him. Then the king said : Let all the inhabitants of the whole earth fear the God of Daniel ; for he is the Saviour, working signs and wonders in the earth ; who hath delivered Daniel out of the lions' den.

This Lesson was intended, in an especial manner, as an instruction to the Catechumens. They were preparing to enrol themselves as Christians ; it was, therefore, necessary that they should have examples put before them, which they might study and imitate. Daniel, cast into the Lions' Den for having despised and destroyed the idol Bel, was the type of a Martyr. This Prophet had confessed the true God in Babylon ; he had put to death a Dragon, to which the people, after Bel had been destroyed, had given their idolatrous worship : nothing less than Daniel's death could appease their indignation. The holy man, full of confidence in God, allowed himself to be thrown into the Lions' Den, thus setting an example of courageous faith to the future Christians: they would imitate him, and, for three centuries, would nobly shed their blood for the establishment of the Church of Christ. In the Roman catacombs, we continually meet with the representation of Daniel surrounded by lions, and many of these paintings date from the ages of Persecution. Thus, the eye of the Catechumens could see what their ear heard,—both told them to be ready for trial and sacrifice.

It is true, the history of Daniel showed them the power of God interfering and delivering him from death; but they were fully aware, that in order to merit a like deliverance, they would have to show a like constancy, and be ready to suffer death, rather than deny their faith. From time to time, a Christian was led to the amphitheatre, and the wild beasts would fawn at his feet; but such miracles only put off the Martyr's sacrifice, and perhaps won others to the faith.

It was the Prophet's courage, and not his victory over the lions, that the Church proposed to her Catechumens. The great thing for them to bear in mind, was this maxim of our Lord: *Fear not them that kill the body, and are not able to kill the soul; but rather fear him that can destroy both soul and body into hell.*[1] We are the descendants of these early Christians; but our faith has not cost us what it cost them. And yet we have a tyrant to try even *ours:* we have to confess our faith, not indeed before Proconsuls or Emperors, but before the World. Let the example of the brave Martyrs send us forth from our Lent with a courageous determination to withstand this tyrant, with his maxims, his pomps, and his works. There has been a truce between him and us, during these days of retirement and penance; but the battle will soon be renewed, and then we must stand the brunt, and show that we are Christians.

GOSPEL.

Sequel of the holy Gospel according to John.	Sequentia sancti Evangelii secundum Joannem.
Ch. VII.	*Cap. VII.*
At that time: Jesus walked in Galilee; for he would not	In illo tempore: Ambulabat Jesus in Galilæam, non

---
[1] St. Matth. x. 28.

enim volebat in Judæam ambulare, quia quærebant eum Judæi interficere. Erat autem in proximo dies festus Judæorum, Scenopegia. Dixerunt autem ad eum fratres ejus: Transi hinc, et vade in Judæam, ut et discipuli tui videant opera tua, quæ facis. Nemo quippe in occulto quid facit, et quærit ipse in palam esse: si hæc facis, manifesta teipsum mundo. Neque enim fratres ejus credebant in eum. Dicit ergo eis Jesus: Tempus meum nondum advenit: tempus autem vestrum semper est paratum. Non potest mundus odisse vos; me autem odit: quia ego testimonium perhibeo de illo, quod opera ejus mala sunt. Vos ascendite ad diem festum hunc, ego autem non ascendo ad diem festum istum: quia meum tempus nondum impletum est. Hæc cum dixisset, ipse mansit in Galilæa. Ut autem ascenderunt fratres ejus, tunc et ipse ascendit ad diem festum non manifeste, sed quasi in occulto. Judæi ergo quærebant eum in die festo, et dicebant: Ubi est ille? et murmur multum erat in turba de eo. Quidam enim dicebant: Quia bonus est. Alii autem dicebant: Non, sed seducit turbas. Nemo tamen palam loquebatur de illo, propter metum Judæorum.

walk in Judea, because the Jews sought to kill him. Now the Jews' feast of Tabernacles was at hand. And his brethren said to him: Depart from hence, and go into Judea, that thy disciples also may see thy works which thou dost. For there is no man that doth anything in secret, and he himself seeketh to be known openly; if thou do these things, manifest thyself to the world. For neither did his brethren believe in him. Then Jesus said to them: My time is not yet come; but your time is always ready. The world cannot hate you; but me it hateth: because I give testimony of it, that the works thereof are evil. Go you up to this festival day, but I go not up to this festival day; because my time is not accomplished. When he had said these things, he himself staid in Galilee. But after his brethren were gone up, then he also went up to the feast, not openly, but as it were in secret. The Jews therefore sought him on the festival day, and said: Where is he? And there was much murmuring among the multitude concerning him. For some said: He is a good man. And others said: No, but he seduceth the people. Yet no man spoke openly of him, for fear of the Jews.

The facts here related refer to an earlier part of

our Lord's life; but the Church proposes them to our consideration to-day, on account of their connection with those given us in the Gospels read to us during the last few days. We learn from these words of St. John, that the Jews were plotting the death of Jesus, not only when this the last Pasch for the Synagogue was approaching, but even so far back as the Feast of Tabernacles, which was kept in September. The Son of God was reduced to the necessity of going from place to place *as it were in secret*: if he would go to Jerusalem, he must take precautions! Let us adore these humiliations of the Man-God, who has deigned to sanctify every position of life, even that of the just man persecuted and obliged to hide himself from his enemies. It would have been an easy matter for him to confound his adversaries by working miracles, such as those which Herod's curiosity sought for; he could have compelled them to treat him with the reverence that was due to him. But this is not God's way; he does not force man to duty; he acts, and then leaves man to recognise his Creator's claims. In order to do this, man must be attentive and humble, he must impose silence on his passions. The divine light shows itself to the soul that thus comports herself. First, she sees the actions, the works, of God; then, she believes, and *wishes* to believe; her happiness, as well as her merit, lies in Faith, and faith will be recompensed in eternity with Light,—with the Vision.

Flesh and blood cannot understand this; they love show and noise. The Son of God, having come down upon this earth, could not subject himself to such an abasement as that of making a parade of his infinite power before men. He had to work miracles, in order to give a guarantee of his mission; but, as Man, everything he did was not to be a miracle. By far the longest period of his life was devoted to the humble duties of a creature; **had it not been so, how should we have learned from him** what we so much needed to know? *His Brethren,* (the Jews gave the name of *Brothers* to all who were collaterally related,) *his Brethren* wished Jesus to make a display of his miraculous power, for some of the glory would have accrued to them. This their ambition caused our Lord to address them in these strong words, upon which we should meditate during this holy season, for, later on, we shall stand in need of the teaching: "The world cannot hate *you;* but *me* it hateth." Let us, therefore, for the time to come, not please the world; its friendship would separate us from Jesus Christ.

Humiliate capita vestra Deo.

Bow down your heads to God.

Da nobis, quæsumus, Domine, perseverantem in tua voluntate famulatum : ut in diebus nostris, et merito et numero, populus tibi serviens augeatur. Per Christum Dominum nostrum. Amen.

Grant us, O Lord, we beseech thee, perseverance in thy service; that in our days, thy faithful may increase both in number and goodness. Through Christ our Lord. Amen.

The following devout Hymn, taken from the ancient Roman-French Missals, may serve us as an expression of the sentiments we entertain towards our loving Redeemer.

HYMN.

Rex Christe factor omnium.
Redemptor et credentium :
Placare votis supplicum
Te laudibus colentium.
　Cujus benigna gratia
Crucis per alma vulnera,

O Jesus! thou King and Creator of all, Redeemer, too, of believers, be appeased by the prayers and praise of thy humble suppliants.
　'Twas thy loving grace that, by the dear wounds of the

Cross, broke so powerfully the fetters forged by our first Parents.

Thou, that art the Creator of the stars, didst deign to assume a body of flesh, and endure the most humiliating sufferings.

Thy hands were tied, that thou mightest loosen sinners, accomplices of a world condemned: thou didst suffer shame, so to cleanse away the manifold sins of the world.

Thou, our Redeemer, art fastened to the Cross, but thou movest the whole earth: thou breathest forth thy mighty Spirit, and the world is buried in darkness.

But soon we see thee shining triumphantly on the high throne of thy Father's glory: do thou, O best of Kings, defend us by the protection of the Holy Spirit. Amen.

Virtute solvit ardua
Primi parentis vincula.

Qui es Creator siderum
Tegmen subisti carneum:
Dignatus es vilissimam
Pati doloris formulam.

Ligatus es ut solveres
Mundi ruentis complices:
Per probra tergens crimina
Quæ mundus auxit plurima.

Cruci redemptor figeris,
Terram sed omnem concutis:
Tradis potentem spiritum,
Nigrescit atque sæculum.

Mox in paternæ gloriæ
Victor resplendens culmine:
Cum Spiritus munimine
Defende nos, Rex optime. Amen.

Let us pay our homage to the holy Cross, in these words of the Greek Liturgy.

HYMN.
(Feria IV. mediæ Septimanæ.)

Thou, O Lord God, the Creator of all things, wast lifted up on the Cross, in the middle of the earth; thou didst draw up to thyself that human nature, which had fallen by the most wicked persuasion of the enemy. Wherefore we pay thee our loyal homage, for thy Passion has strengthened us.

The light of fasting has purified our senses; may we be

Dominus omnium et conditor Deus, in medio terræ in Crucem elevatus es, attrahens ad te eam, quæ pessimo inimici suasu corruerat, humanam naturam. Quapropter sincere te concelebramus, Passione tua roborati.

Mundatis sensibus jejunii lumine, intellectualibus Crucis radiis largissime illustremur, eamque hodie propositam reverenter conspicientes, castis labiis, ore et corde adoremus.

Locum ubi steterunt pedes Domini adoremus, Crucem videlicet divinam; obsecrantes ut animæ nostræ pedes in petra divinorum mandatorum firmentur, et ut gressus ejus, divina gratia in viam pacis dirigantur.

Plaudite omnes fines terræ in hymnis, quando adorari videtis lignum in quo Christus suspensus, et diabolus vulneratus est.

Vivifica Crux hodie proponitur: cum gaudio igitur et timore adoremus Domini Crucem, ut Spiritum Sanctum accipiamus.

Accedens ut te tangam, vivifica Crux, cohorresco et lingua et mente, cernens in te divinum Domini mei sanguinem effusum esse.

Confirma, Domine, Ecclesiam tuam, quam acquisivisti virtute Crucis tuæ; in illa enim inimicum triumphasti, totumque mundum illuminasti.

most brightly enlightened by the spiritual rays of thy Cross. On this day it is exposed to our view; grant, that we may devoutly kiss it, and venerate it in our hymns and hearts.

Let us adore the place where stood his feet, that is, the holy Cross, and beseech him to firmly fix the feet of our soul on the rock of his divine commandments, and, by his holy grace, guide her steps into the way of peace.

Loudly sing your hymns, O all ye ends of the earth, when ye behold men venerating that wood, whereon Christ was fastened, and whereby Satan received his wound.

The life-giving Cross is this day exposed: let us, then, with joy and fear, venerate the Cross of our Lord, that we may receive the Holy Ghost.

O life-giving Cross, my tongue and heart tremble with fear, as I draw nigh to touch thee, for I see the divine Blood of my Lord poured forth upon thee.

Strengthen, O Lord, thy Church, which thou didst purchase to thyself by the power of thy Cross; for by the Cross thou didst triumph over the enemy and enlighten the whole world.

WEDNESDAY

IN PASSION WEEK.

At Rome, the Station is in the Church of Saint Marcellus, Pope and Martyr. This Church was once the house of the holy lady Lucina, who gave it to the Pontiff, that he might consecrate it to God.

COLLECT.

Enlighten, O God of mercy, the hearts of thy people by means of this holy fast; and since all our devotion is the effect of thy bounty, mercifully hear the petitions we make. Through Christ our Lord. Amen.

Sanctificato hoc jejunio, Deus, tuorum corda fidelium miserator illustra: et quibus devotionis præstas affectum, præbe supplicantibus pium benignus auditum. Per Christum Dominum nostrum. Amen.

EPISTLE.

Lesson from the book of Leviticus.

Lectio Libri Levitici.

Ch. XIX.

Cap. XIX.

In those days: The Lord spake to Moses, saying: Speak to all the assembly of the children of Israel, and thou shalt say to them: I am the Lord your God. You shall not steal. You shall not lie: neither shall any man deceive his neighbour. Thou shalt not

In diebus illis: Locutus est Dominus ad Moysen, dicens: Loquere ad omnem cœtum filiorum Israël, et dices ad eos: Ego Dominus Deus vester. Non facietis furtum. Non mentiemini, nec decipiet unusquisque proximum suum. Non perjurabis in nomine meo, nec pollues nomen Dei tui. Ego Dominus. Non facies calumniam, proximo tuo nec vi opprimes eum. Non morabitur opus mercenarii tui apud te usque mane. Non maledices surdo, nec coram cæco pones offendiculum : sed timebis Dominum Deum tuum, quia ego sum Dominus. Non facies quod iniquum est, nec injuste judicabis. Non consideres personam pauperis, nec honores vultum potentis. Juste judica proximo tuo Non eris criminator, nec susurro in populo. Non stabis contra sanguinem proximi tui. Ego Dominus. Non oderis fratrem tuum in corde tuo, sed publice argue eum, ne habeas super illo peccatum. Non quæras ultionem, nec memor eris injuriæ civium tuorum. Diliges amicum tuum sicut teipsum. Ego Dominus. Leges meas custodite. Ego enim sum Dominus Deus vester.

swear falsely by my name, nor profane the name of thy God. I am the Lord. Thou shalt not calumniate thy neighbour, nor oppress him by violence. The wages of him that has been hired by thee, shall not abide with thee until the morning. Thou shalt not speak evil of the deaf, nor put a stumbling block before the blind : but thou shalt fear the Lord thy God, because I am the Lord. Thou shalt not do that which is unjust, nor judge unjustly. Respect not the person of the poor, nor honour the countenance of the mighty. Judge thy neighbour according to justice. Thou shalt not be a detractor nor a whisperer among the people. Thou shalt not stand against the blood of thy neighbour. I am the Lord. Thou shalt not hate thy brother in thy heart, but reprove him openly, lest thou incur sin through him. Seek not revenge, nor be mindful of the injury of thy citizens. Thou shalt love thy friend as thyself. I am the Lord. Keep ye my laws, for I am the Lord your God.

This passage from Leviticus, wherein our duties to our neighbour are so clearly and so fully defined, is read to us to-day, in order that we may see how we fulfil these important duties, and correct whatever short-comings we may discover in ourselves. It is God who here speaks; it is God who commands. Observe that phrase: *I am the Lord*: he repeats it several times, to show us that if we injure our neighbour, He, God himself, will become the avenger.

How strange must not such doctrine have seemed to the Catechumens, who had been brought up in the selfish and heartless principles of Paganism! Here they are told, that all men are Brethren, and that God is the common Father of all, commanding all to love one another with sincere charity, and without distinction of nation or class. Let us Christians resolve to fulfil this precept to the letter: these are days for good resolutions. Let us remember that the commandments we have been reading were given to the Israelite people, many ages before the preaching of the Law of Love. If, then, God exacted from the Jew a cordial love of his fellow-men, when the divine law was written on mere tablets of stone; what will he not require from the Christian, who can now read that Law in the heart of the Man-God, who has come down from heaven and made himself our Brother, in order that we might find it easier and sweeter to fulfil the precept of charity? *Human nature united in his Person to the Divine*, is henceforth sacred; it has become an object of the heavenly Father's love. It was out of fraternal love for this our nature, that Jesus suffered death, teaching us, by his own example, to have such love for our *brethren*, that, if necessary, *we ought to lay down our lives for them*.[1] It is the Beloved Disciple that teaches us this, and he had it from his Divine Master.

GOSPEL.

Sequel of the holy Gospel according to John.	Sequentia sancti Evangelii secundum Joannem.
Ch. X.	*Cap. X.*
At that time: It was the feast of the Dedication at Jerusalem: and it was winter. And Jesus walked in the	In illo tempore: Facta sunt encænia in Jerosolymis: et hiems erat. Et ambulabat Jesus in templo,

[1] I. St. John, iii. 16.

in porticu Salomonis. Circumdederunt ergo eum Judæi, et dicebant ei: Quousque animam nostram tollis? Si tu es Christus, dic nobis palam. Respondit eis Jesus: Loquor vobis, et non creditis. Opera quæ ego facio in nomine Patris mei, hæc testimonium perhibent de me. Sed vos non creditis, quia non estis ex ovibus meis. Oves meæ vocem meam audiunt: et ego cognosco eas, et sequuntur me: et ego vitam æternam do eis: et non peribunt in æternum, et non rapiet eas quisquam de manu mea. Pater meus quod dedit mihi, majus omnibus est: et nemo potest rapere de manu Patris mei. Ego, et Pater unum sumus. Sustulerunt ergo lapides Judæi, ut lapidarent eum. Respondit eis Jesus: Multa bona opera ostendi vobis ex Patre meo; propter quod eorum opus me lapidatis? Responderunt ei Judæi: De bono opere non lapidamus te, sed de blasphemia: et quia tu homo cum sis, facis teipsum Deum. Respondit eis Jesus: Nonne scriptum est in lege vestra: Quia ego dixi, Dii estis? Si illos dixit deos, ad quos sermo Dei factus est, et non potest solvi Scriptura: quem Pater sanctificavit, et misit in mundum, vos dicitis: Quia blasphemas; quia dixi, Filius Dei sum? Si non facio opera Patris mei, nolite credere mihi. Si

temple, in Solomon's porch: the Jews therefore came round about him, and said to him: How long dost thou hold our souls in suspense? If thou be the Christ, tell us plainly. Jesus answered them: I speak to you, and you believe not. The works that I do in the name of my Father, they give testimony of me. But you do not believe because you are not of my sheep. My sheep hear my voice: and I know them, and they follow me: and I give them eternal life: and they shall not perish for ever, and no man shall pluck them out of my hand. That which my Father hath given me, is greater than all: and no man can snatch it out of the hand of my Father. I and the Father are one. The Jews then took up stones to stone him. Jesus answered them: Many good works I have shewed you from my Father; for which of those works do you stone me? The Jews answered him: For a good work we stone thee not, but for blasphemy: and because that thou, being a man, makest thyself God. Jesus answered them: Is it not written in your law: I said you are gods? If he called them gods, to whom the word of God was spoken, and the Scripture cannot be broken; do you say of him, whom the Father hath sanctified and sent into the world: Thou blasphemest; because I said I am the Son of God? If I do not the works of my Father,

believe me not. But if I do, though you will not believe me, believe the works, that you may know, and believe that the Father is in me, and I in the Father.	autem facio, et si mihi non vultis credere, operibus credite, ut cognoscatis, et credatis quia Pater in me est, et ego in Patre.

After the Feast of *Tabernacles* came that of the *Dedication*, and Jesus remained in Jerusalem. The hatred his enemies bore him is greater than ever. They come *round about him*, that they may make him say he is *the Christ*, and then accuse him of claiming a mission which does not belong to him. Jesus deigns not to reply to their question, but tells them that they have seen his *works*, and that these give ample testimony of his being Christ, the Son of God. It is by faith, and by faith alone, that man can here know his God. God manifests himself by his divine works: man sees them, and is bound to believe the truth to which they bear testimony. By thus believing, he has both the certitude of what he believes, and the merit of his believing. The proud Jew rebels against this: he would fain dictate to God how he should act, and sees not that such a pretension is impious and absurd.

But, if Jesus openly declare the truth, he will scandalise these evil-minded men! Be it so: the truth must be preached. Our Lord has others to consult besides them; there are the well-intentioned, and *they* will believe what he teaches. He, therefore, utters these sublime words, whereby he declares, not only that he is Christ, but that he is God: *I and the Father are one.* He knew that this would enrage his enemies; but he had to make himself known to the world, and arm the Church against the false doctrines of heretics, who were to rise up in future ages. One of these is to be Arius, who will teach that Jesus is not God, but only the most perfect of creatures: the Church will answer, that Jesus is *one with the* **Father**,—*consubstantial* to the **Father**: and, then, after causing much trouble and sin, Arianism will die out, and be forgotten. The Jews, mentioned in to-day's Gospel, are the fore-runners of Arius; they understand what our Lord says,—he says he is God; and they seek to stone him. Jesus gives them a fresh grace; he shows them why they should receive what he here teaches: he reminds them, by the Scriptures they knew off by heart, that the name *god* has sometimes been applied, in a limited sense, to men who had certain high offices put upon them by heaven; and then, he bids them think of all the miracles they have seen him work, which so plainly testify to his being assisted by his Father, and once more declares himself to be God, saying: *The Father is in me, and I in the Father.* But men, hardened in obstinacy as these are, cannot be convinced; and the sin they have committed against the Holy Ghost is working its effects. How different is it with the *Sheep* of this divine Shepherd! They *hear his voice;* they *follow him;* he *gives them eternal life; no man shall pluck them out of* his *hand.* Happy *Sheep* indeed! They believe, because they love; and as it is through the heart that Truth gains ascendency over them, so is it by pride of intellect that darkness gets admission into the soul of the unbeliever, and lasts as long as pride lasts. Alas! poor unbeliever! he loves his darkness; he calls it *light;* he blasphemes when he thinks he reasons, just as these Jews crucified the Son of God, that, as they said, they might give glory to God!

Humiliate capita vestra Deo.

Adesto supplicationibus nostris, omnipotens Deus; et quibus fiduciam sperandæ pietatis indulges, con-

Bow down your heads to God.

Hear our prayers and entreaties, O Almighty God, and grant that those to whom thou givest hopes of thy mercy,

may experience the effects of thy usual clemency. Through Christ our Lord. Amen.

suetæ misericordiæ tribue benignus effectum. Per Christum Dominum nostrum. Amen.

The Mozarabic Breviary gives us the following beautiful prayer, which consists of exclamations to our suffering Jesus.

PRAYER.

(Sabbato Dominicæ V. Quadragesimæ.)

℣. O Jesus! thou true Son of God,
℟. Graciously hear us! have mercy on thy suppliant people.
℣. Thou that alone didst save the world by the triumph of thy Cross, do thou, by the Blood thou didst shed, deliver us.
℟. And graciously hear us.
℣. By thy Death, thou didst destroy death; By thy Resurrection, thou didst give us life; for our sakes, thou didst suffer undue punishment.
℟. And graciously hear us.
℣. May we celebrate, in peace, these days of thy Passion, and thereby be consoled by thy sweetness.
℟. And graciously hear us.
℣. Let not them perish, for whom thou didst suffer the Cross; but, by thy Cross, lead them to life everlasting.
℟. And graciously hear us.

℣. Verus Dei Filius Christe,
℟. Exaudi: populo supplicanti miserere.
℣. Qui triumpho Crucis tuæ salvasti solus orbem, tu cruoris tui pœna nos libera.
℟. Et exaudi.
℣. Qui moriens mortem damnas, resurgens vitam præstas, sustinens pro nobis pœnam indebitam.
℟. Et exaudi.
℣. Passionis tuæ dies celebremus indemnes: ut per hoc dulcedo tua nos foveat.
℟. Et exaudi.
℣. Pro quibus passus es crucem, non permittas perire; sed per crucem duc ad vitam perpetuam.
℟. Et exaudi.

Let us now turn towards the Holy Cross. These words of the Greek Church, in her Triodion, will assist our devotion.

HYMN.
(Feria V. mediæ Septimanæ.)

Crucis speciem insinuans, manus, permutato ordine, olim expandit decantatissimus Jacob, benedictionem nepotibus impertiens; simulque salutiferam benedictionem quæ ad nos omnes pertingit indicans.

Te salutiferam armaturam, te invictum trophæum, lætitiæ signum, quo mors occisa est, amplectimur, illustres effecti ejus gloria qui in te, Crux honoratissima, affixus est.

Assistunt incorporearum Virtutum ordines trementes coram ligno vitam præbente. In te enim Christus sanguinem effudit, pretium redemptionis repræsentans, dæmonibus piaculare et capitale, ob perniciem hominibus illatam.

Percussum me hostis gladio sana sanguine tuo, Verbum, et lancea celeriter peccatorum meorum chirographum disrumpe, et in librum vitæ inscribe.

Inferni habitaculum concussisti, ubi in terra defixa es: fidelibus autem fulcrum inconcussum et stabilis protectio effecta es, ô veneranda Crux.

Feraces virtutum effecti decerpamus divini ligni vivificos fructus, quos protulit

When the most praiseworthy Patriarch Jacob, was, of old, about to bless his children, he crossed his arms; in this he represented the Cross, and prefigured that saving blessing which thence came to each of us.

We embrace thee, most venerable Cross, as our armour of salvation, the invincible trophy, the standard of joy, whereby Death was put to death; for we have been made to share in the glory of Him, that was nailed upon thee.

The choirs of the angelic Powers stand in holy awe around thee, O life-giving tree! For it was on thee that Christ shed his Blood, which was the price of our redemption, and which utterly destroyed all those rights that sin had given the devil over mankind.

O Word (made Flesh)! the sword of the enemy hath struck me; heal me by thy Blood. Speedily tear, with thy Spear, the hand-writing of my sins, and write my name in the book of life.

O venerable Cross! when thou wast fixed in the earth, thou didst make to tremble the region of hell; but thou wast made a firm support and unshaken protection to the Faithful.

Being made fruitful in virtue, let us pluck from the divine Tree those life-giving fruits, offered unto us by that rich Vine, Jesus, who lay stretched upon it.

O Jesus! we praise thy immense goodness, as we venerate the Cross, and Spear, and Reed, whereby, O merciful God, thou didst remove the wall of enmity that stood between us and thee.

nobis in hoc extensus Jesus vitis illa fructifera.

Laudamus, Jesu, immensam bonitatem tuam adorantes Crucem, lanceam et arundinem per quam sustulisti, misericors, inimicitiarum medium parietem.

THURSDAY

IN PASSION WEEK.

THE Station at Rome, is in the Church of Saint Apollinaris, who was a disciple of St. Peter, and, afterwards, Bishop of Ravenna, and Martyr.

COLLECT.

Præsta, quæsumus, omnipotens Deus, ut dignitas conditionis humanæ per immoderantiam sauciata, medicinalis parcimoniæ studio reformetur. Per Christum Dominum nostrum. Amen.

Grant, we beseech thee, O Almighty God, that the dignity of human nature, which hath been wounded by excess, may be cured by the practice of healing temperance. Through Christ our Lord. Amen.

EPISTLE.

Lectio Danielis Prophetæ.

Lesson from Daniel the Prophet.

Cap. III.

Ch. III.

In diebus illis: Oravit Azarias Dominum, dicens: Domine Deus noster, ne quæsumus, tradas nos in perpetuum propter nomen tuum, et ne dissipes testamentum tuum: neque auferas misericordiam tuam a nobis propter Abraham dilectum tuum et Isaac

In those days, Azarias prayed to the Lord, saying: O Lord our God, deliver us not up for ever, we beseech thee, for thy name's sake, and abolish not thy covenant: and take not away thy mercy from us, for the sake of Abraham thy beloved, and Isaac thy servant, and Israel thy holy one: to whom thou hast spoken, promising that thou wouldst multiply their seed as the stars of heaven, and as the sand that is on the sea shore. For we, O Lord, are diminished more than any nation, and are brought low in all the earth this day for our sins. Neither is there at this time prince, or leader, or prophet, or holocaust, or sacrifice, or oblation, or incense, or place of first-fruits before thee, that we may find thy mercy: nevertheless, in a contrite heart and humble spirit, let us be accepted. As in holocausts of rams, and bullocks, and as in thousands of fat lambs: so let our sacrifice be made in thy sight this day, that it may please thee: for there is no confusion to them that trust in thee. And now we follow thee with all our heart, and we fear thee, and seek thy face. Put us not to confusion, but deal with us according to thy meekness, and according to the multitude of thy mercies. And deliver us according to thy wonderful works, and give glory to thy name, O Lord; and let all them be confounded that shew evils to thy servants, let them be confounded in all thy might, and let their strength be broken; and let them know that thou art the Lord, the only God, and glorious over all the world, O Lord our God.

servum tuum, et Israël sanctum tuum: quibus locustus es, pollicens quod multiplicares semen eorum sicut stellas cœli, et sicut arenam, quæ est in littore maris: quia, Domine, imminuti sumus plus quam omnes gentes, sumusque humiles in universa terra hodie propter peccata nostra. Et non est in tempore hoc princeps, et dux, et propheta, neque holocaustum, neque sacrificium, neque oblatio, neque incensum, neque locus primitiarum coram te, ut possimus invenire misericordiam tuam: sed in animo contrito, et spiritu humilitatis suscipiamur. Sicut in holocausto arietum, et taurorum, et sicut in millibus agnorum pinguium: sic fiat sacrificium nostrum in conspectu tuo hodie, ut placeat tibi: quoniam non est confusio confidentibus in te. Et nunc sequimur te in toto corde, et timemus te, et quærimus faciem tuam. Ne confundas nos, sed fac nobiscum juxta mansuetudinem tuam, et secundum multitudinem misericordiæ tuæ. Et erue nos in mirabilibus tuis, et da gloriam nomini tuo, Domine: et confundantur omnes quia ostendunt servis tuis mala, confundantur in omnipotentia tua, et robur eorum conteratur; et sciant quia tu es Dominus Deus solus, et gloriosus super orbem terrarum, Domine Deus noster.

Thus did Juda, when captive in Babylon, pour forth her prayers to God, by the mouth of Azarias. Sion was desolate beyond measure; her people were in exile; her solemnities were hushed. Her children were to continue in a strange land for seventy years; after which God would be mindful of them, and lead them, by the hand of Cyrus, back to Jerusalem, when the building of the second Temple would be begun, that Temple which was to receive the Messias within its walls. What crime had Juda committed, that she should be thus severely punished? The Daughter of Sion had fallen into idolatry; she had broken the sacred engagement which made her the Spouse of her God. Her crime, however, was expiated by these seventy years of captivity, and when she returned to the land of her fathers, she never relapsed into the worship of false gods. When the Son of God came to dwell in her, he found her innocent of idolatry. But scarcely had forty years elapsed after the Ascension of this Divine Redeemer, than Juda was again an exile; not, indeed, led captive into Babylon, but dispersed in every nation under the sun, after having first seen the massacre of thousands of her children. This time, it is not merely for seventy years, but for eighteen centuries, that she is without *prince, or leader, or prophet, or holocaust, or sacrifice,* or Temple. Her new crime must be greater than idolatry, for, after all these long ages of suffering and humiliation, the justice of the Father is not appeased! It is, because the blood that was shed, by the Jewish people, on Calvary, was not the blood of a man,—it was the blood of a God. Yes, the very sight of the chastisement inflicted on the murderers proclaims to the world that they were *deicides.* Their crime was an unparalleled one; its punishment is to be so too; it is to last to the end of time, when God, *for the sake of Abraham his beloved, and Isaac his servant, and Jacob his holy one,* will visit Juda with an extraordinary grace, and her conversion will console the Church, whose affliction is then to be great by reason of the apostacy of many of her children. This spectacle of a whole people bearing on itself the curse of God for having crucified the Son of God, should make a Christian tremble for himself. It teaches him, that Divine justice is terrible, and that the Father demands an account of the Blood of his Son, even to the last drop, from those that shed it. Let us lose no time, but go at once, and, in this precious Blood, cleanse ourselves from the share we have had in the sin of the Jews; and, throwing off the chains of iniquity, let us imitate those among them, whom we see, from time to time, separating themselves from their people and returning to the Messias:—let us, also, be converts, and turn to that Jesus, whose hands are stretched out on the Cross, ever ready to receive the humble penitent.

GOSPEL.

Sequel of the holy Gospel according to Luke.

Ch. VII.

At that time: One of the Pharisees desired him to eat with him. And he went into the house of the Pharisee, and sat down to meat. And behold a woman that was in the city, a sinner, when she knew that he sat at meat in the Pharisee's house, brought an alabaster box of ointment; and standing behind at his feet, she began to wash his feet with tears, and wiped them with the hairs of her head, and kissed his feet, and anointed them with the ointment. And the Pharisee, who

Sequentia sancti Evangelii secundum Lucam.

Cap. VII.

In illo tempore: Rogabat Jesum quidam de Pharisæis, ut manducaret cum illo. Et ingressus domum Pharisæi, discubuit. Et ecce mulier, quæ erat in civitate peccatrix, ut cognovit quod accubuisset in domo Pharisæi, attulit alabastrum unguenti; et stans retro secus pedes ejus, lacrymis cœpit rigare pedes ejus, et capillis capitis sui tergebat, et osculabatur pedes ejus, et unguento ungebat. Videns autem Pharisæus, qui vocaverat eum, ait intra se dicens: Hic si esset Propheta, sciret utique, quæ, et qualis est mulier, quæ, tangit eum: quia peccatrix est. Et respondens Jesus, dixit ad illum: Simon, habeo tibi aliquid dicere. At ille ait: Magister, dic. Duo debitores erant cuidem fœneratori: unus debebat denarios quingentos, et alius quinquaginta. Non habentibus illis unde redderent, donavit utrisque. Quis ergo eum plus diligit? Respondens Simon, dixit: Æstimo quia is, cui plus donavit. At ille dixit ei: Recte judicasti. Et conversus ad mulierem, dixit Simoni: Vides hanc mulierem? Intravi in domum tuam: aquam pedibus meis non dedisti; hæc autem lacrymis rigavit pedes meos, et capillis suis tersit. Osculum mihi non dedisti; hæc autem, ex quo intravit, non cessavit osculari pedes meos. Oleo caput meum non unxisti; hæc autem unguento unxit pedes meos. Propter quod dico tibi: Remittuntur ei peccata multa, quoniam dilexit multum. Cui autem minus dimittitur, minus diligit. Dixit autem ad illam: Remittuntur tibi peccata. Et cœperunt qui simul accumbebant, dicere intra se: Quis est hic, qui etiam peccata dimittit? Dixit autem ad mulierem: Fides tua te salvam fecit: vade in pace.

had invited him, seeing it, spoke within himself, saying: This man, if he were a prophet, would know surely who and what manner of woman this is that touches him, that she is a sinner. And Jesus answering, said to him: Simon, I have somewhat to say to thee. But he said: Master, say it. A certain creditor had two debtors; the one owed five hundred pence, and the other fifty. And whereas they had not wherewith to pay, he forgave them both. Which therefore of the two loveth him most? Simon answering, said: I suppose that he to whom he forgave most. And he said to him: Thou hast judged rightly. And turning to the woman, he said unto Simon: Dost thou see this woman? I entered into thy house; thou gavest me no water for my feet, but she with tears hath washed my feet and with her hairs hath wiped them. Thou gavest me no kiss; but she, since she came in, hath not ceased to kiss my feet. My head with oil thou didst not anoint; but she with ointment hath anointed my feet. Wherefore I say to thee: Many sins are forgiven her, because she hath loved much. But to whom less is forgiven, he loveth less. And he said to her: Thy sins are forgiven thee. And they that sat at meat with him began to say within themselves: Who is this, that forgiveth sins also? And he said to the woman: Thy faith hath made thee safe: go in peace.

What consolation there is for us in this Gospel, and how different are the reflections it suggests, from those we were just making upon the Epistle! The event here related does not belong to the time of our Saviour's Passion; but, during these days of mercy, does it not behove us to glorify the meekness of that Divine Heart, which is preparing to grant pardon to countless sinners throughout the world? Besides, is not Magdalene the inseparable Companion of her dear Crucified Master, even to Calvary? Let us, then, study this admirable penitent, this type of love faithful even to death.

Magdalene had led a wicked life: as the Gospel tells us elsewhere,[1] seven devils had taken up their abode within her. But, no sooner has she seen and heard Jesus, than immediately she is filled with a horror for sin; divine love is enkindled within her heart; she has but one desire, and that is to make amends for her past life. Her sins have been public; her conversion must be so too. She has lived in vanity and luxury; she is resolved to give all up. Her perfumes are all to be for her God, her Jesus; that hair of hers, of which she has been so proud, shall serve to wipe his sacred feet; her eyes shall henceforth spend themselves in shedding tears of contrite love. The grace of the Holy Ghost urges her to go to Jesus. He is in the house of a Pharisee, who is giving an entertainment. To go to him now, would be exposing herself to observation. She cares not. Taking with her an ointment of great worth, she makes her way into the feast, throws herself at Jesus' feet, *washes them with her tears, wipes them with the hair of her head, kisses them, anoints them with the ointment.* Jesus himself tells us with what interior sentiments she accompanies these outward acts of respect: but even had he not spoken, her

---

[1] St. Mark, xvi. 9.

tears, her generosity, her position at his feet, tell us enough; she is heart-broken, she is grateful, she is humble: who, but a Pharisee, could have mistaken her?

The Pharisee, then, is shocked! His heart had within it much of that Jewish pride which is soon to crucify the Messias. He looks disdainfully at Magdalene; he is disappointed with his Guest, and murmurs out his conclusion: *This man, if he were a Prophet, would surely know who and what manner of woman this is!* Poor Pharisee!—if he had the spirit of God within him, he would recognise Jesus to be the promised Saviour, by this wonderful condescension shown to a penitent. With all his reputation as a Pharisee, how contemptible he is, compared with this woman! Jesus would give him a useful lesson, and draws the parallel between the two,—Magdalene and the Pharisee:—he passes his own divine judgment on them, and the preference is given to Magdalene. What is it, that has thus transformed her, and made her deserve, not only the pardon, but the praise, of Jesus? Her love: *She hath loved* her Redeemer, *she hath loved* him *much;* and, therefore, she was *forgiven much.* A few hours ago, and this Magdalene loved but the world and its pleasures; now, she cares for nothing, sees nothing, loves nothing, but Jesus: she is a Convert. Henceforward, she keeps close to her Divine Master; she is ambitious to supply his wants; but above all, she longs to see and hear him. When the hour of trial shall come, and his very Apostles dare not be with him, she will follow him to Calvary, stand at the foot of the Cross, and see *Him* die that has made her live.—What an argument for hope is here, even for the worst of sinners! He to whom most is forgiven, is often the most fervent in love! You, then, whose souls are burdened with sins, think of your sins and confess them; but, most of all, think how you may most love. Let your love be in proportion to your pardon, and doubt it not: *Your sins shall be forgiven.*

Bow down your heads to God.
Be propitious, O Lord, we beseech thee, to thy people; that, forsaking what displeaseth thee, they may find comfort in keeping thy law. Through Christ our Lord. Amen.

Humiliate capita vestra Deo.
Esto quæsumus, Domine, propitius plebi tuæ: ut quæ tibi non placent respuentes, tuorum potius repleantur delectationibus mandatorum. Per Christum Dominum nostrum Amen.

Let us close this Thursday of Passion Week with the following devout Hymn, taken from the Mozarabic Breviary.

HYMN.

O Word of the Father, that camest into this world, and wast made Flesh! O Lamb of God, that takest away the sins of the world! to thee do we come, and, in prostrate adoration, beseech thee to give us to drink of the Blood shed for us in thy sacred Passion.

Show unto us the marks of thy divine wounds! Let the invincible Standard of thy glorious Cross be raised on high, and, by its imperishable power, bring salvation to them that believe.

The Reed, the Nails, the Spittle, the Gall, the Crown of

Verbum Patris quod prodiit factum caro;
Agnus Dei peccata mundi auferens:
Ad te venimus cernui, ut inclytum
Bibamus almæ Passionis sanguinem.

Ostende vulnerum sacrorum stigmata:
Exsurgat insignis Crucis fortissimum
Signum, quod in vigore perpetim
Manens, credentibus salvationem conferat.

Arundo, clavi, sputa, potus myrrheus,

Corona spinarum, flagella, lancea,
Impressa sunt damnationis verbera:
Jam nostra pro his cuncta dele crimina.
Fons vulneris sacri riget præcordia,
Lavet cruor, malitiæque contagia:
Sit vita præsens absque omni crimine;
Futura detur in beato munere.
Ut cum resurgendi dies effulserit,
Orbique regni claritas illuxerit,
Sequamur ætheris viam quæ nos trahat
In se receptos jam perennes incolas.
Honor sit æterno Deo, sit gloria
Uni Patri, ejusque soli Filio
Cum Spiritu; quæ Trinitas perenniter
Vivit potens in sæculorum sæculis.
Amen.

Thorns, the Whips, the Spear, —these were the Instruments of thy sufferings: oh! cleanse us by them from all our sins.

May the Blood that gushed from thy sacred Wounds, flow on our hearts and purify them from their stains of guilt, enable us to pass through this world without sin, and give us, in the next, the reward of bliss.

That when the resurrection-day shall break upon the world, brightening it with the splendours of the eternal kingdom, we may ascend by the path that leads above, and dwell in heaven, citizens eternal.

Honour be to the Eternal God! Glory be to the One Father, and to his Only Son, together with the Holy Ghost: —the Almighty Trinity, that liveth unceasingly for ever and ever. Amen.

Let us again borrow from the Greek Church the expression of our devotion to the Holy Cross.

HYMN.
(Feria V. mediæ Septimanæ.)

Securis quam Elisæus ex Jordane retulit, Crucem significabat, qua ex profundo vanitatis retraxisti gentes lætis vocibus cantantes: Benedictus es, Deus patrum nostrorum.

The wood wherewith Eliseus drew the axe from the Jordan, was a figure of thy Cross, O Jesus! wherewith thou didst draw, from the depths of their vanities, the nations that thus sing to thee in joy: Blessed art thou the God of our Fathers!

Let the heavens rejoice together with the earth, as we venerate thy Cross; for it was by thee that Angels and men are united, and sing: Blessed is the Lord our God!

Venerating the Cross of our Lord, and glorifying our Redeemer, who was nailed upon it, let us present him a threefold homage[1]: our Compassion, like the fragrant cypress; our Faith, like the cedar; our Love, like the pine.

Thou didst stretch forth thy hands upon the Cross, to show that 'twas thou didst destroy the sin done by the hand of licentious man. Thou wast wounded with the Spear, that thou mightest wound our foe. Thou didst taste Gall, that thou mightest turn evil pleasures from us. Thy drink was Vinegar, that thou mightest be a joy to each of us.

I have eaten of the Tree of sin, and it was my ruin; I have tasted a pleasure that has caused me death. Bring me to life, O Lord! Raise me from my fall. Make me an adorer of thy Sufferings, a partner in thy Resurrection, a co-heir of them that love thee.

O Cross! thou standard of joy, thou armour invulnerable, thou glory of the Apostles,

Lætantur cum terra cœlestia ob adorationem Crucis tuæ; etenim per te Angeli et homines conjuncti sunt, clamantes: Benedictus Dominus Deus noster.

Compassionem tamquam cupressum suaveolentem, fidem tanquam cedrum, veram charitatem tanquam pinum afferentes.[1] Domine crucem adoremus, glorificantes eum qui in illa affixus est, liberatorem.

Extendisti manus tuas in ligno, incontinentis manus peccatum dissolvens; lancea vulneratus es, eademque inimicum sauciasti. Fel gustasti, et male blandam malitiam exemisti; aceto potatus es, qui omnium lætitia es.

Ligno peccati interemptus sum, gustuque voluptuoso morti traditus. Vivifica me, Domine. Excita jacentem: fac me cruciatuum tuorum adoratorem, et participem divinæ resurrectionis, et cohæredem eorum qui te diligunt.

Gaudii signum, armatura invicta, Apostolorum decus, Pontificum robur, vi-

---

[1] This is an allusion to the tradition, that the Cross was formed of the three kinds of wood here mentioned. (*Translator.*)

res suffice languenti animæ meæ, et dignare me ut te adorem, laudesque tibi decantem, clamans: Omnia opera Domini, laudate Dominum et superexaltate in sæcula.

thou strength of Pontiffs,—supply my languid soul with power, and oh! may I venerate thee, and thus cry out thy praises: "All ye works of the Lord, praise the Lord, and extol him, above all, for ever!"

FRIDAY

IN PASSION WEEK.

THE SEVEN DOLOURS OF THE BLESSED VIRGIN.

The Station, at Rome, is in the Church of Saint Stephen, on Monte Celio. By a sort of prophetic presentiment, this Church of the great Proto-Martyr was chosen as the place where the Faithful were to assemble on the Friday of Passion Week, which was to be, at a future time, the Feast consecrated to the Queen of Martyrs.

COLLECT.

Mercifully, O Lord, we beseech thee, pour forth thy grace into our hearts; that repressing our sins by voluntary mortifications, we may rather suffer for them in this life, than be condemned to eternal torments for them in the next. Through Christ our Lord. Amen.

Cordibus nostris, quæsumus, Domine, gratiam tuam benignus infunde: ut peccata nostra castigatione voluntaria cohibentes, temporaliter potius maceremur, quam suppliciis deputemur æternis. Per Christum Dominum nostrum. Amen.

EPISTLE.

Lesson from Jeremias the Prophet.

Ch. XVII.

In those days, Jeremias said:

Lectio Jeremiæ Prophetæ.

Cap. XVII.

In diebus illis, dixit Jeremias: Domine, omnes qui te derelinquunt, confundentur: recedentes a te, in terra scribentur: quoniam derelinquerunt venam aquatum viventium, Dominum. Sana me, Domine, et sanabor: salvum me fac, et salvus ero: quoniam laus mea tu es. Ecce ipsi dicunt ad me: Ubi est verbum Domini? veniat. Et ego non sum turbatus, te Pastorem sequens: et diem hominis non desideravit, tu scis. Quod egressum est de labiis meis, rectum in conspectu tuo fuit. Non sis tu mihi formidini; spes mea tu in die afflictionis. Confundantur, qui me persequuntur, et non confundar ego: paveant illi, et non paveam ego: induc super eos diem afflictionis, et duplici contritione contere eos, Domine Deus noster.

O Lord, all that forsake thee shall be confounded: they that depart from thee, shall be written in the earth, (*as on sand, from which their names shall soon be effaced,*) because they have forsaken the Lord, the vein of living waters. Heal me, O Lord, and I shall be healed, save me and I shall be saved: for thou art my praise. Behold they say to me: Where is the word of the Lord? let it come. And I am not troubled, following thee for my pastor, and I have not desired the day of man, thou knowest it. That which went out of my lips, hath been right in thy sight. Be not thou a terror unto me; thou art my hope in the day of affliction. Let them be confounded that persecute me, and let me not be confounded: let them be afraid, and let not me be afraid: bring upon them the day of affliction, and with a double destruction destroy them, O Lord our God.

Jeremias is one of the most striking figures of the Messias persecuted by the Jews. It is on this account, that the Church selects from this Prophet so many of her lessons, during these two weeks that are sacred to the Passion. In the passage chosen for to-day's Epistle, we have the complaint addressed to God, by this just man, against those that persecute him; and it is in the name of Christ that he speaks. He says: *They have forsaken the Lord, the vein of living waters.* How forcibly do these words describe the malice, both of the Jews that crucified, and of sinners that still crucify, Jesus our Lord! As to the Jews, they had forgotten the Rock, whence came to them the living water, which quenched their thirst in the desert: or, if they have not forgotten the history of this mysterious Rock, they refuse to take it as the type of the Messias.

And yet, they hear this Jesus *crying out* to them in the streets of Jerusalem, *and saying: If any man thirst, let him come to Me, and drink.*[1] His virtues, his teachings, his miracles, the prophecies that are fulfilled in his person, all claim their confidence in him; they should believe every word he says. But, they are deaf to his invitation; and how many Christians imitate them in their obduracy? How many there are, who once drank at the *vein of living waters*, and afterwards turned away, to seek to quench their thirst in the muddy waters of the world, which can only make them thirst the more! Let them tremble at the punishment that came upon the Jews; for, unless they return to the Lord their God, they must fall into those devouring and eternal flames, where even a drop of water is refused. Jesus, by the mouth of his Prophet, tells the Jews, that *the day of affliction* shall overtake them; and when, later on, he comes to them himself, he forewarns them, that the *tribulation* which is to fall on Jerusalem, in punishment for her deicide, shall be so *great*, that *such hath not been from the beginning of the world until now, neither shall be.*[2] But, if God so rigorously avenged the Blood of his Son against a City, that was, so long a time, the place of the habitation of his glory, and against a people that he had preferred to all others,—will he spare the sinner, who, in spite of the Church's entreaties, continues obstinate in his evil ways? Jerusalem had filled up the measure of her iniquities; we, also, have a *measure* of sin, beyond which the Justice of God will not permit us to go. Let us

---

[1] St. John, vii. 37.   [2] St. Matth. xxiv. 21.

sin no more; let us fill up that other *measure*, the measure of good works. Let us pray for those sinners who are to pass these days of grace without being converted; let us pray, that this Divine Blood, which is to be so generously given to them, but which they are about again to trample upon, let us pray that it may again spare them.

GOSPEL.

Sequentia sancti Evangelii secundum Joannem.	Sequel of the holy Gospel according to John.
Cap. XI.	*Ch. XI.*
In illo tempore : Collegerunt Pontifices et Pharisæi concilium adversus Jesum, et dicebant : Quid facimus, quia hic homo multa signa facit ? Si dimittimus eum sic, omnes credent in eum ; et venient Romani, et tollent nostrum locum et gentem. Unus autem ex ipsis, Caïphas nomine, cum esset pontifex anni illius, dixit eis : Vos nescitis quidquam, nec cogitatis quia expedit vobis ut unus moriatur homo pro populo, et non tota gens pereat. Hoc autem a semetipso non dixit; sed cum esset pontifex anni illius prophetavit, quod Jesus moriturus erat pro gente, et non tantum pro gente, sed ut filios Dei, qui erant dispersi, congregaret in unum. Ab illo ergo die cogitaverunt ut interficerent eum. Jesus ergo jam non in palam ambulabat apud Judæos, sed abiit in regionem juxta desertum, in civitatem quæ dicitur Ephrem,	At that time: the chief priests and Pharisees assembled in council against Jesus, and said : What do we, for this man doth many miracles ? If we let him alone so, all men will believe in him ; and the Romans will come, and take away our place and nation. But one of them, named Caiphas, being the high-priest that year, said to them : You know nothing, neither do you consider that it is expedient for you that one man should die for the people, and that the whole nation perish not. And this he spoke not of himself ; but being the high-priest that year, he prophesied that Jesus should die for the nation, and not only for the nation, but to gather in one the children of God, that were dispersed. From that day therefore they devised to put him to death. Wherefore Jesus walked no more openly among the Jews, but he went unto a country near the desert, unto a city

that is called Ephrem, and there he abode with his disciples.   et ibi morabatur cum discipulis suis.

Jesus is more than ever in danger of losing his life! *The Council* of the nation assembles to devise a plan for his destruction. Listen to these men, slaves of that vilest of passions,—jealousy. They do not deny the miracles of Jesus; therefore, they are in a condition to pass judgment upon him, and the judgment ought to be favourable. But they have not assembled to examine if he be or be not the Messias; it is to discuss the best plan for putting him to death. And what argument will they bring forward to palliate the evident murder they contemplate? Political interests,—their country's good. They argue thus: "If Jesus be longer allowed to appear in public and work miracles, Judea will rise up in rebellion against the Romans, who now govern us, and will proclaim Jesus to be their King; Rome will never allow us, the weakest of her tributaries, to insult her with impunity, and, in order to avenge the outrage offered to the Capitol, her armies will come and exterminate us."—Senseless Councillors! If Jesus had come that he might be King after this world's fashion, all the powers of the earth could not have prevented it. Again,—how is it that these Chief Priests and Pharisees, who know the Scriptures by heart, never once think of that prophecy of Daniel, which fortells, that in seventy weeks of years, after the going forth of the decree for the rebuilding of the Temple, the Christ shall be slain, and the people that shall deny him, shall cease to be His:[1] moreover, that, after this crime, a people, led on by a commander, shall come and destroy Jerusalem; the abomination of desolation shall enter the Holy Place, the temple shall be destroyed, and the deso-

---

[1] Dan., ix. 25.

lation shall last even to the end :[1] how comes it, that this prophecy is lost sight of? Surely, if they thought of it, they would not put Christ to death, for by putting him to death, they ruin their country!

But to return to the Council. The High-Priest, who governed the Synagogue during the last days of the Mosaic Law, is a worthless man, by name Caiphas; he presides over the Council. He puts on the sacred Ephod, and he prophesies; his prophecy is from God, and is true. Let us not be astonished: the veil of the temple is not yet rent asunder; the covenant between God and Juda is not yet broken. Caiphas is a blood-thirsty man, a coward, a sacrilegious wretch; still, he is High-Priest, and God speaks by his mouth. Let us hearken to this Balaam: *Jesus shall die for the nation, and not only for the nation, but to gather in one the children of God, that were dispersed.* Thus, the Synagogue is near her end, and is compelled to prophesy the birth of the Church, and that this birth is to be by the shedding of Jesus' Blood. Here and there, throughout the world, there are *Children of God* who serve him, among the Gentiles, as did the Centurion, Cornelius; but there was no visible bond of union among them. The time is at hand, when the great and only City of God is to appear on the mountain, *and all nations shall flow unto* it.[2] As soon as the Blood of the New Testament shall have been shed, and the Conqueror of death shall have risen from the grave, the day of Pentecost will convoke, not the Jews to the Temple of Jerusalem, but all nations to the Church of Jesus Christ. By that time, Caiphas will have forgotten the prophecy he uttered; he will have ordered his servants to piece together the Veil of the Holy of Holies, which was

---

[1] Dan. ix., 26, 27.   [2] Is., i. 2.

torn in two at the moment of Jesus' death; but this Veil will serve no purpose, for the Holy of Holies will be no longer there; *a clean oblation will be offered up in every place,* the *Sacrifice* of the New Law;[1] and scarcely shall the avengers of Jesus' death have appeared on Mount Olivet, than a voice will be heard in the Sanctuary of the repudiated Temple, saying: "Let us go out from this place!"

Bow down your heads to God.

Grant, we beseech thee, O Almighty God, that we who seek the honour of thy protection, may be delivered from all evil, and serve thee with a secure mind. Through Christ our Lord. Amen.

Humiliate capita vestra Deo.

Concede, quæsumus, omnipotens Deus, ut qui protectionis tuæ gratiam quærimus, liberati a malis omnibus, secura tibi mente serviamus. Per Christum Dominum nostrum. Amen.

THE SEVEN DOLOURS OF OUR LADY.

This Friday of Passion Week is consecrated, in a special manner, to the sufferings which the Holy Mother of God endured at the foot of the Cross. The whole of next week is fully taken up with the celebration of the mysteries of Jesus' Passion; and, although the remembrance of Mary's share in those sufferings is often brought before the Faithful during Holy Week, yet, the thought of what her Son, our Divine Redeemer, goes through for our salvation, so absorbs our attention and love, that it is not then possible to honour, as it deserves, the sublime mystery of the Mother's *Com-passion.*

It was but fitting, therefore, that one day in the

---

[1] Malach., i. 11.

year should be set apart for this sacred duty; and what day could be more appropriate, than the Friday of this Week, which, though sacred to the Passion, admits the celebration of Saints' Feasts, as we have already noticed? As far back as the 15th century, (that is, in the year 1423,) we find the pious Archbishop of Cologne, Theodoric, prescribing this Feast to be kept by his people.[1] It was gradually introduced, and with the connivance of the Holy See, into several other countries; and at length, in the last century, Pope Benedict the Thirteenth, by a decree dated August 22nd, 1727, ordered it to be kept in the whole Church, under the name of *the Feast of the Seven Dolours of the Blessed Virgin Mary*, for, up to that time, it had gone under various names. We will explain the title thus given to it, as also the first origin of the devotion of the Seven Dolours, when our *Liturgical Year* brings us to the Third Sunday of September, the second Feast of Mary's Dolours. What the Church proposes to her children's devotion for this Friday of Passion Week, is that one special Dolour of Mary,—her standing at the Foot of the Cross. Among the various titles given to this Feast,—before it was extended, by the Holy See to the whole Church,—we may mention, *Our Lady of Pity, The Compassion of our Lady*, and the one that was so popular throughout France, *Notre Dame de la Pamoison*. These few historical observations prove that this Feast was dear to the devotion of the people, even before it received the solemn sanction of the Church.

That we may clearly understand the object of this Feast, and spend it, as the Church would have us do, in paying due honour to the Mother of God and of men,—we must recall to our minds this great truth: that God, in the designs of his infinite wisdom, has

---

[1] Labb. *Concil.* t. xiii. p. 365.

willed that Mary should have a share in the work of the world's Redemption. The mystery of the present Feast is one of the applications of this Divine law, a law which reveals to us the whole magnificence of God's *Plan* ; it is also, one of the many realisations of the prophecy, that Satan's pride was to be crushed by a Woman. In the work of our Redemption, there are three interventions of Mary, that is, she is thrice called upon to take part in what God himself did. The first of these was in the Incarnation of the Word, who takes not Flesh in her virginal womb until she has given her consent to become his Mother; and this she gave by that solemn FIAT which blessed the world with a Saviour. The second was in the sacrifice which Jesus consummated on Calvary, where she was present, that she might take part in the expiatory offering. The third was on the day of Pentecost, when she received the Holy Ghost, as did the Apostles, in order that she might effectively labour in the establishment of the Church. We have already explained on the Feast of the Annunciation, the share Mary had in that wonderful mystery of the Incarnation, which God wrought for his own glory and for man's redemption and sanctification. On the Feast of Pentecost we shall speak of the Church commencing and progressing under the active influence of the Mother of God. To-day we must show what part she took in the mystery of her Son's Passion; we must tell the sufferings, *the Dolours*, she endured at the foot of the Cross, and the claims she thereby won to our filial gratitude.

On the fortieth day after the Birth of our Emmanuel, we followed, to the Temple, the happy Mother carrying her Divine Babe in her arms. A venerable old man was there, waiting to receive her Child; and, when he had him in his arms, he proclaimed him to be *the Light of the Gentiles, and the glory of Israel*. But, turning to the Mother, he spoke to her these heart-rending words: *Behold! this Child is set to be a sign that shall be contradicted, and a sword shall pierce thine own soul.* This prophecy of sorrow for the Mother told us that the holy joys of Christmas were over, and that the season of trial, for both Jesus and Mary, had begun. It had, indeed, begun; for, from the night of the Flight into Egypt, up to this present day, when the malice of the Jews is plotting the great crime,— what else has the life of our Jesus been, but the bearing humiliation, insult, persecution, and ingratitude? And if so, what has the Mother gone through?—what ceaseless anxiety? what endless anguish of heart? But, let us pass by all her other sufferings, and come to the morning of the great Friday.

Mary knows, that on the previous night, her Son has been betrayed by one of his Disciples, that is, by one that Jesus had numbered among his intimate friends; she herself had often given him proofs of her maternal affection. After a cruel Agony, her Son has been manacled as a malefactor, and led by armed men to Caiphas, his worst enemy. Thence, they have dragged him before the Roman Governor, whose sanction the Chief Priests and the Scribes must have before they can put Jesus to death. Mary is in Jerusalem; Magdalene, and the other holy women, the friends of Jesus, are with her; but they cannot prevent her from hearing the loud shouts of the people, and if they could, how is such a heart as hers to be slow in its forebodings? The report spreads rapidly through the City that the Roman Governor is being urged to sentence Jesus to be crucified. Whilst the entire populace is on the move towards Calvary, shouting out their blasphemous insults at her Jesus,—will his Mother keep away, she that bore him in her womb, and fed him at her breast? Shall his enemies be eager to glut their eyes with the cruel sight, and his own Mother be afraid to be near him?

The air resounded with the yells of the mob. Joseph of Arimathia, *the noble counsellor*, was not there, neither was the learned Nicodemus; they kept at home, grieving over what was done. The crowd that went before and after the Divine Victim was made up of wretches without hearts, saving only a few who were seen to weep as they went along; they were women; Jesus saw them, and spoke to them. And if these women, from mere sentiments of veneration, or, at most, of gratitude, thus testified their compassion,—would Mary do less? *could* she bear to be elsewhere than close to her Jesus? Our motive for insisting so much upon this point, is that we may show our detestation of that school of modern rationalism, which, regardless of the instincts of a mother's heart and of all tradition, has dared to call in question the Meeting of Jesus and Mary on the way to Calvary. These systematic contradicters are too prudent to deny that Mary was present when Jesus was crucified; the Gospel is too explicit,— *Mary stood near the Cross:*[1] but, they would persuade us, that whilst *the Daughters of Jerusalem* courageously walked after Jesus, Mary went up to Calvary by some secret path! What a heartless insult to the love of the incomparable Mother.

No,—Mary, who is, by excellence, *the Valiant Woman*,[2] was with Jesus as he carried his Cross. And who could describe her anguish and her love, as her eye met that of her Son tottering under his heavy load? Who could tell the affection, and the resignation, of the look he gave her in return? Who could depict the eager and respectful tenderness wherewith Magdalene and the other holy women grouped around this Mother, as she followed her Jesus up Calvary, there to see him crucified and die?

[1] St. John, xix. 25.   [2] Prov. xxxi. 10.

The distance between the Fourth and Tenth *Station* of the *Dolorous Way* is long :—it is marked with Jesus' Blood, and the Mother's tears.

Jesus and Mary have reached the summit of the hill, that is to be the Altar of the holiest and cruelest Sacrifice: but the divine decree permits not the Mother as yet to approach her Son. When the Victim is ready, then She that is to offer him shall come forward. Meanwhile, they nail her Jesus to the Cross; and each blow of the hammer was a wound to Mary's heart. When, at last, she is permitted to approach, accompanied by the Beloved Disciple, (who has made amends for his cowardly flight,) and the disconsolate Magdalene and the other holy women, —what unutterable anguish must have filled the soul of this Mother, when, raising up her eyes, she sees the mangled Body of her Son, stretched upon the Cross, with his face all covered with blood, and his head wreathed with a crown of thorns!

Here, then, is this King of Israel, of whom the Angel had told her such glorious things in his prophecy! Here is that Son of hers, whom she has loved both as her God and as the fruit of her own womb! And who are they that have reduced him to this pitiable state? Men,—for whose sakes, rather than for her own, she conceived him, gave him birth, and nourished him! Oh! if, by one of those miracles, which his Heavenly Father could so easily work, he might be again restored to her! If that Divine Justice, which he has taken upon himself to appease, would be satisfied with what he has already suffered! —but no; he must die; he must breathe forth his blessed Soul after a long and cruel agony.

Mary, then, is at the foot of the Cross, there to witness the death of her Son. He is soon to be separated from her. In three hours' time, all that will be left her of this beloved Jesus will be a lifeless Body, wounded from head to foot. *Our* words are too cold for such a scene as this: let us listen to those of St. Bernard, which the Church has inserted in her Matins of this Feast. "O Blessed Mother! "a sword of sorrow pierced thy soul, and we may "well call thee more than Martyr, for the intensity " of thy compassion surpassed all that a bodily passion "could produce. Could any sword have made thee "smart so much as that word which pierced thy heart, "*reaching unto the division of the soul and the* "*spirit:* 'Woman! behold thy son!' What an ex- "change!—John, for Jesus! the servant, for the Lord! "the disciple, for the Master! the son of Zebedee, " for the Son of God! a mere man, for the very God! " How must not thy most loving heart have been "pierced with the sound of these words, when even " ours, that are hard as stone and steel, break down "as we think of them! Ah! my Brethren, be not "surprised when you are told that Mary was a "Martyr in her soul. Let him alone be surprised, " who has forgotten that St. Paul counts it as one of " the greatest sins of the Gentiles, that they were "*without affection.* Who could say that of Mary? " God forbid it be said of us, the servants of Mary!"[1]

Amidst the shouts and insults vociferated by the enemies of Jesus, Mary's quick ear has heard these words, which tell her, that the only son she is henceforth to have on earth is one of adoption. Her maternal joys of Bethlehem and Nazareth are all gone; they make her present sorrow the bitterer: she was the Mother of a God, and men have taken him from her! Her last and fondest look at her Jesus, her own dearest Jesus, tells her that he is suffering a burning thirst, and she cannot give him to drink! His eyes grow dim; his head droops;—*all is consummated!*

Mary cannot leave the Cross; love brought her

---

[1] Sermon *On the Twelve Stars.*

thither; love keeps her there, whatever may happen! A soldier advances near that hallowed spot; she sees him lift up his spear, and thrust it through the breast of the sacred Corpse. "Ah," cries out St. Bernard, "that thrust is through thy soul, O Blessed Mother! "It could but open his side, but it pierced thy very "soul. *His* Soul was not there; *thine* was, and could "not but be so."[1] No, the undaunted Mother keeps close to the Body of her Son. She watches them as they take it down from the Cross; and when, at last, the friends of Jesus, with all the respect due to both Mother and Son, enable her to embrace it, she raises it upon her lap, and He that once lay upon her knees receiving the homage of the Eastern Kings, now lays there cold, mangled, bleeding, dead! And as she looks upon the wounds of this divine Victim, she gives them the highest honour in the power of creatures,—she kisses them, she bathes them with her tears, she adores them, but oh! with what intensity of loving grief!

The hour is far advanced; and before sunset, he, —Jesus,—the author of life,—must be buried. The Mother puts the whole vehemence of her love into a last kiss, and *oppressed with a bitterness great as is the sea,*[2] she makes over this adorable Body to them that have to embalm and then lay it on the sepulchral slab. The sepulchre is closed; and Mary, —accompanied by John, her adopted son, and Magdalene, and the holy women, and the two disciples that have presided over the Burial,—returns sorrowing to the deicide City.

Now, in all this, there is another mystery besides that of Mary's sufferings. Her dolours at the Foot of the Cross include and imply a truth, which we must not pass by, or we shall not understand the full beauty of to-day's Feast. Why would God

---

[1] Sermon *On the Twelve Stars.* [2] Lament. i. 4, ii. 13,

have her assist in person at such a scene as this of Calvary? Why was not she, as well as Joseph, taken out of this world before this terrible day of Jesus' Death?—Because God had assigned her a great office for that day, and it was to be under the Tree of the Cross that she, the second Eve, was to discharge her office. As the heavenly Father had waited for her consent before he sent his Son into the world; so, likewise, he called for her obedience and devotedness, when the hour came for that Son to be offered up in sacrifice for the world's Redemption. Was not Jesus hers? her Child? her own and dearest treasure? And yet, God gave him not to her, until she had assented to become his Mother; in like manner, he would not take him from her, unless she gave him back.

But, see what this involved, see what a struggle it entailed upon this most loving Heart! It is the injustice, the cruelty, of men that rob her of her Son; how can she, his Mother, ratify, by her consent, the Death of Him, whom she loved with a twofold love,—as her Son, and as her God? But, on the other hand,—if Jesus be not put to death, the human race is left a prey to Satan, sin is not atoned for, and all the honours and joys of her being Mother of God are of no use or blessing to us. This Virgin of Nazareth, this noblest heart, this purest creature, whose affections were never blunted with the selfishness which so easily makes its way into souls that have been wounded by original sin,—what shall she do? Her devotedness to mankind, her conformity with the will of her Son who so vehemently desires the world's salvation, lead her, a second time, to pronounce the solemn FIAT:—she consents to the immolation of her Son. It is not God's justice that takes him from her; it is she herself that gives him up;—but, in return, she is raised to a degree of greatness, which her humility could never have suspected was to be hers:—an ineffable union is made to exist between the two offerings, that of the Incarnate Word and that of Mary; the Blood of the Divine Victim, and the Tears of the Mother, flow together for the redemption of mankind.

We can now understand the conduct and the courage of this Mother of Sorrows. Unlike that other mother, of whom the Scripture speaks,—the unhappy Agar, who, after having sought in vain how she might quench the thirst of her Ismael in the desert, withdrew from him that she might not see him die;—Mary no sooner hears that Jesus is condemned to death, than she rises, hastens to him, and follows him to the place where he is to die. And what is her attitude at the foot of his cross? Does her matchless grief overpower her? Does she swoon? or fall? No: the Evangelist says: "There "*stood* by the Cross of Jesus, his Mother."[1] The sacrificing Priest stands, when offering at the altar: Mary *stood* for such a sacrifice as hers was to be. St. Ambrose,—whose affectionate heart and profound appreciation of the mysteries of religion have revealed to us so many precious traits of Mary's character,—thus speaks of her position at the foot of the Cross: "She *stood* opposite the Cross, gazing, "with maternal love, on the wounds of her Son; and "thus she *stood*, not waiting for her Jesus to die, but "for the world to be saved."[2]

Thus, this Mother of Sorrows, when standing on Calvary, blessed us who deserved but maledictions; she loved us; she sacrificed her Son for our salvation. In spite of all the feelings of her maternal heart, she gave back to the Eternal Father the divine treasure he had entrusted to her keeping. The sword pierced through and through her soul,—but we were saved; and she, though a mere creature, co-

---

[1] St. John, xix. 25.   [2] *In Lucam*, cap. xxiii.

operated with her Son in the work of our salvation. Can we wonder, after this, that Jesus chose this moment for the making her the Mother of men, in the person of John the Evangelist, who represented us? Never had Mary's Heart loved us as she did then; from that time forward, therefore, let this second Eve be the true *Mother of the living*![1] The Sword, by piercing her Immaculate Heart, has given us admission there. For time and eternity, Mary will extend to us the love she has borne for her Son, for she has just heard him saying to her that we are her children. He is *our Lord*, for he has redeemed us; She is *our Lady*, for she generously co-operated in our redemption.

Animated by this confidence, O Mother of Sorrows! we come before thee, on this Feast of thy Dolours, to offer thee our filial love. Jesus, the Blessed Fruit of thy Womb, filled thee with joy as thou gavest him birth; we, thy adopted children, entered into thy Heart by the cruel piercing of the Sword of Suffering. And yet, O Mary! love us, for thou didst co-operate with our Divine Redeemer in saving us. How can we not trust in the love of thy generous Heart, when we know, that, for our salvation, thou didst unite thyself to the Sacrifice of thy Jesus? What proofs hast thou not unceasingly given us of thy maternal tenderness, O Queen of Mercy! O Refuge of Sinners! O untiring Advocate for us in all our miseries! Deign, sweet Mother, to watch over us, during these days of grace. Give us to feel and relish the Passion of thy Son. It was consummated in thy presence; thine own share in it was magnificent! Oh! make us enter into all its mysteries, that so our souls, redeemed by the Blood of thy Son, and helped by thy Tears, may be thoroughly converted to the Lord, and persevere, henceforward, faithful in his service.

[1] Gen., iii. 20.

Let us now recite the devout *Complaint*, whereby the Church unites herself with Mary's Dolours.

SEQUENCE.

Stabat Mater dolorosa
Juxta crucem lacrymosa,
Dum pendebat Filius.
Cujus animam gementem,
Contristatam, et dolentem,
Pertransivit gladius.
O quam tristis et afflicta
Fuit illa benedicta
Mater unigeniti!
Quæ mœrebat, et dolebat,
Pia Mater dum videbat
Nati pœnas inclyti.
Quis est homo qui non fleret,
Matrem Christi si videret
In tanto supplicio?
Quis non posset contristari,
Christi Matrem contemplari
Dolentem cum filio?
Pro peccatis suæ gentis
Vidit Jesum in tormentis,
Et flagellis subditum.
Vidit suum dulcem Natum
Moriendo desolatum,
Dum emisit spiritum.
Eia, Mater, fons amoris,
Me sentire vim doloris
Fac, ut tecum lugeam.

Fac ut ardeat cor meum
In amando Christum Deum,
Ut sibi complaceam.

Sancta Mater, istud agas,
Crucifixi fige plagas
Cordi meo valide.
Tui nati vulnerati,
Tam dignati pro me pati,
Pœnas mecum divide.

Near the Cross, whilst on it hung her Son, the sorrowing Mother stood and wept.
A sword pierced her soul, that sighed, and mourned, and grieved.
Oh! how sad, and how afflicted, was that Blessed Mother of an only Son!
The loving Mother sorrowed and mourned at seeing her divine Son suffer.
Who is there would not weep to see Jesus' Mother in such suffering?
Who is there could contemplate the Mother and the Son in sorrow, and not join his own with theirs?
Mary saw her Jesus tormented and scourged for the sins of his people.
She saw her sweet child abandoned by all, as he breathed forth his soul and died.
Ah, Mother, Fount of love, make me feel the force of sorrow; make me weep with thee!
Make this heart of mine burn with the love of Jesus my God, that so I may content his heart.
Do this, O holy Mother! —deeply stamp the wounds of the Crucified upon my heart.
Let me share with thee the sufferings of thy Son, for it was for me he graciously deigned to be wounded and to suffer.

FEAST OF THE SEVEN DOLOURS.

Make me lovingly weep with thee : make me compassionate with thee our Crucified Jesus, as long as life shall last.

This is my desire,—to stand nigh the Cross with thee, and be a sharer in thy grief.

Peerless Virgin of virgins! be not displeased at my prayer: make me weep with thee.

Make me to carry the death of Jesus; make me a partner of his Passion, an adorer of his Wounds.

Make me to be wounded with his Wounds; make me to be inebriated with the Cross and the Blood of thy Son.

And that I may not suffer the eternal flames, let me be defended by thee, O Virgin, on the Day of Judgment!

O Jesus! when my hour of death comes, let me, by the Mother's aid, come to my crown of victory.

And when my body dies, oh! give to my soul the reward of heaven's glory.

Amen.

Fac me tecum pie flere,
Crucifixo condolere,
Donec ego vixero.

Juxta Crucem tecum stare,
Et me tibi sociare
In planctu desidero.

Virgo virginum præclara,
Mihi jam non sis amara :
Fac me tecum plangere.

Fac ut portem Christi mortem,
Passionis fac consortem,
Et plagas recolere.

Fac me plagis vulnerari,
Fac me cruce inebriari,
Et cruore Filii.

Flammis ne urar succensus,
Per te, Virgo, sim defensus,
In die judicii.

Christe, cum sit hinc exire,
Da per Matrem me venire
Ad palmam victoriæ.

Quando corpus morietur,
Fac ut animæ donetur
Paradisi gloria.

Amen.

Let us recite the concluding stanzas of the Greek Hymn in honour of the Holy Cross.

HYMN.

(Feria IV. mediæ Septimanæ.)

Come, let us devoutly embrace the Cross of our Lord that is exposed before us, for our fasts have made us pure. The Cross is a treasure of

Adeste, Crucem Domini propositam, jejuniis expiati, cum desiderio amplectamur. Est enim thesaurus sanctificationis et potentiæ, per quam laudamus Christum in sæcula.

Hæc Crux tripartita et magna, vilis initio apparens, nunc cœlum tangit virtute sua, hominesque ad Deum semper sursum ducit; per quam laudamus Christum in sæcula.

Honoretur hoc sacratissimum lignum, quod jam olim Propheta in panem Christi immissum esse ab Israëlitis, qui eum crucifixerunt, vaticinatus est; quem superexaltamus in sæcula.

Montes dulcedinem, et colles exsultationem stillate. Ligna campi, cedri Libani, choreas ducite ob hodiernam vivificæ Crucis adorationem. Prophetæ, Martyres, Apostoli et spiritus justorum, exilite.

Respice in populum et in clerum tuum, Domine, qui cum desiderio laudes tuas canit, cujus gratia mortem subiisti. Ne vincat misericordiam tuam infinita multitudo malorum nostrorum, sed salva omnes, o benignissime, per Crucem tuam.

Divina armatura vitæ meæ es, o Crux; in te Dominus ascendens, servavit me. Latere vulnerato fudit sanguinem et aquam, cujus particeps factus exsulto, Christum glorificans.

Divinum Regis sceptrum

holiness and power, and by it we give eternal praise to Christ.

This triple and glorious Cross, contemptible as it seemed at first, now reaches to the very heavens with its power, ever raising and leading men up to God. By it we give eternal praise to Christ.

Honour to this most sacred Wood, which, as the Prophet anciently foretold, was to be put in the bread of Christ, by them that crucified him; to whom be praise above all for ever!

Rain down sweetness, O ye mountains! and ye, O hills, your gladness! Trees of the field, Cedars of Libanus, exult with joy, for on this day we venerate the life-giving Cross. Prophets, Martyrs, Apostles, Spirits of the Just, rejoice!

Look down, O Lord, upon thy people and clergy, who now devoutly sing thy praise, and for whose sakes thou didst suffer death. Let not the countless number of our sins outdo thy mercy, but save us, most loving Jesus, by thy Cross!

O Cross! thou art the sacred armour of my life. My Lord saved me by his ascending upon thee. From his wounded Side there flowed Blood and Water, of which being made a partaker, I exult, and give glory to Christ.

O Cross! thou art the divine sceptre of the King; thou art the strength of them that wage war; it is our confidence in thee that makes us put our enemies to flight. Oh! ever grant to us who honour thee, victory over the Barbarians.

Crux es, exercitus fortitudo; in tua fiducia profligamus hostes; nobis qui te adoramus, semper concede adversus Barbaros victorias.

SATURDAY

IN PASSION WEEK.

To-day, we begin, as does the holy Gospel, to number the days which precede the Death, the Sacrifice, of the Lamb of God. St. John, in the 12th Chapter of his Gospel, tells us that this is the Sixth day before the Pasch.

Jesus is in Bethania, where a feast is being given in his honour. Lazarus, he whom Jesus has restored to life, was present at this repast, which was given in the house of Simon the Leper. Martha is busy looking after the various arrangements; her sister, Mary Magdalene, has a heavenly presentiment that the death and burial of her beloved Master are soon to be, and she has poured upon him a precious perfume. The Holy Gospel, which ever observes such a mysterious reserve with regard to the Mother of Jesus, does not tell us that Mary was at Bethania on this occasion, but there can be no doubt of her being present. The Apostles were also there, and partook of the repast. Whilst the friends of our Saviour were thus grouped around him, in this village, which was about two thousand paces from Jerusalem, the aspect of the faithless City becomes more and more threatening: and yet, though his Disciples are not aware of it, Jesus is to enter the City to-morrow, and in a most public manner. The heart of Mary is a prey to sadness; Magdalene is absorbed in grief; everything announces that the fatal day is near.

The Church has reserved for Monday next the Gospel which relates the history of this Saturday. The reason is, that formerly, and up to the 12th century, there was no Station held on this day in Rome: it was left free, in order that the Pope might rest before the great fatigues of Holy Week, whose long and solemn services were to begin on the morrow. But, although he did not preside over the assembly of the Faithful, he, on this day, had to observe two usages, which had been handed down by tradition, and which had almost become of liturgical importance in the Church at Rome.

During the whole year, the Pope used, every Sunday, to send a portion of the sacred species, consecrated by him, to each of the priests of the presbyterial *Titles*, or parochial Churches, of the City. But it was to-day that this distribution was made for the whole of Holy Week, perhaps on account of to-morrow's long service. We know from the ancient liturgical books of Rome, that it was in the Lateran Consistory that to-day's sacred distribution was made, and it is probable (as the Blessed Cardinal Tommasi and Benedict the Fourteenth tell us,) that the Bishops of the suburbicarian Churches were of the number of those who received it. We have several instances proving that, formerly, Bishops occasionally sent to one another the Blessed Sacrament, as a sign of the union that existed between them. With regard to the priests of the city Parochial Churches, to whom a Particle was sent by the Pope, they put a portion of it in the Chalice before receiving the Precious Blood.

The other custom, peculiar to this day, consisted in giving alms to all the poor. The Pope presided at this distribution, which was no doubt made ample enough to last the whole of the coming Week, when, on account of the long Ceremonies, it would scarcely be possible to attend to individual cases of poverty. The Liturgists of the Middle-Ages allude to the beautiful appropriateness of the Roman Pontiff's distributing alms with his own hand, to the poor, on this day, the same on which Mary Magdalene embalmed, with her perfumes, the feet of Jesus.

Since the 12th century, a Station has been assigned to this Saturday; it takes place in the Church of Saint John *before the Latin Gate.* This ancient basilica is built near the spot where the Beloved Disciple was, by Domitian's order, plunged into the cauldron of boiling oil.

COLLECT.

Proficiat, quæsumus, Domine, plebs tibi dicata piæ devotionis affectu: ut sacris actionibus erudita, quanto majestati tuæ fit gratior, tanto donis potioribus augeatur. Per Christum Dominum nostrum. Amen.

May the people consecrated to thy service, we beseech thee, O Lord, improve in the affections of piety; that instructed by these holy mysteries, they may be so much the more enriched with thy heavenly gifts, as they become more acceptable to thy divine majesty. Through Christ our Lord. Amen.

EPISTLE.

Lectio Jeremiæ prophetæ.

Lesson from Jeremias the Prophet.

Cap. XVIII.

Ch. XVIII.

In diebus illis: Dixerunt impii Judæi ad invicem: Venite, et cogitemus contra Justum cogitationes: non enim peribit Lex a sacerdote, neque consilium a sapiente, nec sermo a propheta: venite, et percutiamus eum lingua, et non

In those days, the wicked Jews said to one another: Come, and let us invent devices against the Just: for the law shall not perish from the priest, nor counsel from the wise, nor the word from the prophet. Come, and let us strike him with the tongue, and let us give no heed to all his words. Give heed to me, O Lord, and hear the voice of my adversaries. Shall evil be rendered for good, because they have digged a pit for my soul? Remember that I have stood in thy sight, to speak good for them, and to turn away thy indignation from them. Therefore deliver up their children to famine, and bring them into the hands of the sword; let their wives be bereaved of children, and widows; and let the husbands be slain by death; let their young men be stabbed with the sword in battle. Let a cry be heard out of their houses; for thou shalt bring the robber upon them suddenly, because they have digged a pit to take me, and have hid snares for my feet. But thou, O Lord, knowest all their counsel against me unto death; forgive not their iniquity, and let not their sin be blotted out from thy sight; let them be overthrown before thy eyes, in the time of thy wrath do thou destroy them, O Lord our God.

attendamus ad universos sermones ejus. Attende, Domine, ad me; et audi vocem adversariorum meorum. Numquid redditur pro bono malum, quia foderunt foveam animæ meæ? Recordare quod steterim in conspectu tuo, ut loquerer pro eis bonum, et averterem indignationem tuam ab eis. Propterea da filios eorum in famem, et deduc eos in manus gladii; fiant uxores eorum absque liberis, et viduæ: et viri earum interficiantur morte: juvenes eorum confodiantur gladio in prælio. Audiatur clamor de domibus eorum: adduces enim super eos latronem repente: quia foderunt foveam ut caperent me, et laqueos absconderunt pedibus meis. Tu autem, Domine, scis omne consilium eorum adversum me in mortem: ne propitieris iniquitati eorum, et peccatum eorum a facie tua non deleatur: fiant corruentes in conspectu tuo, in tempore furoris tui abutere eis, Domine Deus noster.

It makes us tremble to read these awful anathemas, which Jeremias, the figure of Christ, speaks against his enemies, the Jews. This prophecy, which was literally fulfilled at the first destruction of Jerusalem by the Assyrians, received a more terrible fulfilment at the second visitation of God's anger upon this city of malediction. This time, it was not because the Jews had persecuted a Prophet; it was because they had rejected and crucified the very Son of God. It was to their long-expected Messias that they had *rendered evil for good.* It was not a Saint, like Jeremias, that had *spoken good for them* to the Lord, and besought him *to turn away his indignation from them;* the Man-God himself had, without ceasing, made intercession for them, and treated them with the tenderest mercy. But all was in vain; this ungrateful people seemed to hate their divine Benefactor in proportion to his love of them; and at length, in the transport of their fury, they cried out: *His blood be upon us and upon our children!*[1] What a frightful chastisement they entailed on themselves by this imprecation! God heard and remembered it. Alas! the sinner, who knows Jesus and the worth of his Blood, yet who again sheds this precious Blood,—does he not expose himself to the severity of that same Justice, which fell so heavily on the Jews? Let us tremble and pray: let us implore the divine mercy in favour of those many obstinately blind and hardened sinners, who are hastening to destruction. Oh! that by the fervour of our supplications addressed to the merciful Heart of our common Redeemer, we could obtain a reversion of their sentence, and secure them pardon!

GOSPEL.

Sequentia sancti Evangelii secundum Joannem.

Cap. XII.

In illo tempore: Cogitaverunt principes sacerdotum, ut et Lazarum interficerent: quia multi propter illum abibant ex Judæis, et credebant in Jesum. In crastinum autem turba multa, quæ venerat ad diem fes-

Sequel of the holy Gospel according to John.

Ch. XII.

At that time: the chief priests thought to kill Lazarus also, because many of the Jews by reason of him went away, and believed in Jesus. And on the next day a great multitude, that was come to the festival day, when they

---

[1] St. Matth., xxvii. 25.

had heard that Jesus was coming to Jerusalem, took branches of palm trees, and went forth to meet him, and cried: Hosanna, blessed is he that cometh in the name of the Lord, the King of Israel! And Jesus found a young ass, and sat upon it, as it is written: Fear not, daughter of Sion; behold, thy King cometh sitting on an ass's colt. These things his disciples did not know at first; but when Jesus was glorified, they then remembered that these things were written of him, and that they had done these things to him.

The multitude therefore gave testimony, which was with him, when he called Lazarus out of the grave, and raised him from the dead. For which reason also the people came to meet him, because they heard he had done this miracle. The Pharisees therefore said among themselves: Do you see that we prevail nothing? behold, the whole world is gone after him. Now there were certain Gentiles among them that came up to adore on the festival day. These therefore came to Philip, who was of Bethsaida of Galilee, and desired him, saying: Sir, we would see Jesus. Philip cometh, and telleth Andrew. Again Andrew and Philip told Jesus.

But Jesus answered them, saying: The hour is come that the Son of man shall be glorified. Amen, amen, I say

tum, cum audissent quia venit Jesus Jerosolymam: acceperunt ramos palmarum, et processerunt obviam ei, et clamabant: Hosanna: benedictus qui venit in nomine Domine, Rex Israël. Et invenit Jesus asellum, et sedit super eum, sicut scriptum est: Noli timere, filia Sion: ecce Rex tuus venit sedens super pullum asinæ. Hæc non cognoverunt discipuli ejus primum: sed quando glorificatus est Jesus, tunc recordati sunt quia hæc erant scripta de eo: et hæc fecerunt ei.

Testimonium ergo perhibebat turba, quæ erat cum eo quando Lazarum vocavit de monumento, et suscitavit eum a mortuis. Propterea et obviam venit ei turba: quia audierunt eum fecisse hoc signum. Pharisæi ergo dixerunt ad semetipsos: Videtis quia nihil proficimus? Ecce mundus totus post eum abiit. Erant autem quidam Gentiles ex his, qui ascenderant ut adorarent in die festo. Hi ergo accesserunt ad Philippum, qui erat a Bethsaida Galilææ, et rogabant eum, dicentes: Domine, volumus Jesum videre. Venit Philippus, et dicit Andreæ: Andreas rursum et Philippus dixerunt Jesu.

Jesus autem respondit eis, dicens: Venit hora, ut clarificetur Filius hominis. Amen, amen, dico vobis, nisi granum frumenti cadens in terram, mortuum fuerit, ipsum solum manet. Si autem mortuum fuerit, multum fructum affert. Qui amat animam suam, perdet eam: et qui odit animam suam in hoc mundo, in vitam æternam custodit eam. Si quis mihi ministrat, me sequatur: et ubi sum ego, illic et minister meus erit. Si quis mihi ministraverit, honorificabit eum Pater meus. Nunc anima mea turbata est. Et quid dicam? Pater, salvifica me ex hac hora. Sed propterea veni in horam hanc. Pater, clarifica nomen tuum. Venit ergo vox de cœlo: Et clarificavi, et iterum clarificabo. Turba ergo, quæ stabat et audierat, dicebat tonitruum esse factum. Alii dicebant: Angelus ei locutus est.

Respondit Jesus, et dixit: Non propter me hæc vox venit, sed propter vos. Nunc judicium est mundi: nunc princeps hujus mundi ejicietur foras. Et ego si exaltatus fuero a terra, omnia traham ad meipsum (hoc autem dicebat, significans qua morte esset moriturus). Respondit ei turba: Nos audivimus ex Lege, quia Christus manet in æternum: et quomodo tu dicis: Oportet exaltari Filium hominis? Quis est iste Filius hominis? Dixit ergo eis Jesus: Adhuc modicum lumen in vobis est. Ambulate dum lucem habetis, ut non vos tenebræ compre-

to you, unless the grain of wheat falling into the ground die, itself remaining alone. But if it die, it bringeth forth much fruit. He that loveth his life, shall lose it; and he that hateth his life in this world, keepeth it unto life eternal. If any man minister to me, let him follow me; and where I am, there also shall my minister be. If any man minister to me, him will my Father honour. Now is my soul troubled. And what shall I say? Father, save me from this hour. But for this cause I came unto this hour. Father, glorify thy name. A voice therefore came from heaven: I have both glorified it, and will glorify it again. The multitude therefore that stood and heard, said that it thundered. Others said: An Angel spoke to him.

Jesus answered, and said: This voice came not because of me, but for your sakes. Now is the judgment of the world; now shall the prince of this world be cast out. And I, if I be lifted up from the earth, will draw all things to myself. (Now this he said, signifying what death he should die.) The multitude answered him: We have heard out of the law, that Christ abideth for ever; and now sayest thou: The Son of Man must be lifted up? Who is this Son of Man? Jesus therefore said to them: Yet a little while, the light is among you. Walk whilst you have the light, that the darkness overtake you not ; and he that walketh in darkness knoweth not whither he goeth. Whilst you have the light, believe in the light, that you may be the children of light. These things Jesus spoke, and he went away and hid himself from them.

hendant : et qui ambulat in tenebris, nescit quo vadat. Dum lucem habetis, credite in lucem, ut filii lucis sitis. Hæc locutus est Jesus : et abiit, et abscondit se ab eis.

The enemies of Jesus have come to that pitch of hatred, which robs a man of his senses. Lazarus, who has been restored from death to life, is here standing before them; and instead of his resuscitation convincing them of Jesus' being the Messias, it sets them thinking how best to make away with this irresistible witness. O senseless men! that Jesus who raised him to life when dead, can again bring him to life if you murder him.—Jesus' triumphant entry into Jerusalem, which we are solemnly to commemorate to-morrow, adds to their jealousy and hatred. *Behold,* say they, *we prevail nothing: the whole world goes after him.* Alas! this ovation is to be soon followed by one of those reverses to which a populace is so subject. Meanwhile, however, we have *certain Gentiles* who *desire to see Jesus.* It is the beginning of the fulfilment of Jesus' prophecy: *The kingdom of God shall be taken from you, and shall be given to a nation yielding the fruits thereof.*[1] Then shall *the Son of man be glorified;* then shall all nations, by their humble homage to the Crucified, protest against the sinful blindness of the Jews. But, before this comes to pass, it is requisite, that the Divine *Wheat* be cast *into the ground, and die.* Then, the glorious harvest; and the beautiful seed, shall yield a hundredfold.

And yet, Jesus feels, in his human nature, a momentary fear at the thought of this death he is to

[1] St. Matth., xxi. 43.

undergo. It is not the agony in the Garden; it is a *trouble* of soul. Let us listen to his words: *Father! save me from this hour.* It is our God who foresees all that he is about to suffer for our sakes, and it fills him with fear: he asks to be freed from it, though his will has decreed and accepted it. He immediately adds: *But, for this cause I came unto this hour: Father! glorify thy name.* His soul is now calm; he once more accepts the hard conditions of our salvation. After this, his words bespeak a triumph; by virtue of the sacrifice about to be offered, Satan shall be dethroned: *The Prince of this world shall be cast out.* But the defeat of Satan is not the only fruit of our Saviour's immolation:— man, earthly and depraved creature as he is, is to be raised from this earth to heaven. The Son of God is to be the heavenly loadstone, attracting man to himself: *And I, if I be lifted up from the earth, will draw all things to myself.* He forgets his sufferings, and the terrible death which just now *troubled* him; he thinks but of the defeat of our implacable enemy, and of our being saved and glorified by his Cross. These few words reveal the whole Heart of our Redeemer: if we attentively weigh them, they will suffice to inflame us with devotion as we celebrate the ineffable Mysteries of Holy Week.

Humiliate capita vestra Deo.

Tueatur, quæsumus, Domine, dextera tua populum deprecantem, et purificatum dignanter erudiat: ut consolatione præsenti, ad futura bona proficiat. Per Christum Dominum nostrum. Amen.

Bow down your heads to God.

May thy right hand, O Lord, we beseech thee, protect thy people making supplication to thee, and purifying them from their sins, make them wise, that they may make such use of the comforts of this present life, as to arrive at that which is eternal. Through Christ our Lord. Amen.

Let us sue for mercy from the Saviour of our souls, in these words of supplication used in the Gothic Liturgy of Spain.

SUPPLICATION.

(Feria VI. Dominicæ V.)

℣. Have mercy upon, and spare, thy people, O most merciful Lord!

℟. For we have sinned against thee.

℣. Look down, from the throne of thy Cross, upon us miserable creatures, who are fettered by the chains of our passions. Deliver us, O thou our Redeemer, from the punishments we deserve.

℟. For we have sinned against thee.

℣. O thou that wast scourged, ignominiously crucified, and insulted by them that persecuted thee! grant us repentance for our sins.

℟. For we have sinned against thee.

℣. O thou, the just Judge, that wast judged unjustly, and, though innocent, made to suffer the tortures of the Cross! save us from our merited punishments, for thou art our Redeemer.

℟. For we have sinned against thee.

℣. O thou, that heretofore wast silent before the judge! raise up thy voice in pleading for us to thy Father, that we may be happy with thee, our King and Lord.

℣. Miserere, et parce, clementissime Domine, populo tuo.

℟. Quia peccavimus tibi.

℣. De crucis throno aspice nos miseros, et passionum compeditos vinculis nostris absolve, Redemptor, suppliciis.

℟. Quia peccavimus tibi.

℣. Passus flagella, et crucis injuriam, persecutorum sustinens convicia, dona delictis nostris pœnitentiam.

℟. Quia peccavimus tibi.

℣. Qui justus judex, male judicatus es, et pœnas crucis suscepisti innocens; tu nos a pœnis nostris salva redimens.

℟. Quia peccavimus tibi.

℣. Vox tua Patrem pro nobis expostulet, quæ silens fuit olim ante judicem, ut te regnante perfruamur Domino.

℟. Quia peccavimus tibi.   ℟. For we have sinned against thee.

The following sequence, in praise of Mary, is most appropriate for this Saturday of Passion Week. It sweetly blends together the homages we owe to the Cross of Jesus and to the Dolours of Mary. We have taken it from the *Horæ* of the 16th century.

SEQUENCE.

Lignum vitæ quærimus,
Qui vitam amisimus
Fructu ligni vetiti.
　Nec inventum noverit
Qui fructum non viderit
Adhærentem stipiti.
　Fructus per quem vivitur
Pendet, sicut creditur,
Virginis ad ubera.
　Et ad Crucem iterum,
Inter viros scelerum,
Passus quinque vulnera.
　Hic Virgo puerpera,
Hic Crux salutifera :
Ambo ligna mystica.
　Hæc hyssopus humilis,
Illa cedrus nobilis :
Utraque vivifica.
　Positus in medio,
Quo me vertam nescio.
　In hoc dulci dubio,
Dulcis est collatio.
　Hic complexus brachiis,
Modis vagit variis.

　Hic extendit brachia,
Complexurus omnia.

　Charum Mater tenere
Novit hic tenere.
　Charitas sub latere,
Nescit hic latere.
　Hic adhærens pectori,
Pascitur ab ubere.

We, that by the fruit of the forbidden tree, lost our life, now seek the Tree of life.
　He alone hath found this Tree, who sees the Branch whereon is fixed the Fruit.
　Our faith tells us, that the Fruit, that gives us life, hangs on Mary's breast.
　And on the Cross, between two thieves, though, here, he is pierced with five wounds.
　The Virgin-Mother, and the saving Cross,—yea, both are mystic Trees ;
　The Cross, humble as the hyssop ; Mary, noble as the cedar,—both are trees of life.
　Placed between the two, I know not to which to turn.
　O sweet perplexity ! O sweet comparison !
　Here, my Jesus lies, fondled in his Mother's arms, a weeping little Babe ;
　There, with his arms stretched out, calling all to his embrace.
　Here, 'tis a burden sweet to a Mother's love ;
　There, 'tis Love itself, too ardent to be hid.
　Here, leaning on his Mother's heart, he is fed at her breast ;

There, fastened to the tree, he feeds us from his wounds.

The Cross supplies us with the food of its refreshing Fruit;

The Mother forestalls the Cross, feeding the very Fruit, feeding him for us.

This, then, is my decision; —we cannot have the one without the other.

He that chooses the Cross, must have the Mother; for when he comes to the Cross, he will find the Mother standing at the foot.

He that chooses the Mother, meets the Cross as well, for it was whilst standing at the Cross, that the Mother's heart was pierced.

O Jesus! crucified Son of a crucified Mother! look upon us from thy Cross.

O living Fruit! O Fruit of the Tree of life! refresh us with thyself, give us the enjoyment of thine own dear self. Amen.

Hic affixus arbori,
Pascit nos ex vulnere.

Crux ministrat pabula,
Fructu nos reficiens.

Mater est præambula,
Fructum nobis nutriens.

Tandem ad hoc trahitur
Finalis sententia:
Quod nemo consequitur
Unam sine alia.

Qui Crucem elegerit,
Nec sic Matrem deserit:
Cum ad Crucem venerit,
Matrem ibi poterit
Stantem invenire.

Nec qui Matrem elegit,
Crucem prorsus abigit:
Si modum intelligit
Quo per Matrem contigit
Gladium transire.

Fili Matris unica,
Matris crucifixæ,
Nos de Cruce respice,
Fili crucifixe.

Fructus o vivifice,
Fructus ligni vitæ,
Nos teipso refice,
Nobis da frui te.
Amen.

PALM SUNDAY.

| Hodie, si vocem Domini audieritis, nolite obdurare corda vestra. | To-day, if ye shall hear the voice of the Lord, harden not your hearts. |

EARLY in the morning of this day, Jesus sets out for Jerusalem, leaving Mary, his Mother, and the two sisters Martha and Mary Magdalene, and Lazarus, at Bethania. The Mother of Sorrows trembles at seeing her Son thus expose himself to danger, for his enemies are bent upon his destruction; but it is not Death, it is Triumph, that Jesus is to receive to-day in Jerusalem. The Messias, before being nailed to the Cross, is to be proclaimed *King* by the people of the great City; the little children are to make her streets echo with their *Hosannas* to the Son of David; and this in presence of the soldiers of Rome's Emperor, and of the High Priests and Pharisees,—the first, standing under the banner of their Eagles; the second, dumb with rage.

The Prophet Zachary had foretold this Triumph which the Son of Man was to receive a few days before his Passion, and which had been prepared for him from all eternity. *Rejoice greatly, O Daughter of Sion! Shout for joy, O daughter of Jerusalem! Behold thy King will come to thee; the Just and the Saviour. He is poor, and riding upon an ass, and upon a colt, the foal of an ass.*[1] Jesus, knowing that the hour was come for the fulfilment of this prophecy, singles out two from the rest of his Disciples, and bids them lead to him an ass and her colt, which they would find not far off. He had got to Bethphage, on Mount Olivet. The two Disciples lose no time in executing the order given them by their divine Master; and the ass and the colt are soon brought to the place where he stands.

The holy Fathers have explained to us the mystery of these two animals. The ass represents the Jewish people, which had been long under the yoke of the Law; the colt, *upon which*, as the Evangelist says, *no man yet hath sat*,[2] is a figure of the Gentile world, which no one had ever yet brought into subjection. The future of these two people is to be decided in a few days hence: the Jews will be rejected, for having refused to acknowledge Jesus as the Messias; the Gentiles will take their place, be adopted as God's people, and become docile and faithful.

The Disciples spread their garments upon the colt; and our Saviour, that the prophetic figure might be fulfilled, *sat upon him*,[3] and advances towards Jerusalem. As soon as it was known that Jesus was near the City, the Holy Spirit worked in the hearts of those Jews, who had come, from all parts, to celebrate the Feast of the Passover. They go out to meet our Lord, holding palm branches in their hands, and loudly proclaiming him to be *King*.[4] They that had accompanied Jesus from Bethania, join the enthusiastic crowd. Whilst some spread their garments on the way, others cut down boughs from the Palm-trees, and strewed them along the road. *Hosanna* is the triumphant cry, proclaiming to the whole city, that Jesus, *the Son of David*, has made his entrance as her *King*.

[1] Zac., ix. 9.
[2] St. Mark, xi. 2.
[3] *Ibid.*, xi. 7, *and* St. Luke, xix. 35.
[4] St. Luke, xix. 38.

Thus did God, in his power over men's hearts, procure a triumph for his Son, and in the very City, which, a few days after, was to clamour for his Blood. This day was one of glory to our Jesus, and the holy Church would have us renew, each year, the memory of this triumph of the Man-God. Shortly after the Birth of our Emmanuel, we saw the Magi coming from the extreme East, and looking in Jerusalem for the *King of the Jews*, to whom they intended offering their gifts and their adorations: but it is Jerusalem herself that now goes forth to meet this *King*. Each of these events is an acknowledgment of the Kingship of Jesus: the first, from the Gentiles; the second, from the Jews. Both were to pay him this regal homage, before he suffered his Passion. The Inscription to be put upon the Cross, by Pilate's order, will express the Kingly character of the Crucified: *Jesus of Nazareth, King of the Jews*. Pilate,— the Roman Governor, the pagan, the base coward,— has been, unwittingly, the fulfiller of a prophecy; and when the enemies of Jesus insist on the Inscription being altered, Pilate will deign them no answer but this: *What I have written, I have written*. To-day, it is the Jews themselves that proclaim Jesus to be their *King: they* will soon be dispersed, in punishment for their revolt against the *Son of David;* but Jesus is *King*, and will be so for ever. Thus were literally verified the words spoken by the Archangel to Mary, when he announced to her the glories of the Child that was to be born of her: *The Lord God shall give unto him the throne of David, his father; and he shall reign in the house of Jacob for ever*.[1] Jesus begins his reign upon the earth this very day; and though the first Israel is soon to disclaim his rule, a new Israel, formed from the faithful few of the old, shall rise up in every nation of the earth, and

---

[1] St. Luke, i. 32.

become the Kingdom of Christ, a kingdom such as no mere earthly monarch ever coveted in his wildest fancies of ambition.

This is the glorious Mystery which ushers in the Great Week, the Week of Dolours. Holy Church would have us give this momentary consolation to our heart, and hail our Jesus as our *King*. She has so arranged the Service of to-day, that it should express both joy and sorrow; joy, by uniting herself with the loyal Hosannas of the City of David; and sorrow, by compassionating the Passion of her Divine Spouse. The whole *function* is divided into three parts, which we will now proceed to explain.

The first is the blessing of the Palms, and we may have an idea of its importance by the solemnity used by the Church in this sacred rite. One would suppose that the Holy Sacrifice has begun, and is going to be offered up in honour of Jesus' Entry into Jerusalem. Introit, Collect, Epistle, Gradual, Gospel, even a Preface, are said as though we were, as usual, *preparing* for the immolation of the Spotless Lamb; but, after the triple *Sanctus! Sanctus! Sanctus!* the Church suspends these sacrificial formulas, and turns to the Blessing of the Palms. The Prayers she uses for this Blessing are eloquent and full of instruction; and, together, with the sprinkling with Holy Water and the Incensation, impart a virtue to these Branches, which elevates them to the supernatural order, and makes them means for the sanctification of our souls and the protection of our persons and dwellings. The Faithful should hold these Palms in their hands during the procession, and during the reading of the Passion at Mass, and keep them in their homes as an outward expression of their faith, and as a pledge of God's watchful love.

It is scarcely necessary to tell our reader, that the Palms or Olive branches, thus blessed, are carried in memory of those wherewith the people of Jerusalem strewed the road, as our Saviour made his triumphant Entry; but a word on the antiquity of our ceremony will not be superfluous. It began very early in the East. It is probable, that as far as Jerusalem itself is concerned, the custom was estabblished immediately after the Ages of Persecution. St. Cyril, who was Bishop of that City in the 4th century, tells us, that the Palm-tree, from which the people cut the branches when they went out to meet our Saviour, was still to be seen in the Vale of Cedron.[1] Such a circumstance would naturally suggest an annual commemoration of the great event. In the following century, we find this ceremony established, not only in the Churches of the East, but also in the Monasteries of Egypt and Syria. At the beginning of Lent, many of the holy monks obtained permission from their Abbots to retire into the desert, that they might spend the sacred season in strict seclusion; but they were obliged to return to their monasteries for Palm Sunday, as we learn from the Life of St. Euthymius, written by his disciple Cyril.[2] In the West, the introduction of this ceremony was more gradual: the first trace we find of it, is in the Sacramentary of St. Gregory, that is, the end of the 6th, or the beginning of the 7th, century. When the Faith had penetrated into the North, it was not possible to have Palms or Olive branches; they were supplied by branches from other trees. The beautiful prayers used in the Blessing, and which are based on the mysteries expressed by the Palm and Olive trees, are still employed in the blessing of our willow, box, or other branches; and rightly, for they represent the symbolical ones which nature has denied us.

The second of to-day's ceremonies is the Procession, which comes immediately after the Blessing of

---

[1] Cateches. x.   [2] Act. SS.—xx. Januarii.

the Palms. It represents our Saviour's journey to Jerusalem, and his Entry into the City. To make it the more expressive, the Branches that have just been blessed, are held in the hand during it. With the Jews, to hold a branch in one's hand, was a sign of joy. The Divine Law had sanctioned the practice, as we read in the following passage from Leviticus, where God commands his people to keep the Feast of Tabernacles: *And you shall take to you, on the first day, the fruits of the fairest tree, and branches of palm-trees, and boughs of thick trees, and willows of the brook, and you shall rejoice before the Lord your God.*[1] It was, therefore, to testify their delight at seeing Jesus enter within their walls, that the inhabitants, even the little children, of Jerusalem, went forth to meet him with Palms in their hands. Let us, also, go before our King, singing our Hosannas to him as the Conqueror of death, and the Liberator of his people.

During the Middle Ages, it was the custom, in many Churches, to carry the Book of the Holy Gospels in this Procession. The Gospel contains the words of Jesus Christ, and was considered to represent him. The Procession halted at an appointed place, or Station: the Deacon then opened the sacred Volume, and sang from it the passage which describes our Lord's Entry into Jerusalem. This done, the Cross, which, up to this moment, was veiled, was uncovered; each of the clergy advanced towards it, venerated it, and placed at its foot a small portion of the palm he held in his hand. The Procession then returned, preceded by the Cross, which was left unveiled, until all had re-entered the Church. In England and Normandy, as far back as the 11th century, there was practised a holy ceremony, which represented, even more vividly than the one we have just been describing, the scene that was witnessed,

[1] Levit., xxiii. 40.

on this day, at Jerusalem:—the Blessed Sacrament was carried in Procession. The heresy of Berengarius, against the Real Presence of Jesus in the Eucharist, had been broached about that time; and, the tribute of triumphant joy here shown to the Sacred Host, was a distant preparation for the Feast and Procession, which were to be instituted at a later period.

A touching ceremony was also practised in Jerusalem, during to-day's Procession, and, like those just mentioned, was intended to commemorate the event related by the Gospel. The whole community of the Franciscans, (to whose keeping the Holy Places are intrusted,) went, in the morning, to Bethphage. There, the Father Guardian of the Holy Land, vested in pontifical robes, mounted upon an ass, on which garments were laid. Accompanied by the Friars and the Catholics of Jerusalem, all holding Palms in their hands, he entered the City, and alighted at the Church of the Holy Sepulchre, where Mass was celebrated with all possible solemnity. This beautiful ceremony, which dated from the period of the Latin Kingdom in Jerusalem, has been forbidden, for now almost two hundred years, by the Turkish authorities of the City.

We have mentioned these different usages, as we have done others on similar occasions, in order to aid the Faithful to the better understanding of the several mysteries of the Liturgy. In the present instance, they will learn, that, in to-day's Procession the Church wishes us to honour Jesus Christ as though he were really among us, and were receiving the humble tribute of our loyalty. Let us lovingly go forth to meet this *our King, our Saviour, who comes to visit the Daughter of Sion,* as the Prophet has just told us. He is in our midst; it is to him that we pay honour with our Palms;—let us give him our hearts too. He *comes* that he may be our

King; let us welcome him as such, and fervently cry out to him: *Hosanna to the Son of David!*

At the close of the Procession, a ceremony takes place, which is full of the sublimest symbolism. On returning to the church, the doors are found to be shut. The triumphant Procession is stopped; but the songs of joy are continued. A hymn in honour of Christ our King is sung with its joyous chorus; and at length, the Subdeacon strikes the door with the staff of the cross; the door opens, and the people, preceded by the clergy, enter the church, proclaiming the praise of Him, who is our Resurrection and our Life.

This ceremony is intended to represent the entry of Jesus into that Jerusalem, of which the earthly one was but the figure,—the Jerusalem of heaven, which has been opened for us by our Saviour. The sin of our first parents had shut it against us; but Jesus, the King of glory, opened its gates by his Cross, to which every resistance yields. Let us, then, continue to follow in the footsteps of the Son of David, for he is also the Son of God, and he invites us to share his Kingdom with him. Thus, by the Procession, which is commemorative of what happened on this day, the Church raises up our thoughts to the glorious mystery of the Ascension, whereby heaven was made the close of Jesus' mission on earth. Alas! the interval between these two triumphs of our Redeemer are not all days of joy; and no sooner is our Procession over, than the Church, that had laid aside, for a moment, the weight of her grief, falls back into sorrow and mourning.

The third part of to-day's Service is the offering of the Holy Sacrifice. The portions that are sung by the Choir are expressive of the deepest desolation; and the history of our Lord's Passion, which is to be now read by anticipation, gives to the rest of the day that character of sacred gloom, which we all know so well. For the last five or six centuries, the Church has adopted a special chant for this narrative of the holy Gospel. The historian, or the Evangelist, relates the events in a tone that is at once grave and pathetic; the words of our Saviour are sung to a solemn yet sweet melody, which strikingly contrasts with the high dominant of the several other interlocutors and the Jewish populace. During the singing of the Passion, the Faithful should hold their Palms in their hands, and, by this emblem of triumph, protest against the insults offered to Jesus by his enemies. As we listen to each humiliation and suffering, all of which were endured out of love for us, let us offer him our Palm as to our dearest Lord and King. When should we be more adoring, than when he is most suffering?

These are the leading features of this great day. According to our usual plan, we will add to the Prayers and Lessons any instructions that seem to be needed.

This Sunday, besides its liturgical and popular appellation of *Palm Sunday*, has had several other names. Thus, it was called *Hosanna Sunday*, in allusion to the acclamation wherewith the Jews greeted Jesus on his Entry into Jerusalem. Our forefathers used also to call it *Pascha Floridum*, because the Feast of the Pasch (or Easter), which is but eight days off, is to-day in bud, so to speak, and the Faithful could begin from this Sunday to fulfil the precept of Easter Communion. It was in allusion to this name, that the Spaniards, having on the Palm Sunday of 1513, discovered the peninsula on the Gulf of Mexico, called it *Florida*. We also find the name of *Capitilavium* given to this Sunday, because during those times, when it was the custom to defer till Holy Saturday the baptism of infants born during the preceding months, (where such a delay entailed no danger,)—the parents used, on this day, to *wash the heads* of these children, out of respect to the Holy Chrism wherewith they were to be anointed. Later on, this Sunday was, at least in some Churches, called the *Pasch of the Competents*, that is, of the Catechumens, who were admitted to Baptism: they assembled to-day in the Church, and received a special instruction on the Symbol, which had been given to them in the previous scrutiny. In the Gothic Church of Spain, the Symbol was not given till to-day. The Greeks call this Sunday *Baïphoros*, that is, *Palm-Bearing*.

THE BLESSING OF THE PALMS.

It begins with the chanting the following Antiphon, which serves as an Introit.

ANTIPHON.

Hosanna to the Son of David! Blessed is he that cometh in the name of the Lord. O King of Israel! Hosanna in the highest!	Hosanna filio David! Benedictus qui venit in nomine Domine. O Rex Israel! Hosanna in excelsis!

The Priest then sums up, in the following Prayer, the petitions of the Faithful. This is what he asks for his people: that after this short life is over, they may come to that eternal kingdom, which has been prepared for them by Jesus' Death and Resurrection.

℣. The Lord be with you.   ℣. Dominus vobiscum.
℟. And with thy spirit.   ℟. Et cum spiritu tuo.

OREMUS.	LET US PRAY.
Deus quem diligere et amare, justitia est, ineffabilis gratiæ tuæ in nobis dona multiplica; et qui fecisti nos in morte Filii tui sperare quæ credimus, fac nos eodem resurgente pervenire quo tendimus. Qui tecum vivit et regnat in unitate Spiritus Sancti Deus per omnia sæcula sæculorum.	O God, whom to love is true righteousness, multiply in our hearts the gifts of thy holy grace; and since, by the death of thy only Son, thou hast made us to hope for those things which we believe, grant that by his resurrection, we may arrive at the happy end of our journey. Who liveth and reigneth with thee, in the unity of the Holy Ghost, world without end.
℟. Amen.	℟. Amen.

After this Prayer, the Subdeacon chants a passage from the Book of Exodus, which relates how the people of God, after they have gone forth from Egypt, pitch their tents at Elim, beneath the shade of seventy Palm-trees, where also are twelve fountains. Whilst here, they are told by Moses that God is about to send them manna from heaven, and that, on the very next morning, their hunger shall be appeased. These were figures of what is now given to the christian people. The Faithful, by a sincere conversion, have separated themselves from the Egypt of a sinful world. They are offering the Palms of their loyalty and love to Jesus, their King. The Fountains typify the Baptism, which, in a few days hence, is to be administered to our Catechumens. These Fountains are twelve in number; the Twelve articles of the Symbol of our Faith were preached to the world by the Twelve Apostles. And finally, on the *Morning* of Easter Day, Jesus, the Bread of life, the heavenly Manna, will arise from the tomb, and manifest his glory to us.

LESSON.

Lesson from the book of Exodus.

Ch. XV.

In those days, the children of Israel came into Elim, where there were twelve fountains of water, and seventy palm-trees; and they encamped by the waters. And they set forward from Elim; and all the multitude of the children of Israel came into the desert of Sin, which is between Elim and Sinai, the fifteenth day of the second month after they came out of the land of Egypt. And all the congregation of the children of Israel murmured against Moses and Aaron in the wilderness. And the children of Israel said to them: Would to God we had died by the hand of the Lord in the land of Egypt, when we sat over the flesh pots, and ate bread to the full. Why have you brought us into this desert, that you might destroy all the multitude with famine? And the Lord said to Moses: Behold I will rain bread from heaven for you; let the people go forth, and gather what is sufficient for every day, that I may prove them whether they will walk in my law, or no. But the sixth day let them provide for to bring in, and let it be double to that they were wont to gather every day. And Moses and Aaron said to the children of Israel: In the evening you shall know

Lectio libri Exodi.

Cap. XV.

In diebus illis: Venerunt filii Israel in Elim, ubi erant duodecim fontes aquarum, et septuaginta palmæ: et crastrametati sunt juxta aquas. Profectique sunt de Elim: et venit omnis multitudo filiorum Israel in desertum Sin, quod est inter Elim et Sinaï: quintodecimo die mensis secundi, postquam egressi sunt de terra Ægypti. Et murmuravit omnis congregatio filiorum Israel contra Moysen et Aaron in solitudine. Dixeruntque filii Israel ad eos: Utinam mortui essemus per manum Domini in terra Ægypti, quando sedebamus super ollas carnium: et comedebamus panem in saturitate. Cur induxistis nos in desertum istud, ut occideretis omnem multitudinem fame? Dixit autem Dominus ad Moysen: Ecce ego pluam vobis panes de cœlo. Egrediatur populus, et colligat quæ sufficiunt per singulos dies: ut tentem eum, utrum ambulet in lege mea, an non. Die autem sexto parent quod inferant: et sit duplum, quam colligere solebant per singulos dies. Dixeruntque Moyses et Aaron ad omnes filios Israel: Vespere scietis, quod Dominus eduxerit vos de terra

Ægypti: et mane videbitis gloriam Domini.

that the Lord hath brought you forth out of the land of Egypt; and in the morning you shall see the glory of the Lord.

After this Lesson, the choir sings one of the two following Responsories, which commemorate the Passion of our Lord.

RESPONSORY.

℟. Collegerunt Pontifices et Pharisæi concilium, et dixerunt: Quid facimus, quia hic homo multa signa facit? Si dimittimus eum sic, omnes credent in eum: * Et venient Romani, et tollent nostrum locum et gentem.

℣. Unus autem ex illis, Caiphas nomine, cum esset Pontifex anni illius, prophetavit dicens: Expedit vobis, ut unus moriatur homo pro populo, et non tota gens pereat. Ab illo ergo die cogitaverunt interficere eum, dicentes:
* Et venient Romani, et tollent nostrum locum et gentem.

℟. In monte Oliveti oravit ad Patrem: Pater, si fieri potest, transeat a me calix iste. * Spiritus quidem promptus est: caro autem infirma; fiat voluntas tua.

℣. Vigilate et orate, ut non intretis in tentationem.

* Spiritus quidem promptus est: caro autem infirma: fiat voluntas tua.

℟. The chief priest therefore and the Pharisees gathered a council, and said: What are we doing, for this man performeth many wonders? If we let him go on thus, all will believe in him. * And the Romans will come and destroy both our country and people.

℣. But one of them, named Caiphas, being the high priest of that year, said to them: It is for your interest that one man should die for the people, and not the whole nation perish. Therefore from that day they devised to kill him, saying:
* And the Romans will come and destroy both our country and people.

℟. Jesus prayed unto his Father on Mount Olivet: O Father, if it be possible, let this cup pass from me. * The spirit indeed is ready, but the flesh is weak. Thy will be done.

℣. Watch and pray, that ye enter not into temptation.

* The spirit indeed is ready, but the flesh is weak. Thy will be done.

The Deacon then chants, from the Gospel of St. Matthew, the history of Jesus' triumphant Entry into Jerusalem. The *Palms* of the New Testament entwine with those of the Old, in honour of the Man-God, who is the connecting link of both.

GOSPEL.

Sequel of the holy Gospel according to Matthew.

Cap. XXI.

At that time: Jesus drawing near to Jerusalem, and being come to Bethphage, at mount Olivet, he sent two of his disciples, and said to them: Go ye into the village that is over against you, and immediately you shall find an ass tied and a colt with her; loose them and bring them to me. And if any man shall say any thing to you, say ye, that the Lord hath need of them; and forthwith he will let them go. Now all this was done that it might be fulfilled which was spoken by the prophet, saying: Tell ye the daughter of Sion: Behold, thy King cometh to thee, meek, and sitting upon an ass, and a colt, the foal of her that is used to the yoke. And the disciples going, did as Jesus commanded them; and they brought the ass and the colt, and laid their garments upon them, and made him sit thereon. And a very great multitude spread their garments in the way, and others cut down boughs from the trees, and strewed the min the way; and the multitudes

Sequentia sancti Evangelii secundum Matthæum.

Ch. XXI.

In illo tempore: Cum appropinquasset Jesus Jerosolymis et venisset Bethphage, ad montem Oliveti; tunc misit duos discipulos suos, dicens eis: Ite in castellum, quod contra vos est: et statim invenietis asinam alligatam, et pullum cum ea: solvite, et adducite mihi. Et si quis vobis aliquid dixerit: dicite, quia Dominus his opus habet: et confestim dimittet eos. Hoc autem totum factum est, ut adimpleretur quod dictum est per Prophetam dicentem: Dicite filiæ Sion: Ecce Rex tuus venit tibi mansuetus sedens super asinam, et pullum filium subjugalis. Euntes autem discipuli, fecerunt sicut præcepit illis Jesus. Et adduxerunt asinam, et pullum: et imposuerunt super eos vestimenta sua, et eum desuper sedere fecerunt. Plurima autem turba straverunt vestimenta sua in via. Alii autem cædebant ramos de arboribus, et sternebant in via. Turbæ autem quæ præcedebant, et quæ sequebantur, clamabant, dicentes: Hosanna filio David! benedictus qui venit in nomine Domini!

that went before and that followed, cried, saying: Hosanna to the Son of David! Blessed is he that cometh in the name of the Lord!

And now the mystery-speaking Palms are to receive the Church's blessing. The Priest begins by two scriptural allusions: the first is to Noah, who received an olive-branch, when the waters of the deluge had subsided; the second is to Moses, whose people, after quitting Egypt, encamped under the seventy palm-trees. Then, in the solemn tone of the Preface, he calls upon all creatures to give praise to the adorable Name of Jesus, for whom we are preparing the homage of our devoted love. Let us respond to the invitation, and sing with all our hearts: *Holy! Holy! Holy!—Hosanna in excelsis!*

℣. Dominus vobiscum.
℞. Et cum spiritu tuo.

℣. The Lord be with you.
℞. And with thy spirit.

OREMUS.

Auge fidem in te sperantium, Deus, et supplicum preces clementer exaudi: veniat super nos multiplex misericordia tua; benedicantur et hi palmites palmarum, seu olivarum: et sicut in figura Ecclesiæ multiplicasti Noe egredientem de arca, et Moysen exeuntem de Ægypto cum filiis Israel: ita nos portantes palmas, et ramos olivarum bonis actibus occurramus obviam Christo, et per ipsum in gaudium introeamus æternum. Qui tecum vivit et regnat in unitate Spiritus Sancti Deus,

LET US PRAY.

Increase, O God, the faith of them that hope in thee, and mercifully hear the prayers of thy suppliants; let thy manifold mercy come upon us, and let these branches of palm-trees, or olive-trees, be blessed; and as in a figure of the Church thou didst multiply Noah going out of the ark, and Moses going out of Egypt with the children of Israel, so let us, carrying palms and branches of olive-trees, go and meet Christ with good works, and enter through him into eternal joys. Who liveth and reigneth with thee, in the unity of the Holy Ghost, God,

PALM SUNDAY: BLESSING THE PALMS.

℣. For ever and ever.

℟. Amen.
℣. The Lord be with you.
℟. And with thy spirit.
℣. Lift up your hearts.
℟. We have them fixed on God.
℣. Let us give thanks to the Lord our God.
℟. It is meet and just.
It is truly meet and just, right and available to salvation, always and in all places to give thee thanks, O Holy Lord, Almighty Father, Eternal God, who art glorious in the assembly of thy saints. For thy creatures serve thee, because they acknowledge thee for their only Creator and God. And the whole creation praiseth thee, and thy saints bless thee, because they confess with freedom, before the kings and powers of this world, the great name of thy Only Begotten Son. Before whom the Angels and Archangels, the Thrones, and Dominations, stand, and with all the troops of the heavenly host, sing a hymn to thy glory, saying without ceasing:
Holy, Holy, Holy, Lord God of hosts!

Heaven and earth are full of thy glory.
Hosanna in the highest!
Blessed is he that cometh in the name of the Lord.
Hosanna in the highest!

℣. Per omnia sæcula sæculorum.
℟. Amen.
℣. Dominus vobiscum.
℟. Et cum spiritu tuo.
℣. Sursum corda.
℟. Habemus ad Dominum.
℣. Gratias agamus Domino Deo nostro.
℟. Dignum et justum est.
Vere dignum et justum est, æquum et salutare, nos tibi semper et ubique gratias agere, Domine sancte, Pater omnipotens, æterne Deus. Qui gloriaris in consilio sanctorum tuorum. Tibi enim serviunt creaturæ tuæ: quia te solum auctorem et Deum cognoscunt: et omnis factura tua te collaudat, et benedicunt te sancti tui. Quia illud magnum Unigeniti tui nomen, coram regibus et potestatibus hujus sæculi, libera voce confitentur. Cui assistunt Angeli et Archangeli, Throni et Dominationes: cumque omni militia cœlestis exercitus, hymnum gloriæ tuæ concinunt, sine fine dicentes:
Sanctus, Sanctus, Sanctus, Dominus Deus Sabaoth.
Pleni sunt cœli et terra gloria tua.
Hosanna in excelsis.
Benedictus qui venit in nomine Domini.
Hosanna in excelsis.

The Prayers, which now follow, explain the mystery of the Palms, and draw down the blessing of

God upon both them and the Faithful who receive and keep them with proper dispositions.

℣. Dominus vobiscum.
℟. Et cum spiritu tuo.

℣. The Lord be with you.
℟. And with thy spirit.

OREMUS.

Petimus, Domine sancte, Pater omnipotens, æterne Deus: ut hanc creaturam olivæ, quam ex ligni materia prodire jussisti, quamque columba rediens ad arcam, proprio pertulit ore: benedicere, et sanctificare digneris: ut quicumque ex ea receperint, accipiant sibi protectionem animæ et corporis, fiatque, Domine, nostræ salutis remedium, tuæ gratiæ sacramentum. Per Dominum nostrum.
℟. Amen.

LET US PRAY.

We beseech thee, O Holy Lord, Almighty Father, Eternal God, that thou wouldst be pleased to bless and sanctify this creature of the olive tree, which thou madest to shoot out of the substance of the wood, and which the dove, returning to the ark, brought in its bill; that whoever receiveth it, may find protection of soul and body, and that it may prove, O Lord, a saving remedy, and a sacred sign of thy grace. Through, &c.
℟. Amen.

OREMUS.

Deus, qui dispersa congregas, et congregata conservas: qui populis obviam Jesu ramos portantibus benedixisti: benedic etiam hos ramos palmæ et olivæ, quos tui famuli ad honorem nominis tui fideliter suscipiunt: ut in quemcumque locum introducti fuerint, tuam benedictionem habitatores loci illius consequantur: et omni adversitate effugata, dextera tua protegat quos redemit Jesus Christus Filius tuus Dominus noster. Qui tecum.

℟. Amen.

LET US PRAY.

O God, who gatherest what is dispersed, and preservest what is gathered; who didst bless the people, that carried boughs to meet Jesus; bless also these branches of the palm-tree and olive-tree, which thy servants take with faith in honour of thy name; that into whatever place they may be carried, the inhabitants of that place may obtain thy blessing, and thy right hand preserve from all adversity, and protect those that have been redeemed by our Lord Jesus Christ thy Son. Who liveth, &c.
℟. Amen.

PALM SUNDAY: BLESSING THE PALMS.

LET US PRAY.

O God, who by the wonderful order of thy providence wouldst, even in insensible things, show us the manner of our salvation; grant, we beseech thee, that the devout hearts of thy faithful may understand to their benefit the mystical meaning of that ceremony, when the multitude, by direction from heaven, going this day to meet our Redeemer, strewed under his feet palms and olive-branches. The palms represent his triumph over the prince of death; and the olive-branches proclaim, in some manner, the coming of a spiritual unction. For that pious multitude then knew, what was by them signified, that our Redeemer, compassionating the misery of mankind, was to fight for the life of the whole world with the prince of death; and to triumph over him by his own death. And therefore in that action they made use of such things, as might declare both the triumph of his victory, and the riches of his mercy. We also with a firm faith, retaining both the ceremony and its signification, humbly beseech thee, O holy Lord, Almighty Father, Eternal God, through the same Lord Jesus Christ, that we, whom thou hast made his members, gaining by him, and in him, a victory over the empire of death, may deserve to be partakers of his glorious resurrection. Who liveth and reign-

OREMUS.

Deus, qui miro dispositionis ordine, ex rebus etiam insensibilibus, dispensationem nostræ salutis ostendere voluisti : da quæsumus, ut devota tuorum corda fidelium salubriter intelligant, quid mystice designet in facto, quod hodie cœlesti lumine afflata, Redemptori obviam procedens palmarum atque olivarum ramos vestigiis ejus turba substravit. Palmarum igitur rami de mortis principe triumphos exspectant : surculi vero olivarum spiritualem unctionem advenisse quodammodo clamant. Intellexit enim jam tunc illa hominum beata multitudo præfigurari : quia Redemptor noster humanis condolens miseriis, pro totius mundi vita cum mortis principe esset pugnaturus, ac moriendo triumphaturus. Et ideo talia obsequens administravit, quæ in illo et triumphos victoriæ, et misericordiæ pinguedinem declararent. Quod nos quoque plena fide, et factum et significatum retinentes, te Domine sancte, Pater omnipotens, æterne Deus, per eumdem Dominum nostrum Jesum Christum suppliciter exoramus : ut in ipso, atque per ipsum, cujus nos membra fieri voluisti, de mortis imperio victoriam reportantes, ipsius gloriosæ resurrectionis participes esse mereamur. Qui tecum vivit

HOLY WEEK.

et regnat in unitate Spiritus Sancti Deus, per omnia sæcula sæculorum.
℟. Amen.

OREMUS.

Deus qui per olivæ ramum, pacem terris columbam nuntiare jussisti: præsta quæsumus : ut hos olivæ cæterarumque arborum ramos, cœlesti benedictione sanctifices : ut cuncto populo tuo proficiant ad salutem. Per Christum Dominum nostrum.
℟. Amen.

OREMUS.

Benedic quæsumus, Domine, hos palmarum, seu olivarum ramos : et præsta ut quod populus tuus in tui venerationem hodierna die corporaliter agit, hoc spiritualiter summa devotione perficiat, de hoste victoriam reportando, et opus misericordiæ summopere diligendo. Per Dominum.
℟. Amen.

eth with thee, in the unity of the Holy Ghost, world without end.
℟. Amen.

LET US PRAY.

O God, who by an olive branch didst command the dove to proclaim peace to the world; sanctify, we beseech thee, by thy heavenly benediction, these branches of olives and other trees ; that they may be serviceable to all thy people unto salvation. Through, &c.
℟. Amen.

LET US PRAY.

Bless, O Lord, we beseech thee, these branches of the palm-tree, or olive-tree ; and grant that what thy people this day act corporally for thy honour, they may perform the same spiritually with the greatest devotion, by gaining a victory over their enemy, and ardently loving the work of thy mercy. Through, &c.
℟. Amen.

The Priest completes the Blessing of the Palms by sprinkling them with Holy Water and thurifying them with Incense. After which, he adds the following Prayer.

℣. Dominus vobiscum.
℟. Et cum spiritu tuo.

℣. The Lord be with you.
℟. And with thy spirit.

OREMUS.

Deus, qui Filium tuum Jesum Christum Dominum

LET US PRAY.

O God, who, for our salvation, didst send into this

world thy Son Jesus Christ our Lord that he might humble himself to our condition, and call us back to thee: for whom also, as he was coming to Jerusalem, to fulfil the scriptures, a multitude of faithful people, with a zealous devotion, spread their garments together with palm branches in the way: grant, we beseech thee, that we may prepare him the way of faith, out of which the stone of offence and the rock of scandal being removed, our actions may flourish with branches of righteousness, so that we may be worthy to follow his steps. Who liveth and reigneth with thee, in the unity of the Holy Ghost, world without end.

℟. Amen.

nostrum, pro salute nostra in hunc mundum misisti, ut se humiliaret ad nos, et nos revocaret ad te: cui etiam dum Jerusalem veniret, ut adimpleret Scripturas, credentium populorum turba, fidelissima devotione, vestimenta sua cum ramis palmarum in via sternebant: præsta, quæsumus, ut illi fidei viam præparemus: de qua remoto lapide offensionis, et petra scandali, frondeant apud te opera nostra justitiæ ramis: ut ejus vestigia sequi mereamur. Qui tecum vivit et regnat in unitate Spiritus Sancti Deus, per omnia sæcula sæculorum.

℟. Amen.

After this prayer, the Priest distributes the Palms to the Faithful.[1] During the distribution, the Choir reminds us, by the two following Antiphons, of the enthusiasm of the little children of Jerusalem, who, with their Palms in their hands, sang their loud *Hosanna to the Son of David!*

ANTIPHON.

The Hebrew children carrying olive-branches met the Lord, crying out, and saying: Hosanna in the highest!

Pueri Hebræorum portantes ramos olivarum obviaverunt Domino, clamantes, et dicentes: Hosanna in excelsis!

ANTIPHON.

The Hebrew children spread their garments in the way,

Pueri Hebræorum vestimenta prosternebant in via,

---

[1] In receiving the Palm, the Faithful should kiss first the Palm itself, and then the Priest's hand.

et clamabant dicentes: Hosanna filio David; benedictus qui venit in nomine Domini!

and cried out, saying: Hosanna to the Son of David: blessed is he that cometh in the name of the Lord!

As soon as the distribution is over, the Priest concludes this first part of the Service by the following Prayer.

℣. Dominus vobiscum.
℟. Et cum spiritu tuo.

℣. The Lord be with you.
℟. And with thy spirit.

OREMUS.

Omnipotens sempiterne Deus, qui Dominum nostrum Jesum Christum super pullum asinæ sedere fecisti: et turbas populorum vestimenta, vel ramos arborum in via sternere, et Hosanna decantare in laudem ipsius docuisti: da quæsumus, ut illorum innocentiam imitari possimus, et eorum meritum consequi mereamur. Per eumdem Christum Dominum nostrum.
℟. Amen.

LET US PRAY.

O Almighty and Eternal God, who wouldst have our Lord Jesus Christ ride on the colt of an ass, and didst inspire the crowds of people to spread their garments, and branches of trees in the way, and to sing Hosanna to his praise: grant, we beseech thee, that we may imitate their innocence, and deserve to partake of their merits. Through the same Christ our Lord.
℟. Amen.

THE PROCESSION.

The Priest having blessed the Incense,—which, according to the custom of the Church, always heads a Procession and sheds its perfume along the path that is to be taken,—the Deacon turns towards the people, and gives the signal for departure, with these words:

Procedamus in pace.

Let us proceed in peace.

PALM SUNDAY: THE PROCESSION.

The Choir answers:

In the name of Christ. Amen.

In nomine Christi. Amen.

The Procession then advances, the Clergy and people holding the Palms in their hands. The Choir chants the following Antiphons, in honour of Jesus, the King of Israel.

ANTIPHON.

When the Lord drew nigh to Jerusalem, he sent two of his disciples, saying: Go ye into the village that is over against you; and you will find the colt of an ass tied, upon which no man hath sat; loose it, and bring it to me. If any one ask you any questions, say: The Lord wanteth it. They untied, and brought it to Jesus, and laid their garments upon it; and he seated himself on it. Others spread their garments in the way; others cut branches from the trees; and those who followed, cried out, Hosanna! Blessed is he that cometh in the name of the Lord; and blessed be the reign of our father David! Hosanna in the highest! O Son of David, have mercy on us!

Cum appropinquaret Dominus Jerosolymam, misit duos ex dicipulis suis, dicens: Ite in castellum, quod contra vos est: et invenietis pullum asinæ alligatum, super quem nullus hominum sedit: solvite, et adducite mihi. Si quis vos interrogaverit, dicite: Opus Domino est. Solventes adduxerunt ad Jesum; et imposuerunt illi vestimenta sua, et sedit super eum: alii expandebant vestimenta sua in via: alii ramos de arboribus sternebant, et qui sequebantur, clamabant: Hosanna! benedictus qui venit in nomine Domini, et benedictum regnum patris nostri David! Hosanna in excelsis! Miserere nobis, fili David!

ANTIPHON.

When the people heard that Jesus was coming to Jerusalem, they took palm-branches, and went out to meet him: and the children cried out, saying: This is he, who is

Cum audisset populus, quia Jesus venit Jerosolymam, acceperunt ramos palmarum, et exierunt ei obviam, et clamabant pueri dicentes: Hic est, qui venturus est in salutem populi: Hic est salus nostra, et redemptio Israël. Quantus est iste, cui Throni et Dominationes occurrunt! Noli timere, filia Sion! ecce Rex tuus venit tibi, sedens super pullum asinæ, sicut scriptum est. Salve Rex fabricator mundi, qui venisti redimere nos!

come for the salvation of the people. He is our salvation, and the redemption of Israel. How great is he, whom the Thrones and Dominations go out to meet! Fear not, O daughter of Sion: behold thy King cometh to thee sitting on an ass's colt, as it is written. Hail, O King, the Creator of the world, who art come to redeem us!

ANTIPHON.

Ante sex dies solemnis Paschæ, quando venit Dominus in civitatem Jerusalem, occurrerunt ei pueri: et in manibus portabant ramos palmarum: et clamabant voce magna, dicentes: Hosanna in excelsis! Benedictus qui venisti in multitudine misericordiæ tuæ; Hosanna in excelsis!

Six days before the solemnity of the Passover, when the Lord was coming into the city of Jerusalem, the children met him, and carried palm-branches in their hands; and they cried out with a loud voice, saying: Hosanna in the highest: blessed art thou who art come in the multitude of thy mercy: Hosanna in the highest!

ANTIPHON.

Occurrunt turbæ cum floribus et palmis Redemptori obviam: et victori triumphanti digna dant obsequia. Filium Dei ore gentes prædicant: et in laudem Christi voces tonant per nubila: Hosanna in excelsis!

The multitude goeth out to meet their Redeemer with flowers and palms, and payeth the homage due to a triumphant conqueror: the Gentiles proclaim the Son of God: and their voices rend the skies in the praise of Christ: Hosanna in the highest!

ANTIPHON.

Cum Angelis et pueris fideles inveniamur, trium-

Let us faithfully join with the Angels and children, sing-

ing to the Conqueror of death : Hosanna in the highest !	phatori mortis clamantes : Hosanna in excelsis !

ANTIPHON.

A great multitude that was met together at the festival cried out to the Lord : Blessed is he that cometh in the name of the Lord ! Hosanna in the highest !	Turba multa quæ convenerat ad diem festum, clamabat Domino : Benedictus qui venit in nomine Domini ! Hosanna in excelsis !

The Procession is now on its return to the Church : but it cannot enter, for the doors are shut. We have already explained the meaning of this part of the ceremony. Immediately, there are heard voices within the holy place ; they are singing the praises of Christ, our King and Saviour. These chanters represent the holy Angels in heaven, who are greeting the Entry of Jesus into the eternal Jerusalem. Outside the Church, there stands the choir, re-echoing the Hymn of triumph ; but it is man celebrating the Entry of the Son of David into the earthly Jerusalem. The two Choirs are thus kept separated from each other, until, at length, the victorious Cross throws open the door, which represents the gate of heaven, and unites the Church militant with the Church triumphant. The hymn which is sung during this ceremony, was composed by Theodulph, Bishop of Orleans, when prisoner at Angers, by order of Louis the Good. The Church of Rome, by her using the first six stanzas of this short poem, has immortalised it throughout the world.

The Chanters within the Church begin the first stanza, which is repeated by the Choir without, not only after this, but also after each of the following five stanzas.

HYMN.

Gloria, laus et honor tibi sit, Rex Christe Redemptor!
Cui puerile decus prompsit Hosanna pium.
℞. Gloria, laus.
Israël es tu Rex, Davidis et inclyta proles :
Nomine qui in Domini, rex benedicte, venis.

℞. Gloria, laus.
Cœtus in excelsis, te laudat cœlicus omnis,
Et mortalis homo, et cuncta creata simul.
℞. Gloria, laus.
Plebs Hebræa tibi cum palmis obvia venit:
Cum prece, voto, hymnis, adsumus ecce tibi.

℞. Gloria, laus.
Hi tibi passuro solvebant munia laudis ;
Nos tibi regnanti pangimus ecce melos.

℞. Gloria, laus.
Hi placuere tibi, placeat devotio nostra,
Rex bone, rex clemens, cui bona cuncta placent.

℞. Gloria, laus.

Glory, praise, and honour be to thee, O Christ, our King, our Saviour! to whom the innocent children sang their fervent Hosanna.
℞. Glory, praise, &c.
Thou art the King of Israel, the glorious Son of David! Blessed art thou, our King! that comest in the name of the Lord.
℞. Glory, praise, &c.
The whole heavenly host, in the highest heavens above, and men on earth, and all created things, praise thee.
℞. Glory, praise, &c.
The Hebrew people, with Palms, went forth to meet thee : behold! we, too, present ourselves before thee, with our prayers, desires, and hymns.
℞. Glory, praise, &c.
They offered the tribute of their praise to thee, when thou wast about to suffer ; *we* sing our hymn to thee seated on thy throne.
℞. Glory, praise, &c.
They were pleasing to thee ; grant that *our* devotion may also please thee, O dear and merciful King! to whom all is pleasing that is good.
℞. Glory, praise, &c.

As soon as the Choir has sung its Response to the last stanza, the Subdeacon knocks with the Cross at the door, which is immediately opened. In some places, it is the Celebrant himself who performs this ceremony, and whilst doing it, he recites the words of the 23rd Psalm, in which David celebrates the entrance of our Redeemer into heaven, on the day of his Ascension.

The Procession then enters the Church, singing the following Responsory:

RESPONSORY.

℟. As our Lord entered the holy city, the Hebrew children declaring the resurrection of life, * With palm-branches, cried out: Hosanna in the highest!
℣. When the people heard that Jesus was coming to Jerusalem, they went out to meet him.
* With palm-branches, cried out: Hosanna in the highest!

℟. Ingrediente Domino in sanctam civitatem, Hebræorum pueri resurrectionem vitæ pronuntiantes; * Cum ramis palmarum, Hosanna clamabant in excelsis.
℣. Cum audisset populus, quod Jesus veniret Jerosolymam, exierunt obviam ei.
* Cum ramis palmarum, Hosanna clamabant in excelsis.

MASS.

The Station, at Rome, is in the Basilica of Saint John Lateran, the Mother and Mistress of all Churches. The Papal function, however, now takes place at Saint Peter's; but the usual Indulgences are still granted to those who visit the Arch-Basilica.

The Mass of this Sunday retains no vestige of the joy, which characterised the ceremony of the Palms. The Introit is taken from the 21st Psalm, in which the Royal Prophet expresses the anguish of soul suffered by Jesus on the Cross.

INTROIT.

O Lord, keep not thy help far from me; look to my defence; save me from the lion's

Domine, ne longe facias auxilium tuum a me, ad defensionem meam adspice:

220   HOLY WEEK.

libera me de ore leonis, et a cornibus unicornium humilitatem meam.
Ps. Deus, Deus meus, respice in me, quare me dereliquisti? longe a salute mea verba delictorum meorum.
Domine, ne longe.

mouth, and rescue me in my distress, from the horns of unicorns.
Ps. O God, my God, look upon me: why hast thou forsaken me? They are my sins that keep salvation far from me.
Lord, keep not, &c.

In the Collect, the Church prays that we may have grace to imitate the patience and humility of our Saviour. Jesus suffers and humbles himself for us; it is but just that we should work out our salvation by following his example,—that we should suffer, and be humble.

COLLECT.

Omnipotens sempiterne Deus, qui humano generi ad imitandum humilitatis exemplum, Salvatorem nostrum carnem sumere, et crucem subire fecisti: concede propitius: ut et patientiæ ipsius habere documenta, et resurrectionis consortia mereamur. Per eumdem.

O Almighty and Eternal God, who wouldst have our Saviour become man, and suffer on a cross, to give mankind an example of humility; mercifully grant, that we may improve by the example of his patience, and partake of his resurrection. Through the same, &c.

EPISTLE.

Lectio Epistolæ B. Pauli Apostoli ad Philippenses.

Lesson of the Epistle of Saint Paul the Apostle to the Philippians.

Cap. II.

Fratres, hoc enim sentite in vobis, quod et in Christo Jesu. Qui cum in forma Dei esset, non rapinam arbitratus est, esse se æqualem

Ch. II.

Brethren: For let this mind be in you, which was also in Christ Jesus; who being in the form of God, thought it not robbery to be equal with God, but emptied himself, taking the form of a servant, being made in the likeness of men, and in habit found as a man. He humbled himself, becoming obedient unto death, even to the death of the cross. For which cause God also hath exalted him and hath given him a name which is above all names; that in the Name of JESUS *(here, all kneel,)* every knee shall bow, of those that are in heaven, on earth, and under the earth. And that every tongue should confess that the Lord Jesus Christ is in the glory of the Father.

Deo: sed semetipsum exinanivit, formam servi accipiens, in similitudinem hominum factus, et habitu inventus ut homo. Humiliavit semetipsum, factus obediens usque ad mortem, mortem autem crucis. Propter quod et Deus exaltavit illum: et donavit illi nomen, quod est super omne nomen: ut in nomine JESU *(here, all kneel,)* omne genu flectatur, cœlestium, terrestrium, et infernorum: et omnis linguæ confiteatur, quia Dominus Jesus Christus in gloria est Dei Patris.

In obedience to the wishes of the Church, we have knelt down at those words of the Apostle, where he says, that every knee should bow at the Holy Name of Jesus. If there be one time of the Year rather than an other, when the Son of God has a right to our fervent adorations, it is this Week, when we see him insulted in his Passion. Not only should his Sufferings excite us to tender compassion; we should, also, keenly resent the insults that are heaped upon this Jesus of ours, this God of infinite Majesty. Let us strive, by our humble homage, to make him amends for the indignities he suffered in atonement for our pride.

Let us unite with the holy Angels, who, witnessing what he has gone through out of love for man, prostrate themselves, in profoundest adoration, at the sight of his humiliations.

In the Gradual, the Church makes use of the words of the Royal Prophet, who foretells the future *glories* of the victim that dies on Calvary; but he also confesses, that the success permitted to the enemies of Jesus had well nigh shaken his confidence.

GRADUAL.

Tenuisti manum dexteram meam: et in voluntate tua deduxisti me: et cum gloria assumpsisti me.

℣. Quam bonus Israël Deus rectis corde! mei autem pene moti sunt pedus, pene effusi sunt gressus mei: quia zelavi in peccatoribus, pacem peccatorum videns.

Thou hast held me by my right hand, and by thy will thou hast conducted me; and with glory thou hast received me.

℣. How good is the God of Israel, to them that are of a right heart! But my feet were almost moved, my steps had well nigh slipt, because I had a zeal on sinners, seeing the prosperity of sinners.

The Tract consists of several verses taken from the 22nd Psalm, the last words of which were spoken by our Redeemer on the Cross. So clear and explicit are the words of this Psalm, that it might almost be called a history, as well as a prophecy, of the Passion.

TRACT.

Deus, Deus meus, respice in me: quare me dereliquisti?

℣. Longe a salute mea verba delictorum meorum.

℣. Deus meus, clamabo per diem, nec exaudies; in nocte, et non ad insipientiam mihi.

℣. Tu autem in sancto habitas, laus Israël.

℣. In te speraverunt patres nostri: speraverunt et liberasti eos.

℣. Ad te clamaverunt, et salvi facti sunt: in te speraverunt, et non sunt confusi.

O God, my God, look upon me: why hast thou forsaken me?

℣. Far from my salvation are the words of my sins.

℣. O my God, I shall cry by day, and thou wilt not hear; and by night, and it shall not be imputed as folly in me.

℣. But thou dwellest in the holy place, O thou the praise of Israel!

℣. In thee have our fathers hoped: they hoped, and thou hast delivered them.

℣. They cried out to thee, and they were saved: they trusted in thee, and were not confounded.

℣. But I am a worm, and no man : the reproach of men, and the outcast of the people.

℣. All they that saw me, have laughed me to scorn : they have spoken with the lips, and wagged the head.

℣. He hoped in the Lord, (*say they*,) let him deliver him: let him save him, seeing he delighted in him.

℣. They considered me, and viewed me attentively : they divided my garments among them, and cast lots for my vest.

℣. Deliver me from the lion's mouth : and my lowness from the horns of the unicorns.

℣. Ye that fear the Lord, praise him: O all ye of the seed of Jacob, magnify him.

℣. A people that is to come, shall be declared the Lord's : and the heavens shall publish his justice,

℣. To a people to be born, whom the Lord hath made.

℣. Ego autem sum vermis, et non homo : opprobrium hominum, et abjectio plebis.

℣. Omnes qui videbant me, aspernabantur me : locuti sunt labiis, et moverunt caput.

℣. Speravit in Domino, eripiat eum : salvum faciat eum, quoniam vult eum.

℣. Ipsi vero consideraverunt, et conspexerunt me : diviserunt sibi vestimenta mea, et super vestem meam miserunt sortem.

℣. Libera me de ore leonis : et a cornibus unicornium humilitatem meam.

℣. Qui timetis Dominum laudate eum : universum semen Jacob magnificate eum.

℣. Annuntiabitur Domino generatio ventura : et annuntiabunt cœli justitiam ejus.

℣. Populo qui nascetur, quem fecit Dominus.

It is now time that we should hear the history of our Saviour's Passion : but, in order that we may show both heaven and earth that we are not scandalised, as were the Disciples, at the sight of his apparent weakness and the triumph of his enemies, we hold in our hands the Palms, wherewith we have been proclaiming him as our King.

The Church reads, on four different days of this Week, the four Evangelists' narration of the Passion. She begins with that of St. Matthew, who was the first to write the Gospel. To express the sorrow which fills the hearts of the Faithful, the Acolytes do not carry the lights, nor is the Book incensed. Omitting the customary salutation, the Deacon, who is to take the part of the Evangelist, at once begins the mournful history of our Lord's Sufferings and Death.

THE PASSION AND GOSPEL.

Passio Domini nostri Jesu Christi secundum Matthæum.

The Passion of our Lord Jesus Christ, according to Matthew.

Cap. XXVI. et XXVII.

Ch. XXVI. and XXVII.

In illo tempore: Dixit Jesus discipulis suis: Scitis, quia post biduum Pascha fiet: et Filius hominis tradetur, ut crucifigatur. Tunc congregati sunt principes sacerdotum et seniores populi in atrium principis sacerdotum, qui dicebatur Caiphas: et consilium fecerunt, ut Jesum dolo tenerent, et occiderent. Dicebant autem: Non in die festo, ne forte tumultus fieret in populo.

Cum autem Jesus esset in Bethania, in domo Simonis Leprosi, accessit ad eum mulier habens alabastrum unguenti pretiosi: et effudit super caput ipsius recumbentis. Videntes autem discipuli, indignati sunt, dicentes: Ut quid perditio hæc? Potuit enim unguentum istud venundari multo, et dari pauperibus. Sciens autem Jesus, ait illis: Quid molesti estis huic mulieri? Opus enim

At that time: Jesus said to his disciples: You know that after two days shall be the Pasch, and the Son of man shall be delivered up to be crucified. Then were gathered together the chief priests and ancients of the people into the court of the High Priest, who was called Caiphas; and they consulted together, that by subtilty they might apprehend Jesus, and put him to death. But they said: Not on the Festival day, lest perhaps there should be a tumult amongst the people.

And when Jesus was in Bethania, in the house of Simon the Leper, there came to him a woman having an alabaster-box of precious ointment, and poured it on his head as he was at table. And the disciples seeing it, had indignation, saying: To what purpose is this waste? For this might have been sold for much, and given to the poor. And Jesus knowing it, said to them: Why do you trouble this woman? For she has wrought a good work upon me. For the poor you have always with you, but me you have not always. For she, in pouring this ointment upon my body, hath done it for my burial. Amen, I say to you, wheresoever this gospel shall be preached in the whole world, that also which she hath done, shall be told for a memory of her.

Then went one of the twelve, who was called Judas Iscariot, to the chief priests and said to them : What will you give me, and I will deliver him unto you ? But they appointed him thirty pieces of silver. And from thenceforth he sought an opportunity to betray him. And on the first day of the Azymes, the disciples came to Jesus, saying : Where wilt thou that we prepare for thee to eat the Pasch? But Jesus said : Go ye into the city to a certain man, and say to him, The Master saith my time is near at hand. I will keep the Pasch at thy house with my disciples. And the disciples did as Jesus appointed to them, and they prepared the Pasch.

Now when it was evening, he sat down with his twelve disciples; and whilst they were eating, he said : Amen, I say to you, that one of you is about to betray me. And they being very much troubled, began every one to say : Is it I, Lord ? But he answering said : He that dippeth his hand with me in the dish, he

bonum operata est in me. Nam semper pauperes habetis vobiscum : me autem non semper habetis. Mittens enim hæc unguentum hoc in corpus meum, ad sepeliendum me fecit. Amen dico vobis, ubicumque prædicatum fuerit hoc Evangelium in toto mundo, dicetur et quod hæc fecit in memoriam ejus.

Tunc abiit unus de duodecim, qui dicebatur Judas Iscariotes, ad principes sacerdotum : et ait illis : Quid vultis mihi dare, et ego vobis eum tradam ? At illi constituerunt ei triginta argenteos. Et exinde quærebat opportunitatem, ut eum traderet. Prima autem die Azymorum accesserunt discipuli ad Jesum dicentes : Ubi vis paremus tibi comedere Pascha? At Jesus dixit : Ite in civitatem ad quemdam, et dicite ei : Magister dicit : Tempus meum prope est : apud te facio Pascha cum discipulis meis. Et fecerunt discipuli, sicut constituit illis Jesus : et paraverunt Pascha.

Vespere autem facto, discumbebat cum duodecim discipulis suis. Et edentibus illis, dixit : Amen dico vobis : quia unus vestrum me traditurus est. Et contristati valde, cœperunt singuli dicere : Numquid ego sum, Domine ? At ipse respondens, ait : Qui intingit mecum manum in paropside, hic me tradet. Filius quidem hominis vadit, sicut scriptum est de illo. Væ autem homini illi, per quem Filius hominis tradetur. Bonum erat ei, si natus non fuisset homo ille. Respondens autem Judas qui tradidit eum, dixit : Numquid ego sum, Rabbi ? Ait illi : Tu dixisti.

Cœnantibus autem eis, accepit Jesus panem : et benedixit, ac fregit, deditque discipulis suis, et ait : Accipite, et comedite : Hoc est corpus meum. Et accipiens calicem, gratias egit : et dedit illis, dicens : Bibite ex hoc omnes. Hic est enim sanguis meus novi testamenti, qui pro multis effundetur in remissionem peccatorum. Dico autem vobis : Non bibam amodo de hoc genimine vitis usque in diem illum, cum illud bibam vobiscum novum in regno Patris mei.

Et hymno dicto, exierunt in montem Oliveti. Tunc dicit illis Jesus : Omnes vos scandalum patiemini in me, in ista nocte. Scriptum est enim : Percutiam pastorem, et dispergentur oves gregis : postquam autem resurrexero, præcedam vos in Galilæam. Respondens autem Petrus, ait illi : Etsi omnes scandalizati fuerint in te, ego nunquam scandalizabor. Ait illi Jesus : Amen dico tibi quia in hac nocte, antequam gallus cantet, ter me negabis. Ait illi Petrus : Etiam si oportue-

shall betray me. The Son of man indeed goeth, as it is written of him ; but woe to that man, by whom the Son of man shall be betrayed. It were better for him, if that man had not been born. And Judas, that betrayed him, answering said : Is it I, Rabbi ? He saith to him : Thou hast said it.

And whilst they were at supper, Jesus took bread, and blessed, and broke, and gave to his disciples, and said : Take ye, and eat ; this is my body. And taking the chalice he gave thanks, and gave to them, saying : Drink ye all of this ; for this is my blood of the new testament, which shall be shed for many for the remission of sins. And I say to you, I will not drink from henceforth of this fruit of the vine, until that day when I shall drink it new with you in the kingdom of my Father.

And a hymn being said, they went out into mount Olivet. Then Jesus said to them : All you shall be scandalised in me this night. For it is written : "I will strike the shepherd, and the sheep of the flock shall be dispersed." But after I shall be risen again, I will go before you into Galilee. And Peter answering said to him : Although all shall be scandalised in thee, I will never be scandalised. Jesus said to him : Amen, I say to thee, that in this night, before the cock crow, thou wilt deny me thrice. Peter saith to him: Yea, though I should die with thee, I will not deny thee. And in like manner said all the disciples.

Then Jesus came with them into a country place which is called Gethsemani; and he said to his disciples: Sit you here, till I go yonder, and pray. And taking with him Peter and the two sons of Zebedee, he began to grow sorrowful, and to be sad. Then he said to them: My soul is sorrowful even unto death; stay you here and watch with me. And going a little further he fell upon his face, praying, and saying: My Father, if it be possible, let this chalice pass from me. Nevertheless, not as I will, but as thou wilt. And he cometh to his disciples, and findeth them asleep, and he saith to Peter: What! could you not watch one hour with me? Watch ye, and pray that ye enter not into temptation. The spirit indeed is willing, but the flesh is weak. Again the second time he went and prayed, saying: My Father, if this chalice may not pass away, but I must drink it, thy will be done. And he cometh again, and findeth them sleeping; for their eyes were heavy. And leaving them, he went again; and he prayed the third time, saying the self-same words. Then he cometh to his disciples, and saith to them: Sleep ye now, and take your rest; behold the hour is

rit me mori tecum, non te negabo. Similiter et omnes discipuli dixerunt.

Tunc venit Jesus cum illis in villam, quæ dicitur Gethsemani: et dixit discipulis suis: Sedete hic donec vadam illuc, et orem. Et assumpto Petro, et duobus filiis Zebedæi, cœpit contristari, et mœstus esse. Tunc ait illis: Tristis est anima mea usque ad mortem. Sustinete hic et vigilate mecum. Et progressus pusillum, procidit in faciem suam, orans et dicens: Pater mi, si possibile est, transeat a me calix iste. Verumtamen non sicut ego volo, sed sicut tu. Et venit ad discipulos suos, et invenit eos dormientes: et dicit Petro: Sic, non potuistis una hora vigilare mecum? Vigilate, et orate: ut non intretis in tentationem. Spiritus quidem promptus est, caro autem infirma. Iterum secundo abiit, et oravit dicens: Pater mi, si non potest hic calix transire, nisi bibam illum: fiat voluntas tua. Et venit iterum, et invenit eos dormientes. Erant enim oculi eorum gravati. Et relictis illis, iterum abiit: et oravit tertio eumdem sermonem dicens. Tunc venit ad discipulos suos, et dicit illis: Dormite jam, et requiescite. Ecce appropinquavit hora: et Filius hominis tradetur in manus peccatorum. Surgite, eamus: ecce appropinquavit qui me tradet.

Adhuc eo loquente, ecce Judas unus de duodecim venit, et cum eo turba multa cum gladiis et fustibus, missi a principibus sacerdotum, et senioribus populi. Qui autem tradidit eum, dedit illis signum dicens: Quemcumque osculatus fuero, ipse est, tenete eum. Et confestim accedens ad Jesum, dixit: Ave, Rabbi. Et osculatus est eum. Dixitque illi Jesus: Amice, ad quid venisti? Tunc accesserunt, et manus injecerunt in Jesum: et tenuerunt eum. Et ecce unus ex his qui erant cum Jesu, extendens manum, exemit gladium suum: et percutiens servum principis Sacerdotum, amputavit auriculam ejus. Tunc ait illi Jesus: Converte gladium tuum in locum suum. Omnes enim, qui acceperint gladium, gladio peribunt. An putas, quia non possum rogare Patrem meum: et exhibebit mihi modo plus quam duodecim legiones Angelorum? Quomodo ergo implebuntur Scripturæ, quia sic oportet fieri? In illa hora dixit Jesus turbis: Tamquam ad latronem existis cum gladiis et fustibus comprehendere me: quotidie apud vos sedebam docens in Templo: et non me tenuistis. Hoc

at hand, and the Son of man shall be betrayed into the hands of sinners. Rise, let us go: behold he is at hand that will betray me.

As he yet spoke, behold Judas, one of the twelve, came, and with him a great multitude with swords and clubs, sent from the Chief Priests and the ancients of the people. And he that betrayed him, gave them a sign, saying: Whomsoever I shall kiss, that is he, hold him fast. And forthwith coming to Jesus, he said: Hail, Rabbi! And he kissed him. And Jesus said to him: Friend, whereto art thou come? Then they came up, and laid hands on Jesus, and held him. And behold one of them that were with Jesus, stretching forth his hand, drew out his sword; and striking the servant of the High Priest, cut off his ear. Then Jesus said to him: Put up again thy sword into its place; for all that take the sword shall perish with the sword. Thinkest thou that I cannot ask my Father, and he will give me presently more than twelve legions of Angels? How then shall the Scriptures be fulfilled, that so it must be done? In that same hour Jesus said to the multitude: You are come out as it were to a robber, with swords and clubs, to apprehend me. I sat daily with you teaching in the temple, and you laid not hands on me. Now all this was done, that the Scriptures of the prophets might be fulfilled. Then the disciples all leaving him, fled.

But they holding Jesus, led him to Caiphas the High Priest, where the scribes and the ancients were assembled. And Peter followed him afar off, even to the court of the High Priest; and going in, he sat with the servants, that he might see the end. And the chief priests and the whole council sought false witness against Jesus, that they might put him to death; and they found not, whereas many false witnesses had come in. And last of all there came two false witnesses; and they said: This man said, I am able to destroy the temple of God, and after three days to rebuild it. And the High Priest rising up, said to him: Answerest thou nothing to the things which these witness against thee? But Jesus held his peace. And the High Priest said to him: I adjure thee, by the living God, that thou tell us if thou be the Christ the Son of God. Jesus saith to him: Thou hast said it. Nevertheless I say to you, hereafter you shall see the Son of man sitting on the right hand of the power of God, and coming in the clouds of heaven. Then the High Priest rent his garments, saying: He hath blasphemed, what further need have we of witnesses? Behold, now you have heard the blasphemy: what think you?

autem totum factum est, ut adimplerentur Scripturæ Prophetarum. Tunc discipuli omnes, relicto eo, fugerunt. At illi tenentes Jesum duxerunt ad Caipham principem sacerdotum, ubi scribæ et seniores convenerant. Petrus autem sequebatur eum a longe, usque in atrium principis sacerdotum. Et ingressus intro, sedebat cum ministris, ut videret finem. Principes autem sacerdotum, et omne concilium, quærebant falsum testimonium contra Jesum, ut eum morti traderent: et non invenerunt, cum multi falsi testes accessissent. Novissime autem venerunt duo falsi testes, et dixerunt: Hic dixit: Possum destruere Templum Dei, et post triduum reædificare illud. Et surgens princeps sacerdotum, ait ille: Nihil respondes ad ea, quæ isti adversum te testificantur? Jesus autem tacebat. Et princeps sacerdotum ait illi: Adjuro te per Deum vivum, ut dicas nobis, si tu es Christus Filius Dei. Dicit illi Jesus: Tu dixisti. Verumtamen dico vobis, amodo videbitis Filium hominis sedentem a dextris virtutis Dei, et venientem in nubibus cœli. Tunc princeps sacerdotum scidit vestimenta sua, dicens: Blasphemavit. Quid adhuc egemus testibus? Ecce: nunc audistis blasphemiam. Quid vobis videtur? At illi respondentes, dixerunt: Reus est mortis. Tunc expuerunt in faciem suus: et colaphis eum cæciderunt. Alii autem palmas in faciem ejus dederunt dicentes: Prophetiza nobis, Christe, quis est, qui te percussit?

Petrus vero sedebat foris in atrio. Et accessit ad eum una ancilla, dicens: Et tu cum Jesu Galilæo eras. At ille negavit coram omnibus, dicens: Nescio quid dicis. Exeunte autem illo januam, vidit eum alia ancilla: et ait his, qui erant ibi: Et hic erat cum Jesu Nazareno. Et iterum negavit cum juramento: Quia non novi hominem. Et post pusillum accesserunt qui stabant, et dixerunt Petro: Vere et tu ex illis es: nam et loquela tua manifestum te facit. Tunc cœpit detestari et jurare quia non novisset hominem. Et continuo gallus cantavit. Et recordatus est Petrus verbi Jesu quod dixerat: Priusquam gallus cantet, ter me negabis. Et egressus foras, flevit amare.

Mane autem facto, consilium inierunt omnes principes sacerdotum, et seniores populi adversus Jesum, ut eum morti traderent. Et vinctum adduxerunt eum, et tradiderunt Pontio Pilato, præsidi. Tunc videns Judas, qui eum tradidit, quod damnatus esset, pœnitentia ductus, retulit triginta ar-

But they answering, said: He is guilty of death. Then did they spit in his face, and buffet him, and others struck his face with the palms of their hands, saying: Prophesy unto us, O Christ, who is he that struck thee?

But Peter sat without in the court; and there came to him a servant-maid, saying: Thou also wast with Jesus the Galilean. But he denied before them all, saying: I know not what thou sayest. And as he went out of the gate, another maid saw him, and she saith to them that were there: This man also was with Jesus of Nazareth. And again he denied with an oath: That I know not the man. And after a little while they came that stood by, and said to Peter: Surely thou also art one of them; for even thy speech doth discover thee. Then he began to curse and swear that he knew not the man. And immediately the cock crew. And Peter remembered the words of Jesus which he had said: Before the cock crow, thou wilt deny me thrice. And going forth, he wept bitterly.

And when morning was come, all the chief priests and ancients of the people took counsel against Jesus, that they might put him to death. And they brought him bound, and delivered him to Pontius Pilate the governor. Then Judas, who betrayed him, seeing that he was condemned, repenting himself, brought

back the thirty pieces of silver to the chief priests and ancients, saying : I have sinned in betraying innocent blood. But they said : What is that to us? look thou to it. And casting down the pieces of silver in the Temple, he departed, and went and hanged himself with an halter. But the chief priests having taken the pieces of silver, said : It is not lawful to put them into the corbona, because it is the price of blood. And after they had consulted together, they bought with them the potter's field, to be a burying-place for strangers. For this cause that field was called Haceldama, that is, the field of blood, even to this day. Then was fulfilled that which was spoken by Jeremias the prophet, saying : "And they took the thirty pieces of silver, the price of him that was prized, whom they prized of the children of Israel. And they gave them unto the potter's field, as the Lord appointed to me."

And Jesus stood before the governor, and the governor asked him, saying : Art thou the king of the Jews? Jesus saith to him : Thou sayest it. And when he was accused by the chief priests and ancients, he answered nothing. Then Pilate saith to him : Dost thou not hear how great testimonies they allege against thee? And he answered him to never a word ; so that the governor wondered exceedingly.

Now upon the solemn day the governor was accustomed

genteos principibus sacerdotum et senioribus, dicens: Peccavi tradens sanguinem justum. At illi dixerunt : Quid ad nos? Tu videris. Et projectis argenteis in Templo, recessit : et abiens laqueo se suspendit. Principes autem sacerdotum, acceptis argenteis, dixerunt : Non licet eos mittere in corbonam, quia pretium sanguinis est. Consilio autem inito, emerunt ex illis agrum figuli, in sepulturam peregrinorum. Propter hoc vocatus est ager ille Haceldama, hoc est, ager sanguinis, usque in hodiernum diem. Tunc impletum est quod dictum est per Jeremiam prophetam dicentem : Et acceperunt triginta argenteos, pretium appretiati quem appretiaverunt a filiis Israël : et dederunt eos in agrum figuli, sicut constituit mihi Dominus.

Jesus autem stetit ante præsidem. Et interrogavit eum præses dicens : Tu es Rex Judæorum? Dicit illi Jesus : Tu dicis. Et cum accusaretur a principibus sacerdotum et senioribus, nihil respondit. Tunc dicit illi Pilatus : Non audis, quanta adversum te dicunt testimonia? Et non respondit ei ad ullum verbum : ita ut miraretur præses vehementer.

Per diem autem solemnem consueverat præses

populo dimittere unum vinctum, quem voluissent. Habebat autem tunc vinctum insignem, qui dicebatur Barabbas. Congregatis ergo illis, dixit Pilatus: Quem vultis dimittam vobis, Barabbam, an Jesum qui dicitur Christus? Sciebat enim, quod per invidiam tradidissent eum. Sedente autem illo pro tribunali, misit ad eum uxor ejus, dicens: Nihil tibi et justo illi: multa enim passa sum hodie per visum propter eum. Principes autem sacerdotum et seniores persuaserunt populis, ut peterent Barabbam: Jesum vero perderent. Respondens autem præses, ait illis: Quem vultis vobis de duobus dimitti? At illi dixerunt: Barabbam. Dicit illis Pilatus: Quid igitur faciam de Jesu, qui dicitur Christus? Dicunt omnes: Crucifigatur. Ait illis præses: Quid enim mali fecit? At illi magis clamabant dicentes: Crucifigatur.

Videns autem Pilatus, quia nihil proficeret, sed magis tumultus fieret: accepta aqua, lavit manus coram populo, dicens: Innocens ego sum a sanguine justi hujus: vos videritis. Et respondens universus populus, dixit: Sanguis ejus super nos, et super filios nostros. Tunc dimisit illis Barabbam: Je-

to release to the people one prisoner, whom they would. And he had then a notorious prisoner, that was called Barabbas. They therefore being gathered together, Pilate said: Whom will you that I release to you, Barabbas, or Jesus that is called Christ? For he knew that for envy they had delivered him. And as he was sitting in the place of judgment, his wife sent to him, saying: Have thou nothing to do with that just man. For I have suffered many things this day in a dream because of him. But the chief priests and ancients persuaded the people, that they should ask Barabbas, and make Jesus away. And the governor answering, said to them: Whether will you of the two to be released unto you? But they said, Barabbas. Pilate saith to them: What shall I do then with Jesus that is called Christ? They say all: Let him be crucified. The governor said to them: Why, what evil hath he done? But they cried out the more, saying: Let him be crucified.

And Pilate seeing that he prevailed nothing, but that rather a tumult was made; taking water he washed his hands before the people, saying: I am innocent of the blood of this just man: look you to it. And the whole people answering, said: His blood be upon us, and upon our children. Then he released to them Barabbas:

and having scourged Jesus delivered him unto them to be crucified.

Then the soldiers of the governor taking Jesus into the hall, gathered together unto him the whole band; and stripping him, they put a scarlet cloak about him. And platting a crown of thorns, they put it upon his head, and a reed in his right hand. And bowing the knee before him, they mocked him, saying: Hail, king of the Jews. And spitting upon him, they took the reed, and struck his head. And after they had mocked him, they took off the cloak from him, and put on his own garments, and led him away to crucify him.

And going out they met a man of Cyrene, named Simon: him they forced to take up the cross. And they came to the place that is called Golgotha, which is the place of Calvary. And they gave him wine to drink mingled with gall. And when he had tasted, he would not drink. And after they had crucified him, they divided his garments, casting lots: that it might be fulfilled which was spoken by the prophet, saying: "They divided my garments among them; and upon my vesture they cast lots:" and they sat and watched him. And they put over his head his cause written: This is Jesus the King of the Jews. Then were crucified

sum autem flagellatum tradidit eis, ut crucifigeretur.

Tunc milites præsidis suscipientes Jesum in prætorium, congregaverunt ad eum universam cohortem. Et exuentes eum chlamydem coccineam circumdederunt ei. Et plectentes coronam de spinis, posuerunt super caput ejus, et arundinem in dextera ejus. Et genu flexo ante eum, illudebant ei, dicentes : Ave Rex Judæorum! Et exspuentes in eum, acceperunt arundinem, et percutiebant caput ejus. Et postquam illuserunt ei, exuerunt eum chlamyde : et induerunt eum vestimentis ejus, et duxerunt eum ut crucifigerent.

Exeuntes autem, invenerunt hominem Cyrenæum, nomine Simonem. Hunc angariaverunt, ut tolleret crucem ejus. Et venerunt in locum, qui dicitur Golgotha : quod est, Calvariæ locus. Et dederunt ei vinum bibere cum felle mixtum. Et cum gustasset, noluit bibere. Postquam autem crucifixerunt eum, diviserunt vestimenta ejus sortem mittentes : ut impleretur quod dictum est per Prophetam dicentem : Diviserunt sibi vestimenta mea, et super vestem meam miserunt sortem. Et sedentes, servabant eum. Et imposuerunt super caput ejus causam ipsius scriptam: Hic est Jesus Rex Judæorum. Tunc crucifixi sunt cum eo duo latrones, unus a dextris, et unus a sinistris.

Prætereuntes autem blasphemabant eum, moventes capita sua, et dicentes: Vah! qui destruis Templum Dei, et in triduo illud reædificas. Salva temetipsum. Si Filius Dei es, descende de cruce. Similiter et principes sacerdotum illudentes cum scribis et senioribus, dicebant: Alios salvos fecit: seipsum non potest salvum facere. Si Rex Israël est, descendat nunc de cruce, et credimus ei. Confidit in Deo: liberet nunc si vult eum: dixit enim, quia Filius Dei sum. Idipsum autem et latrones, qui crucifixi erant cum eo, improperabant ei.

A sexta autem hora, tenebræ factæ sunt super universam terram, usque ad horam nonam. Et circa horam nonam clamavit Jesus voce magna, dicens: Eli, Eli, lamma sabacthani? Hoc est: Deus meus, Deus meus, ut quid dereliquisti me? Quidam autem illic stantes, et audientes, dicebant: Eliam vocat iste. Et continuo currens unus ex eis acceptam spongiam implevit aceto, et imposuit arundini, et dabat ei bibere. Cæteri vero dicebant: Sine, videamus, an veniat Elias liberans eum. Jesus autem iterum clamans voce magna, emisit spiritum.

with him two thieves; one on the right hand, and one on the left.

And they that passed by, blasphemed him, wagging their heads, and saying: Vah, thou that destroyest the temple of God, and in three days dost rebuild it, save thy own self: if thou be the Son of God, come down from the cross. In like manner also the chief priests, with the scribes and ancients, mocking, said: He saved others; himself he cannot save: if he be the king of Israel, let him now come down from the cross, and we will believe him. He trusted in God: let him now deliver him, if he will have him: for he said: I am the Son of God. And the self same thing the thieves also that were crucified with him, reproached him with.

Now from the sixth hour there was darkness over the whole earth, until the ninth hour. And about the ninth hour Jesus cried with a loud voice, saying: Eli, Eli, lamma sabacthani? that is "my God, "my God, why hast thou for- "saken me?" And some that stood there and heard, said: This man calleth Elias. And immediately one of them running, took a sponge, and filled it with vinegar, and put it on a reed, and gave him to drink. And the others said: Let us see whether Elias will come and deliver him. And Jesus again crying with a loud voice, yielded up the ghost.

Here the Deacon pauses, and honours the Death of our Lord and Saviour by a solemn act of adoration. All the Faithful kneel down, and remain for some time in that position. In many places, it is the custom to prostrate, and kiss the ground. The Deacon then resumes his narration.

And behold the veil of the Temple was rent in two from the top even to the bottom, and the earth quaked, and the rocks were rent. And the graves were opened; and many bodies of the saints that had slept arose; and coming out of the tombs after his resurrection, came into the holy city and appeared to many. Now the centurion, and they that were with him watching Jesus, having seen the earthquake and the things that were done, were sore afraid, saying: Indeed this was the Son of God. And there were there many women afar off who had followed Jesus from Galilee, ministering unto him: among whom was Mary Magdalen, and Mary the mother of James and Joseph, and the mother of the sons of Zebedee. And when it was evening, there came a certain rich man of Arimathea, named Joseph, who also himself was a disciple of Jesus. He went to Pilate, and asked the body of Jesus. Then Pilate commanded that the body should be delivered. And Joseph taking the body, wrapped it up in a clean linen cloth, and laid it in his own new monument, which he had hewn out

Et ecce velum Templi scissum est in duas partes, a summo usque deorsum. Et terra mota est, et petræ scissæ sunt, et monumenta aperta sunt: et multa corpora sanctorum, qui dormierant, surrexerunt. Et exeuntes de monumentis post resurrectionem ejus, venerunt in sanctam civitatem, et apparuerunt multis. Centurio autem, et qui cum eo erant, custodientes Jesum, viso terræ motu, et his quæ fiebant, timuerunt valde, dicentes : Vere Filius Dei erat ista. Erant autem ibi mulieres multæ a longe, quæ secutæ erant Jesum a Galilæa ministrantes ei : inter quas erat Maria Magdalene, et Maria Jacobi et Joseph mater, et mater filiorum Zebedæi. Cum sero autem factum esset, venit quidam homo dives ab Arimathæa, nomine Joseph, qui et ipse discipulus erat Jesu. Hic accessit ad Pilatum, et petiit corpus Jesu. Tunc Pilatus jussit reddi corpus. Et accepto corpore, Joseph involvit illud in sindone munda : et posuit illud in monumento suo novo, quod exciderat in petra. Et advolvit saxum magnum ad

ostium monumenti, et abiit. Erant autem ibi Maria Magdalene, et altera Maria, sedentes contra sepulchrum.	in a rock. And he rolled a great stone to the door of the monument, and went his way. And there was there Mary Magdalen, and the other Mary sitting over against the sepulchre.

That the Mass of this Sunday may not be deprived of that essential rite, which we call the *Gospel*, the Deacon reserves a portion of his narrative; and going to the Altar, he asks the Priest to bless the Incense. Which done, the Deacon himself also having received the Priest's blessing, goes to the place appointed for chanting the Gospel; but the Acolytes do not carry their Lights. After having thurified the book, he thus closes the history of the Passion.

Altera autem die, quæ est post Parasceven, convenerunt principes sacerdotum, et pharisæi ad Pilatum, dicentes: Domine, recordati sumus, quia seductor ille dixit adhuc vivens: Post tres dies resurgam. Jube ergo custodiri sepulchrum usque in diem tertium; ne forte veniant discipuli ejus et furentur eum: et dicant plebi: Surrexit a mortuis. Et erit novissimus error pejor priore. Ait illis Pilatus: Habetis custodiam: ite, et custodite sicut scitis. Illi autem abeuntes, munierunt sepulchrum, signantes lapidem, cum custodibus.	And the next day, which followed the day of preparation, the chief priest and the Pharisees came together to Pilate, saying: Sir, we have remembered, that that seducer said, while he was yet alive: After three days I will rise again. Command therefore the sepulchre to be guarded until the third day: lest perhaps his disciples come and steal him away, and say to the people he is risen from the dead: and the last error shall be worse than the first. Pilate said to them: You have a guard; go, guard it as you know. And they departing, made the sepulchre sure, sealing the stone, and setting guards.

The Offertory is again a prophecy by David. It foretells the state of abandonment, to which our Saviour was to be reduced in the midst of all his

Sufferings, and the cruelty of his enemies, who would feed him with gall and vinegar. Thus is He treated, who is preparing to give us his Body for our food, and his Blood for our drink.

OFFERTORY.

My heart hath expected reproach and misery: and I looked for one that would grieve together with me ; but there was none : and for one that would comfort me, and I found none : they gave me gall for my food, and in my thirst they gave me vinegar to drink.	Improperium exspectavit cor meum, et miseriam : et sustinui qui simul mecum contristaretur, et non fuit : consolantem me quæsivi, et non inveni : et dederunt in escam meam fel, et in siti mea potaverunt me aceto.

The Secret asks of God, that he would impart to his servants the twofold fruit of Jesus' Passion: grace in this life, and glory in the next.

SECRET.

Grant, we beseech thee, O Lord, that what hath been offered in the presence of thy Divine Majesty may procure us the grace of devotion, and effectually obtain a blessed eternity. Through, &c.	Concede, quæsumus, Domine, ut oculis tuæ majestatis munus oblatum, et gratiam nobis devotionis obtineat, et effectum beatæ perennitatis acquirat. Per Dominum.

In the Communion-Anthem, the Church,—after receiving into herself the life of Christ by the chalice of salvation,—calls to our minds that other *Chalice*, which Jesus was to drink, in order that he might gift us with immortality.

COMMUNION.

Father, 'if this cup cannot pass away, but I must drink it, thy will be done.	Pater, si non potest hic calix transire, nisi bibam illum : fiat voluntas tua.

The Church concludes the prayers of the Sacrifice she has just been offering, by asking the remission of sin for all her children, and that they may see fulfilled that longing of their souls,—a share in the glorious Resurrection of Jesus.

POSTCOMMUNION.

Per hujus, Domine, operationem mysterii, et vitia nostra purgentur, et justa desideria compleantur. Per Dominum.	May our vices, O Lord, be destroyed, and our righteous desires fulfilled by the efficacy of these mysteries. Through, &c.

VESPERS.

The Psalms and Antiphons are given in *page* 80.

CAPITULUM.
(Phil. II.)

Fratres, Hoc enim sentite in vobis, quod et in Christo Jesu : qui cum in forma Dei esset, non rapinam arbitratus est esse se æqualem Deo: sed semetipsum exinanivit, formam servi accipiens, in similitudinem hominum factus, et habitu inventus ut homo.	Brethren : For let this mind be in you, which was also in Christ Jesus ; who being in the form of God, thought it not robbery to be equal with God, but emptied himself, taking the form of a servant, being made in the likeness of men, and in habit found as a man.

For the Hymn and Versicle, see *page* 87.

ANTIPHON OF THE *Magnificat*.

Scriptum est enim : Percutiam pastorem, et dispergentur oves gregis : postquam autem resurrexero, præcedam vos in Galilæam : ibi me videbitis, dicit Dominus.	For it is written : I will strike the shepherd, and the sheep of the flock shall be dispersed : but after I shall be risen again, I will go before you into Galilee : there ye shall see me, saith the Lord.

LET US PRAY.	OREMUS.
O Almighty and Eternal God, who wouldst have our Saviour become man, and suffer on a cross, to give mankind an example of humility; mercifully grant that we may improve by the example of his patience, and partake of his resurrection. Through the same, &c.	Omnipotens sempiterne Deus, qui humano generi ad imitandum humilitatis exemplum, Salvatorem nostrum carnem sumere et crucem subire fecisti, concede propitius; ut et patientiæ ipsius habere documenta, et resurrectionis consortia mereamur. Per eumdem.

Let us now go over in our minds the other events, which happened to our Divine Lord on this day of his solemn Entry into Jerusalem. St. Luke tells us, that it was on his approach to the City, that Jesus wept over it, and spoke these touching words: *If thou also hadst known, and that in this thy day, the things that are to thy peace! But now they are hidden from thine eyes. For the days shall come upon thee, and thine enemies shall cast a trench about thee, and compass thee round, and straiten thee on every side, and beat thee flat to the ground, and thy children who are in thee; and they shall not leave in thee a stone upon a stone; because thou hast not known the time of thy visitation.*[1]

A few days ago, we were reading in the holy Gospel, how Jesus wept over the tomb of Lazarus; to-day, he sheds tears over Jerusalem. At Bethania, his weeping was caused by the sight of bodily death, the consequence and punishment of sin; but this death is not irremediable: Jesus is *the resurrection and the life,* and he that *believeth* in Him, *shall live.*[2] Whereas, the state of the unfaithful Jerusalem is a figure of the death of the soul, and from this there is no resurrection, unless the soul, whilst

---

[1] St. Luke, xix. 42-44. [2] St. John, xi. 25.

time is given to her, return to the Author of life. Hence it is, that the tears shed by Jesus, over Jerusalem, are so bitter. Amidst the acclamations which greet his Entry into the City of David, his heart is sad; for he sees that many of her inhabitants will not profit of *the time of her visitation.* Let us console the Heart of our Jesus, and be to him a faithful Jerusalem.

The sacred historian tells us, that Jesus, immediately upon his entrance into the City, went to the Temple, and cast out all them that sold and bought there.[1] This was the second time that he had shown his authority in his Father's House, and no one had dared to resist him. The Chief Priests and Pharisees found fault with him, and accused him to his face of causing confusion by his entry into the City; but our Lord confounded them by the reply he made. It is thus, that in after ages, when it has pleased God to glorify his Son and the Church of his Son, the enemies of both have given vent to their rage; they protested against the triumph, but they could not stop it. But, when God, in the unsearchable ways of his wisdom, allowed persecution and trial to follow these periods of triumph, then did these bitter enemies redouble their efforts to induce the very people, that had cried *Hosanna to the Son of David,* to clamour for his being delivered up and crucified. They succeeded in fomenting persecution, but not in destroying the kingdom of Christ and his Church. The kingdom seemed, at times, to be interrupted in its progress; but the time for another triumph came. Thus will it be to the end; and then, after all these changes from glory to humiliation, and from humiliation to glory, the kingdom of Jesus and his Spouse will gain the last and eternal triumph over

[1] St. Matth., xi. 25.

this world, which would not *know the time of its visitation.*

We learn from St. Matthew,[1] that our Saviour spent the remainder of this day at Bethania. His Blessed Mother and the house of Lazarus were comforted by his return. There was not a single offer of hospitality made to him in Jerusalem, at least, there is no mention in the Gospel of any such being offered. We cannot help making the reflection, as we meditate upon this event of our Lord's life:— an enthusiastic reception is given to him in the morning, he is proclaimed by the people as their King; but, when the evening of that day comes on, there is not one of all those thousands to offer him food or lodging. In the Carmelite Monasteries of St. Teresa's Reform, there is a custom, which has been suggested by this thought, and is intended as a reparation for this ingratitude shown to our Redeemer. A table is placed in the middle of the Refectory; and after the Community have finished their dinner, the food, which was placed upon that table, is distributed among the poor, and Jesus is honoured in them.

We give, as a conclusion to this day, a selection from the Hymn used by the Greek Church on Palm Sunday. It was written by the celebrated hymnographer, Cosmas of Jerusalem.

HYMN.

(In Dominica Palmarum.)

Lo! the God that sitteth in the highest heavens, upon	Qui in altissimis sedet super Cherubim Deus et

---

[1] St. Matth. xxi. 17.

humilia respicit, ecce venit in gloria cum potestate, et replebuntur omnia divina laude ipsius. Pax super Israël, et salutare gentibus.

Clamaverunt in lætitia justorum animæ: Nunc mundo testamentum novum disponitur, et aspersione innovatur populus divini sanguinis.

Genu flexo populi et cum discipulis gaudentes, cum palmis Hosanna filio David clamabant: Superlaudabilis Domine Deus patrum, benedictus es.

Simplex multitudo, adhuc infantilis ætas, ut Deum decet, te rex Israël et Angelorum laudavit: Superlaudabilis Domine Deus patrum, benedictus es.

Juvenum pullum ascendens rex tuus Sion adstitit Christus. Irrationabilem enim idolorum errorum solvere, effrænum impetum compescere omnium gentium advenit, ut cantent: Benedicite, opera, Dominum, et superexaltate in omnia sæcula.

Deus tuus regnavit in sæcula Christus. Iste, ut scriptum est, mitis et salvator, justus redemptor noster venit super pullo equitans, ut audaciam perderet inimicorum non clamantium: Benedicite, opera, Dominum, et superexaltate in omnia sæcula.

the Cherubim, and looketh down on lowly things, cometh in glory and power; all creatures are full of his divine praise. Peace upon Israel, and Salvation to the Gentiles!

The souls of the just cried out with joy: Now is prepared a new Covenant for the world, and mankind is renewed by the sprinkling of the Divine Blood!

The people fell upon their knees, and, rejoicing with the Disciples, sang, with palms in their hands: Hosanna to the Son of David! Praiseworthy and blessed art thou, O Lord God of our fathers!

The simple-hearted people, yea, and little children, (the fittest to adore a God,) praised thee as King of Israel and Angels: Praiseworthy and blessed art thou, O Lord God of our fathers!

O Sion! there came to thee Christ, thy King, seated on a young colt: for he came that he might loosen mankind from the senseless error of idolatry, and tame the wild passions of all nations; that thus they might praise thee, singing: Bless the Lord, all ye his works, and extol him above all for ever!

Christ thy Lord hath reigned for ever. He, as it is written, the meek one, the Saviour, our Just Redeemer, came riding on an ass's colt, that he might destroy the pride of his enemies, who would not sing these words: Bless the Lord, all ye his works, and extol him above all for ever!

PALM SUNDAY: AFTER VESPERS.

The unjust and obstinate Sanhedrim, the usurpers of the Holy Temple, are put to flight; for they had made God's House of prayer a den of thieves, and shut their hearts against the Redeemer, to whom we cry: Bless the Lord, all ye his works, and extol him above all for ever!

God is our Lord, he hath appeared unto us. Appoint a solemn feast, and come, let us rejoice and magnify the Christ, praising him, with palms and branches in our hands: Blessed is he that cometh in the name of the Lord, our Saviour!

Why, O ye Gentiles, have ye raged against the Scriptures? Why, O ye Priests, have ye devised vain things, saying: Who is this, unto whom children, with palms and branches in their hands, cry aloud this praise: Blessed is he that cometh in the name of the Lord, our Saviour?

Why, O ye perverse of heart, have ye thrown stumbling-blocks in the way? Your feet are swift to shed the Blood of the Lord. But he will rise again, that he may save all that cry to him: Blessed is he that cometh in the name of the Lord, our Saviour!

Dissipatur sacri Templi iniquum Synedrium contumacium; orationis enim Dei domum speluncam effecerant latronum, a corde Redemptorem excludentes, cui clamamus: Benedicite, opera, Dominum, et superexaltate in omnia sæcula.

Deus Dominus, et apparuit nobis; constituite diem solémnem, et exsultantes venite, magnificemus Christum, cum palmis et ramis laudibus clamantes: Benedictus qui venit in nomine Domini Salvatoris nostri.

Gentes, ut quid fremuistis in Scripturas? et sacerdotes, ut quid inania meditati estis, dicentes: Quis est iste cui pueri cum palmis et ramis laudibus clamant: Benedictus qui venit in nomine Domini Salvatoris nostri?

Scandala semitas occupantia quid vos ponitis immorigeri? Veloces pedes vestri ad effundendum sanguinem Domini. Sed resurget ut salvet omnes qui clamant: Benedictus qui venit in nomine Domini Salvatoris nostri.

MONDAY

IN HOLY WEEK.

This morning, also, Jesus goes with his Disciples to Jerusalem. He is fasting, for the Gospel tells us, that *he was hungry*.[1] He approaches a fig-tree, which is by the way-side; but finds nothing on it, save leaves only. Jesus, wishing to give us an instruction, curses the fig-tree, which immediately withers away. He would hereby teach us what they are to expect, who have nothing but good desires, and never produce in themselves the fruit of a real conversion. Nor is the allusion to Jerusalem less evident. This City is zealous for the exterior of Divine Worship; but her heart is hard and obstinate, and she is plotting, at this very hour, the death of the Son of God.

The greater portion of the day is spent in the Temple, where Jesus holds long conversations with the Chief Priests and Ancients of the people. His language to them is stronger than ever, and triumphs over all their captious questions. It is principally in the Gospel of St. Matthew,[2] that we shall find these answers of our Redeemer, which so energetically accuse the Jews of their sin of rejecting the Messias, and so plainly foretel the punishment their sin is to bring after it.

[1] St. Matth. xxi. 18.   [2] Chapters xxi. xxii. and xxiii.

At length, Jesus leaves the Temple, and takes the road that leads to Bethania. Having come as far as Mount Olivet, which commands a view of Jerusalem, he sits down, and rests awhile. The Disciples make this an opportunity for asking him, how soon the chastisements he has been speaking of in the Temple will come upon the City. His answer comprises two events: the destruction of Jerusalem, and the final destruction of the world. He thus teaches them that the first is a figure of the second. The time when each is to happen, is to be when the measure of iniquity is filled up. But, with regard to the chastisement that is to befal Jerusalem, he gives this more definite answer: *Amen I say to you: this generation shall not pass, till all these things be done.*[1] History tells us how this prophecy of Jesus was fulfilled: forty years had scarcely elapsed after his Ascension, when the Roman army encamped on this very place where he is now speaking to his Disciples, and laid siege to the ungrateful and wicked City. After giving a prophetic description of that Last Judgment, which is to rectify all the unjust judgments of men, he leaves Mount Olivet, returns to Bethania, and consoles the anxious heart of his most holy Mother.

The Station, at Rome, is in the Church of Saint Praxedes. It was in this Church, that Pope Paschal the Second, in the 9th century, placed two thousand three hundred bodies of holy Martyrs, which he had ordered to be taken out of the Catacombs. The Pillar, to which our Saviour was tied during his scourging, is also here.

---

[1] St. Matth. xxiv. 34.

MASS.

The Introit is taken from the 34th Psalm. Jesus, by these words of the Royal Prophet, prays to his Eternal Father, that he would defend him against his enemies.

INTROIT.

Judica, Domine, nocentes me, expugna impugnantes me : apprehende arma et scutum, et exsurge in adjutorium meum, Domine virtus salutis meæ.	Judge thou, O Lord, them that wrong me ; overthrow them that fight against me : take hold of arms and shield, and rise up to help me, O Lord, my mighty deliverer.
Ps. Effunde frameam, et conclude adversus eos qui persequuntur me : dic animæ meæ : Salus tua ego sum.	*Ps.* Bring out the sword, and shut up the way against them that persecute me ; say to my soul, I am thy salvation.
Judica, Domine.	Judge thou, &c.

In the Collect, the Church teaches us to have recourse to the merits of our Saviour's Passion, in order that we may obtain from God the help we stand in need of amidst our many miseries.

COLLECT.

Da, quæsumus, omnipotens Deus : ut, qui in tot adversis ex nostra infirmitate deficimus, intercedente unigeniti Filii tui Passione respiremus. Qui tecum. .	Grant, we beseech thee, O Almighty God, that we, who through our weakness, faint under so many adversities, may recover by the Passion of thy Only Begotten Son. Who liveth, &c.

Then is added one of the following Collects.

AGAINST THE PERSECUTORS OF THE CHURCH.

Ecclesiæ tuæ, quæsumus, Domine, preces placatus	Mercifully hear, we beseech thee, O Lord, the prayers of

thy Church: that all oppositions and errors being removed, she may serve thee with a secure liberty. Through, &c.

admitte: ut destructis adversitatibus et erroribus universis, secura tibi serviat libertate. Per Dominum.

FOR THE POPE.

O God, the Pastor and Ruler of all the Faithful, look down, in thy mercy, on thy servant N., whom thou hast appointed Pastor over thy Church; and grant, we beseech thee, that both by word and example, he may edify all those that are under his charge; and with the flock intrusted to him, arrive at length at eternal happiness. Through, &c.

Deus, omnium fidelium pastor et rector, famulum tuum N. quem pastorem Ecclesiæ tuæ præesse voluisti propitius respice: da ei, quæsumus, verbo et exemplo, quibus præeest, proficere: ut ad vitam, una cum grege sibi credito, perveniat sempiternam. Per Dominum.

EPISTLE.

Lesson from Isaias the Prophet.

Lectio Isaiæ Prophetæ.

Ch. L.

Cap. L.

In those days, Isaias said: The Lord hath opened my ear, *making known his will to me,* and I do not resist: I have not gone back. I have given my body to the strikers, and my cheeks to them that plucked them: I have not turned away my face from them that rebuked me, and spit upon me. The Lord God is my helper, therefore am I not confounded. He is near that justifieth me, who will contend with me? let us stand together. Who is my adversary? let him come near to me. Behold the Lord God is my helper: who is he that

In diebus illis: Dixit Isaias: Dominus Deus aperuit mihi aurem: ego autem non contradico: retrorsum non abii. Corpus meum dedi percutientibus, et genas meas vellentibus. Faciem meam non averti ab increpantibus et conspuentibus in me. Dominus Deus auxiliator meus, ideo non sum confusus. Ideo posui faciem meam ut petram durissimam: et scio quoniam non confundar. Juxta est qui justificat me: quis contradicet mihi? Stemus simul: quis est adversarius meus? Accedat ad me. Ecce Dominus Deus, auxiliator meus: quis est qui condemnet me? Ecce, omnes quasi vestimentum conterentur: tinea comedet eos. Quis ex vobis timens Dominum, audiens vocem servi sui? Qui ambulavit in tenebris, et non est lumen ei, speret in nomine Domini et innitatur super Deum suum.

shall condemn me? Lo, they shall all be destroyed as a garment, the moth shall eat them up. Who is there among you that feareth the Lord, that heareth the voice of his servant? He that hath walked in darkness, and hath no light, let him hope in the name of the Lord, and lean upon his God.

The Sufferings of our Redeemer, and the patience wherewith he is to bear them, are thus prophesied by Isaias, who is always so explicit on the Passion. Jesus has accepted the office of Victim for the world's salvation; he shrinks from no pain or humiliation: *he turns not his Face from them that strike him and spit upon him.* What reparation can we make to this Infinite Majesty, who, that he might save us, submitted to such outrages as these? Observe these vile and cruel enemies of our Divine Lord: now that they have him in their power, they fear him not. When they came to seize him in the Garden, he had but to speak, and they fell back upon the ground; but he has now permitted them to bind his hands and lead him to the High Priest. They accuse him; they cry out against him; and he answers but a few words. Jesus of Nazareth, the great Teacher, the wonder-worker, has seemingly lost all his influence; they can do what they will with him. It is thus with the sinner; when the thunder-storm is over, and the lightning has not struck him, he regains his courage. The holy Angels look on with amazement at the treatment shown by the Jews to Jesus, and falling down, they adore the Holy Face, which they see thus bruised and defiled: let us, also, prostrate and ask pardon, for *our* sins have outraged that same Face.

But let us hearken to the last words of our Epistle: *He that hath walked in darkness, and hath no light, let him hope in the name of the Lord and lean upon his God.* Who is this but the Gentile, abandoned to sin and idolatry? He knows not what is happening at this very hour in Jerusalem; he knows not that the earth possesses its Saviour, and that this Saviour is being trampled beneath the feet of his own chosen people: but, in a very short time, the light of the Gospel will shine upon this poor Gentile: he will believe; he will obey; he will love his Redeemer, even to the laying down his life for him. Then will be fulfilled the prophecy of the unworthy Pontiff, who prophesied against his will that the death of Jesus would bring salvation to the Gentiles, *by gathering into one* family *the children of God, that* hitherto *had been dispersed.*[1]

In the Gradual, the Royal Prophet again calls down, on the executioners of our Lord, the chastisements they have deserved by their ingratitude and their obstinacy in sin.

The Tract is the one used by the Church on every Monday, Wednesday, and Friday, during Lent. It is a prayer, begging God to bless the works of penance done during this holy Season.

GRADUAL.

Arise, O Lord, and be attentive to my trial; my God and my Lord, undertake my cause.

℣. Draw thy sword, and stop those that are in pursuit of me.

Exsurge, Domine, et intende judicio meo, Deus meus et Dominus meus, in causam meam.

℣. Effunde frameam, et conclude adversus eos qui me persequuntur.

TRACT.

℣. O Lord, deal not with us according to our sins, which

℣. Domine, non secundum peccata nostra, quæ fecimus

[1] St. John, xi. 52.

hos: neque secundum iniquitates nostras retribuas nobis.

℣. Domine, ne memineris iniquitatum nostrarum antiquarum: cito anticipent nos misericordiæ tuæ, quia pauperes facti sumus nimis.

℣. Adjuva nos, Deus salutaris noster: et propter gloriam Nominis tui, Domine, libera nos: et propitius esto peccatis nostris propter Nomen tuum.

we have done, nor reward us according to our iniquities.

℣. O Lord, remember not our former iniquities: let thy mercies speedily prevent us, for we are become exceeding poor.

℣. Help us, O God, our Saviour: and for the glory of thy Name, O Lord, deliver us: and forgive us our sins, for thy Name's sake.

GOSPEL.

Sequentia sancti Evangelii, secundum Joannem.

Sequel of the holy Gospel according to John.

Cap. XII.

Ch. XII.

Ante sex dies Paschæ venit Jesus Bethaniam, ubi Lazarus fuerat mortuus, quem suscitavit Jesus. Fecerunt autem ei cœnam ibi: et Martha ministrabat; Lazarus vero unus erat ex discumbentibus cum eo. Maria ergo accepit libram unguenti nardi pistici pretiosi: et unxit pedes Jesu, et extersit pedes ejus capillis suis; et domus impleta est ex odore unguenti. Dixit ergo unus ex discipulis ejus, Judas Iscariotes, qui erat eum traditurus: Quare hoc unguentum non væniit trecentis denariis, et datum est egenis? Dixit autem hoc non quia de egenis pertinebat ad eum: sed quia fur erat, et loculos habens, ea quæ mitteban-

Jesus, six days before the Pasch, came to Bethania, where Lazarus had been dead, whom Jesus raised to life. And they made him a supper there; and Martha served, but Lazarus was one of them that were at table with him. Mary therefore took a pound of ointment of right spikenard, of great price, and anointed the feet of Jesus, and wiped his feet with her hair: and the house was filled with the odour of the ointment. Then one of his disciples, Judas Iscariot, he that was about to betray him, said: Why was not this ointment sold for three hundred pence, and given to the poor? Now he said this, not because he cared for the poor, but because he was a thief, and, having the purse, carried the things that were put therein. Jesus therefore said: Let her alone, that she may keep it against the day of my burial; for the poor you have always with you, but me you have not always. A great multitude therefore of the Jews knew that he was there; and they came not for Jesus' sake only, but that they might see Lazarus, whom he had raised from the dead.

tur, portabat. Dixit ergo Jesus: Sinite illam, ut in diem sepulturæ meæ servet illud. Pauperes enim semper habetis vobiscum: me autem non semper habetis. Cognovit ergo turba multa ex Judæis, quia illic est: et venerunt, non propter Jesum tantum, sed ut Lazarum viderent, quem suscitavit a mortuis.

As we have already said, the event related in this passage of the Gospel took place on Saturday, the eve of Palm Sunday; but, as formerly there was no Station for that day, the reading of this Gospel was deferred till the following Monday. The Church brings this episode of the last days of our Saviour before us, because it enables us to have a clearer understanding of the history of the Passion.

Mary Magdalene, whose conversion was the subject of our meditation a few days back, is a prominent figure in the Passion and Resurrection of her Divine Master. She is the type of a soul that has been purified by grace, and then admitted to the enjoyment of God's choicest favours. It is of importance that we study her in each of the several phases, through which divine grace led her. We have already seen how she keeps close to her Saviour and supplies his sacred wants; elsewhere, we shall find Jesus giving the preference to her over her sister Martha, and this because Mary chose a better part than Martha; but now, during these days of Passiontide, it is her tender love for Jesus that makes her dear to us. She knows that the Jews are plotting Jesus' death; the Holy Ghost, who guides her through the different degrees of perfection, inspires her, on the occasion mentioned in to-day's Gospel, to the performance of an action which prophesied what she most dreaded.

One of the three gifts offered by the Magi to the Divine Infant, was Myrrh; it is an emblem of death, and the Gospel tells us that it was used at the Burial of our Lord. Magdalene, on the day of her conversion, testified the earnestness of her change of heart by pouring on the feet of Jesus the most precious of her perfumes. She gives him, to-day, the same proof of her love. Her divine Master is invited by Simon the Leper to a feast: his Blessed Mother and his Disciples are among the guests: Martha is busy, looking after the *service.* Outwardly, there is no disturbance; but inwardly, there are sad forebodings. During the repast, Magdalene is seen entering the room, holding in her hand a vase of precious spikenard. She advances towards Jesus, kneels at his feet, anoints them with the perfume, and wipes them with her hair, as on the previous occasion.

Jesus lay on one of those couches, which were used by the Eastern people during their repasts. Magdalene, therefore, could easily take her favourite place at Jesus' feet, and give him the same proof of her love as she had already done in the Pharisee's house. The Evangelist does not say that this time, she shed tears. St. Matthew,[1] and St. Mark[2] add, that she poured the ointment on his head also. Whether or no Magdalene herself understood the full import of what the Holy Ghost inspired her to do, the Gospel does not say; but Jesus himself revealed the mystery to his Disciples, and we gather from his words that this action of Magdalene was, in a certain manner, the commencement of his Passion: *She, in pouring this ointment upon my body, hath done it for my burial*[3].

The fragrance of the Ointment fills the whole

---

[1] St. Matth., xxvi. 7. [2] St. Mark, xiv. 3. [3] St. Matth., xxvi. 12.

house. One of the Disciples, Judas Iscariot, dares to protest against this *waste*, as he calls it. His base avarice deprives him of feeling and respect for his Divine Master. His opinion was shared in by several of the other Disciples, for they were still carnal-minded. For several reasons Jesus permits Magdalene's generosity to be thus blamed. And firstly, he wishes to announce his approaching death, which is mystically expressed by the pouring of this ointment upon his body. Then, too, he would glorify Magdalene; and he therefore tells them that are present, that her tender and ardent love shall be rewarded, and that her name shall be celebrated in every country, wheresoever the Gospel shall be preached[1]. And lastly, he would console those whose generous love prompts them to be liberal in their gifts to his Altars, for what he here says of Magdalene is, in reality, a defence for them, when they are accused of spending too much over the *beauty of God's House.*

Let us prize each of these divine teachings. Let us love to honour Jesus, both in his own person, and in his poor. Let us honour Magdalene, and imitate her devotion to the Passion and Death of our Lord. In fine, let us prepare our perfumes for our Divine Master: there must be the *Myrrh* of the Magi, which signifies penance, and the precious *Spikenard* of Magdalene, which is the emblem of generous and compassionating love.

In the Offertory, our Redeemer implores his Eternal Father to deliver him from his enemies, and to fulfil the decrees regarding the salvation of mankind.

OFFERTORY.

| Deliver me from my enemies, O Lord; to thee have I | Eripe me de inimicis meis, Domine: ad te con- |

[1] St. Matth., xxvi. 13.

fugi, doce me facere volun- fled, teach me to do thy will,
tatem tuam: quia Deus because thou art my God,
meus es tu.

The Secret tells us the wonderful power of the Sacred Mysteries. Not only does this Sacrifice purify our souls; it also raises them to perfect union with Him who is their Creator.

SECRET.

Hæc sacrificia nos, om- Grant, O Almighty God,
nipotens Deus, potenti vir- that being purified by the
tute mundatos, ad suum powerful virtue of this sacri-
faciant puriores venire prin- fice, we may arrive with greater
cipium. Per Dominum. purity to the author and in-
stitutor thereof. Through, &c.

Then is added one of the following Prayers:

AGAINST THE PERSECUTORS OF THE CHURCH.

Protege nos, Domine, tuis Protect us, O Lord, while
mysteriis servientes: ut we assist at thy sacred mys-
divinis rebus inhærentes, et teries: that being employed
corpore tibi famulemur et in acts of religion, we may
mente. Per Dominum. serve thee both in body and
mind. Through, &c.

FOR THE POPE.

Oblatis, quæsumus, Do- Be appeased, O Lord, with
mine, placare muneribus: the offering we have made:
et famulum tuum N. quem and cease not to protect thy
pastorem Ecclesiæ tuæ Servant N., whom thou hast
præesse voluisti, assidua been pleased to appoint Pastor
protectione guberna. Per over thy Church. Through,
Dominum. &c.

After the Faithful have partaken of the Divine Mystery, there is read, in the Communion-Anthem, a malediction against the enemies of our Saviour. Thus does God act in his government of the world: they who refuse his mercy, cannot escape his justice.

COMMUNION.

Let them blush and be ashamed, who rejoice at my misfortunes ; let them be covered with shame and confusion, who speak maliciously against me.

Erubescant, et revereantur simul, qui gratulantur malis meis : induantur pudore et reverentia, qui maligna loquuntur adversus me.

The Church concludes her Prayers of this morning's Sacrifice, by begging that her children may persevere in the holy fervour, which they have received at its very source.

POSTCOMMUNION.

Let thy holy mysteries, O Lord, inspire us with divine fervour ; that we may delight both in their effect and celebration. Through, &c.

Præbeant nobis, Domine, divinum tua Sancta fervorem ; quo eorum pariter et actu delectemur et fructu. Per Dominum.

To this is added one of the following :

AGAINST THE PERSECUTORS OF THE CHURCH.

We beseech thee, O Lord our God, not to leave exposed to the dangers of human life, those whom thou hast permitted to partake of these divine mysteries. Through, &c.

Quæsumus, Domine Deus noster : ut quos divina tribuis participatione gaudere, humanis non sinas subjacere periculis. Per Dominum.

FOR THE POPE.

May the participation of this divine Sacrament protect us, we beseech thee, O Lord ; and always procure safety and defence to thy Servant N., whom thou hast appointed Pastor over thy Church, together with the flock committed to his charge. Through, &c.

Hæc nos, quæsumus, Domine, divini sacramenti perceptio protegat: et famulum tuum N. quem pastorem Ecclesiæ tuæ præesse voluisti, una cum commisso sibi grege salvet semper, et muniat. Per Dominum.

256 HOLY WEEK.

OREMUS.

Humiliate capita vestra Deo.

Adjuva nos, Deus salutaris noster; et ad beneficia recolenda, quibus nos instaurare dignatus es, tribue venire gaudentes. Per Dominum.

LET US PRAY.

Bow down your heads to God.

Help us, O God, our salvation; and grant that we may celebrate with joy the memory of these benefits, by which thou hast been pleased to redeem us. Through, &c.

As an appropriate conclusion to this day, we may use the following beautiful Prayer, taken from the ancient Gallican Liturgy:

PRAYER.
(Oratio ad Sextam.)

Christe Deus, Adonaï magne, nos tecum quasi huic mundo crucifige; ut vita tua in nobis sit: nostraque peccata super te pone, ut ea crucifigas: nos quoque ad teipsum trahe, cum pro nobis exaltatus es a terra, ut nos eripias ab adultero tyranno: quia licet carne et vitiis diabolo noxii sumus; tibi tamen, non illi optamus servire: et sub tuo jure vivere desideramus, et a te gubernari rogamus; qui nos mortales et a morte invasos, per mortem crucis liberare voluisti. Pro quo singulari beneficio hodierna tibi nostra famulatur devotio: teque nunc hodie supplices adoramus, imploramus, invocamus; ut ad nos properes, virtus æterna Deus: quod nobis proficiat tua crux, triumphans scilicet de mundo in nobis per

O great and Sovereign Lord! (Adonaï!) Christ our God! crucify us, with thyself, to this world, that so thy life may be in us. Take upon thee our sins, that thou mayst crucify them. Draw us unto thyself, since it was for our sakes that thou wast raised up from the earth; and thus snatch us from the power of the unclean tyrant: for, though by flesh and our sins, we be exposed to the insults of the devil, yet do we desire to serve, not him, but thee. We would be thy subjects; we ask to be governed by thee; for, by thy death on the cross, thou didst deliver us, who are mortals and surrounded by death. It is to bless thee for this wonderful favour, that we this day offer thee our devoted service; and humbly adoring thee, we now implore and beseech thee, to hasten to our assistance, O thou our God, the Eternal and Almighty! Let thy Cross thus profit us unto good, that thou, by its power, mayst triumph over the world in us, and thine own mercy restore us, by thy might and grace, to the ancient blessing. O thou, whose power hath turned the future into the past, and whose presence maketh the past to be present,—grant, that thy Passion may avail us to salvation, as though it were accomplished now on this very day. May the drops of thy holy Blood, which heretofore fell upon the earth from the Cross, be our present salvation: may it wash away all the sins of our earthly nature, and be, so to say, commingled with the earth of our body, rendering it all thine, since we, by our reconciliation with thee, our Head, have been made one body with thee. Thou that ever reignest with the Father and the Holy Ghost, now begin to reign over us, O God-Man, Christ Jesus, King for ever and ever!

crucis virtutem: atque tua pietas nobis illud antiquum restituat beneficium, virtute scilicet et gratia: qui per potentiam futura præterita; per præsentiam facis similiter præterita præsentia: redde, ut nobis tua Passio salutaris sit, quasi præsens et hodierna; et sic nobis hodie, illa gutta sancti sanguinis super terram olim de cruce stillantis, sit salus: ut omnia terræ nostræ delicta lavans, et corporis nostri humo quodam modo immixta, nos de terra tuos efficiat; nos quoque tibi quasi corpus idem reconciliati capitis. Qui regnas cum Patre semper et Spiritu Sancto; nunc nobis regnare incipe, Homo Deus, Christi Jesu, Rex in sæcula sæculorum.

TUESDAY

IN HOLY WEEK.

TO-DAY, again, our Saviour sets out in the morning for Jerusalem. His intention is to repair to the temple, and continue his yesterday's teachings. It is evident that his mission on earth is fast drawing to its close. He says to his Disciples: *You know that after two days shall be the Pasch, and the Son of Man shall be delivered up to be crucified.*[1]

On the road from Bethania to Jerusalem, the Disciples are surprised at seeing the fig-tree, which their Divine Master had yesterday cursed, now dead. Addressing himself to Jesus, Peter says: *Rabbi, behold, the fig-tree, which thou didst curse, is withered away.*[2] In order to teach us that the whole of material nature is subservient to the spiritual element, when this last is united to God by faith,—Jesus replies: *Have the faith of God. Amen I say to you, that whosoever shall say to this mountain: Be thou removed and cast into the sea! and shall not stagger in his heart, but believe, that whatsoever he saith shall be done, it shall be done unto him.*[3]

Having entered the City, Jesus directs his steps towards the Temple. No sooner has he entered, than the Chief Priests, the Scribes, and the Ancients of the people, accost him with these words: *By what authority dost thou these things? and who has given*

---

[1] St Matth., xxvi. 2.   [2] St. Mark, xi. 21.
[3] *Idem, ibid.*, 22, 23.

thee this authority, that thou shouldst do these things?[1] We shall find our Lord's answer given in the Gospel. Our object is to mention the leading events of the last days of our Redeemer on earth; the holy Volume will supply the details.

As on the two preceding days, Jesus leaves the City towards evening: he passes over Mount Olivet, and returns to Bethania, where he finds his Blessed Mother and his devoted friends.

In to-day's Mass, the Church reads the history of the Passion according to St. Mark, who wrote his Gospel the next after St. Matthew: hence it is, that the second place is assigned to him. His account of the Passion is shorter than St. Matthew's, of which it would often seem to be a summary; and yet certain details are peculiar to this Evangelist, and prove him to have been an eye-witness. Our readers are aware that St. Mark was the disciple of St. Peter, and that his Gospel was written under the very eye of the Prince of the Apostles.

In Rome, the Station for to-day is in the Church of St. Prisca, which is said to have been the house of Aquila and his wife Prisca, to whom St. Paul sends his salutations, in his Epistle to the Romans. In the 3rd century, Pope St. Eutychian had translated thither, on account of the sameness of the name, the body of St. Prisca, a Virgin and Martyr of Rome.

MASS.

Three days hence, and the Cross will be lifted up on Calvary, bearing upon itself the Author of our Salvation. The Church, in the Introit of to-day's Mass, bids us at once pay our homage to this trophy of our victory, and *glory* in it.

[1] St. Mark, xi. 28.

INTROIT.

Nos autem gloriari oportet in cruce Domini nostri Jesu Christi : in quo est salus, vita, et resurrectio nostra, per quem salvati, et liberati sumus.	We ought to glory in the Cross of our Lord Jesus Christ, in whom is our salvation, life, and resurrection; by whom we have been saved and delivered.
Ps. Deus misereatur nostri, et benedicat nobis : illuminet vultum suum super nos, et misereatur nostri.	*Ps.* May God have mercy on us, and bless us; may his countenance shine upon us, and may he have mercy on us.
Nos autem.	We ought, &c.

In the Collect, the Church prays that the sacred anniversaries of our Saviour's Passion may be to us a source of pardon; and that they may work in us a full reconciliation with the Divine Justice.

COLLECT.

Omnipotens sempiterne Deus, da nobis ita Dominicæ Passionis sacramenta peragere, ut indulgentiam percipere mereamur. Per eumdem.	O Almighty and everlasting God, grant that we may so celebrate the mysteries of our Lord's Passion, as to obtain thy pardon. Through the same, &c.

For the other Collects, see *page* 246.

EPISTLE.

Lectio Jeremiæ Prophetæ.	Lesson from Jeremias the Prophet.
Cap. XI.	*Ch. XI.*
In diebus illis : Dixit Jeremias : Domine, demonstrasti mihi, et cognovi; tunc ostendisti mihi studia eorum. Et ego quasi agnus	In those days : Jeremias said : Thou, O Lord, hast shewed me, and I have known : then thou shewedst me their doings. And I was as a meek

lamb, that is carried to be a victim; and I knew not that they had devised counsels against me, saying: Let us put wood on his bread, and cut him off from the land of the living, and let his name be remembered no more. But thou, O Lord of Sabaoth, who judgest justly, and triest the reins of the heart, let me see thy revenge on them; for to thee I have revealed my cause, O Lord, my God!	mansuetus, qui portatur ad victimam : et non cognovi quia cogitaverunt super me consilia, dicentes: Venite, mittamus lignum in panem ejus, et eradamus eum de terra viventium, et nomen ejus non memoretur amplius. Tu autem, Domine Sabaoth, qui judicas juste, et probas renes et corda, videam ultionem tuam ex eis : tibi enim revelavi causam meam, Domine Deus meus.

Again, we have the plaintive words of Jeremias: he gives us the very words used by his enemies, when they conspired his death. It is evident, however, that the Prophet is here a figure of one greater than himself. *Let us*, say these enemies, *put wood upon his bread:* that is, let us put poisonous wood into what he eats, that so we may cause his death. This is the literal sense of these words, as applied to the Prophet; but how much more truly were they fulfilled in our Redeemer! He tells us, that his Divine Flesh is the *True Bread* that came down from heaven. This *Bread,* this Body of the Man-God, is bruised, torn, and wounded ; the Jews nail it to the *Wood;* so that, it is, in a manner, made one with the *Wood,* and the *Wood* is all covered with Jesus' Blood. This Lamb of God was immolated on the Wood of the Cross : it is by his immolation, that we have had given to us a Sacrifice, which is worthy of God ; and it is by this Sacrifice, that we participate in the *Bread* of Heaven, the Flesh of the Lamb, our true Pasch.

The Gradual, which is taken from the 34th Psalm, shows us the humility and meekness of our Jesus under his sufferings. How they contrast with the haughty pride of his enemies!

GRADUAL.

Ego autem, dum mihi molesti essent, induebam me cilicio, et humiliabam in jejunio animam meam : et oratio mea in sinu meo convertetur.

℣. Judica, Domine, nocentes me, expugna impugnantes me : apprehende arma et scutum, et exsurge in adjutorium mihi.

When they were troublesome to me, I clothed myself with hair-cloth, and I humbled my soul with fasting; and I will yet continue to pour forth my prayer in my bosom.

℣. Judge thou, O Lord, them that wrong me, overthrow them that fight against me; take hold of arms and shield, and rise to help me.

After the Gradual, is sung the Passion according to Saint Mark. The same ceremonies are observed as during the Passion, which was read to us on Sunday, excepting only what regarded the Palms.

THE PASSION AND GOSPEL.

Passio Domini nostri Jesu Christi secundum Marcum.

Cap. XIV. et XV.

In illo tempore : Erat Pascha, et Azyma post biduum : et quærebant summi sacerdotes et scribæ quomodo Jesum dolo tenerent, et occiderent. Dicebant autem : Non in die festo ne forte tumultus fieret in populo.

Et cum esset Jesus Bethaniæ in domo Simonis Leprosi, et recumberet : venit mulier habens alabastrum unguenti nardi spicati pretiosi, et fracto alabastro, effudit super caput ejus. Erant autem quidam indigne ferentes intra semetipsos,

The Passion of our Lord Jesus Christ according to Mark.

Ch. XIV. and XV.

At that time, The Feast of the Pasch and of Azymes was after two days; and the chief priests and the scribes sought how they might by some wile lay hold on Jesus, and kill him. But they said : Not on the festival day, lest there should be a tumult among the people.

And when Jesus was in Bethania, in the house of Simon the Leper, and was at meat, there came a woman having an alabaster box of ointment of precious spikenard; and breaking the alabaster box, she poured it out upon his head. Now there were some that had indignation within themselves, and said: Why was this waste of the ointment made? For this ointment might have been sold for more than three hundred pence, and given to the poor. And they murmured against her. But Jesus said: Let her alone, why do you molest her? She hath wrought a good work upon me. For the poor you have always with you, and whensoever you will, you may do them good; but me you have not always. What she had, she hath done; she is come beforehand to anoint my body for the burial. Amen I say to you, wheresoever this gospel shall be preached in the whole world, that also which she hath done shall be told for a memorial of her.

And Judas Iscariot, one of the twelve, went to the chief priests, to betray him to them. Who hearing it were glad; and promised to give him money. And he sought how he might conveniently betray him.

Now on the first day of the unleavened bread, when they sacrificed the Pasch, the disciples say to him: Whither wilt thou that we go and prepare for thee to eat the Pasch? And he sendeth two of his disciples, and saith to them: Go ye into the city, and there shall meet you, a man carrying a pitcher of water; follow him, and whithersoever he shall go in, say to the master of the house: The Master saith: Where is my refectory, that I

et dicentes: Ut quid perditio ista unguenti facta est? Poterat enim unguentum istud venundari plus quam trecentis denariis, et dari pauperibus. Et fremebant in eam. Jesus autem dixit: Sinite eam: quid illi molesti estis? Bonum opus operata est in me. Semper enim pauperes habetis vobiscum, et cum volueritis, potestis illis benefacere: me autem non semper habetis. Quod habuit hæc, fecit: prævenit ungere corpus meum in sepulturam. Amen dico vobis: Ubicumque prædicatum fuerit evangelium istud in universo mundo, et quod fecit hæc, narrabitur in memoriam ejus.

Et Judas Iscariotes unus de duodecim abiit ad summos sacerdotes, ut proderet eum illis. Qui audientes, gavisi sunt: et promiserunt ei pecuniam se daturos. Et quærebat, quomodo illum opportune traderet.

Et primo die Azymorum, quando Pascha immolabant, dicunt ei discipuli: Quo vis eamus, et paremus tibi, ut manduces Pascha? Et mittit duos ex discipulis suis, et dicit eis: Ite in civitatem: et occurret vobis homo lagenam aquæ bajulans; sequimini eum: et quocumque introierit, dicite domino domus, quia Magister dicit: Ubi est refectio mea, ubi Pascha cum discipulis meis manducem? Et ipse vobis demonstrabit cœnaculum grande, stratum, et illic parate nobis. Et abierunt discipuli ejus, et venerunt in civitatem; et invenerunt sicut dixerat illis, et paraverunt Pascha.

Vespere autem facto, venit cum duodecim. Et discumbentibus eis, et manducantibus ait Jesus: Amen dico vobis, quia unus ex vobis tradet me, qui manducat mecum. At illi cœperunt contristari, et dicere ei singulatim: Numquid ego? Qui ait illis: Unus ex duodecim, qui intingit mecum manum in catino. Et Filius quidem hominis vadit, sicut scriptum est de eo? Væ autem homini illi, per quem Filius hominis tradetur. Bonum erat ei, si non esset natus homo ille. Et manducantibus illis, accepit Jesus panem: et benedicens fregit, et dedit eis, et ait: Sumite: Hoc est corpus meum. Et accepto calice, gratias agens dedit eis: et biberunt ex illo omnes. Et ait illis: Hic est sanguis meus novi testamenti, qui pro multis effundetur. Amen dico vobis: quia non bibam de hoc genimine vitis, usque in diem illum, cum illud bibam novum in regno Dei.

Et hymno dicto, exierunt in montem Olivarum. Et ait eis Jesus: Omnes scandalizabimini in me, in nocte

may eat the Pasch with my disciples? And he will shew you a large dining room furnished; and there prepare ye for us. And his disciples went their way, and came into the city; and they found as he had told them, and they prepared the Pasch.

And when evening was come, he cometh with the twelve. And when they were at table eating, Jesus saith: Amen I say to you, one of you that eateth with me shall betray me. But they began to be sorrowful, and to say to him one by one: Is it I? Who saith to them: One of the twelve, who dippeth his hand in the dish with me. And the Son of Man indeed goeth, as it is written of him; but wo to that man by whom the Son of Man shall be betrayed. It were better for him, if that man had not been born. And whilst they were eating, Jesus took bread: and blessing, broke, and gave to them, and said: Take ye, this is my body. And having taken the chalice, giving thanks, he gave it to them, and they all drank of it; and he said to them: This is my blood of the new testament, which shall be shed for many. Amen I say to you, that I will drink no more of this fruit of the vine, until that day when I shall drink it new in the kingdom of God.

And when they had sung an hymn, they went forth to the mount of Olives. And Jesus saith to them: You will all be scandalized in my regard this night; for it is written: "I will strike the shepherd, "and the sheep shall be dis- "persed." But after I shall be risen again, I will go before you into Galilee. But Peter saith to him: Although all shall be scandalized in thee, yet not I. And Jesus saith to him: Amen I say to thee, to-day, even in this night, before the cock crow twice, thou shalt deny me thrice. But he spoke the more vehemently: Although I should die together with thee, I will not deny thee. And in like manner also said they all.

And they came to a farm called Gethsemani. And he saith to his disciples: Sit you here, while I pray. And he taketh Peter, and James, and John with him; and he began to fear and to be heavy. And he saith to them: My soul is sorrowful even unto death; stay you here, and watch. And when he had gone forward a little, he fell flat on the ground; and he prayed that, if it might be, the hour might pass from him: and he saith: Abba, Father, all things are possible to thee, remove this chalice from me; but not what I will, but what thou wilt. And he cometh, and findeth them sleeping. And he saith to Peter: Simon, sleepest thou? couldst thou not watch one hour? Watch ye, and pray, that ye enter not into temptation. The spirit indeed is willing, but the flesh is weak. And going

ista: quia scriptum est. Percutiam pastorem, et dispergentur oves; sed postquam resurrexero, præcedam vos in Galilæam. Petrus autem ait illi: Et si omnes scandalizati fuerint in te, sed non ego. Et ait illi Jesus: Amen dico tibi, quia tu hodie in nocte hac, priusquam gallus vocem bis dederit, ter me es negaturus. At ille amplius loquebatur: Et si oportuerit me simul commori tibi, non te negabo. Similiter autem et omnes dicebant.

Et veniunt in prædium, cui nomen Gethsemani, et ait discipulis suis: Sedete hic donec orem. Et assumit Petrum, et Jacobum et Joannem secum: et cœpit pavere, et tædere. Et ait illis: Tristis est anima mea usque ad mortem. Sustinete hic, et vigilate. Et cum processisset paululum, procidit super terram: et orabat, ut si fieri posset, transiret ab eo hora: et dixit: Abba Pater, omnia tibi possibilia sunt: transfer calicem hunc a me. Sed non quod ego volo: sed quod tu. Et venit, et invenit eos dormientes. Et ait Petro: Simon dormis? Non potuisti una hora vigilare? Vigilate, et orate, ut non intretis in tentationem. Spiritus quidem promptus est, caro vero infirma. Et iterum abiens oravit, eumdem sermonem dicens. Et reversus, denuo invenit eos dormientes (erant enim oculi eorum gravati), et ignorabant quid responderent ei. Et venit tertio, et ait illis: Dormite jam, et requiescite. Sufficit: venit hora: ecce Filius hominis tradetur in manus peccatorum. Surgite, eamus: ecce, qui me tradet, prope est.

Et adhuc eo loquente venit Judas Iscariotes unus de duodecim, et cum illo turba multa cum gladiis et lignis, missi a summis sacerdotibus, et scribis, et senioribus. Dederat autem traditor ejus signum eis, dicens: Quemcumque osculatus fuero, ipse est: tenete eum, et ducite caute. Et cum venisset, statim accedens ad eum, ait: Ave Rabbi! Et osculatus est eum. At illi manus injecerunt in eum, et tenuerunt eum. Unus autem quidam de circumstantibus educens gladium, percussit servum summi sacerdotis: et amputavit illi auriculam. Et respondens Jesus ait illis: Tamquam ad latronem existis cum gladiis et lignis comprehendere me: quotidie eram apud vos in templo docens, et non me tenuistis. Sed ut impleantur Scripturæ. Tunc discipuli ejus relinquentes eum, omnes fugerunt. Adolescens autem quidam sequebatur eum amictus sindone super

away again, he prayed, saying the same words. And when he returned, he found them again asleep, (for their eyes were heavy,) and they knew not what to answer him. And he cometh the third time, and saith to them: Sleep ye now, and take your rest. It is enough, the hour is come; behold the Son of man shall be betrayed into the hands of sinners. Rise up, let us go. Behold he that will betray me is at hand.

And while he was yet speaking, cometh Judas Iscariot, one of the twelve, and with him a great multitude with swords and staves, from the chief priests, and the scribes, and the ancients. And he that betrayed him had given them a sign, saying: Whomsoever I shall kiss, that is he, lay hold on him, and lead him away carefully. And when he was come, immediately going up to him, he saith: Hail Rabbi! And he kissed him. But they laid hands on him, and held him. And one of them that stood by, drawing a sword, struck a servant of the chief priest, and cut off his ear. And Jesus answering, said to them: Are you come out as to a robber with swords and staves to apprehend me? I was daily with you in the temple teaching, and you did not lay hands on me. But, that the scripture may be fulfilled. Then his disciples leaving him, all fled away. And a certain young man followed him, having a linen cloth cast about his naked body; and they laid hold on him. But he casting off the linen cloth, fled from them naked.

And they brought Jesus to the High Priest; and all the priests and the scribes and the ancients were assembled together. And Peter followed him afar off even into the place of the High Priest; and he sat with the servants at the fire and warmed himself. And the chief priests and all the council sought for evidence against Jesus that they might put him to death, and they found none. For many bore false witness against him, and their evidences were not agreeing. And some rising up, bore false witness against him, saying: We heard him say: I will destroy this temple made with hands, and within three days I will build another not made with hands. And their witness did not agree.

And the High Priest rising up in the midst, asked Jesus, saying: Answerest thou nothing to the things that are laid to thy charge by these men? But he held his peace, and answered nothing. Again the High Priest asked him, and said to him: Art thou Christ the Son of the Blessed God? and Jesus said to him: I am. And you shall see the Son of Man sitting on the right hand of the power of God, and

nudo : et tenuerunt eum. At ille rejecta sindone, nudus profugit ab eis.

Et adduxerunt Jesum ad summum sacerdotem : et convenerunt omnes sacerdotes, et scribæ et seniores. Petrus autem a longe secutus est eum usque intro in atrium summi sacerdotis : et sedebat cum ministris ad ignem, et calefaciebat se. Summi vero sacerdotes et omne concilium, quærebant adversus Jesum testimonium, ut eum morti traderent : nec inveniebant. Multi enim testimonium falsum dicebant adversus eum : et convenientia testimonia non erant. Et quidam surgentes, falsum testimonium ferebant adversus eum, dicentes: Quoniam nos audivimus eum dicentem : Ego dissolvam templum hoc manufactum : et per triduum, aliud non manufactum ædificabo. Et non erat conveniens testimonium illorum.

Et exsurgens summus sacerdos in medium, interrogavit Jesum, dicens : Non respondes quidquam ad ea, quæ tibi objiciuntur ab his? Ille autem tacebat, et nihil respondit. Rursum summus sacerdos interrogabat eum, et dixit ei : Tu es Christus Filius Dei benedicti? Jesus autem dixit illi : Ego sum. Et videbitis Filium hominis sedentem a dextris virtutis Dei, et venientem cum nubibus cœli. Summus autem sacerdos scindens vestimenta sua, ait: Quid adhuc desideramus testes? Audistis blasphemiam. Quid vobis videtur? Qui omnes condemnaverunt eum esse reum mortis. Et cœperunt quidam conspuére eum, et velare faciem ejus, et colaphis eum cædere, et dicere ei: Prophetiza. Et ministri alapis eum cædebant.

Et cum esset Petrus in atrio deorsum, venit una ex ancillis summi sacerdotis: et cum vidisset Petrum calefacientem se, aspiciens illum, ait: Et tu cum Jesu Nazareno eras. At ille negavit, dicens: Neque scio, neque novi quid dicas. Et exiit foras ante atrium: et gallus cantavit. Rursus autem, cum vidisset illum ancilla, cæpit dicere circumstantibus: Quia hic ex illis est. At ille iterum negavit. Et post pusillum, rursus qui astabant, dicebant Petro: Vere ex illis es: nam et Galilæus es. Ille autem cœpit anathematizare et jurare: quia nescio hominem istum quem dicitis. Et statim gallus iterum cantavit. Et recordatus est Petrus verbi, quod dixerat ei Jesus: Priusquam gallus cantet bis, ter me negabis. Et cœpit flere.

Et confestim mane concilium facientes summi sacerdotes cum senioribus, et

coming in the clouds of heaven. Then the High Priest rending his garments saith: What need we any further witnesses? You have heard the blasphemy. What think you? Who all condemned him to be guilty of death. And some began to spit on him, and to cover his face, and to buffet him, and to say to him: Prophesy! And the servants struck him with the palms of their hands.

Now when Peter was in the court below, there cometh to him one of the maid servants of the High Priest; and when she had seen Peter warming himself, looking on him, she saith: Thou also wast with Jesus of Nazareth. But he denied, saying: I neither know nor understand what thou sayest. And he went forth before the court, and the cock crew. And again a maid-servant seeing him, began to say to the standers-by: This is one of them. But he denied again. And after a while, they that stood by said again to Peter: Surely thou art one of them, for thou also art a Galilean. But he began to curse and swear, saying: I know not this man of whom you speak. And immediately the cock crew again. And Peter remembered the word that Jesus had said to him: Before the cock crow twice, thou shalt deny me thrice. And he began to weep.

And straightway in the morning, the chief priests holding a consultation with the ancients and the scribes, and the whole council, binding Jesus, led him away, and delivered him to Pilate. And Pilate asked him: Art thou the king of the Jews? But he answering, saith to him: Thou sayest it. And the chief priests accused him in many things. And Pilate again asked him, saying: Answerest thou nothing? behold in how many things they accuse thee. But Jesus still answered nothing; so that Pilate wondered.

Now on the festival day he was wont to release unto them one of the prisoners, whomsoever they demanded. And there was one called Barabbas, who was put in prison with some seditious men, who in the sedition had committed murder. And when the multitude was come up, they began to desire that he would do as he had ever done unto them. And Pilate answered them, and said: Will you that I release to you the King of the Jews? For he knew that the chief priests had delivered him up out of envy. But the chief priests moved the people that he should rather release Barabbas to them. And Pilate again answering, saith to them: What will you then that I do with the King of the Jews? But they again cried out: Crucify him. And Pilate saith to them: Why, what evil hath he done? But they cried out the more: Crucify him.

And Pilate being willing to satisfy the people, released to them Barabbas, and delivered

scribis, et universo concilio, vincientes Jesum, duxerunt et tradiderunt Pilato. Et interrogavit eum Pilatus: Tu es Rex Judæorum? At ille respondens, ait illi: Tu dicis. Et accusabant eum summi sacerdotes in multis. Pilatus autem rursum interrogavit eum, dicens: Non respondes quidquam? Vide, in quantis te accusant. Jesus autem amplius nihil respondit: ita ut miraretur Pilatus.

Per diem autem festum solebat dimittere illis unum ex vinctis quemcumque petiissent. Erat autem qui dicebatur Barabbas, qui cum seditiosis erat vinctus, qui in seditione fecerat homicidium. Et cum ascendisset turba, cœpit rogare, sicut semper faciebat illis. Pilatus autem respondit eis, et dixit: Vultis dimittam vobis Regem Judæorum? Sciebat enim, quod per invidiam tradidissent eum summi sacerdotes. Pontifices autem concitaverunt turbam ut magis Barabbam dimitteret eis. Pilatus autem iterum respondens, ait illis: Quid ergo vultis faciam Regi Judæorum? At illi iterum clamaverunt: Crucifige eum. Pilatus vero dicebat illis: Quid enim mali fecit? At illi magis clamabant: Crufige eum.

Pilatus autem volens populo satisfacere, dimisit illis Barabbam, et tradidit

Jesum flagellis cæsum, ut crucifigeretur. Milites autem duxerunt eum in atrium prætorii, et convocant totam cohortem: et induunt eum purpura, et imponunt ei plectentes spineam coronam. Et cœperunt salutare eum: Ave, Rex Judæorum. Et percutiebant caput ejus arundine: et conspuebant eum, et ponentes genua, adorabant eum.

Et postquam illuserunt ei, exuerunt illum purpura, et induerunt eum vestimentis suis, et educunt illum, ut crucifigerent eum. Et angariaverunt prætereuntem quempiam Simonem Cyrenæum venientem de villa, patrem Alexandri et Rufi, ut tolleret crucem ejus. Et perducunt illum in Golgotha locum: quod est interpretatum, Calvariæ locus. Et dabant ei bibere myrrhatum vinum: et non accepit. Et crucifigentes eum diviserunt vestimenta ejus, mittentes sortem super eis, quis quid tolleret. Erat autem hora tertia: et crucifixerunt eum. Et erat titulus causæ ejus inscriptus: Rex Judæorum. Et cum eo crucifigunt duos latrones: unum a dextris, et alium a sinistris ejus. Et impleta est Scriptura, quæ dicit: Et cum iniquis reputatus est.

Et prætereuntes blasphemabant eum, moventes ca-

up Jesus, when he had scourged him, to be crucified. And the soldiers led him away into the court of the palace, and they called together the whole band; and they clothed him with purple, and platting a crown of thorns, they put it upon him. And they began to salute him: Hail, king of the Jews. And they struck his head with a reed, and they did spit on him; and bowing their knees, they adored him.

And after they had mocked him, they took off the purple from him, and put his own garments on him, and they led him out to crucify him. And they forced one Simon, a Cyrenean, who passed by, coming out of the country, the father of Alexander and of Rufus, to take up his cross. And they bring him into the place called Golgotha, which being interpreted is, The place of Calvary. And they gave him to drink wine mingled with myrrh; but he took it not. And crucifying him, they divided his garments casting lots for them, what every man should take. And it was the third hour, and they crucified him. And the inscription of his cause was written over, The King of the Jews. And with him they crucified two thieves, the one on his right hand and the other on his left. And the scripture was fulfilled which saith: "And with the wicked he "was reputed."

And they that passed by blasphemed him, wagging

their heads, and saying: Vah, thou that destroyest the Temple of God, and in three days buildest it up again, save thyself, coming down from the cross. In like manner also the chief priests with the scribes mocking, said one to another: He saved others, himself he cannot save. Let Christ the King of Israel come down from the cross, that we may see and believe. And they that were crucified with him reviled him.

And when the sixth hour was come, there was darkness over the whole earth until the ninth hour; and at the ninth hour Jesus cried out with a loud voice, saying: Eloï, Eloï, lamma sabacthani? which is, being interpreted: My God, my God, why hast thou forsaken me? And some of the standers-by hearing, said: Behold, he calleth Elias. And one running and filling a sponge with vinegar, and putting it upon a reed, gave him to drink, saying: Stay, let us see if Elias will come to take him down. And Jesus having cried out with a loud voice, gave up the ghost.

pita sua, et dicentes: Vah, qui destruis Templum Dei et in tribus diebus reædificas: salvum fac temetipsum, descendens de cruce. Similiter et summi sacerdotes illudentes, ad alterutrum cum scribis dicebant: Alios salvos fecit, seipsum non potest salvum facere. Christus Rex Israel descendat nunc de cruce, ut videamus, et credamus. Et qui cum eo crucifixi erant, conviciabantur ei.

Et facta hora sexta, tenebræ factæ sunt per totam terram, usque in horam nonam. Et hora nona exclamavit Jesus voce magna, dicens: Eloï, Eloï, lamma sabacthani? Quod est interpretatum: Deus meus, Deus meus, ut quid dereliquisti me? Et quidam de circumstantibus audientes dicebant: Ecce, Eliam vocat. Currens autem unus, et implens spongiam aceto, circumponensque calamo, potum dabat ei, dicens: Sinite videamus si veniat Elias ad deponendum eum. Jesus autem emissa voce magna, exspiravit.

Here a pause is made, as on Palm Sunday. All kneel down, and if such be custom of the place, prostrate and kiss the ground.

And the veil of the temple was rent in two from the top to the bottom; and the centurion who stood over against him, seeing that crying out in

Et velum templi scissum est in duo, a summo usque deorsum. Videns autem centurio, qui ex adverso stabat, quia sic clamans expirasset, ait: Vere hic homo Filius Dei erat. Erant autem et mulieres de longe aspicientes: inter quas erat Maria Magdalene, et Maria Jacobi minoris, et Joseph mater, et Salome: et cum esset in Galilæa, sequebantur eum, et ministrabant ei: et aliæ multæ, quæ simul cum eo ascenderant Jerosolymam.

this manner he gave up the ghost, said: Indeed this man was the Son of God. And there were also women looking on afar off, among whom was Mary Magdalen, and Mary the Mother of James the Less, and of Joseph, and Salome; who also when he was in Galilee followed him, and ministered to him, and many other women that came up with him to Jerusalem.

Here, the Deacon presents the Incense to the Priest, that it may be blessed; and, after having himself received a blessing, he terminates the Passion, observing the ceremonies which are used at the singing of the Gospel in a High Mass.

Et quum jam sero esset factum (quia erat Parasceve, quod est ante Sabbatum) venit Joseph ab Arimathæa, nobilis decurio, qui et ipse erat exspectans regnum Dei. Et audacter introivit ad Pilatum, et petiit corpus Jesu. Pilatus autem mirabatur si jam obiisset. Et accersito centurione, interrogavit eum, si jam mortuus esset. Et cum cognovisset a centurione, donavit corpus Joseph. Joseph autem mercatus sindonem, et deponens eum, involvit sindone: et posuit eum in monumento, quod erat excisum de petra, et advolvit lapidem ad ostium monumenti.

And when the evening was now come, (because it was the Parasceve, that is, the day before the Sabbath,) Joseph of Arimathea, a noble counsellor, who was also himself looking for the kingdom of God, came and went in boldly to Pilate, and begged the body of Jesus. But Pilate wondered that he should be already dead; and sending for the centurion, he asked him if he were already dead. And when he had understood it by the centurion, he gave the body to Joseph. And Joseph buying fine linen, and taking him down, wrapped him up in the fine linen, and laid him in a sepulchre which was hewn out of a rock, and he rolled a stone to the door of the sepulchre.

TUESDAY IN HOLY WEEK. 273

At the Offertory, the Messias asks his Eternal Father to defend him from the enemies that are preparing his destruction.

OFFERTORY.

Keep me, O Lord, from the hands of the sinful man ; and from unjust men deliver me.	Custodi me, Domine, de manu peccatoris : et ab hominibus iniquis eripe me.

In the Secret, the Church offers to the Majesty of God the tribute of our fasts, in union with the Holy Host on our Altar, and from which they derive all their merit and efficacy.

SECRET.

May these sacrifices, O Lord, we beseech thee, which are accompanied with healing fasts, mercifully repair us. Through, &c.	Sacrificia nos, quæsumus, Domine, propensius ista restaurent : quæ medicinalibus sunt instituta jejuniis. Per Dominum.

For the other Secrets, see *page* 254.

The words of the Psalmist, used by the Church in her Communion-Anthem, show us the blasphemous daring of our Saviour's enemies, as also the dispositions in which this dear Jesus himself was during his sacred Passion.

COMMUNION.

The judges in the gate spoke against me, and they that drank wine made songs against me. But I poured forth my prayer to thee, O Lord : it is	Adversum me exercebantur, qui sedebant in porta : et in me psallebant, qui bibebant vinum : ego vero orationem meam ad te, Do-

mine : tempus beneplaciti Deus, in multitudine misericordiæ tuæ.

time, O God, to shew thy good will to me, according to the multitude of thy mercies.

In the Postcommunion, the Church prays, that, by the merits of the Sacrifice she has just offered, we may obtain the perfect cure of our spiritual infirmities; for the Blood of the Lamb takes away the sins of the world.

POSTCOMMUNION.[1]

Sanctificationibus tuis, omnipotens Deus, et vitia nostra curentur : et remedia nobis sempiterna proveniant. Per Dominum.

May these thy holy mysteries, O Almighty God, both cure our vices and become an eternal remedy to us. Through, &c.

See the other Postcommunions in *page* 255.

OREMUS.

LET US PRAY.

Humiliate capita vestra Deo.
Tua nos misericordia, Deus, et ab omni subreptione vetustatis expurget, et capaces sanctæ novitatis efficiat. Per Dominum.

Bow down your heads to God.
May thy mercy, O God, purify us from the corruption of the old man, and enable us to put on the new. Through, &c.

We may close this day, by saying these few verses, taken from a Hymn of the Greek Church on the Passion of our Lord.

HYMN.

(In Parasceve.)

The life-giving Wound of thy Side, O Jesus! like the fountain that sprang from Eden, waters the spiritual garden of thy Church. Thence, dividing itself into the four Gospels, as into so many master-streams, it freshens the world, gladdens creation, and teaches all nations to bow down in faith, and venerate thy Kingdom.

Thou wast crucified for me, that thou mightest be to me as a fountain, pouring out forgiveness upon me. Thou wast wounded in thy Side, that thou mightest open to me the sources of life. Thou wast nailed to the Cross, that I, confessing the greatness of thy power in the depth of thy Passion, might sing to thee, O Christ, thou giver of life: Glory be to thy Cross and Passion, O Saviour!

Thou, O Christ, didst, on thy Cross, tear the hand-writing that was against us. Thou wast numbered among the dead, and there didst bind down the tyrant, and, by thy Resurrection, didst set us all free from the chains of death. It is thy Resurrection that has given us light, O God, thou lover of mankind! To thee do we sing: Remember us, also, O Saviour, in thy Kingdom!

To thee, most merciful Lord, we bring thy Mother, that she

Vitale latus tuum, tanquam fons ex Eden scaturiens, Ecclesiam tuam, Christe, tanquam rationalem hortum adaquat: inde tanquam in quædam initia se dividens in quatuor Evangelia: mundum irrigans; creaturam lætificans, gentesque fideliter docens venerari regnum tuum.

Crucifixus es propter me; ut velut ex fonte mihi effunderes remissionem. Punctus es in latere, ut mihi vitæ scaturigines aperires; clavis confixus es, ut ego in passionum tuarum profundo altitudinem tuæ potentiæ confessus, clamem ad te, vitæ largitor Christe: Gloria Cruci tuæ, Salvator, ac Passioni tuæ.

Chirographum nostrum in cruce dirupisti, Christe: et inter mortuos reputatus, tyrannum illic ligasti, liberatis omnibus ex vinculis mortis resurrectione tua. Per quam illuminati sumus, o amans hominum Domine! tibique clamamus: Memento et nostri Salvator in Regno tuo.

Tuam, Christe, Matrem, quæ te in carne sine virili

semine peperit, et vere virgo etiam post partum incorrupta permansit; hanc tibi adducimus ad intercessionem, Domine multum misericors : ut offensarum condonationem jugiter largiaris iis qui clamant : Memento et nostri Domine in Regno tuo.

may intercede for us,—she that conceived thee and was a Virgin, she that gave thee birth, and was a spotless Virgin. May her prayers obtain from thee the unceasing pardon of sin to all that cry out to thee : Remember us, also, O Lord, in thy Kingdom !

WEDNESDAY

IN HOLY WEEK.

THE Chief Priests and the Ancients of the people, are met to-day, in one of the rooms adjoining the Temple, for the purpose of deliberating on the best means of putting Jesus to death. Several plans are discussed. Would it be prudent to lay hands upon him at this season of the Feast of the Pasch, when the City is filled with strangers, who have received a favourable impression of Jesus from the solemn ovation given to him three days back? Then, too, are there not a great number of the inhabitants of Jerusalem, who took part in that triumph, and whose enthusiastic admiration of Jesus might excite them to rise up in his defence? These considerations persuade them not to have recourse to any violent measure, at least for the present, as a sedition among the people might be the consequence, and its promoters, even were they to escape being ill-treated by the people, would be brought before the tribunal of the Roman Governor, Pontius Pilate. They, therefore, come to the resolution of letting the Feast pass quietly over, before apprehending Jesus.

But these blood-thirsty men are making all these calculations as though they were the masters. They are, if they will, shrewd assassins, who put off their murder to a more convenient day: but the Divine decrees,—which, from all eternity, have prepared a Sacrifice for the world's salvation,—have fixed this very year's Pasch as the day of the Sacrifice, and, to-morrow evening, the holy City will re-echo with the trumpets, which proclaim the opening of the Feast. The figurative Lamb is now to make way for the true one; the Pasch of this year will substitute the reality for the type; and Jesus' Blood, shed by the hands of wicked priests, is soon to flow simultaneously with that of victims, which have only been hitherto acceptable to God, because they prefigured the Sacrifice of Calvary. The Jewish priesthood is about to be its own executioner, by immolating Him, whose Blood is to abrogate the Ancient Alliance, and perpetuate the New one.

But how are Jesus' enemies to get possession of their divine Victim, so as to avoid a disturbance in the City? There is only one plan that could succeed, and they have not thought of it: it is treachery. Just at the close of their deliberations, they are told that one of Jesus' Disciples seeks admission. They admit him, and he says to them: *What will you give me, and I will deliver him unto you?*[1] They are delighted at this proposition: and yet, how is it, that they, *doctors of the law,* forget that this infamous bargain between themselves and Judas has all been foretold by David, in the 108th Psalm? They know the Scriptures from beginning to end;—how comes it, that they forget the words of the Prophet, who even mentions the sum of *thirty pieces of silver.*[2] Judas asks them what they will give him; and they give him thirty pieces of silver! All is arranged: to-morrow, Jesus will be in Jerusalem, eating the Pasch with his Disciples. In the evening, he will go, as usual, to the Garden on Mount Olivet. But how shall they, who are sent to seize him, be able to distinguish him from his Disciples? Judas will lead the way; he will show them which is Jesus, by going up to him and kissing him!

---

[1] St. Matth. xxvi. 15. [2] *Idem*, xxvii. 9. Zach. xi. 12.

Such is the impious scheme devised on this day, within the precincts of the Temple of Jerusalem. To testify her detestation at it, and to make atonement to the Son of God for the outrage thus offered him, the Holy Church, from the earliest ages, consecrated the Wednesday of every week to penance. In our own times, the Fast of Lent begins on a Wednesday; and when the Church ordained that we should commence each of the four Seasons of the year with Fasting, Wednesday was chosen to be one of the three days thus consecrated to bodily mortification.

On this day, in the Roman Church, was held the sixth Scrutiny, for the admission of Catechumens to Baptism. Those, upon whom there had been previous doubts, were now added to the number of the chosen ones, if they were found worthy. There were two Lessons read in the Mass, as on the day of the great Scrutiny, the Wednesday of the fourth Week of Lent. As usual, the Catechumens left the Church, after the Gospel; but, as soon as the Holy Sacrifice was over, they were brought back by the Door-Keeper, and one of the Priests addressed them in these words: " On Saturday next, the Eve of Easter, " at *such an hour*, you will assemble in the Lateran " Basilica, for the seventh Scrutiny; you will then " recite the Symbol, which you must have learned; " and lastly, you will receive, by God's help, the " sacred laver of regeneration. Prepare yourselves, " zealously and humbly, by persevering fasts and " prayers, in order that, having been buried, by this " holy Baptism, together with Jesus Christ, you may " rise again with him, unto life everlasting. Amen."

At Rome, the Station for to-day is in the Basilica of Saint Mary Major. Let us compassionate with our Holy Mother, whose Heart is filled with poignant grief at the foresight of the Sacrifice, which is preparing.

MASS.

The Church commences her chants with one to the glory of the Holy Name of Jesus, outraged as it is, on this day, by them that plot his Death. This Name, which was given him by heaven, and signifies that he is our *Saviour*, is now being blasphemed by his enemies: in a few hours, their crime will bring its full meaning before us, for his Death will have worked the *Salvation* of the world.

INTROIT.

In nomine Jesu omne genu flectatur, cœlestium, terrestrium, et infernorum: quia Dominus factus est obediens usque ad mortem, mortem autem crucis: ideo Dominus Jesus Christus in gloria est Dei Patris.

Ps. Domine, exaudi orationem meam: et clamor meus ad te veniat.
In nomine.

At the name of Jesus every knee should bow, of those that are in heaven, on earth, and under the earth; because the Lord became obedient unto death, even the death of the cross: therefore the Lord Jesus Christ is in the glory of God the Father.

Ps. O Lord, hear my prayer, and let my cry come unto thee.
At the name, &c.

In the first Collect, the Church acknowledges to God, that her children have sinned against him: but she reminds him of the *Passion*, endured for their sakes, by his Only Begotten Son, and this revives her hope.

OREMUS.

℣. Flectamus genua.
℟. Levate.
Præsta, quæsumus, omnipotens Deus: ut qui nostris excessibus incessanter affligimur, per unigeniti Filii

LET US PRAY.

℣. Let us keeel down.
℟. Stand up again.
Grant, we beseech thee, O Almighty God, that we, who continually are punished for our excesses, may be de-

livered by the Passion of thy Only Begotten Son. Who liveth, &c.

tui Passionem liberemur. Qui tecum.

Lesson from Isaias the Prophet.

Lectio Isaiæ prophetæ.

Ch. LXII. and LXIII.

Cap. LXII. et LXIII.

Thus saith the Lord God: Tell the daughter of Sion: Behold thy Saviour cometh. Who is this that cometh from Edom, with dyed garments from Bosra, this beautiful one in his robe, walking in the greatness of his strength? I, that speak justice, and am a defender to save. Why then is thy apparel red, and thy garments like them that tread in the wine-press? I have trodden the wine-press alone, and of the Gentiles there is not a man with me; I have trampled on them in my indignation, and have trodden them down in my wrath, and their blood is sprinkled upon my garments, and I have stained all my apparel. For the day of vengeance is in my heart, the year of my redemption is come. I looked about, and there was none to help; I sought, and there was none to give aid; and my own arm hath saved me, and my indignation itself hath helped me. And I have trodden down the people in my wrath, and made them drunk in my indignation, and have brought down their strength to the earth. I will remember the tender mercies of the Lord, the praise of the Lord, for all the things

Hæc dicit Dominus Deus: Dicite filiæ Sion : Ecce Salvator tuus venit, ecce merces ejus cum eo. Quis est iste, qui venit de Edom, tinctis vestibus de Bosra? Iste formosus in stola sua, gradiens in multitudine fortitudinis suæ. Ego, qui loquor justitiam : et propugnator sum ad salvandum. Quare ergo rubrum est indumentum tuum, et vestimenta tua sicut calcantium in torculari? Torcular calcavi solus : et de gentibus non est vir mecum. Calcavi eos in furore meo : et conculcavi eos in ira mea. Et aspersus est sanguis eorum super vestimenta mea, et omnia indumenta mea inquinavi. Dies enim ultionis in corde meo : annus redemptionis meæ venit. Circumspexi, et non erat auxiliator: et quæsivi, et non fuit qui adjuvaret. Et salvavit mihi brachium meum : et indignatio mea ipsa auxiliata est mihi. Et conculcavi populos in furore meo : et inebriavi eos in indignatione mea, et detraxi in terram virtutem eorum. Miserationem Domini recordabor, laudem

| Domini super omnibus, quæ reddidit nobis Dominus Deus noster. | that the Lord hath bestowed on us. |

How terrible is this our *Defender*, who tramples his enemies beneath his feet, as they that *tread in the wine-press*; so that their *blood* is *sprinkled upon his garments!* But is not this the fittest time for us to proclaim his power, now that he is being treated with ignominy, and sold to his enemies by one of his Disciples? These humiliations will soon pass away; he will rise in glory, and his might will be shown by the chastisements, wherewith he will crush them that now persecute him. Jerusalem will stone them that shall preach in his name; she will be a cruel step-mother to those true Israelites, who, docile to the teaching of the Prophets, have recognised Jesus as the promised Messias. The Synagogue will seek to stifle the Church in her infancy; but no sooner shall the Church, shaking the dust from her feet, turn from Jerusalem to the Gentiles, than the vengeance of Christ will fall on the City, which bought, betrayed, and crucified him. Her citizens will have to pay dearly for these crimes. We learn from the Jewish historian, Josephus, (who was an eye-witness to the siege,) that the fire which was raging in one of the streets, was quenched by the torrents of their blood. Thus were fulfilled the threats pronounced by our Lord against this faithless City, as he sat on Mount Olivet, the day after his triumphant Entry.

And yet, the destruction of Jerusalem was but a faint image of the terrible destruction which is to befal the world at the last day. Jesus, who is now despised and insulted by sinners, will then appear on the clouds of heaven, and reparation will be made for all these outrages. Now he suffers himself to be betrayed, scoffed at, and spit upon; but, when *the day of vengeance is come*, happy they that have served him, and have compassionated with him in his humiliations and sufferings! Wo to them, that have treated him with contempt! Wo to them, who not content with their own refusing to bear his yoke, have led others to rebel against him! For he is King; he came into this world that he might reign over it; and they that despise his Mercy, shall not escape his Justice.

The Gradual, which immediately follows upon this sublime passage from Isaias, is a prayer addressed by Jesus to his Eternal Father: the words are taken from one of the Psalms.

GRADUAL.

Turn not away thy face from thy servant, for I am in trouble : hear me speedily.	Ne avertas faciem tuam a puero tuo, quoniam tribulor : velociter exaudi me.
℣. Save me, O God, for the waters are come in even unto my soul ; I stick fast in the mire of the deep, and there is no sure standing.	℣. Salvum me fac, Deus, quoniam intraverunt aquæ usque ad animam meam : infixus sum in limo profundi, et non est substantia.

In the second Collect, the Church again reminds our Heavenly Father of the Death, which his Divine Son deigned to suffer, in order to set us free from the yoke of Satan; she prays that we may have a share in the glorious *Resurrection* of this our Redeemer.

COLLECT.

O God, who wouldst have thy Son suffer on the Cross, to deliver us from the power of the enemy ; grant that we thy servants, may obtain the grace of his resurrection. Through the same, &c.	Deus, qui pro nobis Filium tuum Crucis patibulum subire voluisti, ut inimici a nobis expelleres potestatem : concede nobis famulis tuis, ut resurrectionis gratiam consequamur. Per eumdem.

For the other Collects, see *page* 246.

EPISTLE.

Lectio Isaiæ Prophetæ.

Cap. LIII.

In diebus illis : Dixit Isaias : Domine, quis credit auditui nostro ; et brachium Domini cui revelatum est ? Et ascendet sicut virgultum coram eo : et sicut radix de terra sitienti. Non est species ei, neque decor. Et vidimus eum : et non erat aspectus, et desideravimus eum : despectum, et novissimum virorum, virum dolorum, et scientem infirmitatem. Et quasi absconditus vultus ejus, et despectus : unde nec reputavimus eum. Vere languores nostros ipse tulit : et dolores nostros ipse portavit. Et nos putavimus eum quasi leprosum, et percussum a Deo, et humiliatum. Ipse autem vulneratus est propter iniquitates nostras : attritus est propter scelera nostra : disciplina pacis nostræ super eum : et livore ejus sanati sumus. Omnes nos quasi oves erravimus : unusquisque in viam suam declinavit : et posuit Dominus in eo iniquitatem omnium nostrum. Oblatus est, quia ipse voluit : et non aperuit os suum. Sicut ovis ad occisionem ducetur ; et quasi agnus coram tondente se, obmutescet : et non aperiet os suum. De angus-

Lesson from Isaias the Prophet.

Ch. LIII.

In those days : Isaias said : Who hath believed our report ? and to whom is the arm of the Lord revealed ? And he shall grow up as a tender plant before him, and as a root out of a thirsty ground. There is no beauty in him, nor comeliness. And we have seen him, and there was no sightliness that we should be desirous of him ; despised, and the most abject of men, a man of sorrows, and acquainted with infirmity. And his look was as it were hidden and despised; whereupon we esteemed him not. Surely he hath borne our infirmities, and carried our sorrows. And we have thought him as it were a leper, and as one struck by God and afflicted. But he was wounded for our iniquities, he was bruised for our sins ; the chastisement of our peace was upon him, and by his bruises we are healed. All we like sheep have gone astray, every one hath turned aside into his own way ; and the Lord hath laid upon him the iniquity of us all. He was offered because it was his own will, and he opened not his mouth. He shall be led as a sheep to the slaughter, and shall be dumb as a lamb before his shearer ; and he shall not open his mouth. He was taken away from distress, and from judgment. Who shall declare his generation? because he is cut off out of the land of the living. For the wickedness of my people have I struck him. And he shall give the ungodly for his burial, and the rich for his death; because he hath done no iniquity, neither was there deceit in his mouth. And the Lord was pleased to bruise him in infirmity. If he shall lay down his life for sin, he shall see a longlived seed, and the will of the Lord shall be prosperous in his hand. Because his soul hath laboured, he shall see and be filled; by his knowledge shall this my just servant justify many, and he shall bear their iniquities. Therefore will I distribute to him very many, and he shall divide the spoils of the strong, because he hath delivered his soul unto death, and was reputed with the wicked; and he hath borne the sins of many, and hath prayed for the transgressors.

tia, et de judicio sublatus est. Generationem ejus quis enarrabit? Quia abscissus est de terra viventium. Propter scelus populi mei percussi eum. Et dabit impios pro sepultura, et divitem pro morte sua: eo quod iniquitatem non fecerit, neque dolus inventus fuerit in ore ejus. Et Dominus voluit conterere eum in infirmitate. Si posuerit pro peccato animam suam, videbit semen longævum: et voluntas Domini in manu ejus dirigetur. Pro eo quod laboravit anima ejus, videbit, et saturabitur. In scientia sua justificabit ipse justus servus meus multos: et iniquitates eorum ipse portabit. Ideo dispertiam ei plurimos, et fortium dividet spolia: pro eo quod tradidit in mortem animam suam, et cum sceleratis reputatus est. Et ipse peccata multorum tulit: et pro transgressoribus rogavit.

Again it is Isaias that instructs us, not indeed upon the triumph which our Emmanuel is to win over his enemies, but upon the sufferings of *the Man of Sorrows*. So explicit is his description of our Lord's Passion, that the holy Fathers have called him the fifth Evangelist. What could be more sublimely plaintive than the language here used by the son of Amos? And we, after hearing both the Old and New Testament upon the sufferings which Jesus went through for our sins,—how shall we sufficiently love this dear Redeemer, who *bore our infirmities and carried our Sorrows*, so as to look *as a leper, and as one struck by God, and afflicted?*

We are healed by his bruises! O heavenly Physician, that takes upon himself the sufferings of them he comes to cure! But not only was he *bruised* for our sins; he was also *slaughtered as a lamb:* and this not merely as a Victim submitting to the inflexible justice of his Father who *hath laid upon him the iniquity of us all*, but, (as the Prophet here assures us,) *because it was his own will.* His love for us, as well as his submission to his Father, led him to the great Sacrifice. Observe, too, how he refuses to defend himself before Pilate, who could so easily deliver him from his enemies: *He shall be dumb as a lamb before his shearers, and he shall not open his mouth.* Let us love and adore this divine Silence, which works our Salvation. Let us not pass over an iota of the devotedness which Jesus shows us,— a devotedness which never could have existed, save in the Heart of a God. Oh! how much he has loved us,—his children, the purchase of his Blood, his *Seed*, as the Prophet here calls us. O Holy Church! thou *long-lived Seed* of Jesus, that *laid down his life!*—thou art dear to him, for he bought thee at a great price. Faithful Souls! give him love for love. Sinners! be converted to this your Saviour; his Blood will restore you to life, for if *we have all gone astray like sheep*, remember what is added: *The Lord hath laid upon him the iniquity of us all.* There is no sinner, however great may be his crimes; there is no heretic, or infidel, who has not his share in this precious Blood, whose infinite merit is such, that it could redeem a million worlds, more guilty even than our own.

The Tract, which follows this Lesson, is taken from the 101st Psalm, in which the Royal Prophet expresses the sufferings of body and mind endured by Jesus, in his human Nature.

TRACT.

Hear, O Lord, my prayer, and let my cry come unto thee.
℣. Turn not away thy face from me, in the day when I am in trouble, incline thine ear to me.
℣. In what day soever I shall call upon thee, hear me speedily.
℣. For my days are vanished like smoke : and my bones are as if they were fried in a frying-pan.
℣. I am smitten as grass, and my heart is withered, because I forgot to eat my bread.
℣. Thou, O Lord, arising, wilt have mercy on Sion, for the time to have mercy on her is come.

Domine, exaudi orationem meam, et clamor meus ad te veniat.
℣. Ne avertas faciem tuam a me, in quacumque die tribulor, inclina ad me aurem tuam.
℣. In quacumque die invocavero, velociter exaudi me.
℣. Quia defecerunt sicut fumus dies mei : et ossa mea sicut in frixorio confrixa sunt.
℣. Percussus sum sicut fœnum, et aruit cor meum, quia oblitus sum manducare panem meum.
℣. Tu exsurgens, Domine, misereberis Sion, quia venit tempus miserendi ejus.

The Church then gives us the history of the Passion according to St. Luke. This Evangelist mentions several details not given by Saints Matthew and Mark, which will assist us to a fuller understanding of the divine mystery of the Sufferings and Sacrifice of the Man-God.

THE PASSION AND GOSPEL.

The Passion of our Lord Jesus Christ according to Luke.

Passio Domini nostri Jesu Christi secundum Lucam.

Ch. XXII. and XXIII.

Cap. XXII. et XXIII.

At that time : The feast of Unleavened Bread, which is called the Pasch, was at hand. And the chief priests and the scribes sought how they might

In illo tempore : Appropinquabat dies festus Azymorum, qui dicitur Pascha : et quærebant principes sacerdotum et scribæ, quomodo Jesum interficerent: timebant vero plebem. Intravit autem Satanas in Judam, qui cognominabatur Iscariotes, unum de duodecim; et abiit et locutus est cum principibus sacerdotum et magistratibus, quemadmodum illum traderet eis. Et gavisi sunt: et pacti sunt pecuniam illi dare. Et spopondit. Et quærebat opportunitatem ut traderet illum sine turbis.

Venit autem dies Azymorum, in qua necesse erat occidi Pascha. Et misit Petrum et Joannem, dicens: Euntes parate nobis Pascha, ut manducemus. At illi dixerunt: Ubi vis paremus? Et dixit ad eos: Ecce introeuntibus vobis in civitatem, occurret vobis homo quidam amphoram aquæ portans; sequimini eum in domum, in quam intrat, et dicetis patrifamilias domus: Dicit tibi Magister: Ubi est diversorium, ubi Pascha cum discipulis meis manducem? Et ipse ostendet vobis cœnaculum magnum stratum, et ibi parate.

Euntes autem invenerunt sicut dixit illis: et paraverunt Pascha. Et cum facta esset hora, discubuit, et duodecim Apostoli cum eo: et ait illis: Desiderio desideravi hoc Pascha manducare vobiscum, antequam patiar. Dico enim vobis: quia ex hoc non

put Jesus to death; but they feared the people. And Satan entered into Judas, who was surnamed Iscariot, one of the twelve; and he went, and discoursed with the chief priests and the magistrates, how he might betray him to them. And they were glad, and covenanted to give him money. And he promised; and he sought opportunity to betray him in the absence of the multitude.

And the day of the unleavened bread came, on which it was necessary that the Pasch should be killed. And he sent Peter and John, saying: Go and prepare us the Pasch, that we may eat. But they said: Where wilt thou that we prepare? And he said to them: Behold, as you go into the city, there shall meet you a man carrying a pitcher of water; follow him into the house where he entereth in, and you shall say to the good man of the house: The Master saith to thee: Where is the guest-chamber, where I may eat the Pasch with my disciples? and he will shew you a large dining-room furnished; and there prepare.

And they going, found as he had said to them, and they made ready the Pasch; and when the hour was come, he sat down, and the twelve apostles with him. And he said to them: With desire I have desired to eat this Pasch with you before I suffer. For I say to you, that from this time I will not eat it, till it be fulfilled in the kingdom of God. And having taken the chalice he gave thanks, and said: Take and divide it among you. For I say to you, that I will not drink of the fruit of the vine, till the kingdom of God come. And taking bread, he gave thanks, and brake, and gave to them, saying: This is my Body, which is given to you: do this for a commemoration of me. In like manner the chalice also, after he had supped, saying: This is the chalice, the new testament of my Blood, which shall be shed for you. But yet behold, the hand of him that betrayeth me is with me on the table. And the Son of Man indeed goeth according to that which is determined; but yet wo to that man by whom he shall be betrayed. And they began to enquire among themselves which of them it was that should do this thing.

And there was also a strife amongst them, which of them should seem to be greater. And he said to them: The kings of the Gentiles lord it over them; and they that have power over them, are called beneficent. But you not so; but he that is the greater among you, let him be as the younger; and he that is the leader, as he that serveth. For which is greater, he that sitteth at table, or he that serveth? Is not he that sitteth at table? But I am in the midst of you, as he that serveth; and you are they who

manducabo illud, donec impleatur in regno Dei. Et accepto calice, gratias egit, et dixit: Accipite, et dividite inter vos. Dico enim vobis: quod non bibam de generatione vitis, donec regnum Dei veniat. Et accepto pane, gratias egit, et fregit, et dedit eis, dicens: Hoc est corpus meum, quod pro vobis datur. Hoc facite in meam commemorationem. Similiter et calicem, postquam cœnavit, dicens: Hic est calix novum testamentum in sanguine meo, qui pro vobis fundetur. Verumtamen ecce manus tradentis me, mecum est in mensa. Et quidem Filius hominis, secundum quod definitum est, vadit: verumtamen væ homini illi, per quem tradetur. Et ipsi cœperunt quærere inter se, quis esset ex eis, qui hoc facturus esset.

Facta est autem et contentio inter eos, quis eorum videretur esse major. Dixit autem eis: Reges gentium dominantur eorum: et qui potestatem habent super eos, benefici vocantur. Vos autem non sic: sed qui major est in vobis fiat sicut minor; et qui præcessor est, sicut ministrator. Nam quis major est, qui recumbit, an qui ministrat? Nonne qui recumbit? Ego autem in medio vestrum sum, sicut qui ministrat: vos autem estis, qui permansistis mecum in tentationibus meis.

Et ego dispono vobis, sicut disposuit mihi Pater meus regnum : ut edatis et bibatis super mensam meam in regno meo, et sedeatis super thronos, judicantes duodecim tribus Israël. Ait autem Dominus : Simon, Simon, ecce Satanas expetivit vos, ut cribraret sicut triticum. Ego autem rogavi pro te, ut non deficiat fides tua : et tu aliquando conversus, confirma fratres tuos. Qui dixit ei : Domine, tecum paratus sum, et in carcerem et in mortem ire. At ille dixit : Dico tibi Petre, non cantabit hodie gallus, donec ter abneges nosse me. Et dixit eis : Quando misi vos sine sacculo et pera et calceamentis, numquid aliquid defuit vobis? At illi dixerunt: Nihil. Dixit ergo eis: Sed nunc, qui habet, sacculum tollat similiter et peram. Et qui non habet, vendat tunicam suam et emat gladium. Dico enim vobis, quoniam adhuc hoc, quod scriptum est, oportet impleri in me: Et cum iniquis deputatus est. Etenim ea quæ sunt de me, finem habent. At illi dixerunt : Domine, ecce duo gladii hic. At ille dixit eis : Satis est.

Et egressus ibat secundum consuetudinem in montem Olivarum : secuti sunt autem illum et discipuli. Et cum pervenisset ad locum, dixit illis : Orate, ne intretis

have continued with me in my temptations. And I dispose to you, as my Father hath disposed to me, a kingdom : that you may eat and drink at my table in my kingdom ; and may sit upon thrones judging the twelve tribes of Israel. And the Lord said : Simon, Simon, behold Satan hath desired to have you, that he may sift you as wheat. But I have prayed for thee that thy faith fail not : and thou, being once converted, confirm thy brethren. Who said to him: Lord, I am ready to go with thee, both into prison, and to death. And he said : I say to thee, Peter, the cock shall not crow this day, till thou thrice deniest that thou knowest me. And he said to them : When I sent you without purse, and scrip, and shoes, did you want any thing? But they said : Nothing. Then said he to them : But now he that hath a purse, let him take it, and likewise a scrip : and he that hath no sword, let him sell his coat, and buy one. For I say to you, that this that is written must yet be fulfilled in me, "And he was reckoned among "the wicked :" for the things concerning me have an end. But they said : Lord, here are two swords. And he said to them : It is enough.

And going out, he went according to his custom to the mount of Olives. And his disciples also followed him. And when he was come to the place, he said to them : Pray,

WEDNESDAY IN HOLY WEEK.

lest you enter into temptation. And he was withdrawn away from them a stone's cast; and kneeling down he prayed, saying: Father, if thou wilt, remove this chalice from me; but yet not my will, but thine be done. And there appeared to him an Angel from heaven, strengthening him. And being in an agony, he prayed the longer. And his sweat became as drops of blood trickling down upon the ground. And when he rose up from prayer, and was come to his disciples, he found them sleeping for sorrow. And he said to them: Why sleep you? Arise, pray, lest you enter into temptation.

As he was yet speaking, behold a multitude; and he that was called Judas, one of the twelve, went before them, and drew near to Jesus to kiss him. And Jesus said to him: Judas, dost thou betray the Son of Man with a kiss? And they that were about him, seeing what would follow, said to him: Lord, shall we strike with the sword? And one of them struck the servant of the High Priest, and cut off his right ear. But Jesus answering, said: Suffer ye thus far. And when he had touched his ear, he healed him. And Jesus said to the chief priests and magistrates of the temple, and the ancients that were come to him: Are you come out, as it were against a thief, with swords and clubs? When I was daily with you in the temple, you did not stretch forth your hands against me.

in tentationem. Et ipse avulsus est ab eis, quantum jactus est lapidis, et positis genibus orabat, dicens: Pater, si vis, transfer calicem istum a me: verumtamen non mea voluntas, sed tua fiat. Apparuit autem illi Angelus de cœlo, confortans eum. Et factus in agonia, prolixius orabat. Et factus est sudor ejus sicut guttæ sanguinis decurrentis in terram. Et cum surrexisset ab oratione, et venisset ad discipulos suos, invenit eos dormientes præ tristitia, et ait illis: Quid dormitis? Surgite, orate, ne intretis in tentationem.

Adhuc eo loquente, ecce turba: et qui vocabatur Judas, unus de duodecim, antecedebat eos: et appropinquavit Jesu, ut oscularetur eum. Jesus autem dixit illi: Juda, osculo Filium hominis tradis? Videntes autem hi, qui circa ipsum erant, quod futurum erat, dixerunt ei: Domine, si percutimus in gladio? Et percussit unus ex illis servum principis sacerdotum: et amputavit auriculam ejus dexteram. Respondens autem Jesus, ait: Sinite usque huc. Et cum tetigisset auriculam ejus, sanavit eum. Dixit autem Jesus ad eos qui venerant ad se, principes sacerdotum et magistratus Templi, et seniores: Quasi ad latronem existis cum gladiis et fustibus. Cum quotidie vobiscum fuerim in Templo, non extendistis manus in me. Sed hæc est hora vestra, et potestas tenebrarum.

Comprehendentes autem eum, duxerunt ad domum principis sacerdotum. Petrus vero sequebatur a longe. Accenso autem igne in medio atrii, et circumsedentibus illis, erat Petrus in medio eorum. Quem cum vidisset ancilla quædam sedentem ad lumen, et eum fuisset intuita, dixit: Et hic cum illo erat. At ille negavit eum, dicens: Mulier, non novi illum. Et post pusillum alius videns eum, dixit: Et tu de illis es. Petrus vero ait: O homo, non sum. Et intervallo facto quasi horæ unius, alius quidam affirmabat, dicens: Vere et hic cum illo erat: nam et Galilæus est. Et ait Petrus: Homo, nescio quid dicis. Et continuo, adhuc illo loquente, cantavit gallus. Et conversus Dominus respexit Petrum. Et recordatus est Petrus verbi Domini, sicut dixerat: Quia priusquam gallus cantet, ter me negabis. Et egressus foras Petrus, flevit amare.

Et viri qui tenebant eum, illudebant ei, cædentes. Et velaverunt eum: et percutiebant faciem ejus, et interrogabant eum, dicentes: Prophetiza, quis est qui te percussit? Et alia multa blasphemantes dicebant in eum. Et ut factus est dies, convenerunt seniores plebis, et principes

But this is your hour, and the power of darkness.

And apprehending him, they led him to the High Priest's house: but Peter followed afar off. And when they had kindled a fire in the midst of the hall, and were sitting about it, Peter was in the midst of them. Whom when a certain servant maid had seen sitting at the light, and had earnestly beheld him, she said: This man also was with him. But he denied, saying: Woman, I know him not. And after a little while, another seeing him, said: Thou also art one of them. But Peter said: O man, I am not. And after the space as it were of one hour, another certain man affirmed, saying: Of a truth this man was also with him: for he is also a Galilean. And Peter said: Man, I know not what thou sayest. And immediately as he was yet speaking, the cock crew. And the Lord turning looked on Peter. And Peter remembered the word of the Lord, as he had said: Before the cock crow, thou shalt deny me thrice. And Peter going out wept bitterly.

And the men that held him, mocked him, and struck him. And they blindfolded him, and smote him on the face. And they asked him, saying: Prophesy, who is it that struck thee? And blaspheming, many other things they said against him. And as soon as it was day, the ancients of the people, and the chief priests,

WEDNESDAY IN HOLY WEEK.

and scribes came together, and they brought him into their council, saying: If thou be the Christ, tell us. And he said to them: If I shall tell you, you will not believe me; and if I shall also ask you, you will not answer me, nor let me go. But hereafter the Son of man shall be sitting on the right hand of the power of God. Then said they all: Art thou the Son of God? And he said: You say that I am. And they said: What need we any further testimony? For ourselves have heard it from his own mouth.

And the whole multitude of them rose up, and led him away to Pilate. And they began to accuse him, saying: We have found this man perverting our nation, and forbidding to give tribute to Cæsar, and saying that he is Christ the King. And Pilate asked him, saying: Art thou the King of the Jews? But he answering, said: Thou sayest it. But Pilate said to the chief priests and to the multitude: I find no cause in this man. But they were more earnest, saying: He stirreth up the people, teaching throughout all Judea, beginning from Galilee to this place. But Pilate hearing Galilee, asked if the man were of Galilee? And when he understood that he was of Herod's jurisdiction, he sent him away to Herod, who himself was also at Jerusalem in those days. And Herod

sacerdotum et scribæ, et duxerunt illum in concilium suum, dicentes: Si tu es Christus, dic nobis. Et ait illis: Si vobis dixero, non credetis mihi: si autem et interrogavero, non respondebitis mihi, neque dimittetis. Ex hoc autem erit Filius hominis sedens a dextris virtutis Dei. Dixerunt autem omnes: Tu ergo es Filius Dei? Qui ait: Vos dicitis, quia ego sum. At illi dixerunt: Quid adhuc desideramus testimonium? Ipsi enim audivimus de ore ejus.

Et surgens omnis multitudo eorum, duxerunt illum ad Pilatum. Cœperunt autem illum accusare, dicentes: Hunc invenimus subvertentem gentem nostram, et prohibentem tributa dare Cæsari, et dicentem se Christum regem esse. Pilatus autem interrogavit eum, dicens: Tu es Rex Judæorum? At ille respondens, ait: Tu dicis. Ait autem Pilatus ad principes sacerdotum et turbas: Nihil invenio causæ in hoc homine. At illi invalescebant, dicentes: Commovet populum, docens per universam Judæam, incipiens a Galilæa usque huc. Pilatus autem audiens Galilæam, interrogavit, si homo Galilæus esset. Et ut cognovit, quod de Herodis potestate esset, remisit eum ad Herodem, qui et ipse Jerosolymis erat illis diebus. Herodes autem viso Jesu, gavisus est valde. Erat enim cupiens ex multo tempore videre eum, eo quod audierat multa de eo: et sperabat signum aliquod videre ab eo fieri. Interrogabat autem eum multis sermonibus. At ipse nihil illi respondebat. Stabant autem principes sacerdotum et scribæ constanter accusantes eum : sprevit autem illum Herodes cum exercitu suo : et illusit indutum veste alba, et remisit ad Pilatum. Et facti sunt amici Herodes et Pilatus in ipsa die : nam antea inimici erant ad invicem. Pilatus autem convocatis principibus sacerdotum, et magistratibus, et plebe, dixit ad illos : Obtulistis mihi hunc hominem, quasi avertentem populum : et ecce ego coram vobis interrogans nullam causam inveni in homine isto ex his, in quibus eum accusatis. Sed neque Herodes : nam remisi vos ad illum : et ecce, nihil dignum morte actum est ei. Emendatum ergo illum dimittam.

Necesse autem habebat dimittere eis, per diem festum, unum. Exclamavit autem simul universa turba, dicens : Tolle hunc, et dimitte nobis Barabbam. Qui erat, propter seditionem quamdam factam in civitate et homicidium, missus in carcerem. Iterum autem Pilatus locutus est ad eos, volens dimittere

seeing Jesus was very glad, for he was desirous of a long time to see him, because he had heard many things of him : and he hoped to see some sign wrought by him. And he questioned him with many words. But he answered him nothing. And the chief priests and the scribes stood by, earnestly accusing him. And Herod with his army set him at naught, and mocked him, putting on him a white garment, and sent him back to Pilate. And Herod and Pilate were made friends that same day ; for before they were enemies to one another. Then Pilate calling together the chief priests, and the magistrates, and the people, said to them : You have brought this man to me as one that perverteth the people : and, behold I, having examined him before you, find no cause in this man touching those things wherein you accuse him. No, nor Herod neither. For I sent you to him, and behold, nothing worthy of death is done to him. I will chastise him therefore and release him.

Now of necessity he was to release unto them one upon the feast day. But the whole multitude together cried out at once, saying : Away with this man, and release unto us Barabbas. Who, for a certain sedition made in the city, and for a murder, was cast into prison. And Pilate again spoke to them, desiring to release Jesus. But they cried out again, saying: Crucify him, crucify him. And he said to them the third time: Why, what evil hath this man done? I find no cause of death in him. I will chastise him therefore, and let him go. But they were instant with loud voices requiring that he might be crucified; and their voices prevailed. And Pilate gave sentence that it should be as they required. And he released unto them him who for murder and sedition had been cast into prison, whom they had desired: but Jesus he delivered up to their will.

And as they led him away, they laid hold on one Simon of Cyrene, coming from the country: and they laid the cross on him to carry after Jesus. And there followed him a great multitude of people, and of women, who bewailed and lamented him. But Jesus turning to them, said: Daughters of Jerusalem, weep not over me, but weep for yourselves, and for your children. For behold the days shall come, wherein they will say, Blessed are the barren, and the wombs that have not borne, and the paps that have not given suck. Then shall they begin to say to the mountains: Fall upon us; and to the hills: Cover us. For if in the green wood they do these things, what shall be done in the dry? And there were also two other malefactors led with him, to be put to death.

Jesum. At illi succlamabant, dicentes: Crucifige, crucifige eum. Ille autem tertio dixit ad illos: Quid enim mali fecit iste? Nullam causam mortis invenio in eo. Corripiam ergo illum, et dimittam. At illi instabant vocibus magnis postulantes, ut crucifigeretur: et invalescebant voces eorum. Et Pilatus adjudicavit fieri petitionem eorum. Dimisit autem illis eum, qui propter homicidium et seditionem missus fuerat in carcerem, quem petebant: Jesum vero tradidit voluntati eorum.

Et cum ducerent eum, apprehenderunt Simonem quemdam Cyrenensem venientem de villa, et imposuerunt illi crucem portare post Jesum. Sequebatur autem illum multa turba populi, et mulierum, quæ plangebant et lamentabantur eum. Conversus autem ad illas Jesus, dixit: Filiæ Jerusalem, nolite flere super me: sed super vos ipsas flete, et super filios vestros. Quoniam ecce venient dies, in quibus dicent: Beatæ steriles, et ventres qui non genuerunt, et ubera quæ non lactaverunt. Tunc incipient dicere montibus: Cadite super nos: et collibus: Operite nos. Quia si in viridi ligno hæc faciunt; in arido quid fiet? Ducebantur autem et alii duo nequam cum eo, ut interficerentur.

Et postquam venerunt in locum, qui vocatur Calvariæ, ibi crucifixerunt eum: et latrones unum a dextris, et alterum a sinistris. Jesus autem dicebat: Pater, dimitte illis: non enim sciunt quid faciunt. Dividentes vero vestimenta ejus, miserunt sortes. Et stabat populus spectans, et deridebant eum principes cum eis, dicentes: Alios salvos fecit: se salvum faciat, si hic est Christus, Dei electus. Illudebant autem ei et milites, accedentes, et acetum offerentes ei et dicentes: Si tu es Rex Judæorum, salvum te fac. Erat autem et superscriptio scripta super eum litteris græcis, et latinis, et hebraicis: Hic est Rex Judæorum.

Unus autem de his, qui pendebant, latronibus, blasphemabat eum, dicens: Si tu es Christus, salvum fac temetipsum, et nos. Respondens autem alter, increpabat eum, dicens: Neque tu times Deum, quod in eadem damnatione es. Et nos quidem juste, nam digna factis recipimus: hic vero nihil mali gessit. Et dicebat ad Jesum: Domine, memento mei, cum veneris in regnum tuum. Et dixit illi Jesus: Amen dico tibi: Hodie mecum eris in Paradiso.

Erat autem fere hora sexta: et tenebræ factæ sunt in universam terram, usque in horam nonam. Et obscuratus est sol: et velum Tem-

And when they were come to the place which is called Calvary, they crucified him there; and the robbers, one on the right hand, and the other on the left. And Jesus said: Father forgive them, for they know not what they do. But they dividing his garments, cast lots. And the people stood beholding, and the rulers with them derided him, saying: He saved others; let him save himself, if he be Christ, the elect of God. And the soldiers also mocked him, coming to him, and offering him vinegar, and saying: If thou be the King of the Jews, save thyself. And there was also a superscription written over him in letters of Greek, and Latin, and Hebrew: This is the King of the Jews.

And one of the robbers who were hanged, blasphemed him, saying: If thou be Christ, save thyself and us. But the other answering, rebuked him, saying: Neither dost thou fear God, seeing thou art under the same condemnation. And we indeed justly, for we receive the due reward of our deeds; but this man hath done no evil. And he said to Jesus: Lord, remember me when thou shalt come into thy kingdom. And Jesus said to him: Amen I say to thee, this day thou shalt be with me in paradise.

And it was almost the sixth hour; and there was darkness over all the earth until the ninth hour. And the sun was darkened; and the veil of the

Temple was rent in the midst. And Jesus crying with a loud voice, said: Father, into thy hands I commend my spirit. And saying this, he gave up the ghost.	pli scissum est medium. Et clamans voce magna Jesus ait: Pater, in manus tuas commendo spiritum meum. Et hæc dicens, exspiravit.

Here, a pause is made, as on Palm Sunday. All kneel down, and if such be the custom of the place, they prostrate and kiss the ground.

Now the centurion seeing what was done, glorified God, saying: Indeed this was a just man. And all the multitude of them that were come together to that sight, and saw the things that were done, returned striking their breast. And all his acquaintance, and the women that had followed him from Galilee, stood afar off, beholding these things.	Videns autem centurio quod factum fuerat, glorificavit Deum, dicens: Vere hic homo justus erat. Et omnis turba eorum, qui simul aderant ad spectaculum istud, et videbant quæ fiebant, percutientes pectora sua, revertebantur. Stabant autem omnes noti ejus a longe et mulieres, quæ secutæ eum erant a Galilæa, hæc videntes.

Here, the Deacon offers the Incense to the Priest, that he may bless it; and, having himself received a blessing, he concludes the history of the Passion, observing the ceremonies used for singing the Gospel at High Mass.

And behold there was a man named Joseph, who was a counsellor, a good and just man, (the same had not consented to their counsel and doing,) of Arimathea, a city of Judea, who also himself looked for the kingdom of God. This man went to Pilate and begged the body of Jesus. And taking him down he wrapped him in fine linen,	Et ecce vir nomine Joseph, qui erat decurio, vir bonus et justus; hic non consenserat consilio et actibus eorum: ab Arimathæa civitate Judææ: qui exspectabat et ipse regnum Dei. Hic accessit ad Pilatum, et petiit corpus Jesu. Et depositum involvit sindone: et posuit eum in monumento exciso, in quo

nondum quisquam positus fuerat.

and laid him in a sepulchre that was hewed in stone, wherein never yet any man had been laid.

The words of the Offertory are those of Jesus, suppliantly beseeching his Eternal Father not to turn away his face from his own Son, who is a prey to every suffering, both of body and mind.

OFFERTORY.

Domine, exaudi orationem meam: et clamor meus ad te perveniat: ne avertas faciem tuam a me.

Hear, O Lord, my prayer; and let my cry come to thee: turn not away thy face from me.

In the Secret, the Church prays that we may have a tender devotion for the Holy Sacrifice of the Mass, in which the Passion of our Saviour is daily commemorated.

SECRET.

Suscipe, quæsumus, Domine, munus oblatum, et dignanter operare: ut quod Passionis Filii tui Domini nostri mysterio gerimus, piis affectibus consequamur. Per eumdem.

Accept, O Lord, we beseech thee, the offerings we have made; and mercifully grant that we may receive, with pious sentiments, what we celebrate in the mystery of the Passion of our Lord. Through the same, &c.

For the other Secrets, see *page* 254.

The Church takes her Communion-Anthem from the same Psalm, which supplied her with the Tract and Offertory, namely the 101st.

COMMUNION.

Potum meum cum fletu

I mingled my drink with

weeping; for having lifted me up, thou hast thrown me down, and I am withered like grass; but thou, O Lord, endurest for ever: thou shalt arise, and have mercy on Sion; because the time to have mercy on her is come.

temperabam: quia elevans allisisti me: et ego sicut fœnum arui: tu autem, Domine, in æternum permanes: tu exsurgens misereberis Sion, quia venit tempus miserendi ejus.

The Death of Jesus should be to us an unceasing motive for confidence in the divine mercy. This confidence is one of the first conditions of our salvation. The Church asks it for us in the Postcommunion.

POSTCOMMUNION.

Grant, O Almighty God, that we may have a lively hope, that thou hast given us eternal life by the temporal death of thy Son, represented in these adorable mysteries. Through the same, &c.

Largire sensibus nostris, omnipotens Deus: ut, per temporalem Filii tui mortem, quam mysteria veneranda testantur, vitam te nobis dedisse perpetuam confidamus. Per eumdem.

See the other Postcommunions in the Mass for Monday, *page* 255.

LET US PRAY.   OREMUS.

Bow down your heads to God.
Look down, O Lord, we beseech thee, on this thy family, for which our Lord Jesus Christ hesitated not to be delivered into the hands of wicked men, and undergo the punishment of the Cross. Who liveth, &c.

Humiliate capita vestra Deo.
Respice, quæsumus, Domine, super hanc familiam tuam: pro qua Dominus noster Jesus Christus non dubitavit manibus tradi nocentium, et crucis subire tormentum. Qui tecum.

THE OFFICE OF TENEBRÆ.

On this and the two following days, the Church anticipates the Night-Office; she celebrates it on the previous evening of each day, and this in order that the Faithful may be present at it. The Matins and Lauds of Maundy Thursday are, therefore, said this afternoon. The Faithful should make every effort to assist at this solemn Office, seeing it is on their account that the Church has changed her usual hours. As to the merit there is in joining in it, there can be no doubt, but that it is to be preferred to any private devotions. The surest means for obtaining favours from God, and winning him to our requests, is to approach him through the Church. And as regards the feelings of devotion wherewith we ought to celebrate the mysteries of these three great Days, the Offices of the Church are, ordinarily speaking, a surer and richer source than the Exercises of Piety composed by men. The soul that feeds on the words and ceremonies of the holy Liturgy, will be all the more disposed to profit by the private devotions she practises at home. The prayer of the Church will thus become the basis, whereon is built the edifice of christian piety during these glorious Anniversaries of our Redemption; and we shall be imitating our forefathers who lived in the Ages of Faith, and who were such admirable Christians, because they lived the life of the Church, by means of the sacred Liturgy.

The Office of Tenebræ for to-day is given below, on Maundy Thursday; the "*Night Office,*" *page* 304.

As an appropriate exercise for the close of this day, we offer our readers the following stanzas from a Hymn of the Greek Liturgy: they allude to the mysteries we have been explaining.

HYMN.

(In Parasceve.)

On this day, Judas leaves his Master, and takes the devil for his guide. The love of money blinds him. He fell from the light, he became darkened; for how could he be said to see, who sold the Light for thirty pieces of silver? But to us he has risen, he that suffered for the world: let us thus cry out unto him: Glory be to thee, that didst endure thy Passion, and hadst compassion, for mankind!

What was it, O Judas! that led thee to betray Jesus? Had he cut thee off from the number of his Apostles? Had he deprived thee of the gift of healing the sick? When he supped with his Apostles, did he drive thee from table? When he washed their feet, did he pass thee by? And yet, thou wast unmindful of these great favours! Thy ungrateful plot has branded thee with infamy: but his incomparable patience and great mercy are worthy of praise.

Say, O ye unjust ones! what is it ye have heard from our Saviour? Did he not expound unto you the Law and the Prophets? Why, therefore, have ye plotted how to

Hodie Judas Magistrum derelinquit, et diabolum assumit: obcæcatur passione amoris pecuniæ; decidit a lumine, obscuratus est ille. Quomodo namque videre poterat ille qui Luminare vendidit triginta argenteis? Sed nobis exortus est ille, qui passus est pro mundo. Ad quem clamemus: Qui passus, et compassus es hominibus, gloria tibi.

Quænam te ratio, Juda, Salvatoris proditorem effecit? Numquid ille ab Apostolorum te choro segregavit? Numquid sanitatum te gratia privavit? Numquid cum cœnaret una cum illis, a mensa te expulit? Numquid aliorum cum lavisset, pedes tuos neglexit? O quantorum factus es immemor beneficiorum! et tuum sane consilium ingratum infamia notatur: illius autem prædicatur incomparabilis patientia et misericordia magna.

Dicite iniqui quidnam a Salvatore nostro audistis? Nonne Legem ac documenta Prophetarum exposuit? Quomodo ergo Verbum quod ex Deo est, et nostras animas redimit, Pilato tradere cogitastis?

Crucifigatur, clamabant ii qui tuis semper muneribus fuerant delectati; petebantque ut malefactorem acciperent pro benefactore interfectores illi justorum. Sed tacebas, Christe, eorum proterviam sustinens: volens pati, nosque salvare, ut hominum amans.

Loquendi libertatem non habemus propter multa peccata nostra; tu ex te genitum exora, Virgo Deipara: multum enim valet deprecatio Matris apud clementiam Domini. Ne despicias peccatorum supplicationes, o castissima; quia misericors est et potens ad salvandum, is qui pro nobis etiam pati sustinuit.

deliver up to Pilate the Word that is from God, and that came to redeem our souls?

They that had enjoyed thy unceasing gifts cried out: *Let him be crucified!* These murderers of such as were innocent, sought thee, that they might treat thee, their benefactor, as an evil-doer. But thou, O Christ! didst bear their wickedness with silence, for thou being the lover of mankind, didst desire to suffer for and save us.

We are prevented from speaking by the multitude of our sins: do thou, O Virgin-Mother of God! pray for us to Him that was born of thee, for the Mother's prayer avails much with the mercy of our Lord. Despise not, O most pure Virgin! the prayers of sinners, for he that refused not even to suffer for us, is merciful, and is able to save us.

We subjoin the following beautiful Preface from the Ambrosian Missal: it expresses, in a most touching manner, the sentiments which a Christian should have within him on this vigil of our Lord's Supper.

PREFACE.

Dignum et justum est, æquum et salutare, nos tibi semper hic et ubique gratias agere, Domine sancte, Pater omnipotens, æterne Deus, per Christum Dominum nostrum, qui innocens pro impiis voluit pati, et pro sceleratis indebite con-

It is meet and just, right and available to salvation, that we should ever, here and in all places, give thanks to thee, O Holy Lord, Almighty Father, Eternal God, through Christ our Lord: who, being innocent, willed to suffer for sinners, and be unjustly con-

WEDNESDAY IN HOLY WEEK.

demned for the guilty. His Death wiped away our crimes, and his Resurrection opened for us the gates of heaven. Through him we beseech thy clemency, that, to-day, thou cleanse us from our sins, and, to-morrow, feed us on the banquet of the venerable Supper; that, to-day, thou receive the confession of our faults, and, to-morrow, grant us the increase of spiritual gifts; that, to-day, thou receive the offering of our fasts, but, to-morrow, introduce us to the feast of the most holy Supper. Through the same Christ our Lord. Amen.

demnari. Cujus mors delicta nostra detersit, et resurrectio Paradisi fores nobis reseravit. Per quem tuam pietatem suppliciter exoramus; ut nos hodie a peccatis emacules; cras vero venerabilis Cœnæ dapibus saties; hodie acceptes nostrorum confessionem delictorum: cras vero tribuas spiritualium incrementa donorum; hodie jejuniorum nostrorum vota suscipias; cras vero nos ad sanctissimæ Cœnæ convivium introducas. Per eumdem Christum Dominum nostrum. Amen.

MAUNDY THURSDAY.

THE NIGHT OFFICE.

THE Office of Matins and Lauds, for the last three days of Holy Week, differs, in many things, from that of the rest of the year. All is sad and mournful, as though it were a funeral-service: nothing could more emphatically express the grief that now weighs down the heart of our holy mother the Church. Throughout all the Office of Thursday, Friday, and Saturday, she forbids herself the use of those formulas of joy and hope, wherewith, on all other days, she begins her praise of God. The *Domine, labia mea aperies (O Lord, thou shalt open my lips):* the *Deus, in adjutorium meum intende (Incline unto mine aid, O God):* the *Gloria Patri,* at the end of the Psalms, Canticles, and Responsories:—all are taken away. So likewise are those soul-stirring additions, which have been gradually made, in the different ages; and nothing is left, but what is essential to the form of the Divine Office:— Psalms, Lessons, and Chants expressive of grief. Each Canonical Hour ends with the Psalm *Miserere,* and with a commemoration of the Death and Cross of our Redeemer.

The name of *Tenebræ* has been given to the Matins and Lauds of the last three days of Holy Week, because this Office used formerly to be celebrated during the night: and even when the hour was anticipated, the name of *Tenebræ* was kept up for another reason; namely, that it began with daylight, but ended after the sun had set. There is an impressive ceremony, peculiar to this Office, which tends to perpetuate its name. There is placed in the Sanctuary, near the Altar, a large triangular candlestick, holding fifteen candles. These candles, and the six that are on the Altar, are of yellow wax, as in the Office for the Dead. At the end of each Psalm or Canticle, one of these fifteen candles is extinguished; but the one, which is placed at the top of the Triangle, is left lighted. During the singing of the *Benedictus*, at Lauds, the Six candles on the Altar are also put out. Then the Master of Ceremonies takes the lighted candle from the Triangle, and holds it upon the Altar, whilst the Choir repeats the antiphon after the Canticle: after which, he hides it behind the Altar during the recitation of the *Miserere* and the Prayer, which follows the Psalm. As soon as this Prayer is finished, a noise is made with the seats of the stalls in the choir, which continues until the candle is brought from behind the Altar, and shows, by its light, that the Office of *Tenebræ* is over.

Let us now study the meaning of these ceremonies. The glory of the Son of God was obscured, and, so to say, eclipsed, by the ignominies he endured during his Passion. He, *the Light of the world*, powerful in word and work, who, but a few days ago, was proclaimed King by the citizens of Jerusalem, is now robbed of all his honours; he is, says Isaias, *the Man of sorrows,—a leper;*[1] he is, says the Royal Prophet, *a worm of the earth, and no man;*[2] he is, as he says of himself, an object of shame even to his own Disciples, for they are all *scandalised* in him,[3]

---

[1] Is. liii. 3, 4.   [2] Ps. xxi. 7.   [3] St. Mark, xiv. 27.

PASSIONTIDE.   X

and abandon him, yea, even Peter protests that he never knew him. This desertion on the part of his Apostles and Disciples is expressed by the candles being extinguished, one after the other, not only on the Triangle, but on the Altar itself. But Jesus, our *Light*, though despised and hidden, is not extinguished. This is signified by the Candle which is momentarily placed on the Altar; it figures our Redeemer suffering and dying on Calvary. In order to express his burial, the candle is hid behind the Altar; its light disappears. A confused noise is heard in the House of God, where all is now darkness. This noise and gloom express the convulsions of nature, when Jesus expired on the Cross;—the earth shook, the rocks were split, the dead came forth from their tombs. But the candle suddenly reappears; its light is as fair as ever; the noise is hushed, and homage is paid to the Conqueror of Death.

After having given these general explanations, we now offer the Faithful the text of the Liturgy, to which we subjoin a few words of commentary, where we think it needed.

MATINS.

After the *Pater, Ave,* and *Credo,* have been said secretly, the first Nocturn begins as follows.

THE FIRST NOCTURN.

The *first* Psalm was written by David, when obliged to flee from the persecution of his son Absalom, who sought his death. It refers to Christ, and describes various incidents of his Passion. The *gall* and *vinegar,* here mentioned, show us that this

Psalm is prophetic, for David never received any such treatment from his enemies.

ANT. The zeal of thy house hath eaten me up; and the reproaches of them that reproached thee, are fallen upon me.	ANT. Zelus domus tuæ comedit me, et opprobria exprobrantium tibi ceciderunt super me.

PSALM 68.

Save me, O God : for the waters are come in even unto my soul.	Salvum me fac, Deus : * quoniam intraverunt aquæ usque ad animam meam.
I stick fast in the mire of the deep : and there is no sure standing.	Infixus sum in limo profundi : * et non est substantia.
I am come into the depth of the sea : and a tempest hath overwhelmed me.	Veni in altitudinem maris : * et tempestas demersit me.
I have laboured with crying : my jaws are become hoarse : my eyes have failed, whilst I hope in my God.	Laboravi clamans, raucæ factæ sunt fauces meæ : * defecerunt oculi mei, dum spero in Deum meum.
They are multiplied above the hairs of my head, who hate me without cause.	Multiplicati sunt super capillos capitis mei : * qui oderunt me gratis.
My enemies are grown strong, who have wrongfully persecuted me : then did I pay that which I took not away.	Confortati sunt qui persecuti sunt me inimici mei injuste : * quæ non rapui, tunc exsolvebam.
O God, thou knowest my foolishness, and my offences, *the offences which I have taken upon myself*, are not hid from thee.	Deus, tu scis insipientiam meam : * et delicta mea a te non sunt abscondita.
Let them not be ashamed for me, who look for thee, O Lord, the Lord of hosts.	Non erubescant in me, qui exspectant te, Domine : * Domine virtutum.
Let them not be confounded on my account, who seek thee, O God of Israel.	Non confundantur super me : * qui quærunt te, Deus Israel.
Because for thy sake I have	Quoniam propter te sus-

tinui opprobrium : * operuit confusio faciem meum.

Extraneus factus sum fratribus meis : * et peregrinus filiis matris meæ.

Quoniam zelus domus tuæ comedit me : * et opprobria exprobrantium tibi ceciderunt super me.

Et operui in jejunio animam meam : * et factum est in opprobrium mihi.

Et posui vestimentum meum cilicium : * et factus sum illis in parabolam.

Adversum me loquebantur qui sedebant in porta : * et in me psallebant qui bibebant vinum.

Ego vero orationem meam ad te, Domine : * tempus beneplaciti Deus.

In multitudine misericordiæ tuæ exaudi me : * in veritate salutis tuæ.

Eripe me de luto, ut non infigar : * libera me ab iis qui oderunt me, et de profundis aquarum.

Non me demergat tempestas aquæ, neque absorbeat me profundum : * neque urgeat super me puteus os suum.

Exaudi me, Domine, quoniam benigna est misericordia tua : * secundum multitudinem miserationum tuarum respice in me.

Et ne avertas faciem tuam a puero tuo : * quoniam tribulor, velociter exaudi me.

Intende animæ meæ et li-

borne reproach : shame hath covered my face.

I am become a stranger to my brethren, and an alien to the sons of my mother.

For the zeal of thy house hath eaten me up : and the reproaches of them that reproached thee, are fallen upon me.

And I covered my soul in fasting : and it made a reproach to me.

And I made hair-cloth my garment : and I became a byeword to them.

They that sat in the gate spoke against me : and they that drank wine made me their song.

But as for me, my prayer is to thee, O Lord : for the time of thy good pleasure, O God.

In the multitude of thy mercy hear me in the truth of thy salvation.

Draw me out of the mire, that I may not stick fast : deliver me from them that hate me, and out of the deep waters.

Let not the tempest of water drown me, nor the deep swallow me up : and let not the pit shut her mouth upon me.

Hear me, O Lord, for thy mercy is kind : look upon me according to the multitude of thy tender mercies.

And turn not away thy face from thy servant : for I am in trouble, hear me speedily.

Attend to my soul, and deliver it; save me because of my enemies.

Thou knowest my reproach, and my confusion, and my shame.

In thy sight are all they that afflict me; my heart hath experienced reproach and misery.

And I looked for one that would grieve together with me, but there was none: and for one that would comfort me, and I found none.

And they gave me gall for my food, and in my thirst they gave me vinegar to drink.

Let their table become as a snare before them, and a recompense, and a stumbling block.

Let their eyes be darkened that they see not: and their back, bow thou down always.

Pour out thy indignation upon them: and let thy wrathful anger take hold of them.

Let their habitation be made desolate: and let there be none to dwell in their tabernacles.

Because they have persecuted him whom thou hast smitten: and they have added to the grief of my wounds.

Add thou iniquity upon their iniquity: and let them not come into thy justice.

Let them be blotted out of the book of the living: and with the just let them not be written.

But I am poor and sorrowful: thy salvation, O God, hath set me up.

bera eam: * propter inimicos meos eripe me.

Tu scis improperium meum, et confusionem meam: * et reverentiam meam.

In conspectu tuo sunt omnes qui tribulant me: * improperium exspectavit cor meum et miseriam.

Et sustinui qui simul contristaretur, et non fuit: * et qui consolaretur, et non inveni.

Et dederunt in escam meam fel: * et in siti mea potaverunt me aceto.

Fiat mensa eorum coram ipsis in laqueum, * et in retributiones, et in scandalum.

Obscurentur oculi eorum ne videant: * et dorsum eorum semper incurva.

Effunde super eos iram tuam: * et furor irae tuae comprehendat eos.

Fiat habitatio eorum deserta: * et in tabernaculis eorum non sit qui inhabitet.

Quoniam quem tu percussisti, persecuti sunt; * et super dolorem vulnerum meorum addiderunt.

Appone iniquitatem super iniquitatem eorum; * et non intrent in justitiam tuam.

Deleantur de libro viventium: * et cum justis non scribantur.

Ego sum pauper et dolens: * salus tua Deus suscepit me.

Laudabo nomen Dei cum cantico : * et magnificabo eum in laude.	I will praise the name of God with a canticle : and I will magnify him with praise.
Et placebit Deo super vitulum novellum : * cornua producentem et ungulas.	And it shall please God better than a young calf, that bringeth forth horns and hoofs.
Videant pauperes et lætentur : * quærite Deum, et vivet anima vestra.	Let the poor see and rejoice : Seek ye God, and your soul shall live.
Quoniam exaudivit pauperes Dominus : * et vinctos suos non despexit.	For the Lord hath heard the poor, and hath not despised his prisoners.
Laudent illum cœli et terra : * mare et omnia reptilia in eis.	Let the heavens and the earth praise him ; the sea, and every thing that creepeth therein.
Quoniam Deus salvam faciet Sion : * et ædificabuntur civitates Juda.	For God will save Sion ; and the cities of Juda shall be built up.
Et inhabitabunt ibi : * et hæreditate acquirent eam.	And they shall dwell there, and acquire it by inheritance.
Et semen servorum ejus possidebit eam : * et qui diligunt nomen ejus habitabunt in ea.	And the seed of his servants shall possess it : and they that love his name shall dwell therein.
ANT. Zelus domus tuæ comedit me, et opprobria exprobrantium tibi ceciderunt super me.	ANT. The zeal of thy house hath eaten me up ; and the reproaches of them that reproached thee, are fallen upon me.

The *second* Psalm was written by David, under the same circumstances as the previous one. He begs God to defend him against the enemies that are seeking to destroy him. This Psalm is prophetic of the lot reserved to the Messias.

ANT. Avertantur retrorsum, et erubescant, qui cogitant mihi mala.	ANT. Let them that devise evils against me be turned back, and let them blush for shame.

PSALM 69.

O God, come to my assistance : O Lord, make haste to help me.

Let them be confounded and ashamed that seek my soul.

Let them be turned backward, and blush for shame, that desire evils to me.

Let them be presently turned away blushing for shame that say to me : 'Tis well, 'tis well.

Let all that seek thee rejoice and be glad in thee : and let such as love thy salvation say always : The Lord be magnified.

But I am needy and poor; O God, help me.

Thou art my helper and my deliverer : O Lord, make no delay.

ANT. Let them that devise evils against me, be turned back, and let them blush for shame.

Deus in adjutorium meum intende : * Domine ad adjuvandum me festina.

Confundantur et revereantur: * qui quærunt animam meam.

Avertantur retrorsum, et erubescant : * qui volunt mihi mala.

Avertantur statim erubescentes : * qui dicunt mihi : Euge, euge.

Exsultent et lætentur in te omnes qui quærunt te : * et dicant semper : Magnificetur Dominus, qui diligunt salutare tuum.

Ego vero egenus et pauper sum : * Deus adjuva me.

Adjutor meus et liberator meus es tu : * Domine ne moreris.

ANT. Avertantur retrorsum, et erubescant, qui cogitant mihi mala.

The *third* Psalm refers to the same period of David's life; but whilst it describes the dangers to which this holy king was exposed, it also expresses the wonderful confidence he had that God would crown him with victory over all his enemies. In its prophetic signification, this Psalm shows us how the Man-God, even in the lowest depths of his anguish, confided in his Father's help.

ANT. Deliver me, O my God, out of the hand of the sinner.

ANT. Deus meus, eripe me de manu peccatoris.

PSALM 70.

In te Domine speravi, non confundar in æternum: * in justitia tua libera me, et eripe me.

Inclina ad me aurem tuam: * et salva me.

Esto mihi in Deum protectorem et in locum munitum: * ut salvum me facias.

Quoniam firmamentum meum: * et refugium meum es tu.

Deus meus, eripe me de manu peccatoris: * et de manu contra legem agentis et iniqui.

Quoniam tu es patientia mea, Domine: * Domine, spes mea a juventute mea.

In te confirmatus sum ex utero: * de ventre matris meæ tu es protector meus.

In te cantatio mea semper: * tamquam prodigium factus sum multis; et tu adjutor fortis.

Repleatur os meum laude, ut cantem gloriam tuam: * tota die magnitudinem tuam.

Ne projicias me in tempore senectutis: * cum defecerit virtus mea, ne derelinquas me.

Quia dixerunt inimici mei mihi: * et qui custodiebant animam meam consilium fecerunt in unum.

Dicentes: Deus dereliquit eum, persequimini et com-

In thee, O Lord, I have hoped, let me never be put to confusion: deliver me in thy justice, and rescue me.

Incline thine ear unto me, and save me.

Be thou unto me a God, a protector, and a place of strength, that thou mayest make me safe.

For thou art my firmament and my refuge.

Deliver me, O my God, out of the hand of the sinner, and out of the hand of the transgressor of the law, and of the unjust.

For thou art my patience, O Lord: my hope, O Lord, from my youth.

By thee have I been confirmed from the womb: from my mother's womb thou art my protector.

Of thee shall I continually sing: I am become unto many as a wonder: but thou art a strong helper.

Let my mouth be filled with praise, that I may sing thy glory: thy greatness all the day long.

Cast me not off in the time of old age, when my strength shall fail, do not thou forsake me.

For my enemies have spoken against me; and they that watched my soul have consulted together,

Saying: God hath forsaken him; pursue and take him,

for there is none to deliver him.

O God, be not thou far from me: O my God, make haste to my help.

Let them be confounded and come to nothing that detract my soul: Let them be covered with confusion and shame that seek my hurt.

But I will always hope: and will add to all thy praise.

My mouth shall show forth thy justice: thy salvation all the day long.

Because I have not known learning, I will enter into the powers of the Lord: O Lord, I will be mindful of thy justice alone.

Thou hast taught me, O God, from my youth, and till now I will declare thy wonderful works.

And unto old age and grey hairs, O God, forsake me not.

Until I show forth thy arm to all the generation that is to come.

Thy power, and thy justice, O God, even to the highest, great things thou hast done; O God, who is like to thee?

How great troubles hast thou showed me, many and grievous: and turning thou hast brought me to life, and hast brought me back again from the depths of the earth.

Thou hast multiplied thy magnificence; and turning to me, thou hast comforted me.

I will also give praise to thee: I will extol thy truth

prehendite eum: * quia non est qui eripiat.

Deus ne elongeris a me:* Deus meus in auxilium meum respice.

Confundantur et deficiant detrahentes animæ meæ: * operiantur confusione et pudore, qui quærunt mala mihi.

Ego autem semper sperabo: * et adjiciam super omnem laudem tuam.

Os meum annuntiavit justitiam tuam: * tota die salutare tuum.

Quoniam non cognovi literaturam, introibo in potentias Domini:* Domine, memorabor justitiæ tuæ solius.

Deus docuisti me a juventute mea: * et usque nunc pronuntiabo mirabilia tua.

Et usque in senectam et senium: * Deus ne derelinquas me.

Donec annuntiem brachium tuum: * generationi omni, quæ ventura est.

Potentiam tuam, et justitiam tuam Deus usque in altissima, quæ fecisti magnalia: * Deus quis similis tibi?

Quantas ostendisti mihi tribulationes multas et malas: et conversus vivificasti me:* et de abyssis terræ iterum reduxisti me.

Multiplicasti magnificentiam tuam: * et conversus consolatus es me.

Nam et ego confitebor tibi in vasis psalmi veritatem

tuam : * Deus, psallam tibi in cithara, Sanctus Israël.

with the instruments of psaltery : O God, I will sing to thee with the harp, thou holy one of Israel.

Exsultabunt labia mea cum cantavero tibi : * et anima mea, quam redemisti.

My lips shall greatly rejoice when I shall sing to thee : and my soul which thou hast redeemed.

Sed et lingua mea tota die meditabitur justitiam tuam : * cum confusi et reveriti fuerint qui quærunt mala mihi.

Yea and my tongue also shall meditate on thy justice all the day : when they shall be confounded and put to shame that seek evils to me.

ANT. Deus meus, eripe me de manu peccatoris.

ANT. Deliver me, O my God, out of the hand of the sinner.

℣. Avertantur retrorsum, et erubescant.

℣. Let them be turned back, and let them blush for shame.

℟. Qui cogitant mihi mala.

℟. That devise evil things against me.

Here is said the *Pater noster*, but all in secret.

The Lessons of the first Nocturn, for each of these three days, are taken from the Lamentations of Jeremias, which describe the miserable state of Jerusalem, when, in punishment for her idolatry, her people were led captive into Babylon. How visibly is the anger of God shown in these ruins of the great City, over which Jeremias pours forth his inspired words of mourning! And yet, this first disaster was but a figure of a more terrible one to come. When the Assyrians took Jerusalem, and well nigh reduced her to a wilderness, she lost not her name; and the very Prophet, who laments over her destruction, had foretold that the desolation was not to last beyond seventy years. But, in her second destruction, the faithless City forfeited even her name. Rebuilt by her conquerors, she went, for two hundred years, under the name of *Ælia*

Adriana; and when, after peace was granted to the Church, she was again called *Jerusalem*, it was not a restitution of honour to Juda, but a homage that was paid to the God of the Christians, whom Juda had crucified in her capital. Neither St. Helen's and Constantine's devotedness, nor the heroism of the Crusaders, could raise Jerusalem to the position of even a second-rate City; she is doomed to be a slave, and a slave to infidels, to all but the very end of time. She drew this frightful curse upon herself by the crimes she committed against the Son of God; and nothing could give us a better idea of the enormity of those crimes, than the plaintive words of such a Prophet as Jeremias. This is the reason that his Lamentations are chosen for the Lessons of Tenebræ. The mournful chant, to which they are sung, is probably the one used by the Jews themselves. The names of the letters of the Hebrew alphabet, which divide the stanzas of this inspired Elegy, show us that it was written by the Prophet as an Acrostic. The Jewish custom of singing these Lamentations has been retained in the Christian Church.

FIRST LESSON.

Here beginneth the Lamentation of Jeremias the Prophet.	Incipit Lamentatio Jeremiæ Prophetæ.
Ch. I.	*Cap. I.*
ALEPH. How doth the city sit solitary, that was full of people: how is the mistress of nations become as a widow: the princess of provinces made tributary?	ALEPH. Quomodo sedet sola civitas plena populo? facta est quasi vidua domina gentium, princeps provinciarum facta est sub tributo.
BETH. Weeping she hath wept in the night, and her tears are on her cheeks: there is none to comfort her among all them that were dear to her:	BETH. Plorans ploravit in nocte, et lacrymæ ejus in maxillis ejus: non est qui consoletur eam ex omnibus charis ejus. Omnes amici

ejus spreverunt eam, et facti sunt ei inimici.

GHIMEL. Migravit Judas propter afflictionem, et multitudinem servitutis: habitavit inter gentes, nec invenit requiem. Omnes persecutores ejus apprehenderunt eam inter angustias.

DALETH. Viæ Sion lugent, eo quod non sint qui veniant ad solemnitatem: omnes portæ ejus destructæ, sacerdotes ejus gementes, virgines ejus squalidæ, et ipsa oppressa amaritudine.

HE. Facti sunt hostes ejus in capite, inimici ejus locupletati sunt: quia Dominus locutus est super eam propter multitudinem iniquitatum ejus. Parvuli ejus ducti sunt in captivitatem, ante faciem tribulantis.

Jerusalem, Jerusalem, convertere ad Dominum Deum tuum.

℟. In monte Oliveti oravit ad Patrem: Pater, si fieri potest, transeat a me calix iste: * Spiritus quidem promptus est, caro autem infirma.

℣. Vigilate, et orate, ut non intretis in tentationem.

* Spiritus quidem promptus est; caro autem infirma.

all her friends have despised her, and are become her enemies.

GHIMEL. Juda hath removed her dwelling place because of her affliction, and the greatness of her bondage: she hath dwelt among the nations, and she hath found no rest: her persecutors have taken her in the midst of straits.

DALETH. The ways of Sion mourn, because there are none that come to the solemn feast: all her gates are broken down: her priests sigh, her virgins are in affliction, and she is oppressed with bitterness.

HE. Her adversaries are become her lords, her enemies are enriched: because the Lord hath spoken against her for the multitude of her iniquities: her children are led into captivity, before the face of the oppressor.

Jerusalem, Jerusalem, be converted to the Lord thy God.

℟. He prayed to his Father on Mount Olivet: Father, if it be possible, let this chalice pass from me: * The spirit, indeed, is willing, but the flesh is weak.

℣. Watch and pray, that ye may not enter into temptation.

* The Spirit, indeed, is willing, but the flesh is weak.

SECOND LESSON.

VAU. Et egressus est a filia Sion omnis decor ejus:

VAU. And from the daughter of Sion all her beauty is

departed: her princes are become like rams that find no pasture; and they are gone away without strength before the face of the pursuer.

ZAIN. Jerusalem hath remembered the days of her affliction and transgression of all her desirable things, which she had from the days of old, when her people fell in the enemy's hand, and there was no helper: the enemies have seen her, and have mocked at her Sabbaths.

HETH. Jerusalem hath grievously sinned, therefore is she become vagabond: all that honoured her, have despised her, because they have seen her shame: but she sighed and turned backward.

TETH. Her filthiness is on her feet, and she hath not remembered her end: she is wonderfully cast down, not having a comforter: behold, O Lord, my affliction, because the enemy is lifted up.

Jerusalem, Jerusalem, be converted to the Lord thy God.

℟. My soul is sorrowful even to death: stay here, and watch with me: now ye shall see a multitude, that will surround me: * Ye shall take to flight, and I will go to be sacrificed for you.

℣. Behold the hour is at hand, when the Son of Man shall be delivered into the hands of sinners.

* Ye shall take to flight, and

facti sunt principes ejus velut arietes non invenientes pascua, et abierunt absque fortitudine, ante faciem subsequentis.

ZAÏN. Recordata est Jerusalem dierum afflictionis suæ, et prævaricationis omnium desiderabilium suorum, quæ habuerat a diebus antiquis, cum caderet populus ejus in manu hostili, et non esset auxiliator. Viderunt eam hostes, et deriserunt sabbata ejus.

HETH. Peccatum peccavit Jerusalem; propterea instabilis facta est. Omnes qui glorificabant eam, spreverunt illam: quia viderunt ignominiam ejus. Ipsa autem gemens conversa est retrorsum.

TETH. Sordes ejus in pedibus ejus, nec recordata est finis sui. Deposita est vehementer, non habens consolatorem. Vide, Domine, afflictionem meam: quoniam erectus est inimicus.

Jerusalem, Jerusalem, convertere ad Dominum Deum tuum.

℟. Tristis est anima mea usque ad mortem: sustinete hic, et vigilate mecum: nunc videbitis turbam quæ circumdabit me: * Vos fugam capietis, et ego vadam immolari pro vobis.

℣. Ecce appropinquat hora, et Filius hominis tradetur in manus peccatorum.

* Vos fugam capietis, et

ego vadam immolari pro vobis. | I will go to be sacrificed for you.

THIRD LESSON.

IOD. Manum suam misit hostis ad omnia desiderabilia ejus: quia vidit gentes ingressas sanctuarium suum, de quibus præceperas ne intrarent in ecclesiam tuam.

JOD. The enemy hath put out his hand to all her desirable things: for she hath seen the Gentiles enter into her sanctuary, of whom thou gavest commandment that they should not enter into thy church.

CAPH. Omnis populus ejus gemens, et quærens panem, dederunt pretiosa quæque pro cibo ad refocillandam animam. Vide, Domine, et considera, quoniam facta sum vilis.

CAPH. All her people sigh, they seek bread: they have given all their precious things for food to relieve the soul. See, O Lord, and consider, for I am become vile.

LAMED. O vos omnes, qui transitis per viam, attendite, et videte si est dolor sicut dolor meus: quoniam vindemiavit me, ut locutus est Dominus in die iræ furoris sui.

LAMED. O all ye that pass by the way, attend, and see if there be any sorrow like to my sorrow: for he hath made a vintage of me, as the Lord spoke in the day of his fierce anger.

MEM. De excelso misit ignem in ossibus meis, et erudivit me: expandit rete pedibus meis, convertit me retrorsum: posuit me desolatam, tota die mœrore confectam.

MEM. From above he hath sent fire into my bones, and hath chastised me: he hath spread a net for my feet, he hath turned me back; he hath made me destitute, and spent with sorrow all the day long.

NUN. Vigilavit jugum iniquitatum mearum: in manu ejus convolutæ sunt, et impositæ collo meo: infirmata est virtus mea: dedit me Dominus in manu, de qua non potero surgere.

NUN. The yoke of my iniquities hath watched for me: they are folded together in his hand, and put on my neck: my strength is weakened: the Lord hath delivered me into a hand, out of which I am not able to rise.

Jerusalem, Jerusalem, convertere ad Dominum Deum tuum.

Jerusalem, Jerusalem, be converted to the Lord thy God.

℞. Lo! we have seen him as one not having beauty nor comeliness; there is no sightliness in him: he hath borne our sins, and grieves for us: and he was wounded for our iniquities: * By his wounds we have been healed.

℣. Surely he hath borne our infirmities, and carried our sorrows.
* By his wounds we have been healed.
Here is repeated: Lo! we have seen.

℞. Ecce vidimus eum non habentem speciem, neque decorem; aspectus ejus in eo non est: hic peccata nostra portavit, et pro nobis dolet: ipse autem vulneratus est propter iniquitates nostras: * Cujus livore sanati sumus.

℣. Vere languores nostros ipse tulit, et dolores nostros ipse portavit.
* Cujus livore sanati sumus.
Here is repeated: Ecce vidimus.

THE SECOND NOCTURN.

The *fourth* Psalm, which celebrates, in such glowing terms, the glories of the Son of David, would seem, at first sight, to be inappropriate for this office, which commemorates only his humiliations. We sang this fine Canticle on the night of our Emmanuel's birth at Bethlehem; how comes it to be among our present chants, which are all so sorrowful? The Church has chosen it, because one of the glories here prophesied of Jesus is, that *he shall deliver the poor from the mighty; and the needy that had no helper.* Mankind is this *poor* one; Satan is the *mighty* one; Jesus is about to *deliver* us from his power, by suffering what we have deserved by our sins.

ANT. The Lord hath delivered the poor from the mighty; and the needy that had no helper.

ANT. Liberavit Dominus pauperem a potente, et inopem, cui non erat adjutor.

PSALM 71.

Give to the king thy judgment, O God; and to the king's son thy justice.
To judge thy people with justice, and thy poor with judgment.

Deus judicium tuum regi da: * et justitiam tuam filio regis.
Judicare populum tuum in justitia: * et pauperes tuos in judicio.

Suscipiant montes pacem populo: * et colles justitiam.	Let the mountains receive peace for the people, and the hills justice.
Judicabit pauperes populi, et salvos faciet filios pauperum: * et humiliabit calumniatorem.	He shall judge the poor of the people, and he shall save the children of the poor, and he shall humble the oppressor.
Et permanebit cum sole, et ante lunam: * in generatione et generationem.	And his kingdom on earth shall continue with the sun; and before the moon, throughout all generations.
Descendet sicut pluvia in vellus: * et sicut stillicidia stillantia super terram.	He shall come down like rain upon the fleece: and as showers falling gently upon the earth.
Orietur in diebus ejus justitia, et abundantia pacis: * donec auferatur luna.	In his days justice shall spring up, and abundance of peace: till the moon be taken away.
Et dominabitur a mari usque ad mare: * et a flumine usque ad terminos orbis terrarum.	And he shall rule from sea to sea: and from the river *Jordan* to the ends of the earth.
Coram illo procident Æthiopes: * et inimici ejus terram lingent.	Before him the Ethiopians shall fall down: and his enemies shall lick the ground.
Reges Tharsis et insulæ munera offerent: * reges Arabum et Saba dona adducent.	The kings of Tharsis and the islands shall offer presents: the kings of the Arabians and of Saba shall bring gifts.
Et adorabunt eum omnes reges terræ: * omnes gentes servient ei.	And all kings of the earth shall adore him; all nations shall serve him.
Quia liberabit pauperem a potente: * et pauperem cui non erat adjutor.	For he shall deliver the poor from the mighty: and the needy that had no helper.
Parcet pauperi et inopi: * et animas pauperum salvas faciet.	He shall spare the *human race, which is* poor and needy: and he shall save the souls of the poor.
Ex usuris et iniquitate redimet animas eorum: * et honorabile nomen eorum coram illo.	He shall redeem their souls from the usuries and iniquity of *Satan:* and their name shall be honourable in his sight.
Et vivet, et dabitur ei de	And he shall live, and to

him shall be given of the gold of Arabia: for him they shall always adore; they shall bless him all the day.

He is the Bread of Life; therefore, under his reign, there shall be a firmament on the earth, on the tops of mountains: above Libanus shall the fruit thereof be exalted: and they of the city shall flourish like the grass of the earth.

Let his name be blessed for evermore: his name continueth before the sun.

And in him shall all the tribes of the earth be blessed: all nations shall magnify him.

Blessed be the Lord the God of Israel, who alone doth wonderful things.

And blessed be the name of his majesty for ever: and the whole earth shall be filled with his majesty. So be it. So be it.

ANT. The Lord hath delivered the poor from the mighty; and the needy that had no helper.

auro Arabiæ, et adorabunt de ipso semper: * tota die; benedicent ei.

Et erit firmamentum in terra in summis montium, superextolletur super Libanum fructus ejus: * et florebunt de civitate sicut fœnum terræ.

Sit nomen ejus benedictum in sæcula: * ante solem permanet nomen ejus.

Et benedicentur in ipso omnes tribus terræ: * omnes gentes magnificabunt eum.

Benedictus Dominus Deus Israel: * qui facit mirabilia solus.

Et benedictum nomen majestatis ejus in æternum: * et replebitur majestate ejus omnis terra: fiat, fiat.

ANT. Liberavit Dominus pauperem a potente, et inopem, cui non erat adjutor.

The *fifth* Psalm conveys a moral teaching, which, if listened to, would correct many a false judgment of the world. It often happens that men are shaken at seeing the wicked prosperous, and the virtuous afflicted. It was the temptation which overcame the Apostles, when, seeing their Divine Master in the hands of his enemies, they lost their faith in him as the Messias. The Psalmist owns that he himself was troubled by the same kind of thought; but God enlightened him to see the truth: it is, that if Divine Providence permit iniquity to triumph for a time, the day is sure to come, when he will punish the wicked, and avenge the just that have suffered persecution.

ANT. Cogitaverunt impii, et locuti sunt nequitiam: iniquitatem in excelso locuti sunt.

ANT. The ungodly have thought and spoken wickedness: they have spoken iniquity on high.

PSALM 72.

Quam bonus Israel Deus:* his qui recto sunt corde.

How good is God to Israel, to them that are of a right heart!

Mei autem pene moti sunt pedes: * pene effusi sunt gressus mei:

But my feet were almost moved; my steps had well nigh slipt:

Quia zelavi super iniquos, * pacem peccatorum videns.

Because I had a zeal on occasion of the wicked, seeing the prosperity of sinners.

Quia non est respectus morti eorum: * et firmamentum in plaga eorum.

For there is no regard to their death; nor is there strength in their stripes.

In labore hominum non sunt: * et cum hominibus non flagellabuntur.

They are not in the labour of men; neither shall they be scourged like other men.

Ideo tenuit eos superbia: * operti sunt iniquitate et impietate sua.

Therefore pride hath held them fast: they are covered with their iniquity and their wickedness.

Prodiit quasi ex adipe iniquitas eorum: * transierunt in affectum cordis.

Their iniquity hath come forth, as it were from fatness: they have passed into the affection of the heart.

Cogitaverunt, et locuti sunt nequitiam: * iniquitatem in excelso locuti sunt.

They have thought and spoken wickedness: they have spoken iniquity on high.

Posuerunt in cœlum os suum: * et lingua eorum transivit in terra.

They have set their mouth against heaven: and their tongue hath passed through the earth.

Ideo convertetur populus meus hic: * et dies pleni invenientur in eis.

Therefore will my people return here: and full days shall be found in them.

Et dixerunt. Quomodo scit Deus: * et si est scientia in excelso?

And they said: How doth God know, and is there knowledge in the Most High?

Behold these are sinners; and yet abounding in the world, they have obtained riches.

And I said: Then have I in vain justified my heart, and washed my hands among the innocent.

And I have been scourged all the day, and my chastisement hath been in the mornings.

If I said: I will speak thus: behold I should condemn the generation of thy children.

I studied that I might know this thing: it is as labour in my sight:

Until I go into the sanctuary of God, and understand concerning their last ends.

But indeed for deceits thou hast put it to them: when they were lifted up, thou hast cast them down.

How are they brought to desolation! they have suddenly ceased to be: they have perished by reason of their iniquity.

As the dream of them that awake, O Lord, so in thy city thou shalt bring their image to nothing.

For my heart hath been inflamed, and my reins have been changed: and I am brought to nothing, and I knew not.

I am become as a beast before thee: and I am always with thee.

Thou hast held me by my right hand: and by thy will thou hast conducted me: and with glory thou hast received me.

Ecce ipsi peccatores, et abundantes in sæculo: * obtinuerunt divitias.

Et dixi: Ergo sine causa justificavi cor meum: * et lavi inter innocentes manus meas.

Et fui flagellatu stota die: * et castigatio mea in matutinis.

Si dicebam: Narrabo sic: * ecce nationem filiorum tuorum reprobavi.

Existimabam ut cognoscerem hoc: * labor est ante me:

Donec intrem in sanctuarium Dei: * et intelligam in novissimis eorum.

Verumtamen propter dolos posuisti eis: * dejecisti eos dum allevarentur.

Quomodo facti sunt in desolationem, subito defecerunt: * perierunt propter iniquitatem suam.

Velut somnium surgentium, Domine: * in civitate tua imaginem ipsorum ad nihilum rediges.

Quia inflammatum est cor meum, et renes mei commutati sunt: * et ego ad nihilum redactus sum, et nescivi.

Ut jumentum factus sum apud te: * et ego semper tecum.

Tenuisti manum dexteram meam: et in voluntate tua deduxisti me: * et cum gloria suscepisti me.

Quid enim mihi est in cœlo : * et a te quid volui super terram?

Defecit caro mea, et cor meum : * Deus cordis mei, et pars mea Deus in æternum.

Quia ecce, qui elongant se a te, peribunt : * perdidisti omnes, qui fornicantur abs te.

Mihi autem adhærere Deo bonum est : * ponere in Domino Deo spem meam.

Ut annuntiem omnes prædicationes tuas : * in portis filiæ Sion.

ANT. Cogitaverunt impii, et locuti sunt nequitiam : iniquitatem in excelso locuti sunt.

For what have I in heaven? and besides thee, what do I desire upon earth?

For thee my flesh and my heart hath fainted away : thou art the God of my heart, and the God that is my portion for ever.

For behold they that go far from thee shall perish : thou hast destroyed all them that are disloyal to thee.

But it is good for me to stick close to my God, to put my hope in the Lord God.

That I may declare all thy praises in the gates of the daughter of Sion.

ANT. The ungodly have thought and spoken wickedness : they have spoken iniquity on high.

The *sixth* Psalm is a reproach made to the enemies of the Divine Worship. The Jews used it, for many ages, against the Gentiles; the Christians now apply it to the Synagogue, which, after having crucified the Son of God, did its utmost to destroy his Church, by putting many of her children to death, and forbidding the Apostles to preach the name of Christ.

ANT. Exsurge, Domine, et judica causam meam.

ANT. Arise, O Lord, and judge my cause.

PSALM 73.

Ut quid Deus repulisti in finem : * iratus est furor tuus super oves pascuæ tuæ?

Memor esto congregationis tuæ : * quam possedisti ab initio.

Redemisti virgam hæredi-

O God, why hast thou cast us off unto the end? why is thy wrath enkindled against the sheep of thy pasture?

Remember thy congregation, which thou hast possessed from the beginning.

The sceptre of thy inheritance which thou hast redeemed: Mount Sion, in which thou hast dwelt.

Lift up thy hands against their pride unto the end : see what things the enemy hath done wickedly in the sanctuary.

And they that hate thee have made their boasts, in the midst of thy solemnity.

They have set up their ensigns for signs ; and they knew not: both in the going out and on the highest top.

As with axes in a wood of trees, they have cut down at once the gates thereof : with axe and hatchet they have brought it down.

They have set fire to thy sanctuary : they have defiled the dwelling-place of thy name on the earth.

They said in their heart, the whole kindred of them together : Let us abolish all the festival days of God from the land.

Our signs we have not seen, there is now no prophet : and he will know us no more.

How long, O God, shall the enemy reproach ? Is the adversary to provoke thy name for ever ?

Why dost thou turn away thy hand ; and thy right hand out of the midst of thy bosom for ever ?

But God is our king before ages : he hath wrought salvation in the midst of the earth.

Thou by thy strength didst make the sea firm : thou didst crush the heads of the dragons in the waters.

tatis tuæ : * mons Sion in quo habitasti in eo.

Leva manus tuas in superbias eorum in finem : * quanta malignatus est inimicus in sancto.

Et gloriati sunt qui oderunt te : * in medio solemnitatis tuæ.

Posuerunt signa sua, signa : * et non cognoverunt sicut in exitu super summum.

Quasi in silva lignorum securibus exciderunt januas ejus in idipsum : * in securi et ascia dejecerunt eam.

Incenderunt igni sanctuarium tuum : * in terra polluerunt tabernaculum nominis tui.

Dixerunt in corde suo cognatio eorum simul : * Quiescere faciamus omnes dies festos Dei a terra.

Signa nostra non vidimus, jam non est propheta : * et nos non cognoscet amplius.

Usquequo Deus improperabit inimicus : * irritat adversarius nomen tuum in finem ?

Ut quid avertis manum tuam, et dexteram tuam : * de medio sinu tuo in finem ?

Deus autem Rex noster ante sæcula : * operatus est salutem in medio terræ.

Tu confirmasti in virtute tua mare : * contribulasti capita draconum in aquis.

Tu confregisti capita draconis : * dedisti eum escam populis Æthiopum.

Tu dirupisti fontes, et torrentes : * tu siccasti fluvios Ethan.

Tuus est dies, et tua est nox : * tu fabricatus es auroram et solem.

Tu fecisti omnes terminos terræ : * æstatem et ver tu plasmasti ea.

Memor esto hujus, inimicus improperavit Domino: * et populus iisipiens incitavit nomen tuum.

Ne tradas bestiis animas confitentes tibi : * et animas pauperum tuorum ne obliviscaris in finem.

Respice in testamentum tuum : * quia repleti sunt, qui obscurati sunt, terræ domibus iniquitatum.

Ne avertatur humilis factus confusus : * pauper et inops laudabunt nomen tuum.

Exsurge Deus judica causam tuam : * memor esto improperiorum tuorum, eorum quæ ab insipiente sunt tota die.

Ne obliviscaris voces inimicorum tuorum : * superbia eorum qui te oderunt, ascendit semper.

ANT. Exsurge, Domine, et judica causam meam.

℣. Deus meus, eripe me de manu peccatoris.

Thou hast broken the heads of the dragon : thou hast given him to be meat for the Ethiopian people.

Thou hast broken up the fountains, and the torrents : thou hast dried up the Ethan rivers.

Thine is the day, and thine is the night : thou hast made the moon and the sun.

Thou hast made all the borders of the earth : the summer and the spring were formed by thee.

Remember this, the enemy hath reproached the Lord : and a foolish people hath provoked thy name.

Deliver not up to beasts the souls that confess to thee : and forget not to the end the souls of thy poor.

Have regard to thy covenant : for they that are obscure of the earth have been filled with the dwellings of iniquity.

Let not the humble be turned away with confusion : the poor and needy shall praise thy name.

Arise, O God, judge thy own cause : remember the reproaches with which the foolish man hath reproached thee all the day.

Forget not the voices of thy enemies : the pride of them that hate thee ascendeth continually.

ANT. Arise, O Lord, and judge my cause.

℣. O my God, deliver me out of the hand of the sinner.

MAUNDY THURSDAY: TENEBRÆ.

℟. And out of the hand of the transgressor of the law, and of the unjust.

℟. Et de manu contra legem agentis et iniqui.

Here is said, in secret, the *Pater noster*.

For the Lessons of the second Nocturn, the Church reads, each of these three days, a passage from St. Augustine's *Enarrations* on the Psalms, which are prophetic of our Lord's Passion.

FOURTH LESSON.

From the treatise of Saint Augustine, Bishop, upon the Psalms.

Ex tractatu Sancti Augustini Episcopi super Psalmos.

Ps. LIV.

Ps. LIV.

Hear my prayer, O God, and despise not my petition: attend to me and hear me. These are the words of a man in trouble, solicitude, and affliction. He prays in his great sufferings, desiring to be freed from some evil. Let us now see what evil he lies under: and when he has told it to us, let us acknowledge ourselves in it: that by partaking of the affliction, we may join in his prayer. *I am become sorrowful in my exercise,* says he, *and I am troubled.* Where is he become *sorrowful?* where is he *troubled?* He says, *In my exercise.* He speaks of the wicked men whom he suffers, and calls such suffering of wicked men his *exercise.* Think not that the wicked are in the world for nothing, and that God works no good with them. Every wicked man lives, either to

Exaudi, Deus, orationem meam, et ne despexeris deprecationem meam: intende mihi, et exaudi me. Satagentis, solliciti, in tribulatione positi verba sunt ista. Orat multa patiens, de malo liberari desiderans. Superest ut videamus in quo malo sit; et cum dicere cœperit, agnoscamus ibi nos esse: ut communicata tribulatione, conjungamus orationem. Contristatus sum, inquit, in exercitatione mea, et conturbatus sum. Ubi contristatus? ubi conturbatus? In exercitatione mea, inquit. Homines malos, quos patitur, commemoratus est: eamdemque passionem malorum hominum, exercitationem suam dixit. Ne putetis gratis esse malos in hoc mundo, et nihil boni de illis agere Deum. Omnis malus, aut ideo vivit, ut corrigatur: aut ideo vivit, ut per illum bonus exerceatur.

℟. Amicus meus osculi me tradidit signo: quem osculatus fuero, ipse est, tenete eum: hoc malum fecit signum, qui per osculum adimplevit homicidium. * Infelix prætermisit pretium sanguinis, et in fine laqueo se suspendit.

℣. Bonum erat ei, si natus non fuisset homo ille.

* Infelix prætermisit pretium sanguinis, et in fine laqueo se suspendit.

amend his life, or to *exercise* the good man.

℟. My friend hath betrayed me by the sign of a kiss: Whom I shall kiss, that is He; hold him fast: this was the wicked sign given by him, who committed murder by a kiss. * The unhappy wretch returned the price of Blood, and, in the end, hanged himself.

℣. It had been well for that man, had he never been born.

* The unhappy wretch returned the price of Blood, and, in the end, hanged himself.

FIFTH LESSON.

Utinam ergo qui nos modo exercent, convertantur, et nobiscum exerceantur: tamen quamdiu ita sunt, ut exerceant nos, non eos oderimus: quia in eo quod malus est quis eorum, utrum usque in finem perseveraturus sit, ignoramus. Et plerumque cum tibi videris odisse inimicum, fratrem odisti, et nescis. Diabolus, et angeli ejus in Scripturis sanctis manifestati sunt nobis, quod ad ignem æternum sint destinati: ipsorum tantum desperanda est correctio, contra quos habemus occultam luctam: ad quam luctam nos armat Apostolus, dicens: Non est nobis colluctatio adversus carnem et sanguinem: id est, non adversus homines quos videtis, sed adversus principes, et potestates, et

Would to God, then, they that now *exercise* us were converted and *exercised* with us: but let us not hate them, though they continue to *exercise* us; for we know not whether they will persevere to the end in their wickedness. And many times, when you imagine that you hate your enemy, it is your brother you hate, though you are ignorant of it. The holy Scriptures plainly show us that the devil and his angels are doomed to eternal fire. It is only *their* amendment we may despair of, with whom we wage an invisible war; for which the apostle arms us, saying: *Our conflict is not with flesh and blood*, that is not with the men you see before your eyes, *but with the princes, and powers, and rulers of the world of this darkness*. And lest by his saying, *of the world*, you might think perhaps, that the devils are rulers of heaven and earth, he added, *of this darkness*. By *the world*, then, he meant the lovers of the world : by the *world*, he meant the impious and the wicked : by the *world*, he meant that which the gospel speaks of : *And the world knew him not.*

℟. Judas, the impious trader, betrayed his Lord with a kiss; He, as an innocent Lamb, refused not the kiss to Judas : * Who, for a few pence, delivered Christ up to the Jews.

℣. It would have been better for him, had he not been born.

* Who, for a few pence, delivered Christ up to the Jews.

rectores mundi, tenebrarum harum. Ne forte cum dixisset, mundi, intelligeres dæmones esse rectores cœli et terræ : mundi dixit, tenebrarum harum: mundi dixit amatorum mundi : mundi dixit, impiorum et iniquorum : mundi dixit, de quo dicit Evangelium : Et mundus eum non cognovit.

℟. Judas mercator pessimus osculo petiit Dominum: ille ut agnus innocens non negavit Judæ osculum : * Denariorum numero Christum Judæis tradidit.

℣. Melius illi erat, si natus non fuisset.

* Denariorum numero Christum Judæis tradidit.

SIXTH LESSON.

For I have seen injustice and strife in the city. See the glory of the Cross ! That Cross, that was an object of derision to his enemies, is now placed on the foreheads of kings. The effect is a proof of his power : he conquered the world not by the sword, but by the wood. The wood of the Cross was thought a subject of scorn by his enemies, who, as they stood before it, shook their heads and said : *If he be the Son of God, let him come down from the Cross.* He stretched forth his hand to an unbelieving and seditious people. For if he is just that lives by faith, he is unjust that has not faith. By

Quoniam vidi iniquitatem et contradictionem in civitate. Attende gloriam Crucis ipsius. Jam in fronte regum crux illa fixa est, cui inimici insultaverunt. Effectus probavit virtutem : domuit orbem non ferro, sed ligno. Lignum crucis contumeliis dignum visum est inimicis, et ante ipsum lignum stantes caput agitabant, et dicebant : Si Filius Dei est, descendat de cruce. Extendebat ille manus suas ad populum non credentem, et contradicentem. Si enim justus est qui ex fide vivit, iniquus est qui non habet fidem. Quod ergo hic ait, iniquitatem, perfidiam in telliga. Videbat ergo Dominus in civitate iniquitatem et contradictionem, et extendebat manus suas ad populum non credentem: et tamen ipsos exspectans dicebat: Pater, ignosce illis, quia nesciunt quid faciunt.

injustice then here you must understand infidelity. Our Lord, therefore, *saw injustice and strife in the city,* and stretched forth his hands to an unbelieving and seditious people: and yet he waited for them, saying: *Father, forgive them, for they know not what they do.*

℟. Unus ex discipulis meis tradet me hodie: væ illi per quem tradar ego! * Melius illi erat, si natus non fuisset.

℟. One of my Disciples will this day betray me: wo to him, by whom I shall be betrayed! * It had been better for him, if he had not been born.

℣. Qui intingit mecum manum in paropside, hic me traditurus est in manus peccatorum.
* Melius illi erat, si natus non fuisset.
Here is repeated: Unus ex discipulis meis.

℣. He that dips his hand with me in the dish, he it is that is about to betray me into the hands of sinners.
* It had been better for him, if he had not been born.
Here is repeated: One of my Disciples.

THIRD NOCTURN.

The *seventh* Psalm declares the vengeance of God on those that excite his anger. It shows us what will happen to the Synagogue: after having obliged the Messias to drink the bitter chalice of his Passion, its own turn shall come, and it shall drink the *cup* of God's wrath, even to the very *dregs thereof*.

ANT. Dixi iniquis: Nolite loqui adversus Deum iniquitatem.

ANT. I said to the wicked: Speak not iniquity against God.

PSALM 74.

Confitebimur tibi Deus: * confitebimur, et invocabimus nomen tuum.
Narrabimus mirabilia tua: * cum accepero tempus, ego justitias judicabo.

We will praise thee, O God: we will praise, and we will call upon thy name.
We will relate thy wondrous works: when, says the Lord, I shall take a time, I will judge justice.

The earth is melted and all that dwell therein: I have established the pillars thereof.

I said to the wicked: Do not act wickedly: and to the sinners: Lift not up the horn.

Lift not up your horn on high: speak not iniquity against God.

For neither from the east, nor from the west, nor from the desert hills: for God is the judge.

One he putteth down, and another he lifteth up. For in the hand of the Lord there is a cup of strong wine full of mixture.

And he hath poured it out from this to that: but the dregs thereof are not emptied: all the sinners of the earth shall drink.

But I will declare for ever: I will sing to the God of Jacob.

And I will break all the horns of sinners: but the horns of the just shall be exalted.

ANT. I said to the wicked: Speak not iniquity against God.

Liquefacta est terra, et omnes qui habitant in ea: *ego confirmavi columnas ejus.

Dixi iniquis: Nolite inique agere: *et delinquentibus: Nolite exaltare cornu.

Nolite extollere in altum cornu vestrum: *Nolite loqui adversus Deum iniquitatem.

Quia neque ab oriente, neque ab occidente, neque a desertis montibus: *quoniam Deus judex est.

Hunc humiliat, et hunc exaltat: *quia calix in manu Domini vini meri plenus mixto.

Et inclinavit ex hoc in hoc: verumtamen fæx ejus non est exinanita: *bibent omnes peccatores terræ.

Ego autem annuntiabo in sæculum: *cantabo Deo Jacob.

Et omnia cornua peccatorum confringam: *et exaltabuntur cornua justi.

ANT. Dixi iniquis: Nolite loqui adversus Deum iniquitatem.

The *eighth* Psalm was written after David had conquered his enemies. He speaks of the *peace* that was restored to *Sion,* and of the sudden vengeance of God that overtook the wicked. The enemies of our Saviour were *sleeping their sleep;* when, suddenly, *the earth trembled,* and *God arose* to *judge* them.

ANT. The earth trembled, and was still, when God arose in judgment.

ANT. Terra tremuit et quievit, dum exsurgeret in judicio Deus.

PSALM 75.

Notus in Judæa Deus : * in Israël magnum nomen ejus.

Et factus est in pace locus ejus : * et habitatio ejus in Sion.

Ibi confregit potentias arcuum : * scutum, gladium, et bellum.

Illuminans tu mirabiliter a montibus æternis : * turbati sunt omnes insipientes corde.

Dormierunt somnum suum : * et nihil invenerunt omnes viri divitiarum in manibus suis.

Ab increpatione tua Deus Jacob : * dormitaverunt qui ascenderunt equos.

Tu terribilis es, et quis resistet tibi : * ex tunc ira tua.

De cœlo auditum fecisti judicium : * terra tremuit et quievit,

Cum exsurgeret in judicium Deus : * ut salvos faceret omnes mansuetos terræ.

Quoniam cogitatio hominis confitebitur tibi : * et reliquiæ cogitationis diem festum agent tibi.

Vovete et reddite Domino Deo vestro : * omnes qui in circuitu ejus affertis munera.

Terribili et ei qui aufert spiritum principum, * terribili apud reges terræ.

ANT. Terra tremuit et quievit, dum exsurgeret in judicio Deus.

In Judea God is known, his name is great in Israel.

And his place is in peace, and his abode in Sion.

There hath he broken the power of bows, the shield, the sword, and the battle.

Thou enlightenest wonderfully from the everlasting hills : all the foolish of heart were troubled.

They have slept their sleep: and all the men of riches have found nothing in their hands.

At thy rebuke, O God of Jacob, they have all slumbered that mounted on horseback.

Thou art terrible, and who shall resist thee? from that time thy wrath.

Thou hast caused judgment to be heard from heaven : the earth trembled and was still.

When God arose in judgment, to save all the meek of the earth.

For the thought of man shall give praise to thee : and the remainders of the thought shall keep holyday to thee.

Vow ye, and pray to the Lord your God : all you that round about him bring presents.

To him that is terrible, even to him who taketh away the spirit of princes ; to the terrible with the kings of the earth.

ANT. The earth trembled, and was still, when God arose in judgment.

The *ninth* Psalm tells us of David's tribulation

when his son Absalom,—the type of the Jewish people,—raised the standard of revolt against him. The Royal Prophet, who is the figure of Christ, loses not his confidence in the midst of his trials. The recollection of the wonderful works wrought by God in favour of His people, animates his courage, and he feels that this same merciful God will deliver him.

ANT. In the day of my tribulation, I sought God with my hands *raised up in prayer*.

ANT. In die tribulationis meæ Deum exquisivi manibus meis.

PSALM 76.

I cried to the Lord with my voice; to God with my voice, and he gave ear to me.

In the day of my trouble I sought God: with my hands lifted up to him in the night, and I was not deceived.

My soul refused to be comforted; I remembered God, and was delighted, and was exercised, and my spirit swooned away.

My eyes prevented the watches: I was troubled, and I spoke not.

I thought upon the days of old: and I had in my mind the eternal years.

And I meditated in the night with my own heart, and I was exercised, and I swept my spirit.

Will God then cast off for ever? or will he never be more favourable again?

Or will he cut off his mercy for ever, from generation to generation?

Or will God forget to show

Voce mea ad Dominum clamavi: * voce mea ad Deum, et intendit mihi.

In die tribulationis meæ Deum exquisivi, manibus meis nocte contra eum : * et non sum deceptus.

Renuit consolari anima mea: * memor fui Dei, et delectatus sum, et exercitatus sum, et defecit spiritus meus.

Anticipaverunt vigilias oculi mei : * turbatus sum, et non sum locutus.

Cogitavi dies antiquos : * et annos æternos in mente habui.

Et meditatus sum nocte cum corde meo: * et exercitabar, et scopebam spiritum meum.

Numquid in æternum projiciet Deus : * aut non apponet ut complacitior sit adhuc?

Aut in finem misericordiam suam abscindet : * a generatione in generationem?

Aut obliviscetur misereri

Deus: * aut continebit in ira sua misericordias suas?

Et dixi: nunc cœpi: * hæc mutatio dexteræ Excelsi.

Memor fui operum Domini: * quia memor ero ab initio mirabilium tuorum.

Et meditabor in omnibus operibus tuis: * et in adinventionibus tuis exercebor.

Deus in sancto via tua: quis Deus magnus sicut Deus, noster? * Tu es Deus, qui facis mirabilia.

Notum fecisti in populis virtutem tuam: * redemisti in brachio tuo populum tuum, filios Jacob et Joseph.

Viderunt te aquæ Deus, viderunt, te aquæ: * et timuerunt, et turbatæ sunt abyssi.

Multitudo sonitus aquarum: * vocem dederunt nubes.

Etenim sagittæ tuæ transeunt: * vox tonitrui tui in rota.

Illuxerunt coruscationes tuæ orbi terræ: * commota est et contremuit terra.

In mari via tua, et semitæ tuæ in aquis multis: * et vestigia tua non cognoscentur.

Deduxisti sicut oves populum tuum: * in manu Moysi et Aaron.

ANT. In die tribulationis meæ Deum exquisivi manibus meis.

℣. Exsurge, Domine.

mercy? or will he in his anger shut up his mercies?

And I said: Now have I begun: this is the change of the right hand of the Most High.

I remembered the works of the Lord; for I will be mindful of thy wonders from the beginning.

And I will meditate on all thy works; and will be employed in thy inventions.

Thy way, O God, is in the holy place: who is the great God like our God? Thou art the God that dost wonders.

Thou hast made thy power known among the nations: with thy arm thou hast redeemed thy people, the children of Jacob and Joseph.

The waters saw thee, O God, the waters saw thee; and they were afraid, and the depths were troubled.

Great was the noise of the waters: the clouds sent out a sound.

For thy arrows pass: the voice of thy thunder in a wheel.

Thy lightnings enlightened the world, the earth shook and trembled.

Thy way is in the sea, and thy paths in many waters; and thy footsteps shall not be known.

Thou hast conducted thy people like sheep, by the hand of Moses and Aaron.

ANT. In the day of my tribulation, I sought God with my hands *raised up in prayer.*

℣. Arise, O Lord.

℞. And judge my cause. ℞. Et judica causam meam.

Here is said the *Pater noster*, in secret.

The Lessons of the third Nocturn are taken from St. Paul. After having reproved the Faithful of Corinth for the abuses which had crept into their assemblies, he relates the institution of the Holy Eucharist, which took place to-day (Thursday); and after showing us the dispositions, wherewith we should approach the Holy Table, he speaks of the enormity of the crime of an unworthy Communion.

SEVENTH LESSON.

From the first Epistle of Saint Paul, the Apostle, to the Corinthians.

Ch. XI.

Now this I ordain: not praising you, that you come together, not for the better, but for the worse. For first of all I hear that when you come together in the church, there are divisions among you, and in part I believe it. For there must be, also, heresies; that they also, who are approved, may be made manifest among you. When you come together therefore into one place, it is not now to eat the Lord's Supper. For every one taketh before his own supper to eat. And one indeed is hungry, and another is drunk. What, have you not houses to eat and drink in? Or despise ye the Church of God, and put them to shame that have not? What shall I say to you? Do I praise you? In this I praise you not.

De Epistola prima Beati Pauli Apostoli ad Corinthios.

Cap. XI.

Hoc autem præcipio: non laudans quod non in melius, sed in deterius convenitis. Primum quidem convenientibus vobis in ecclesiam, audio scissuras esse inter vos, et ex parte credo. Nam oportet et hæreses esse, ut et qui probati sunt, manifesti fiant in vobis. Convenientibus ergo vobis in unum, jam non est Dominicam Cœnam manducare. Unusquisque enim suam cœnam præsumit ad manducandum. Et alius quidem esurit, alius autem ebrius est. Numquid domos non habetis ad manducandum et bibendum? Aut Ecclesiam Dei contemnitis, et confunditis eos qui non habent? Quid dicam vobis? Laudo vos? In hoc non laudo.

℞. Eram quasi agnus innocens: ductus sum ad immolandum, et nesciebam: consilium fecerunt inimici mei adversum me, dicentes: * Venite mittamus lignum in panem ejus, et eradamus eum de terra viventium.

℣. Omnes inimici mei adversum me cogitabant mala mihi: verbum iniquum mandaverunt adversum me, dicentes:

* Venite, mittamus lignum in panem ejus, et eradamus eum de terra viventium.

℞. I was like an innocent Lamb; I was led to be sacrificed, and I knew it not: my enemies conspired against me, saying: * Come, let us put wood into his bread, and root him out of the land of the living.

℣. All my enemies devised evil things against me: they uttered a wicked speech against me, saying:

* Come, let us put wood into his bread, and root him out of the land of the living.

EIGHTH LESSON.

Ego enim accepi a Domino, quod et tradidi vobis, quoniam Dominus Jesus, in qua nocte tradebatur, accepit panem, et gratias agens fregit, et dixit: Accipite, et manducate: hoc est Corpus meum, quod pro vobis tradetur: hoc facite in meam commemorationem. Similiter et calicem post quam cœnavit dicens: Hic calix novum testamentum est in meo Sanguine. Hoc facite quotiescumque bibetis, in meam commemorationem. Quotiescumque enim manducabitis panem hunc, et calicem bibetis, mortem Domini annuntiabitis donec veniat.

℞. Una hora non potuistis vigilare mecum, qui exhortabamini mori pro me?

For I have received of the Lord that which also I delivered to you, that the Lord Jesus, the same night in which he was betrayed, took bread, and giving thanks, broke it and said: Take ye, and eat: this is my body which shall be delivered for you: this do for the commemoration of me. In like manner also the chalice, after he had supped, saying: This chalice is the new testament in my Blood: this do ye, as often as you shall drink it, for the commemoration of me. For as often as you shall eat this bread, and drink this chalice, you shall show the death of the Lord until he comes.

℞. Could ye not watch one hour with me, ye that exhorted each other to die for me? * Or see ye not how Judas sleepeth not, but maketh speed to deliver me up to the Jews?

℣. Why sleep ye? Arise, and pray, lest ye enter into temptation.
* Or see ye not how Judas sleepeth not, but maketh speed to deliver me up to the Jews?

℣. Quid dormitis? Surgite, et orate, ne intretis in tentationem.
* Vel Judam non videtis, quomodo non dormit, sed festinat tradere me Judæis?

NINTH LESSON.

Wherefore whosoever shall eat this bread, or drink the chalice of the Lord unworthily, shall be guilty of the body and of the blood of the Lord. But let a man prove himself: and so let him eat of that bread, and drink of the chalice. For he that eateth and drinketh unworthily, eateth and drinketh judgment to himself, not discerning the body of the Lord. Therefore are there many infirm and weak among you, and many sleep. But if we would judge ourselves, we should not be judged. But whilst we are judged, we are chastised by the Lord, that we be not condemned with this world. Wherefore, my brethren, when you come together to eat, wait for one another. If any man be hungry let him eat at home; that you come not together unto judgment. And the rest I will set in order when I come.

℟. The ancients of the people consulted together, * How they might, by craft, apprehend Jesus, and kill him: they went forth, with swords and clubs, as to a thief.
℣. The Priests and Pharisees held a council.

Itaque quicumque manducaverit panem hunc, vel biberit calicem Domini indigne, reus erit Corporis et Sanguinis Domini. Probet autem seipsum homo; et sic de pane illo edat, et de calice bibat. Qui enim manducat et bibit indigne, judicium sibi manducat et bibit, non dijudicans Corpus Domini. Ideo inter vos multi infirmi et imbecilles, et dormiunt multi. Quod si nosmetipsos dijudicaremus, non utique judicaremur. Dum judicamur autem, a Domino corripimur, ut non cum hoc mundo damnemur. Itaque fratres mei, cum convenitis ad manducandum, invicem exspectate. Si quis esurit, domi manducet: ut non in judicium conveniatis. Cætera autem, cum venero, disponam.

℟. Seniores populi consilium fecerunt, * Ut Jesum dolo tenerent, et occiderent: cum gladiis et fustibus exierunt tamquam ad latronem.
℣. Collegerunt Pontifices et Pharisæi concilium.

* Ut Jesum dolo tenerent, et occiderent: cum gladiis et fustibus exierunt tanquam ad latronem.

Here is repeated: Seniores populi.

* How they might, by craft, apprehend Jesus, and kill him: they went forth, with swords and clubs, as to a thief.

Here is repeated: The ancients.

LAUDS.

The *first* Psalm is the one written by David after his sin, in which he so feelingly and so humbly breathes forth his repentance. The Church invariably makes use of this Psalm, when she sues to God for *mercy;* and of all the canticles of the Royal Prophet, there is not one which is so familiar to the Faithful as this.

ANT. Justificeris, Domine, in sermonibus tuis, et vincas cum judicaris.

ANT. Be thou justified, O Lord, in thy words, and overcome, when thou art judged.

PSALM 50.

Miserere mei, Deus: * secundum magnam misericordiam tuam.

Et secundum multitudinem miserationum tuarum: * dele iniquitatem meam.

Amplius lava me ab iniquitate mea: * et a peccato meo munda me.

Quoniam iniquitatem meam ego cognosco: * et peccatum meum contra me est semper.

Tibi soli peccavi, et malum coram te feci: * ut justificeris in sermonibus tuis, et vincas cum judicaris.

Have mercy on me, O God, according to thy great mercy.

And according to the multitude of thy tender mercies, blot out my iniquities.

Wash me yet more from my iniquity: and cleanse me from my sin.

For I know my iniquity: and my sin is always before me.

To thee only have I sinned, and have done evil before thee: *I confess it: do thou pardon me*, that thou mayest be justified in thy words, and mayest overcome when thou art judged.

For behold I was conceived in iniquities: and in sins did my mother conceive me.

For behold thou hast loved truth: the uncertain and hidden things of thy wisdom thou hast made manifest to me.

Thou shalt sprinkle me with hyssop, *as is a leper*, and I shall be cleansed: thou shalt wash me, and I shall be made whiter than snow.

To my hearing thou shalt give joy and gladness: and the bones that have been humbled shall rejoice.

Turn away thy face from my sins: and blot out all my iniquities.

Create a clean heart in me, O God: and renew a right spirit within my bowels.

Cast me not away from thy face: and take not thy holy Spirit from me.

Restore unto me the joy of thy salvation: and strengthen me with a perfect spirit.

I will teach the unjust thy ways: and the wicked shall be converted to thee.

Deliver me from blood, O God, the God of my salvation: and my tongue shall extol thy justice.

O Lord, thou wilt open my lips: and my mouth shall declare thy praise.

For if thou hadst desired sacrifice, I would indeed have given it: with burnt-offerings thou wilt not be delighted.

A sacrifice to God is an afflicted spirit: a contrite and humble heart, O God, thou wilt not despise.

Ecce enim in iniquitatibus conceptus sum: * et in peccatis concepit me mater mea.

Ecce enim veritatem dilexisti: * incerta et occulta sapientiæ tuæ manifestasti mihi.

Asperges me hyssopo, et mundabor: * lavabis me, et super nivem dealbabor.

Auditui meo dabis gaudium et lætitiam :* et exsultabunt ossa humiliata.

Averte faciem tuam a peccatis meis: * et omnes iniquitates meas dele.

Cor mundum crea in me, Deus: * et spiritum rectum innova in visceribus meis.

Ne projicias me a facie tua: * et spiritum sanctum tuum ne auferas a me.

Redde mihi lætitiam salutaris tuæ: * et spiritu principali confirma me.

Docebo iniquos vitas tuas: * et impii ad te convertentur.

Libera me de sanguinibus Deus, Deus salutis meæ: * et exsultabit lingua mea justitiam tuam.

Domine, labia mea aperies: et os meum annuntiabit laudem tuam.

Quoniam si voluisses sacrificium dedissem utique :* holocaustis non delectaberis.

Sacrificium Deo spiritus contribulatus: * cor contritem et humiliatum, Deus, non despicies.

Benigne fac Domine in bona voluntate tua Sion : * ut ædificentur muri Jerusalem.

Junc acceptabis sacrificium justitiæ, oblationes, et holocausta : * tunc imponent super altare tuum vitulos.

ANT. Justificeris,Domine, in sermonibus tuis, et vincas cum judicaris.

Deal favourably, O Lord, in thy good-will with Sion : that the walls of Jerusalem may be built up.

Then shalt thou accept the sacrifice of justice, oblations and whole burnt-offering : then shall they lay calves upon thy altar.

ANT. Be thou justified, O Lord, in thy words, and overcome, when thou art judged.

The *second* Psalm is one of those which is fixed for the Thursday of each week : it is a prayer suitable for the morning. The Psalmist confesses the nothingness of man, and the shortness of his life : he asks God to bless the actions of the day. The Faithful must not forget that the Office of Lauds is the morning service, and its being said over night, during these three days, is exceptional.

ANT. Dominus tamquam ovis ad victimam ductus est, et non aperuit os suum.

ANT. The Lord was led as a sheep to the slaughter, and he opened not his mouth.

PSALM 89.

Domine, refugium factus es nobis : * a generatione in generationem.

Priusquam montes fierent, aut formaretur terra et orbis : * a sæculo et usque in sæculum tu es Deus.

Ne avertas hominem in humilitatem : * et dixisti : Convertimini, filii hominum.

Quoniam mille anni ante oculos tuos : * tanquam dies hesterna quæ præteriit.

Lord, thou hast been our refuge : from generation to generation.

Before the mountains were made, or the earth and the world was formed ; from eternity and to eternity thou art God.

Turn not man away to be brought low ; and thou hast said : Be converted, O ye sons of men.

For a thousand years, in thy sight, are but as yesterday which is past and gone.

And as a watch in the night: as things that are counted nothing, so shall thy years be.

In the morning, man shall grow up like grass, in the morning he shall flourish and pass away: in the evening he shall fall, grow dry, and wither.

For in thy wrath we are quickly consumed: and are troubled in thy indignation.

Thou hast set our iniquities before thy eyes: our life in the light of thy countenance.

For all our days are spent: and in thy wrath we have fainted away.

Our years shall be considered as a spider: the days of our years in them are threescore and ten years.

But if in the strong they be fourscore years: and what is more of them is labour and sorrow.

For mildness is come upon us; and we shall be corrected.

Who knoweth the power of thy anger: and, for thy fear, can number thy wrath?

So make thy right hand known: and make us learned in heart in wisdom.

Return, O Lord, how long? and be entreated in favour of thy servants.

We are filled in the morning with thy mercy: and we are rejoiced, and are delighted all our days.

We have rejoiced for the day in which thou hast humbled us: for the years in which we have seen evils.

Et custodia in nocte:* quæ pro nihilo habentur, eorum anni erunt.

Mane sicut herba transeat, mane floreat, et transeat: * vespere decidat, induret, et arescat.

Quia defecimus in ira tua: * et in furore tuo turbati sumus.

Posuisti iniquitates nostras in conspectu tuo: * sæculum nostrum in illuminatione vultus tui.

Quoniam omnes dies nostri defecerunt: * et in ira tua defecimus.

Anni nostri sicut aranea meditabuntur: * dies annorum nostrorum in ipsis septuaginta anni.

Si autem in potentatibus, octoginta anni: * et amplius eorum labor et dolor.

Quoniam supervenit mansuetudo: * et corripiemur.

Quis novit potestatem iræ tuæ: * et præ timore tuo iram tuam dinumerare?

Dexteram tuam sic notam fac: * et eruditos corde in sapientia.

Convertere, Domine, usquequo: * et deprecabilis esto super servos tuos.

Repleti sumus mane misericordia tua: * et exsultavimus, et delectati sumus omnibus diebus nostris.

Lætati sumus pro diebus, quibus nos humiliasti: * annis, quibus vidimus mala.

Respice in servos tuos, et in opera tua : * et dirige filios eorum.	Look upon thy servants, and upon their works : and direct their children.
Et sit splendor Domini Dei nostri super nos, et opera manuum nostrarum dirige super nos : * et opus manuum nostrarum dirige.	And let the brightness of the Lord our God be upon us, and direct thou the works of our hands over us : yea, the work of our hands do thou direct.
ANT. Dominus tanquam ovis ad victimam ductus est, et non aperuit os suum.	ANT. The Lord was led as a sheep to the slaughter, and he opened not his mouth.

The *third* Psalm is the one that is said every day in Lauds, and the Church would not make these three days an exception. It is the prayer of the soul, turning towards her God at the dawn of day, and assuring him of her confidence and love. It is always joined to the 66th Psalm, in which the Royal Prophet prays to God, at the rising of the sun, to bless the world with the rays of his divine mercy.

ANT. Contritum est cor meum in medio mei, contremuerunt omnia ossa mea.	ANT. My heart is broken within me ; all my bones have trembled.

PSALM 62.

Deus, Deus meus : * ad te de luce vigilo.	O God, my God, to thee do I watch at break of day.
Sitivit in te anima mea : * quam multipliciter tibi caro mea.	For thee my soul hath thirsted : for thee my flesh, O how many ways !
In terra deserta, et invia, et inaquosa : * sic in sancto apparui tibi, ut viderem virtutem tuam, et gloriam tuam.	In a desert land, and where there is no way, and no water : so in the sanctuary have I come before thee, to see thy power and thy glory.
Quoniam melior est misericordia tua super vitas : * labia mea laudabunt te.	For thy mercy is better than lives : thee my lips shall praise.
Sic benedicam te in vita mea : * et in nomine tuo lavabo manus meas.	Thus will I bless thee all my life long : and in thy name I will lift up my hands.

Let my soul be filled as with marrow and fatness: and my mouth shall praise thee with joyful lips.

If I have remembered thee on my bed, I will meditate on thee in the morning: because thou hast been my helper.

And I will rejoice under the covert of thy wings: my soul hath stuck close to thee: thy right hand hath received me.

But they have sought my soul in vain, they shall go into the lower parts of the earth: they shall be delivered into the hands of the sword, they shall be the portions of foxes.

But the *just man, being delivered from danger, like a* king shall rejoice in God: all they shall be praised that swear by him: because the mouth is stopped of them that speak wicked things.

Sicut adipe et pinguedine repleatur anima mea: * et labiis exsultationis laudabit os meum.

Si memor fui tui super stratum meum, in matutinis meditabor in te: * quia fuisti adjutor meus.

Et in velamento alarum tuarum exsultabo, adhæsit anima mea post te: * me suscepit dextera tua.

Ipsi vero in vanum quæsierunt animam meam, introibunt in inferiora terræ: * tradentur in manus gladii, partes vulpium erunt.

Rex vero lætabitur in Deo, laudabuntur omnes qui jurant in eo: * quia obstructum est os loquentium iniqua.

PSALM 66.

May God have mercy on us, and bless us: may he cause the light of his countenance to shine upon us, and may he have mercy on us.

That we may know thy way upon earth, thy salvation in all nations.

Let people confess to thee, O God: let all people give praise to thee.

Let the nations be glad and rejoice: for thou judgest the people with justice, and directest the nations upon earth.

Deus misereatur nostri, et benedicat nobis: * illuminet vultum suum super nos, et misereatur nostri.

Ut cognoscamus in terra viam tuam: * in omnibus gentibus salutare tuum.

Confiteantur tibi populi Deus: * confiteantur tibi populi omnes.

Lætentur et exsultent gentes: * quoniam judicas populos in æquitate, et gentes in terra dirigis.

Confiteantur tibi populi Deus: confiteantur tibi populi omnes: * terra dedit fructum suum.	Let the people, O God, confess to thee, let all the people give praise to thee. The earth hath yielded her fruit.
Benedicat nos Deus, Deus noster, benedicat nos Deus: * et metuant eum omnes fines terræ.	May God, our own God, bless us, may God bless us: and all the ends of the earth fear him.
Ant. Contritum est cor meum in medio mei, contremuerunt omnia ossa mea.	Ant. My heart is broken within me; all my bones have trembled.

The sublime Canticle of Moses, which was sung after the passage through the Red Sea, forms part of Thursday's Lauds during the whole year. It is peculiarly appropriate now, when our Catechumens are about to receive holy Baptism. The Font will be their Red Sea, wherein all their sins will be drowned, as the Egyptians of old. The Israelites, after having offered the sacrifice of the Paschal Lamb, passed safely between the waves: our Catechumens will come to the laver of regeneration full of hope in the Sacrifice of the True Lamb, for his Blood has imparted to the element of Water the power of purifying the soul.

Ant. Exhortatus es in virtute tua, et in refectione sancta tua, Domine.	Ant. Thou hast encouraged us by thy power, and by thy holy refreshment, O Lord!

CANTICLE OF MOSES.

(Exod. XV.)

Cantemus Domino: gloriose enim magnificatus est: * equum et ascensorem dejecit in mare.	Let us sing to the Lord: for he is gloriously magnified: the horse and the rider he hath thrown into the sea.
Fortitudo mea et laus mea Dominus: * et factus est mihi in salutem.	The Lord is my strength and my praise: and he is become salvation to me.

He is my God, and I will glorify him: the God of my father, and I will exalt him.

The Lord is as a man of war, Almighty is his name. Pharaoh's chariots and his army he hath cast into the sea.

His chosen captains are drowned in the Red Sea. The depths have covered them, they are sunk to the bottom like a stone.

Thy right hand, O Lord, is magnified in strength; thy right hand, O Lord, hath slain the enemy. And in the multitude of thy power thou hast put down thy adversaries.

Thou hast sent thy wrath, which hath devoured them like stubble. And with the blast of thy anger the waters were gathered together.

The flowing water stood, the depths were gathered together in the midst of the sea.

The enemy said: I will pursue and overtake, I will divide the spoils, my soul shall have its fill.

I will draw my sword, my hand shall slay them.

Thy wind blew, and the sea covered them: they sunk as lead in the mighty waters.

Who is like to thee among the strong, O Lord? who is like to thee, glorious in holiness, terrible and praiseworthy, doing wonders?

Thou stretchedst forth thy hand, and the earth swallowed them. In thy mercy thou

Iste Deus meus, et glorificabo eum : * Deus patris mei, et exaltabo eum.

Dominus quasi vir pugnator, Omnipotens nomen ejus : * currus Pharaonis, et exercitum ejus projecit in mare.

Electi principes ejus submersi sunt in mari rubro : * abyssi operuerunt eos, descenderunt in profundum quasi lapis.

Dextera tua, Domine, magnificata est in fortitudine : dextera tua, Domine, percussit inimicum : * et in multitudine gloriæ tuæ deposuisti adversarios tuos.

Misisti iram tuam, quæ devoravit eos sicut stipulam : * et in spiritu furoris tui congregatæ sunt aquæ.

Stetit unda fluens : * congregatæ sunt abyssi in medio mari.

Dixit inimicus : persequar et comprehendam : * dividam spolia, implebitur anima mea.

Evaginabo gladium meum : * interficiat eos manus mea.

Flavit spiritus tuus, et operuit eos mare : * submersi sunt quasi plumbum in aquis vehementibus.

Quis similis tui in fortibus, Domine : * quis similis tui, magnificus in sanctitate, terribilis atque laudabilis, faciens mirabilia?

Extendisti manum tuam, et devoravit eos terra : * dux fuisti in misericordia tua populo quem rede-misti.

Et portasti eum in fortitudine tua : * ad habitaculum sanctum tuum.

Ascenderunt populi et irati sunt : * dolores obtinuerunt habitatores Philisthiim.

Tunc conturbati sunt principes Edom, robustos Moab obtinuit tremor : * obriguerunt omnes habitatores Chanaan.

Irruat super eos formido et pavor : * in magnitudine brachii tui.

Fiant immobiles quasi lapis, donec pertranseat populus tuus, Domine : * donec pertranseat populus tuus iste, quem possedisti.

Introduces eos, et plantabis in monte hæreditatis tuæ : * firmissimo habitaculo tuo, quod operatus es, Domine :

Sanctuarium tuum, Domine, quod firmaverunt manus tuæ : * Dominus regnabit in æternum, et ultra.

Ingressus est enim eques Pharao cum curribus et equitibus ejus in mare : * et reduxit super eos Dominus aquas maris.

Filii autem Israël ambulaverunt per siccum : * in medio ejus.

ANT. Exhortatus es in virtute tua, et in refectione sancta tua Domine.

hast been a leader to the people whom thou hast redeemed :

And in thy strength thou hast carried them to thy holy habitation.

Nations rose up, and were angry : sorrows took hold of the inhabitants of Philisthiim.

Then were the princes of Edom troubled, trembling seized on the stout men of Moab : all the inhabitants of Canaan became stiff.

Let fear and dread fall upon them, in the greatness of thy arm.

Let them become immoveable as a stone, until thy people, O Lord, pass by; until this thy people pass by, which thou hast possessed.

Thou shalt bring them in and plant them in the mountain of thy inheritance, in thy most firm habitation, which thou hast made, O Lord :

Thy sanctuary, O Lord, which thy hands have established. The Lord shall reign for ever and ever.

For Pharaoh went in on horseback with his chariots and horsemen into the sea : and the Lord brought back upon them the waters of the sea.

But the children of Israel walked on dry ground in the midst thereof.

ANT. Thou hast encouraged us by thy power, and by thy holy refreshment, O Lord !

The *last* Psalm, which is always said at Lauds, is

composed of the last three of the Psaltery. Their theme is the *praise* of God, and this portion of the canonical office is called, on that account, *Lauds*.

ANT. He was offered because it was his own will, and he bore himself our sins.

ANT. Oblatus est quia ipse voluit, et peccata nostra ipse portavit.

PSALM 148.

Praise ye the Lord from the heavens : praise ye him in the high places.

Praise ye him, all his Angels : praise ye him all his hosts.

Praise ye him, O sun and moon : praise him all ye stars and light.

Praise him ye heavens of heavens : and let all the waters that are above the heavens praise the name of the Lord.

For he spoke, and they were made ; he commanded, and they were created.

He hath established them for ever, and for ages of ages : he hath made a decree, and it shall not pass away.

Praise the Lord from the earth, ye dragons, and all ye deeps.

Fire, hail, snow, ice, stormy winds, which fulfil his word.

Mountains and all hills, fruitful trees, and all cedars.

Beasts and all cattle : serpents and feathered fowls.

Laudate Dominum de cœlis : * laudate eum in excelsis.

Laudate eum omnes Angeli ejus : * laudate eum omnes virtutes ejus.

Laudate eum sol et luna : * laudate eum omnes stellæ et lumen.

Laudate eum cœli cœlorum : * et aquæ omnes, quæ super cœlos sunt, laudent nomen Domini.

Quia ipse dixit, et facta sunt : * ipse mandavit, et creata sunt.

Statuit ea in æternum, et in sæculum sæculi : * præceptum posuit, et non præteribit.

Laudate Dominum de terra : * dracones et omnes abyssi.

Ignis, grando, nix, glacies, spiritus procellarum : * quæ faciunt verbum ejus.

Montes et omnes colles : * ligna fructifera, et omnes cedri.

Bestiæ et universa pecora : * serpentes et volucres pennatæ.

Reges terræ, et omnes populi : * principes et omnes judices terræ.

Juvenes et virgines : senes cum junioribus laudent nomen Domini : * quia exaltatum est nomen ejus solius.

Confessio ejus super cœlum et terram : * et exaltavit cornu populi sui.

Hymnus omnibus sanctis ejus : * filiis Israël, populo appropinquanti sibi.

Kings of the earth, and all people : princes and all judges of the earth.

Young men and maidens : let the old with the younger praise the name of the Lord : for his name alone is exalted.

The praise of him is above heaven and earth : and he hath exalted the horn of his people.

A hymn to all his saints ; to the children of Israel, a people approaching to him.

PSALM 149.

Cantate Domino canticum novum : * laus ejus in ecclesia sanctorum.

Lætetur Israël in eo qui fecit eum : * et filii Sion exsultent in rege suo.

Laudent nomen ejus in choro : * in tympano, et psalterio psallant ei.

Quia beneplacitum est Domino in populo suo : * et exaltabit mansuetos in salutem.

Exsultabunt sancti in gloria : * lætabuntur in cubilibus suis.

Exsultationes Dei in gutture eorum : * et gladii ancipites in manibus eorum.

Ad faciendam vindictam in nationibus : * increpationes in populis.

Ad alligandos reges eorum in compedibus : * et nobiles eorum in manicis ferreis.

Sing ye to the Lord a new canticle : let his praise be in the church of the saints.

Let Israel rejoice in him that made him : and let the children of Sion be joyful in their king.

Let them praise his name in choir : let them sing to him with the timbrel and the psaltery.

For the Lord is well pleased with his people : and he will exalt the meek unto salvation.

The saints shall rejoice in glory : they shall be joyful in their beds.

The high praises of God shall be in their mouth : and two-edged swords in their hands.

To execute vengeance upon the nations, chastisements among the people.

To bind their kings with fetters, and their nobles with manacles of iron.

PSALM 150.

To execute upon them the judgment that is written: this glory is to all his saints.

Ut faciant in eis judicium conscriptum : * gloria hæc est omnibus sanctis ejus.

Praise ye the Lord in his holy places : praise ye him in the firmament of his power.

Praise ye him for his mighty acts: praise ye him according to the multitude of his greatness.

Praise him with sound of trumpet: praise him with psaltery and harp.

Praise him with timbrel and choir : praise him with strings and organs.

Praise him on high-sounding cymbals : praise him on cymbals of joy : let every spirit praise the Lord.

Laudate Dominum in sanctis ejus : * laudate eum in firmamento virtutis ejus.

Laudate eum in virtutibus ejus : * laudate eum secundum multitudinem magnitudinis ejus.

Laudate eum in sono tubæ : * laudate eum in psalterio et cithara.

Laudate eum in tympano et choro : * laudate eum in chordis et organo.

Laudate eum in cymbalis benesonantibus : laudate eum in cymbalis jubilationis : * omnis spiritus laudet Dominum.

ANT. He was offered because it was his own will, and he bore himself our sins.

℣. The man of my peace, in whom I trusted ;

℞. Who eat my bread, hath greatly supplanted me.

ANT. Oblatus est quia ipse voluit, et peccata nostra ipse portavit.

℣. Homo pacis meæ, in quo speravi.

℞. Qui edebat panes meos, ampliavit adversum me supplantationem.

The Church now intones the sweet Canticle of Zachary, which she repeats every morning. Its joyous accents strangely contrast with the sadness caused in us by the Passion of our Jesus, the Sun of Justice. It was during these very days, that *the remission of sins* was wrought *through the bowels of the mercy of our God;* but the Divine *Orient* rises not upon us *from on high* and in his splendour; he is about to set on Calvary by the cruelest of deaths. Let us weep for ourselves, whilst we weep for Him; but let us look forward to his Resurrection, which is to be *ours* also.

ANT. Traditor autem dedit eis signum, dicens: Quem osculatus fuero, ipse est, tenete eum.

ANT. But the traitor gave them a sign, saying: He that I shall kiss, that is He; hold him fast.

CANTICLE OF ZACHARY.

(*St. Luke, I.*)

Benedictus Dominus Deus Israël : * quia visitavit, et fecit redemptionem plebis suæ :

Et erexit cornu salutis nobis : * in domo David pueri sui.

Sicut locutus est per os sanctorum, * qui a sæculo sunt Prophetarum ejus :

Salutem ex inimicis nostris : * et de manu omnium qui oderunt nos.

Ad faciendam misericordiam cum patribus nostris : * et memorari testamenti sui sancti.

Jusjurandum, quod juravit ad Abraham patrem nostrum : * daturum se nobis.

Ut sine timore, de manu inimicorum nostrorum liberati : * serviamus illi.

In sanctitate et justitia coram ipso : * omnibus diebus nostris.

Et tu puer, propheta Altissimi vocaberis : * præibis enim ante faciem Domini parare vias ejus.

Ad dandam scientiam salutis plebi ejus : * in remissionem peccatorum eorum.

Per viscera misericordiæ Dei nostri : * in quibus visitavit nos Oriens ex alto.

Blessed be the Lord God of Israel, because he hath visited and wrought the redemption of his people :

And hath raised up a horn of salvation to us, in the house of David his servant.

As he spoke by the mouth of his holy Prophets, who are from the beginning :

Salvation from our enemies, and from the hand of all that hate us.

To perform mercy to our fathers ; and to remember his holy covenant.

The oath which he swore to Abraham our father, that he would grant to us.

That being delivered from the hands of our enemies, we may serve him without fear.

In holiness and justice before him, all our days.

And thou, child, shalt be called the prophet of the Highest : for thou shalt go before the face of the Lord to prepare his ways.

To give knowledge of salvation to his people, unto the remission of their sins.

Through the bowels of the mercy of our God : in which the Orient from on high hath visited us :

To enlighten them that sit in darkness, and in the shadow of death: to direct our feet in the way of peace.	Illuminare his, qui in tenebris et in umbra mortis sedent: * ad dirigendos pedes nostros in viam pacis.
ANT. But the traitor gave them a sign, saying: He that I shall kiss, that is He; hold him fast.	ANT. Traditor autem dedit eis signum, dicens: Quem osculatus fuero, ipse est, tenete eum.

As soon as the Antiphon is finished, the Choir sings, to a most plaintive chant, the following words, which are continually on the lips of the Church during these three days:

℣. Christ became, for our sakes, obedient unto death.	℣. Christus factus est pro nobis obediens usque ad mortem.

Immediately after this is said, in secret, the *Pater noster*, which is followed by the Psalm *Miserere* (*page* 338): it is recited with a suppressed voice, by alternate choirs. Finally, the first in dignity says the following Prayer.

Look down, O Lord, we beseech thee, upon this thy family, for which our Lord Jesus Christ hesitated not to be delivered into the hands of wicked men, and undergo the punishment of the Cross:	Respice, quæsumus, Domine, super hanc familiam tuam, pro qua Dominus noster Jesus Christus non dubitavit manibus tradi nocentium, et crucis subire tormentum:

(*then, the rest in secret:*)

Who liveth and reigneth with thee, in the unity of the Holy Ghost, God, world without end, amen.	Qui tecum vivit et regnat, in unitate Spiritus Sancti, Deus, per omnia sæcula sæculorum, amen.

The gradual putting out the candles,—the taking the one that is left lighted, its being concealed and then shown again,—the noise which is made at the end,—all these ceremonies have been already explained: see *page* 305.

THE MORNING.

This is the first day of the *Azymes*, or *Feast of the Unleavened Bread*. At sun-set, the Jews must eat the *Pasch* in Jerusalem. Jesus is still in Bethania; but he will return to the City before the hour for the Paschal supper. The Law commands this; and, until he has abrogated the Law by the shedding of his Blood, he wishes to observe its ordinances. He therefore sends two of his Disciples to get everything ready for the Pasch, without, however, telling them the great Mystery, wherewith it is to terminate. We who know it, and that it was at this Last Supper that was instituted the Sacrament of the Eucharist, we can understand why he sends Peter and John, in preference to any of the other Disciples, to prepare what is needed[1]. Peter, who was the first to confess the Divinity of Jesus, represents Faith: and John, who leaned upon the breast of the Man-God, represents Love. The mystery, which is to be instituted at to-night's Supper, is revealed to Love by Faith. It is this that Jesus would have us learn from his choice of the two Apostles; but they themselves see not the intention of their Master.

Jesus, who knew all things, tells them by what sign they are to know the house, which he intends to honour with his presence: they have but to follow a man, whom they will see carrying a pitcher of water. The house to which this man is going, belongs to a rich Jew, who recognises Jesus as the Messias. The two Apostles apprise him of their Master's wishes; and immediately he puts at their disposal a large and richly furnished room. It was fitting, that the place,

[1] St. Luke, xxii. 8.

where the most august Mystery was to be instituted, should be something above common. This Room, where the reality was to be substituted for all the ancient figures, was far superior to the Temple of Jerusalem. In it was to be erected the first Altar for the offering up of the *clean oblation*, foretold by the Prophet:[1] in it was to commence the Christian Priesthood: in it, finally, fifty days later on, the Church of Christ, collected together and visited by the Holy Ghost, was to make herself known to the world, and promulgate the new and universal Covenant of God with men. This favoured sanctuary of our Faith, is still venerated on Mount Sion. The Infidels have profaned it by their false worship, for even they look on it as a sacred place; but as though Divine Providence, which has mercifully preserved unto us so many traces of our Redeemer, would give us an earnest of better days to come,—this venerable sanctuary has been recently thrown open to several Priests of the Church, and they have even been permitted to offer up the Holy Sacrifice in the very place where the Eucharist was instituted.

During the course of the day, Jesus has entered Jerusalem, with the rest of his Disciples: he has found all things prepared.

The Paschal Lamb, after being first presented in the Temple, has been brought to the house, where Jesus is to celebrate the Supper: it is prepared, together with the wild lettuce and the unleavened bread. In a few hours, the Divine Master and his Disciples will be standing round the table, their loins girt, and staves in their hands; and, for the last time, they will observe the solemn rite prescribed by God to his people, when they first went forth from Egypt.

But let us wait for the hour of Mass, before going further into the details of this Last Supper. Mean-

[1] Malach. i. 11.

while, let us seek edification and instruction in two holy functions, which belong to this great day. The first is the *Reconciliation of Penitents*, which, although not now in use, needs to be described, in order that our readers may have a proper idea of the Lenten Liturgy. The second is the *Consecration of the Holy Oils*, which is a ceremony confined to Cathedral Churches, but so interesting to the Faithful, that we should have scrupled to have excluded it from our volume. After having briefly described these, we will return to the history of the Institution of the Blessed Sacrament, and assist at Mass. Then we shall have to speak of the preparation for the Mass of the Presanctified for to-morrow's service, of the Stripping the Altars, and of the *Mandatum*, or Washing of the Feet. We proceed, therefore, to explain these several ceremonies, which make Maundy Thursday to be one of the most sacred days of the Liturgical Year.

THE RECONCILIATION OF PENITENTS.

Three solemn Masses were anciently celebrated on this day; and the first was preceded by the absolution of the public Penitents, and their re-admission into the Church. The following was the order of the service for the Reconciliation of Penitents. They presented themselves at the Church-door, clad in penitential garb, and bare-footed. The hair of both head and beard had been allowed to grow from Ash Wednesday, the day on which they had received their penance. The Bishop recited, in the sanctuary, the seven Psalms, in which David expresses his sorrow for having offended God. These were followed by the Litany of the Saints.

During these prayers, the Penitents were prostrate in the porch, for entrance into the Church was forbidden them. Thrice during the Litany, the Bishop deputed some of the clergy to go and visit them, in his name, and bear them words of hope and consolation. The first time, two Sub-Deacons went to them and said: *As I live, saith the Lord, I will not the death of the sinner, but rather that he be converted and live.* The second time, two other Sub-Deacons were sent, with this message: *Thus saith the Lord: Do penance; for the kingdom of heaven is at hand.* Finally, a Deacon was commissioned to go to them, and say: *Lift up your heads; lo! your redemption is nigh.*

After these announcements of approaching pardon, the Bishop left the Sanctuary and went towards the Penitents, as far as half way down the centre nave, where was prepared a seat, turned towards the door which led into the porch, where the Penitents were still lying prostrate. The Pontiff being seated the Archdeacon addressed him in these words:

Venerable Pontiff! The acceptable time has come, the day of God's mercy and of man's salvation, when death was destroyed, and eternal life began. This is the time, when, in the vineyard of the Lord of Sabaoth, new plants are to be set, and the detestableness of the old growth is to be pruned away. For though there be no period of time, which is not rich in the goodness and mercy of God, yet now indulgence produces a more abundant remission of sins, and grace yields a more plentiful number of the regenerated. Those that are regenerated add to our ranks; those that return, increase our numbers. There is a laver of water; there is a laver of tears. From the one, there is joy because of the admittance of them that are called; from the other, there is gladness because of them that repent. Therefore it is, that these thy suppliant servants,—after having fallen into sundry kinds of sins, by the neglect of the divine commandments, and the transgression of the moral law,—humbled and prostrate, cry out to the Lord in these words of the Prophet: *We have sinned: we have done unjustly; we have committed iniquity: have mercy on us, O Lord!* It has not been in vain, that they have heard the words of the Gospel: *Blessed are they that mourn; for they shall be comforted.* As it is written, they have eaten the bread of sorrow; they have watered their couch with tears; they have afflicted their hearts with mourning, and their bodies with fasting, that thus they might recover the health of soul, which they had lost. The grace of penance, therefore, is one; but it profits each one that receives it, and gives help to all in common.

The Bishop then rose, and advanced towards the Penitents. He spoke to them concerning the mercy of God, and how they should live for the time to come. After this exhortation, he thus addressed them: *Come, come, come, my children! I will teach you the fear of the Lord.* The Choir then sang this Antiphon, taken from the 33rd Psalm: *Come ye to him, and be enlightened, and your faces shall not be confounded.* Hereupon, the Penitents got up, and, coming to the Bishop, threw themselves at his feet. The Archpriest then pleaded for them in these words:

Make good in them, O Apostolic Pontiff, all that has been corrupted in them by the temptation of the devil! By the merit of thy prayers and intercession, and by the grace of the divine reconciliation, bring these men nigh unto God. Thus, they who, heretofore, suffered by the sins they committed, may now be happy in the hope, that, having overcome the author of their death, they may please the Lord, in the land of the living.

The Bishop answered: *Knowest thou, if they be worthy of reconciliation?* The Archpriest replied: *I know, and bear witness, that they are worthy.* A Deacon then ordered the Penitents to rise. This done, the Bishop took one of them by the hand, who did the same to his neighbour; and thus all, hand in hand, followed the Bishop to the place prepared in the centre of the nave. Meanwhile, the Choir sang the following Antiphons: *I say unto you, there is joy to the Angels of God over one sinner doing penance. It behoveth thee, my son, to rejoice; for thy brother was dead, and has come to life again; he was lost, and is found.* The Bishop then offered up to God this prayer, which he sang to the solemn tone of the Preface.

It is truly meet and just, right and available to salvation, that we should always and in all places give thanks to thee, O Holy Lord, Almighty Father, Eternal God, through Christ our Lord: Whom thou, O Almighty Father, didst will should be born among us by an ineffable Birth, that so he might pay to thee, his Eternal Father, the debt contracted by Adam, and put our death to death by his own, and bear our wounds in his own flesh, and cleanse away our stains by his Blood; hereby enabling us, who had fallen by the envy of the old enemy, to rise again by his mercy. Through him, O Lord, we suppliantly beseech and pray thee that thou mayest graciously hear us making intercession for the sins of others, who are not worthy to plead for our own. Do thou, O most merciful Lord, recal to thyself, with thy wonted goodness, these thy servants, who have separated themselves from thee by their sins. For neither didst thou reject the most wicked Achab when he humbled himself before thee, but didst avert from him the punishment he had deserved. So, likewise, didst thou graciously hear Peter, when he wept, and didst afterwards give to him the keys of the kingdom of heaven; and thou didst promise the reward of that same kingdom to the Thief when he trusted in thee. Therefore, O most merciful Lord! mercifully welcome back these for whom we offer to thee our prayers, and restore them to the bosom of the Church, that the enemy may not triumph over them, but that they may be reconciled unto thee by thy co-equal Son, and by Him be cleansed from their guilt, and graciously admitted by Him to the banquet of thy most Holy Supper. May he in such wise refresh them by his Flesh and Blood, as to lead them, after this life's course is run, to the kingdom of heaven.

After this Prayer, all, both clergy and laity, prostrated themselves, together with the Penitents, before the Divine Majesty, and recited the three Psalms which begin with the word *Miserere*, (that is, the 50th, the 55th, and the 56th). The Bishop then stood up, and said over the Penitents, (who remained prostrate, as did also all the assistants,) six Prayers, from which we select the following sentences.

Give ear, O Lord, to our supplications, and mercifully hear me, though I myself need mercy above all others. Thou hast chosen me to be the minister of this work, not from any merits thou didst see in me, but by the pure gift of thy grace. Grant me courage to fulfil my office, and do thou work, by my ministry, the effects of thine own mercy. It is thou that didst bring back, on thy shoulders, the lost sheep to the fold, and that didst mercifully hear the prayers of the Publican: do thou, also, restore to life these thy servants, whom thou wouldst not have die unto thee. O thou, who abandonest not them that are gone astray, receive these who have returned to thee. We beseech thee, O Lord, let the tearful sighs of these thy servants move thee to clemency: heal their wounds: stretch out thy saving hand to them, and raise them up. Permit not thy Church to be injured in any of her members: let not thy flock suffer loss; let not the enemy exult over the destruction of any of thy family, nor the second death lay hold of them that have been regenerated in the laver of salvation. Pardon, O Lord, these that confess their sins to thee: let them not fall into the punishments of the future judgment to come; let them never know the horrors of darkness, or the torments of the flames of hell. They have returned from the way of error to the path of justice; let them not be again wounded, but maintain ever within themselves both what thy grace hath conferred upon them, and what thy mercy hath reformed within them.

Having said these Prayers, the Bishop stretched forth his hands over the Penitents, and pronounced the Reconciliation, in this solemn formula:

May our Lord Jesus Christ, who vouchsafed to take away the sins of the whole world by delivering himself up for us, and shedding his spotless Blood; who, also, said unto his Disciples: whatsoever ye shall bind on earth, shall be bound also in heaven; and whatsoever ye shall loose on earth, shall be loosed also in heaven: and who hath numbered me, though unworthy, among these his ministers: may he deign, by the intercession of Mary, the Mother of God, of the blessed Archangel Michael, of holy Peter the Apostle, (to whom he gave the power of binding and loosing,) and of all the Saints, to absolve you, by the merits of his Blood shed for the remission of sins, from all whatsoever you have negligently committed in thought, or word, or action; and, having loosed you from the bonds of sin, may he graciously lead you to the kingdom of heaven. Who, with God the

Father, and the Holy Ghost, liveth and reigneth for ever and ever. Amen.

The Bishop then advanced towards the Penitents, who were still lying prostrate: he sprinkled them with holy water, and thurified them. Finally, he addressed them in these words of the Apostle: *Arise, ye that sleep! arise from the dead, and Christ shall enlighten you!* The Penitents stood up; and, in order to express the joy they felt at being reconciled with their God, they immediately went and changed their penitential garb for one more in accordance with gladness, and with the Holy Communion they were now to receive together with the rest of the Faithful.

This Reconciliation of Penitents has given rise to the magnificent ceremony, which takes place at Rome on this day,—*the Papal Benediction.* After Mass, the Sovereign Pontiff, vested in cope, and wearing the tiara, goes to the balcony over the centre door of the Vatican Basilica. In the Piazza of Saint Peter's, there stands an immense crowd of people, come from every country of the world, awaiting the appearance of the Vicar of Christ, who is about to grant them the remission of the punishment due to their sins. One of the Prelates, who surround the Pope's throne, recites the usual form of the Confession of Sins; he recites it in the name of the assembly below, whom one and the same holy Faith has thus brought before the Father of the Christian World. After a few seconds of silence, the Pontiff beseeches God to show the riches of his Mercy upon the multitude, who have already purified their conscience in the Tribunal of reconciliation; he invokes upon them the assistance of the holy Apostles Peter and Paul; and then rising, he raises up his hands to heaven, as though to draw thence the treasures of eternal indulgence; and immediately lowering them, he blesses the assembled multitude. This *Blessing*,[1] which grants a Plenary Indulgence to all that have fulfilled the requisite conditions, was, originally, given only on Maundy Thursday; afterwards, it was given also on Easter Sunday; and again, later on, was extended to two other days in the year, namely, the Ascension (at Saint John Lateran), and the Assumption (at Saint Mary Major).

THE BLESSING

OF THE

HOLY OILS.

The second Mass which used, formerly, to be said on Maundy Thursday, was that of the Blessing of the Holy Oils. This holy function, which takes place but once each year, requires a Bishop as the consecrator. For now many centuries, this great ceremony is celebrated at the single Mass, which is said, on this day, in commemoration of our Lord's Supper. As this Blessing only takes place in Cathedral Churches, we will not enter into each detail; and yet we would not deprive our readers of what they ought to know with regard to the Holy Oils. Faith teaches us, that, as we are regenerated by water, so are we confirmed and fortified by oil; and that Oil is one of the chief elements chosen by the Divine Author of the Sacraments, whereby to signify and produce grace in our souls.

The reason of the Church's selecting Maundy Thursday for the Blessing of the Holy Oils, was that

[1] It is incorrectly called a Blessing *Urbi et Orbi*, inasmuch as it is only given to the Faithful who are present at it.

they would be so much needed for the Baptism of the neophytes on Easter Eve. It behoves the Faithful to understand the mystery of those sacred elements. We will, therefore, briefly explain it to them, in order that we may excite their hearts to gratitude to our Blessed Lord, who has made material things the instruments of grace, and, by his Blood, has given them the sacramental power which resides within them.

The first of the Holy Oils, that is, the first that is blessed by the Bishop, is the one called the *Oil of the Sick*. It is the matter of the Sacrament of Extreme Unction. It takes away, from the dying Christian, the remnants of sin; it strengthens him in his last combat; and, by the supernatural power it possesses, sometimes restores to him the health of the body. Formerly, it used to be blessed on any day of the year, as often as required: but, later on, its Blessing was fixed for this day, that thus the three Oils might be blessed all together. The Faithful should assist, with much devotion, at this ceremony; for the element that is thus sanctified, is one day to anoint and purify their bodies, sinking under sickness. Let them, as they see it being blessed, think upon their last hour, and praise the infinite goodness of their Saviour, "whose blood streams so plentifully through "this precious fluid."[1]

The noblest of the three Oils is the Chrism, and its consecration is more solemn, and fuller of mystery, than those of the other two. It is by the Chrism that the Holy Ghost imprints his indelible seal on the Christian, that has already been made a member of Christ by Baptism. The Water gives us our spiritual birth; the Chrism gives us strength; and, until such time as we have received its holy anointing, we have not as yet the perfect character of a Christian.

---

[1] Bossuet, *Oraison funèbre d'Henriette d'Angleterre*.

Anointed with this holy Oil, the Faithful has a visible sign given him of his being a member of the Man-God, whose name of *Christ* signifies the *unction* he has received both as King and Pontiff. This consecration of a Christian by Chrism is so much in accordance with the spirit of our holy Religion, that, immediately after Baptism, the child receives upon its head an anointing, (though it is not a sacramental one,) of this Oil, to show that he is already a sharer of the kingly character of Jesus Christ.

In order to express, by an outward sign, the sacredness of Chrism, an Apostolic tradition requires the Bishop to mix Balm with it. This Balm represents what the Apostle calls *the good odour of Christ*,[1] of whom it is written: *We will run after thee, to the odour of thy ointments*.[2] The scarcity and high price of other perfumes has obliged the Latin Church to be content with Balm alone in the mixture of holy Chrism: but in the Eastern Church, where the climate is more favourable than ours, three and thirty species of precious perfumes are put into the Oil, and it thus becomes an ointment of exquisite fragrance.

The holy Chrism, besides its sacramental use in Confirmation, and its being put upon the head of the newly baptised, is also used by the Church in the consecration of her Bishops, in the consecration of Chalices and Altars, in the blessing of Bells, and in the Dedication of a Church, in which last most imposing ceremony, the Bishop pours out the Chrism on the twelve crosses, which are to attest to all succeeding ages, the glory of God's House.

The third of the holy Oils is that which is called the *Oil of Catechumens*. Though it be not the matter of any Sacrament, it is, nevertheless, an Apostolic institution. Its blessing is less solemn than that of the Chrism, but more so than that of the Oil of the

---

[1] I. Cor. ii. 15.   [2] Cant. i. 3.

Sick. The Oil of Catechumens is used in the ceremonies of Baptism, for the anointing the breast and shoulders. It is also used for the anointing a Priest's hands in Ordination, and for the coronation of a King or Queen.

These few words of explanation will give the Faithful some idea of the importance of the Blessing of the holy Oils. By this threefold Blessing, says St. Fortunatus, (in the beautiful Hymn, which is used during the ceremony,) the Bishop acquits the debt he owes, and which none but he can pay.

The holy Church seldom employs such pomp as she does on this occasion. Twelve Priests, seven Deacons, and seven Subdeacons, are present. The *Roman Pontifical* tells us, that the twelve Priests assist as witnesses and co-operators of the holy Chrism. The Mass commences, and goes on as far as the Prayer of the Canon, which immediately precedes the *Pater noster*. The Bishop then leaves the Altar, and goes to the place prepared for the Blessing. The first phial of Oil that is brought to him, is that which is intended for the sick. He prefaces the blessing, by pronouncing the words of exorcism over this oil, in order to drive from it the influence of the wicked spirits, who, out of hatred for man, are ever seeking to infest the creatures given to us for our use. This done, he blesses it in these words:

We beseech thee, O Lord, send forth from heaven thy Holy Spirit the Paraclete upon this rich juice of the olive, which thou hast graciously produced from the green wood, for the solace of both mind and body. By thy holy blessing, may all they that are anointed with this ointment of heavenly virtue, receive help to mind and body; may it remove from them all pains, all infirmities, and all sickness of mind and body, for it was with oil that thou didst anoint thy Priests, Kings, Prophets, and Martyrs. May this, being blessed by thee, O Lord, become unto us an ointment of perfection, and abide within our whole being. In the name of our Lord Jesus Christ.

One of the seven Subdeacons then carries the phial back, and the Bishop returns to the Altar, and continues the Mass. As soon as he has given Holy Communion to the clergy, he returns to the place prepared for the blessing of the Oils. The twelve Priests, the seven Deacons, and the seven Subdeacons, repair to the place where the other two phials have been put. One contains the oil, which is to become the Chrism of salvation; the other, the oil which is to be sanctified as the oil of Catechumens. The procession is soon seen returning towards the Pontiff. The two phials are carried by two Deacons; a Subdeacon carries the vase of Balm. The Bishop begins by blessing the Balm: he calls it " the fragrant " tear of dry bark,—the oozing of a favoured branch, " that gives us the priestly unction." Before proceeding to bless the oil of the Chrism, he thrice breathes upon it, in the form of a cross. The twelve Priests do the same. The Gospel tells us that our Blessed Saviour used this same ceremony over his Apostles. It signifies the power of the Holy Ghost, and expresses his name, which is *The Spirit.* This Holy Spirit is about to make this oil become an instrument of his Divine power. The Bishop first prepares it for the heavenly dignity, by exorcising it. He then celebrates the praises of the Chrism, by this magnificent Preface, which has been handed down to us from the earliest ages of our faith.

It is truly meet and just, right available to salvation, that we should always, and in all places, give thanks to thee, O Holy Lord, Almighty Father, Eternal God: who, in the beginning, among the rest of thy bounteous gifts, didst command the earth to yield fruitbearing trees, among which should be the olive, which produces this most rich liquor, and whose fruit was to serve for the making holy Chrism. Hence it was, that David, foreknowing, by a prophetic spirit, the Sacraments of thy grace, sang that our faces were to be made glad with oil: and when the sins of the world were expiated of old, by the deluge, a dove announced that peace was restored to the earth, by bearing an olive-branch, the type of the gift to come, which has been manifested in these latter ages; for after the waters of Baptism have washed away the sins of men, this anointing of oil gave us joy and calm. Hence, too, thou didst command thy servant Moses to ordain his brother Aaron priest, by pouring oil upon him, after he had been cleansed with water. A greater honour still was, that when thy Son, our Lord Jesus Christ, bade John baptise him in the waters of the Jordan, thou didst send upon him the Holy Ghost in the form of a dove; that thus, by a voice that bore testimony, thou mightest designate thine Only Begotten Son, in whom thou wast well pleased, and mightest prove, beyond all doubt, that this was the fulfilment of what the Prophet David had foretold, when he sang, that he was to be anointed with the oil of gladness above his fellows. We, therefore, beseech thee, O Holy Lord, Almighty Father, Eternal God, through the same Jesus Christ, thy Son, our Lord, that thou vouchsafe to sanctify, by thy blessing, this thy creature oil, and infuse into it the virtue of the Holy Ghost, through the co-operating power of Christ, thy Son, from whose name it hath borrowed its own of *Chrism*, and wherewith thou didst anoint the Priests, Kings, Prophets, and Martyrs. Raise this Chrism into a Sacrament of perfect salvation and life, to them that are to be renewed by the spiritual laver of Baptism. That thus, the corruption of their first birth being absorbed by the infusion of this holy anointing, they may become a holy temple, redolent with the fragrance of the innocence of holy living. According to what thou hast appointed in this mystery, bestow upon them the honour of kings, priests, and prophets, by vesting them in the robe of incorruption. May this oil be to them, that are born again from water and the Holy Ghost, a Chrism of salvation, making them partakers of life everlasting, and co-heirs of heavenly glory.

The Bishop then takes the Balm; and having mixed it, on a paten, with a little oil, he pours it into the Phial. The consecration of the Chrism thus completed, he salutes it with these words: *Hail, O Holy Chrism!* This he does with the intention of honouring the Holy Ghost, who is to work by this sacramental oil. The same is done by each of the twelve Priests.

The Bishop then proceeds to bless the Oil of

Catechumens. After having breathed upon it, and pronounced the exorcism, (as before, in the blessing of the holy Chrism,) he says this Prayer:

O God, the rewarder of every spiritual increase and growth! who strengthenest the beginnings of weakly souls by the power of the Holy Ghost: we beseech thee, O Lord, that thou vouchsafe to pour out thy blessing upon this oil, and grant to them, that come to the laver of holy regeneration, the cleansing of soul and body, by the anointing they receive from this thy creature; that so, if there should be any stains fixed upon them by their spiritual enemies, they may be effaced by the touch of this holy oil. May the wicked spirits find no room there; may the powers, that have been put to flight, have no further sway; may there be no lurking place left to insidious evil ones. May thy servants that come to the faith, and are to be cleansed by the operation of thy Holy Spirit, find in this anointing a preparation for that salvation, which they are to receive in the Sacrament of Baptism, by the birth of a heavenly regeneration. Through our Lord Jesus Christ, thy Son, who is to come to judge the living, and the dead, and the world by fire. Amen.

The Bishop then salutes the Oil, on which he has conferred these wonderful prerogatives, saying: *Hail, O holy Oil!* The same act of reverence is repeated by each of the Priests. One of the deacons takes the Chrism, an other the Oil of Catechumens, and a procession is again formed for taking them to the place prepared for them. They are covered with veils of silk;—the holy Chrism, with white; the Oil of Catechumens, with purple.

We will conclude our outline of this imposing ceremony, by giving our readers the beautiful Hymn, composed in the 6th century, by St. Venantius Fortunatus, Bishop of Poitiers. The Church has adopted it for the two processions, which we have already described.

HYMN.

O Redeemer of mankind! receive the hymn of them that sing thy praise.
Repeat: O Redeemer.
O Judge of the dead! thou only hope of men! hear the prayers of them that carry the emblem of the gift of peace.
O Redeemer.
A tree made fruitful by the fostering sun, produced this oil that is now to be blessed, which we, the adorers of his holy name, bring to the Saviour of the world.
O Redeemer.
The mitred Pontiff, too, standing humbly before the altar, is about to pay his debt, by consecrating the Chrism.
O Redeemer.
O King of the everlasting kingdom! deign to consecrate this oil, this instrument of life, that breaks the demon's power.
O Redeemer.
Men and women are renovated by the unction of the Chrism; and their glorious dignity, that had been wounded, is healed by the same.
O Redeemer.
When the soul is washed in the sacred font, her crimes are put to flight: and holiest graces come upon them, whose brow is anointed with this oil.
O Redeemer.
O thou the Son of the Eternal Father, and Son of

O Redemptor, sume carmen temet concinentium.
Repeat: O Redemptor.
Audi, judex mortuorum,
Una spes mortalium,
Audi voces proferentum
Donum pacis prævium.
O Redemptor.
Arbor fœta alma luce
Hoc sacrandum protulit:
Fert hoc prona præsens turba
Salvatori sæculi.

O Redemptor.
Stans ad aram immo supplex
Infulatus Pontifex,
Debitum persolvit omne,
Consecrato Chrismate.
O Redemptor.
Consecrare tu dignare,
Rex perennis patriæ,
Hoc olivum, signum vivum
Jura contra dæmonum.

O Redemptor.
Ut novetur sexus omnis
Unctione Chrismatis,
Ut sanetur sauciata
Dignitatis gloria.

O Redemptor.
Lota mente sacro fonte
Aufugantur crimina:
Uncta fronte, sacrosancta
Influunt charismata.

O Redemptor.
Corde natus ex Parentis,
Alvum implens Virginis,

Præsta lucem, claude mortem Chrismatis consortibus.	the Virgin-Mother! grant light and life to us whom thou hast made to share in thine own anointing.
O Redemptor.	O Redeemer.
Sit hæc dies festa nobis Sæculorum sæculis: Sit sacrata, digna laude, Nec senescat tempore.	May this day be to us an everlasting feast. May it be sacred, praiseworthy, nor grow old with time.
O Redemptor.	O Redeemer.

THE MASS OF MAUNDY THURSDAY.

The Church intends, on this day, to renew, in a most solemn manner, the mystery of the Last Supper: for our Lord himself, on this occasion of the institution of the Blessed Sacrament, said to his Apostles: *Do this for a Commemoration of me.*[1] Let us, therefore, resume the Gospel narrative.

Jesus is in the Supper chamber, where the Paschal Lamb is to be eaten. All the Apostles are with him; Judas is there, also, but his crime is not known to the rest. Jesus approaches the table, on which the Lamb is served. His Disciples stand around him. The ceremonies prescribed by God to Moses are religiously observed. At the beginning of the repast, Jesus speaks these words to his Apostles: *With desire I have desired to eat this Pasch with you, before I suffer.*[1] In saying this, he does not imply that the Pasch of this year is intrinsically better than those that have preceded it; but, that it is dearer to him, inasmuch as it is to give rise to the institution of the new Pasch, which he has prepared for mankind, and which he is now going to give them as his last gift: for as St. John says, *having loved his*

---

[1] St. Luke, xxii. 15.

own who were in the world, he loved them unto the end.[1]

During the repast, Jesus, who reads the hearts of all men, utters these words, which cause great consternation among the Disciples: *Amen I say to you, that one of you is about to betray me:—he that dippeth his hand with me in the dish, he shall betray me.*[2] The sadness, with which he speaks, is enough to soften any heart; and Judas, who knows his Master's goodness, feels that they imply a merciful pardon, if he will but ask it. But no: the passion of avarice has enslaved his soul, and he, like the rest of the Apostles, says to Jesus: *Is it I, Rabbi?* Jesus answers him in a whisper, in order not to compromise him before his brethren: *Thou hast said it!* But Judas yields not. He intends to remain with Jesus, until the hour comes for betraying him. Thus, the august mystery, which is on the point of being celebrated, is to be insulted by his presence!

The legal repast is over. It is followed by a feast, which again brings the Disciples around their Divine Master. It was the custom in the East, that guests should repose two and two on couches round the table; these have been provided by the disciple, who has placed his house at Jesus' service. John is on the same couch as Jesus, so that it is easy for him to lean his head upon his Master's breast. Peter is on the next couch, on the other side of Jesus, who is thus between the two Disciples, whom he had sent, in the morning, to prepare the Pasch, and who, as we have already observed, represent Faith and Love This second repast is a sorrowful one, in consequence of Jesus having told the guests, that one of them is a traitor. The innocent and affectionate John is overwhelmed with grief, and seeks consolation on the Heart of this dear Lord, whom some one is about to deliver to his enemies.

[1] St. John, xiii. 1. [2] St. Matth. xxvi. 21, 23.

But the Apostles little expect a *third* Supper. Jesus has not told them of his intention; but he had made a promise, and he would fulfil it before his Passion. Speaking, one day, to the people, he had said: *I am the Living Bread which came down from heaven: if any man eat of this Bread, he shall live for ever, and the Bread that I will give, is my Flesh for the life of the world.* * * * *My Flesh is meat indeed, and my Blood is drink indeed. He that eateth my Flesh and drinketh my Blood, abideth in me, and I in him.*[1] The time has come for the fulfilment of this his loving promise. But as it was both his Flesh and his Blood that he promised us, he waited till the time of his sacrifice. His Passion has begun; he is sold to his enemies; his life is already in their hands;—he may at once, therefore, offer himself in sacrifice, and give to his Disciples the very Flesh and Blood of the Victim.

As soon as the second repast was over, Jesus suddenly rises, and, to the astonishment of his Apostles, takes off his upper garment, girds himself, as a servant, with a towel, pours water into a basin, and prepares to wash the feet of the guests. It was the custom, in the East, to wash one's feet, before taking part in a feast; it was considered as the very extreme of hospitality, when the master of the house himself did this service to his guest. Jesus is about to regale his Apostles with a Divine Banquet; he wishes to treat them with every possible mark of welcome and attention. But in this, as in every other action of his, there is a fund of instruction: he would teach us, by what he is now doing, how great is the purity, wherewith we should approach the Holy Table. *He that is washed,* says he, *needeth not but to wash his feet;*[2] as though he would say: "The holiness of "this Table is such, that they who come to it, should

---

[1] St. John, vi. 51, 52, 54, 56, 57.   [2] *Idem*, xiii. 10.

"not only be free from grievous sins, but they should, "moreover, strive to cleanse their souls from those "lesser faults, which come from contact with the "world, and are like the dust that covers the feet of "one that walks on the high-way." We will explain further on, the other teachings conveyed by this action of our Lord.

It is with Peter, the future Head of his Church, that Jesus begins. The Apostle protests; he declares that he will never permit his Master to humble himself so low as this: but he is obliged to yield. The other Apostles, (who, as Peter himself, are reclining upon their couches,) receive the same mark of love: Jesus comes to each of them in turn, and washes their feet. Judas is not excepted: he has just received a second warning from his merciful Master; for Jesus, addressing himself to all the Apostles, said to them: *You are clean; but not all*:[1] but the reproach produced no effect upon this hardened heart. Having finished washing the feet of the Twelve, Jesus resumes his place, side by side with John.

Then taking a piece of the unleavened bread, that had remained over from the feast, he raises his eyes to heaven, blesses the bread, breaks it, and distributes it to his Disciples, saying to them: *Take ye, and eat; this is my Body.*[2] The Apostles take the bread, which is now changed into the Body of their Divine Master; they eat;—and Jesus is, now, not only with them, but in them. But, as this sacred mystery is not only the most holy of the Sacraments, but, moreover, a true Sacrifice; and as a Sacrifice requires the shedding of blood;—our Jesus takes the cup, and changing the wine into his own Blood, he passes it round to his Disciples, saying to them: *Drink ye, all, of this; for this is my Blood of the new testament, which shall be shed for many, unto remission*

---

[1] St. John, xiii. 10.   [2] St. Matth. xxvi. 26.

of sins.[1] The Apostles drink from the sacred chalice thus proffered them; when it comes to Judas, he too, partakes of it, but he drinks his own damnation, as he ate his own *judgment*, when he received the Bread of Life.[2] Jesus, however, mercifully offers the traitor another grace, by saying, as he gives the Cup to his Disciples: *The hand of him that betrayeth me is with me on the table.*[3]

Peter is struck by Jesus thus frequently alluding to the crime, which is to be committed by one of the Twelve. He is determined to find out who the traitor is. Not daring himself to ask Jesus, at whose right hand he is sitting, he makes a sign to John, who is on the other side, and begs him to put the question. John leans on Jesus' breast, and says to him in a whisper: *Lord, who is it?* Jesus answers him in an equally suppressed tone: *He to whom I shall reach bread dipped.* And having taken one of the pieces of bread that remained over from the repast, he *dipped* it, and gave it to Judas. It was one more grace offered and refused, for the Evangelist adds: *And after the morsel, Satan entered into him.*[4] Jesus again addresses him, saying: *That which thou dost, do quickly.*[5] The wretch then leaves the room, and sets about the perpetration of his crime.

Such is the history of the Last Supper, of which we celebrate the anniversary on this day. But there is one circumstance of the deepest interest to us, and to which we have, so far, only made an indirect allusion. The institution of the Holy Eucharist, both as a *Sacrament* and *Sacrifice*, is followed by another,—the institution of a new *Priesthood.* How could our Saviour have said: *Except you eat the Flesh of the Son of Man, and*

---

[1] St. Matth. xxvi. 27, 28.　　[2] I. Cor. xi. 29.
[3] St. Luke, xxii. 21.　[4] St. John, xiii. 27.　[5] *Id. ibid.*

drink his Blood, you shall not have life in you,[1]—unless he had resolved to establish a ministry upon earth, whereby he would renew, even to the end of time, the great Mystery he thus commands us to receive? He begins it to-day, in the Cenacle. The twelve Apostles are the first to partake of it: but observe what he says to them: *Do this for a commemoration of me.*[2] By these words, he gives them power to change bread into his Body, and wine into his Blood; and this sublime power shall be perpetuated in the Church, by holy Ordination, even to the end of the world. Jesus will continue to operate, by the ministry of mortal and sinful men, the Mystery of the Last Supper. By thus enriching his Church with the one and perpetual Sacrifice, he also gives us the means of *abiding in him*, for he gives us, as he promised, the *Bread of heaven.* To-day, then, we keep the anniversary, not only of the Institution of the Holy Eucharist, but, also, of the equally wonderful Institution of the *Christian Priesthood.*

To offer the Faithful an outward expression of the greatness and the unity of this Supper, which our Saviour gave to his Disciples, and, through them, to us,—the Church forbids her Priests to say private Masses on this day, except in cases of necessity. She would have but one Sacrifice to be offered in each church, at which the other Priests are to assist, and receive Holy Communion from the hands of the Celebrant. When approaching the Altar, they put on the Stole, the emblem of their Priesthood.

The Mass of Maundy Thursday is one of the most solemn of the Year; and although the Feast of Corpus Christi is the day for the solemn honouring the mystery of the Holy Eucharist,—still, the Church

---

[1] St. John, vi. 54.   [2] St. Luke, xxii. 19.

would have the anniversary of the Last Supper to be celebrated with all possible splendour. The colour of the vestments is white, as it is for Christmas Day and Easter Sunday; the decorations of the Altar and Sanctuary all bespeak joy: and yet, there are several ceremonies during this Mass, which show that the holy Spouse of Christ has not forgotten the Passion of her Jesus, and that this joy is but transient. The Priest entones the Angelic Hymn, *Glory be to God in the highest!* and the Bells ring forth a joyous peal, which continues during the whole singing of the heavenly Canticle: but, from that moment, they remain silent, and their long silence produces, in every heart, a sentiment of holy mournfulness. But why does the Church deprive us, for so many hours, of the grand melody of these sweet bells, whose voices cheer us during the rest of the year? It is to show us, that this world lost all its melody and joy when its Saviour suffered and was crucified. Moreover, she would hereby remind us, how the Apostles, (who were the heralds of Christ, and are figured by the Bells, whose ringing summons the Faithful to the House of God,) fled from their Divine Master and left him a prey to his enemies.

The Holy Sacrifice continues as usual; but at the solemn moment of the Elevation of the Holy Host and the Chalice of Salvation, the Bell is silent, and, outside the Church, there is not given to the neighbourhood the usual signal of the descent of Jesus upon the Altar. When the time of the holy Communion is near, the Priest does not give the Kiss of *Peace* to the Deacon, who, according to the Apostolic tradition, should transmit it, by the Subdeacon, to those that are about to communicate. Our thoughts turn to the traitor Judas, who, on this very day, profaned the sign of friendship by making it an instrument of death. It is out of detestation for this crime, that the Church omits, to-day, the sign of fraternal charity,—it would too painfully remind us of sacrilegious hypocrisy.

Another rite, peculiar to to-day, is the Priest's consecrating two Hosts during the Mass. One of these he receives in Communion; the other he reserves, and reverently places it in a Chalice, which he covers with a veil. The reason of this is, that, to-morrow, the Church suspends the daily Sacrifice. Such is the impression produced by the anniversary of our Saviour's Death, that the Church dares not to renew, upon her Altars, the immolation which was then offered on Calvary:—or rather, her renewal of it will be by the fixing all her thoughts on the terrible scene of that Friday Noon. The Host reserved from to-day's Mass, will be her morrow's participation. This rite is called the Mass *of the Presanctified*, because, in it, the Priest does not consecrate, but only receives the Host consecrated on the previous day. Formerly, as we shall explain more fully further on, the holy Sacrifice was not offered up on Holy Saturday, and yet the Mass *of the Presanctified* was not celebrated, as it was on the Friday.

But, although the Church suspends, for a few short hours, the oblation of the perpetual Sacrifice,—she would not that her Divine Spouse should lose aught of the homage, that is due to him in the Sacrament of his Love. Catholic piety has found a means of changing these trying hours into a tribute of devotion to the Holy Eucharist. In every Church is prepared a richly ornamented side-chapel or pavilion, where, after to-day's Mass, the Church places the Body of her Divine Lord. Though veiled from their view, the Faithful will visit him in this his holy resting-place, pay him their most humble adorations, and present him their most fervent supplications. *Wheresoever the Body shall be, there shall the eagles be gathered together.*[1] In every part of the Catholic world, a concert of prayer, more loving and earnest than at any other period of the Year, will be offered to our Jesus, in reparation for the outrages he underwent, during these very hours, from the Jews. Around this anticipated Tomb will be united both his long-tried and fervent servants, and those who are newly converted, or are preparing for their reconciliation.

At Rome, the Station is in the Lateran Basilica. The *metropolitan* Church both of the Holy City and the World was deservedly chosen for this great Day of the Reconciliation of Sinners and the Consecration of the Chrism. The Papal function, however, now takes place at the Vatican; and, as we have already stated, the Apostolic Benediction is given by the Sovereign Pontiff from the *loggia* of Saint Peter's.

MASS.

In the Introit, the Church makes use of the words of St. Paul, in praise of the Cross of Christ. She is filled with gratitude for this her Redeemer, who has made himself our *Salvation,* by dying for us; our *Life,* by the Bread of Heaven he has given us; and our *Resurrection,* by his having risen from the grave.

INTROIT.

Nos autem gloriari oportet in cruce Domini nostri Jesu Christi, in quo est salus, vita, et resurrectio nostra: per quem salvati, et liberati sumus.	We ought to glory in the cross of our Lord Jesus Christ: in whom is our salvation, life, and resurrection: by whom we have been saved and delivered.
Ps. Deus misereatur nostri, et benedicat nobis, illu-	*Ps.* May God have mercy on us, and bless us: may his

---
[1] St. Matth. xxiv. 28.

countenance shine upon us, minet vultum suum super
and may he have mercy on us. nos, et misereatur nostri.
We ought. Nos autem.

In the Collect, the Church reminds us of Judas
and the Good Thief: both are guilty: and yet, the
one is condemned, the other is pardoned. She
prays for us to God, that the Passion of his Son,
(during which were thus shown the Divine Justice
and Mercy,) may procure us the forgiveness of our
sins, and the fulness of grace.

COLLECT.

O God, from whom both Judas received the punishment of his sin, and the Thief the reward of his confession : grant us the effects of thy mercy; that as our Lord Jesus Christ, at the time of his Passion, bestowed on both different rewards according to their merits; so, having destroyed the old man in us, he may give us grace to rise again with him. Who liveth, &c.	Deus, a quo et Judas reatus sui poenam, et confessionis suae latro praemium sumpsit : concede nobis tuae propitiationis effectum: ut sicut in passione sua Jesus Christus Dominus noster diversa utrisque intulit stipendia meritorum, ita nobis, ablato vetustatis errore, resurrectionis suae gratiam largiatur. Qui tecum.

EPISTLE.

Lesson of the Epistle of Saint Paul the Apostle to the Corinthians.   Lectio Epistolae beati Pauli Apostoli ad Corinthios.

I. Ch. XI.   *I. Cap. XI.*

Brethren: When you come therefore together into one place, it is not now to eat the Lord's supper. For every one taketh before his own supper to eat. And one indeed is hungry, and another is drunk. What, have you not houses to eat and drink in? Or despise   Fratres: Convenientibus vobis in unum, jam non est Dominicam Coenam manducare. Unusquisque enim suam coenam praesumit ad manducandum. Et alius quidem esurit: alius autem ebrius est. Numquid domos non habetis ad manducandum et bibendum? Aut Ecclesiam Dei contemnitis, et confunditis eos, qui non habent? Quid dicam vobis? Laudo vos? In hoc non laudo. Ego enim accepi a Domino, quod et tradidi vobis: quoniam Dominus Jesus in qua nocte tradebatur, accepit panem, et gratias agens fregit, et dixit: Accipite et manducate: hoc est Corpus meum, quod pro vobis tradetur; hoc facite in meam commemorationem. Similiter et calicem postquam cœnavit, dicens: Hic calix novum testamentum est in meo Sanguine. Hoc facite quotiescumque bibetis, in meam commemorationem. Quotiescumque enim manducabitis panem hunc, et calicem bibetis, mortem Domini annuntiabitis donec veniat. Itaque quicumque manducaverit panem hunc, vel biberit calicem Domini indigne, reus erit Corporis et Sanguinis Domini. Probet autem seipsum homo, et sic de pane illo edat, et de calice bibat. Qui enim manducat et bibit indigne, judicium sibi manducat et bibit, non dijudicans Corpus Domini. Ideo inter vos multi infirmi et imbecilles, et dormiunt multi. Quod si nosmetipsos dijudicaremus, non utique judicaremur. Dum judicamur autem, a Domino corripimur, ut non cum hoc mundo damnemur.

ye the Church of God, and put them to shame that have not? What shall I say to you? Do I praise you? In this I praise you not. For I have received of the Lord that which also I delivered to you, that the Lord Jesus, the same night in which he was betrayed, took bread, and giving thanks, broke, and said: Take ye and eat: this is my Body which shall be delivered for you: this do for the commemoration of me. In like manner also the chalice, after he had supped, saying: This Chalice is the New Testament in my Blood: this do ye, as often as ye shall drink it, for the commemoration of me. For as often as you shall eat this bread, or drink the chalice, you shall show the death of the Lord, until he come. Therefore whosoever shall eat this bread or drink the chalice of the Lord unworthily, shall be guilty of the Body and Blood of the Lord. But let a man prove himself, and so let him eat of that bread, and drink of the chalice. For he that eateth and drinketh unworthily, eateth and drinketh judgment to himself, not discerning the Body of the Lord. Therefore are there many infirm and weak among you, and many sleep. But if we would judge ourselves, we should not be judged. But whilst we are judged, we are chastised by the Lord, that we be not condemned with this world.

After having rebuked the Christians of Corinth for the abuses into which they had fallen at the Feasts, (called *Agape*,) which had been introduced by a spirit of fraternal charity, but were soon abolished,—the holy Apostle relates the history of the Last Supper. His account, which corresponds throughout with that given by the Evangelists, rests upon the testimony of our Blessed Saviour himself, who deigned to appear to him, and instruct him, in person, after his conversion. The Apostle does not omit to give the words, whereby our Lord empowered his Apostles to renew what he himself had done: he tells us, that as often as the Priest consecrates the Body and Blood of Christ, he *shows the Death of the Lord*, thus expressing the oneness there is between the Sacrifice of the Cross and that of the Altar. We have explained this important doctrine in the 6th Chapter of the introduction to this present Volume. The consequence to be drawn from this teaching is evident; it is contained in these words of the Apostle: *Let a man prove himself, and so let him eat of that bread and drink of the chalice.* What could be more just, than that having to be initiated in so intimate a manner, with the Mystery of the Redemption, and contract so close a union with the Divine Victim,—we should banish from our hearts sin and affection to sin? *He that eateth my Flesh and drinketh my Blood, abideth in me, and I in him,* says our Lord.[1] Could there be a closer union? God and man *abiding* in each other! Oh! how carefully ought we not to purify our soul, and render our will conformable with the will of Jesus, before approaching this Divine Banquet, to which he invites us! Let us beseech him to prepare us himself, as he did his Apostles, by washing their feet. He will grant us our request, not only to-day, but as often

---

[1] St. John, vi. 57.

as we go to Holy Communion, provided we are docile to his grace.

The Gradual is made up of those admirable words, which the Church so often repeats during these three days, and by which St. Paul warms us to gratitude towards the Son of God, who delivered himself up for us.

GRADUAL.

Christus factus est pro nobis obediens usque ad mortem, mortem autem crucis.
℣. Propter quod et Deus exaltavit illum, et dedit illi nomen, quod est super omne nomen.

Christ became, for our sakes, obedient unto death, even to the death of the Cross.
℣. For which cause, God also hath exalted him, and hath given him a name, which is above all names.

GOSPEL.

Sequentia sancti Evangelii secundum Joannem.
Cap. XIII.
Ante diem festum Paschæ, sciens Jesus, quia venit hora ejus, ut transeat ex hoc mundo ad Patrem: cum dilexisset suos, qui erant in mundo, in finem dilexit eos. Et cœna facta, cum diabolus jam misisset in cor, ut traderet eum Judas Simonis Iscariotæ: sciens quia omnia dedit ei Pater in manus, et quia a Deo exivit et ad Deum vadit, surgit a cœna, et ponit vestimenta sua. Et cum accepisset linteum, præcinxit se. Deinde misit aquam in pelvim, et cœpit lavare pedes discipulorum, et exter-

Sequel of the holy Gospel according to John.
Ch. XIII.
Before the festival day of the Pasch, Jesus knowing that his hour was come that he should pass out of this world to the Father: having loved his own who were in the world, he loved them unto the end. And when supper was done, (the devil having now put it into the heart of Judas Iscariot, the son of Simon, to betray him,) knowing that the Father had given him all things into his hands, and that he came from God, and goeth to God: he riseth from supper, and layeth aside his garments, and having taken a towel, girded himself. After that, he

putteth water into a basin, and began to wash the feet of the disciples, and to wipe them with the towel wherewith he was girded. He cometh therefore to Simon Peter. And Peter saith to him: Lord, dost thou wash my feet? Jesus answered, and said to him: What I do, thou knowest not now, but thou shalt know hereafter. Peter saith to him: Thou shalt never wash my feet. Jesus answered him: If I wash thee not, thou shalt have no part with me. Simon Peter saith to him: Lord not only my feet, but also my hands and my head. Jesus saith to him: He that is washed, needeth not but to wash his feet, but is clean wholly. And you are clean, but not all. For he knew who he was that would betray him: therefore he said: You are not all clean. Then after he had washed their feet, and taken his garments, being set down again, he said to them: Know you what I have done to you? You call me Master, and Lord: and you say well, for so I am. If then I, being your Lord and Master, have washed your feet; you also ought to wash one another's feet. For I have given you an example, that as I have done to you, so do you also.

gere linteo, quo erat præcinctus. Venit ergo ad Simonen Petrum, et dicit ei Petrus: Domine, tu mihi lavas pedes? Respondit Jesus, et dixit ei: Quod ego facio, tu nescis modo: scies autem postea. Dicit ei Petrus: Non lavabis mihi pedes in æternum. Respondit ei Jesus: Si non lavero te, non habebis partem mecum. Dicit ei Simon Petrus: Domine, non tantum pedes meos, sed et manus et caput. Dicit ei Jesus: Qui lotus est, non indiget nisi ut pedes lavet, sed est mundus totus. Et vos mundi estis, sed non omnes. Sciebat enim quisnam esset qui traderet eum; propterea dixit: Non estis mundi omnes. Postquam ergo lavit pedes eorum, accepit vestimenta sua: et cum recubuisset iterum, dixit eis: Scitis quid fecerim vobis? Vos vocatis me Magister et Domine: et bene dicitis: sum etenim. Si ergo ego lavi pedes vestros, Dominus et Magister, et vos debetis alter alterius lavare pedes. Exemplum enim dedi vobis, ut quemadmodum ego feci vobis, ita et vos faciatis.

Our Saviour's washing the feet of his Disciples before permitting them to partake of his Divine Mystery, conveys an instruction to us. The Apostle has just been telling us, that we should *prove ourselves*: and here, we have Jesus saying to his Disciples: *You are clean.* It is true, he adds: *but not all:* just as the Apostle assures us, that there are some who render themselves *guilty of the Body and Blood of the Lord.* God forbid we should ever be of the number! Let us *prove* ourselves; let us sound the depths of our conscience, before approaching the Holy Table. Mortal sin, and the affection to mortal sin, would change the Bread of Life into a deadly poison for our souls. But, if respect for the holiness of God, who is about to enter within us by Holy Communion, should make us shudder at the thought of our receiving him in the state of mortal sin, which robs the soul of the image of God and gives her that of Satan,—ought not that same respect urge us to purify our souls from venial sins, which dim the beauty of grace? *He,* says our Saviour, *that is washed, needeth not but to wash his feet.* The *feet* are those earthly attachments, which so often lead us to the brink of sin. Let us watch over our senses, and the affections of our hearts. Let us wash away these stains by a sincere confession, by penance, by sorrow, and by humility; that thus we may worthily receive the Adorable Sacrament, and derive from it the fulness of its power and grace.

In the Offertory-Antiphon, the Soul,—confiding in the promise made to her by Christ, that he will feed her with the Bread of Life,—gives way to a transport of joy. She praises her God for this Divine nourishment, which keeps death from them that eat.

OFFERTORY.

Dextera Domini fecit virtutem, dextera Domini exaltavit me: non moriar, sed vivam, et narrabo opera Domini.

The right hand of the Lord hath displayed its might: the right hand of the Lord hath raised me up; I shall not die, but live, and publish the works of the Lord.

In the Secret, the Church reminds our Heavenly Father, that it was on this very day, that was instituted the august Sacrifice which she is now celebrating.

SECRET.

We beseech thee, O Holy Lord, Almighty Father, Eternal God, that our Lord Jesus Christ, thy Son, may make our sacrifice acceptable to thee, who on this day commanded his disciples to celebrate it in memory of him. Who liveth, &c.	Ipse tibi, quæsumus, Domine sancte, Pater omnipotens, æterne Deus, sacrificium nostrum reddat acceptum, qui Discipulis suis in sui commemorationem hoc fieri hodierna traditione monstravit, Jesus Christus Filius tuus Dominus noster : Qui tecum.

After the Priest has received under both kinds, he puts into a Chalice the Host reserved for to-morrow: he then gives Communion to the Clergy, and, afterwards, to the Laity. As soon as the Communion is finished, the Choir sings the following Antiphon, which tells us how Jesus prepared his Disciples for the great Mystery by humbly washing their feet.

COMMUNION.

The Lord Jesus, after he had supped with his disciples, washed their feet, and said to them : Do you understand what I have done to you, I your Lord and Master? I have set you an example, that you may do the same.	Dominus Jesus postquam cœnavit cum Discipulis suis, lavit pedes eorum, et ait illis: Scitis quid fecerim vobis, ego Dominus et Magister? Exemplum dedi vobis, ut et vos ita faciatis.

Our holy Mother prays for us in the Postcommunion, that we may preserve in ourselves, for all eternity, the Divine Gift just bestowed upon us.

POSTCOMMUNION.

Refecti vitalibus alimentis, quæsumus, Domine Deus noster: ut quod tempore nostræ mortalitatis exsequimur, immortalitatis tuæ munere consequamur. Per Dominum.	We beseech thee, O Lord, our God, that being nourished with this life-giving food, we may receive by thy grace, in immortal glory, what we celebrate in this mortal life. Through, &c.

As soon as the Mass is over, a Procession is formed to the place prepared for the sacred Host, which is to be reserved for the morrow. The Celebrant carries it beneath a canopy, as on the Feast of Corpus Christi; it is not however exposed, as on that day of its Triumph, but concealed in a chalice closely veiled. Let us adore this Divine Sun of Justice, whose rising at Bethlehem brought gladness to our hearts: he is now near his setting: a few hours more, and his Light will be eclipsed. Our earth will then be buried in gloom, until, on the third day, he will rise again with renewed splendour.

During the Procession, the Choir sings the well-known Hymn of the Blessed Sacrament.

HYMN.

Pange, lingua, gloriosi Corporis mysterium, Sanguinisque pretiosi, Quem in mundi pretium, Fructus ventris generosi, Rex effudit gentium.	Sing, my tongue, the Mystery of the glorious Body and precious Blood!—that Blood which the King of all nations, the Fruit of Mary's womb, shed for the world's redemption.
Nobis datus, nobis natus Ex intacta Virgine, Et in mundo conversatus, Sparso verbi semine, Sui moras incolatus Miro clausit ordine.	He gave himself to us; for us was he born from a pure Virgin; he lived among men, sowing the seed of his word, and closed his career on earth by a gift of wondrous love.

MAUNDY THURSDAY: MASS.

On the night of the Last Supper, he assembled his Brethren around him ; and having observed the law, and eaten the Pasch prescribed, he, with his own hands, gave himself to the Twelve, as their Food.

The Word made Flesh changes bread, by his word, into his own Flesh, and the wine becomes the Blood of Christ. Our senses fail us here : but Faith has power to take all wavering from the Christian heart.

Let us, therefore, venerate this great Sacrament in prostrate adoration ! Let the ancient form give place to the new rite ! Let Faith supply what the senses cannot give.

Be praise and jubilee to the Father and the Son ! Salvation, honour, power, yea and benediction, be to them ; and to the Spirit that proceeds from both, be one co-equal praise ! Amen.

In supremæ nocte cœnæ Recumbens cum fratribus, Observata lege plene Cibis in legalibus, Cibum turbæ duodenæ Se dat suis manibus.

Verbum caro, panem verum
Verbo carnem efficit :
Fitque sanguis Christi merum :
Et si sensus deficit,
Ad firmandum cor sincerum
Sola fides sufficit.

Tantum ergo Sacramentum
Veneremur cernui :
Et antiquum documentum
Novo cedat ritui :
Præstet fides supplementum
Sensuum defectui.

Genitori, Genitoque Laus et jubilatio,
Salus, honor, virtus quoque
Sit et benedictio :
Procedenti ab utroque
Compar sit laudatio. Amen.

Having reached the place prepared, the Priest places the Chalice upon the Altar, and censes the Sacred Host. The Deacon takes the Chalice, and puts it in the Tabernacle. After a short prayer in silence, the Procession returns to the Choir, and Vespers are immediately begun. This Office, which, on Feast Days, is celebrated with so much solemnity, is, to-day and to-morrow, deprived of everything that betokens joy. The Psalms are recited, without the slightest chant or even inflexion. The Church, as a disconsolate widow, mourns the loss of her Jesus.

VESPERS.

Pater and *Ave* are said in secret.

The *first* Psalm alludes to the *Chalice of Salvation*, which Jesus prepared for his Church by shedding his Blood for our redemption. It was on this day, at his Last Supper, that he gave her the *Chalice* of the New Testament.

ANT. Calicem salutaris accipiam, et nomen Domini invocabo.

ANT. I will take the Chalice of salvation, and I will call upon the name of the Lord.

PSALM 115.

Credidi, propter quod locutus sum : * ego autem humiliatus sum nimis.

Ego dixi in excessu meo : * omnis homo mendax.

Quid retribuam Domino : * pro omnibus quæ retribuit mihi ?

Calicem salutaris accipiam : * et nomen Domini invocabo.

Vota mea Domino reddam coram omni populo ejus : * pretiosa in conspectu Domini mors sanctorum ejus.

O Domine, quia ego servus tuus : * ego servus tuus, et filius ancillæ tuæ.

Dirupisti vincula mea : * tibi sacrificabo hostiam laudis, et nomen Domini invocabo.

Vota mea Domino reddam in conspectu omnis populi ejus : * in atriis domus Domini, in [medio tui Jerusalem.

I have believed, therefore have I spoken: but I have been humbled exceedingly.

I said in my excess : every man is a liar.

What shall I render to the Lord for all the things that he hath rendered to me ?

I will take the chalice of salvation : and I will call upon the name of the Lord.

I will pay my vows to the Lord before all his people : precious in the sight of the Lord is the death of his saints.

O Lord, for I am thy servant : I am thy servant, and the son of thy handmaid.

Thou hast broken my bonds : I will sacrifice to thee the sacrifice of praise, and I will call upon the name of the Lord.

I will pay my vows to the Lord in the sight of all his people : in the courts of the house of the Lord, in the midst of thee, O Jerusalem.

ANT. I will take the Chalice of salvation, and I will call upon the name of the Lord.

ANT. Calicem salutaris accipiam, et nomen Domini invocabo.

The *second* Psalm shows us our Lord patiently bearing the calumnies of his enemies, and the trials of his earthly *sojourn*.

ANT. With them that hated peace, I was peaceable : when I spoke to them, they fought against me without cause.

ANT. Cum his qui oderunt pacem, eram pacificus : dum loquebar illis, impugnabant me gratis.

PSALM 119.

In my trouble, I cried to the Lord, and he heard me.

O Lord, deliver my soul from wicked lips, and a deceitful tongue.

What shall be given to thee, or what shall be added to thee, to a deceitful tongue ?

The sharp arrows of the mighty, with coals that lay waste.

Wo is me that my sojourning is prolonged : I have dwelt with the inhabitants of Cedar: my soul has been long a sojourner.

With them that hated peace I was peaceable : when I spoke to them, they fought against me without cause.

ANT. With them that hated peace, I was peaceable : when I spoke to them, they fought against me without cause.

Ad Dominum cum tribularer, clamavi : * et exaudivit me.

Domine, libera animam meam a labiis iniquis : * et a lingua dolosa.

Quid detur tibi, aut quid apponatur tibi : * ad linguam dolosam ?

Sagittæ potentis acutæ :* cum carbonibus desolatoriis.

Heu mihi quia incolatus meus prolongatus est ! habitavi cum habitantibus Cedar : * multum incola fuit anima mea.

Cum his qui oderunt pacem, eram pacificus : * dmu loquebar illis, impugnabant me gratis.

ANT. Cum his qui oderunt pacem, eram pacificus : dum loquebar illis, impugnabant me gratis.

In the *third* Psalm, the Messias complains of the perfidy of Judas, and of the persecutions he met with from the Synagogue.

ANT. From unjust men, deliver me, O Lord !

ANT. Ab hominibus iniquis libera me, Domine.

PSALM 139.

Eripe me, Domine, ab homine malo : * a viro iniquo eripe me.

Qui cogitaverunt iniquitates in corde : * tota die constituebant prælia.

Acuerunt linguas suas sicut serpentis : * venenum aspidum sub labiis eorum.

Custodi me, Domine, de manu peccatoris : * et ab hominibus iniquis eripe me.

Qui cogitaverunt supplantare gressus meos : * absconderunt superbi laqueum mihi.

Et funes extenderunt in laqueum : * juxta iter scandalum posuerunt mihi.

Dixi Domino : Deus meus es tu : * exaudi, Domine, vocem deprecationis meæ.

Domine, Domine, virtus salutis meæ : * obumbrasti super caput meum in die belli.

Ne tradas me Domine, a desiderio meo peccatori : * cogitaverunt contra me, ne derelinquas me, ne forte exaltentur.

Caput circuitus eorum : * labor labiorum ipsorum operiet eos.

Cadent super eos carbones, in ignem dejicies eos : * in miseriis non subsistent.

Vir linguosus non dirigetur in terra : * virum injus-

Deliver me, O Lord, from the evil man : rescue me from the unjust man.

Who have devised iniquities in their hearts : all the day long they designed battles.

They have sharpened their tongues like a serpent : the venom of asps is under their lips.

Keep me, O Lord, from the hands of the wicked : and from unjust men deliver me.

Who have proposed to supplant my steps : the proud have hid a net for me.

And they have stretched out cords for a snare : they have laid for me a stumbling-block by the way side.

I said to the Lord : Thou art my God : hear, O Lord, the voice of my supplication.

O Lord, O Lord, the strength of my salvation : thou hast overshadowed my head in the day of battle.

Give me not up, O Lord, from my desire to the wicked : they have plotted against me; do not thou forsake me, lest they should triumph.

The head of their compassing me about : the labour of their lips shall overwhelm them.

Burning coals shall fall upon them ; thou wilt cast them down into the fire : in miseries they shall not be able to stand.

A man full of tongue shall not be established in the earth :

evils shall catch the unjust man unto destruction.

I know that the Lord will do justice to the needy, and will revenge the poor.

But as for the just, they shall give glory to thy name: and the upright shall dwell with thy countenance.

ANT. From unjust men, deliver me, O Lord!

tum mala capient in interitu.

Cognovi quia faciet Dominus judicium inopis: * et vindictam pauperum.

Verumtamen justi confitebuntur nomini tuo: * et habitabunt recti cum vulto tuo.

ANT. Ab hominibus iniquis libera me, Domine.

The *fourth* Psalm represents our Saviour offering his prayer to God as *evening incense:* his *hands* are stretched out upon the Cross. His *bones* are disjointed; the tomb, (which the Psalmist here calls *hell,*) is soon to receive him as its victim; and yet, he hopes in the promised aid.

ANT. Keep me from the snare which they have laid for me, and from the stumblingblocks of them that work iniquity.

ANT. Custodi me a laqueo, quem statuerunt mihi, et a scandalis operantium iniquitatem.

PSALM 140.

I have cried out to thee, O Lord, hear me: hearken to my voice when I cry to thee.

Let my prayer be directed as incense in thy sight: the lifting up of my hands as an evening sacrifice.

Set a watch, O Lord, before my mouth: and a door round my lips.

Incline not my heart to evil words: to make excuses for sins.

With men that work iniquity: and I will not communicate with the choicest of them.

Domine, clamavi ad te, exaudi me: * intende voci meæ cum clamavero ad te.

Dirigatur oratio mea sicut incensum in conspectu tuo: * elevatio manuum mearum, sacrificium vespertinum.

Pone, Domine, custodiam ori meo: * et ostium circumstantiæ labiis meis.

Non declines cor meum in verba malitiæ, * ad excusandas excusationes in peccatis.

Cum hominibus operantibus iniquitatem: * et non communicabo cum electis eorum.

Corripiet me justus in misericordia, et increpabit me : * oleum autem peccatoris non impinguet caput meum.	The just man shall correct me in mercy, and reprove me : but let not the oil of the sinner fatten my head.
Quoniam adhuc et oratio mea in beneplacitis eorum : * absorpti sunt juncti petræ judices eorum.	For my prayer also shall still be against the things with which they are well pleased : their judges falling upon the rock have been swallowed up.
Audient verba mea quoniam potuerunt : * sicut crassitudo terræ erupta est super terram.	They shall hear my words, for they have prevailed ; as when the thickness of the earth is broken up upon the ground.
Dissipata sunt ossa nostra secus infernum : * quia ad te Domine, Domine oculi mei : in te speravi, non auferas animam meam.	Our bones are scattered by the side of hell ; but on thee, O Lord, Lord, are my eyes : in thee have I put my trust, take not away my soul.
Custodi me a laqueo quem statuerunt mihi : * et a scandalis operantium iniquitatem.	Keep me from the snare, which they have laid for me, and from the stumbling-blocks of them that work iniquity.
Cadent in retiaculo ejus peccatores : * singulariter sum ego, donec transeam.	The wicked shall fall in his net : I am alone until I pass.
ANT. Custodi me a laqueo, quem statuerunt mihi, et a scandalis operantium iniquitatem.	ANT. Keep me from the snare which they have laid for me, and from the stumbling-blocks of them that work iniquity.

In the *fifth* Psalm, the Messias complains of his being abandoned by all. No one takes his part ; his enemies have him in their power, and are determined he shall not escape. He turns towards his Eternal Father, and beseeches him to deliver him from *the prison* of the tomb, into which he is soon to descend.

ANT. Considerabam ad dexteram, et videbam ; et non erat qui cognosceret me.	ANT. I looked on my right hand, and beheld ; and there was no one that would know me.

PSALM 141.

I cried to the Lord with my voice : with my voice I made supplication to the Lord.

In his sight I pour out my prayer : and before him I declare my trouble.

When my spirit failed me, then thou knowest my paths.

In this way wherein I walked, they have had a snare for me.

I looked on my right hand, and beheld : and there was no one that would know me.

Flight hath perished from me : and there is no one that hath regard to my soul.

I cried to thee, O Lord ; I said : Thou art my hope, my portion in the land of the living.

Attend to my supplication : for I am brought very low.

Deliver me from my persecutors, for they are stronger than I.

Bring my soul out of prison, that I may praise thy name : the just wait for me until thou reward me.

ANT. I looked on my right hand, and beheld : and there was no one that would know me.

Voce mea ad Dominum clamavi : * voce mea ad Dominum deprecatus sum.

Effundo in conspectu ejus orationem meam : * et tribulationem meam ante ipsum pronuntio.

In deficiendo ex me spiritum meum : * et tu cognovisti semitas meas.

In via hac qua ambulabam : * abconderunt laqueum mihi.

Considerabam ad dexteram, et videbam : * et non erat qui cognosceret me.

Periit fuga a me : * et non est qui requirat animam meam.

Clamavi ad te, Domine : * dixi : Tu es spes mea, portio mea in terra viventium.

Intende ad deprecationem meam : * quia humiliatus sum nimis.

Libera me a persequentibus me : * quia confortati sunt super me.

Educ de custodia animam meam ad confitendum nomini tuo : * me exspectant justi, donec retribuas mihi.

ANT. Considerabam ad dexteram, et videbam ; et non erat qui cognosceret me.

ANTIPHON OF THE *Magnificat.*

ANT. As they were at Supper, Jesus took bread, and blessed it, and broke it, and gave it to his Disciples.

ANT. Cœnantibus autem illis, accepit Jesus panem et benedixit, ac fregit, deditque discipulis suis.

Then is said the Canticle *Magnificat*, (see *page* 88.) The Antiphon is repeated, and then is added the following Versicle:

℣. Christus factus est pro nobis obediens usque ad mortem.

℣. Christ became, for our sakes, obedient unto death.

After the *Pater noster* has been said secretly, the Psalm *Miserere* (*page* 388) is recited with a suppressed voice. The following prayer concludes the Vespers.

Respice, quæsumus, Domine, super hanc familiam tuam, pro qua Dominus noster Jesus Christus non dubitavit manibus tradi nocentium, et crucis subire tormentum.

Look down, O Lord, we beseech thee, on this thy family, for which our Lord Jesus Christ hesitated not to be delivered into the hands of wicked men, and undergo the punishment of the Cross.

(*Then, the rest in secret :*)

Qui tecum vivit et regnat in unitate Spiritus Sancti, Deus, per omnia sæcula sæculorum, amen.

Who liveth and reigneth with thee, in the unity of the Holy Ghost, God, world without end, amen.

THE STRIPPING THE ALTARS.

As soon as Vespers are over, the Celebrant returns to the Sanctuary, assisted by the Deacon and Subdeacon. He goes to the Altar, and takes off the cloths and ornaments. This ceremony signifies the suspension of the Holy Sacrifice. The Altar should be left in this denuded state, until the daily offering can be again presented to the Divine Majesty; that is, when the Spouse of the holy Church shall arise from the Grave, the Conqueror of

Death. He is now in the Hands of his enemies, the Jews, who are about to strip him of his garments, just as we strip the Altar. He is to be exposed naked to the insults of the rabble: and for this reason, the Psalm selected to be recited during this mournful ceremony is the 21st, wherein the Messias speaks of the Roman Soldiers' dividing his garments among them.

ANT. They parted my garments among them, and upon my vesture they cast lots.

ANT. Diviserunt sibi vestimenta mea, et super vestem meam miserunt sortem.

PSALM 21.

O God, my God, look upon me: why hast thou forsaken me? Far from my salvation are the words of my sins.

O my God, I shall cry by day, and thou wilt not hear: and by night, and it shall not be reputed as folly in me.

But thou dwellest in the holy place, the praise of Israel.

In thee have our fathers hoped: they have hoped and thou hast delivered them.

They cried to thee, and they were saved: they trusted in thee, and were not confounded.

But I am a worm, and no man: the reproach of men, and the outcast of the people.

All they that saw me have laughed me to scorn: they have spoken with the lips, and wagged the head.

He hoped in the Lord, let him deliver him: let him save him, seeing he delighted in him.

For thou art he that hast

Deus, Deus meus, respice in me: quare me dereliquisti: * Longe a salute mea verba delictorum meorum.

Deus meus, clamabo per diem, et non exaudies: * et nocte, et non ad insipientiam mihi.

Tu autem in sancto habitus: * Laus Israël.

In te speraverunt patres nostri: * speraverunt, et liberasti eos.

Ad te clamaverunt, et salvi facti sunt: * in te speraverunt, et non sunt confusi.

Ego autem sum vermis, et non homo: * opprobrium hominum, et abjectio plebis.

Omnes videntes me deriserunt me: * locuti sunt labiis, et moverunt caput.

Speravit in Domino, eripiat eum: * salvum faciat eum, quoniam vult eum.

Quoniam tu es, qui extraxisti me de ventre : * spes mea ab uberibus matris meæ. In te projectus sum ex utero.

De ventre matris meæ Deus meus es tu : * ne discesseris a me.

Quoniam tribulatio proxima est : * quoniam non est qui adjuvet.

Circumdederunt me vituli multi : * tauri pingues obsederunt me.

Aperuerunt super me os suum : * sicut leo rapiens et rugiens.

Sicut aqua effusus sum : * et dispersa sunt omnia ossa me.

Factum est cor meum tamquam cera liquescens : * in medio ventris mei.

Aruit tamquam testa virtus mea, et lingua mea, adhæsit faucibus meis : * et in pulverem mortis deduxisti me.

Quoniam circumdederunt me canes multi : * concilium malignantium obsedit me.

Foderunt manus meas et pedes meos : * dinumeraverunt omnia ossa mea.

Ipsi vero consideraverunt et inspexerunt me : * diviserunt sibi vestimenta mea, et super vestem meam miserunt sortem.

Tu autem, Domine, ne elongaveris auxilium tuum a me : * ad defensionem meam conspice.

Erue a framea, Deus, animam meam : * et de manu canis unicam meam.

drawn me out of the womb : my hope from the breasts of my mother. I was cast upon thee from the womb.

From my mother's womb thou art my God, depart not from me.

For tribulation is very near : for there is none to help me.

Many calves have surrounded me : fat bulls have besieged me.

They have opened their mouths against me, as a lion ravening and roaring.

I am poured out like water : and all my bones are scattered.

My heart is become like wax melting in the midst of my bowels.

My strength is dried up like a potsherd, and my tongue hath cleaven to my jaws : and thou hast brought me down into the dust of death.

For many dogs have encompassed me : the council of the malignant hath besieged me.

They have dug my hands and feet : they have numbered all my bones.

And they have looked and stared upon me : they parted my garments amongst them, and upon my vesture they cast lots.

But thou, O Lord, remove not thy help to a distance from me : look towards my defence.

Deliver, O God, my soul from the sword : my only one from the hand of the dog.

Save me from the lion's mouth: and my lowness from the horns of the unicorns.

I will declare thy name to my brethren: in the midst of the church will I praise thee.

Ye that fear the Lord, praise him: all ye the seed of Jacob, glorify him.

Let all the seed of Israel fear him: because he hath not slighted nor despised the supplication of the poor man.

Neither hath he turned away his face from me: and when I cried to him he heard me.

With thee is my praise in the great church: I will pay vows in the sight of them that fear him.

The poor shall eat, and shall be filled, and they shall praise the Lord that seek him: their hearts shall live for ever and ever.

All the ends of the earth shall remember, and shall be converted to the Lord.

And all the kindreds of the Gentiles shall adore in his sight.

For the kingdom is the Lord's: and he shall have dominion over the nations.

All the fat ones of the earth have eaten and have adored: all they that go down to the earth, shall fall before him.

And to him my soul shall live: and my seed shall serve him.

There shall be declared to the Lord a generation to come: and the heavens shall show

Salva me ex ore leonis: * et a cornibus unicornium humilitatem meam.

Narrabo nomen tuum fratribus meis: * in medio ecclesiæ laudabo te.

Qui timetis Dominum, laudate eum: * universum semen Jacob, glorificate eum.

Timeat eum omne semen Israël: * quoniam non sprevit, neque despexit deprecationem pauperis.

Nec avertit faciem suam a me: et cum clamarem ad eum, exaudivit me.

Apud te laus mea in ecclesia magna: * vota mea reddam in conspectu timentium eum.

Edent pauperes, et saturabuntur, et laudabunt Dominum qui requirunt eum: * vivent corda eorum in sæculum sæculi.

Reminiscentur, et convertentur ad Dominum: * universi fines terræ.

Et adorabunt in conspectu ejus: * universæ familiæ gentium.

Quoniam Domini est regnum: * et ipse dominabitur gentium.

Manducaverunt, et adoraverunt omnes pingues terræ: * in conspectu ejus cadent omnes, qui descendunt in terram.

Et anima mea illi vivet:* et semen meum serviet ipsi.

Annuntiabitur Domino generatio ventura: * et annuntiabunt cœli justitiam

ejus, populo qui nascetur quem fecit Dominus.	forth his justice to a people that shall be born, which the Lord hath made.
ANT. Diviserunt sibi vestimenta mea, et super vestem meam miserunt sortem.	ANT. They parted my garments among them, and upon my vesture they cast lots.

After having stripped the High Altar, the Celebrant takes off the Cloths from the other Altars that are in the Church. An air of desolation pervades the Temple of God. The very Tabernacle has lost its Divine Guest. The Ciborium, (in which the Blessed Sacrament is reserved for Viaticum,) has been taken to the place, where reposes the Chalice containing the Body of our Lord. The Majesty of our God has withdrawn to that mysterious Sanctuary, into which we enter not but with silence and compunction.

It was the custom, in some Churches, for the Priest to wash, in the afternoon, the Altars with wine and water, which he sprinkled upon them with a branch of hyssop. This ceremony, (which has now ceased to be observed in almost every Church, excepting at St. Peter's, in Rome,) was intended as a homage offered to our Blessed Lord, in return for the humility, wherewith he deigned to wash the feet of his Disciples. We find it so explained by St. Isidore of Seville,[1] and St. Eligius, Bishop of Noyon.[2]

THE WASHING OF THE FEET.

After having, on this day, washed the feet of his Disciples, Jesus said to them: *Know ye what I have done to you? You call me Master and Lord: and you say well, for so I am. If then I, being your*

---

[1] De Ecclesiasticis Officiis, lib. I. cap. xxviii.
[2] Homil. viii. *De Cœna Domini.*

Lord and Master, have washed your feet; you, also, ought to wash one an other's feet. For I have given you an example, that as I have done to you, so you do also.[1] Although the meaning of these words is, that after the example of our Divine Master, we should practise works of fraternal charity towards our neighbour,—yet the literal imitation of this our Saviour's act has always been observed in the Church.

At the commencement, it was almost a daily practice. St. Paul, when mentioning the qualities which should adorn the Christian Widow, includes that of *washing the feet of the Saints*,[2] that is, of the Faithful. We find this act of humble charity practised in the Ages of Persecution, and even later. The *Acts of the Saints* of the first six centuries, and the Homilies and Writings of the Holy Fathers, are filled with allusions to it. Afterwards, charity grew cold, and this particular way of exercising it was confined, almost exclusively, to Monasteries. Still, from time to time, it was practised elsewhere. We occasionally find Kings and Queens setting this example of humility. The holy King Robert of France, and, later, St. Louis, used frequently to wash the feet of the poor. The holy Queens, St. Margarite of Scotland, and St. Elizabeth of Hungary, did the same. The Church, with that spirit which makes her treasure up every recommendation of her Divine Lord, has introduced this act of humility into her Liturgy, and it is to-day that she puts the great lesson before her children. In every Church of any importance, the Prelate, or Superior, honours our Saviour's condescension by the ceremony, called *the Washing of the Feet*. The Bishops throughout the world follow the example set them by the Sovereign Pontiff, who performs this ceremony in the Vatican. Yea, there are still

---

[1] St. John, xiii. 12-15.   [2] I. Tim. v. 10.

to be found Kings and Queens who, on this day, wash the feet of the poor, and give them abundant alms.

The Twelve Apostles are represented by the twelve poor, who, according to the most general practice, are chosen for this ceremony. The Pope, however, washes the feet of thirteen Priests of as many different countries; and this is the reason of the *Ceremonial* requiring this number for Cathedral Churches. But, why *thirteen?* Some have interpreted it thus: that it represented the full number of the Apostolic College, which is thirteen, for St. Matthias was elected in Judas' place, and our Lord himself, after his Ascension, called St. Paul to be an Apostle. Other authors, however, among whom the learned Pope Benedict the Fourteenth,[1] assert, that the reason of this number being chosen was the miracle related in the life of St. Gregory the Great. This holy Pope used, every day, to wash the feet of twelve poor men, whom he afterwards invited to his own table. One day, a thirteenth was present:—it was an Angel, whom God had sent, that he might thereby testify how dear to him was the charity of his Servant.

The Ceremony of the *Washing of the Feet* is, also, called the *Mandatum*, from the first word of the first Antiphon. After the Deacon has chanted the Gospel of the Mass of Maundy Thursday (*page* 380,) the Celebrant takes off the Cope, girds himself with a towel, and, kneeling down, begins to wash the feet of those who have been chosen. He kisses the right foot of each one, after having washed it. Meanwhile, the Choir sings the following Antiphons:

ANT. Mandatum novum do vobis: ut diligatis invi-	ANT. I give you a new commandment: that ye love

[1] *De Festis D. N. J. C.*—Lib. L Cap. vi. No. 57.

one another, as I have loved you, says our Lord. ℣. Blessed are the immaculate in the way; who walk in the law of the Lord. I give, &c.

ANT. After our Lord was risen from supper, he put water into a basin, and began to wash the feet of his disciples; to whom he gave this example. ℣. Great is the Lord, and exceedingly to be praised: in the city of our God, in his holy mountain. After, &c.

ANT. Our Lord Jesus, after he had supped with his disciples, washed their feet, and said to them: Know you what I your Lord and Master have done to you? I have given you an example, that ye also may do the same. ℣. Thou hast blessed, O Lord, thy land: thou hast delivered Jacob from captivity. Our Lord, &c.

ANT. Lord, dost thou wash my feet? Jesus answered, and said to him: If I shall not wash thy feet, thou shalt have no part with me. ℣. He came to Simon Peter, and Peter said to him: Lord, &c. ℣. What I do thou knowest not now: but thou shalt know it afterwards. Lord, &c.

ANT. If I your Lord and Master have washed your feet: how much more ought you to wash the feet of one another? ℣. Hear these things, all ye nations: hearken to them, all ye that inhabit the world. If I, &c.

ANT. In this all shall know that ye are my disciples, if ye

cem sicut dilexi vos, dicit Dominus. ℣. Beati immaculati in via: * qui ambulant in lege domini. Mandatum.

ANT. Postquam surrexit Dominus a cœna, misit aquam in pelvim, et cœpit lavare pedes discipulorum suorum: hoc exemplum reliquit eis. ℣. Magnus Dominus et laudabilis nimis: * in civitate Dei nostri, in monte sancto ejus. Postquam.

ANT. Dominus Jesus, postquam cœnavit cum discipulis suis, lavit pedes eorum, et ait illis: Scitis quid fecerim vobis ego Dominus et Magister? Exemplum dedi vobis, ut et vos ita faciatis. ℣. Benedixisti, Domine, terram tuam; * avertisti captivitatem Jacob. Dominus.

ANT. Domine, tu mihi lavas pedes! Respondit Jesus, et dixit ei: Si non lavero tibi pedes, non habebis partem mecum. ℣. Venit ergo ad Simonem Petrum, * et dixit ei Petrus: Domine. ℣. Quod ego facio tu nescis modo: scies autem postea. Domine.

ANT. Si ego Dominus et Magister vester lavi vobis pedes: quanto magis debetis alter alterius lavare pedes! ℣. Audite hæc, omnes gentes: * auribus percipite qui habitatis orbem. Si ego.

ANT. In hoc cognoscent omnes quia discipuli mei

estis, si dilectionem habueritis ad invicem. ℣. Dixit Jesus discipulis suis. In hoc.

ANT. Maneant in vobis fides, spes, charitas, tria hæc: major autem horum est charitas. ℣. Nunc autem manent fides, spes, charitas, tria hæc: * major horum est charitas. Maneant.

ANT. Benedicta sit sancta Trinitas atque indivisa unitas: confitebimur ei, quia fecit nobiscum misericordiam suam. ℣. Benedicamus Patrem et Filium, * cum Sancto Spiritu. ℣. Quam dilecta tabernacula tua, Domine virtutum! * concupiscit et deficit anima mea in atria Domini. Benedicta.

have a love for one another. ℣. Said Jesus to his disciples. In this, &c.

ANT. Let these three, Faith, Hope, and Charity, remain in you: but the greatest of them is charity. ℣. But now remain Faith, Hope, and Charity, these three: but the greatest of them is charity. Let, &c.

ANT. Blessed be the holy Trinity and undivided Unity: we will praise him because he has shown us his mercy. ℣. Let us bless the Father and the Son, with the Holy Ghost. ℣. How lovely are thy tabernacles, O Lord of Hosts: my soul desires and longs after the house of the Lord. Blessed, &c.

After these Antiphons, the Choir sings the following Canticle. It is a fervent exhortation to Fraternal Charity, of which the Washing of the Feet is a symbol.

CANTICLE.

Ubi charitas, et amor, Deus ibi est.
℣. Congregavit nos in unum Christi amor.
℣. Exsultemus, et in ipso jucundemur.
℣. Timeamus, et amemus Deum vivum.
℣. Et ex corde diligamus nos sincero.

Ubi charitas et amor, Deus ibi est.

Where charity and love are, there is God.
℣. The love of Christ hath gathered us together.
℣. Let us rejoice in him, and be glad.
℣. Let us fear and love the living God.
℣. And let us love one the other with a sincere heart.

Where charity and love are, there is God.

MAUNDY THURSDAY: WASHING OF FEET.

℣. When, therefore, we are gathered together,
℟. Let us take heed we be not divided in mind.
℣. Let wicked quarrels and contentions be at an end,
℟. And let Christ our God dwell among us.

Where charity and love are, there is God.
℣. Let us, also, with the Blessed, see
℟. Thy face in glory, O Christ our God!
℣. There to possess an immense and happy joy,
℟. For endless ages. Amen.

℣. Simul ergo cum in unum congregamur,
℟. Ne nos mente dividamur caveamus.
℣. Cessent jurgia maligna, cessent lites,
℟. Et in medio nostri sit Christus Deus.

Ubi charitas et amor, Deus ibi est.
℣. Simul quoque cum beatis videamus,
℟. Glorianter, vultum tuum, Christe Deus.
℣. Gaudium, quod est immensum, atque probum,
℟. Sæcula per infinita sæculorum. Amen.

The Celebrant having resumed his Cope, the ceremony concludes with the following prayers:

Our Father. Pater Noster.

The rest of the Lord's Prayer is said in silence, as far as the last two petitions.

℣. And lead us not into temptation.
℟. But deliver us from evil.
℣. Thou hast commanded, O Lord,
℟. That thy precept be exactly observed.
℣. Thou hast washed the feet of thy disciples.
℟. Despise not the work of thy hands.

℣. Et ne nos inducas in tentationem.
℟. Sed libera nos a malo.
℣. Tu mandasti mandata tua, Domine,
℟. Custodiri nimis.
℣. Tu lavasti pedes discipulorum tuorum.
℟. Opera manuum tuarum ne despicias.

℣. Domine, exaudi orationem meam.
℟. Et clamor meus ad te veniat.
℣. Dominus vobiscum.
℟. Et cum spiritu tuo.

℣. O Lord, hear my prayer.
℟. And let my cry come unto thee.
℣. The Lord be with you.
℟. And with thy spirit.

OREMUS.

Adesto, Domine, quæsumus, officio servitutis nostræ et quia tu discipulis tuis pedes lavare dignatus es, ne despicias opera manuum tuarum, quæ nobis retinenda mandasti: ut sicut hic nobis, et a nobis exteriora abluuntur inquinamenta, sic a te omnium nostrum interiora laventur peccata. Quod ipse præstare digneris, qui vivis et regnas Deus per omnia sæcula sæculorum.
℟. Amen.

LET US PRAY.

Accept, O Lord, we beseech thee, this duty of our service, and since thou didst vouchsafe to wash the feet of thy disciples, despise not the work of thy hands, which thou hast commanded us to imitate: that as here the outward stains are washed away by us and from us, so the inward sins of us all may be blotted out by thee. Which be thou pleased to grant, who livest and reignest one God for ever and ever.
℟. Amen.

THE OFFICE OF TENEBRÆ.

At a late hour in the afternoon, the Night Office of Good Friday is anticipated, as was done yesterday. The Faithful repair to the Church at the time specified. Let them remember, that the Bells are not rung from this till Saturday.

The Office of Tenebræ for Good Friday is given below, *page* 414.

THE EVENING.

Judas has left the Cenacle, and, profiting of the darkness, has reached the place where the enemies of his Saviour are assembled. Jesus then turns to his faithful Apostles, and says to them: *Now is the Son of Man glorified.*[1] Yes, his Passion is to be followed by triumph and glory; and the Passion has already begun, for Judas has commenced his work of betraying him. Meanwhile, the Apostles,—forgetting the trouble, into which they had been thrown by Jesus' telling them, that one of the Twelve was about to betray him,—begin to dispute among themselves, *which of them should seem to be greater?*[2] They have not forgotten the words spoken by Jesus to Peter, when he made him the Rock, on which he would build his Church; and here, at the Supper, they have seen their Divine Master wash the feet of Peter first. On the other hand, John's affectionate familiarity with Jesus, during this same Supper, has made some of them argue, that he who was most *loved*, would be most *honoured*.

Jesus puts an end to this dispute, by giving to these future Pastors of his Church a lesson of humility. There shall, it is true, be a Head among them; but, says our Redeemer, *let him that is the greater among you, become as the younger; and he that is the leader, as he that serveth.* He bids them look at him: he is their Master, and yet, says he, *I am in the midst of you, as he that serveth.*[3] Then turning towards Peter, he thus addresses him: *Simon, Simon! behold Satan hath desired to have you, that he may sift you as wheat. But I have prayed for thee, that thy faith fail not: and thou, being once converted, confirm thy Brethren.*[4] This last interview is, as it were, our Saviour's Testament; he provides for his Church, before leaving her. The Apostles are to be Peter's *Brethren*, but Peter is to be their *Head*. This sublime dignity is to be enhanced by the humility of him that enjoys it: he shall be "The Servant of the Servants of God." The Apostolic College is to be exposed to the fury of hell; but

---

[1] St. John, xiii. 31.
[2] St. Luke, xxii. 24.
[3] St. Luke, xxii. 26, 27.
[4] *Ibid.*, 31, 32.

Peter alone is to *confirm* his Brethren in the faith. His teaching shall ever be conformable to Divine Truth; it shall be ever Infallible: Jesus has prayed that it may be so. Such a prayer is all-powerful; and thereby, the Church, ever docile to the voice of Peter, shall for ever maintain the doctrine of Christ.

Jesus, after having provided for the future of his Church by the words he addressed to Peter, thus speaks affectionately to all the eleven: *Little children! yet a little while I am with you. Love one an other. By this shall all men know that ye are my disciples, if ye have love one for an other.* Peter says to him: *Lord! whither goest thou?—Whither I go,* answers Jesus, *thou canst not now follow me; but thou shalt follow hereafter.—Why cannot I follow thee now?* again asks Peter: *I will lay down my life for thee.—Wilt thou,* replies Jesus, *lay down thy life for me? Amen, amen, I say to thee: the cock shall not crow, till thou deny me thrice.*[1] Peter's love for Jesus had too much of the human about it, for it was not based on humility. Presumption comes from pride: it almost always results in a fall. In order to prepare Peter for his future ministry of pardon, as also to give us a useful lesson, God permits that *he,* who was soon to be made Prince of the Apostles, should fall into a most grievous and humiliating sin.

But let us return to the instructions contained in the last words spoken by our Jesus before he leaves his disciples. *I am,* says he, *the Way, the Truth, and the Life. If you love me, keep my commandments. I will ask the Father, and he shall give you another Paraclete, that he may abide with you for ever. I will not leave you orphans; I will come to you. Peace I leave with you, my peace I give unto you: not as the world giveth, do I give unto you. Let not your*

---

[1] St. John, xiii. 33-38.

heart be troubled, nor let it be afraid. If you loved me, you would indeed be glad, because I go to the Father. I will not now speak many things with you, for the prince of this world cometh, and in me he hath not anything. But that the world may know that I love the Father, and as the Father hath given me commandment, so do I,—arise, let us go hence.[1] Deeply impressed by these words, the Disciples arise, and, after the hymn of thanksgiving has been said, they accompany Jesus to Mount Olivet.

He continues his instructions as they go along. He takes occasion from their passing by a Vine to speak of the effect produced by divine grace in the soul of man. *I am the true vine*, he says, *and my Father is the husbandman. Every branch in me, that beareth not fruit, he will take away, and every one that beareth fruit, he will purge it, that it may bring forth more fruit. Abide in me, and I in you. As the branch cannot bear fruit of itself, unless it abide in the vine; so neither can you, unless you abide in me. I am the Vine, you are the branches: he that abideth in me, and I in him, the same beareth much fruit: for without me you can do nothing. If any one abideth not in me, he shall be cast forth as a branch, and shall wither, and they shall gather him up, and cast him into the fire, and he burneth. You have not chosen me: but I have chosen you, and have appointed you, that you should go, and should bring forth fruit, and your fruit should remain.*[2]

He next speaks to them of the persecutions that await them, and of the hatred the world will have of them. He renews the promise he had made them of the Holy Spirit, the Comforter, and tells them that it is to their advantage that he himself should leave them. He assures them, that they shall obtain whatever they ask of the Father in his name. *The*

---

[1] St. John, xiv. [2] St. John, xv.

Father, he adds, *loveth you, because you have loved me, and have believed that I came out from God. I came forth from the Father, and am come into the world: again I leave the world, and I go to the Father.* The *Disciples say to him : Now we know that thou knowest all things, and thou needest not that any man should ask thee. By this we believe that thou comest forth from God.—Do you now believe?* answered Jesus: *behold! the hour cometh, and it is now come, that you shall be scattered every man to his own, and shall leave me alone.*[1] *All you shall be scandalised in me this night: for it is written: "I will strike the shepherd, "and the sheep of the flock shall be dispersed." But after I shall be risen again, I will go before you into Galilee*[2]

Peter again protests that he will be faithful to his Master; the rest may abandon him, if they will, but *he* will keep with him to the last! It should, indeed, be so, for he has received so much more from Jesus than the others have: but he is again humbled by being told of his coming speedy fall. Jesus then calmly raising up his eyes to heaven, says: *Father! the hour is come; glorify thy Son, that thy Son may glorify thee. I have finished the work which thou gavest me to do; I have manifested thy name to the men whom thou hast given me. They have known that I came out from thee, and they have believed that thou didst send me. I pray for them; I pray not for the world. And now I am not in the world, and these are in the world, and I come to thee. Holy Father! keep them in thy name, whom thou hast given me; that they may be one, as we also are. While I was with them, I kept them in thy name. Those whom thou gavest me, have I kept; and none of them is lost, but the son of perdition, that the Scripture may be fulfilled. I have given them thy word; and the world hath hated them,*

---

[1] St. John, xvi.   [2] St. Matth..xxvi. 31, 32.

because they are not of the world, as I also am not of the world. I pray not that thou shouldst take them out of the world, but that thou shouldst keep them from evil. Not for them only do I pray, but for them also who, through their word, shall believe in me: that they all may be one, as thou, Father! in me, and I in thee: that they also may be one in us: that the world may know, that thou hast sent me. Father! I will, that where I am, they also, whom thou hast given me, may be with me; that they may see the glory which thou hast given me, because thou hast loved me before the creation of the world. Just Father! the world hath not known me; but I have known thee, and these have known that thou hast sent me. And I have made known thy name to them, and will make it known, that the love, wherewith thou hast loved me, may be in them, and I in them.[1]

Such are the out-pourings of the loving Heart of our Jesus, as he crosses the Brook Cedron, and ascends, with his Disciples, the Mount of Olives. Having come as far as Gethsemani, he goes into a garden, whither he had often led his Apostles and rested there with them. Suddenly, his Soul is overpowered with grief; his Human Nature experiences, as it were, a suspension of that beatitude, which results from its union with the Divinity. This his Humanity will be interiorly supported, even to the very last moment of his Passion; but it must bear everything that it is possible for it to bear. Jesus feels such intense sadness, that the very presence of his Disciples is insupportable; he leaves them, taking with him only Peter, James, and John, who, a short time before, had been witnesses of his glorious Transfiguration:—will they show greater courage than the rest, when they see their Divine Master in the hands of his enemies? His words

[1] St. John, xvii.

show them what a sudden change has come over
him. He whose language was, a few moments before, so calm, his look so serene, and his tone of voice
so sweet,—now says to them: *My soul is sorrowful
even unto death: stay you here, and watch with
me.*[1]

He leaves them, and goes to a grotto, which is
about a stone's throw distant. Even to this day it
exists, perpetuating the memory of the terrible
event. There does our Jesus prostrate himself, and
prays, saying: *Father! all things are possible to thee.
Remove this chalice from me:—but, not what I will,
but what thou wilt.*[2] Whilst thus praying, a Sweat
of Blood flows from his body and bathes the
ground. It is not merely a swooning,—it is an
Agony, that he suffers. God sends help to his sinking frame, and it is an Angel that is intrusted with
the office. Jesus is treated as man; his Humanity,
exhausted as it is, is to receive no other sensible aid
than that which is now brought him by an Angel,
(whom tradition affirms to have been Gabriel.)
Hereupon he rises, and again accepts the *Chalice* prepared for him. But what a *Chalice!*—every pain
that body and soul can suffer; the sins of the whole
world taken upon himself, and crying out vengeance
against him; the ingratitude of men, many of whom
will make his Sacrifice useless. Jesus has to accept
all this, and at the very time, when he seems to be
left to his Human Nature. The power of the Divinity, which is in him, supports him; but it does not
prevent him from feeling every suffering, just as
though he had been mere Man. He begins his
Prayer by asking, that the Chalice may be taken
from him; he ends it by saying to his Father: *Not
my will, but thine be done!*[3]

---

[1] St. Matth. xxvi. 38. [2] St. Mark, xiv. 36.
[3] St. Luke, xxii. 42.

Jesus then rises, leaving the earth covered with the Blood of his Agony:—it is the first Bloodshedding of his Passion. He goes to his three Disciples, and, finding them asleep, says to them: *What! could you not watch one hour with me?*[1] This was the beginning of that feature of his sufferings, which consists in his being abandoned. He twice returns to the grotto, and repeats his sorrowful, but submissive, prayer; twice he returns to his Disciples, whom he had asked to watch near him, but, at each time, finds them asleep. At length, he speaks to them, saying: *Sleep ye now, and take your rest! Behold, the hour is at hand, and the Son of Man shall be betrayed into the hands of sinners.* Then resuming the energy of his divine courage, he adds: *Rise! let us go! Behold, he is at hand that will betray me!*[2]

Whilst speaking these last few words, a numerous body of armed men enter the Garden with torches in their hands. Judas is at their head. The betrayal is made by a profanation of the sign of friendship. *Judas! dost thou betray the Son of Man with a kiss?*[3] These piercing words should have made the traitor throw himself at his Master's feet, and ask pardon; but it was too late: he feared the soldiers. But the servants of the High Priest cannot lay hands on Jesus, unless he, their Victim, permit them to do so. With one single word, he casts them prostrate on the ground. Then permitting them to rise, he says to them, with all the majesty of a King: *If you seek Me, let these go their way. You are come out, as it were against a thief, with swords and clubs. When I was daily with you in the Temple, you did not stretch forth your hands against me: but this is your hour, and the power of darkness.* Then turning to Peter, who had drawn and used his sword, he says

---

[1] St. Matth. xxvi. 40.   [2] *Id. ibid.* 46.
[3] St. Luke, xxii. 48.

to him: *Thinkest thou, that I cannot ask my Father, and he will give me presently twelve legions of Angels? How then shall the Scriptures be fulfilled?*[1]

And now, Jesus permits himself to be led. Whereupon, his Apostles run away in fear. Peter and another Disciple follow him, but as far off as they can. The soldiers lead Jesus by the same road, along which he had passed on the previous Sunday, when the people met him, with palm and olive branches in their hands. They cross the brook Cedron; and there is a tradition of the Church of Jerusalem, that the soldiers as they passed the bridge, threw Jesus into the water. Thus was fulfilled the prophecy of David: *He shall drink of the torrent in the way.*[2]

They reach the City walls. The gate is opened, and the divine Prisoner enters. It is night, and the inhabitants know not the crime that has been committed. It is only on the morrow, that they will learn, that Jesus of Nazareth, the great Prophet, has fallen into the hands of the Chief Priests and Pharisees. The night is far advanced; but many hours must elapse before the dawn of day. The enemies of Jesus have arranged to take him, in the morning, to Pontius Pilate, and accuse him as being a disturber of the peace: but in the meanwhile, they intend to condemn him as guilty in matters of *religion!* Their tribunal has authority to judge in cases of this nature, only they cannot pass sentence of death upon a culprit, how guilty soever they may prove him. They, consequently, hurry Jesus to Annas, the father-in-law of the High Priest Caiphas. Here is to take place the first examination. These blood-thirsty men have spent these hours in sleepless anxiety. They have counted the very minutes since the departure of their minions for Mount Olivet. They are not without some doubt as to whether their plot

---
[1] St. John, xviii. 8. St. Luke, xxii. 52, 53. St. Matth. xxvi. 53.
[2] Ps. cix. 7.

will succeed. At last, their Victim is brought before them, and he shall not escape their vengeance!

Here let us interrupt our History of the Passion, till the morrow shall bring us to the solemn hour, when the great Mystery of our instruction and salvation was accomplished. What a day is this that we have been spending! How full of Jesus' love! He has given us his Body and Blood to be our Food; he has instituted the Priesthood of the New Testament; he has poured out upon the world the sublimest instructions of his loving Heart. We have seen him struggling with the feelings of human weakness, as he beheld the Chalice of the Passion that was prepared for him; but he triumphed over all, in order to save *us*. We have seen him betrayed, fettered, and led captive into the holy City, there to consummate his Sacrifice. Let us adore and love this Jesus, who might have saved us by one and the least of all these humiliations; but whose love for us was not satisfied unless he drank, to the very dregs, the Chalice he had accepted from his Father.

The following beautiful Preface of the Gothic Missal of Spain will assist us in our devotion towards the Mysteries we have been celebrating.

ILLATION.

It is meet and just, that we should give thanks to thee, O Holy Lord, Almighty Father! and to Jesus Christ thy Son. We have been fostered by his Humanity, exalted by his humility, set free by his betrayal, redeemed by his punishment, saved by his Cross, cleansed by his Blood, fed by his Flesh. He, on this day, delivered himself for us; and loosened the bonds of our sin. He showed to his

Dignum et justum est: nos tibi, Domine sancte, Pater omnipotens, gratias agere: et Jesu Christo Filio tuo. Cujus nos humanitas colligit: humilitas erigit: traditio solvit: pœna redimit: crux salvificat: sanguis emaculat: caro saginat. Qui seipsum pro nobis hodie tradidit; et culpæ nostræ vincula relaxavit. Qui ad commendandam fidelibus bonitatis suæ, humilitatisque magnificentiam, etiam traditoris sui non dedignatus est pedes abluere: cujus jam manus prævidebat in scelere. Sed quid mirum: si dum ministerium formæ servilis voluntariæ morti vicinus adimplet, posuit vestimenta sua: qui cum in forma Dei esset, semetipsum exinanivit? Quid mirum si præcinxit se linteo: qui formam servi accipiens, habitu est inventus ut homo? Quid mirum si misit aquam in pelvim: unde lavaret pedes discipulorum: qui in terra sanguinem suum fudit: quo immunditias dilueret peccatorum? quid mirum, si linteo quo erat præcinctus, pedes quos laverat tersit: qui carne qua erat indutus evangelistarum vestigia confirmavit? Et linteo quidem ut se præcingeret: posuit vestimenta quæ habebat: ut autem formam servi acciperet: quando semetipsum exinanivit: non quod habebat deposuit: sed quod non habebat accepit. Crucifigendus sane suis expoliatus est vestimentis: et mortuus involutus est linteis: et tota illa ejus passio credentium est facta purgatio. Passurus igitur exitia; præmisit obsequia. Non solum eis pro quibus subiturus venerat mortem; sed etiam illi qui fuerat traditurus illum ad mortem. Tanta quippe est humanæ humilitatis utilitas: ut eam suo commendaret exemplo

Faithful people the riches of his goodness and humility, by deigning to wash the feet of his very betrayer, whose hand he already perceived to be engaged in his wicked deed. But, what wonder, that he, on the eve of his voluntary Death, when about to do the work of a servant, should take off his garments,—he, who *being in the form of God*, had *emptied himself?* What wonder, that *he* should gird himself with a towel, who, *taking the form of a servant, was found in the habit of man?* What wonder that *he* should put water into a basin, for the washing the feet of his Disciples, who shed his Blood upon the earth for the cleansing away the defilements of sinners? What wonder that with the towel, wherewith he was girt, he should wipe the feet he had washed, *he* that with the Flesh, wherewith he had clothed himself, had strengthened the feet of them that were to preach his Gospel? Before girding himself with the towel, he took off the garments he wore; but, when he took the form of a servant, and *emptied himself,* he laid not aside what he had, but assumed what he had not. When he was crucified, he was stripped of his garments, and when dead, was wrapped in linen: and his whole Passion was a purification of them that believe. When, therefore, he was on the eve of his sufferings, he prepared for them by benefits, given not only to them for whom he

MAUNDY THURSDAY. 413

was about to suffer Death, but even to him who was about to betray him unto Death. Such, indeed, is the importance of humility to man, that the very majesty of God taught it him by his own example. Proud man would have been for ever lost, had not the humble God found him: and thus, he that had been ruined by the pride of the seducer, was saved by the humility of the most loving Redeemer, to whom deservedly all the Angels and Archangels cry out daily without ceasing, saying with one voice: *Holy! Holy! Holy!*

divina sublimitas. Quia homo superbus in æternum periret : nisi illum Deus humilis inveniret. Ut qui periret superbia deceptoris : salvaretur humilitate piissimi redemptoris. Cui merito omnes Angeli et Archangeli non cessant clamare quotidie : una voce dicentes: *Sanctus, sanctus, sanctus.*

GOOD FRIDAY.

THE NIGHT OFFICE.

The ceremonies used by the Church for the *Office of Tenebræ* having been already explained, we deem it unnecessary to repeat our instructions. The reader may refer to them, should he require to refresh his memory. They are given in *pages* 304–306.

THE FIRST NOCTURN.

The *first* Psalm, after having spoken of the Eternal Generation of the Son of God, prophesies his Kingship over the Nations, and the vengeance he will take on his enemies, at the last day. As this magnificent Canticle also foretells the revolt of earthly Princes against Christ, the Church uses it on this day, when the Synagogue has plotted his Death.

ANT. Adstiterunt reges terræ, et principes convenerunt in unum, adversus Dominum, et adversus Christum ejus.	ANT. The kings of the earth stood up, and the princes met together, against the Lord, and against his Christ.

PSALM 2.

Quare fremuerunt Gentes : * et populi meditati sunt inania ?	Why have the Gentiles raged, and the people devised vain things ?
Astiterunt reges terræ, et principes convenerunt in unum : * adversus Dominum, et adversus Christum ejus.	The kings of the earth stood up, and the princes met together, against the Lord, and against his Christ.

GOOD FRIDAY: TENEBRÆ. 415

They said: Let us break their bonds asunder: and let us cast away their yoke from us.

He that dwelleth in heaven shall laugh at them: and the Lord shall deride them.

Then shall he speak to them in his anger: and trouble them in his rage.

But I am appointed king by him over Sion his holy mountain, preaching his commandment.

The Lord hath said to me: Thou art my son, this day have I begotten thee.

Ask of me, and I will give thee the Gentiles for thy inheritance: and the utmost parts of the earth for thy possession.

Thou shalt rule them with a rod of iron: and shalt break them in pieces like a potter's vessel.

And now, O ye kings, understand: receive instruction, you that judge the earth.

Serve ye the Lord with fear: and rejoice unto him with trembling.

Embrace discipline, lest at any time the Lord be angry: and you perish from the just way.

When his wrath shall be kindled in a short time, blessed are all they that trust in him.

ANT. The kings of the earth stood up, and the princes met together, against the Lord and against his Christ.

Dirumpamus vincula eorum : * et projiciamus a nobis jugum ipsorum.

Qui habitat in cœlis irridebit eos : * et Dominus subsannabit eos.

Tunc loquetur ad eos in ira sua : * et in furore suo conturbabit eos.

Ego autem constitutus sum rex ab eo super Sion montem sanctum ejus : * prædicans præceptum ejus.

Dominus dixit ad me : * Filius meus es tu, ego hodie genui te.

Postula a me, et dabo tibi Gentes hæreditatem tuam : * et possessionem tuam terminos terræ.

Reges eos in virga ferrea: * et tamquam vas figuli confringes eos.

Et nunc reges intelligite: * erudimini qui judicatis terram.

Servite Domino in timore: * et exsultate ei cum tremore.

Apprehendite disciplinam, ne quando irascatur Dominus : * et pereatis de via justa.

Cum exarserit in brevi ira ejus : * beati omnes qui confidunt in eo.

ANT. Adstiterunt reges terræ, et principes convenerunt in unum, adversus Dominum, et adversus Christum ejus.

The *second* Psalm is pre-eminently the Psalm of

the Passion. The first verse contains one of the Seven Words spoken by our Saviour on the Cross. The rest of the Psalm mentions so many circumstances of the Passion, and with such clearness, that we almost seem to be reading the account of an eye-witness. Thus it tells us, among other particulars of our Lord's sufferings, of his Hands and Feet being pierced, of his body being violently stretched upon the Cross, of his Garments being divided, of Lots being cast for his Vesture, of his Agony, and of his being insulted by them that crucified him.

ANT. Diviserunt sibi vestimenta mea, et super vestem meam miserunt sortem.

ANT. They parted my garments among them, and upon my vesture they cast lots.

PSALM 21.

Deus, Deus meus, respice in me: quare me dereliquisti: * Longe a salute mea verba delictorum meorum.

Deus meus, clamabo per diem, et non exaudies: * et nocte, et non ad insipientiam mihi.

Tu autem in sancto habitas: * Laus Israel.

In te speraverunt patres nostri: * speraverunt, et liberasti eos.

Ad te clamaverunt, et salvi facti sunt: * in te speraverunt, et non sunt confusi.

Ego autem sum vermis, et non homo: * opprobrium hominum, et abjectio plebis.

Omnes videntes me deriserunt me: * locuti sunt

O God, my God, look upon me: why hast thou forsaken me? Far from my salvation are the words of my sins.

O my God, I shall cry by day, and thou wilt not hear: and by night, and it shall not be reputed as folly in me.

But thou dwellest in the holy place, the praise of Israel.

In thee have our fathers hoped: they have hoped and thou hast delivered them.

They cried to thee, and they were saved: they trusted in thee, and were not confounded.

But I am a worm, and no man: the reproach of men, and the outcast of the people.

All they that saw me have laughed me to scorn: they have

spoken with the lips, and wagged the head.

They said: He hoped in the Lord, let him deliver him: let him save him, seeing he delighted in him.

For thou art he that hast drawn me out of the womb: my hope from the breasts of my mother. I was cast upon thee from the womb.

From my mother's womb thou art my God, depart not from me.

For tribulation is very near: for there is none to help me.

Many calves have surrounded me: fat bulls have besieged me.

They have opened their mouths against me, as a lion ravening and roaring.

I am poured out like water: and all my bones are scattered.

My heart is become like wax melting in the midst of my bowels.

My strength is dried up like a potsherd, and my tongue hath cleaven to my jaws: and thou hast brought me down into the dust of death.

For many dogs have encompassed me: the council of the malignant hath besieged me.

They have dug my hands and feet: they have numbered all my bones.

And they have looked and stared upon me: they parted my garments among them, and upon my vesture they cast lots.

But thou, O Lord, remove

labiis, et moverunt caput.

Speravit in Domino, eripiat eum: * salvum faciat eum, quoniam vult eum.

Quoniam tu es, qui extraxisti me de ventre: * spes mea ab uberibus matris meæ. In te projectus sum ex utero.

De ventre matris meæ Deus meus es tu: * ne discesseris a me.

Quoniam tribulatio proxima est: * quoniam non est qui adjuvet.

Circumdederunt me vituli multi: * tauri pingues obsederunt me.

Aperuerunt super me os suum: * sicut leo rapiens et rugiens.

Sicut aqua effusus sum: * et dispersa sunt omnia ossa mea.

Factum est cor meum tamquam cera liquescens: * in medio ventris mei.

Aruit tamquam testa virtus mea, et lingua mea, adhæsit faucibus meis: * et in pulverem mortis deduxisti me.

Quoniam circumdederunt me canes multi: * concilium malignantium obsedit me.

Foderunt manus meas et pedes meos: * dinumeraverunt omnia ossa mea.

Ipsi vero consideraverunt et inspexerunt me: * diviserunt sibi vestimenta mea, et super vestem meam miserunt sortem.

Tu autem, Domine, ne

elongaveris auxilium tuum a me : * ad defensionem meam conspice.

Erue a framea, Deus, animam meam : * et de manu canis unicam meam.

Salva me ex ore leonis : * et a cornibus unicornium humilitatem meam.

Narrabo nomen tuum fratribus meis : * in medio ecclesiæ laudabo te.

Qui timetis Dominum, laudate eum : * universum semen Jacob, glorificate eum.

Timeat eum omne semen Israel : * quoniam non sprevit, neque despexit deprecationem pauperis.

Nec avertit faciem suam a me : * et cum clamarem ad eum, exaudivit me.

Apud te laus me in ecclesia magna : * vota mea reddam in conspectu timentium eum.

Edent pauperes et saturabuntur : et laudabunt Dominum qui requirunt eum : * vivent corda eorum in sæculum sæculi.

Reminiscentur et convertentur ad Dominum : * universi fines terræ.

Et adorabunt in conspectu ejus : * universæ familiæ Gentium.

Quoniam Domini est regnum : * et ipse dominabitur Gentium.

Manducaverunt et adoraverunt omnes pingues terræ: * in conspectu ejus cadent omnes qui descendunt in terram.

not thy help to a distance from me : look towards my defence.

Deliver, O God, my soul from the sword : my only one from the hand of the dog.

Save me from the lion's mouth : and my lowness from the horns of the unicorns.

I will declare thy name to my brethren : in the midst of the church will I praise thee.

Ye that fear the Lord, praise him : all ye the seed of Jacob, glorify him.

Let all the seed of Israel fear him : because he hath not slighted nor despised the supplication of the poor man.

Neither hath he turned away his face from me : and when I cried to him he heard me.

With thee is my praise in the great church : I will pay my vows in the sight of them that fear him.

The poor shall eat and shall be filled : and they shall praise the Lord that seek him: their hearts shall live for ever and ever.

All the ends of the earth shall remember and shall be converted to the Lord.

And all the kindreds of the Gentiles shall adore in his sight.

For the kingdom is the Lord's : and he shall have dominion over the nations.

All the fat ones of the earth have eaten and have adored : all they that go down to the earth shall fall before him.

And to him my soul shall live: and my seed shall serve him.	Et anima mea illi vivet: * et semen meum serviet ipsi.
There shall be declared to the Lord a generation to come: and the heavens shall show forth his justice to a people that shall be born, which the Lord hath made.	Annuntiabitur Domino generatio ventura: * et annuntiabunt cœli justitiam ejus populo qui nascetur, quem fecit Dominus.
ANT. They parted my garments among them, and upon my vesture they cast lots.	ANT. Diviserunt sibi vestimenta mea: et super vestem meam miserunt sortem.

The *third* Psalm was composed by David, when feeling the persecution of Saul. It shows us how this holy Prophet kept up his confidence in the Lord, in spite of all the dangers that threatened him. David is here a figure of Christ in his Passion.

ANT. Unjust witnesses have risen up against me, and iniquity hath belied itself.	ANT. Insurrexerunt in me testes iniqui, et mentita est iniquitas sibi.

PSALM 26.

The Lord is my light and my salvation, whom shall I fear?	Dominus illuminatio mea, et salus mea: * quem timebo?
The Lord is the protector of my life, of whom shall I be afraid?	Dominus protector vitæ meæ: * a quo trepidabo?
Whilst the wicked draw near against me, to eat my flesh.	Dum appropriant super me nocentes: * ut edant carnes meas.
My enemies that troubled me have been weakened, and have fallen.	Qui tribulant me inimici mei: * ipsi infirmati sunt et ceciderunt.
If armies in camp should stand together against me, my heart shall not fear.	Si consistant adversum me castra: * non timebit cor meum.
If a battle should rise up against me, in this will I be confident.	Si exsurgat adversum me prælium: * in hoc ego sperabo.
One thing have I asked of the Lord, this will I seek	Unam petii a Domino, hanc requiram: * ut inha-

after, that I may dwell in the house of the Lord all the days of my life.

That I may see the delight of the Lord, and may visit his temple.

For he hath hid me in his tabernacle : in the day of evils he hath protected me in the secret place of his tabernacle.

He hath exalted me upon a rock : and now he hath lifted up my head above my enemies.

I have gone round, and have offered up in his tabernacle a sacrifice of jubilation : I will sing, and recite a psalm to the Lord.

Hear, O Lord, my voice, with which I have cried to thee : have mercy on me, and hear me.

My heart hath said to thee, my face hath sought thee : thy face, O Lord, will I still seek.

Turn not away thy face from me : decline not in thy wrath from thy servant.

Be thou my helper : forsake me not, do not thou despise me, O God my Saviour.

For my father and my mother have left me : but the Lord hath taken me up.

Set me, O Lord, a law in thy way: and guide me in the right path, because of my enemies.

Deliver me not over to the will of them that trouble me : for unjust witnesses have risen up against me and iniquity hath belied itself.

bitem in domo Domini omnibus diebus vitæ meæ.

Ut videam voluptatem Domini : * et visitem templum ejus.

Quoniam abscondit me in tabernaculo suo : * in die malorum protexit me in abscondito tabernaculi sui.

In petra exaltavit me : * et nunc exaltavit caput meum super inimicos meos.

Circuivi, et immolavi in tabernaculo ejus hostiam vociferationis : * cantabo, et psalmum dicam Domino.

Exaudi, Domine, vocem meam, qua clamavi ad te : * miserere mei, et exaudi me.

Tibi dixit cor meum exquisivit te facies mea : * faciem tuam, Domine, requiram.

Nec avertas faciem tuam a me : * ne declines in ira a servo tuo.

Adjutor meus esto : * ne derelinquas me, neque despicias me, Deus salutaris meus.

Quoniam pater meus et mater mea dereliquerunt me : * Dominus autem assumpsit me.

Legem pone mihi, Domine, in via tua: * et dirige me in semitam rectam propter inimicos meos.

Ne tradideris me in animas tribulantium me : * quoniam insurrexerunt in me testes iniqui, et mentita est iniquitas sibi.

I believe to see the good things of the Lord in the land of the living.	Credo videre bona Domini : * in terra viventium.
Expect the Lord, do manfully: and let thy heart take courage, and wait thou for the Lord.	Exspecta Dominum, viriliter age: * et confortetur cor tuum, et sustine Dominum.
ANT. Unjust witnesses have risen up against me, and iniquity hath belied itself.	ANT. Insurrexerunt in me testes iniqui, et mentita est iniquitas sibi.
℣. They parted my garments among them.	℣. Diviserunt sibi vestimenta mea.
℟. And upon my vesture they cast lots.	℟. Et super vestem meam miserunt sortem.

The Lessons of the First Nocturn are to-day, also, taken from the Lamentations of Jeremias. We have, already (*page* 314,) explained why the Church reads them on these three days. The first two of the following Lessons refer to the destruction of Jerusalem; the third we will explain in its proper place.

FIRST LESSON.

From the Lamentation of Jeremias the Prophet.	De Lamentatione Jeremiæ Prophetæ.
Ch. II.	*Cap. II.*
HETH. The Lord hath purposed to destroy the wall of the daughter of Sion: he hath stretched out his line, and hath not withdrawn his hand from destroying: and the bulwark hath mourned, and the wall hath been destroyed together.	HETH. Cogitavit Dominus dissipare murum filiæ Sion : tetendit funiculum suum, et non avertit manum suam a perditione : luxitque antemurale, et murus pariter dissipatus est.
TETH. Her gates are sunk into the ground: he hath destroyed and broken her bars: her king and her princes are among the Gentiles. The law is no more, and her prophets have found no vision from the Lord.	TETH. Defixæ sunt in terra portæ ejus, perdidit et contrivit vectes ejus, regem ejus, et principes ejus, in gentibus. Non est lex: et prophetæ ejus non invenerunt visionem a Domino.

Jod. Sederunt in terra, conticuerunt senes filiæ Sion: consperserunt cinere capita sua, accincti sunt ciliciis, abjecerunt in terram capita sua virgines Jerusalem.

Caph. Defecerunt præ lacrymis oculi mei, conturbata sunt viscera mea. Effusum est in terra jecur meum super contritione filiæ populi mei, cum deficeret parvulus et lactens in plateis oppidi.

Jerusalem, Jerusalem, convertere ad Dominum Deum tuum.

℞. Omnes amici mei dereliquerunt me, et prævaluerunt insidiantes mihi: tradidit me quem diligebam. * Et terribilibus oculis plaga crudeli percutientes, aceto potabant me.

℣. Inter iniquos projecerunt me: et non pepercerunt animæ suæ.

* Et terribilibus oculis plaga crudeli percutientes, aceto potabant me.

Jod. The ancients of the daughter of Sion sit upon the ground, they have held their peace; they have sprinkled their heads with dust, they are girded with hair-cloth: the virgins of Jerusalem hang down their heads to the ground.

Caph. My eyes have failed with weeping, my bowels are troubled. My liver is poured out upon the earth, for the destruction of the daughter of my people, when the children and the sucklings fainted away in the streets of the city.

Jerusalem, Jerusalem, be converted to the Lord thy God.

℞. All my friends have forsaken me, and they that lay in ambush for me prevailed: he whom I loved has betrayed me. * And they, with terrible looks striking me with a cruel wound, gave me vinegar to drink.

℣. They cast me out among the wicked, and spared not my life.

* And they, with terrible looks striking me with a cruel wound, gave me vinegar to drink.

SECOND LESSON.

Lamed. Matribus suis dixerunt: Ubi est triticum et vinum? cum deficerent quasi vulnerati in plateis civitatis, cum exhalarent animas suas in sinu matrum suarum.

Mem. Cui comparabo te, vel cui assimilabo te filia Jerusalem? cui exæquabo

Lamed. They said to their mother: Where is corn and wine? when they fainted away as the wounded in the streets of the city: when they breathed out their souls in the bosoms of their mothers.

Mem. To what shall I compare thee? or to what shall I liken thee, O daughter of Jerusalem? to what shall I equal thee, that I may comfort thee, O virgin daughter of Sion? For great as the sea is thy destruction: who shall heal thee?

NUN. Thy prophets have seen false and foolish things for thee, and they have not laid open thy iniquity, to excite thee to penance: but they have seen for thee false revelations and banishments.

SAMECH. All they that passed by the way have clapped their hands at thee: they have hissed and wagged their head at the daughter of Jerusalem, saying: Is this the city of perfect beauty, the joy of all the earth?

Jerusalem, Jerusalem, be converted to the Lord thy God.

℟. The veil of the temple was rent, * And all the earth shook: the thief cried out from the cross, saying: Remember me, O Lord, when thou shalt come into thy kingdom.

℣. The rocks were split, and the monuments opened, and many bodies of the saints that were dead rose out of them.

* And all the earth shook: the thief cried out from the cross, saying: Remember me, O Lord, when thou shalt come into thy kingdom.

te, et consolabor te, virgo filia Sion? Magna est enim velut mare contritio tua: quis medebitur tui?

NUN. Prophetæ tui viderunt tibi falsa et stulta: nec aperiebant iniquitatem tuam, ut te ad pœnitentiam provocarent. Viderunt autem tibi assumptiones falsas, et ejectiones.

SAMECH. Plauserunt super te manibus omnes transeuntes per viam: sibilaverunt, et moverunt caput suum super filiam Jerusalem: Hæccine est urbs, dicentes, perfecti decoris, gaudium universæ terræ?

Jerusalem, Jerusalem, convertere ad Dominum Deum tuum.

℟. Velum templi scissum est, * Et omnis terra tremuit: latro de cruce clamabat, dicens: Memento mei, Domine, dum veneris in regnum tuum.

℣. Petræ scissæ sunt, et monumenta aperta sunt, et multa corpora sanctorum, qui dormierant, surrexerunt.

* Et omnis terra tremuit: latro de cruce clamabat, dicens: Memento mei, Domine, dum veneris in regnum tuum.

In the third Lesson, which now follows, Jeremias passes to an other subject. According to the usage of the Prophets, he leaves Jerusalem to speak of Him who is the expectation of Israel,—the Messias. But it is not of the glory of the Messias that he now speaks: it is of the sufferings he endures: he has made himself the object of God's severest justice, by taking upon himself the sins of the whole world.

THIRD LESSON.

ALEPH. Ego vir videns paupertatem meam, in virga indignationis ejus.

ALEPH. Me minavit et ad duxit in tenebras, et non in lucem.

ALEPH. Tantum in me vertit, et convertit manum suam tota die.

BETH. Vetustam fecit pellem meam et carnem meam: contrivit ossa mea.

BETH. Ædificavit in gyro meo, et circumdedit me felle et labore.

BETH. In tenebrosis collocavit me, quasi mortuos sempiternos.

GHIMEL. Circumædificavit adversum me, ut non egrediar: aggravavit compedem meum.

GHIMEL. Sed et cum clamavero et rogavero, exclusit orationem meam.

GHIMEL. Conclusit vias meas lapidibus quadris, semitas meas subvertit.

Jerusalem, Jerusalem, convertere ad Dominum Deum tuum.

℟. Vinea mea electa, ego te plantavi: * Quomodo conversa es in amaritudinem ut me crucifigeres, et Barabbam dimitteres?

℣. Sepivi te, et lapides elegi ex te, et ædificavi turrim.

ALEPH. I am the man that see my poverty by the rod of his indignation.

ALEPH. He hath led me, and brought me into darkness, and not into light.

ALEPH. Only against me he hath turned, and turned his hand all the day.

BETH. My skin and my flesh he hath made old, he hath broken my bones.

BETH. He hath built round about me, and he hath compassed me with gall and labour.

BETH. He hath set me in dark places as those that are dead for ever.

GHIMEL. He hath built against me round about, that I may not get out: he hath made my fetters heavy.

GHIMEL. Yea, and when I cry and entreat, he hath shut out my prayer.

GHIMEL. He hath shut up my ways with square stones, he hath turned my paths upside down.

Jerusalem, Jerusalem, be converted to the Lord thy God.

℟. O my chosen vineyard, it is I that have planted thee: * How art thou become so bitter, that thou shouldst crucify me, and release Barabbas?

℣. I have hedged thee in, and picked the stones out of thee, and have built a tower.

* How art thou become so bitter, that thou shouldst crucify me, and release Barabbas?

Here is repeated: O my chosen.

* Quomodo conversa es in amaritudinem ut me crucifigeres, et Barabbam dimitteres?

Here is repeated: Vinea mea.

THE SECOND NOCTURN.

In the *fourth* Psalm, David humbly acknowledges that the rebellion of his son Absalom was a just punishment of the sins he himself had committed. He is a figure of the Messias, who, in his Agony, confesses that the *iniquities*, which he has taken upon himself, are a *heavy burthen* upon him, that his *heart is troubled*, and that his *strength hath left* him.

ANT. They used violence that sought my soul.

ANT. Vim faciebant, qui quærebant animam meam.

PSALM 37.

Rebuke me not, O Lord, in thy indignation: nor chastise me in thy wrath.

For thy arrows are fastened in me: and thy hand hath been strong upon me.

There is no health in my flesh, because of thy wrath: there is no peace for my bones, because of my sins.

For my iniquities are gone over my head: and as a heavy burthen are become heavy upon me.

My sores are putrefied and corrupted, because of my foolishness.

I am become miserable, and am bowed down even to the

Domine, ne in furore tuo arguas me: * neque in ira tua corripias me.

Quoniam sagittæ tuæ infixæ sunt mihi: * et confirmasti super me manum tuam.

Non est sanitas in carne mea a facie iræ tuæ: * non est pax ossibus meis a facie peccatorum meorum.

Quoniam iniquitates meæ supergressæ sunt caput meum: * et sicut onus grave gravatæ sunt super me.

Putruerunt, et corruptæ sunt cicatrices meæ: * a facie insipientiæ meæ.

Miser factus sum, et curvatus sum usque in finem:

* tota die contristatus ingrediebar.

Quoniam lumbi mei impleti sunt illusionibus : * et non est sanitas in carne mea.

Afflictus sum, et humiliatus sum nimis : * rugiebam a gemitu cordis mei.

Domine, ante te omne desiderium meum : * et gemitus meus a te non est absconditus.

Cor meum conturbatum est, dereliquit me virtus mea : * et lumen oculorum meorum, et ipsum non est mecum.

Amici mei et proximi mei : * adversum me appropinquaverunt et steterunt.

Et qui juxta me erant, de longe steterunt : * et vim faciebant qui quærebant animam meam.

Et qui inquirebant mala mihi, locuti sunt vanitates : * et dolos tota die meditabantur.

Ego autem tamquam surdus non audiebam : * et sicut mutus non aperiens os suum.

Et factus sum sicut homo non audiens : * et non habens in ore suo redargutiones.

Quoniam in te Domine, speravi : * tu exaudies me, Domine Deus meus.

Quia dixi : Nequando supergaudeant mihi inimici mei : * et dum commoventur pedes mei super me magna locuti sunt.

Quoniam ego in flagella

end : I walked sorrowful all the day long.

For my loins are filled with illusions : and there is no health in my flesh.

I am afflicted and humbled exceedingly : I roared with the groaning of my heart.

Lord, all my desire is before thee : and my groaning is not hid from thee.

My heart is troubled, my strength hath left me : and the light of my eyes itself is not with me.

My friends and my neighbours have drawn near, and stood against me.

And they that were near me stood afar off : and they that sought my soul used violence.

And they that sought evils to me spoke vain things : and studied deceits all the day long.

But I, as a deaf man, heard not : and was as a dumb man not opening his mouth.

And I became as a man that heareth not : and that hath no reproofs in his mouth.

For in thee, O Lord, have I hoped : thou wilt hear me, O Lord my God.

For I said : Lest at any time my enemies rejoice over me : and whilst my feet are moved, they speak great things against me.

For I am ready for scourges:

and my sorrow is continually before me.

For I will declare my iniquity: and I will think for my sin.

But my enemies live, and are stronger than I: and they that hate me wrongfully are multiplied.

They that render evil for good, have detracted me, because I followed goodness.

Forsake me not, O Lord my God: do not thou depart from me.

Attend unto my help, O Lord, the God of my salvation.

ANT. They used violence that sought my soul.

paratus sum: * et dolor meus in conspectu meo semper.

Quoniam iniquitatem meam annuntiabo: * et cogitabo pro peccato meo.

Inimici autem mei vivunt, et confirmati sunt super me: * et multiplicati sunt qui oderunt me inique.

Qui retribuunt mala pro bonis detrahebant mihi: * quoniam sequebar bonitatem.

Ne derelinquas me, Domine Deus meus: * ne discesseris a me.

Intende in adjutorium meum: * Domine, Deus salutis meæ.

ANT. Vim faciebant, qui quærebant animam meam.

The *fifth* Psalm also represents David, under persecution, as the figure of the Messias. But there is one verse in it, which refers only to Christ, and not to David: it is the tenth, wherein it is said: *Burnt-offerings and sin-offerings thou didst not require: then said I: " Behold I come !"*

ANT. Let them be confounded and ashamed that seek after my soul, to take it away.

ANT. Confundantur et revereantur, qui quærunt animam meam, ut auferant eam.

PSALM 39.

With expectation I have waited for the Lord, and he was attentive to me.

And he heard my prayers, and he brought me out of the pit of misery, and the mire of dregs.

Exspectans exspectavi Domini: * et intendit mihi.

Et exaudivit preces meas: * et eduxit me de lacu miseriæ et de luto fæcis.

Et statuit super petram pedes meos : * et direxit gressus meos.

Et immisit in os meum canticum novum : * carmen Deo nostro.

Videbunt multi, et timebunt : * et sperabunt in Domino.

Beatus vir, cujus est nomen Domini spes ejus : * et non respexit in vanitates et insanias falsas.

Multa fecisti tu Domine Deus meus, mirabilia tua: * et cogitationibus tuis non est qui similis sit tibi.

Annuntiavi, et locutus sum : * multiplicati sunt super numerum.

Sacrificium et oblationem noluisti : * aures autem perfecisti mihi.

Holocaustum et pro peccato non postulasti: * tunc dixi : Ecce venio.

In capite libri scriptum est de me, ut facerem voluntatem tuam : * Deus meus, volui, et legem tuam in medio cordis mei.

Annuntiavi justitiam tuam in ecclesia magna : * ecce labia mea non prohibebo : Domine, tu scisti.

Justitiam tuam non abscondi in corde meo : * veritatem tuam et salutare tuum dixi.

Non abscondi misericordiam tuam, et veritatem tuam : * a concilio multo.

Tu autem, Domine, ne longe facias miserationes

And he set my feet upon a rock, and directed my steps.

And he put a new canticle into my mouth, a song to our God.

Many shall see this, and shall fear : and they shall hope in the Lord.

Blessed is the man whose trust is in the name of the Lord : and who hath not had regard to vanities and lying follies.

Thou hast multiplied thy wonderful works, O Lord my God : and in thy thoughts there is no one like to thee.

I have declared, and I have spoken : they are multiplied above number.

Sacrifice and oblation thou didst not desire : but thou hast pierced ears for me.

Burnt-offerings and sin-offerings thou didst not require : then said I : Behold I come.

In the head of the book it was written of me, that I should do thy will : O my God, I have desired it, and thy law in the midst of my heart.

I have declared thy justice in the great church : lo I will not restrain my lips : O Lord, thou knowest it.

I have not hid thy justice within my heart. I have declared thy truth and thy salvation.

I have not concealed thy mercy and thy truth from the great council.

Withhold not thou, O Lord, thy tender mercies from me :

thy mercy and thy truth have always upheld me.

For evils without number have surrounded me: my iniquities have overtaken me, and I was not able to see.

They are multiplied above the hairs of my head: and my heart hath forsaken me.

Be pleased, O Lord, to deliver me: look down, O Lord, to help me.

Let them be confounded and ashamed together, that seek after my soul, to take it away.

Let them be turned backward, and be ashamed, that desire evils to me.

Let them immediately bear their confusion that say to me: 'Tis well, 'tis well.

Let all that seek thee rejoice and be glad in thee: and let such as love thy salvation, say always, The Lord be magnified.

But I am a beggar and poor: the Lord is careful for me.

Thou art my helper and my protector: O my God, be not slack.

ANT. Let them be confounded and ashamed that seek after my soul, to take it away.

tuas a me: * misericordia tua et veritas tua semper susceperunt me.

Quoniam circumdederunt me mala, quorum non est numerus: * comprehenderunt me iniquitates meæ, et non potui ut viderem.

Multiplicatæ sunt super capillos capitis mei: * et cor meum dereliquit me.

Complaceat tibi Domine, ut eruas me: * Domine, ad adjuvandum me respice.

Confundantur et revereantur simul, qui quærunt animam meam: * ut auferant eam.

Convertantur retrorsum et revereantur: * qui volunt mihi mala.

Ferant confestim confusionem suam: * qui dicunt mihi: Euge, euge.

Exsultent et lætentur super te omnes quærentes te: * et dicant semper: Magnificetur Dominus, qui diligunt salutare tuum.

Ego autem mendicus sum, et pauper: * Dominus solicitus est mei.

Adjutor meus et protector meus tu es: * Deus meus, ne tardaveris.

ANT. Confundantur et revereantur, qui quærunt animam meam, ut auferant eam.

In the *sixth* Psalm, David, persecuted by Saul, is a figure of our Saviour, against whom the Synagogue prepares its wicked plots.

ANT. Strangers have risen

ANT. Alieni insurrexerunt in me, et fortes quæsierunt animam meam.

up against me, and the mighty have sought after my soul.

PSALM 53.

Deus, in nomine tuo salvum me fac : * et in virtute tua judica me.

Deus, exaudi orationem meam : * auribus percipe verba oris mei.

Quoniam alieni insurrexerunt adversum me, et fortes quæsierunt animam meam : * et non posuerunt Deum ante conspectum suum.

Ecce enim Deus adjuvat me : * et Dominus susceptor est animæ meæ.

Averte mala inimicis meis : * et in veritate tua disperde illos.

Voluntarie sacrificabo tibi : * et confitebor nomini tuo, Domine, quoniam bonum est.

Quoniam ex omni tribulatione eripuisti me : * et super inimicos meos despexit oculus meus.

ANT. Alieni insurrexerunt in me, et fortes quæsierunt animam meam.

℣. Insurrexerunt in me testes iniqui.

℟. Et mentita est iniquitas sibi.

Save me, O God, by thy name, and judge me in thy strength.

O God, hear my prayer : give ear to the words of my mouth.

For strangers have risen up against me : and the mighty have sought after my soul : and they have not set God before their eyes.

For behold God is my helper : and the Lord is the protector of my soul.

Turn back the evils upon my enemies : and cut them off in thy truth.

I will freely sacrifice to thee, and will give praise, O God, to thy name : because it is good.

For thou hast delivered me out of all trouble : and my eye hath looked down upon my enemies.

ANT. Strangers have risen up against me, and the mighty have sought after my soul.

℣. Unjust witnesses have risen up against me.

℟. And iniquity hath belied itself.

Here is said, in secret, the *Pater noster*.

For the Second Nocturn Lessons the Church continues the *Enarrations* of St. Augustine, on the Psalms prophetic of our Lord's Passion.

From the treatise of Saint Augustine, Bishop, upon the Psalms.

Ex tractatu Sancti Augustini Episcopi, super Psalmos.

Ps. LXIII.

Ps. LXIII.

FOURTH LESSON.

Thou hast protected me, O God, from the assembly of the wicked, from the multitude of those that work iniquity. Now let us behold our head himself. Many martyrs have suffered such torments, but nothing is so conspicuous as the head of the martyrs; there we see better what they endured. He was *protected from the multitude of the wicked:* that is, God protected himself; the Son, and the Man assumed by the Son, protected his own flesh. For he is the Son of Man, and the Son of God: the Son of God because of the form of God: the Son of Man because of the form of a servant, having it in his power to lay down his life, and take it up again. What could his enemies do against him? They killed his body, but they did not kill his soul. Take notice, then. It signified little for our Lord to exhort the martyrs by word, if he had not fortified them by his example.

℟. Ye are come out to take me, as a thief, with swords and clubs. * I was daily with you in the Temple teaching, and ye did not apprehend me: and lo! ye scourge me, and lead me to be crucified.

Protexisti me, Deus, aconventu malignantium, a multitudine operantium iniquitatem. Jam ipsum caput nostrum intueamur. Multi martyres talia passi sunt, sed nihil sic elucet, quomodo caput martyrum: ibi melius intuemur, quod illi experti sunt. Protectus est a multitudine malignantium: protegente se Deo, protegente carnem suam ipso Filio, et hominem quem gerebat, quia Filius hominis est, et Filius Dei est: Filius Dei, propter formam Dei: Filius hominis, propter formam servi, habens in potestate ponere animam suam, et recipere eam. Quid ei potuerunt facere inimici? Occiderunt corpus, animam non occiderunt. Intendite. Parum ergo erat, Dominum hortari martyres verbo, nisi firmaret exemplo.

℟. Tamquam ad latronem existis cum gladiis et fustibus comprehendere me. * Quotidie apud vos eram in Templo docens, et non me tenuistis: et ecce flagellatum ducitis ad crucifigendum.

℣. Cumque injecissent manus in Jesum, et tenuissent eum, dixit ad eos :

* Quotidie apud vos eram in Templo docens, et non me tenuistis ; et ecce flagellatum ducitis ad crucifigendum.

℣. And when they had laid hands on Jesus, and taken him, he said to them :

* I was daily with you in the Temple teaching, and ye did not apprehend me : and lo! ye scourge me, and lead me to be crucified.

FIFTH LESSON.

Nostis qui conventus erat malignantium Judæorum, et quæ multitudo erat operantium iniquitatem ? Quam iniquitatem ? Quia voluerunt occidere Dominum Jesum Christum. Tanta opera bona, inquit, ostendi vobis ; propter quod horum me vultis occidere ? Pertulit omnes infirmos eorum, curavit omnes languidos eorum, prædicavit regnum cœlorum, non tacuit vitia eorum, ut ipsa potius eis displicerent, non medicus, a quo sanabantur. His omnibus curationibus ejus ingrati, tamquam multa febre phrenetici, insanientes in medicum qui venerat curare eos, excogitaverunt consilium perdendi eum, tamquam ibi volentes probare, utrum vere homo sit qui mori possit, an aliquid super homines sit, et mori se non permittat. Verbum ipsorum agnoscimus in Sapientia Salomonis. Morte turpissima, inquiunt, condemnemus eum : interrogemus eum : erit enim respectus in sermonibus illius Si enim vere Filius Dei est, liberet eum.

You know what was the *assembly of the wicked* Jews, and what the *multitude of those that work iniquity.* But what was that *iniquity ?* It was that they intended to kill our Lord Jesus Christ. *I have done,* saith he, *so many good works among you: for which of them will you kill me ?* He bore with all their weaknesses, he cured all their sick, he preached the kingdom of heaven, he concealed not their crimes, that they might rather hate them, than the physician that healed them. Yet such was their ingratitude for all these cures, that like men raving in a high fever, they raged against the physician that came to cure them, and formed a design of destroying him : as if they had a mind to try whether he was a real man that could die, or something above men, and would not die. We find their words in the Wisdom of Solomon : *Let us condemn him,* say they, *to a most shameful death. Let us examine him : for regard will be had to his words. If he is truly the Son of God, let him deliver him.*

℞. Darkness covered the earth, whilst the Jews crucified Jesus: and about the ninth hour, Jesus cried out with a loud voice : My God ! why hast thou forsaken me ? * And bowing down his head, he gave up the ghost.

℣. Jesus crying out with a loud voice said : Father ! into thy hands I commend my spirit !

* And bowing down his head, he gave up the ghost.

℞. Tenebræ factæ sunt, dum crucifixissent Jesum Judæi : et circa horam nonam exclamavit Jesus voce magna : Deus meus, ut quid me dereliquisti ? * Et inclinato capite, emisit spiritum.

℣. Exclamans Jesus voce magna ait : Pater, in manus tuas commendo spiritum meum.

* Et inclinato capite, emisit spiritum.

SIXTH LESSON.

They sharpened their tongues like a sword. Let not the Jews say : "We did not kill Christ :" for they delivered him up to Pilate, the judge, that they might seem innocent of his death. Thus when Pilate had said to them : *Put him to death yourselves :* they answered : *It is not lawful for us to put any man to death.* Hereby, they pretended to throw the injustice of their crime upon a judge that was a man : but could they deceive a Judge that is God? What Pilate did, made him partaker of their crime : but in comparison with them, he was much more innocent. For he laboured what he could to get him out of their hands ; and for that reason ordered him to be scourged and shown to them. This he did to our Lord, not by way of persecution, but to satisfy their rage ; that the sight of him in that condition might move them to pity, and make them desist

Exacuerunt tamquam gladium linguas suas. Non dicant Judæi : Non occidimus Christum. Etenim propterea eum dederunt judici Pilato, ut quasi ipsi a morte ejus viderentur immunes. Nam cum ʻdixisset eis Pilatus : Vos eum occidite ; responderunt : Nobis non licet occidere quemquam. Iniquitatem facinoris sui in judicem hominem refundere volebant : sed numquid Deum judicem fallebant ? Quod fecit Pilatus, in eo ipso quod fecit, aliquantum particeps fuit : sed in comparatione illorum, multo ipse innocentior. Institit enim quantum potuit, ut illum ex eorum manibus liberaret : nam propterea flagellatum produxit ad eos. Non persequendo Dominum flagellavit, sed eorum furori satisfacere volens : ut vel jam mitescerent, et desinerent velle occidere, cum flagellatum viderent. Fecit et hoc.

2 F

At ubi perseverarunt, nostis illum lavisse manus, et dixisse quod ipse non fecisset, mundum se esse a morte illius. Fecit tamen. Sed si reus, quia fecit vel invitus: illi innocentes, qui coegerunt ut faceret? Nullo modo. Sed ille dixit in eum sententiam, et jussit eum crucifigi, et quasi ipse occidit: et vos, o Judæi, occidistis. Unde occidistis? Gladio linguæ; acuistis enim linguas vestras. Et quando percussistis, nisi quando clamastis: Crucifige, crucifige?

℞. Animam meam dilectam tradidi in manus iniquorum, et facta est mihi hæreditas mea sicut leo in silva: dedit contra me voces adversarius, dicens: Congregamini, et properate ad devorandum illum. Posuerunt me in deserto solitudinis, et luxit super me omnis terra: * Quia non est inventus qui me agnosceret, et faceret bene.

℣. Insurrexerunt in me viri absque misericordia, et non pepercerunt animæ meæ.

* Quia non est inventus qui me agnosceret, et faceret bene.

Here is repeated: Animam meam dilectam.

from desiring his death. All this he did. But when they still persisted, you know that he washed his hands, and said, that he had no hand in it, that he was innocent of his death. And yet he really put him to death. But if he was guilty for doing so against his will: are they innocent that forced him to it? By no means. He pronounced sentence upon him, and commanded him to be crucified, and so might be said to kill him: but you, O Jews, *you* also killed him. How? With the sword of your tongues: for *ye sharpened your tongues.* And when gave you the stroke, but when you cried out: *Crucify him, crucify him?*

℞. I have delivered my beloved soul into the hands of the wicked, and my inheritance is become to me like a lion in the forest: my adversary gave out his words against me, saying: Come together, and make haste to devour him. They placed me in a solitary desert, and all the earth mourned for me: * Because there was none found that would know me, and do good unto me.

℣. Men without mercy rose up against me, and they spared not my life.

* Because there was none found that would know me, and do good unto me.

Here is repeated: I have delivered.

THIRD NOCTURN.

The *seventh* Psalm was composed by David at the time when he was being persecuted by Saul. The Prophet, by describing the fury of his own persecutors, shows us what kind of men were the enemies of the Messias.

ANT. From them that rise up against me, deliver me, O Lord; for they are in possession of my soul.

ANT. Ab insurgentibus in me libera me, Domine, quia occupaverunt animam meam.

PSALM 58.

Deliver me from my enemies, O my God: and defend me from them that rise up against me.

Deliver me from them that work iniquity: and save me from bloody men.

For behold they have caught my soul: the mighty have rushed in upon me.

Neither is it for my iniquity, nor for my sin, O Lord: without iniquity have I run and directed my steps.

Rise up thou to meet me, and behold: even thou, O Lord, the God of hosts, the God of Israel.

Attend to visit all the nations: have no mercy on all them that work iniquity.

They shall return at evening, and shall suffer hunger like dogs: and shall go round about the city.

Behold they shall speak with their mouth, and a sword is in their lips: for who, say they, hath heard us?

Eripe me de inimicis meis Deus meus: * et ab insurgentibus in me, libera me.

Eripe me de operantibus iniquitatem: * et de viris sanguinum salva me.

Quia ecce ceperunt animam meam: * irruerunt in me fortes.

Neque iniquitas mea, neque peccatum meum, Domine: * sine iniquitate cucurri, et direxi.

Exsurge in occursum meum, et vide: * et tu, Domine, Deus virtutum, Deus Israël.

Intende ad visitandas omnes Gentes: * non miserearis omnibus qui operantur iniquitatem.

Convertentur ad vesperam, et famem patientur ut canes: * et circuibunt civitatem.

Ecce loquentur in ore suo, et gladius in labiis eorum: * quoniam quis audivit?

Et tu, Domine, deridebis eos : * ad nihilum deduces omnes Gentes.

Fortitudinem meam ad te custodiam, quia Deus, susceptor meus es : * Deus meus, misericordia ejus præveniet me.

Deus ostendit mihi super inimicos meos, ne occidas eos : * nequando obliviscantur populi mei.

Disperge illos in virtute tua : * et depone eos protector meus, Domine.

Delictum oris eorum sermonem labiorum ipsorum : * et comprehendantur in superbia sua.

Et de execratione et mendacio annuntiabuntur in consummatione : * in ira consummationis, et non erunt.

Et scient quia Deus dominabitur Jacob : * et finium terræ.

Convertentur ad vesperam, et famem patientur ut canes: * et circuibunt civitatem.

Ipsi dispergentur ad manducandum : * si vero non fuerint saturati, et murmurabunt.

Ego autem cantabo fortitudinem tuam : * et exaltabo mane misericordiam tuam.

Quia factus es susceptor meus : * et refugium meum, in die tribulationis meæ.

Adjutor meus tibi psallam, quia Deus susceptor

But thou, O Lord, shalt laugh at them : thou shalt bring all the nations to nothing.

I will keep my strength to thee, for thou art my protector : my God, his mercy shall prevent me.

God shall let me see over my enemies : slay them not, lest at any time my people forget.

Scatter them by thy power: and bring them down, O Lord, my protector.

For the sin of their mouth, and the word of their lips : and let them be taken in their pride.

And for their cursing and lying they shall be talked of, when they are consumed : when they are consumed by thy wrath, and they shall be no more.

And they shall know that God will rule Jacob : and all the ends of the earth.

They shall return at evening, and shall suffer hunger like dogs : and shall go round about the city.

They shall be scattered abroad to eat : and shall murmur if they be not filled.

But I will sing thy strength : and will extol thy mercy in the morning.

For thou art become my support and my refuge, in the day of my trouble.

Unto thee, O my helper, will I sing, for thou art God,

my defence: my God, my mercy.

ANT. From them that rise up against me, deliver me, O Lord; for they are in possession of my soul.

meus es: * Deus meus, misericordia mea.

ANT. Ab insurgentibus in me libera me, Domine, quia occupaverunt animam meam.

In the *eighth* Psalm, the Royal Prophet shows us the Messias threatened with death, and complaining of his Disciples having abandoned him.

ANT. Thou hast put away my acquaintance far from me: I was delivered up, and I escaped not.

ANT. Longe fecisti notos meos a me: traditus sum, et non egrediebar.

PSALM 87.

O Lord, the God of my salvation, I have cried in the day, and in the night before thee.

Let my prayer come in before thee: incline thy ear to my petition.

For my soul is filled with evils: and my life hath drawn nigh to hell.

I am counted among them that go down to the pit: I am become as a man without help, free among the dead.

Like the slain sleeping in the sepulchres, whom thou rememberest no more: and they are cast off from thy hand.

They have laid me in the lower pit: in the dark places and in the shadow of death.

Thy wrath is strong over me: and all thy waves thou hast brought in upon me.

Thou hast put away my

Domine, Deus salutis meæ: * in die clamavi, et nocte coram te.

Intret in conspectu tuo oratio mea: * inclina aurem tuam ad precem meam.

Quia repleta est malis anima mea: et vita mea inferno appropinquavit.

Æstimatus sum cum descendentibus in lacum: * factus sum sicut homo sine adjutorio, inter mortuos liber.

Sicut vulnerati dormientes in sepulchris, quorum non es memor amplius: * et ipsi de manu tua repulsi sunt.

Posuerunt me in lacu inferiori: * in tenebrosis, et in umbra mortis.

Super me confirmatus est furor tuus: * et omnes fluctus tuos induxisti super me.

Longe fecisti notos meos

a me : * posuerunt me abominationem sibi.

Traditus sum, et non egrediebar : * oculi mei languerunt præ inopia.

Clamavi ad te, Domine, tota die : * expandi ad te manus meas.

Numquid mortuis facies mirabilia : * aut medici suscitabunt, et confitebuntur tibi ?

Numquid narrabit aliquis in sepulchro misericordiam tuam : * et veritatem tuam in perditione ?

Numquid cognoscentur in tenebris mirabilia tua : * et justitia tua in terra oblivionis ?

Et ego ad te, Domine, clamavi : * et mane oratio mea præveniet te.

Ut quid, Domine, repellis orationem meam : * avertis faciem tuam a me ?

Pauper sum ego, et in laboribus a juventute mea :* exaltatus autem, humiliatus sum et conturbatus.

In me transierunt iræ tuæ: * et terrores tui conturbaverunt me.

Circumdederunt me sicut aqua tota die : * circumdederunt me simul.

Elongasti a me amicum et proximum : * et notos meos a miseria.

ANT. Longe fecisti notos meos a me : traditus sum, et non egrediebar.

acquaintance far from me : they have set me an abomination to themselves.

I was delivered up, and came not forth : my eyes languished through poverty.

All the day I cried to thee, O Lord : I stretched out my hands to thee.

Wilt thou show wonders to the dead : or shall physicians raise to life, and give praise to thee ?

Shall any one in the sepulchre declare thy mercy, and thy truth in destruction ?

Shall thy wonders be known in the dark : and thy justice in the land of forgetfulness ?

But I, O Lord, have cried to thee : and in the morning my prayer shall prevent thee.

Lord, why castest thou off my prayer : why turnest thou away thy face from me ?

I am poor, and in labours from my youth : and being exalted, have been humbled and troubled.

Thy wrath hath come upon me : and thy terrors have troubled me.

They have come round about me like water all the day : they have compassed me about together.

Friend and neighbour thou hast put far from me : and my acquaintance because of misery.

ANT. Thou hast put away my acquaintance far from me : I was delivered up, and I escaped not.

The *ninth* Psalm invokes the vengeance of God upon the unjust judges, who shed the blood of the innocent Jesus, and forget that there is One in heaven who is witness of *their* injustice and of *his* immolation. The High Priests, the Doctors of the Law, the dastardly Pontius Pilate, are here described as unjust judges, upon whose heads will fall the wrath of heaven.

Ant. They will hunt after the soul of the Just; and will condemn innocent Blood.

Ant. Captabunt in animam justi, et sanguinem innocentem condemnabunt.

PSALM 93.

The Lord is the God to whom revenge belongeth: the God of revenge hath acted freely.

Lift up thyself, thou that judgeth the earth: render a reward to the proud.

How long shall the wicked, O Lord, how long shall the wicked make their boast?

How long shall they utter and speak wrong things: how long shall the workers of iniquity talk?

Thy people, O Lord, they have brought low: and they have afflicted thy inheritance.

They have slain the widow and the stranger: and they have murdered the fatherless.

And they have said: The Lord shall not see: neither shall the God of Jacob understand.

Understand, ye senseless among the people: and you fools be wise at last.

He that planted the ear, shall he not hear: or he that formed the eye, doth he not consider?

Deus ultionum Dominus: * Deus ultionum libere egit.

Exaltare qui judicas terram: * redde retributionem superbis.

Usquequo peccatores Domine: * usquequo peccatores gloriabuntur?

Effabuntur et loquentur iniquitatem: * loquentur omnes qui operantur injustitiam?

Populum tuum, Domine, humiliaverunt: * et hæreditatem tuam vexaverunt.

Viduam et advenam interfecerunt: * et pupillos occiderunt.

Et dixerunt: Non videbit Dominus: * nec intelliget Deus Jacob.

Intelligite insipientes in populo: * et stulti aliquando sapite.

Qui plantavit aurem, non audiet: * aut qui finxit oculum, non considerat?

Qui corripit gentes, non arguet : * qui docet hominem scientiam ?

Dominus scit cogitationes hominum : * quoniam vanæ sunt.

Beatus homo, quem tu erudieris, Domine : * et de lege tua docueris eum.

Ut mitiges ei a diebus malis : * donec fodiatur peccatori fovea.

Quia non repellet Dominus plebem suam : * et hæreditatem suam non derelinquet.

Quoadusque justitia convertatur in judicium : * et qui juxta illam omnes qui recto sunt corde.

Quis consurget mihi adversus malignantes : * aut quis stabit mecum adversus operantes iniquitatem ?

Nisi quia Dominus adjuvit me : * paulo minus habitasset in inferno anima mea.

Si dicebam : Motus est pes meus : * misericordia tua, Domine, adjuvabat me.

Secundum multitudinem dolorum meorum in corde meo : * consolationes tuæ lætificaverunt animam meam.

Numquid adhæret tibi sedes iniquitatis : * qui fingis laborem in præcepto ?

Captabunt in animam justi : * et sanguinem innocentem condemnabunt.

Et factus est mihi Dominus in refugium : * et Deus meus in adjutorium spei meæ.

Et reddet illis iniquita-

He that chastiseth nations, shall he not rebuke : he that teacheth man knowledge ?

The Lord knoweth the thoughts of men, that they are vain.

Blessed is the man whom thou shalt instruct, O Lord : and shalt teach him out of thy law.

That thou mayest give him rest from the evil days : till a pit be dug for the wicked.

For the Lord will not cast off his people : neither will he forsake his own inheritance.

Until justice be turned into judgment : and they that are near it are all the upright in heart.

Who shall rise up for me against the evil doers ? or who shall stand with me against the workers of iniquity ?

Unless the Lord had been my helper : my soul had almost dwelt in hell.

If I said : My foot is moved: thy mercy, O Lord, assisted me.

According to the multitude of my sorrows in my heart : thy comforts have given joy to my soul.

Doth the seat of iniquity stick to thee : who framest labour in commandment ?

They will hunt after the soul of the just : and will condemn innocent blood.

But the Lord is my refuge : and my God the help of my hope.

And he will render to them

their iniquity: and in their malice he will destroy them: yea, the Lord our God will destroy them.

ANT. They will hunt after the soul of the Just; and will condemn innocent Blood.

℣. They have spoken against me with a deceitful tongue.

℟. And they have compassed me about with words of hatred, and have fought against me without cause.

tem ipsorum: et in malitia eorum disperdet eos: * disperdet illos Dominus Deus noster.

ANT. Captabunt in animam justi, et sanguinem innocentem condemnabunt.

℣. Locuti sunt adversum me lingua dolosa.

℟. Et sermonibus odii circumdederunt me, et expugnaverunt me gratis.

Here is said the *Pater noster*, in secret.

For the Lessons of this Nocturn, the Church has selected a passage from the Epistle to the Hebrews, where St. Paul speaks of the Son of God having become our High Priest and Mediator with the Father, by the shedding of his Blood. This precious Blood blots out our sins, and opens heaven to us, which Adam's sin had closed against us.

SEVENTH LESSON.

From the Epistle of St. Paul the Apostle to the Hebrews.
Ch. IV. and V.

Let us haste therefore to enter into that rest: lest any man fall into the same example of unbelief. For the word of God is living and effectual and more piercing than any two-edged sword, and reaching unto the division of the soul and the spirit, of the joints also, and the marrow, and is a discerner of the thoughts and intents of the heart. Neither is there any creature invisible in his sight: but all

De Epistola B. Pauli Apostoli ad Hebræos.
Cap. IV. et V.

Festinemus ingredi in illam requiem: ut ne in idipsum quis incidat incredulitatis exemplum. Vivus est enim sermo Dei, et efficax, et penetrabilior omni gladio ancipiti: et pertingens usque ad divisionem animæ ac spiritus, compagum quoque ac medullarum, et discretor cogitationum et intentionum cordis. Et non est ulla creatura invisibilis in conspectu ejus: omnia autem nuda et aperta sunt oculis ejus, ad quem nobis sermo. Habentes ergo Pontificem magnum, qui penetravit cœlis, Jesum Filium Dei, teneamus confessionem. Non enim habemus Pontificem qui non possit compati infirmitatibus nostris: tentatum autem per omnia pro similitudine absque peccato.

℟. Tradiderunt me in manus impiorum, et inter iniquos projecerunt me, et non pepercerunt animæ meæ: congregati sunt adversum me fortes; * Et sicut gigantes steterunt contra me.

℣. Alieni insurrexerunt adversum me, et fortes quæsierunt animam meam.

* Et sicut gigantes steterunt contra me.

things are naked and open to the eyes of him, to whom our speech is. Seeing then that we have a great High Priest that hath passed into the heavens, Jesus the Son of God, let us hold fast our confession. For we have not a High Priest who cannot have compassion on our infirmities: but one tempted in all things like as we are, without sin.

℟. They delivered me into the hands of the impious, and cast me out among the wicked, and spared not my life: the powerful gathered together against me; * And like giants they stood against me.

℣. Strangers have risen up against me, and the mighty have sought my soul.

* And like giants they stood against me.

EIGHTH LESSON.

Adeamus ergo cum fiducia ad thronum gratiæ: ut misericordiam consequamur, et gratiam inveniamus in auxilio opportuno. Omnis namque Pontifex ex hominibus assumptus, pro hominibus constituitur in iis quæ sunt ad Deum, ut offerat dona et sacrificia pro peccatis: qui condolere possit iis qui ignorant et errant: quoniam et ipse circumdatus est infirmitate. Et propterea debet, quemadmodum pro populo, ita etiam et pro semetipso offerre pro peccatis.

Let us go therefore with confidence to the throne of grace: that we may obtain mercy, and find grace in seasonable aid. For every High Priest taken from among men, is appointed for men in the things that appertain to God, that he may offer up gifts and sacrifices for sins: who can have compassion on them that are ignorant, and that err: because he himself also is compassed with infirmity. And therefore he ought, as for the people, so also for himself, to offer for sins.

℟. The wicked man betrayed Jesus to the chief priests and elders of the people : * But Peter followed him afar off, that he might see the end.
℣. And they led him to Caiphas the high priest, where the Scribes and Pharisees were met together.
* But Peter followed him afar off, that he might see the end.

℟. Jesum tradidit impius summis principibus sacerdotum, et senioribus populi: * Petrus autem sequebatur eum a longe, ut videret finem.
℣. Adduxerunt autem eum ad Caïpham principem sacerdotum, ubi Scribæ et Pharisæi convenerant.
* Petrus autem sequebatur eum a longe, ut videret finem.

NINTH LESSON.

Neither doth any man take the honour to himself, but he that is called by God, as Aaron was. So also Christ did not glorify himself to be made a high priest : but he that said to him : Thou art my Son, this day have I begotten thee. As he saith also in another place : Thou art a priest for ever according to the order of Melchisedech. Who in the days of his flesh, offering up prayers and supplications, with a strong cry and tears, to him that was able to save him from death, was heard for his reverence: and whereas indeed he was the Son of God, he learned obedience by the things which he suffered : and being consummated, he became the cause of eternal salvation to all that obey him, called by God a high-priest according to the order of Melchisedech.

℟. My eyes are darkened by my tears : for he is far from me that comforted me. See

Nec quisquam sumit sibi honorem sed qui vocatur a Deo, tanquam Aaron. Sic et Christus non semetipsum clarificavit ut pontifex fieret : sed qui locutus est ad eum : Filius meus es tu, ego hodie genui te. Quemadmodum et in alio loco dicit: Tu es sacerdos in æternum secundum ordinem Melchisedech. Qui in diebus carnis suæ, preces supplicationesque ad eum, qui possit illum salvum facere a morte, cum clamore valido et lacrymis offerens, exauditus est pro sua reverentia. Et quidem cum esset Filius Dei, didicit ex iis, quæ passus est, obedientiam : et consummatus, factus est omnibus obtemperantibus sibi, causa salutis æternæ, appellatus a Deo pontifex juxta ordinem Melchisedech.

℟. Caligaverunt oculi mei a fletu meo : quia elongatus est a me, qui consolabatur

444 HOLY WEEK.

me. Videte omnes populi,
* Si est dolor similis sicut
dolor meus.
℣. O vos omnes qui transitis per viam, attendite, et videte.
* Si est dolor similis sicut dolor meus.
Here is repeated: Caligaverunt oculi mei.

all ye people, * If there be sorrow like unto my sorrow.
℣. O all ye that pass by the way, behold and see,
* If there be sorrow like unto my sorrow.
Here is repeated': My eyes are darkened.

LAUDS.

The *first* Psalm of Lauds is the *Miserere*, as yesterday, *page* 338. It is sung to the following Antiphon:

ANT. Proprio Filio suo non pepercit Deus, sed pro nobis omnibus tradidit illum.

ANT. God spared not his own Son, but delivered him up for us all.

The *second* Psalm is one of those that was composed by David during the time of Absalom's rebellion. It is one of the Psalms of Friday's ferial Lauds throughout the year; and is appropriate to the mystery of to-day, inasmuch as it expresses how the Messias was abandoned by his Disciples, and how confidently he hoped in God.

ANT. Anxiatus es super me spiritus meus, in me turbatum est cor meum.

ANT. My spirit is in anguish within me, my heart within me is troubled.

PSALM 142.

Domine, exaudi orationem meam: auribus percipe obsecrationem meam in veritate tua: * exaudi me in tua justitia.
Et non intres in judicium cum servo tuo: * quia non

Hear, O Lord, my prayer, give ear to my supplication in thy truth: hear me in thy justice.
And enter not into judgment with thy servant: for in

thy sight no man living shall be justified.

For the enemy hath persecuted my soul: he hath brought down my life to the earth.

He hath made me to dwell in darkness, as those that have been dead of old; and my spirit is in anguish within me, my heart within me is troubled.

I remembered the days of old, I meditated on all thy works. I mused upon the works of thy hands.

I stretched forth my hands to thee: my soul is as earth without water unto thee.

Hear me speedily, O Lord: my spirit hath fainted away.

Turn not away thy face from me: lest I be like unto them that go down into the pit.

Cause me to hear thy mercy in the morning: for in thee have I hoped.

Make the way known to me wherein I should walk: for I have lifted up my soul to thee.

Deliver me from my enemies, O Lord, to thee have I fled: teach me to do thy will, for thou art my God.

Thy good spirit shall lead me into the right land: for thy name's sake, O Lord, thou wilt quicken me in thy justice.

Thou wilt bring my soul out of troubles: and in thy mercy thou wilt destroy my enemies.

justificabitur in conspectu tuo omnis vivens.

Quia persecutus est inimicus animam meam: * humiliavit in terra vitam meam.

Collocavit me in obscuris sicut mortuos sæculi: * et anxiatus est super me spiritus meus, in me turbatum est cor meum.

Memor fui dierum antiquorum, meditatus sum in omnibus operibus tuis: * in factis manuum tuarum meditabar.

Expandi manus meas ad te: * anima mea sicut terra sine aqua tibi.

Velociter exaudi me, Domine: * defecit spiritus meus.

Non avertas faciem tuam a me: * et similis ero descendentibus in lacum.

Auditam fac mihi mane misericordiam tuam: * quia in te speravi.

Notam fac mihi viam in qua ambulem: * quia ad te levavi animam meam.

Eripe me de inimicis meis, Domine, ad te confugi: * doce me facere voluntatem tuam, quia Deus meus es tu.

Spiritus tuus bonus deducet me in terram rectam: * propter nomen tuum, Domine, vivificabis me in æquitate tua.

Educes de tribulatione animam meam: * et in misericordia tua disperdes inimicos meos.

Et perdes omnes qui tribulant animam meam: * quoniam ego servus tuus sum.	And thou wilt cut off all them that afflict my soul: for I am thy servant.
ANT. Anxiatus est super me spiritus meus, in me turbatum est cor meum.	ANT. My spirit is in anguish within me, my heart within me is troubled.

The *third* Psalm is the *Deus, Deus meus*, which is given in *page* 342. The following is its Antiphon:

ANT. Ait latro ad latronem: Nos quidem digna factis recipimus; hic autem quid fecit? Memento mei, Domine, dum veneris in regnum tuum.	ANT. The thief said to the thief: We, indeed, receive the due reward of our deeds; but what has this Man done? Remember me, O Lord, when thou shalt come into thy kingdom.

The following Canticle is that of the Prophet Habacuc, and comes in the Lauds of every Friday, (when a Feria,) throughout the year. It celebrates the victory of Christ over his enemies, when he shall come to judge the world. It forms a sublime contrast with the humiliations which the Man-God suffers on this the day of his Death.

ANT. Cum conturbata fuerit anima mea, Domine, misericordiæ memor eris.	ANT. When my soul shall be in trouble, O Lord! thou wilt be mindful of thy mercy.

CANTICLE OF HABACUC.

Domine, audivi auditionem tuam: * et timui.	O Lord, I heard what thou madest me hear, and was afraid.
Domine, opus tuum: * in medio annorum vivifica illud.	O Lord, thy work in the midst of the years bring it to life.
In medio annorum notum facies: * cum iratus fueris, misericordiæ recordaberis.	In the midst of the years thou shalt make it known: when thou art angry, thou wilt remember mercy.
Deus ab austro veniet: * et Sanctus de monte Pharan.	God will come from the south, and the Holy One from mount Pharan.

His glory covered the heavens: and the earth is full of his praise.

His brightness shall be as the light: horns are in his hands.

There is his strength hid: death shall go before his face.

And the devil shall go forth before his feet: he stood and measured the earth.

He beheld, and melted the nations: and the ancient mountains were crushed to pieces.

The hills of the world were bowed down, by the journeys of his eternity.

I saw the tents of Æthiopia for their iniquity: the curtains of the land of Madian shall be troubled.

Wast thou angry, O Lord, with the rivers? or was thy wrath upon the rivers? or thy indignation in the sea?

Who wilt ride upon thy horses, and thy chariots are salvation.

Thou wilt surely take up thy bow, according to the oaths which thou hast spoken to the tribes.

Thou wilt divide the rivers of the earth: the mountains saw thee and were grieved: the great body of waters passed away.

The deep put forth its voice: the deep lifted up its hands.

The sun and the moon stood still in their habitation, in the light of thy arrows, they shall go in the brightness of thy glittering spear.

Operuit cœlos gloria ejus: * et laudis ejus plena est terra.

Splendor ejus ut lux erit: * cornua in manibus ejus.

Ibi abscondita est fortitudo ejus: * ante faciem ejus ibit mors.

Et egredietur diabolus ante pedes ejus: * stetit et mensus est terram.

Aspexit, et dissolvit Gentes: * et contriti sunt montes sæculi.

Incurvati sunt colles mundi: * ab itineribus æternitatis ejus.

Pro iniquitate vide tentoria Æthiopiæ: * turbabuntur pelles terræ Madian.

Numquid in fluminibus iratus es, Domine: * aut in fluminibus furor tuus, vel in mari indignatio tua?

Qui ascendes super equos tuos: * et quadrigæ tuæ salvatio.

Suscitans suscitabis arcum tuum: * juramenta tribubus, quæ locutus es.

Fluvios scindes terræ: viderunt te et doluerunt montes: * gurges aquarum transiit.

Dedit abyssus vocem suam: * altitudo manus suas levavit.

Sol et luna steterunt in habitaculo suo: * in luce sagittarum tuarum, ibunt in splendore fulgurantis hastæ tuæ.

In fremitu conculcabis terram : * et in furore obstupefacies Gentes.

Egressus es in salutem populi tui : * in salutem cum Christo tuo.

Percussisti caput de domo impii : * denudasti fundamentum ejus usque ad collum.

Maledixisti sceptris ejus, capiti bellatorum ejus : * venientibus ut turbo ad dispergendum me.

Exsultatio eorum : * sicut ejus qui devorat pauperem in abscondito.

Viam fecisti in mari equis tuis : * in luto aquarum multarum.

Audivi, et conturbatus est venter meus : * a voce contremuerunt labia mea.

Ingrediatur putredo in ossibus meis : * et subter me scateat.

Ut requiescam in die tribulationis: * ut ascendam ad populum accinctum nostrum.

Ficus enim non florebit: * et non erit germen in vineis.

Mentietur opus olivæ : * et arva non afferent cibum.

Abscindetur de ovili pecus : * non erit armentum in præsepibus.

Ego autem in Domino gaudebo : * et exsultabo in Deo Jesu meo.

Deus Dominus fortitudo mea : * et ponet pedes meos quasi cervorum.

In thy anger thou wilt tread the earth under foot : in thy wrath thou wilt astonish the nations.

Thou wentest forth for the salvation of thy people, for salvation with thy Christ.

Thou struckest the head of the house of the wicked : thou hast laid bare his foundation even to the neck.

Thou hast cursed their sceptres, the head of his warriors, them that came out as a whirlwind to scatter me.

Their joy was like that of him that devoureth the poor man in secret.

Thou madest a way in the sea for thy horses, in the mud of many waters.

I have heard, and my bowels were troubled : my lips trembled at the voice.

Let rottenness enter into my bones, and swarm under me.

That I may rest in the day of tribulation : that I may go up to our people that are girded.

For the fig-tree shall not blossom : and there shall be no spring in the vines.

The labour of the olive-tree shall fail : and the fields shall yield no food.

The flock shall be cut off from the fold : and there shall be no herd in the stalls.

But I will rejoice in the Lord : and I will rejoice in God my Jesus.

The Lord God is my strength : and he will make my feet like the feet of harts.

And he, the conqueror, will lead me upon my high places, singing psalms.

ANT. When my soul shall be in trouble, O Lord! thou wilt be mindful of thy mercy.

Et super excelsa mea deducet me victor : * in psalmis canentem.

ANT. Cum conturbata fuerit anima mea, Domine, misericordiæ memor eris.

The *last* Psalm of Lauds is *Laudate Dominum de cœlis*, which is given above, *page* 347. The following is its Antiphon:

ANT. Remember me, O Lord, when thou shalt come into thy kingdom.

℣. He hath made me to dwell in darkness,

℟. As them that have been dead of old.

ANT. Memento mei Domine, dum veneris in regnum tuum.

℣. Collocavit me in obscuris.

℟. Sicut mortuos sæculi.

After this Versicle, is sung the Canticle *Benedictus*, (see *page* 350,) with the following Antiphon:

ANT. They put over his head his cause written : Jesus of Nazareth King of the Jews.

ANT. Posuerunt super caput ejus causam ipsius scriptam: Jesus Nazarenus Rex Judæorum.

This Antiphon having been repeated after the Canticle, the Choir sings, to a touching melody, the following words. She repeats them at the end of all the Canonical Hours of these three days, adding to them each day. The addition for to-day is, that the Death which our Saviour deigned to suffer for us was the most disgraceful and painful of all deaths,— *the Death of the Cross.*

℣. Christ became, for our sakes, obedient unto death, even to the death of the Cross.

℣. Christus factus est pro nobis obediens usque ad mortem, mortem autem Crucis.

Then is said, in secret, the *Pater noster*, which is followed by the *Miserere, (page* 338*).* This Psalm is not sung, but only recited, as explained in yesterday's Tenebræ. As soon as the *Miserere* is finished, the following Prayer is said by the first in dignity:

Look down, O Lord, we beseech thee, upon this thy family, for which our Lord Jesus Christ hesitated not to be delivered into the hands of wicked men, and undergo the punishment of the Cross.	Respice, quæsumus, Domine, super hanc familiam tuam, pro qua Dominus noster Jesus Christus non dubitavit manibus tradi nocentium, et crucis subire tormentum.

(then the rest in secret:)

Who liveth and reigneth with thee, in the unity of the Holy Ghost, God, world without end, amen.	Qui tecum vivit et regnat, in unitate Spiritus Sancti, Deus, per omnia sæcula sæculorum, amen.

THE MORNING.

The sun has risen upon Jerusalem. But the Priests and Scribes have not waited all this time without venting their anger upon Jesus. Annas, who was the first to receive the divine Captive, has had him taken to his son-in-law Caiphas, the High Priest. Here he is put through a series of insulting questions, which disdaining to answer, he receives a blow from one of the High Priest's servants. False witnesses had been already prepared: they now come forward, and depose their lies against Him who is the very Truth:—but their testimony is contradictory. Then, Caiphas, seeing that this plan for convicting Jesus of blasphemy is only serving to expose his accomplices, turns to another. He asks him a question, which will oblige our Lord to make an answer; and in this answer, he, Caiphas, will discover blasphemy, and blasphemy would bring Jesus under the power of the Synagogue. This is the question: *I adjure thee, by the living God, that thou tell us, if thou be the Christ the Son of God?*[1] Our Saviour, in order to teach us that we should show respect to those who are in authority, breaks the silence he has hitherto observed, and answers: *Thou hast said it: I am: and hereafter ye shall see the Son of Man sitting on the right hand of the power of God, and coming in the clouds of heaven.*[2] Hereupon, the impious Pontiff rises, rends his garments, and exclaims: *He hath blasphemed! What further need have we of witnesses? Behold! now ye have heard the blasphemy: what think ye?* The whole place resounds with the cry: *He is guilty of death!*[3]

The Son of God has come down upon the earth, in order to restore man to Life; and yet, here we have this creature of death daring to summon his Divine Benefactor before a human tribunal, and condemning him to Death! And Jesus is silent! and bears with these presumptuous, these ungrateful, blasphemers! Well may we exclaim, in the words, wherewith the Greek Church frequently interrupts to-day's reading of the Passion: "Glory be to thy Patience, O Lord!"

Scarcely have the terrible words, *He is guilty of death,* been uttered, than the servants of the High Priest rush upon Jesus. They spit upon him, and blindfolding him, they strike him, saying: *Prophesy! who is it struck thee?*[4] Thus does the Synagogue treat the Messias, who, they say, is to be their glory! And yet, these outrages, frightful as they are, are but the beginning of what our Redeemer has to go through.

But there is something far more trying than all this to the heart of Jesus, and it is happening at this very time. Peter has made his way as far as the court of the High Priest's Palace! He is recognised by the bystanders as a Galilean, and one of Jesus'

---

[1] St. Matth. xxvi. 63.
[2] *Idem, ibid,* 64.—St. Mark, xiv. 62.
[3] St. Matth. xxvi. 65,66.
[4] St. Luke, xxii. 64.

Disciples. The Apostle trembles for his life;—he denies his Master, and affirms, with an oath, that he does not even know him. What a sad example is here of the punishment of presumption! But, Jesus has mercy on his Apostle. The servants of the High Priest lead him to the place, near where Peter is standing; he casts upon him a look of reproach and pardon; Peter immediately goes forth, and weeps bitterly. From this hour forward, he can do nothing but lament his sin; and it is only on Easter Morning, when Jesus shall appear to him after his Resurrection, that he will admit any consolation to his afflicted heart. Let us make him our model, now that we are spending these hours, with our holy Mother the Church, in contemplating the Passion of Jesus. Peter withdraws, because he fears his own weakness; let us remain to the end, for what have we to fear? May our Jesus give us one of those looks, which can change the hardest and worst of hearts!

Meanwhile, the day-dawn breaks upon the City, and the chief Priests make arrangements for taking Jesus before the Roman Governor. They themselves have found him guilty; they have condemned him as a Blasphemer, and, according to the law of Moses, a Blasphemer must be stoned to death: but they cannot apply the law: Jerusalem is no longer free, or governed by her own laws. The power over life and death may only be exercised by her conquerors, and that in the name of Cæsar. How is it, that these Priests and Scribes can go through all this, and never once remember the prophecy of Jacob,—that the Messias would come, when the sceptre should be taken away from Juda?[1] They know off by heart, they are the appointed guardians of those Prophecies, which describe the death to which this Messias is to be put,—and yet, they are the very ones who bring

---

[1] Gen. xlix. 10.

it about! How is all this?—They are blind, and it is Jealousy that blinds them.

The rumour of Jesus' having been seized during the night, and that he is on the point of being led before the Roman Governor, rapidly spreads through the City, and reaches Judas' ear. This wretched man had a passion for money, but there was nothing to make him desire the death of his Divine Master. He knew Jesus' supernatural power. He perhaps flattered himself, that He who could command nature and the elements, would easily escape from the hands of his enemies. But now when he sees that he does *not* escape, and that he is to be condemned to death,—he runs to the Temple, and gives back the thirty pieces of silver to the Chief Priests. Is it that he is converted? and is about to ask his Master to pardon him? Alas! no: despair has possession of him, and he puts an end to his existence. The recollection of all the merciful solicitations made to him, yesterday, by Jesus, both during the Last Supper, and in the Garden, gives him no confidence; it only serves to increase his despair. Surely, he well knew what a merciful Saviour he had to deal with! And yet, he despairs, and this at the very time when the Blood, which washes away the sins of the whole world, is about to be shed! He is lost, because he despaired.

The Chief Priests, taking Jesus with them, present themselves at the Governor's Palace, demanding audience for a case of importance. Pilate comes forward, and peevishly asks them: *What accusation bring ye against this man?*—They answered: *If he were not a malefactor, we would not have delivered him up to thee.* It is very evident from these first words, that Pilate has a contempt for these Jewish Priests; it is not less evident that they are determined to gain their cause. *Take him you,* says Pilate, *and judge him according to your Law.*—

The Chief Priests answered: *It is not lawful for us to put any man to death.*[1]

Pilate leaves the Hall, in order to speak with these men. He returns, and commands Jesus to be brought in. The son of God and the representative of the pagan world are face to face. Pilate begins by asking him: *Art thou the King of the Jews?*—To this Jesus thus replies: *My Kingdom is not of this world. If my Kingdom were of this world, my servants would certainly strive that I should not be delivered to the Jews. But, now, my Kingdom is not from hence.—Art thou a King, then?* says Pilate.—*Thou sayest,* answers Jesus, *that I am a King.* Having, by these last words, confessed his august dignity, our Lord offers a grace to this Roman; he tells him, that there is something worthier of Man's ambition than earthly honours. *For this,* says Jesus, *was I born, and for this came I into the world; that I should give testimony to the Truth. Every one that is of the Truth, heareth my voice.*—*What is Truth?* asks Pilate; but without waiting for the answer, he leaves Jesus, for he is anxious to have done with this case. He returns to the Jews, and says to them: *I find no cause in him.*[2]—Pilate fancies that this Jesus must be a leader of some Jewish sect, whose teachings give offence to the Chief Priests, but which are not worth his examining into them; yet at the same time, he is convinced that he is a harmless man, and that it would be foolish and unjust to accuse him of disturbing the state.

Scarcely has Pilate expressed his opinion in favour of Jesus, than a long list of accusations is brought up against him by the Chief Priests. Pilate is astonished at Jesus' making no reply, and says to him: *Dost thou not hear how great testimonies they allege*

[1] St. John, xviii. 29, 30, 31. [2] *Id. ibid.* 33, 36, 37, 38.

against thee?[1]—These words are kindly meant, but Jesus still remains silent: they, however, excite his enemies to fresh fury, and they cry out: *He stirreth up the people, teaching throughout all Judea, beginning from Galilee, even to this place.*[2] This word *Galilee* suggests a new idea to Pilate. Herod, the Tetrarch of Galilee, happens to be in Jerusalem at this very time. Jesus is his subject; he must be sent to him. Thus Pilate will get rid of a troublesome case, and this act of courteous deference will re-establish a good understanding between himself and Herod.

The Saviour is therefore dragged through the streets of Jerusalem, from Pilate's house to Herod's palace. His enemies follow him with relentless fury; but Jesus still observes his noble silence. Herod, the murderer of John the Baptist, insults him, and ordering him to be clothed in a white garment, as a Fool, he sends him back to Pilate. Another plan for ridding himself of this troublesome case, now strikes the Roman Governor. At the feast of the Pasch, he had the power of granting pardon to any one criminal the people may select. They are assembled together at the court-gates. He feels sure, that their choice will fall upon Jesus, for it is but a few days ago that they led him in triumph through the City: besides, he intends to make the alternative one who is an object of execration to the whole people; he is a murderer, and his name Barabbas. *Whom will you that I release to you?* says Pilate: *Barabbas, or Jesus, that is called the Christ?*—He has not long to wait for the answer: the crowd exclaim: *Not this man, but Barabbas!—What then,* replies Pilate, *shall I do with Jesus, that is called the Christ?—Crucify him?—Why, what evil hath he done? I will chastise him, therefore,*

---

[1] St. Matth. xxvii. 13.   [2] St. Luke, xxiii. 5.

and let him go.—But they growing irritated at this, cry out so much the louder: *Crucify him! Crucify him!*[1]

Pilate's cowardly subterfuge has failed, and left him in a more difficult position than he was before. His putting the innocent on a level with a murderer was, in itself, a gross injustice; and yet, he has not gone far enough for a people that is blind with passion. Neither does his promise to chastise Jesus satisfy them: they want more than his Blood: they insist on his Death!

Here let us pause, and offer our Saviour a reparation for the insult he here receives. He is put in competition with a murderer, and the murderer is preferred! Pilate makes an attempt to save Jesus: but, on what terms!—he must be put on a footing with a vile wretch, and, even so, be worsted! Those very lips that, a few days back, sang " Hosannah to the Son of David," now clamour for his Crucifixion! The City Magistrate and Governor pronounces him innocent; and yet, he condemns him to be scourged, because he fears a disturbance!

Jesus is made over to the soldiers, to be scourged. They rudely strip him of his garments, and tie him to the pillar, which is kept for this kind of torture. Fiercely do they strike him; the blood flows down his sacred Body. Let us adore this the second Bloodshedding of our Jesus, whereby he expiates for the sins we and the whole world have committed by the flesh. This Scourging is by the hands of Gentiles: the Jews delivered him up to be punished, and the Romans were the executioners:—thus have we all had our share in the awful Deicide!

At last, the soldiers are tired; they loosen their Victim;—but it is not out of anything like pity. Their cruelty is going to rest, and their rest is

---

[1] St. Matth. xxvii.—St. Luke, xxiii.—St. John, xviii.

derision. Jesus has been called "King of the Jews:" a King, say they, must have a Crown! Accordingly they make one for the Son of David! It is of Thorns. They press it violently upon his head, and this is the third Bloodshedding of our Redeemer. Then, that they may make their scoffing perfect, the soldiers throw a scarlet cloak over his shoulders, and put a reed, for a sceptre, into his hand; and bending their knee before him, they thus salute him: *Hail, King of the Jews!*—This insulting homage is accompanied with blows upon his face; they spit upon him; and, from time to time, take the reed from his hand, wherewith to strike the Thorns deeper into his head.

Here, the Christian prostrates himself before his Saviour, and says to him with a heart full of compassion and veneration: "Yes! my Jesus! Thou art King of the Jews! Thou art the Son of David, and therefore our Messias and our Redeemer! Israel, that has so lately proclaimed thee King, now unkings thee; the Gentiles scoff at thy Royalty, making it a subject for keener insult:—but reign thou must and over both Jews and Gentiles: over the Jews, by thy justice, for they are soon to feel the sceptre of thy revenge; over the Gentiles, by thy mercy, for thine Apostles are soon to lead them to thy feet. Receive, dearest King! our homage and submission! Reign now and for ever over our hearts, yea, over our whole being!"

Thus mangled and bleeding, holding the reed in his hand, and with the scarlet tatters on his shoulders, Jesus is led back to Pilate. It is just the sight that will soften the hearts of the people; at least, Pilate thinks so; and taking him with him to a balcony of the palace, he shows him to the crowd below, saying: *Behold the Man!*[1] Little did Pilate know all that these few words conveyed! He says not: "Behold

---

[1] St. John, xix. 5.

Jesus!"—nor, "Behold the King of the Jews!" he says: *Behold the Man!*—Man!—the Christian understands the full force of the word thus applied to our Redeemer. Adam, the first Man, rebelled against God, and, by his sin, deranged the whole work of the Creator: as a punishment for his pride and intemperance, the flesh tyrannised over the spirit; the very earth was cursed, and thorns were to be its growth. Jesus, the New Man, comes into this world, bearing upon him, not the reality, but the appearance, the likeness, of sin: in him, the work of the Creator regains its primeval order; but the change was not wrought without violence. To teach us, that the flesh must be brought into subjection to the spirit, Jesus' Flesh was torn by the scourges: to teach us, that pride must give way to humility, the only Crown that Jesus wears is made of Thorns. Yes,—*Behold Man!*—the triumph of the spirit over the flesh, the triumph of humility over pride.

Like the tiger that grows fiercer as he sees blood, so is Israel at the sight of Jesus after his scourging. *Crucify him! Crucify him!*—the cry is still the same.—*Take him you*, says Pilate, *and crucify him; for I find no cause in him.* And yet, he has ordered him to be scourged enough to cause his death! Here is another device of the base coward; but it, too, fails. The Jews have their answer ready: they put forward the right granted by the Romans to the nations that are tributary to the Empire. *We have*, say they, *a law, and according to the law he ought to die; because he made himself the Son of God.* Disconcerted by the reply, Pilate takes Jesus aside into the hall, and says to him: *Whence art thou?* Jesus is silent; Pilate was not worthy to hear the answer to his question. This silence irritates him. *Speakest thou not to me?* says he. *Knowest thou not, that I have power to crucify thee, and I have power to release thee?* Here Jesus deigns to speak; and he speaks, in order to teach us that every power of government, even where pagans are in question, comes from God, and not from a pretended social compact: *Thou shouldst not have any power against me, unless it were given thee from above. Therefore, he that hath delivered me to thee, hath the greater sin.*[1]

This dignified reply produces an impression upon Pilate : he resolves to make another attempt to save Jesus. But the people vociferate a threat which alarms him : *If thou release this man, thou art not Cæsar's friend ; for whosoever maketh himself a King, speaketh against Cæsar.* Still, he is determined to try and pacify the crowd. He leaves the hall, sits upon the judgment-seat, orders Jesus to be placed near him, and thus pleads for him : *Behold your King!* as though he would say, " What have you or Cæsar to fear from such a pitiable object as this ?" The argument was unavailing, and only provokes the cry : *Away with him! Away with him! Crucify him!* As though he did not believe them to be in earnest, Pilate says to them : *Shall I crucify your King?* This time the Chief Priests give the answer : *We have no king but Cæsar.*[2] When the very Ministers of God can talk thus, religion is at an end. *No king but Cæsar!*—then, the sceptre is taken from Juda, and Jerusalem is cast off, and the Messias is come!

Pilate, seeing that nothing can quell the tumult, and that his honour as Governor is at stake, decides on making Jesus over to his enemies. Though against his own inclination, he passes the Sentence, which is to cause him such remorse of conscience that he will afterwards seek relief in suicide. He takes a tablet, and with a *style*, writes the Inscription which is to be fastened to the Cross. The people demand that two thieves should be crucified

---

[1] St. John, xix.   [2] *Id. ibid.*

at the same time,—it would be an additional insult to Jesus: this, too, he grants, fulfilling the prophecy of Isaias: *And with the wicked was he reputed.*[1] Having thus defiled his soul with the most heinous of crimes, Pilate washes his hands before the people, and says to them: *I am innocent of the blood of this just man; look ye to it!* They answer him with this terrible self-imprecation: *His blood be upon us and upon our children!*[2] The mark of *Parricide* here fastens on this ungrateful and sacrilegious people; Cain-like, they shall wander fugitives on the earth. Eighteen hundred years have passed since then; slavery, misery, and contempt, have been their portion; but the *mark* is still upon them. Let us Gentiles,—upon whom this *Blood* of Jesus has fallen as the dew of heaven's mercy,—let us return fervent thanks to the goodness of our heavenly Father, who *hath so loved the world, as to give it his Only Begotten Son.*[3] Let us give thanks to the Son, who, seeing that our iniquities could not be blotted out save by his Blood, shed it, on this day, even to the very last drop.

Here commences "The Way of the Cross;" the House of Pilate, where our Jesus receives the sentence of Death, is the First Station. Our Redeemer is consigned, by the Governor's order, into the hands of the Jews. The Soldiers seize him, and drag him from the Court. They strip him of the scarlet cloak, and bid him clothe himself with his own garments, as before the Scourging. The Cross is ready and they put it on his wounded shoulders. The place where the new Isaac loads himself with the wood of his sacrifice, is the Second Station. To Calvary!— this is the word of command, and it is obeyed: soldiers, executioners, priests, scribes, people,—these form the procession. Jesus moves slowly on; but, after a few paces, exhausted by the loss of Blood and

---

[1] Is. liii. 12. [2] St. Matth. xxvii. 24, 25. [3] St. John, iii. 16.

by his Sufferings, he falls under the weight of his Cross. It is the first fall, and marks the Third Station.

He falls, not so much by the weight of his Cross, as by that of our sins! The Soldiers roughly lay their hands on him, and force him up again. Scarcely has he resumed his steps, than he is met by his afflicted Mother. The *Valiant Woman*, whose love is stronger than death, was not to be absent at such an hour as this. She must see her Son, follow him, keep close to him, even to his last breath. No tongue could tell the poignancy of her grief. The anxiety she has endured during the last few days has exhausted her strength. All the Sufferings of Jesus have been made known to her by a divine revelation; she has shared each one of them with him. But, now, she cannot endure to be absent, and makes her way through the crowd. The Sacrifice is nigh its consummation; no human power could keep such a Mother from her Jesus. The faithful Magdalene is by her side, bathed in tears; John, Mary, (the mother of James the Less) and Salome, (the mother of John,) are also with her: *they* weep for their Divine Master, *she* for her Son. Jesus sees her, but cannot comfort her, for all this is but the beginning of what he is to endure. Oh! what an additional suffering was this for his loving Heart,—to see his Mother agonizing with sorrow! The executioners observe the Mother of their Victim, but it would be too much mercy in them to allow her to speak to him; she may follow, if she please, with the crowd; it is more than she could have expected, to have been allowed this *Meeting*, which we venerate as the Fourth Station of the Way of the Cross.

But from this to the last there is a long distance, for there is a law, that criminals are to be executed outside the City Walls. The Jews are afraid of Jesus' expiring before reaching the place of Sacrifice. Just at this time, they behold a man coming from the country; his name is Simon of Cyrene; they order him to help Jesus to carry his Cross. It is out of a motive of cruelty to our Lord, but it gives Simon the honour of sharing with him the fatigue of bearing the instrument of the world's salvation. The spot where this happens is the Fifth Station.

A little farther on, an incident occurs which strikes the executioners themselves with astonishment. A woman makes her way through the crowd, and setting the soldiers at defiance, comes close up to Jesus. She holds her veil in her hands, and with it respectfully wipes the Face of our Lord, for it is covered with blood, sweat, and spittle. She loves Jesus, and cares not what may happen to her, so she can offer him this slight comfort. Her love receives its reward:—she finds her Veil miraculously impressed with the likeness of Jesus' Face. This courageous act of Veronica marks the Sixth Station of the Way of the Cross.

Jesus grows weaker at each step:—he falls a second time: it is the Seventh Station. Again do the soldiers violently raise him up, and push him along the road. It is easy to follow in his footsteps, for a streak of Blood shows where he has passed. A group of women is following close behind the soldiers; they heed not the insults heaped upon them; their compassion makes them brave. But the last brutal treatment shown to Jesus is more than they can bear in silence; they utter a cry of pitiful lamentation. Our Saviour is pleased with these women, who, in spite of the weakness of their sex, are showing more courage than all the men of Jerusalem put together. He affectionately turns towards them, and tells them what a terrible chastisement is to follow the crime they are now witnessing. The Chief Priests and Scribes recognise the dignity of the Prophet that had so often spoken to them: they listen with indignation, and, at this the Eighth Station of the great Way, they hear these words: *Daughters of Jerusalem! weep not over me, but weep for yourselves and for your children. For behold the days shall come, wherein they will say: Blessed are the barren, and the wombs that have not borne, and the paps that have not given suck. Then shall they begin to say to the mountains: Fall upon us! And to the hills: Cover us!*[1]

At last, they reach the foot of the hill. Calvary is steep; but is the place of Jesus' Sacrifice. He begins the ascent, but falls a third time: the hallowed spot is counted as the Ninth Station. A third time the soldiers force Jesus to rise and continue his painful journey to the summit of the hill, which is to serve as the Altar for the holocaust that is to surpass all others in holiness and power. The executioners' seize the Cross and lay it upon the ground, preparatory to their nailing the Divine Victim to it. According to a custom, practised both by the Romans and the Jews, a cup containing wine and myrrh is offered to Jesus. This drink, which had the bitterness of gall, was given as a narcotic, in order to deaden, in some degree, the feeling of the criminal, and lessen his pain. Jesus raises to his lips the cup, which was proffered him rather from custom than from any idea of kindness; but he drinks not its contents, for he wishes to feel the full intensity of the sufferings he accepts for our sakes. Then the executioners, having violently stripped him of his garments, which had fastened to his wounds, lead him to the Cross. The place where he was thus stripped of his garments, and where the cup of bitter drink was presented to him, is venerated as the Tenth Station of the Way of the Cross. The first nine, from Pilate's hall to the foot of Calvary, are still to be seen in the streets of

---

[1] St. Luke, xxiii. 27-31.

Jerusalem; but the Tenth and the remaining four are in the interior of the Church of Holy Sepulchre, whose spacious walls inclose the spot where the last mysteries of the Passion were accomplished.

But we must here interrupt our history: we have already anticipated the hours of this great Friday, and we shall have to return, later on, to the hill of Calvary. It is time to assist at the service of our holy Mother the Church, in which she celebrates the Death of her Divine Spouse. We must not wait for the usual summons of the Bells; they are silent; we must listen to the call of our faith and devotion. Let us, then, repair to the House of God.

THE MORNING SERVICE.

The Service of this morning consists of four parts, which we now proceed to explain. First of all, we have the Lessons; next, the Prayers; thirdly, the Veneration of the Cross; and lastly, the Mass of the Presanctified. These solemn and unusual rites announce to the Faithful the sacredness of this Day, as also the suspension of the daily Sacrifice, for which they are substituted. The Altar is stripped; the Cross is covered with a black veil; the Candles are of yellow wax;—everything in the Sanctuary bespeaks mournfulness. As soon as the Choir have recited None, the Celebrant and sacred Ministers approach the Altar; their black Vestments denote the grief of holy Church. Being come to the foot of the Altar, they prostrate, and pray in silence, whilst the Acolytes cover the Altar with a single cloth, instead of the three which are always required when Mass is celebrated. The Celebrant and Ministers then rise, and the Lessons are begun.

THE LESSONS.

The first portion of this morning's function consists of two prophetic passages from the Old Testament, and of the Passion according to St. John. The passage from the Prophet Osee tells us of the merciful designs of God in favour of his new people, the Gentiles, who were dead, and who, nevertheless, were to rise again, *in three days*, with Christ, whom they do not so much as yet know. *Ephraim* and *Juda* are to be treated otherwise: their material sacrifices have not been acceptable to a God, who loves *mercy* above every other gift, and rejects the offerings of those whose hearts are filled with bitterness.

LESSON.

(Osee, Chap. VI.)

Thus saith the Lord: In their affliction they will rise early to me. Come, and let us return to the Lord: For he hath taken us, and he will heal us: he will strike, and he will cure us. He will revive us after two days; on the third day he will raise us up, and we shall live in his sight. We shall know, and we shall follow on, that we may know the Lord. His going forth is prepared as the morning light, and he will come to us as the early and the latter rain to the earth. What shall I do to thee, O Ephraim? what shall I do to thee, O Juda? Your mercy is as a morning cloud, and as the dew that goeth away in the morning. For this reason have I hewed them by the prophets, I have slain

Hæc dicit Dominus: In tribulatione sua mane consurgent ad me. Venite, et revertamur ad Dominum: quia ipse cepit, et sanabit nos: percutiet, et curabit nos. Vivificabit nos post duos dies: in die tertia suscitabit nos, et vivemus in conspectu ejus. Sciemus sequemurque, ut cognoscamus Dominum. Quasi diluculum præparatus est egressus ejus; et veniet quasi imber nobis temporaneus et serotinus terræ. Quid faciam tibi Ephraïm? Quid faciam tibi Juda? Misericordia vestra quasi nubes matutina: et quasi ros mane pertransiens. Propter hoc dolavi in prophetis, et occidi eos in verbis oris mei: et judicia tua, quasi lux, egredientur. Quia misericordiam volui, et non sacrificium : et scientiam Dei, plus quam holocausta.

them by the words of my mouth ; and thy judgments shall go forth as the light. For I desired mercy, and not sacrifice ; and the knowledge of God more than holocausts.

The Tract is taken from the Canticle of the Prophet Habacuc, and which we have already sung at Lauds. It foretells the second coming of Christ, when he shall come, in glory and majesty, to judge them that have crucified him.

TRACT.

Domine, audivi auditum tuum, et timui : consideravi opera tua, et expavi.

℣. In medio duorum animalium innotesceris : dum appropinquaverint anni, cognosceris : dum advenerit tempus, ostenderis.

℣. In eo, dum conturbata fuerit anima mea : in ira misericordiæ memor eris.

℣. Deus a Libano veniet, et sanctus de monte umbroso et condenso.

℣. Operuit cœlos majestas ejus : et laudis ejus plena est terra.

Lord, I have heard thy works, and was afraid : I considered thy works, and trembled.

℣. Thou wilt appear between two animals ; when the years draw near, thou wilt be known ; when the time shall come, thou wilt be shown.

℣. When my soul shall be in trouble, even in thy wrath thou wilt remember thy mercy.

℣. God will come from Libanus, and the Holy One from the dark mountain.

℣. His majesty hath clouded the heavens ; and the earth is full of his praise.

The Church sums up, in the following Collect, the prayers of her children. She reminds our heavenly Father of his justice towards Judas and his mercy towards the Good Thief, and begs, that every remnant of the old man may be removed from us, and we rise again with our Lord Jesus Christ.

GOOD FRIDAY: MORNING SERVICE.

The Deacon says:

Let us kneel down. Flectamus genua.

The Subdeacon:

Stand up again. Levate.

COLLECT.

O God, from whom both Judas received the punishment of his sin, and the Thief the reward of his confession: grant us the effects of thy mercy; that as our Lord Jesus Christ, at the time of his Passion, bestowed on both different rewards according to their merits: so, having destroyed the old man within us, he may give us grace to rise again with him. Who liveth, &c.

Deus, a quo et Judas reatus sui pœnam, et confessionis suæ latro præmium sumpsit: concede nobis tuæ propitationis effectum: ut, sicut in passione sua Jesus Christus Dominus noster diversa utrisque intulit stipendia meritorum; ita nobis, ablato vetustatis errore, resurrectionis suæ gratiam largiatur. Qui tecum.

The second Lesson now follows. It is taken from the book of Exodus, and describes to us the ancient rite of the Paschal Lamb, which was the figure of the reality that is given to us to-day. It is to be a Lamb without spot or *blemish*. Its blood has the power of preserving from death those whose dwellings are sprinkled with it. It is not only to be immolated; it is to be eaten by them that have been saved by it. It is to be the food of the wayfarer; and they who partake of it must stand whilst they eat, like unto men who have no time to lose during this passing life. Its immolation is the signal of the Pasch;—the immolation of our Emmanuel, the Lamb of God, is the signal of *our* Pasch.

LESSON.

(Exod. Chap. XII.)

In those days: The Lord said to Moses and Aaron in

In diebus illis: Dixit Dominus ad Moysen et Aaron

in terra Ægypti: Mensis iste vobis principium mensium: primus erit in mensibus anni. Loquimini ad universum cœtum filiorum Israël, et dicite eis: Decima die mensis hujus tollat unusquisque agnum per familias et domos suas. Sin autem minor est numerus, ut sufficere possit ad vescendum agnum, assumet vicinum suum, qui junctus est domui suæ: juxta numerum animarum, quæ sufficere possunt ad esum agni. Erit autem agnus absque macula, masculus, anniculus: juxta quem ritum tolletis et hœdum. Et servabitis eum usque ad quartam decimam diem mensis hujus. Immolabitque eum universa multitudo filiorum Israël ad vesperam. Et sument de sanguine ejus: ac ponent super utrumque postem, et in superliminaribus domorum, in quibus comedent illum. Et edent carnes nocte illa assas igni, et azymos panes, cum lactucis agrestibus. Non comedetis ex eo crudum quid, nec coctum aqua: sed tantum assum igni. Caput cum pedibus ejus et intestinis vorabitis: nec remanebit quidquam ex eo usque mane. Si quid residuum fuerit, igne comburetis. Sic autem comedetis illum. Renes vestros accingetis: et calceamenta habebitis in pedibus, tenentes baculos in manibus: et comedetis festinanter. Est enim

the land of Egypt: This month shall be to you the beginning of months: it shall be the first in the months of the year. Speak ye to the whole assembly of the children of Israel, and say to them: On the tenth day of this month, let every man take a lamb by their families and houses. But if the number be less than may suffice to eat the lamb, he shall take unto him his neighbour that joineth to his house, according to the number of souls which may be enough to eat the lamb. And it shall be a lamb without blemish, a male of one year; according to which rite also he shall kill a kid. And you shall keep it unto the fourteenth day of this month: and the whole multitude of the children of Israel shall sacrifice it in the evening. And they shall take of the blood thereof, and put it upon both the sideposts, and on the upper door posts of the houses, wherein they shall eat it. And they shall eat the flesh that night roasted at the fire, and unleavened bread, with wild lettuce. You shall not eat thereof any thing raw, nor boiled in water, but only roasted at the fire: you shall eat the head with the feet and entrails thereof. Neither shall there remain any thing of it until morning. If there be any thing left, you shall burn it with fire. And thus you shall eat it: you shall gird your reins, and you shall have shoes on your feet, holding staves in your hands, and you shall eat in haste: for it is the Phase (that is, the Passage) of the Lord.

Phase, id est Transitus, Domini.

This magnificent prophecy is followed by a Tract taken from the 139th Psalm, in which the Church represents our Redeemer, (who has been betrayed into the hands of his enemies,) praying to his Eternal Father.

TRACT.

Deliver me, O Lord, from the evil man: rescue me from the unjust man.

℣. Who have devised iniquities in their hearts; all the day long they designed battles.

℣. They have sharpened their tongues like a serpent: the venom of asps is under their lips.

℣. Keep me, O Lord, from the hand of the wicked, and from unjust men deliver me.

℣. Who have proposed to supplant my steps: the proud have hid a net for me.

℣. And they have stretched out cords for a snare: they have laid for me a stumbling block by the way side.

℣. I said to the Lord: thou art my God; hear, O Lord, the voice of my supplication.

℣. O Lord, Lord, the might of my salvation: cover thou my head in the day of battle.

℣. Give me not up, O Lord, from my desire to the wicked:

Eripe me Domine ab homine malo: a viro iniquo libera me.

℣. Qui cogitaverunt malitias in corde: tota die constituebant prælia.

℣. Acuerunt linguas suas sicut serpentis: venenum aspidum sub labiis eorum.

℣. Custodi me Domine de manu peccatoris: et ab hominibus iniquis libera me.

℣. Qui cogitaverunt supplantare gressus meos: absconderunt superbi laqueum mihi.

℣. Et funes extenderunt in laqueum pedibus meis: juxta iter scandalum posuerunt mihi.

℣. Dixi Domino: Deus meus es tu: exaudi Domine vocem orationis meæ.

℣. Domine, Domine, virtus salutis meæ, obumbra caput meum in die belli.

℣. Ne tradas me a desiderio meo peccatori: cogitaverunt adversus me, ne derelinquas me, ne unquam exaltentur.

℣. Caput circuitus eorum: labor labiorum ipsorum operiet eos.

℣. Verumtamen justi confitebuntur nomini tuo: et habitabunt recti cum vultu tuo.

they have plotted against me, do not thou forsake me, lest they should triumph.

℣. The head of their compassing me about: the labour of their lips shall overwhelm them.

℣. But as for the just they shall give glory to thy name; and the upright shall dwell with thy countenance.

The Prophets have prepared us for the fulfilment of their types. Holy Church is now going to relate to us the history of our Saviour's Passion. It is St. John, the fourth of the Evangelists, and an eye-witness of what took place on Calvary, who is about to describe to us the last moments of Jesus' mortal life. Let us be all attention, and beg our Lord to give us something of that devotion, which filled the soul of his Beloved Disciple as he stood at the foot of the Cross.

THE PASSION.

Passio Domini nostri Jesu Christi secundum Joannem.

The Passion of our Lord Jesus Christ according to John.

Cap. XVIII. XIX.

Ch. XVIII. XIX.

In illo tempore: Egressus est Jesus cum discipulis suis, trans torrentem Cedron, ubi erat hortus, in quem introivit ipse, et discipuli ejus. Sciebat autem et Judas, qui tradebat eum, locum: quia frequenter Jesus convenerat illuc cum discipulis suis. Judas ergo cum accepisset cohortem, et a pontificibus et pharisæis

At that time: Jesus went with his disciples over the brook Cedron, where there was a garden, into which he entered with his disciples. And Judas also, who betrayed him, knew the place; because Jesus had often resorted thither together with his disciples. Judas therefore having received a band of soldiers, and servants from the chief priests and the Pharisees, cometh thither with lanterns and torches and weapons. Jesus therefore knowing all things that should come upon him, went forth, and said to them: Whom seek ye? They answered him: Jesus of Nazareth. Jesus saith to them: I am he. And Judas also, who betrayed him, stood with them. As soon therefore as he had said to them: I am he: they went backward and fell to the ground. Again therefore he asked them: Whom seek ye? And they said: Jesus of Nazareth. Jesus answered: I have told you, that I am he. If therefore you seek me, let these go their way. That the word might be fulfilled which he said: Of them whom thou hast given me, I have not lost any one. Then Simon Peter, having a sword, drew it: and struck a servant of the High Priest, and cut off his right ear. And the name of the servant was Malchus. Jesus then said to Peter: Put up thy sword into the scabbard. The chalice which my Father hath given me, shall I not drink it?

Then the band, and the tribune, and the servants of the Jews took Jesus, and they bound him, and they led him away to Annas first, for he was father-in-law to Caiphas, who was the High Priest of that year. Now Caiphas was he who had given the counsel to the Jews: That it was expedient that one man should die for the people. And Simon Peter followed Jesus, and so did

ministros: venit illuc cum laternis, et facibus, et armis. Jesus itaque sciens omnia, quæ ventura erant super eum, processit, et dixit eis; Quem quæritis? Responderunt ei: Jesum Nazarenum. Dicit eis Jesus: Ego sum. Stabat autem et Judas, qui tradebat eum, cum ipsis. Ut ergo dixit eis: Ego sum: abierunt retrorsum et ceciderunt in terram. Iterum ergo interrogavit eos: Quem quæritis? Illi autem dixerunt: Jesum Nazarenum. Respondit Jesus: Dixi vobis, quia ego sum. Si ergo me quæritis, sinite hos abire. Ut impleretur sermo, quem dixit: Quia quos dedisti mihi, non perdidi ex eis quemquam. Simon ergo Petrus habens gladium, eduxit eum, et percussit pontificis servum, et abscidit auriculam ejus dexteram. Erat autem nomen servo Malchus. Dixit ergo Jesus Petro: Mitte gladium tuum in vaginam. Calicem, quem dedit mihi Pater, non bibam illum?

Cohors ergo et tribunus et ministri Judæorum comprehenderunt Jesum, et ligaverunt eum, et adduxerunt eum ad Annam primum. Erat enim socer Caiphæ, qui erat Pontifex anni illius. Erat autem Caiphas, qui consilium dederat Judæis: Quia expedit unum hominem mori pro populo. Sequebatur autem Jesum Simon Petrus, et alius discipulus. Discipulus autem ille erat notus Pontifici : et introivit cum Jesus in atrium Pontificis. Petrus autem stabat ad ostium foris. Exivit ergo discipulus alius, qui erat notus Pontifici : et dixit ostiariæ, et introduxit Petrum. Dicit ergo Petro ancilla ostiaria : Numquid et tu ex discipulis es hominis istius? Dicit ille : Non sum. Stabant autem servi et ministri ad prunas, quia frigus erat : et calefaciebant se. Erat autem cum eis et Petrus stans, et calefaciens se.

Pontifex ergo interrogavit Jesum de discipulis suis, et de doctrina ejus. Respondit ei Jesus: Ego palam locutus sum mundo. Ego semper docui in synagoga, et in templo, quo omnes Judæi conveniunt : et in occulto locutus sum nihil. Quid me interrogas? Interroga eos qui audierunt quid locutus sim ipsis : ecce hi sciunt quæ dixerim ego. Hæc autem cum dixisset, unus assistens ministrorum dedit alapam Jesu, dicens : Sic respondes Pontifici? Respondit ei Jesus : Si male locutus sum, testimonium perhibe de malo : si autem bene, quid me cædis? Et misit eum Annas ligatum ad Caipham Pontificem. Erat autem Simon Petrus stans, et calefaciens se. Dixerunt ergo ei : Numquid et tu ex

another disciple. And that disciple was known to the High Priest, and went in with Jesus into the court of the High Priest. But Peter stood at the door without. The other disciple therefore, who was known to the High Priest, went out, and spoke to the porteress, and brought in Peter. And the maid that was porteress, saith to Peter : Art not thou also one of this man's disciples? He saith : I am not. Now the servants and officers stood at a fire of coals, because it was cold, and warmed themselves. And with them was Peter also standing and warming himself.

The High Priest then asked Jesus of his disciples and of his doctrine. Jesus answered him : I have spoken openly to the world : I have always taught in the synagogue, and in the temple whither all the Jews resort ; and in secret I have spoken nothing. Why askest thou me? ask them who have heard what I have spoken unto them : behold they know what things I have said. And when he had said these things, one of the officers standing by, gave Jesus a blow, saying : Answerest thou the High Priest so? Jesus answered him : If I have spoken evil, give testimony of the evil : but if well, why strikest thou me? And Annas sent him bound to Caiphas the High Priest. And Simon Peter was standing and warming himself. They said there-

GOOD FRIDAY: MORNING SERVICE. 473

fore to him: Art not thou also one of his disciples? He denied it, and said: I am not. One of the servants of the High Priest (a kinsman to him whose ear Peter cut off) saith to him: Did not I see thee in the garden with him? Then Peter again denied: and immediately the cock crew.

Then they led Jesus from Caiphas to the governor's hall. And it was morning; and they went not into the hall, that they might not be defiled, but that they might eat the Pasch. Pilate therefore went out to them and said: What accusation bring you against this man? They answered and said to him: If he were not a malefactor we would not have delivered him up to thee. Pilate then said to them: Take him you, and judge him according to your law. The Jews therefore said to him: It is not lawful for us to put any man to death. That the word of Jesus might be fulfilled which he said, signifying what death he should die. Pilate therefore went into the hall again, and called Jesus, and said to him: Art thou the king of the Jews? Jesus answered: Sayest thou this thing of thyself, or have others told it thee of me? Pilate answered: Am I a Jew? Thy own nation, and the chief priests have delivered thee up to me: what hast thou done? Jesus answered: My kingdom is not of this world. If my kingdom were of this world, my servants would certainly

discipulis ejus es? Negavit ille, et dixit: Non sum. Dicit ei unus ex servis Pontificis, cognatus ejus cujus abscidit Petrus auriculam: Nonne ego te vidi in horto cum illo? Iterum ergo negavit Petrus: et statim gallus cantavit.

Adducunt ergo Jesum a Caïpha in prætorium. Erat autem mane. Et ipsi non introierunt in prætorium, ut non contaminarentur: sed ut manducarent Pascha. Exivit ergo Pilatus ad eos foras, et dixit: Quam accusationem affertis adversus hominem hunc? Responderunt, et dixerunt ei: Si non esset hic malefactor, non tibi tradidissemus eum. Dixit ergo eis Pilatus: Accipite eum vos; et secundum legem vestram judicate eum. Dixerunt ergo ei Judæi: Nobis non licet interficere quemquam. Ut sermo Jesu impleretur, quem dixit, significans, qua morte esset moriturus. Introivit ergo iterum in prætorium Pilatus; et vocavit Jesum, et dixit ei: Tu es Rex Judæorum? Respondit Jesus: A temetipso hoc dicis, an alii dixerunt tibi de me? Respondit Pilatus: Numquid ego Judæus sum? Gens tua, et pontifices tradiderunt te mihi. Quid fecisti? Respondit Jesus: Regnum meum non est de hoc mundo. Si ex hoc mundo esset regnum meum, ministri mei utique decertarent, ut non traderer Judæis. Nunc autem regnum meum non est hinc. Dixit itaque ei Pilatus: Ergo Rex es tu? Respondit Jesus: Tu dicis, quia Rex sum ego. Ego in hoc natus sum, et ad hoc veni in mundum: ut testimonium perhibeam veritati. Omnis qui est ex veritate, audit vocem meam. Dicit ei Pilatus: Quid est veritas? Et cum hoc dixisset, iterum exivit ad Judæos, et dicit eis: Ego nullam invenio in eo causam. Est autem consuetudo vobis, ut unum dimittam vobis in Pascha. Vultis ergo dimittam vobis Regem Judæorum? Clamaverunt ergo rursum omnes dicentes: Non hunc, sed Barabbam. Erat autem Barabbas latro.

Tunc ergo apprehendit Pilatus Jesum, et flagellavit. Et milites plectentes coronam de spinis, imposuerunt capiti ejus, et veste purpurea circumdederunt eum. Et veniebant ad eum, et dicebant: Ave, Rex Judæorum. Et dabant ei alapas. Exivit ergo iterum Pilatus foras, et dicit eis: Ecce adduco vobis eum foras, ut cognoscatis quia nullam invenio in eo causam. Exivit ergo Jesus portans coronam spineam et purpureum vestimentum. Et dicit eis: Ecce Homo. Cum ergo vidissent eum pontifices et ministri, clamabant, dicentes: Crucifige, crucifige eum. Dicit

strive that I should not be delivered to the Jews: but now my kingdom is not from hence. Pilate therefore said to him: Art thou a king then? Jesus answered: Thou sayest that I am a king. For this was I born, and for this I came into the world; that I should give testimony to the truth. Every one that is of the truth, heareth my voice. Pilate saith to him: What is the truth? And when he had said this, he went out again to the Jews, and said to them: I find no cause in him. But you have a custom that I should release one unto you at the Pasch: will you therefore that I release unto you the king of the Jews? Then cried they all again, saying: Not this man, but Barabbas. Now Barabbas was a robber.

Then therefore Pilate took Jesus, and scourged him. And the soldiers platting a crown of thorns, put it upon his head: and they put on him a purple garment. And they came to him, and said: Hail, king of the Jews. And they gave him blows: Pilate therefore went forth again, and saith to them: Behold I bring him forth unto you, that you may know that I find no cause in him. Jesus therefore came forth bearing the crown of thorns, and the purple garment. And he saith to them: Behold the man. When the chief priests therefore and the servants had seen him, they cried out, saying: Crucify him, crucify him. Pilate saith to them: Take him you, and crucify him: for I find no cause in him. The Jews answered him: We have a law; and according to that law he ought to die, because he made himself the Son of God. When Pilate therefore had heard this saying, he feared the more. And he entered into the hall again; and he said to Jesus: Whence art thou? But Jesus gave him no answer. Pilate therefore saith to him: Speakest thou not to me? knowest thou not that I have power to crucify thee, and I have power to release thee? Jesus answered: Thou shouldst not have any power against me, unless it were given thee from above. Therefore he that hath delivered me to thee, hath the greater sin. And from thenceforth Pilate sought to release him. But the Jews cried out, saying: If thou release this man, thou art not Cæsar's friend. For whosoever maketh himself a king, speaketh against Cæsar. Now when Pilate had heard these words, he brought Jesus forth: and sat down in the judgment-seat in the place that is called Lithostrotos; and in the Hebrew, Gabbatha.

And it was the parasceve of the Pasch, about the sixth hour, and he saith to the Jews: Behold your king. But they cried out: Away with him, away with him, crucify him. Pilate saith to them: Shall I crucify your king? The chief priests answered: We have no king but Cæsar. Then therefore he de-

eis Pilatus: Accipite eum vos, et crucifigite. Ego enim non invenio in eo causam. Responderunt ei Judæi: Nos legem habemus, et secundum legem debet mori: quia Filium Dei se fecit. Cum ergo audisset Pilatus hunc sermonem, magis timuit. Et ingressus est prætorium iterum: et dixit ad Jesum: Unde es tu? Jesus autem responsum non dedit ei. Dicit ergo ei Pilatus: Mihi non loqueris? Nescis, quia potestatem habeo crucifigere te, et potestatem habeo dimittere te? Respondit Jesus: Non haberes potestatem adversum me ullam, nisi tibi datum esset desuper. Propterea qui me tradidit tibi, majus peccatum habet. Et exinde quærebat Pilatus dimittere eum. Judæi autem clamabant, dicentes: Si hunc dimittis, non es amicus Cæsaris. Omnis enim qui se regem facit, contradicit Cæsari. Pilatus autem cum audisset hos sermones, adduxit foras Jesum, et sedit pro tribunali in loco qui dicitur Lithostrotos, hebraïce autem Gabbatha.

Erat autem parasceve Paschæ, hora quasi sexta. Et dicit Judæis: Ecce rex vester. Illi autem clamabant: Tolle, tolle, crucifige eum. Dicit eis Pilatus: Regem vestrum crucifigam? Responderunt pontifices: Non habemus regem, nisi Cæsarem. Tunc ergo tradidit eis illum, ut crucifigeretur. Susceperunt autem Jesum: et eduxerunt. Et bajulans sibi crucem, exivit in eum qui dicitur Calvariæ locum, hebraïce autem Golgotha, ubi crucifixerunt eum, et cum eo alios duos hinc et hinc, medium autem Jesum. Scripsit autem et titulum Pilatus: et posuit super crucem. Erat autem scriptum: Jesus Nazarenus, Rex Judæorum. Hunc ergo titulem multi Judæorum legerunt: quia prope civitatem erat locus, ubi crucifixus est Jesus. Et erat scriptum hebraïce, græce, et latine. Dicebant ergo Pilato pontifices Judæorum: Noli scribere: Rex Judæorum: sed quia ipse dixit, Rex sum Judæorum. Respondit Pilatus: Quod scripsi, scripsi. Milites ergo cum crucifixissent eum, acceperunt vestimenta ejus (et fecerunt quatuor partes, unicuique militi partem) et tunicam. Erat autem tunica inconsutilis, desuper contexta per totum. Dixerunt ergo ad invicem: Non scindamus eam, sed sortiamur de illa cujus sit. Ut scriptura impleretur, dicens: Partiti sunt vestimenta mea sibi, et in vestem meam miserunt sortem. Et milites quidem hæc fecerunt.

Stabant autem juxta crucem Jesu mater ejus, et soror matris ejus, Maria Cleo-

livered him to them to be crucified. And they took Jesus, and led him forth. And bearing his own cross, he went forth to that place which is called Calvary, but in Hebrew, Golgotha, where they crucified him, and with him two others, one on each side, and Jesus in the midst. And Pilate wrote a title also: and he put it upon the cross. And the writing was, Jesus of Nazareth the King of the Jews. This title therefore many of the Jews did read: because the place where Jesus was crucified was nigh to the city; and it was written in Hebrew, in Greek, and in Latin. Then the chief priests of the Jews said to Pilate: Write not, The King of the Jews; but that he said, I am the King of the Jews. Pilate answered: What I have written, I have written. The soldiers therefore when they had crucified him, took his garments (and they made four parts, to every soldier a part,) and also his coat. Now the coat was without seam, woven from the top throughout. They said then one to another: Let us not cut it, but let us cast lots for it whose it shall be; that the scripture might be fulfilled which saith: "They have parted my garments among them, and upon my vesture they have cast lots." And the soldiers indeed did these things.

Now there stood by the cross of Jesus, his mother, and his mother's sister, Mary of Cleophas, and Mary Magdalene. When Jesus therefore had seen his mother, and the disciple standing whom he loved, he saith to his mother: Woman behold thy Son. After that, he saith to the disciple: Behold thy mother. And from that hour the disciple took her to his own. Afterwards Jesus knowing that all things were now accomplished, that the scripture might be fulfilled, said: I thirst. Now there was a vessel set there full of vinegar. And they putting a sponge full of vinegar about hyssop, put it to his mouth. Jesus, therefore, when he had taken the vinegar, said: It is consummated. And bowing his head, he gave up the ghost.

phæ, et Maria Magdalene. Cum vidisset ergo Jesus matrem et discipulum stantem, quem diligebat, dicit matri suæ: Mulier, ecce filius tuus. Deinde dicit discipulo: Ecce mater tua. Et ex illa hora accepit eam discipulus in sua. Postea sciens Jesus, quia omnia consumata sunt: ut consummaretur Scriptura, dicit: Sitio. Vas ergo erat positum aceto plenum. Illi autem spongiam plenam aceto, hyssopo circumponentes, obtulerunt ori ejus. Cum ergo accepisset Jesus acetum, dixit: Consummatum est. Et inclinato capite, tradidit spiritum.

Here, a pause is made, as on Palm Sunday.

All kneel down, and, if such be the custom of the place, they prostrate and kiss the ground.

Then the Jews, (because it was the Parasceve,) that the bodies might not remain upon the cross on the sabbath-day, (for that was a great sabbath-day,) besought Pilate that their legs might be broken, and that they might be taken away. The soldiers therefore came; and they broke the legs of the first, and of the other, that was crucified with him. But after they came to Jesus, when they saw that he was already dead, they did not break his legs. But one of the soldiers with a spear

Judæi ergo (quoniam Parasceve erat), ut non remanerent in cruce corpora sabbato (erat enim magnus dies ille sabbati), rogaverunt Pilatum, ut frangerentur eorum crura, et tollerentur. Venerunt ergo milites: et primi quidem fregerunt crura, et alterius qui crucifixus est cum eo. Ad Jesum autem cum venissent, ut viderunt eum jam mortuum, non fregerunt ejus crura; sed unus militum lancea latus ejus aperuit, et continuo exivit sanguis et

aqua. Et qui vidit, testimonium perhibuit : et verum est testimonium ejus. Et ille scit, quia vera dicit, ut et vos credatis. Facta sunt enim hæc, ut scriptura impleretur : Os non comminuetis ex eo. Et iterum alia scriptura dicit : Videbunt in quem transfixerunt.	opened his side, and immediately there came out blood and water. And he that saw it, hath given testimony ; and his testimony is true. And he knoweth that he saith true ; that you also may believe. For these things were done that the scripture might be fulfilled: "You shall not break a bone of him." And again another scripture saith : "They shall look on him whom they pierced."

Here, the Deacon kneels at the foot of the Altar, and prays, in silence, that there may descend upon him the blessing of God; but he does not ask the blessing, as usual, from the Celebrant, either upon the incense or himself. Neither do the Acolytes hold their torches whilst he sings the Gospel. The Sub-deacon does not offer the Missal to the Priest, at the end of the Gospel. The omission of all these ceremonies is expressive of the grief which fills the soul of the Spouse of Christ, the Church.

Post hæc autem rogavit Pilatum Joseph ab Arimathæa (eo quod esset discipulus Jesu, occultus autem propter metum Judæorum) ut tolleret corpus Jesu. Et permisit Pilatus. Venit ergo, et tulit corpus Jesu. Venit autem et Nicodemus, qui venerat ad Jesum nocte primum, ferens mixturam myrrhæ et aloes, quasi libras centum. Acceperunt ergo corpus Jesu, et ligaverunt illud linteis cum aromatibus, sicut mos est Judæis sepelire. Erat autem in loco, ubi crucifixus est, hortus ; et in	After these things, Joseph of Arimathea (because he was a disciple of Jesus, but secretly for fear of the Jews,) besought Pilate that he might take the body of Jesus. And Pilate gave leave. He came therefore and took away the body of Jesus. And Nicodemus also came, he who at the first came to Jesus by night, bringing a mixture of myrrh and aloes, about one hundred pound weight. They took therefore the body of Jesus, and bound it in linen cloths with the spices, as the manner of the Jews is to

bury. Now there was in the place where he was crucified, a garden; and in the garden a new sepulchre, wherein no man had yet been laid. There, therefore, because of the Parasceve of the Jews, they laid Jesus, because the sepulchre was nigh at hand.	horto monumentum novum, in quo nondum quisquam positus erat. Ibi ergo propter Parasceven Judæorum, quia juxta erat monumentum, posuerunt Jesum.

THE PRAYERS.

Having thus described to us the Passion and Death of her Divine Spouse, the Church would follow the example set her by this the Mediator of the world. St. Paul tells us, that our Jesus, when dying on the Cross, *offered up* to his Eternal Father, and this for all mankind, *prayers and supplications, with a strong cry and tears*.[1] Therefore it is, that, from the earliest ages, the Church has presented to the Divine Majesty, upon this day, a solemn formula of "Prayers," in which she intercedes for the necessities of the whole world. How truly is she the Mother of men, and the affectionate Spouse of Jesus! None, not even the Jews, are excluded from this her intercession, which she makes, under the shadow of the Cross, to the Father of all ages.

Each of these "Prayers" is prefaced by a few words, which show its object. The Deacon then bids the Faithful kneel down; and the Subdeacon tells them to rise, and unite in the Prayer made by the Priest.

Let us pray, most dearly beloved brethren, for the holy Church of God, that the Lord God would be pleased to grant it peace, maintain it in union, and	Oremus dilectissimi nobis, pro Ecclesia sancta Dei: ut eam Deus et Dominus noster, pacificare, adunare, et custodire dignetur toto orbe terrarum: subjiciens

[1] Heb. v. 7.

ei principatus, et potestates : detque nobis quietam et tranquillam vitam degentibus, glorificare Deum Patrem omnipotentem.

preserve it all over the earth. That he would likewise bring into her bosom the princes and potentates of the whole world, and grant us peace and tranquillity in this life, and to glorify God the Father Almighty.

OREMUS.

LET US PRAY.

The Deacon: Flectamus genua.
The Subdeacon: Levate.

The Deacon: Let us kneel down.
The Subdeacon: Stand up again.

Omnipotens sempiterne Deus, qui gloriam tuam omnibus in Christo gentibus revelasti : custodi opera misericordiæ tuæ : ut Ecclesia tua toto orbe diffusa, stabili fide in confessione tui Nominis perseveret. Per eumdem.

O Almighty and Eternal God, who, by Christ, hast revealed thy glory to all nations ; preserve the works of thine own mercy, that thy Church, which is spread over the whole world, may persevere with a constant faith in the confession of thy name. Through the same, *&c.*

℞. Amen.

℞. Amen.

Oremus et pro beatissimo Papa nostro N. ut Deus Dominus noster, qui elegit eum in ordine Episcopatus, salvum atque incolumem custodiat Ecclesiæ suæ sanctæ, ad regendum populum sanctum Dei.

Let us pray also for our most holy Father, Pope N., that our Lord God, who hath made choice of him in the order of the Episcopacy, may preserve him in health and safety for the good of his holy Church, and to govern the holy people of God.

OREMUS.

LET US PRAY.

The Deacon: Flectamus genua.
The Subdeacon: Levate.

The Deacon: Let us kneel down.
The Subdeacon: Stand up again.

Omnipotens sempiterne Deus, cujus judicio universa fundantur : respice propitius ad preces nostras, et

O Almighty and Eternal God, by whose appointment all things are established and maintained ; mercifully regard

GOOD FRIDAY: MORNING SERVICE.

our prayers, and by thy goodness preserve the Prelate chosen to govern us; that the Christian people who are governed by thy authority, may increase the merits of their faith under so great a Pontiff. Through, &c.
℞. Amen.

Let us also pray for all Bishops, Priests, Deacons, Subdeacons, Acolytes, Exorcists, Readers, Doorkeepers, Confessors, Virgins, Widows, and for all the holy people of God.

electum nobis Antistitem tua pietate conserva: ut Christiana plebs, quæ te gubernatur auctore, sub tanto Pontifice, credulitatis suæ meritis augeatur. Per Dominum.
℞. Amen.

Oremus et pro omnibus Episcopis, Presbyteris, Diaconibus, Subdiaconibus, Acolythis, Exorcistis, Lectoribus, Ostiariis, Confessoribus, Virginibus, Viduis: et pro omni populo sancto Dei.

LET US PRAY.

The Deacon: Let us kneel down.
The Subdeacon: Stand up again.

O Almighty and Eternal God, by whose spirit the whole body of the Church is sanctified and governed; hear our prayers for all Orders thereof; that, by the assistance of thy grace, thou mayest be served by every rank and condition. Through, &c.
℞. Amen.

OREMUS.

The Deacon: Flectamus genua.
The Subdeacon: Levate.

Omnipotens sempiterne Deus, cujus Spiritu totum corpus Ecclesiæ sanctificatur et regitur: exaudi nos pro universis Ordinibus supplicantes: ut gratiæ tuæ munere, ab omnibus tibi gradibus fideliter serviatur. Per Dominum.
℞. Amen.

The Church of Rome, in the following "Prayer," had in view the Emperor of Germany, who was formerly the head of the germanic confederation, and, in the Middle Ages, was intrusted, by the Church, with the charge of propagating the Faith among the northern nations. This "Prayer" is now omitted, excepting in those countries, which are subject to Austria.

Let us pray also for the most Christian Emperor N.,

Oremus et pro christianissimo Imperatore nostro

N. ut Deus et Dominus noster subditas illi faciat omnes barbaras nationes, ad nostram perpetuam pacem.

OREMUS.
The Deacon: Flectamus genua.
The Subdeacon: Levate.

Omnipotens sempiterne Deus, in cujus manu sunt omnium potestates, et omnium jura regnorum : respice ad Romanum benignus Imperium : ut gentes, quæ in sua feritate confidunt, potentiæ tuæ dextera comprimantur. Per Dominum.
℟. Amen.

Oremus et pro catechumenis nostris : ut Deus et Dominus noster adaperiat aures præcordiorum ipsorum, januamque misericordiæ : ut per lavacrum regenerationis, accepta remissione omnium peccatorum, et ipsi inveniantur in Christo Jesu Domino nostro.

LET US PRAY.
The Deacon: Flectamus genua.
The Subdeacon: Levate.

Omnipotens sempiterne Deus, qui Ecclesiam tuam nova semper prole fœcundas : auge fidem et intellectum catechumenis nostris : ut renati fonte baptismatis, adoptionis tuæ filiis aggregentur. Per Dominum.

that the Lord God may reduce to his obedience all barbarous nations for our perpetual peace.

LET US PRAY.
The Deacon: Let us kneel down.
The Subdeacon: Stand up again.

O Almighty and Eternal God, in whose hands are the power and right of all kingdoms, graciously look down on the Roman Empire : that those nations who confide in their own haughtiness and strength, may be reduced by the power of thy right hand.
℟. Amen.

Let us pray also for our Catechumens, that our Lord God may open for them the ears of their hearts, and the gates of mercy ; that having received the remission of sin by the laver of regeneration, they may also belong to our Lord Jesus Christ.

OREMUS.
The Deacon: Let us kneel down.
The Subdeacon: Stand up again.

O Almighty and Eternal God, who continually makest the church fruitful in new children, increase the faith and understanding of our Catechumens, that, being again born at the font of baptism, they may be joined to thy adopted children. Through, &c.

℞. Amen.

Let us pray, most dearly beloved brethren, to God the Father Almighty, that he would purge the world of all errors, cure diseases, drive away famine, open prisons, break chains, grant a safe return to travellers, health to the sick, and a secure harbour to such as are at sea.

LET US PRAY.

The Deacon: Let us kneel down.

The Subdeacon: Stand up again.

O Almighty and Eternal God, the comfort of the afflicted, and the strength of those that labour; let the prayers of all such as call upon thee in tribulation, come to thee; that all, with joy, may find the effects of thy mercy in their necessities. Through, &c.

℞. Amen.

Let us pray also for all heretics and schismatics, that our Lord God would be pleased to deliver them from all their errors, and call them back to our Holy Mother the Catholic and Apostolic Church.

LET US PRAY.

The Deacon: Let us kneel down.

The Subdeacon: Stand up again.

O Almighty and eternal God, who savest all and wouldst have none to perish; look down on those souls that

℞. Amen.

Oremus, dilectissimi nobis, Deum Patrem omnipotentem, ut cunctis mundum purget erroribus : morbos auferat : famem depellat : aperiat carceres : vincula dissolvat : peregrinantibus reditum, infirmantibus sanitatem, navigantibus portum salutis indulgeat.

OREMUS.

The Deacon: Flectamus genua.

The Subdeacon: Levate.

Omnipotens sempiterne Deus, mœstorum consolatio, laborantium fortitudo, perveniant ad te preces de quacumque tribulatione clamantium : ut omnes sibi in necessitatibus suis misericordiam tuam gaudeant adfuisse. Per Dominum.

℞. Amen.

Oremus et pro hæreticis et schismaticis : ut Deus et Dominus noster eruat eos ab erroribus universis : et ad sanctam matrem Ecclesiam Catholicam atque Apostolicam revocare dignetur.

OREMUS.

The Deacon: Flectamus genua.

The Subdeacon: Levate.

Omnipotens sempiterne Deus, qui salvas omnes, et neminem vis perire : respice ad animas diabolica fraude deceptas: ut omni hæretica pravitate deposita, errantium corda resipiscant, et ad veritatis tuæ redeant unitatem. Per Dominum.

℟. Amen.

Oremus et pro perfidis Judæis: ut Deus et Dominus noster auferat velamen de cordibus eorum, ut et ipsi agnoscant Jesum Christum Dominum nostrum.

are seduced by the deceits of the devil; that the hearts of all those who err, laying aside all heretical malice, may repent and return to the unity of the truth. Through, &c.

℟. Amen.

Let us pray also for the perfidious Jews; that the Lord God would withdraw the veil from their hearts, that they also may acknowledge our Lord Jesus Christ thy Son.

Here, the Deacon does not invite the Faithful to kneel. The Church has no hesitation in offering up a "Prayer" for the descendants of Jesus' executioners, but, in doing so, she refrains from genuflecting: because this mark of adoration was turned by the Jews into an insult against our Lord during the Passion. She prays for his scoffers; but she shrinks from repeating the act wherewith they scoffed him.

Omnipotens sempiterne Deus, qui etiam Judaicam perfidiam a tua misericordia non repellis: exaudi preces nostras, quas pro illius populi obcæcatione deferimus: ut agnita veritatis tuæ luce, quæ Christus est, a suis tenebris eruantur. Per eumdem Dominum.

℟. Amen.

Oremus et pro paganis: ut Deus omnipotens auferat iniquitatem a cordibus eorum: ut relictis idolis suis, convertantur ad Deum vivum et verum, et unicum Filium ejus Jesum Christum, Deum et Dominum nostrum.

O Almighty and Eternal God, who deniest not thy mercy even to the perfidious Jews; hear our prayers which we pour forth for the blindness of that people; that by acknowledging the light of thy truth, which is the Christ, they may be brought out of their darkness. Through the same, &c.

℟. Amen.

Let us pray also for the pagans, that Almighty God would remove all iniquity from their hearts; that quitting their idols, they may be converted to the true and living God, and his only Son, Jesus Christ our Lord.

LET US PRAY.

The Deacon: Let us kneel down.
The Subdeacon: Stand up again.

O Almighty and Eternal God, who seekest not the death of sinners, but that they should live; mercifully hear our prayers, and deliver them from their idolatry: and, to the praise and glory of thy name, admit them into thy holy Church. Through, &c.

℟. Amen.

OREMUS.

The Deacon: Flectamus genua.
The Subdeacon: Levate.

Omnipotens sempiterne Deus, qui non mortem peccatorum, sed vitam semper inquiris: suscipe propitius orationem nostram: et libera eos ab idolorum cultura: et aggrega Ecclesiæ tuæ sanctæ, ad laudem et gloriam Nominis tui. Per Dominum.

℟. Amen.

THE VENERATION OF THE CROSS.

The "Prayers" are ended. The charity and zeal of the Church have embraced the whole universe of men, invoking upon them the merciful effusion of that precious Blood, which is now flowing from the Wounds of her Crucified Lord. She turns next to her faithful Children. Filled with holy indignation at the humiliations heaped upon her Jesus, she invites us to an act of solemn reparation: it is to consist in our venerating that Cross, which our Divine Lord has borne to the summit of Calvary, and to which he is to be fastened with nails. The Cross is *a stumbling-block to the Jews, and foolishness to the Gentiles;*[1] but to us Christians, it is the trophy of Jesus' victory, and the instrument of the world's Redemption. It is worthy of our deepest veneration, because of the honour conferred upon it by the Son of God:—he consecrated it by his own Blood, he worked our salvation by its means. No time could be more appropriate than this for the honouring it with the humble tribute of our veneration.

[1] I. Cor. i. 23.

The holy ceremony of venerating the Cross on Good Friday was first instituted at Jerusalem, in the 4th century. Owing to the pious zeal of the Empress St. Helen, the True Cross had then recently been discovered, to the immense joy of the whole Church. The Faithful, as might be expected, were desirous to see the precious Relic, and, accordingly, it was exposed every Good Friday. This brought a very great number of pilgrims to Jerusalem; and yet how few, comparatively, could hope to have the happiness of such a visit, or witness the magnificent ceremony? An imitation of what was done, on this day, at Jerusalem, was a natural result of these pious desires. It was about the 7th century, that the practice of publicly venerating the Cross on Good Friday was introduced into other Churches. True, it was but an image of the True Cross that these other Churches could show to the people; but as the respect that is paid to the True Cross refers to Christ himself, the Faithful could offer him a like homage of adoration, even though not having present before their eyes the sacred Wood which had been consecrated by the Blood of Jesus. Such was the origin of the imposing ceremony, at which holy Church now invites us to assist.

The Celebrant takes off the Chasuble, which is the badge of the Priesthood; it is in order that the Reparation, which he is to be first to offer to our outraged Jesus, may be made with all possible humility. He then stands on the step near the Epistle side of the Altar, and turns his face towards the people. The Deacon takes down the Cross from the Altar, and gives it to the Celebrant, who then unveils the upper part as far as the arms. He raises it a little, and sings these words:

| Ecce lignum Crucis; | Behold the wood of the Cross; |

Then he continues, joined by the Deacon and Subdeacon:

| on which hung the salvation of the world. | in quo salus mundi pependit. |

The people then kneel down, and venerate the Cross, while the Choir sings these words:

| Come, let us adore. | Venite adoremus. |

This first exposition, which is made at the side of the Altar, and in a low tone of voice, represents the first preaching of the Cross, that, namely, which the Apostles made, when, for fear of the Jews, they dared not to speak of the great Mystery except to the few faithful Disciples of Jesus. For the same reason, the Priest but slightly elevates the Cross. The homage here paid to it is intended as a reparation for the insults and injuries offered to our Redeemer in the house of Caiphas.

The Priest then comes to the front of the step, and is thus nearer to the people. He unveils the right arm of the Cross, and holds up the holy Sign of our Redemption higher than the first time. He then sings, and on a higher note:

| Behold the wood of the Cross; | Ecce lignum Crucis; |

Then he continues, joined by the Deacon and Subdeacon:

| on which hung the salvation of the world. | in quo salus mundi pependit. |

The people then fall upon their knees, and continue in that posture, whilst the Choir sings:

| Come, let us adore. | Venite adoremus. |

This second elevation of the holy Cross signifies the Apostles' extending their preaching the mystery of our Redemption to the Jews, after the descent of the Holy Ghost; by which preaching they made many thousand converts, and planted the Church in the very midst of the Synagogue. It is intended as a reparation to our Saviour, for the treatment he received in the Court of Pilate.

The Priest then advances to the middle of the Altar, and, with his face still turned towards the people, he removes the veil entirely from the Cross. He elevates it more than he did the two preceding times, and triumphantly sings on a still higher note:

Ecce lignum Crucis ;   Behold the wood of the Cross ;

The Deacon and Subdeacon here unite their voices with his:

in quo salus mundi pendit.   on which hung the salvation of the world.

The people fall down upon their knees, and the Choir sings:

Venite adoremus.   Come, let us adore.

This third and unreserved manifestation represents the mystery of the Cross being preached to the whole earth, when the Apostles, after being rejected by the majority of the Jewish people, turned towards the Gentiles, and preached Jesus Crucified, even far beyond the limits of the Roman Empire. It is intended as a Reparation to our Lord for the outrages offered to him on Calvary.

There is also another teaching embodied in this ceremony of holy Church. By this gradual unveiling of the Cross, she would express to us the contrast of the Jewish and the Christian view. The one finds nothing in Christ Crucified but shame and ignominy: the other discovers in him *the power and the wisdom of God*.[1] Honour, then, and veneration to his Cross! The veil is removed by Faith. Unveiled let it be upon our Altar, for He that died upon it is soon to triumph by a glorious Resurrection! Yea, let every Crucifix in our Church be unveiled, and every Altar beam once more with the vision of the glorious Standard!

But the Church is not satisfied with showing her Children the Cross that has saved them; she would have them approach, and kiss it. The Priest leads the way. He has already taken off his Chasuble; he now takes off his shoes also, and then advances towards the place where he has put the Crucifix. He makes three genuflexions at intervals, and finally kisses the Cross. The Deacon and Subdeacon follow him, then the clergy, and lastly the people.

The chants which are used during this ceremony are exceedingly fine. First of all, there are the *Improperia*, that is, the *Reproaches* made by our Saviour to the Jews. Each of the first three stanzas of this plaintive Hymn is followed by the *Trisagion*, or Prayer to the Thrice Holy God, who, as Man, suffers death for us. Oh! let us fervently proclaim him to be *The Holy, The Immortal!* This form of prayer was used at Constantinople, so far back as the fifth Century. The Roman Church adopted it, retaining even the original Greek words, to which, however, she adds a Latin translation. The rest of this beautiful chant contains the comparison made by our Lord, between the favours he has bestowed

---

[1] I. Cor. i. 24.

upon the Jewish people, and the injuries he has received from them in return.

THE "IMPROPERIA," OR "REPROACHES."

Popule meus, quid feci tibi, aut in quo contristavi te? Responde mihi. Quia eduxi te de terra Ægypti! parasti crucem Salvatori tuo.

My people, what have I done to thee? or in what have I grieved thee? Answer me. Because I brought thee out of the land of Egypt, thou hast prepared a Cross for thy Saviour.

Agios o Theos.
Sanctus Deus.
Agios ischyros.
Sanctus fortis.
Agios athanatos, eleison imas.
Sanctus immortalis, miserere nobis.

O Holy God!
O Holy God!
O Holy and Strong!
O Holy and Strong!
O Holy and Immortal! have mercy on us.
O Holy and Immortal! have mercy on us.

Quia eduxi te per desertum quadraginta annis: et manna cibavi te, et introduxi te in terram satis bonam, parasti crucem Salvatori tuo.

Because I was thy guide through the desert for forty years, and fed thee with manna, and brought thee into an excellent land, thou hast prepared a cross for thy Saviour.

Agios o Theos, &c.

O Holy God, &c.

Quid ultra debui facere tibi, et non feci? Ego quidem plantavi te vineam meam speciosissimam: et tu facta es mihi nimis amara: aceto namque sitim meam potasti: et lancea perforasti latus Salvatori tuo.

What more should I have done to thee, and have not done? I have planted thee for my most beautiful vineyard: and thou hast proved very bitter to me, for in my thirst thou gavest me vinegar to drink; and piercedst the side of thy Saviour with a spear,

Agios o Theos, &c.

O Holy God, &c.

GOOD FRIDAY: MORNING SERVICE.

For thy sake I scourged Egypt with her first-born; and thou hast delivered me up to be scourged.

My people, what have I done to thee? or in what have I grieved thee? Answer me.

Ego propter te flagellavi Ægyptum cum primogenitis suis: et tu me flagellatum tradidisti.

Popule meus, quid feci tibi, aut in quo contristavi te? Responde mihi.

I led thee out of Egypt, having drowned Pharaoh in the Red Sea; and thou hast delivered me up to the chief priests.

My people, &c.

Ego eduxi te de Ægypto, demerso Pharaone in mare Rubrum: et tu me tradidisti principibus sacerdotum.

Popule meus, &c.

I opened the sea before thee; and thou hast opened my side with a spear.

My people, &c.

Ego ante te aperui mare: et tu aperuisti lancea latus meum.

Popule meus, &c.

I went before thee in a pillar of cloud; and thou hast brought me to the court of Pilate.

My people, &c.

Ego ante te præivi in columna nubis: et tu me duxisti ad prætorium Pilati.

Popule meus, &c.

I fed thee with manna in the desert; and thou hast beaten me with buffets and stripes.

My people, &c.

Ego te pavi manna per desertum: et tu me cæcidisti alapis et flagellis.

Popule meus, &c.

I gave thee wholesome water to drink out of the rock, and thou hast given me for my drink gall and vinegar.

My people, &c.

Ego te potavi aquâ salutis de petra: et tu me potasti felle et aceto.

Popule meus, &c.

For thy sake I smote the king of Canaan; and thou

Ego propter te Chananæorum reges percussi: et tu

percussisti arundine caput meum.
 Popule meus, &c.

hast smote my head with a cane.
 My people, &c.

 Ego dedi tibi sceptrum regale : et tu dedisti capiti meo spineam coronam.
 Popule meus, &c.

 I gave thee a royal sceptre, and thou hast given to my head a crown of thorns.
 My people, &c.

 Ego te exaltavi magna virtute : et tu me suspendisti in patibulo crucis.
 Popule meus, &c.

 By great might I raised thee on high ; and thou hast hanged me on the gibbet of the Cross.
 My people, &c.

The *Improperia* are followed by this solemn Antiphon, in which the two great Mysteries are blended together: the Crucifixion and the Resurrection. This union eloquently expresses the Triumph of our Redeemer.

 Crucem tuam adoramus, Domine : et sanctam Resurrectionem tuam laudamus, et glorificamus : ecce enim propter lignum venit gaudium in universo mundo.
 Ps. Deus misereatur nostri, et benedicat nobis : illuminet vultum suum super nos, et misereatur nostri.
 Then, is repeated: Crucem tuam, &c.

 We adore thy Cross, O Lord, and we praise and glorify thy holy Resurrection, for by the wood of the Cross the whole earth is filled with joy.
 Ps. May God have mercy on us and bless us ; may his countenance shine upon us, and may he have mercy on us.
 Then, is repeated: We adore, &c.

If the Adoration of the Cross is not yet finished, the following Hymn is sung. It was composed by Mamertus Claudianus, in the 6th century. One of the stanzas is repeated after each six verses, as the burden of the Hymn.

HYMN.

O Faithful Cross! thou noblest of all trees. No forest yields thy like, in leaf, or flower, or fruit. Sweet is the Wood, that hath nails so sweet, and bears so sweet a weight!	Crux fidelis, inter omnes, Arbor una nobilis: Nulla silva talem profert, Fronde, flore, germine. Dulce lignum, dulces clavos, Dulce pondus sustinet.
O sing, my tongue, the victory of the glorious combat! Tell how was won the noble triumph on the trophy of the Cross, and how the world's Redeemer, when immolated, conquered. *Repeat:* O faithful Cross.	Pange lingua gloriosi Lauream certaminis, Et super crucis trophæo Dic triumphum nobilem; Qualiter Redemptor orbis Immolatus vicerit. *Repeat:* Crux fidelis.
Our Creator compassionated his creature, our First Parent, when being deceived, he became a victim of death by eating the fatal fruit: and even then he chose the *Tree*, whereby to make good the evils brought on us by that other tree *Repeat:* Sweet is the Wood.	De parentis protoplasti Fraude factor condolens, Quando pomi noxialis In necem morsu ruit, Ipse lignum tunc notavit, Damna ligni ut solveret. *Repeat:* Dulce lignum.
This was the plan designed for our salvation,—that artifice divine should foil the artifice of Satan, the arch-seducer; and turn the very instrument, wherewith the enemy had wounded us, into our remedy. *Repeat:* O faithful Cross.	Hoc opus nostræ salutis Ordo depoposcerat, Multiformis proditoris Ars ut artem falleret; Et medelam ferret inde, Hostis unde læserat. *Repeat:* Crux fidelis.
When, therefore, the fulness	Quando venit ergo sacri

Plenitudo temporis, Missus est ab arce Patris Natus orbis conditor; Atque ventre virginali Carne amictus prodiit.

Repeat: Dulce lignum.

of God's time had come, the Son, by whom the world was made, was sent from heaven; and having clothed himself with our flesh, in the Virgin's womb, he came among us.

Repeat: Sweet is the Wood.

Vagit infans, inter arcta Conditus præsepia: Membra pannis involuta Virgo mater alligat, Et Dei manus, pedesque Stricta cingit fascia.
Repeat: Crux fidelis.

He lies a weeping Babe in a little crib. His Virgin Mother swathes his limbs with clothes. The hands and feet of God are tied with bands!

Repeat: O faithful Cross.

Lustra sex qui jam peregit, Tempus implens corporis: Sponte libera Redemptor Passioni deditus: Agnus in crucis levatur Immolandus stipite.
Repeat: Dulce lignum.

Thirty years he lived on earth, and his mortal life was nigh its end. He, our Redeemer, willingly gave himself up to his Passion; He, the Lamb of Sacrifice, was raised upon the Cross.
Repeat: Sweet is the Wood.

Felle potus, ecce languit; Spina, clavi, lancea, Mite corpus perforarunt; Unda manat et cruor: Terra, pontus, astra, mundus Quo lavantur flumine.

Repeat: Crux fidelis.

His drink is gall;—his strength is gone; his tender flesh is pierced with thorns, and nails, and spear; and from it flows a stream of water and blood, wherewith the earth and sea, the stars and world, are washed.
Repeat: O faithful Cross.

Flecte ramos arbor alta, Tensa laxa viscera: Et rigor lentescat ille, Quem dedit nativitas: Et superni membra Regis Tende miti stipite.
Repeat: Dulce lignum.

Bow down thy branches, lofty Tree! unstring thy sinews, soften thine inborn hardness, and gently welcome the body of our Almighty King!
Repeat: Sweet is the Wood.

Thou alone wast found worthy to bear the Victim of the world! Thou wast the Ark that led this ship-wrecked world into the haven of salvation! The sacred Blood that flowed from the Lamb covered and anointed thee.
Repeat: O faithful Cross.

Sola digna tu fuisti Ferre mundi victimam, Atque portum præparare Arca mundo naufrago: Quam sacer cruor perunxit, Fusus Agni corpore.
Repeat: Crux fidelis.

To the Blessed Trinity be glory everlasting! To the Father, Son, and Holy Ghost, be equal praise! May heaven and earth praise the Name of the Triune God! Amen.
Repeat: Sweet is the Wood!

Sempiterna sit beatæ Trinitati gloria; Æqua Patri, Filioque, Par decus Paraclito; Unius Trinique nomen Laudet universitas. Amen.
Repeat: Dulce lignum.

Towards the end of the Veneration of the Cross, the Candles are lighted, and the Deacon spreads a Corporal upon the Altar, for the Blessed Sacrament is to be placed there. As soon as the Faithful have finished their Adoration, the Priest takes the Cross and replaces it over the Altar.

MASS OF THE PRESANCTIFIED.

So vividly is the Church impressed with the remembrance of the great Sacrifice offered, to-day, on Calvary, that she refrains from renewing, on her Altars, the immolation of the Divine Victim: she contents herself with partaking of the sacred mystery by Communion. Formerly, the Clergy and Laity were also permitted to communicate; but the present discipline is that only the Priest shall receive. After the Priest has resumed his Chasuble, the Clergy go in procession to the Altar, where the consecrated Host has been reserved since yesterday's Mass. The Deacon takes the Chalice which contains it, and places it on the Altar. The Priest, having offered the homage of his adoration to our Redeemer, takes into his hands the Chalice, wherein *He* is inclosed, whom heaven and earth cannot contain. The Clergy, with lighted tapers in their hands, return to the high Altar, and sing, during the procession, the Hymn of the Cross.

HYMN.

Vexilla Regis prodeunt;
Fulget Crucis mysterium,
Qua Vita mortem pertulit,
Et morte vitam protulit.

The Standard of our King comes forth: the mystery of the Cross shines upon us,— that Cross on which Life suffered death, and by his Death gave life.

Quæ vulnerata lanceæ
Mucrone diro, criminum
Ut nos lavaret sordibus
Manavit unda et sanguine.

He was pierced with the cruel Spear, that, by the Water and the Blood, which flowed from the wound, he might cleanse us from sin.

Impleta sunt quæ concinit
David fideli carmine,
Dicendo nationibus:
Regnavit a ligno Deus.

Here, on the Cross was fulfilled the prophecy foretold in David's truthful words: "God hath reigned from the Tree."

Arbor decora et fulgida,
Ornata regis purpura,
Electa digno stipite
Tam sancta membra tangere.

O fair and shining Tree! beautified by the scarlet of the King, and chosen as the noble trunk that was to touch such sacred limbs!

Beata cujus brachiis
Pretium pependit sæculi,
Statera facta corporis,
Tulitque prædam tartari.

O blessed Tree! on whose arms hung the ransom of the world! It was the balance, wherein was placed the Body of Jesus, and thereby hell lost its prey.

O Crux, ave spes unica,
Hoc Passionis tempore,
Piis adauge gratiam,
Reisque dele crimina.

Hail, O Cross! our only hope! During these days of the Passion, increase to the good their grace, and cleanse sinners from their guilt.

Te, fons salutis, Trinitas,
Collaudet omnis spiritus:
Quibus Crucis victoriam
Largiris, adde præmium.
  Amen.

May every spirit praise thee, O Holy Trinity, thou Fount of Salvation! and by the Cross, whereby thou gavest us victory, give us, too, our recompense. Amen.

GOOD FRIDAY: MORNING SERVICE. 497

As soon as the Priest has reached the Altar, the Deacon receives the Sacred Host upon a Paten, and pours wine and water into the Chalice. Let us reverently fix our eyes upon the Altar. The Priest censes the offerings and the Altar, as usual; but, to express the grief which now fills the soul of the Church, he himself is not thurified. He says, secretly, the following prayers :

May this incense, which hath been blessed by thee, O Lord, ascend unto thee ; and may thy mercy descend upon us.	Incensum istud, a te benedictum, ascendat ad te, Domine : et descendat super nos misericordia tua.
Let my prayer, O Lord, ascend like incense in thy sight. May the lifting up of my hands be like the evening sacrifice. Place, O Lord, a guard upon my mouth, and a gate of prudence before my lips ; that my heart may not incline to evil words, to make excuses in sins.	Dirigatur, Domine, oratio mea, sicut incensum in conspectu tuo. Elevatio manuum mearum sacrificium vespertinum. Pone, Domine, custodiam ori meo, et ostium circumstantiæ labiis meis ; ut non declinet cor meum in verba malitiæ, ad excusandas excusationes in peccatis.

Giving the thurible to the Deacon, he says :

May the Lord kindle within us the fire of his love, and the flame of everlasting charity. Amen.	Accendat in nobis Dominus ignem sui amoris, et flammam æternæ charitatis. Amen.

Here, he washes his hands, and then returns to the middle of the Altar, where he says the following prayer in secret :

Receive us, O Lord, coming to thee in the spirit of humility, and with a contrite heart : and grant that the sacrifice of this day may be so celebrated by us, as to be well pleasing unto thee, O Lord our God !	In spiritu humilitatis, et in animo contrito suscipiamur a te, Domine : et sic fiat sacrificium nostrum in conspecto tuo hodie, ut placeat tibi, Domine Deus.

He then turns towards the people, and asks their prayers, saying:

Orate fratres: ut meum ac vestrum sacrificium acceptabile fiat apud Deum Patrem Omnipotentem.	Brethren, pray: that this my sacrifice and yours may be acceptable to God the Father Almighty.

The usual answer, *Suscipiat*, is omitted: and the Celebrant immediately sings, on the Ferial tone, the *Pater noster*. Let us join, with earnest confidence, in the seven petitions. Our Jesus, with his arms extended on the Cross, is now offering them, for us, to his Eternal Father. This is the solemn hour, when every prayer offered to heaven, through his mediation, is sure to be granted.

Pater noster, qui es in cœlis, sanctificetur nomen tuum; adveniat regnum tuum; fiat voluntas tua sicut in cœlo, et in terra; panem nostrum quotidianum da nobis hodie; et dimitte nobis debita nostra, sicut et nos dimittimus debitoribus nostris; et ne nos inducas in tentationem.	Our Father, who art in heaven, hallowed be thy name; thy kingdom come; thy will be done on earth, as it is in heaven; give us this day our daily bread; and forgive us our trespasses, as we forgive them that trespass against us; and lead us not into temptation.
℟. Sed libera nos a malo.	℟. But deliver us from evil.

The Celebrant having answered *Amen*, in secret, says aloud the following Prayer, which is always secretly said in every Mass. He there prays that we may be delivered from every evil, set free from sin, and established in peace.

Libera nos, quæsumus, Domine, ab omnibus malis, præteritis, præsentibus, et futuris; et intercedente beata et gloriosa semper Virgine Dei Genitrice Maria, cum beatis apostolis tuis	Deliver us, we beseech thee, O Lord, from all evils, past, present, and to come: and by the intercession of the blessed and ever glorious Virgin Mary Mother of God, and of the holy apostles Peter and Paul,

GOOD FRIDAY: MORNING SERVICE. 499

and of Andrew, and of all the Saints, mercifully grant peace in our days, that through the assistance of thy mercy, we may be always free from sin, and secure from all disturbance. Through the same Jesus Christ, thy Son our Lord, who with thee and the Holy Ghost liveth and reigneth God: world without end.

℞. Amen.

Petro et Paulo, atque Andrea, et omnibus sanctis, da propitius pacem in diebus nostris, ut ope misericordiæ tuæ adjuti, et a peccato simus semper liberi, et ab omni perturbatione securi. Per eumdem Dominum nostrum Jesum Christum Filium tuum, qui tecum vivit et regnat, in unitate Spiritus Sancti, Deus : per omnia sæcula sæculorum.

℞. Amen.

But before receiving the Sacred Host in holy Communion, the Priest invites us to adore it. Taking, then, in his right hand, the adorable Body of our Redeemer, he raises it on high, as he, our Jesus, was raised up on the Cross. The Faithful, who are kneeling during this part of the Service, bow down in profound adoration before their Crucified Lord.

The Priest then divides the Host into three parts, one of which he puts into the Chalice, that thus he may sanctify the wine and water, which he is to take after having communicated. The wine is not changed into the Blood of Jesus by contact with the consecrated particle; but it thereby receives a very special benediction, similar to that which attached to the garments worn by our Saviour.

After this, the Celebrant recites, in secret, the last of the three prayers, which precede Communion; and then, taking the two portions of the host into his left hand, he says thrice:

Lord, I am not worthy that thou shouldst enter under my roof : say but the word, and my soul shall be healed.

Domine, non sum dignus ut intres sub tectum meum ; sed tantum dic verbo, et sanabitur anima mea.

He then communicates. After which, he takes also the wine and water, and the sacred particle which he had put into the Chalice. He then washes his fingers, returns to the middle of the Altar, and says, in secret, the following prayer:

Quod ore sumpsimus, Domine, purâmente capiamus, ut de munere temporali fiat nobis remedium sempiternum.	Grant, O Lord, that what we have taken with our mouth, we may receive with a pure mind; that of a temporal gift it may become to us an eternal remedy.

Thus terminates the *Mass of the Presanctified.* The Priest, with the sacred Ministers, makes a genuflexion, at the foot of the Altar, to the Cross, and retires to the Sacristy. The Choir immediately begin Vespers, which are simply recited.

VESPERS.

After the *Pater* and *Ave* have been said in secret, the five Antiphons and Psalms of yesterday are recited: *page* 386. The *Magnificat* has the following Antiphon:

ANTIPHON OF THE *Magnificat*.

ANT. Cum accepisset Jesus acetum, dixit: Consummatum est. Et inclinato capite, emisit spiritum.	ANT. When Jesus had taken the vinegar, he said: It is consummated. And bowing his head, he gave up the ghost.

Then is said the Canticle *Magnificat,* (see *page* 88). The Antiphon is repeated, and the following Versicle is added:

℣. Christus factus est pro nobis obediens usque ad mortem, mortem autem crucis.	℣. Christ became, for our sakes, obedient unto death, even to the death of the Cross.

This is followed by the *Pater noster*, in secret; after which, the Psalm *Miserere (page 338)* is recited with a suppressed voice; and then, the prayer *Respice.*

Look down, O Lord, we beseech thee, on this thy family, for which our Lord Jesus Christ hesitated not to be delivered into the hands of wicked men, and undergo the punishment of the Cross.	Respice quæsumus, Domine, super hanc familiam tuam pro qua Dominus noster Jesus Christus non dubitavit manibus tradi nocentium et crucis subire tormentum.

(then the rest in secret :)

Who liveth and reigneth with thee, in the unity of the Holy Ghost, God, world without end, amen.	Qui tecum vivit et regnat, in unitate Spiritus Sancti, Deus, per omnia sæcula sæculorum, amen.

AFTERNOON.

Holy Church will soon be calling us once more to join with her in the holy Offices: meanwhile, let us, as it behoves us, keep our hearts and thoughts upon our Redeemer, for these are the very Hours when he wrought our Salvation. Our morning's meditation brought us to Calvary, where we were considering how the executioners stripped Jesus of his clothes, preparatory to their nailing him to the Cross. Let us reverently assist at the consummation of the Sacrifice, which he offers, for us, to the Justice of his Eternal Father.

The executioners led Jesus to the spot where the Cross is lying on the ground: it is the Eleventh Station. Like a lamb destined for a holocaust, he lays himself on the wood that is to serve as the Altar. They violently stretch his hands and feet to the places marked for them, and fasten them with nails to the wood. The Blood gushes forth from these four life-giving founts, wherein our souls are to find their purification. This is the fourth Bloodshedding. Mary hears the strokes of the hammer, and every blow wounds her heart. Magdalene's grief is intensified by her incapability of helping her tortured Master. Jesus is heard to speak: it is his first Word on Calvary: *Father forgive them, for they know not what they do!*[1] O infinite goodness of our Creator! He has come into this world, which is the work of his hands, and men nail him to a Cross: and on that Cross he prays for them, and in his prayer he seems to excuse them!

The Victim is fastened to the wood, whereon he is to die. But the Cross is not to be left, as it is, lying on the ground. Isaias has foretold that the *Root of Jesse* is to be raised up as a *Standard* of all nations.[2] Yes, our Crucified God must be raised up, and, by that elevation, purify the polluted atmosphere of this world, infested as it is by the spirits of wickedness. He is the Mediator between God and men; he is our High Priest; our Intercessor;—he is *lifted up*[3] between earth and heaven, making *reconciliation* between them.[4] Not far from the spot where the Cross now lies on the ground, they have made a hole in the rock, wherein to fix it, so that all may have a sight of Him that hangs upon it. It is the Twelfth Station. It needs a great effort to raise and plant the Tree of the world's Redemption. The soldiers lift it up, and then, with impatient vehemence, let it fall into the hole. The shock tears the four wounds. Oh! see him now exposed naked before the multitude, this good Jesus who is come to clothe the nakedness that sin has caused in us!—The soldiers have done their work, and now they claim his Garments.

[1] St. Luke, xxiii. 34.
[2] Is. xi. 10.
[3] St. John, xii. 32.
[4] Rom. v. 11.

They tear them into four lots, and each takes a share: but a strange feeling induces them to respect his Tunic, which was without a seam, and, as we are told by a pious tradition, was woven by the hand of his Blessed Mother. *Let us not cut it,* say they: *but let us cast lots for it, whose it shall be.*[1] It is a symbol of the unity of the Church, which is never to be broken under any pretext whatsoever.

Above our Redeemer's head there are written these words, in hebrew, greek, and latin: JESUS OF NAZARETH, KING OF THE JEWS. The people read this Inscription, and say it to each other; without wishing it, they are once more proclaiming the Royalty of the Son of David. The enemies of Jesus are quick enough to perceive this: they hasten to Pilate, and beseech him to have the Title changed. The only answer he deigns to make them is: *What I have written, I have written.*[2] The Holy Fathers have noticed a circumstance of the Crucifixion, which expresses, how this King of the Jews is, indeed, rejected by his chosen people, but that he will reign all the more gloriously over the Nations of the earth, whom the Father has given to him for his inheritance. The circumstance we allude to is this: the soldiers, when fixing the Cross in the rock, have so placed it, that Jesus has his back to Jerusalem, and is stretching out his arms towards the countries of the west. The Sun of Truth is setting on the deicide City, and rising upon the new Jerusalem, that proud Rome, which feels that she is destined to be "The Eternal City," yet knows not that she is to be so by the Cross.

The Tree of our Salvation, as it falls into the hole prepared for it, strikes against a tomb:—and the Tomb is that of our First Parent. The blood of the Redeemer flows down the Cross, and falls upon a skull: it is the skull of Adam, whose sin has called for this

[1] St. John, xix. 24.   [2] *Ibid.* 22.

great expiation. In his mercy, the Son of God wills that the instrument, wherewith he has gained pardon for the guilty world, should rest amidst the very bones of him that first caused its guilt. Thus is Satan confounded: the creation is not, as he has hitherto thought, turned, by his own artifice, to the shame of its Creator. The hill, on which is raised the Standard of our Salvation, is called *Calvary*, which signifies a *skull*. Here, according to the tradition of the Jews, was buried our First Parent, the first Sinner. Among the Holy Fathers of the early Ages, who have handed down this interesting tradition to us, we may cite St. Basil, St. Ambrose, St. John Chrysostom, St. Epiphanius, St. Jerome. Origen, too, who had such opportunities of knowing the Jewish traditions, mentions this among the number. At a very early period, Christian Art introduced the custom of placing a human skull at the feet of Jesus' image on the Cross: it was done to commemorate the great fact, to which we have been alluding.

But let us look up and see this Jesus of ours, whose life is so soon to end upon this instrument of torture. Here we behold him exposed to the view of the Jewish people, *as the Serpent was, of old, lifted up, by Moses, in the desert*.[1] His enemies pass before him, making insulting gestures, and saying: *Vah! thou that destroyest the temple of God, and in three days dost rebuild it,—save thine own self! If thou be the Son of God, come down from the cross!*[2] The Chief Priests and the Ancients continue the blasphemy, but adding their own emphasis to it: *He saved others; himself he cannot save! If he be King of Israel, let him now come down from the cross, and we will believe in him. He trusted in God; let him now deliver him, if he will have him; for he said: I*

---

[1] St. John, iii. 14. [2] St. Matth. xxvii. 40.

am the Son of God.[1] The two thieves, who were crucified with him, insulted him in like manner.

Never had God conferred on his creatures a blessing comparable to this: and yet, never did man so boldly insult his God! Let us Christians, who adore *Him* whom the Jews blaspheme, offer him, at this moment, the Reparation he so infinitely deserves. These impious men cite his own words, and turn them against him:—let *us* reverently remind our Jesus of an expression he once deigned to use, which should fill us with hope: *And I, if I be lifted up from the earth, will draw all things to myself.*[2] Sweet Jesus! the time is come: thou art *lifted up from the earth:* fulfil thy promise,—*draw* us to thyself! Alas! this *earth* has such hold upon us, we are chained fast to it by so many ties; self-love fetters us; and when we attempt to fly towards thee, our flight is checked. Oh! break our chains, and *draw* us to thyself, that we may at length reach thee, and thou be consoled by the conquest of our souls!

It is the Sixth hour, or, as we call it, mid-day. The sun immediately withdraws his light, and darkness covers the face of the earth. The stars appear in the heavens, and a gloomy silence pervades throughout the world. It is said, that the celebrated Denys the Areopagite of Athens, who was afterwards a disciple of St. Paul, exclaimed, on witnessing this awful eclipse: "Either the God of nature is suffering, or the world is coming to an end." Phlegon, a pagan author, who wrote a century after, tells us, that this sudden darkness spread consternation throughout the Roman Empire, and that the Astronomers owned it baffled all their calculations.

So terrible an indication of the wrath of heaven produced a panic of fear among the spectators on Calvary. Blasphemers are struck dumb, and the

---

[1] St. Matth. xxvii. 42, 43. [2] St. John, xii. 32.

blasphemies of them, that were just now insulting our Redeemer, cease. All is silent as death. The Thief, whose cross was at the right of Jesus', feels himself touched with repentance and hope. Turning to his companion, he upbraids him for what he had been saying: *Dost thou not fear God, seeing thou art under the same condemnation? And we, indeed, justly, for we receive the due reward of our deeds: but this Man hath done no evil.*[1] Jesus defended by a Thief, at the very time that he is being insulted by them who boast that they know every iota of God's Law, and are sitting in the Chair of Moses! Nothing could give us a clearer idea of the blindness, to which the Synagogue has voluntarily brought itself. This poor criminal, whose name is Dimas, represents the Gentile world, which now is steeped in ignorance and crime, yet is soon to be cleansed from all its abominations by confessing Jesus Crucified to be the Son of God. Turning his head towards our Saviour's Cross, he thus prays to him: *Lord! remember me, when thou shalt come into thy kingdom! He* believes Jesus to be King; and the Chief Priests and Ancients were, but a moment ago, making jests with this King! Dimas sees the divine calmness and dignity of the innocent Victim: it is evidence enough; he gives him his faith, and begs a remembrance from him when the day of his glory comes. Grace has made him a true *Christian:* and who can doubt, but that the grace was asked and obtained for him by Mary, the Mother of Mercy, who is now uniting herself in sacrifice together with her Jesus? Jesus is pleased to find in this poor criminal the faith he had vainly sought for from Israel: he thus grants his humble prayer: *Amen I say to thee, this day thou shalt be with me in Paradise.*[2] It is the second of Jesus' Words on the Cross. The happy penitent is filled with joy,

---

[1] St. Luke, xxiii. 40, 41. [2] St. Luke, xxiii. 42, 43.

and awaits in patient silence the blissful moment when death shall set him free.

Meanwhile, Mary draws near to the Cross, whereon hangs her Son. She recognises him, in spite of all the darkness; her love was her light. The eclipse has dispersed the crowd; all is silent; and the Soldiers can find no reason for keeping the afflicted Mother from approaching her Son. Jesus looks with tenderest affection upon Mary; the sight of her sorrow is a new grief to his sacred Heart. He is dying, and his Mother cannot console or embrace him. Magdalene, too, is there, distracted with grief. Those feet, which, a few days before, she had anointed with her most precious perfumes, are now pierced through with nails, and the Blood is clotting round the wounds. They are near enough to the ground for her to reach and bathe them with her tears; but her tears cannot stay the pain. She is come to see the Death of Him that forgave her all her sins. John, the Beloved Disciple, the only Apostle that has followed Jesus to Calvary, is overwhelmed with sorrow. He thinks of the favour bestowed upon him last night, when he rested his head on the Breast of this dear Master,—and the remembrance intensifies his grief. He grieves for the Son, he grieves for the Mother. He little knows the reward he is soon to receive for this his love! Mary of Cleophas has followed the Holy Mother up to the foot of the Cross. At some distance off, there stands a group of women, who loved Jesus, and had ministered unto him during his life.[1]

The silence is again broken: Jesus speaks his third Word, and it is to his Mother: but he does not call her by that dear name, for it would redouble her pain: *Woman! he says, behold thy son!* Then looking upon John, he says to him: *Son! behold thy Mother!*[2] What an exchange was here for

[1] St. Matth. xxvii. 55. [2] St. John, xix. 26, 27.

Mary! but, O what a blessing it brought upon John, and through him to all mankind!—the Mother of God was made *our* Mother! This was the subject of our meditation on the Friday of Passion Week: let us, to-day, gratefully receive this last Testament of our Jesus, who, having by his Incarnation made us the adopted Children of his Heavenly Father, now, in his dying moments, makes us Children of his own Blessed Mother.

It is close upon the Ninth hour,—the third hour after mid-day,—and it is the one fixed by the eternal decree of God for the Death of Jesus. The feeling of abandonment, which had caused our Redeemer to suffer an Agony in the Garden, now returns. He has taken upon himself the sins of mankind: the whole weight of God's justice now presses on his soul. The bitter Chalice of God's anger, which he is drinking to the very dregs, extorts from his lips this plaintive cry: *My God! My God! Why hast thou forsaken me?*[1] It is the fourth Word. He does not say *My Father!* He speaks as though he were but a poor Sinner, trembling before the judgment-seat of God. A burning thirst elicits from him the fifth Word: *I thirst.*[2] Whereupon, one of the soldiers presents to his dying lips a sponge full of vinegar; and this is all the refreshment he receives from that earth, on which he daily pours a heavenly dew, and to which he has given ever-flowing fountains and rivers.

The moment is at length come, when Jesus is to yield up his Soul to his Father. He has fulfilled every single prophecy that had been foretold of him, even that of his receiving vinegar when parched with thirst. He therefore speaks this his sixth Word: *It is consummated!*[3] He has, then, but to die; his Death is to put the finishing stroke to our

---

[1] St. Matth. xxvii. 46. [2] St. John, xix. 28.
[3] St. John, xix. 30.

Redemption, as the Prophets assure us. But he must die as God. This man, worn out by suffering, exhausted by his three hours' agony, whose few words were scarce audible to them that stood round his Cross,—now utters a loud cry, which is heard at a great distance off, and fills the Centurion, who commands the guard, with fear and astonishment:— *Father! into thy hands I commend my spirit!*[1] This is his seventh and last Word; after which he bows down his head, and dies.

At this awful moment, the sun re-appears in the heavens, and darkness ceases: but the earth is shaken by an earthquake, and the rocks are split. The space between the Cross of Jesus and that of the bad Thief is violently rent asunder, and the opening is shown to this day. The Jewish Priests, who are in the Temple, are terrified at seeing the Veil, which hides the Holy of Holies, torn from top to bottom: the time for figures and types is over, the great realities are come. Many holy personages arise from their graves, and return to life. But it is in hell itself that the Death of Jesus is most felt. Satan now sees who *He* is, against whom He has excited all this persecution. He sees, that the Blood which he has caused to be shed, has saved mankind and opened the gates of heaven. This Jesus, whom he dared to tempt in the desert, he now recognises as the Son of God, whose precious Blood has purchased for men a Redemption that was refused to the rebel Angels!

O Jesus! Son of the Eternal Father! we adore thee now lying dead on the wood of thy Sacrifice. Thy bitter Death has given us Life. Like those Jews who saw thee expire, and returned to Jerusalem striking their breasts,—we, also, confess that it is our sins have caused thy Death. Thou hast loved

---

[1] St. Luke, xxiii. 46.

us, as none but a God could love. Henceforth, we must be thine, and serve thee, as creatures redeemed at the infinite price of thy Blood. Thou art our God; we are thy people. Accept, we beseech thee, our most loving thanks for this final proof of thy goodness towards us. Thy holy Church now silently invites us to celebrate thy praise. We leave Calvary for a time; but will soon return thither, to assist at thy holy Burial. Mary, thy Mother, remains immoveable at the foot of thy Cross. Magdalene clings to thy feet. John and the holy women stand around thee. Once more, dearest Jesus! we adore thy sacred Body, thy precious Blood, and thy holy Cross, that have brought us Salvation.

THE OFFICE OF TENEBRÆ.

At a late hour in the afternoon, the Night Office of Holy Saturday is anticipated, as on the two previous days. The Faithful are not summoned to the Church by the bells, for, as we have already explained, they are not rung till the *Gloria in excelsis* of tomorrow's Mass.

The Office of Tenebræ for Holy Saturday is given below, *page* 519.

THE EVENING.

Let us return to Calvary, and there close this mournful day. We left Mary there, with Magdalene and other holy women, and the Beloved Disciple John. An hour has scarcely elapsed since Jesus died, when a troop of soldiers, led on by a Centurion, come up the hill, breaking the silence with their tramp and voices. They are sent by Pilate. The Chief Priests lost no time in returning to the Governor's house; and he, at their request, has sent these men to break the legs of the three Crucified, detach them from their crosses, and bury them before night. The Jews count the days of their week from sunset; so that *the great Sabbath-day of the Parasceve* is close upon them. The soldiers come to the Crosses; they begin with the two thieves, and put an end to their sufferings and life by breaking their legs. Dimas dies in saintly dispositions, for the promise made to him by Jesus is his consolation: his companion dies blaspheming. The soldiers now advance towards Jesus:—Mary's heart sinks within her:— what fresh outrage are these men about to offer to the lifeless and bleeding body of her Son? On inspection, they find that he is dead; but, that no doubt may be left, and no blame for neglect of orders fall upon them, one of the company raises up his spear and thrusts it into the right Side of the divine Victim, even to the Heart; and when he draws his spear out, there gushes forth a stream of Water and Blood. This is the fifth Bloodshedding, and the fifth Wound inflicted on our Jesus upon the Cross. The Church honours this mystery on the Feast of the Sacred Heart; let us reserve our reflections till then.

The soul of the Holy Mother is pierced by this cruel Spear; and they that are with her redouble their sobs and tears. How is this terrible day to end? Who shall take the Body of her Jesus from his Cross? Who will enable her to give it a last embrace? The soldiers return to the City, and with them Longinus,—he that pierced Jesus' Side, but is already feeling within himself the workings of that faith, for which he is one day to lay down his life as a Martyr. But lo! two other men are seen coming towards the Cross: they are not enemies, they are faithful Disciples of Jesus: one is the wealthy counsellor Joseph of Arimathea; the other is Nicodemus, a ruler among the Jews. Mary gratefully welcomes their arrival: they are come to take the body of Jesus from the Cross, and give it an honourable burial. They have the requisite authorisation, for

Pilate has given permission to Joseph to take *the Body of Jesus*.[1]

They lose no time in doing so, for the sun is near to setting, and then begins the Sabbath. Within a few yards from where stands the Cross, at the foot of the hillock which forms the summit of Calvary, there is a garden, and in this garden a sepulchre cut into the rock. No one has yet been buried in this tomb. It is to be Jesus' Sepulchre. Hither Joseph and Nicodemus carry the sacred Body: they lay it upon a slab of stone, near to the Sepulchre. It is here that Mary receives into her arms the Body of her Jesus: she kisses each wound, and bathes it with her tears. John, Magdalene, and all that are present, compassionate the holy Mother. She resigns it into the hands of the two Disciples, for they have but a few moments left. Upon this slab, which, even to this day, is called the *Stone of the Anointing*, and designates the Thirteenth Station of the way of the Cross, Joseph unfolds a piece of *fine linen*,[2] and Nicodemus, whose servants have brought *a hundred pound weight of myrrh and aloes*,[3] makes every arrangement for the embalming. They reverently wash the Body, for it was covered with Blood; they remove the Crown of Thorns from the Head; and, after embalming it with their perfumes, they wrap it in the Winding-Sheet. Mary gives a last embrace to the remains of her Jesus, who is now hidden under these swathing-bands of the Tomb.

Joseph and Nicodemus take the Body into their arms, and enter the Sepulchre. It is the Fourteenth Station of the Way of the Cross. It consists of two open cells; it is into the one on the right hand that they enter, and there, in a cavity cut into the side of the rock, they lay the Body of Jesus. They then

---

[1] St. John, xix. 38.   [2] St. Mark, xv. 46.
[3] St. John, xix. 39.

retire; and, with the assistance of their servants, they close up the entrance of the Sepulchre with a large square stone, which Pilate, at the request of the Jews, orders to be fastened with his own seal, and guarded by a patrol of soldiers.

The sun is just setting; *the great Sabbath*, with its severe legal prescriptions, is just about to begin. Magdalene and the other women carefully notice the place where Jesus' Body has been laid, and return with all speed to Jerusalem, that they may have time to purchase and prepare a quantity of materials for a more careful embalming of the Body early on the Sunday morning, that is, immediately after the Sabbath is over. The holy Mother takes a farewell-look at the Tomb wherein lies her Jesus, and then follows the rest into the City. John, her adopted son, keeps close to her. He is the guardian of Her, who, without ceasing to be Mother of God, has been made, also, Mother of Men. But oh! how much this second Maternity cost her! She was standing at the Foot of the Cross, seeing her Jesus die, when she received us as her children. Let us imitate St. John, and keep our Blessed Mother company during these trying hours which she has to pass before her Son is risen from the Grave.

How, O most merciful Redeemer! shall we leave thy Holy Sepulchre, without offering thee the tribute of our adoration and repentance? Death, which is the consequence of sin, has extended its dominion over thee, for thou didst submit thyself to the sentence pronounced against thee, and wouldst become like to us even to the humiliation of the tomb. It was thy love for us, that led to all this! What return can we make thee? The holy Angels stand around thy Body, thus lying in its rocky grave. They are lost in amazement at thy having loved, to such an excess as this, thy poor ungrateful creature,—man. Thou hadst made them, as well as us, out of nothing, and they loved thee with all the intensity of their mighty spirits; but the sight of thy Tomb reveals to them a fresh abyss of thine infinite goodness:—thou hast suffered death, not for their fallen fellow-angels, but for us men, who are so inferior to the Angels!—Oh! what a bond of love between us and thee must result from this Sacrifice of thy Life for us! Thou hast died, O Jesus, for us!—we must, henceforth, live for thee. We promise it upon this Tomb, which, alas! is the handiwork of our sins. We, too, wish to die to sin, and live to grace. For the time to come, we will follow thy precepts and thine examples; we will avoid sin, which has made us accomplices in thy Passion and Death. We will courageously bear, in union with thine own, the crosses of this life: they are indeed light compared with thine, but our weakness makes them heavy. And our death, too,—when the moment comes for us to undergo that sentence which even thou didst submit to,—we will accept it with resignation. Terrible as that last hour is to nature, our faith tells us, that thy Death has merited for it graces rich enough to make it sweet. Thy Death, dearest Jesus! has made *our* death become but a passing into life: and as, now, we leave thy holy Sepulchre with the certain hope of speedily seeing thee glorious in thy Resurrection; so, when our body descends into the tomb, our soul shall confidently mount up to thee, and there blissfully await the day of the Resurrection of the flesh made pure by the humiliation *of the grave.*

We will close our day by offering to our readers the following stanzas from the Greek Liturgy of Good Friday.

HYMN.

(In Parasceve.)

To-day, is poised upon a Cross, He that poised the earth upon the waters. He that is the King of Angels, is wreathed with a Crown of Thorns. He that covereth the heaven with clouds, is covered with a mock scarlet robe. He that, in the Jordan, set Adam free, is buffeted. The Spouse of the Church is pierced with Nails. The Son of the Virgin is wounded with a Spear. O Jesus! we adore thy Sufferings. Show unto us, also, thy glorious Resurrection.

Mary, the Mother, saw her Lamb dragged to the slaughter, and, in company with other women, followed him, saying: "Whither goest thou, my Son? "Wherefore this hurried step? "Is it to a second marriage-"feast at Cana that thou thus "hastenest, there to turn water "into wine? Must I come "with thee, my Son? or must "I wait thy return? O Word "of the Father! speak one "word to me. Pass me not "by in silence, O thou, my "Child and my God! who "didst make me thy Virgin-"Mother!"

For our sakes, O Jesus! thou didst permit thy whole sacred Body to be ignominiously tortured: thy head, with thorns; thy face, with spittle; thy cheeks, with blows; thy mouth, with vinegar and gall; thine ears, with impious blasphe-

Hodie in cruce appenditur, qui super aquas terram appendit: corona spinea circumdatur rex Angelorum: falsa purpura operitur, qui operit cœlum nubibus: alapam suscipit, qui in Jordane libertati dedit Adamum: clavis confixus est sponsus Ecclesiæ: lancea punctus est filius Virginis. Adoramus passiones tuas, Christe. Et ostende nobis etiam gloriosam resurrectionem tuam.

Intuens agna agnum suum trahi ad occisionem; sequebatur Maria afflicta una cum aliis mulieribus, hæc clamans: Quo progrederis, nate? Cujus rei gratia velocem cursum perficis? Num aliæ nuptiæ rursus fiunt in Cana; et eo tu nunc festinas, ut eis ex aqua vinum facias? Tecum veniam, nate; an te potius exspectabo? Da mihi verbum, o Verbum: ne silens me prætereas, qui me castam servasti filius et Deus meus.

Singula sanctæ carnis tuæ membra ignominiam propter nos sustinuerunt; spinas caput; facies sputa; maxilla alapas; os aceto mistum fel in gustu; impias blasphemias aures; dorsum flagellationem; et manus arundinem; totiusque corporis extensioues in cruce; artus clavos; et latus lanceam. Qui passus es pro nobis, et patiens liberos nos fecisti; quique amore erga homines una nobiscum te demisisti, nosque sublimasti, omnipotens Salvator, miserere nostri.

Hodie in cruce te suspensum, o Verbum, inculpata Virgo spectans, maternis visceribus mœrens, corde vulnerabatur amare, et gemens dolenter ex animæ profundo flebiliter exclamabat: Heu me, Divine Nate! heu me, o lux mundi! cur ex oculis meis abscessisti, Agne Dei? Inde incorporeorum Spirituum exercitus tremore corripiebantur, dicentes: Incomprehensibilis Domine, gloria tibi.

Domine, ascendente te in crucem, timor et tremor cecidit in creaturam: et terram quidem prohibebas absorbere eos, qui te crucifigebant: inferno autem permittebas remittere vinctos. Judex vivorum, et mortuorum venisti, ut vitam præstares et non mortem: amans hominum, gloria tibi.

mies; thy back, with scourges; thy hand, with a reed; thy whole body, with the cross; thy hands and feet, with nails; thy side, with a spear. O Almighty Saviour! who didst suffer for us, and, by thy sufferings, didst make us free! O thou, that out of love for man, didst humble thyself with us, that thus thou mightest exalt us!—have mercy on us!

To-day, the sinless Virgin saw thee, O Word! hanging on the Cross: she wept over thee with a mother's love: her heart was cruelly wounded: and thus, with doleful sobs and tears, she spake from her inmost soul: "Alas! my Di-"vine Son! Alas! thou Light "of the World! why hast thou "departed from my sight, O "Lamb of God?"—The Angel host was seized with trembling, and said: "Glory be "to thee, O incomprehensible "Lord!"

Fear and trembling fell upon thy creatures, O Lord, when thou didst ascend thy Cross. Yet wouldst thou not permit the earth to swallow up them that crucified thee; nay, thou gavest leave to death to set its captives free. Thou camest into the world, O Judge of the living and the dead! that thou mightest bring, not death, but life. Glory be to thee, O Lover of mankind!

The ancient Gallican Liturgy contains, in to-day's Office, the following eloquent and devout prayer.

PRAYER.

(Oratio ad Nonam.)

O saving hour of the Passion! O hour of None, favoured with richest graces! O hour of hours! O beloved Spouse of souls, kiss us at this hour from thy Cross, for the Cross is the trophy of thy victory. Yea, we beseech, grant us thy kiss, grant us thy salvation, O admirable Conqueror! O heavenly Charioteer! O good God! O most glorious Champion! Do thou, O all-seeing Jesus, speak to our hearts, and say: "Hail, all "hail! Be vigorous, act man- "fully, be courageous!" Thou, O Lord, that didst these things of old, canst thou not the same now? Thou canst, yea, thou canst, for thou art all-powerful. Thou canst, most loving Jesus! thou canst do beyond what we can think. And whereas nothing is impossible to thee, O Almighty God, our Jesus! kiss us, we beseech thee, Beloved Lord, who didst triumphantly return to the Father, with whom thou wast and art, for ever, one ; for thy kiss is sweet, thy breasts are better than wine, and are fragrant with the best ointments. Thy name is as oil poured out, therefore have our souls loved thee. The righteous, whom thou drawest to thee, love thee. Thy couch is strewed with flowers, the Cross is thy trophy. Coming in scarlet, at this Hour, from,

O salutaris hora Passionis, o magna maximarum gratiarum Nona hodierna, maxima horarum hora. Hac nunc tu, noster dilecte Sponse, osculare de cruce, licet post crucis trophæum. Osculare, precamur ; salutare tuum impertire nobis, triumphator mirabilis, auriga supreme, Deus pie, gloriosissime propugnator. Avete, valete, invalescite et viriliter agite, confortamini dicito, loquere cordibus nostris inspector Christe. An qui olim hæc fecisti, nunc eadem non potes facere? potes utique, potes ; quia omnipotens es : potes, amantissime, potes facere quod non possumus cogitare : quia nihil tibi impossibile est, Deus omnipotens, Jesus, osculare, quæso, dilectissime, qui triumphans regressus es ad Patrem, cum quo semper eras et permanes unus ; quia osculum tuum dulce est, et ubera tua vino dulciora, fragrantia optimis unguentis ; et nomen tuum super oleum, quem adolescentulæ dilexerunt : quem recti diligunt, quos trahis post te : cujus lectus floridus, cujus trophæum crux. Qui hac hora rubens de Edom, de cruce, tinctis vestibus de Bosra, solus quasi calcator magni illius torcularis ad cœlos ascendisti: cui occurrunt Angeli, Archangeli dicentes : Quis est iste qui ascendit, tinctis vestibus de Bosra? Quibus te interrogantibus : Quare ergo rubrum est vestimentum tuum? respondisti : Torcular calcavi solus, et vir de gentibus non fuit mecum. Vere, Salvator, vere rubrum est tuum propter nos corpus : rubrum est sanguine uvæ ; lavasti enim in vino stolam tuam, et pallium tuum in sanguine uvæ : qui es Deus solus, crucifixus pro nobis, quos antiqua prævaricatio morti tradidit : cujus vulnere omnium innumera peccatorum vulnera sanata sunt. Et nos, pie crucifixe Christe, cum tuis redime ; salva, pia bonitas Deus. Qui regnas cum Patre et Spiritu Sancto, unus in æternum et in sæcula sæculorum.

Edom, thy Cross,—coming with dyed garments from Bosra, treading alone that great wine-press,—thou didst ascend to heaven. The Angels and Archangels go out to meet thee, and they say: "Who is this that cometh up, "with dyed garments, from "Bosra?" They ask thee : "Why, then, is thy apparel "red?" Thou answerest : "I "have trodden the wine-press "alone : and of the Gentiles, "there is not a man with me." Truly, O Saviour ! truly is thy body red for our sakes : it is red with the blood of the Grape, for thou hast washed thy robe in Wine, and thy garment in the blood of the Grape. Thou alone art God, crucified for us, whom the ancient sin had delivered over to death ; and by thy Wounds, the countless sins of all men have been healed. O loving crucified Jesus ! put us among the number of thy redeemed. Save us, O loving goodness ! our God ! who with the Father and Holy Ghost, reignest one God for ever, yea for ever and ever.

HOLY SATURDAY.

THE NIGHT OFFICE.

The Ceremonies used by the Church for the *Office of Tenebræ* having been already explained, we deem it unnecessary to repeat our instructions. The reader may refer to them, should he require to refresh his memory. They are given in *pages* 304-306.

Pater noster, Ave, and *Credo,* in secret.

THE FIRST NOCTURN.

The *first* Psalm is one which the Church daily recites in her Compline, because it expresses the confidence wherewith the Christian takes his rest. She uses it in to-day's Tenebræ, to remind us of the *Rest* taken by Christ in his Sepulchre, where he *sleeps* with the assurance of wakening to a glorious Resurrection.

ANT. In peace, in the self-same, I will sleep, and I will take my rest.	ANT. In pace, in idipsum, dormiam et requiescam.

PSALM 4.

When I called upon him, the God of my justice heard me: when I was in distress thou hast enlarged me.	Cum invocarem, exaudivit me Deus justitiæ meæ : * in tribulatione dilatasti mihi.

Miserere mei : * et exaudi orationem meam.	Have mercy upon me, and hear my prayer.
Filii hominum usquequo gravi corde : * ut quid diligitis vanitatem, et quæritis mendacium ?	O ye sons of men, how long will ye be dull of heart ? why do you love vanity, and seek after lying ?
Et scitote quoniam mirivicavit Dominus sanctum suum : * Dominus exaudiet me, cum clamavero ad eum.	Know ye also that the Lord hath made his Holy One wonderful : the Lord will hear me when I shall cry unto him.
Irascimini, et nolite peccare : * quæ dicitis in cordibus vestris, in cubilibus vestris compungimini.	Be ye angry and sin not : the things you say in your hearts, be sorry for them on your beds.
Sacrificate sacrificium justitiæ, et sperate in Domino : * multi dicunt : Quis ostendit nobis bona ?	Offer up the sacrifice of justice and trust in the Lord : many say : Who showeth us good things ?
Signatum est super nos lumen vultus tui, Domine : * dedisti lætitiam in corde meo.	The light of thy countenance, O Lord, is signed upon us : thou hast given gladness in my heart.
A fructu frumenti, vini et olei sui : * multiplicati sunt.	By the fruit of their corn, their wine and oil, they are multiplied.
In pace in idipsum : * dormiam et requiescam.	In peace, in the self-same I will sleep, and I will take my rest.
Quoniam tu, Domine, singulariter in spe : * constituisti me.	For thou, O Lord, singularly hast settled me in hope.
ANT. In pace in idipsum, dormiam et requiescam.	ANT. In peace, in the self-same, I will sleep, and I will take my rest.

The *second* Psalm speaks of the happiness that is in reserve for the just man, and of the *rest* which is to be the reward of his labours. The Church applies it to Christ, the *Just* One, by excellence, who went about doing good.

ANT. Habitabit in tabernaculo tuo : requiescet in monte sancto tuo.	ANT. He shall dwell in thy tabernacle : he shall rest in thy holy hill.

PSALM 14.

Lord, who shall dwell in thy tabernacle? or who shall rest in thy holy hill?

He that walketh without blemish, and worketh justice.

He that speaketh truth in his heart, who hath not used deceit in his tongue.

Nor hath done evil to his neighbour, nor taken up a reproach against his neighbours.

In his sight the malignant is brought to nothing : but he glorifieth them that fear the Lord.

He that sweareth to his neighbour, and deceiveth not : he that hath not put out his money to usury, nor taken bribes against the innocent :

He that doth these things, shall not be moved for ever.

ANT. He shall dwell in thy tabernacle : he shall rest in thy holy hill.

Domine, quis habitabit in tabernaculo tuo : * aut quis requiescet in monte sancto tuo ?

Qui ingreditur sine macula : * et operatur justitiam.

Qui loquitur veritatem in corde suo : * qui non egit dolum in lingua sua.

Nec fecit proximo suo malum : * et opprobrium non accepit adversus proximos suos.

Ad nihilum deductus est in conspectu ejus malignus : * timentes autem Dominum glorificat.

Qui jurat proximo suo, et non decipit : * qui pecuniam suam non dedit ad usuram, et munera super innocentem non accepit :

Qui facit hæc, * non movebitur in æternum.

ANT. Habitabit in tabernaculo tuo, requiescet in monte sancto tuo.

The *third* Psalm, composed by David, during his exile under Saul, is a prophecy of our Saviour's Resurrection, and was quoted as such by St. Peter, in his address to the Jews, on the day of Pentecost. He that speaks in this Psalm, says, that his *flesh shall rest in hope,* and that the Lord *will not give him to see corruption.* This was not verified in David, but in Christ.

ANT. My flesh shall rest in hope.

ANT. Caro mea requiescet in spe.

PSALM 15.

Conserva me, Domine, quoniam speravi in te : * dixi Domino, Deus meus es tu quoniam bonorum meorum non eges.

Sanctis qui sunt in terra ejus : * mirificavit omnes voluntates meas in eis.

Multiplicatæ sunt infirmitates eorum : * postea acceleraverunt.

Non congregabo conventicula eorum de sanguinibus : * nec memor ero nominum eorum per labia mea.

Dominus pars hæreditatis meæ et calicis mei : * tu es qui restitues hæreditatem meam mihi.

Funes ceciderunt mihi in præclaris : * etenim hæreditas mea præclara est mihi.

Benedicam Dominum, qui tribuit mihi intellectum :* insuper et usque ad noctem increpuerunt me renes mei.

Providebam Dominum in conspectu meo semper :* quoniam a dextris est mihi ne commovear.

Propter hoc lætatum est cor meum, et exsultavit lingua mea : * insuper et caro mea requiescet in spe.

Quoniam non derelinques animam meam in inferno :* nec dabis Sanctum tuum videre corruptionem.

Notas mihi fecisti vias vitæ, adimplebis me lætitia cum vultu tuo : * delectationes in dextera tua usque in finem.

Preserve me, O Lord, for I have put my trust in thee. I have said to the Lord : thou art my God, for thou hast no need of my goods.

To the saints who are in his land, he hath made wonderful all my desires in them.

Their infirmities were multiplied : afterwards they made haste.

I will not gather together their meetings for blood offerings : nor will I be mindful of their names by my lips.

The Lord is the portion of my inheritance and of my cup : it is thou that wilt restore my inheritance to me.

The lines are fallen unto me in goodly places : for my inheritance is goodly to me.

I will bless the Lord, who hath given me understanding: moreover my reins also have corrected me even till night.

I set the Lord always in my sight : for he is at my right-hand that I be not moved.

Therefore my heart hath been glad and my tongue hath rejoiced : moreover my flesh also shall rest in hope.

Because thou wilt not leave my soul in hell : nor wilt thou give thy Holy One to see corruption.

Thou hast made known to me the ways of life, thou shalt fill me with joy with thy countenance : at thy right-hand are delights even to the end.

ANT. My flesh shall rest in hope.	ANT. Caro mea requiescet in spe.
℣. In peace, in the self-same.	℣. In pace in idipsum.
℟. I will sleep, and I will take my rest.	℟. Dormiam et requiescam.

The *Pater noster* is here recited, in secret.

The Lessons of the First Nocturn are again taken from the Lamentations of Jeremias. The first refers to our Saviour. It speaks of his fidelity to his Father, and of his resignation. It foretells the buffets he received during his Passion.

FIRST LESSON.

From the Lamentations of Jeremias the Prophet.	De Lamentatione Jeremiæ Prophetæ.
Chap. III.	*Cap. III.*
HETH. The mercies of the Lord that we are not consumed: because his tender mercies have not failed.	HETH. Misericordiæ Domini, quia non sumus consumpti: quia non defecerunt miserationes ejus.
HETH. They are new every morning, great is thy faithfulness.	HETH. Novi diluculo, multa est fides tua.
HETH. The Lord is my portion, said my soul: therefore will I wait for him.	HETH. Pars mea Dominus, dixit anima mea: propterea exspectabo eum.
TETH. The Lord is good to them that hope in him, to the soul that seeketh him.	TETH. Bonus est Dominus sperantibus in eum, animæ quærenti illum.
TETH. It is good to wait with silence for the salvation of God.	TETH. Bonum est præstolari cum silentio salutare Dei.
TETH. It is good for a man when he hath borne the yoke from his youth.	TETH. Bonum est viro, cum portaverit jugum ab adolescentia sua.
JOD. He shall sit solitary, and hold his peace: because he hath taken it up upon himself.	JOD. Sedebit solitarius, et tacebit: quia levavit super se.

JOD. Ponet in pulvere os suum, si forte sit spes.

JOD. Dabit percutienti se maxillam, saturabitur opprobriis.

Jerusalem, Jerusalem, convertere ad Dominum Deum tuum.

℟. Sicut ovis ad occisionem ductus est, et dum male tractaretur, non aperuit os suum : traditus est ad mortem : * Ut vivificaret populum suum.

℣. Tradidit in mortem animam suam, et inter sceleratos reputatus est.

* Ut vivificaret populum suum.

JOD. He shall put his mouth in the dust, if so be there may be hope.

JOD. He shall give his cheek to him that striketh him, he shall be filled with reproaches.

Jerusalem, Jerusalem, be converted to the Lord thy God.

℟. He was led like a sheep to the slaughter; and whilst he was ill-used, he opened not his mouth : he was condemned to death, * That he might give life to his people.

℣. He delivered up himself to death, and was reckoned among the wicked.

* That he might give life to his people.

The second Lesson is an elegy upon Jerusalem. The grievousness of the sins of this ungrateful City is expressed in forcible terms.

SECOND LESSON.

ALEPH. Quomodo obscuratum est aurum, mutatus est color optimus, dispersi sunt lapides sanctuarii in capite omnium platearum?

BETH. Filii Sion inclyti, et amicti auro primo : quomodo reputati sunt in vasa testea, opus manuum figuli?

GHIMEL. Sed et lamiæ nudaverunt mammam, lactaverunt catulos suos, filia populi mei crudelis, quasi struthio in deserto.

ALEPH. How is the gold become dim, the finest color is changed, the stones of the sanctuary are scattered in the top of every street?

BETH. The noble sons of Sion, and they that were clothed with the best gold : how are they esteemed as earthen vessels, the work of the potter's hands?

GHIMEL. Even the sea monsters have drawn out the breast, they have given suck to their young : the daughter of my people is cruel, like the ostrich in the desert.

HOLY SATURDAY: TENEBRÆ.

DALETH. The tongue of the sucking child hath stuck to the roof of his mouth for thirst: the little ones have asked for bread, and there was none to break it unto them.

HE. They that were fed delicately, have died in the streets: they that were brought up in scarlet, have embraced the dung.

VAU. And the iniquity of the daughter of my people is made greater than the sin of Sodom, which was overthrown in a moment, and hands took nothing in her.

Jerusalem, Jerusalem, be converted to the Lord thy God.

℟. Arise, Jerusalem, and put off thy garments of joy: put on ashes and hair-cloth: * For in thee was slain the Saviour of Israel.

℣. Let tears run down like a torrent day and night, and let not the apple of thine eye cease.

* For in thee was slain the Saviour of Israel.

DALETH. Adhæsit lingua lactentis ad palatum ejus in siti: parvuli petierunt panem, et non erat qui frangeret eis.

HE. Qui vescebantur voluptuose interierunt in viis; qui nutriebantur in croceis, amplexati sunt stercora.

VAU. Et major effecta est iniquitas filiæ populi mei peccato Sodomorum: quæ subversa est in momento, et non ceperunt in ea manus.

Jerusalem, Jerusalem, convertere ad Dominum Deum tuum.

℟. Jerusalem, surge, et exue te vestibus jucunditatis: induere cinere et cilicio: * Quia in te occisus est Salvator Israël.

℣. Deduc quasi torrentem lacrymas per diem et noctem, et non taceat pupilla oculi tui.

* Quia in te occisus est Salvator Israël.

The third Lesson is a portion of the Prayer made by the Prophet for the Jewish people, after they had been led into captivity. It gives us a faithful, but terrible, description of their miseries after they had committed the crime of Deicide.

THIRD LESSON.

Here beginneth the Prayer of Jeremias the Prophet.

Ch. V.

Remember, O Lord, what is come upon us: consider and

Incipit Oratio Jeremiæ Prophetæ.

Cap. V.

Recordare Domine quid acciderit nobis: intuere,

et respice opprobrium nostrum. Hæreditas nostra versa est ad alienos, domus nostræ ad extraneos. Pupilli facti sumus absque patre: matres nostræ quasi viduæ. Aquam nostram pecunia bibimus: ligna nostra pretio comparavimus. Cervicibus nostris minabamur: lassis non dabatur requies. Ægypto dedimus manum, et Assyriis, ut saturaremur pane. Patres nostri peccaverunt, et non sunt: et nos iniquitates eorum portavimus. Servi dominati sunt nostri: non fuit qui redimeret de manu eorum. In animabus nostris afferebamus panem nobis, a facie gladii in deserto. Pellis nostra quasi clibanus, exusta est a facie tempestatum famis. Mulieres in Sion humiliaverunt, et virgines in civitatibus Juda.

Jerusalem, Jerusalem, convertere ad Dominum Deum tuum.

℟. Plange quasi virgo plebs mea: ululate pastores in cinere et cilicio: * Quia venit dies Domini magna et amara valde.

℣. Accingite vos sacerdotes, et plangite: ministri altaris, aspergite vos cinere.

* Quia venit dies Domini magna, et amare valde.

Here, is repeated: Plange.

behold our reproach. Our inheritance is turned to aliens: our houses to strangers. We are become orphans without a father, our mothers are as widows. We have drunk our water for money: we have bought our wood. We were dragged by the necks, we were weary and no rest was given us. We have given our hand to Egypt, and to the Assyrians, that we might be satisfied with bread. Our fathers have sinned, and are not: and we have borne their iniquities. Servants have ruled over us: and there was none to redeem us out of their hand. We fetched our bread at the peril of our lives, because of the sword in the desert. Our skin was burnt as an oven, by reason of the violence of the famine. They oppressed the women in Sion, and the virgins in the cities of Juda.

Jerusalem, Jerusalem, be converted to the Lord thy God.

℟. Mourn, O my people, as a virgin: howl, ye shepherds, in ashes and hair cloth: * For the great and exceeding bitter day of the Lord is coming.

℣. Gird yourselves, ye priests and mourn; sprinkle yourselves with ashes, ye ministers of the altar.

* For the great and exceeding bitter day of the Lord is coming.

Here, is repeated: Mourn, O my people.

SECOND NOCTURN.

The *fourth* Psalm speaks of the triumphant entry which the Son of God, after having risen from his Tomb, shall make into heaven.

ANT. Be ye lifted up, O ye eternal gates, and the King of glory shall enter in.

ANT. Elevamini portæ æternales, et introibit Rex gloriæ.

PSALM 23.

The earth is the Lord's and the fulness thereof; the world, and all they that dwell therein.

For he hath founded it upon the seas: and hath prepared it upon the rivers.

Who shall ascend into the mountain of the Lord? or who shall stand in his holy place?

The innocent in hands, and clean of heart, who hath not taken his soul in vain, nor sworn deceitfully to his neighbour.

He shall receive a blessing from the Lord: and mercy from God his Saviour.

This is the generation of them that seek him, of them that seek the face of the God of Jacob.

Lift up your gates, O ye princes, and be ye lifted up, O eternal gates: and the King of glory shall enter in.

Who is this King of glory? the Lord, who is strong and mighty, the Lord mighty in battle.

Lift up your gates, O ye princes, and be ye lifted up, O eternal gates, and the King of glory shall enter in.

Who is this King of glory? the Lord of hosts, he is the King of glory.

Domini est terra, et plenitudo ejus: * orbis terrarum, et universi qui habitant in eo.

Quia ipse super maria fundavit eum: * et super flumina præparavit eum.

Quis ascendet in montem Domini: * aut quis stabit in loco sancto ejus?

Innocens manibus et mundo corde: * qui non accepit in vano animam suam, nec juravit in dolo proximo suo.

Hic accipiet benedictionem a Domino: * et misericordiam a Deo salutari suo.

Hæc est generatio quærentium eum: * quærentium faciem Dei Jacob.

Attolite portas principes vestras, et elevamini portæ æternales: * et introibit Rex gloriæ.

Quis est iste Rex gloriæ: * Dominus fortis et potens, Dominus potens in prælio.

Attolite portas principes vestras, et elevamini portæ æternales: * et introibit Rex gloriæ.

Quis est iste Rex gloriæ? * Dominus virtutum, ipse est Rex gloriæ.

ANT. Elevamini portæ æternales, et introibit Rex gloriæ.

ANT. Be ye lifted up, O eternal gates, and the King of glory shall enter in.

The *fifth* Psalm was sung in yesterday's Office, and expressed the confidence in his Father's love and assistance, which never left our Jesus during his Passion: we repeat it to-day, because it speaks of his speedy deliverance. The Church changes the Antiphon, which gave us the words of our Saviour, complaining of his false witnesses, into the following, wherein we have our Divine Master telling us, that he is soon to be *in the land of the living.*

ANT. Credo videre bona Domini in terra viventium.

ANT. I believe to see the good things of the Lord in the land of the living.

PSALM 26.

Dominus illuminatio mea et salus mea: * quem timebo?

Dominus protector vitæ mea: * a quo trepidabo?

Dum appropriant super me nocentes: * ut edant carnes meas.

Qui tribulant me inimici mei: * ipsi infirmati sunt et ceciderunt.

Si consistant adversum me castra: * non timebit cor meum.

Si exsurgat adversum me prælium: * in hoc ego sperabo.

Unam petii a Domino, hanc requiram: * ut inhabitem in domo Domini omnibus diebus vitæ meæ.

Ut videam voluptatem Domini: * et visitem templum ejus.

Quoniam abscondit me in tabernaculo suo: * in die

The Lord is my light and my salvation, whom shall I fear?

The Lord is the protector of my life, of whom shall I be afraid?

Whilst the wicked draw near against me, to eat my flesh.

My enemies that troubled me have been weakened, and have fallen.

If armies in camp should stand together against me, my heart shall not fear.

If a battle should rise up against me, in this will I be confident.

One thing have I asked of the Lord, this will I seek after, that I may dwell in the house of the Lord all the days of my life.

That I may see the delight of the Lord, and may visit his temple.

For he hath hid me in his tabernacle: in the day of evils,

he hath protected me in the secret place of his tabernacle.

He hath exalted me upon a rock : and now he hath lifted up my head above my enemies.

I have gone round, and have offered up in his tabernacle a sacrifice of jubilation : I will sing, and recite a psalm to the Lord.

Hear, O Lord, my voice with which I have cried to thee : have mercy on me, and hear me.

My heart hath said to thee, my face hath sought thee : thy face, O Lord, will I still seek.

Turn not away thy face from me : decline not in thy wrath from thy servant.

Be thou my helper : forsake me not, do not thou despise me, O God my Saviour.

For my father and my mother have left me : but the Lord hath taken me up.

Set me, O Lord, a law in the way : and guide me in the right path, because of my enemies.

Deliver me not over to the will of them that trouble me : for unjust witnesses have risen up against me and inquity hath belied itself.

I believe to see the good things of the Lord in the land of the living.

Expect the Lord, do manfully : and let thy heart take courage, and wait thou for the Lord.

ANT. I believe to see the

malorum protexit me in abscondito tabernaculi sui.

In petra exaltavit me : * et nunc exaltavit caput meum super inimicos meos.

Circuivi, et immolavi in tabernaculo ejus hostiam vociferationis : * cantabo, et psalmum dicam Domino.

Exaudi, Domine, vocem meam, qua clamavi ad te : * miserere mei, et exaudi me.

Tibi dixit cor meum, exquisivit te facies mea : * faciem tuam, Domine, requiram.

Nec avertas faciem tuam a me : * ne declines in ira a servo tuo.

Adjutor meus esto : * ne derelinquas me, neque despicias me, Deus salutaris meus.

Quoniam pater meus et mater mea dereliquerunt me : * Dominus autem assumpsit me.

Legem pone mihi, Domine, in via tua : * et dirige me in semitam rectam propter inimicos meos.

Ne tradideris me in animas tribulantium me : * quoniam insurrexerunt in me testes iniqui, et mentita est iniquitas sibi.

Credo videre bona Domini : * in terra viventium.

Exspecta Dominum viriliter age : * et confortetur cor tuum, et sustine Dominum.

ANT. Credo videre bona

Domini in terra viven-
tium.

good things of the Lord in the
land of the living.

The *sixth* Psalm tells us, that Jesus, the divine
Captive of Death, will soon rise from the grave.
The Prophet speaks of the *weeping*, which shall last
till *evening*, and of the *gladness*, that shall follow in
the *morning*.

ANT. Domine abstraxisti ab inferis animam meam.

ANT. O Lord, thou hast brought forth my soul from hell.

PSALM 29.

Exaltabo te Domine, quoniam suscepisti me: * nec delectasti inimicos meos super me.

Domine Deus meus, clamavi ad te: * et sanasti me.

Domine eduxisti ab inferno animam meam: * salvasti me a descendentibus in lacum.

Psallite Domino sancti ejus: * et confitemini memoriæ sanctitatis ejus.

Quoniam ira in indignatione ejus: * et vita in voluntate ejus.

Ad vesperum demorabitur fletus: * et ad matutinum lætitia.

Ego autem dixi in abundantia mea: * Non movebor in æternum.

Domine in voluntate tua: * præstitisti decori meo virtutem.

Avertisti faciem tuam a me: * et factus sum conturbatus.

I will extol thee, O Lord, for thou hast upheld me: and hast not made my enemies to rejoice over me.

O Lord, my God, I have cried to thee, and thou hast healed me.

Thou hast brought forth, O Lord, my soul from hell: thou hast saved me from them that go down into the pit.

Sing to the Lord, O you his saints: and give praise to the memory of his holiness.

For wrath is in his indignation: and life in his good will.

In the evening, weeping shall have place: and in the morning, gladness.

And in my abundance I said: I shall never be moved.

O Lord, in thy favour, thou gavest strength to my beauty.

Thou turnedst away thy face from me, and I became troubled.

To thee, O Lord, will I cry: and I will make supplication to my God.

What profit is there in my blood, whilst I go down to corruption?

Shall dust confess to thee, or declare thy truth?

The Lord hath heard, and hath had mercy on me: the Lord became my helper.

Thou hast turned for me my mourning into joy: thou hast cut my sackcloth, and hast compassed me with gladness.

To the end that my glory may sing to thee, and I may not regret. O Lord my God, I will give praise to thee for ever.

ANT. O Lord, thou hast brought forth my soul from hell.

℣. But thou, O Lord, have mercy on me.

℟. And raise me up again, and I will requite them.

Ad te, Domine, clamabo: * et ad Deum meum deprecabor.

Quæ utilitas in sanguine meo: * dum descendo in corruptionem?

Numquid confitebitur tibi pulvis: * aut annuntiabit veritatem tuam?

Audivit Dominus, et misertus est mei: * Dominus factus est adjutor meus.

Convertisti planctum meum in gaudium mihi: * conscidisti saccum meum, et circumdedisti me lætitia.

Ut cantet tibi gloria mea, et non compungar: * Domine Deus meus, in æternum confitebor tibi.

ANT. Domine abstraxisti ab inferis animam meam.

℣. Tu autem, Domine, miserere mei.

℟. Et resuscita me, et retribuam eis.

The *Pater noster* is here recited, in secret.

For the second Nocturn Lessons, the Church continues the *Enarrations* of St. Augustine on the Psalms prophetic of our Lord's Passion.

From the treatise of Saint Augustine, Bishop, on the Psalms.

Ex tractatu sancti Augustini Episcopi super Psalmos.

FOURTH LESSON.

Man shall come to the deep heart, and God shall be exalted. They said, Who will see us? They failed in making diligent search for wicked designs.

Accedet homo ad cor altum, et exaltabitur Deus. Illi dixerunt: Quis nos videbit? Defecerunt scrutantes scrutationes, consilia mala. Accessit homo ad ipsa consilia: passus est se teneri ut homo. Non enim teneretur nisi homo, aut videretur nisi homo, aut cæderetur nisi homo, aut crucifigeretur, aut moreretur nisi homo. Accessit ergo homo ad illas omnes passiones, quæ in illo nihil valerent, nisi esset homo. Sed si ille non esset homo, non liberaretur homo. Accessit homo ad cor altum, id est, cor secretum, objiciens aspectibus humanis hominem, servans intus Deum, celans formam Dei, in qua æqualis est Patri, et offerens formam servi, qua minor est Patre.

Christ, as *Man*, came to those designs, and suffered himself to be seized on as a *Man*. For he could not be seized on if he were not *Man*, nor seen, if he were not *Man*, nor scourged, if he were not *Man*, nor crucified, nor die, if he were not *Man*. As *Man*, therefore, he came to all these sufferings, which could have no effect on him, if he were not *Man*. But if he had not been *Man*, man could not have been redeemed. *Man came to the deep heart*, that is, the secret heart, exposing his humanity to human view, but hiding his divinity: concealing the form of God, by which he is equal to the Father; and offering the form of the servant, by which he is inferior to the Father.

℞. Recessit Pastor noster, fons aquæ vivæ, ad cujus transitum sol obscuratus est: * Nam et ille captus est, qui captivum tenebat primum hominem: hodie portas mortis et seras pariter Salvator noster disrupit.

℣. Destruxit quidem claustra inferni, et subvertit potentias diaboli.

* Nam et ille captus est qui captivum tenebat primum hominem: hodie portas mortis et seras pariter Salvator noster disrupit.

℞. Our Shepherd, the fountain of living water, is gone; at whose departure, the sun was darkened. * For *he* is taken, who made the first man a prisoner. To day our Saviour broke the gates and bolts of death.

℣. He, indeed, destroyed the prisons of hell, and overthrew the powers of the devil.

* For *he* is taken, who made the first man a prisoner. To-day our Saviour broke the gates and bolts of death.

FIFTH LESSON.

Quo perduxerunt illas scrutationes suas, quas perscrutantes defecerunt, ut

How far did they carry this their *diligent search*, in which they *failed* so much, that when our Lord was dead and buried, they placed guards at the sepulchre? For they said to Pilate: This seducer, (by which name our Lord Jesus Christ was called, for the comfort of his servants, when they are called seducers,) this seducer, say they to Pilate, whilst he was yet living, said: After three days I will rise again. Command therefore the sepulchre to be guarded until the third day, lest perhaps his disciples come and steal him away, and say to the people, he is risen from the dead: and the last error will be worse than the first. Pilate saith to them: Ye have a guard, go, and guard him as ye know. And they went away and secured the sepulchre with guards, sealing up the stone.

℞. O all ye, that pass by the way, attend and see, * If there be sorrow like unto my sorrow.

℣. Attend all ye people, and see my sorrow.

* If there be sorrow like unto my sorrow.

etiam mortuo Domino et sepulto, custodes ponerent ad sepulchrum. Dixerunt enim Pilato: Seductor ille. Hoc appellabatur nomine Dominus Jesus Christus, ad solatium servorum suorum, quando dicuntur seductores. Ergo illi Pilato: Seductor ille, inquiunt, dixit adhuc vivens: Post tres dies resurgam. Jube itaque custodiri sepulchrum usque in diem tertium, ne forte veniant discipuli ejus, et furentur eum, et dicant plebi: Surrexit a mortuis: et erit novissimus error pejor priore. Ait illis Pilatus: Habetis custodiam; ite, custodite sicut scitis. Illi autem abeuntes, munierunt sepulchrum, signantes lapidem cum custodibus.

℞. O vos omnes, qui transitis per viam, attendite et videte, * Si est dolor similis sicut dolor meus.

℣. Attendite universi populi, et videte dolorem meum.

* Si est dolor similis sicut dolor meus.

SIXTH LESSON.

They placed soldiers to guard the sepulchre. The earth shook, and the Lord rose again: such miracles were done at the sepulchre, that the very soldiers that came as guards might be witnesses of it, if they would declare the truth. But that

Posuerunt custodes milites ad sepulchrum. Concussa terra Dominus resurrexit: miracula facta sunt talia circa sepulchrum, ut et ipsi milites qui custodes advenerant, testes fierent, si vellent vera nuntiare. Sed avaritia illa, quæ captivavit discipulum comitem Christi, captivavit et militem custodem sepulchri. Damus, inquiunt, vobis pecuniam, et dicite, quia, vobis dormientibus, venerunt discipuli ejus, et abstulerunt eum. Vere defecerunt scrutantes scrutationes. Quid est quod dixisti, o infelix astutia? Tantumne deseris lucem consilii pietatis, et in profunda versutia demergeris, ut hoc dicas : Dicite, quia, vobis dormientibus, venerunt discipuli ejus, et abstulerunt eum? Dormientes testes adhibes : vere tu ipse obdormisti, qui scrutando talia defecisti.

℣. Ecce quomodo moritur justus, et nemo percipit corde : et viri justi tolluntur et nemo considerat : a facie iniquitatis sublatus est Justus : * Et erit in pace memoria ejus.

℣. Tamquam agnus coram tondente se obmutuit, et non aperuit os suum : de angustia, et de judicio sublatus est.
* Et erit in pace memoria ejus.
Here is repeated: Ecce quomodo.

covetousness which possessed the disciple that was the companion of Christ, blinded also the soldiers that were the guards of his sepulchre. We will give you money, said they: and say, that whilst ye were asleep, his disciples came and took him away : They truly *failed*, in *making diligent search*. What is it thou hast said, O wretched craft? Dost thou shut thy eyes against the light of prudence and piety, and plunge thyself so deep in cunning, as to say this : Say that whilst ye were asleep, his disciples came and took him away? Dost thou produce *sleeping* witnesses? Certainly thou thyself *sleepest*, that *failedst* in *making search* after such things.

℣. Behold! how the Just One dieth, and there is none that taketh it to heart : and just men are taken away and no one considereth it : the Just One is taken away because of iniquity : * And his memory shall be in peace.

℣. He was silent, as a lamb under his shearer, and he opened not his mouth : he was taken away from distress and judgment.
* And his memory shall be in peace.
Here is repeated : Behold!

THIRD NOCTURN.

The *seventh* Psalm is the one we sang yesterday, when commemorating the persecution our Saviour met with from the Jews. We repeat it, to-day, because of his approaching triumph, for the Eternal Father is his *helper* and *protector*.

ANT. God is my helper, and the Lord is the protector of my soul.	ANT. Deus adjuvat me, et Dominus susceptor est animæ meæ.

PSALM 53.

Save me, O God, by thy name, and judge me in thy strength.	Deus, in nomine tuo salvum me fac : * et in virtute tua judica me.
O God, hear my prayer : give ear to the words of my mouth.	Deus, exaudi orationem meam : * auribus percipe verba oris mei.
For strangers have risen up against me : and the mighty have sought after my soul : and they have not set God before their eyes.	Quoniam alieni insurrexerunt adversum me, et fortes quæsierunt animam meam : * et non proposuerunt Deum ante conspectum suum.
For behold God is my helper : and the Lord is the protector of my soul.	Ecce enim Deus adjuvat me : * et Dominus susceptor est animæ meæ.
Turn back the evils upon my enemies : and cut them off in thy truth.	Averte mala inimicis meis : * et in veritate tua disperde illos.
I will freely sacrifice to thee, and will give praise, O God, to thy name : because it is good.	Voluntarie sacrificabo tibi : * et confitebor nomini tuo, Domine, quoniam bonum est.
For thou hast delivered me out of all trouble : and my eye hath looked down upon my enemies.	Quoniam ex omni tribulatione eripuisti me : * et super inimicos meos despexit oculus meus.
ANT. God is my helper, and the Lord is the protector of my soul.	ANT. Deus adjuvat me, et Dominus susceptor est animæ meæ.

The *eighth* Psalm is one that was sung in the *Tenebræ* for Maundy Thursday: then, it was an allusion to the divine vengeance that was to fall on the enemies of Jesus ; to-day, we must rejoice in its prophecy of the sleep of *peace,* which this Saviour of ours is taking *in Sion.* A few more hours, and he will *rise* from his Tomb. His enemies, who boast of having him in their power, will find, on awaking, that they have *nothing in their hands.* The earth shall *tremble,* and our Lord shall *arise,* an object of terror to his enemies, but a *Saviour to the meek,* that is, to the humble and faithful ones, who will then *praise* him as the God ever faithful to his word.

ANT. In pace factus est locus ejus, et in Sion habitatio ejus.

ANT. His place is in peace, and his abode in Sion.

PSALM 75.

Notus in Judæa Deus : * in Israël magnum nomen ejus.

In Judea God is known, his name is great in Israel.

Et factus est in pace locus ejus : * et habitatio ejus in Sion.

And his place is in peace, and his abode in Sion.

Ibi confregit potentias arcuum : * scutum, gladium, et bellum.

There hath he broken the power of bows, the shield, the sword, and the battle.

Illuminans tu mirabiliter a montibus æternis : * turbati sunt omnes insipientes corde.

Thou enlightenest wonderfully from the everlasting hills : all the foolish of heart were troubled.

Dormierunt somnum suum : * et nihil invenerunt omnes viri divitiarum in manibus suis.

They have slept their sleep : and all the men of riches have found nothing in their hands.

Ab increpatione tua, Deus Jacob : * dormitaverunt qui ascenderunt equos.

At thy rebuke, O God of Jacob, they have all slumbered that mounted on horseback.

Tu terribilis es, et quis resistet tibi : * ex tunc ira tua.

Thou art terrible, and who shall resist thee? from that time thy wrath.

De cœlo auditum fecisti judicium : * terra tremuit et quievit.

Thou hast caused judgment to be heard from heaven: the earth trembled and was still.

When God arose in judgment, to save all the meek of the earth.
For the thought of man shall give praise to thee : and the remainders of the thought shall keep holyday to thee.
Vow ye, and pray to the Lord your God : all you that round about him bring presents.
To him that is terrible, even to him who taketh away the spirit of princes ; to the terrible with the kings of the earth.
ANT. His place is in peace, and his abode in Sion.

Cum exsurgeret in judicium Deus: * ut salvos faceret omnes mansuetos terræ.
Quoniam cogitatio hominis confitebitur tibi : * et reliquiæ cogitationis diem festum agent tibi.
Vovete et reddite Domino Deo vestro : * omnes qui in circuitu ejus affertis munera.
Terribili et ei qui aufert spiritum principum : * terribili apud reges terræ.
ANT. In pace factus est locus ejus, et in Sion habitatio ejus.

The *ninth* Psalm is repeated from yesterday's Office. It shows us our Saviour praying to his Father, that he will raise him, and *free him* from *among the dead*. The time fixed for his *lying in the darkness* of the *sepulchre* is over, the hour of his Resurrection to *Life* is at hand.

ANT. I am become as a man without help, *whose life is set free, and he now numbered* among the dead.

ANT. Factus sum sicut homo sine adjutorio, inter mortuos liber.

PSALM 87.

O Lord, the God of my salvation, I have cried in the day, and in the night before thee.
Let my prayer come in before thee : incline thy ear to my petition.
For my soul is filled with evils : and my life hath drawn nigh to hell.

Domine, Deus salutis meæ, * in die clamavi, et nocte coram te.
Intret in conspectu tuo oratio mea : * inclina aurem tuam ad precem meam.
Quia repleta est malis anima mea : * et vita mea inferno appropinquavit.

Æstimatus sum cum descendentibus in lacum : * factus sum sicut homo sine adjutorio, inter mortuos liber.

Sicut vulnerati dormientes in sepulchris, quorum non es memor amplius : * et ipsi de manu tua repulsi sunt.

Posuerunt me in lacu inferiori : * in tenebrosis, et in umbra mortis.

Super me confirmatus est furor tuus : * et omnes fluctus tuos induxisti super me.

Longe fecisti notos meos a me : * posuerunt me abominationem sibi.

Traditus sum, et non egrediebar : * oculi mei languerunt præ inopia.

Clamavi ad te, Domine tota die : * expandi ad te manus meas.

Numquid mortuis facies mirabilia : * aut medici suscitabunt, et confitebuntur tibi.

Numquid narrabit aliquis in sepulchro misericordiam tuam : * et veritatem tuam in perditione ?

Numquid cognoscentur in tenebris mirabilia tua : * et justitia tua in terra oblivionis ?

Et ego ad te, Domine, clamavi : * et mane oratio mea præveniet te.

Ut quid, Domine, repellis orationem meam : * avertis faciem tuam a me ?

Pauper sum ego, et in la-

I am counted among them that go down to the pit : I am become as a man without help, free among the dead.

Like the slain sleeping in the sepulchres, whom thou rememberest no more : and they are cast off from thy hand.

They have laid me in the lower pit : in the dark places, and in the shadow of death.

Thy wrath is strong over me : and all thy waves thou hast brought in upon me.

Thou hast put away my acquaintance far from me : they have set me an abomination to themselves.

I was delivered up, and came not forth : my eyes languished through poverty.

All the day I cried to thee, O Lord : I stretched out my hands to thee.

Wilt thou show wonders to the dead : or shall physicians raise to life, and give praise to thee ?

Shall any one in the sepulchre declare thy mercy, and thy truth in destruction ?

Shall thy wonders be known in the dark : and thy justice in the land of forgetfulness ?

But I, O Lord, have cried to thee : and in the morning my prayer shall prevent thee.

Lord, why castest thou off my prayer : why turnest thou away thy face from me.

I am poor, and in labours

from my youth: and being exalted, have been humbled and troubled.

Thy wrath hath come upon me: and thy terrors have troubled me.

They have come round about me like water all the day: they have compassed me about together.

Friend and neighbour thou hast put far from me: and my acquaintance because of misery.

ANT. I am become as a man without help, whose life is set *free, and he now numbered* among the dead.

℣. His place is in peace.

℟. And his abode in Sion.

boribus a juventute mea: * exaltatus autem, humilitatus sum et conturbatus.

In me transierunt iræ tuæ: * et terrores tui conturbaverunt me.

Circumdederunt me sicut aqua tota die: * circumdederunt me simul.

Elongasti a me amicum et proximum: * et notos meos a miseria.

ANT. Factus sum sicut homo sine adjutorio, inter mortuos liber.

℣. In pace factus est locus ejus.

℟. Et in Sion habitatio ejus.

Here *Pater noster* is recited, in secret.

The third Nocturn Lessons are again from the Epistle to the Hebrews. In the passage chosen for to-day, the Apostle shows us the divine efficacy of the Blood of Jesus, and how his *Testament*, or Last Will, could not be applied to us, save by his *Death*.

SEVENTH LESSON.

From the Epistle of Saint Paul to the Hebrews.

Cap. IX.

Christ being come a High Priest of the good things to come, by a greater and more perfect tabernacle not made with hands, that is, not of this creation: neither by the blood of goats, nor of calves, but by his own Blood, entered once into the holies having

De Epistola beati Pauli Apostoli ad Hebræos.

Ch. IX.

Christus assistens Pontifex futurorum bonorum; per amplius et perfectius tabernaculum non manu factum, id est non hujus creationis; neque per sanguinem hircorum aut vitulorum, sed per proprium Sanguinem introivit semel in Sancta, æterna redemptione inventa. Si enim sanguis hircorum et taurorum, et cinis vitulæ aspersus inquinatos sanctificat ad emundationem carnis: quanto magis Sanguis Christi qui per Spiritum Sanctum semetipsum obtulit immaculatum Deo, emundabit conscientiam nostram ab operibus mortuis, ad serviendum Deo viventi?

℟. Adstiterunt reges terræ, et principes convenerunt in unum, * Adversus Dominum, et adversus Christum ejus.

℣. Quare fremuerunt gentes, et populi meditati sunt inania?

* Adversus Dominum, et adversus Christum ejus.

obtained eternal redemption. For if the blood of goats and of oxen, and the ashes of an heifer being sprinkled, sanctify such as are defiled, to the cleansing of the flesh: how much more shall the Blood of Christ, who through the Holy Ghost offered himself without spot to God, cleanse our conscience from dead works, to serve the living God?

℟. The kings of the earth stood, and the princes met together, * Against the Lord, and against his Christ.

℣. Why have the Gentiles raged, and the people devised vain things?

* Against the Lord, and against his Christ.

EIGHTH LESSON.

Et ideo novi Testamenti mediator est: ut morte intercedente, in redemptionem earum prævaricationum, quæ erant sub priori testamento, repromissionem accipiant, qui vocati sunt æternæ hæreditatis. Ubi enim testamentum est, mors necesse est intercedat testatoris. Testamentum enim in mortuis confirmatum est; alioquin nondum valet, dum vivit qui testatus est. Unde nec primum quidem sine sanguine dedicatum est.

℟. Æstimatus sum cum descendentibus in lacum.

And therefore he is the mediator of the new testament: that by means of his death, for the redemption of those transgressions which were under the former testament, they that are called may receive the promise of eternal inheritance. For where there is a testament, the death of a testator must of necessity come in. For a testament is of force, after men are dead: otherwise it is as yet of no strength, whilst the testator liveth. Whereupon neither was the first indeed dedicated without blood.

℟. I am counted among them that go down to the pit.

* I am become as a man without help, free among the dead.

℣. They have laid me in the lower pit, in the dark places, and in the shadow of death.

* I am become as a man without help, free among the dead.

* Factus sum sicut homo sine adjutorio, inter mortuos liber.

℣. Posuerunt me in lacu inferiori, in tenebrosis, et in umbra mortis.

* Factus sum sicut homo sine adjutorio, inter mortuos liber.

NINTH LESSON.

For when every commandment of the law had been read by Moses to all the people, he took the blood of calves and goats, with water and scarlet wool and hyssop, and sprinkled both the book itself and all the people, saying: This is the blood of the testament, which God hath enjoined to you. The tabernacle also, and all the vessels of the ministry, in like manner, he sprinkled with blood. And almost all things, according to the law, are cleansed with blood: and without shedding of blood there is no remission.

℞. Having buried our Lord, they sealed up the Sepulchre, rolling a stone before the entrance of the Sepulchre: * Placing soldiers to guard him.

℣. The chief priests went to Pilate, and sought his permission. .

* Placing soldiers to guard him.

Here, is repeated: Having buried.

Lecto enim omni mandato legis a Moyse universo populo, accipiens sanguinem vitulorum et hircorum, cum aqua et lana coccinea et hyssopo; ipsum quoque librum et omnem populum aspersit, dicens: Hic sanguis testamenti, quod mandavit ad vos Deus. Etiam tabernaculum, et omnia vasa ministerii sanguine similiter aspersit. Et omnia pene in sanguine secundum legem mundantur: et sine sanguinis effusione non fit remissio.

℞. Sepulto Domino, signatum est monumentum, volventes lapidem ad ostium monumenti: * Ponentes milites, qui custodirent illum.

℣. Accedentes principes sacerdotum ad Pilatum, petierunt illum.

* Ponentes milites, qui custodirent illum.

Here, is repeated: Sepulto Domino.

LAUDS.

The *first* Psalm of Lauds is the *Miserere*, (*page* 338.) Its Antiphon is the following:

ANT. O mors, ero mors tua: morsus tuus ero, inferne.

ANT. O Death! I will be thy death. O Hell! I will be thy ruin.

The *second* Psalm is one of those that were composed by David, when he was in banishment. He here expresses the desire and hope of again seeing his country. He is a figure of our Saviour when lying in the grave, and longing for the day of his Resurrection.

ANT. Plangent eum quasi unigenitum; quia innocens Dominus occisus est.

ANT. They shall mourn for him as for an only son; because the innocent Lord is slain.

PSALM 42.

Judica me, Deus, et discerne causam meam de gente non sancta: * ab homine iniquo et doloso erue me.

Quia tu es Deus fortitudo mea: * quare me repulisti, et quare tristis incedo, dum affligit me inimicus?

Emitte lucem tuam et veritatem tuam: * ipsa me deduxerunt, et adduxerunt in montem sanctum tuum, et in tabernacula tua.

Et introibo ad altare Dei: * ad Deum qui lætificat juventutem meam.

Judge me, O God, and distinguish my cause from the nation that is not holy: deliver me from the unjust and deceitful man.

For thou art God my strength: why hast thou cast me off? and why do I go sorrowful whilst the enemy afflicteth me?

Send forth thy light and thy truth: they have conducted me, and brought me unto thy holy hill, and into thy tabernacles.

And I will go into the altar of God: to God who giveth joy to my youth.

To thee, O God, my God, I will give praise upon the harp: why art thou sad, O my soul, and why dost thou disquiet me?	Confitebor tibi in cithara Deus, Deus meus: * quare tristis es, anima mea, et quare conturbas me?
Hope in God, for I will still give praise to him: the salvation of my countenance and my God.	Spera in Deo, quoniam adhuc confitebor illi: * salutare vultus mei, et Deus meus.
ANT. They shall mourn for him as for an only son; because the innocent Lord is slain.	ANT. Plangent eum quasi unigenitum; quia innocens Dominus occisus est.

The *third* Psalm is the *Deus, Deus meus*, (*page* 342.) Its Antiphon is as follows:

ANT. Attend, all ye people, and see my sorrow.	ANT. Attendite universi populi, et videte dolorem meum.

The Canticle of Ezechias, which is always sung in Tuesday's Lauds, is here substituted for that of Deuteronomy, which is the proper one for Saturdays, but which is not in harmony with to-day's mystery. Ezechias, lying on his sick bed, and praying God to restore him to health, is a figure of Christ in his Tomb, beseeching his Father to give him a speedy Resurrection to life.

ANT. From the gate of the tomb, O Lord, deliver my soul.	ANT. A porta inferi erue Domine animam meam.

THE CANTICLE OF EZECHIAS.
(Is. XXXVIII.)

I said in the midst of my days I shall go to the gates of hell.	Ego dixi: in dimidio dierum meorum: * vadam ad portas inferi.
I sought for the residue of my years: I said, I shall not see the Lord God in the land of the living.	Quæsivi residuum annorum meorum: * dixi: Non videbo Dominum Deum in terra viventium.

Non aspiciam hominem ultra : * et habitatorem quietis.

Generatio mea ablata est, et convoluta est a me : * quasi tabernaculum pastorum.

Precisa est velut a texente, vita mea, dum adhuc ordirer, succidit me : * de mane usque ad vesperam finies me.

Sperabam usque ad mane: * quasi leo sic contrivit omnia ossa mea.

De mane usque ad vesperam finies me : * sicut pullus hirundinis sic clamabo meditabor ut columba.

Attenuati sunt oculi mei: * suspicientes in excelsum.

Domine, vim patior, responde pro me : * Quid dicam, aut quid respondebit mihi, cum ispe fecerit ?

Recogitabo tibi omnes annos meos : * in amaritudine animæ meæ.

Domine, si sic vivitur, et in talibus, vita spiritus mei, corripies me, et vivificabis me : * ecce in pace amaritudo mea amarissima.

Tu autem eruisti animam meam ut non periret : * projecisti post tergum tuum omnia peccata mea.

Quia non infernus confitebitur tibi, neque mors laudabit te : * non exspectabunt qui desendunt in lacum veritatem tuam.

Vivens, vivens, ipse con-

I shall behold man no more, nor the inhabitant of rest.

My generation is at an end, and it is rolled away from me as a shepherd's tent.

My life is cut off as by a weaver ; whilst I was but beginning, he cut me off : from morning even till night thou wilt make an end of me.

I hoped till morning : as a lion so hath he broken my bones.

From morning even till night thou wilt make an end of me : I will cry like young swallow, I will meditate like a dove.

My eyes are weakened with looking upward.

Lord, I suffer violence, answer thou for me. What shall I say, or what shall he answer for me, whereas he himself hath done it ?

I will recount to thee all my years, in the bitterness of my soul.

O Lord, if man's life be such, and the life of my spirit be in such things as these, thou shalt correct me, and make me to live. Behold in peace is my bitterness most bitter.

But thou hast delivered my soul that it should not perish : thou hast cast all my sins behind thy back.

For hell shall not confess to thee, neither shall death praise thee : nor shall they that go down into the pit look for thy truth.

The living, the living, he

HOLY SATURDAY: TENEBRÆ. 545

shall give praise to thee, as I do this day: the father shall make thy truth known to the children.

O Lord, save me, and we will sing our psalms all the days of our life, in the house of the Lord.

ANT. From the gate of the tomb, O Lord, deliver my soul.

fitebitur tibi, sicut et ego hodie: * pater filiis notam faciet veritatem tuam.

Domine, salvum me fac: * et psalmos nostros cantabimus cunctis diebus vitæ nostræ in domo Domini.

ANT. A porta inferi erue, Domine, animam meam.

The *last* Psalm of Lauds is the *Laudate Dominum de cœlis*, (*page* 347.) Its Antiphon is the following:

ANT. O all ye that pass by the way, attend and see, if there be sorrow like unto my sorrow.

℣. My flesh shall rest in hope.

℟. And thou wilt not suffer thy Holy One to see corruption.

ANT. O vos omnes qui transitis per viam, attendite et videte, si est dolor sicut dolor meus.

℣. Caro mea requiescet in spe.

℟. Et non dabis Sanctum tuum videre corruptionem.

After this Versicle, the *Benedictus* (*page* 350,) is sung, to the following Antiphon:

ANT. The women, sitting near the Tomb, mourned, weeping for the Lord.

ANT. Mulieres sedentes ad monumentum lamentabantur, flentes Dominum.

The Antiphon having been repeated after the Canticle, the Choir sings, to a touching melody, the following words. She repeats them at the end of all the Canonical Hours of these three days. But, to-day she is not satisfied with announcing the Death of her Jesus: she adds the remaining words of the Apostle, wherein he tells us of the glory of the Man-God, the Conqueror of the Tomb.

546   HOLY WEEK.

℣. Christus factus est pro nobis obediens usque ad mortem, mortem autem crucis :

Propter quod et Deus exaltavit illum, et dedit illi nomen quod est super omne nomen.

℣. Christ became, for our sakes, obedient unto death, even to the death of the Cross:

For which cause, God also hath exalted him, and hath given him a Name, which is above all names.

Then is said, in secret, the *Pater noster*, which is followed by the *Miserere (page 338)*. As soon as the Psalm is finished, the following Prayer is recited by the first in dignity :

Respice, quæsumus, Domine, super hanc familiam tuam, pro qua Dominus noster Jesus Christus non dubitavit manibus tradi nocentium, et crucis subire tormentum.

Look down, O Lord, we beseech thee, on this thy family, for which our Lord Jesus Christ hesitated not to be delivered into the hands of wicked men, and undergo the punishment of the Cross.

(Then the rest in secret:)

Qui tecum vivit et regnat in unitate Spiritus Sancti, Deus, per omnia sæcula sæculorum, amen.

Who liveth and reigneth with thee, in the unity of the Holy Ghost, God, world without end, amen.

THE MORNING.

A night has passed over the Tomb, wherein lies buried the Body of the Man-God. Death is triumphant in that silent cave, and holds captive Him that gives life to every creature :—but his triumph will soon be at an end. The Soldiers may watch, as best they will, over that Grave : they cannot hold Jesus prisoner, as soon as the moment fixed for his Resurrection comes. The holy Angels are there, profoundly adoring the lifeless Body of Him, whose Blood is to *reconcile all things, both on earth, and in heaven.*[1] This Body, though, for a brief interval, separated from the Soul, is still united to the Person of the Son of God; so, likewise, the Soul, during its separation from the Body, has not, for an instant, lost its union with the Word. The Divinity remains also united with the Blood that lies sprinkled on Calvary, and which, at the moment of the Resurrection of the Man-God, is to enter once more into his sacred veins.

Let us, also, return to the Sepulchre, and adore the Body of our Buried Jesus. Now, at last, we understand what sin has done: *By sin, death entered into the world; and it passed upon all men.*[2] Though Jesus *knew no sin*,[3] yet has he permitted Death to have dominion over him, in order that he might make it less bitter to us, and, by his Resurrection, restore unto us that eternal life, of which we had been deprived by sin. How gratefully we should appreciate this Death of our Jesus! By becoming Incarnate, he became a *Servant*;[4] his Death was a still deeper humiliation. The sight of this Tomb, wherein his Body lies lifeless and cold, teaches us something far more important than the power of death:—it reveals to us the immense, the incomprehensible love of God for man. He knew that we were to gain by his humiliations;—the greater *his* humiliations, the greater our exaltation: this was his principle, and it led him to what seems like an excess! Let us, then, love this sacred Sepulchre, which is to give us Life. We have thanked him for having died for us upon the Cross; let us thank him, but most feelingly, for having humbled himself, for our sakes, even to the Tomb!

And now, let us visit the Holy Mother, who has passed the night in Jerusalem, going over, in saddest

---

[1] Coloss. i. 20.
[2] Rom. v. 12.
[3] II. Cor. v. 21.
[4] Philipp. ii. 7.

memory, the scenes she has witnessed. Her Jesus has been a Victim to every possible insult and cruelty: he has been crucified: his precious Blood has flowed in torrents from those Five Wounds: he is dead, and now lies buried in yonder Tomb, as though he were but a mere man, yea the most abject of men. How many tears have fallen, during these long hours, from the eyes of the Daughter of David! and yet, her Son has not come back to her! Near her is Magdalene; heart-broken by yesterday's events, she has no words to tell her grief, for Jesus is gone, and, as she thinks, for ever. The other Women, less loved by Jesus than Magdalene, yet, still, dear to him, stand round the disconsolate Mother. They have braved every insult and danger in order to remain on Calvary till all was over, and they intend returning thither with Magdalene, as soon as the Sabbath is over, to honour the Tomb and the Body of Jesus.

John, the adopted son of Mary, and the Beloved Disciple of Jesus, is oppressed with sorrow. Others, also, of the Apostles and Disciples visit the house of mourning. Peter, penitent and humble, fears not to appear before the Mother of Mercy. Among the Disciples, are Joseph of Arimathea and Nicodemus. We may easily imagine the conversation,—it is on the Sufferings and Death of Jesus, and on the ingratitude of the Jews. The Church, in the 7th Responsory of to-day's *Tenebræ*, represents these men as saying: " Behold! how the Just One dieth, and there " is none that taketh it to heart. Iniquity has had " its way. He was silent as a Lamb under his shearer, " and he opened not his mouth. He was taken away " from distress and judgment: but his memory shall " be in peace."

Thus speak the men!—the women are thinking of their morrow's visit to the Sepulchre! The saintliness of Jesus, his goodness, his power, his Sufferings, his Death,—everything is remembered, except his Resurrection, which they had often heard him say should certainly and speedily take place. Mary alone lives in expectation of his triumph. In her was verified that expression of the Holy Ghost, where, speaking of the Valiant Woman, he says : *Her lamp shall not be put out in the night.*[1] Her courage fails not, because she knows that the Sepulchre must yield up its Dead, and her Jesus will rise again to Life. St. Paul tells us that our religion is vain, unless we have faith in the mystery of our Saviour's Resurrection ;—where was this faith on the day after our Lord's Death ? In one heart only,—and that was Mary's. As it was her chaste womb, that had held within it Him, whom heaven and earth cannot contain,—so on this day, by her firm and unwavering faith, she resumes within her single self the whole Church. How sacred is this *Saturday*, which, notwithstanding all its sadness, is such a day of glory to the Mother of Jesus! It is on this account that the Church has consecrated to Mary the Saturday of every week.

But it is time to repair to the House of God. The Bells are still silent : our faith must speak to us, and make us eager to assist at the grand Mysteries, which the Liturgy is about to celebrate. Surely, the christian sentiment must be dead in them who can be willingly absent from their Church on such a morning as this. No, it cannot be, that we, who have followed the celebration of the Mysteries of our Religion thus far, can flag now, and lose the graces of this Morning's magnificent Service.

[1] Prov. xxxi. 18.

THE MORNING SERVICE.

It was the practice of the Church, and one that had been handed down from the earliest Ages, that the Sacrifice of the Mass should not be offered up either yesterday or to-day. Yesterday, the anniversary of Jesus' Death, was exclusively devoted to the remembrance of the Mystery of Calvary, and a holy fear kept the Church from renewing that Sacrifice upon her Altars. For the same reason, she abstained to-day, also, from its celebration. The Burial of Christ is a sequel of his Passion : and during these hours when his Body lay lifeless in the Tomb, it was fitting that the Sacrifice, wherein he is offered as the glorious and Risen Jesus, should be suspended. Even the Greek Church, which never fasts on the Saturdays of Lent, follows the practice of the Latin Church for this Saturday : she not only fasts, but she even omits the celebration of the *Mass of the Presanctified*.

Such, we repeat, was the discipline of the Latin Church for nearly a thousand years : but about the 11th century, an important change began to be introduced with regard to the celebration of Mass on Holy Saturday. The Mass which, hitherto, had been celebrated during the Night preceding Easter Sunday,—then began to be anticipated, on the Saturday; but it was always considered as the Mass of the hour of our Lord's Resurrection, and not as the Mass of Holy Saturday. The relaxations, that had been introduced with regard to Fasting, were the occasion of this change in the Liturgy. In the first ages, the Faithful watched the whole night in the Church, awaiting the hour when our Lord rose triumphant from the Tomb. They also assisted at the solemn administration of Baptism to the Catechumens, which so sublimely expressed the passing from spiritual death to the life of grace. There was no other *Vigil* in the whole Year, which was so solemnly observed as this: but it lost a great portion of its interest, when the necessity of baptising Adults was removed by Christianity having triumphed wheresoever it had been preached. The Orientals have kept up the ancient tradition to this day: but, in the West, dating from the 11th century, the Mass of the Resurrection Hour has been gradually anticipated, until it has been brought even to the morning of Holy Saturday. Durandus of Menda, who wrote his *Rational of the Divine Offices*, towards the close of the 13th century, tells us, that in his time, there were very few Churches which observed the primitive custom: even these soon conformed to the general practice of the Latin Church.

As a result of this change, there is an apparent contradiction between the mystery of Holy Saturday and the Divine Service which is celebrated upon it; Christ is still in the Tomb, and yet we are celebrating his Resurrection: the hours preceding Mass are mournful,—and before mid-day, the paschal joy will have filled our hearts. We will conform to the present order of the Holy Liturgy, thus entering into the spirit of the Church, who has thought proper to give her children a foretaste of the joys of Easter. We will give a general view of the solemn Service, at which we are going to assist; afterwards, we will explain each portion, as it comes.

The great object of the whole of to-day's Service, and the centre to which every one of the ceremonies converges,—is the Baptism of the Catechumens. The Faithful must keep this incessantly before them, or they will be at a loss how to understand or profit by the Liturgy of to-day. First of all, there is the Blessing of the new Fire, and the Incense. This is followed by the Blessing of the Paschal Candle. Immediately after this, are read the Twelve Prophecies, which have reference to the mysteries of to-day's Service. As soon as the Prophecies are finished, a procession is formed to the Baptistery, and the Water is blessed. The matter of Baptism thus prepared, the Catechumens receive the Sacrament of Regeneration. Confirmation is then administered to them by the Bishop. Immediately after this, the Holy Sacrifice is celebrated in honour of our Lord's Resurrection, and the Neophytes partake of the Divine Mysteries. Finally, the joyous Vesper-Office comes in, and brings to a termination the longest and most trying Service of the Latin Liturgy. In order to assist our readers to enter fully into its spirit, we will go back a thousand years, and imagine ourselves to be celebrating this solemn Eve of Easter in one of the ancient Cathedrals of Italy, or of our own dear land.

At Rome, the Station is at Saint John Lateran, the Mother and Mistress of all Churches. The Sacrament of Regeneration is administered in the Baptistery of Constantine. The sight of these venerable Sanctuaries carries us back in thought to the 4th century; there, each year, holy Baptism is conferred upon some adult; and a numerous Ordination adds its own to the sacred pomp of this day, whose liturgy, as we have just said, is the richest of the whole year.

THE BLESSING OF THE NEW FIRE AND INCENSE.

Last Wednesday, the Catechumens were told to present themselves at the Church, for the hour of to-day's Tierce, (that is, nine o'clock in the morning). It is the final Scrutiny. The Priests are there to receive them; they who have not previously been examined upon the Symbol, are now questioned. The Lord's Prayer, and the biblical attributes of the four Evangelists, having been explained, one of the Priests dismisses the Candidates for Baptism, bidding them spend the interval in recollection and prayer.

At the hour of None, (our three o'clock in the afternoon,) the Bishop and all the Clergy repair to the Church, and Holy Saturday Vigil begins from this moment. The first ceremony consists in the blessing the new fire, which is to furnish light for the whole Service. It was the daily custom, in the first Ages of the Church, to strike a light from a flint, before Vespers: from this the lamps and candles were lighted for the celebration of that Hour, and the light thus procured was kept up in the Church till the Vespers of the following day. The Church of Rome observed this custom with great solemnity on Maundy Thursday morning, and the new fire received a special blessing. We learn from a letter written, in the 8th century, by Pope St. Zachary to St. Boniface, Archbishop of Mayence,—that three lamps were lighted from this fire, which were then removed to some safe place, and care was taken that their light was kept in. It was from these lamps that the light for Holy Saturday Night was taken. In the following century, under St. Leo the Fourth, whose Pontificate lasted from 847 to 855, the custom of every day procuring new fire from a flint was extended also to Holy Saturday.

It is not difficult to understand the meaning of this ceremony, which is now not observed by the Latin Church save on this day. Our Lord said of himself: *I am the Light of the world.*[1] Light, then, is an image of the Son of God. Stone, also, is one of the types under which the Scriptures speak to us of the Messias. St. Peter[2] and St. Paul,[3] quoting the words of the Prophet Isaias,[4] speak of Jesus as *the Corner-Stone.* The spark which is struck from the

---

[1] St. John, viii. 12.
[2] I. St. Peter, ii. 6.
[3] Eph. ii. 20.
[4] Is. xxviii. 16.

flint represents our Lord rising from his rock-hewn Sepulchre, through the Stone that had been rolled against it.

It is fitting, therefore, that this fire, which is to provide light for the Paschal Candle, as well as for those that are upon the Altar, should receive a special blessing, and be triumphantly shown to the Faithful. All the Lamps in the Church have been extinguished; formerly, the Faithful used to put out the fires in their houses, before going to the Church : they lighted them, on their return, with light taken from the blessed Fire, which they received as a symbol of our Lord's Resurrection. Let us not here omit to notice, that the putting out of all the lights in the Church is a symbol of the abrogation of the Old Law, which ended with the rending of the Veil of the Temple ; and that the new Fire represents the preaching of the New Law, whereby our Lord Jesus Christ, the Light of the World, fulfilled all the figures of the ancient Covenant.

In order to help our readers to enter more fully into the mystery of the ceremony we are describing, we will here mention a miracle which was witnessed for many centuries. The clergy and people of Jerusalem assembled for the Service of Easter Eve in the Church of Holy Sepulchre. After waiting for some time in silence, one of the lamps that were suspended over our Lord's Tomb, was miraculously lighted. The other lamps and torches throughout the Church were lighted from this, and the Faithful took its holy flame with them to their homes. It would seem, that this annual miracle first began after the Saracens had taken possession of Jerusalem ; God so ordaining, that it might be a proof to these Infidels of the Divinity of the Christian Religion. The historians of those times, who have written upon the Latin Kingdom of Jerusalem, all speak of this miracle as of an incontestable fact; and when Pope Urban the

Second went to France, there to preach the first Crusade, he brought forward this Miracle as one of the motives, which should inspire the Faithful with zeal for the defence of the Sepulchre of Christ. When our Lord, in the unsearchable ways of his justice, permitted Jerusalem to be re-conquered by the Infidels, the Miracle ceased, nor has it ever been witnessed from that time. Our readers have no doubt heard of the scandalous scene, which is now repeated every Holy Saturday in the Church of Holy Sepulchre in Jerusalem: we allude to the deception practised by the schismatic Greek Priests, whereby they persuade their deluded people that their ingenious trick for lighting a lamp is the continuation of the Miracle.

The Church also blesses the five grains of Incense, which are to be used in this Morning's Service. They represent the perfumes prepared by Magdalene and her holy companions for the embalming the Body of Jesus. The Prayer said by the Bishop, when blessing the Incense, not only shows us the connection there is between it and the Light, but it also teaches us what is the power these several sacred objects have against the wicked spirits.

The Bishop and his attendants go, in procession, from the Church to the place where he is to bless the Fire and Incense. The Fire, as we have already said, is the symbol of our Lord Jesus Christ; and the Sepulchre, whence he is to rise to life, is outside the walls of Jerusalem. The holy Women and the Apostles, when they go to the Sepulchre, will have to go forth from the City.

The Bishop, having come to the appointed place, blesses the Fire by the following Prayers.

℣. The Lord be with you.	℣. Dominus vobiscum.
℟. And with thy spirit.	℟. Et cum spiritu tuo.
LET US PRAY.	OREMUS.
O God, who by thy Son, the	Deus, qui per Filium tu-

um, angularem scilicet lapidem, claritatis tuæ ignem fidelibus contulisti, productum e silice, nostris profuturum usibus, novum hunc ignem sanctifica; et concede nobis, ita per hæc festa Paschalia cœlestibus desideriis inflammari; ut ad perpetuæ claritatis, puris mentibus, valeamus festa pertingere. Per eumdem Christum Dominum nostrum.
℟. Amen.

corner-stone, hast bestowed on the faithful the fire of thy brightness; sanctify this new fire produced from a flint for our use: and grant, that during this Paschal festival, we may be so inflamed with heavenly desires, that with pure minds we may come to the solemnity of eternal splendour. Through the same Christ our Lord.
℟. Amen.

OREMUS.

Domine Deus, Pater omnipotens, lumen indeficiens, qui es conditor omnium luminum: benedic hoc lumen, quod a te sanctificatum atque benedictum est, qui illuminasti omnem mundum: ut ab eo lumine accendamur, atque illuminemur igne claritatis tuæ; et sicut illuminasti Moysen exeuntem de Ægypto, ita illumines corda et sensus nostros; ut ad vitam et lucem æternam pervenire mereamur. Per Christum Dominum nostrum.
℟. Amen.

LET US PRAY.

O Lord God, Almighty Father, never failing light, who art the author of all light: bless this light, that is blessed and sanctified by thee, who hast enlightened the whole world: that we may be enlightened by that light, and inflamed with the fire of thy brightness: and as thou didst give light to Moses, when he went out of Egypt, so illumine our hearts and senses, that we may obtain light and life everlasting. Through Christ our Lord.
℟. Amen.

OREMUS.

Domine sancte, Pater omnipotens, æterne Deus, benedicentibus nobis hunc ignem in nomine tuo, et unigeniti Filii tui Dei ac Domini nostri Jesu Christi, et Spiritus Sancti, cooperare digneris, et adjuva nos

LET US PRAY.

O Holy Lord, Almighty Father, Eternal God: vouchsafe to co-operate with us, who bless this fire in thy name, and in that of thy only Son Christ Jesus, our Lord and God, and of the Holy Ghost: assist us against the fiery darts

of the enemy, and illumine us with thy heavenly grace. Who livest and reignest with the same only Son and Holy Ghost, one God, for ever and ever.
℞. Amen.

contra ignita tela inimici, et illustra gratia cœlesti. Qui vivis et regnas cum eodem Unigenito tuo et Spiritu Sancto, Deus, per omnia sæcula sæculorum.
℞. Amen.

The Bishop then blesses the Incense, thus addressing himself in prayer to God:

Pour forth, we beseech thee, O Almighty God, thy abundant blessing on this Incense: and kindle, O invisible regenerator, the brightness of this night: that not only the sacrifice that is offered this night may shine by the secret mixture of thy light; but also into whatever place any thing of this mysterious sanctification shall be brought, there, by the power of thy majesty, all the malicious artifices of the devil may be defeated. Through Christ our Lord.

℞. Amen.

Veniat, quæsumus, omnipotens Deus, super hoc incensum largæ tuæ benedictionis infusio: et hunc nocturnum splendorem invisibilis regenerator accende: ut non solum sacrificium, quod hac nocte litatum est, arcana luminis tui admixtione refulgeat: sed in quocumque loco ex hujus sanctificationis mysterio aliquid fuerit deportatum, expulsa diabolicæ fraudis nequitia, virtus tuæ Majestatis assistat. Per Christum Dominum nostrum.
℞. Amen.

After these prayers, an Acolyte puts some of the blessed Fire into the thurible. The Bishop then censes the Fire and the Incense, after having first sprinkled them with holy water. An other of the Acolytes lights a candle from the blessed Fire, that the new light may be brought into the Church. The Deacon then vests in a white Dalmatic. This festive colour, which contrasts so strongly with the purple cope worn by the Bishop, is worn on account of the joyful ministry which the Deacon is about to fulfil. He takes into his right hand a Reed, on the top of which is placed a triple-branched candle. The Reed is in memory of our Lord's Passion: it also expresses the weakness of the Human Nature, which he assumed to himself by the Incarnation. The three-branch candle signifies the blessed Trinity, of which the Incarnate Word is the Second Person.

The Procession returns. Having entered the Church, the Deacon, after advancing a few steps, lowers the Reed, and the Acolyte, who carries the new light, lights one of the three branches of the candle. The Deacon then kneels, as do also all the clergy and people. Raising the light on high, he sings these words:

Lumen Christi. The Light of Christ!

All answer:

Deo gratias. Thanks be to God!

This first showing of the Light expresses the revelation made to us, by Jesus, of the Divinity of the Father. *No one,* says he, *knoweth the Father, but the Son, and he to whom it shall please the Son to reveal him.*[1]

After this, all rise, and the Procession advances as far as mid-way up the Church. Here, the Deacon again lowers the Reed, and a second branch of the Candle is lighted by the Acolyte. The same ceremonies are observed as before, and the Deacon sings on a higher note:

Lumen Christi. The Light of Christ!

The whole assembly answers:

Deo gratias. Thanks be to God!

---

[1] St. Matth. xi. 27.

This second showing of the Light signifies the world's receiving the knowledge of the Divinity of the Son; he appeared and dwelt among us, and, with his own sacred lips, taught us that he was God, equal to the Father in all things.

The procession continues as far as the Altar-steps. The third branch of the Candle on the Reed is lighted, and the Deacon once more sings, but on a still higher and gladder note:

The Light of Christ!   Lumen Christi.

Again, the response is made:

Thanks be to God!   Deo gratias.

This third showing of the Light signifies the revelation of the Divinity of the Holy Ghost, which was made to us by our Saviour when he commanded his Apostles to do what the Church is to do this very Night: *Teach ye all nations, baptising them in the name of the Father, and of the Son, and of the Holy Ghost.*[1] It is, then, by Jesus, who is *the Light of the world*, that mankind has been taught to know the Blessed Trinity. The Bishop, before administering Baptism to the Catechumens, will ask them if they believe in this great Mystery. During the whole of this Night's Service, they will have before their eyes the expressive symbol of the Trinity,—the three-branch Candle.

This, then, is the first use to which the new Fire is put:—to proclaim the Holy Trinity. It is next to publish the glory of the Incarnate Word, by lighting up the glorious symbol which is now to be brought before us. The Bishop is seated on his throne. The Deacon kneels before him, and asks a

---

[1] St. Matth. xxviii. 19.

blessing, before beginning the great work intrusted to him. The Pontiff thus blesses him.

| Dominus sit in corde tuo, et in labiis tuis : ut digne et competenter annunties suum Paschale præconium. In nomine Patris, et Filii, et Spiritus Sancti. Amen. | The Lord be in thy heart and lips, that thou mayest worthily and fitly proclaim his Paschal praise. In the name of the Father, and of the Son, and of the Holy Ghost. Amen. |

Thus prepared, the Deacon rises, and goes to the Ambo. The Acolytes, holding the triple Candle and the five grains of Incense, are standing at his side. Near the Ambo is a marble pillar, on which is fixed the Paschal Candle.

THE PASCHAL CANDLE.

The sun is setting, and our earth will soon be mantled in darkness. The Church has provided a torch, which is to spread its light upon us during the whole of this long Vigil. It is of an unusual size. It stands alone, and is of a pillar-like form. It is the symbol of Christ. Before being lighted, its scriptural type is the pillar of a cloud, which hid the Israelites when they went out from Egypt; under this form, it is the figure of our Lord, when lying lifeless in the tomb. When lighted, we must see in it both the pillar of fire, which guided the people of God, and the glory of our Jesus risen from his grave. Our holy mother the Church, would have us enthusiastically love this glorious symbol, and speaks its praises to us in all the magnificence of her inspired eloquence. As early as the beginning of the 5th century, Pope St. Zozimus extended to all the Churches of the City of Rome, the privilege of blessing the Paschal Candle, although Baptism was administered no where but in the Baptistery of St. John Lateran. The object of this grant was, that all

HOLY SATURDAY: MORNING SERVICE. 561

the Faithful might share in the holy impressions which so solemn a rite is intended to produce. It was for the same intention that, later, every Church, even though it had no Baptismal Font, was permitted to have the Blessing of the Paschal Candle.

The Deacon proclaims the Easter Solemnity to the people, whilst chanting the praises of this sacred object: and whilst celebrating the glory of Him, whose emblem it is, he becomes the herald of the Resurrection. The Altar, the Sanctuary, the Bishop, all are in the sombre colour of the Lenten rite; the Deacon alone is vested in white. At other times, he would not presume to raise his voice as he is now going to do, in the solemn tone of a Preface: but this is the Eve of the Resurrection, and the Deacon, as the interpreters of the Liturgy tell us, represents Magdalene and the holy women, on whom our Lord conferred the honour of being the first to know his Resurrection, and to whom he gave the mission of preaching to the very Apostles, that he had risen from the dead, and would meet them in Galilee.

But let us listen to the thrilling *Exsultet* of our Deacon, and learn from him the joys that await us on this wonderful Night.

Let now the heavenly troops of Angels rejoice: let the divine mysteries be joyfully celebrated: and let a sacred trumpet proclaim the victory of so great a King. Let the earth also be filled with joy, being illuminated with such resplendent rays; and let it be sensible that the darkness, which overspread the whole world, is chased away by the splendour of our eternal King. Let our Mother, the Church, be also glad finding herself adorned with the rays of so great a	Exsultet jam angelica turba cœlorum; exsultent divina mysteria: et pro tanti Regis victoria, tuba insonet salutaris. Gaudeat et tellus tantis irradiata fulgoribus: et æterni Regis splendore illustrata, totius orbis se sentiat amisisse caliginem. Lætetur et mater Ecclesia, tanti luminis adornata fulgoribus: et magnis populorum vocibus hæc aula resultet. Quapropter adstantes vos, fratres charissimi, ad tam miram hujus sancti

luminis claritatem, una mecum, quæso, Dei omnipotentis misericordiam invocate. Ut qui me non meis meritis intra Levitarum numerum dignatus est aggregare : luminis sui claritatem infundens, Cerei hujus laudem implere perficiat. Per Dominum nostrum Jesum Christum Filium suum : qui cum eo vivit et regnat in unitate Spiritus Sancti Deus, per omnia sæcula sæculorum.

℟. Amen.
℣. Domimus vobiscum.
℟. Et cum spiritu tuo.
℣. Sursum corda.
℟. Habemus ad Dominum.
℣. Gratias agamus Domino Deo nostro.
℟. Dignum et justum est.

Vere dignum et justum est invisibilem Deum Patrem omnipotentem, Filiumque ejus unigenitum, Dominum nostrum Jesum Christum, toto cordis ac mentis affectu, et vocis ministerio personare. Qui pro nobis æterno Patri Adæ debitum solvit : et veteris piaculi cautionem pio cruore detersit. Hæc sunt enim festa Paschalia, in quibus verus ille Agnus occiditur, cujus sanguine postes fidelium consecrantur.

Hæc nox est, in qua primum patres nostros filios Israël eductos de Ægypto, light : and let this temple resound with the joyful acclamations of the people. Wherefore, beloved brethren, you who are now present at the admirable brightness of this holy light, I beseech you to invoke with me the mercy of Almighty God. That he, who has been pleased, above my desert, to admit me into the number of his Levites, will, by an infusion of his light upon me, enable me to celebrate the praises of this Candle. Through our Lord Jesus Christ his Son, who, with him and the Holy Ghost, liveth and reigneth one God for ever and ever.

℟. Amen.
℣. The Lord be with you.
℟. And with thy spirit.
℣. Lift up your hearts.
℟. We have them fixed on God.
℣. Let us give thanks to the Lord our God.
℟. It is meet and just.

It is truly meet and just to proclaim with all the affection of our heart and soul, and with the sound of our voice, the invisible God the Father Almighty, and his only Son our Lord Jesus Christ. Who paid for us to his eternal Father, the debt of Adam : and by his sacred blood cancelled the guilt contracted by original sin. For this is the Paschal solemnity, in which the true Lamb was slain, by whose Blood the doors of the faithful are consecrated.

This is the Night in which thou formerly broughtest forth our forefathers the children of

Israel out of Egypt, leading them dry-foot through the Red Sea. This, then, is the Night which dissipated the darkness of sin, by the light of the pillar. This is the Night, which now delivers all over the world those that believe in Christ, from the vices of the world, and darkness of sin, restores them to grace, and clothes them with sanctity. This is the Night in which Christ broke the chains of death, and ascended conqueror from hell. For it availed us nothing to be born, unless it had availed us to be redeemed.

O how admirable is thy goodness towards us! O how inestimable is thy love! Thou hast delivered up thy Son to redeem a slave. O truly necessary sin of Adam, which the death of Christ has blotted out! O happy fault, that merited such and so great a Redeemer!

O truly blessed Night, which alone deserved to know the time and hour when Christ rose again from hell. This is the Night of which it is written: *And the Night shall be as light as the day, and the Night is my illumination in my delights.* Therefore the santification of this Night blots out crimes, washes away sins, and restores innocence to sinners, and joy to the sorrowful. It banishes enmities, produces concord, and humbles empires.

mare Rubrum sicco vestigio transire fecisti. Hæc igitur nox est, quæ peccatorum tenebras columnæ illuminatione purgavit. Hæc nox est, quæ hodie per universum mundum, in Christo credentes, a vitiis sæculi, et caligine peccatorum segregatos reddit gratiæ, sociat sanctitati. Hæc nox est in qua destructis vinculis mortis, Christus ab inferis victor ascendit. Nihil enim nobis nasci profuit, nisi redimi profuisset.

O mira circa nos tuæ pietatis dignatio! O inæstimabilis dilectio charitatis! ut servum redimeres, filium tradidisti. O certe necessarium Adæ peccatum, quod Christi morte deletum est! O felix culpa, quæ talem ac tantum meruit habere redemptorem!

O vere beata nox, quæ sola meruit scire tempus et horam, in qua Christus ab inferis resurrexit. Hæc nox est, de qua scriptum est: Et nox sicut dies illuminabitur; et: Nox illuminatio mea in deliciis meis. Hujus igitur santificatio noctis, fugat scelera, culpas lavat: et reddit innocentiam lapsis, et mæstis lætitiam. Fugat odia, concordiam parat, et curvat imperia.

Here the Deacon pauses, and taking the five grains

of Incense, he fixes them in the Candle in the form of a Cross. They represent the Five Wounds received by our Lord upon the Cross; as also, the perfumes which Magdalene and her companions had prepared for embalming his Body in the Tomb. Thus far, as we have already explained, the Paschal Candle is the figure of the Man-God not yet glorified by the Resurrection.

In hujus igitur noctis gratia, suscipe, sancte Pater, incensi hujus sacrificium vespertinum quod tibi in hac Cerei oblatione solemni, per ministrorum manus de operibus apum, sacrosancta reddit Ecclesia. Sed jam columnæ hujus præconia novimus, quam in honorem Dei rutilans ignis accendit.	Therefore on this sacred Night, receive, O holy Father, the evening sacrifice of this incense, which thy holy church by the hands of her ministers, presents to thee in the solemn oblation of this wax Candle made out of the labour of bees. And now we know the excellence of this pillar, which the sparkling fire lights for the honour of God.

After these words, the Deacon again pauses, and taking the Reed which holds the triple candle, he lights the Paschal Candle with one of its branches. This signifies the instant of our Lord's Resurrection, when the divine power restored his Body to life, by uniting with it the Soul which death had separated. The glorious Symbol of Christ, our Light, is now perfect; and holy Church exults in the thought of soon beholding her heavenly Spouse triumph over death.

Qui licet sit divisus in partes, mutuati tamen luminis detrimenta non novit. Alitur enim liquantibus ceris, quas in substantiam pretiosæ hujus lampadis, apis mater eduxit.	Which fire, though now divided, suffers no loss from the communication of its light. Because it is fed by the melted wax, which its mother, the bee, made for the composition of the precious torch.

Here are lighted, from the new fire, the lamps of the Church. They are lighted after the Paschal

HOLY SATURDAY : MORNING SERVICE. 565

Candle, to signify, that Jesus' Resurrection was made known gradually. It also tells us, that *our* Resurrection is to be a consequence and a likeness of that of our Saviour, who opens to us the way, whereby, after having, like him, passed through the tomb, we shall enter into life everlasting.

O truly blessed Night! which plundered the Egyptians, and enriched the Hebrews. A Night, in which things heavenly are united with those of earth, and divine with human. We beseech thee therefore, O Lord, that this Candle, consecrated to the honour of thy name, may continue burning to dissipate the darkness of this night. And being accepted as a sweet-smelling savour, may be united with the celestial lights. Let the morning-star find it burning. I mean that Star which never sets. Who being returned from hell, shone with brightness on mankind.

We beseech thee therefore, O Lord, to grant us peaceable times during these Paschal solemnities, and with thy constant protection to rule, govern, and preserve us thy servants, and all the clergy, and the devout people, together with our holy Father Pope *N.*, and our Bishop *N.*[1] (Regard also our most devout Emperor: and since thou knowest, O God, the desires of his heart, grant by the ineffable grace of thy goodness and mercy, that he

O vere beata nox quæ exspoliavit Ægyptios, ditavit Hebræos. Nox, in qua terrenis cœlestia, humanis divina junguntur. Oramus ergo te Domine : ut Cereus iste in honorem tui nominis consecratus, ad noctis hujus caliginem destruendam, indeficiens perseveret. Et in odorem suavitatis acceptus, supernis luminaribus misceatur. Flammas ejus Lucifer matutinus inveniat. Ille, inquam, Lucifer, qui nescit occasum. Ille, qui regressus ab inferis, humano generi serenus illuxit.

Precamur ergo te Domine: ut nos famulos tuos, omnemque clerum, et devotissimum populum : una cum beatissimo Papa nostro N. et Antistite nostro N. quiete temporum concessa, in his Paschalibus gaudiis, assidua protectione regere, gubernare, et conservare digneris. (Respice etiam ad devotissimum Imperatorem nostrum N., cujus tu, Deus, desiderii vota prænoscens, ineffabili pietatis et misericordiæ tuæ

---

[1] The words here put in parentheses are only said in those countries, which are subject to the Emperor of Austria. See above, *page* 481.

munere, tranquillum perpetuæ pacis accommoda: et cœlestem victoriam cum omni populo suo.) Per eumdem Dominum nostrum Jesum Christum Fillium tuum: qui tecum vivit et regnat in unitate Spiritus Sancti Deus, per omnia sæcula sæculorum.

℞. Amen.

may enjoy with all his people the tranquillity of perpetual peace and heavenly victory.) Through the same Lord Jesus Christ thy Son: who, with thee and the Holy Ghost, liveth and reigneth one God for ever and ever.

℞. Amen.

Here, the Deacon takes off the white Dalmatic, vests in purple, and returns to the Bishop. Then begin the *Prophecies* from the Old Testament.

THE PROPHECIES.

The Torch of the Resurrection now sheds its light from the Ambo throughout the holy place, and gladdens the hearts of the Faithful. How solemn a preparation for what is now to engage our attention, —the Baptism of the Catechumens, whose instruction and progress in good works we have followed with such interest during the past forty days! They are assembled together under the outward porch of the Church. The Priests are performing over them the preparatory rites, which embody such profound teaching, and were instituted by the Apostles. First of all, the sign of the cross is made upon their foreheads; and then, the Priest, imposing his hand upon the head of each Catechumen, adjures Satan to depart from this soul and body, and give place to Christ. Imitating thus our Redeemer, the Priest then touches with his spittle the ears, saying: "Be ye opened!" He does the same to the nostrils, and says: "Breathe ye in the sweetness of fragrance!" The Neophyte is next anointed, on the breast and between the shoulders, with the Oil of Catechumens: but, as this ceremony expresses his having to fight the spiritual combat, the Priest first receives from him the promise to renounce Satan, with his works and pomps.

These rites are performed first over the men, and then over the women. The children of Christian parents are also admitted to take their place among the Catechumens. If any of these latter be labouring under any sickness, and have notwithstanding come to the Church in order to receive, to-night, the grace of Regeneration,—a Priest says over them a Prayer, in which he fervently begs of God to heal them, and confound the malice of Satan.

These ceremonies, which are called the *Catechisation*, occupy a considerable portion of time, on account of the great number of the aspirants to Baptism. It is for this reason, that the Bishop came to the Church at the hour of None (three o'clock in the afternoon), and that the great Vigil began so early. Whilst these rites are being administered to the Catechumens, the rest of the Faithful are listening to appropriate passages from the Scripture, which are being read from the Ambo, and which are the complement of the Lenten Instructions.

These Lessons are twelve in number: but in the venerable Basilica, where we are now supposing ourselves to be, we may say they are twenty-four, since each of the Twelve is read in Latin first, and then in Greek. In order to fix the attention, and excite the devotion, of her children to what she reads to them, the Church, after each Lesson, recites a Prayer, which sums up the doctrine expressed in the preceding Prophecy. To some of them is added an appropriate Canticle from the Old Testament, and it is sung, by the whole assembly, to the well known melody of the *Tract*. The aspirants to Baptism, as soon as they have received the ceremonies of *Catechisation*, are allowed to enter the Church, where, in the place assigned to them, they listen to the Lessons, and join in the Prayers:—how could they better continue their preparation for the great Sacrament? And yet, there is an aspect of mournfulness about this portion of the Service, which tells us that the longed-for hour is not yet come. Frequent genuflexions, and the sombre coloured Vestments, strongly contrast with the beautiful flame of the Paschal Torch, which sheds its silent beams of light upon the Faithful. Their hearts are still throbbing with the emotions excited within them by the *Exsultet:* they are impatient to see their Jesus' Resurrection fulfilled in the Baptism of the Catechumens.

FIRST PROPHECY.

(Genesis, CHAP. I.)

This first Lesson speaks to us of the *Creation,* of the *Spirit of God moving over the waters,* of the separation of *light from darkness,* and of *Man's* being made to the likeness of his God. This work of the Creator had been deranged and spoiled by Satan's malice. The time is come, when it is to recover all its beauty. The Holy Ghost is about to effect this regeneration by *Water;* Christ, our *Light,* is going to rise from the darkness of the tomb; the image of God is to re-appear in Man, for he is to be cleansed by the Blood of his Redeemer, who is the new *Adam,* that came down from heaven, in order to re-instate, in all his rights, the old and earthly Adam.

In principio creavit Deus cœlum et terram. Terra autem erat inanis, et vacua: et tenebræ erant super faciem abyssi: et Spiritus Dei ferebatur super aquas. Dixitque Deus: Fiat lux. Et facta est lux. Et vidit Deus lucem, quod esset bona; et divisit lucem a tenebris. Appellavitque lucem, Di-

In the beginning God created heaven and earth. And the earth was void and empty, and darkness was upon the face of the deep; and the Spirit of God moved over the waters. And God said: Be light made. And light was made. And God saw the light that it was good: and he divided the light from the darkness. And he called the light day, and the darkness night; and there was evening and morning one day.

And God said: Let there be a firmament made amidst the waters: and let it divide the waters from the waters. And God made a firmament, and divided the waters that were under the firmament from those that were above the firmament. And it was so. And God called the firmament, Heaven: and the evening and morning were the second day.

God also said: Let the waters that are under the heaven be gathered together into one place: and let the dry land appear. And it was so done. And God called the dry land Earth: and the gathering together of the waters he called Seas. And God saw that it was good. And he said: Let the earth bring forth the green herb, and such as may seed, and the fruit tree yielding fruit after its kind, which may have seed in itself upon the earth. And it was so done. And the earth brought forth the green herb, and such as yieldeth seed according to its kind, and the tree that beareth fruit, having seed each one according to its kind. And God saw that it was good. And the evening and the morning were the third day.

And God said: Let there be lights made in the firmament of heaven, to divide the day and the night, and let them

em: et tenebras, Noctem. Factumque est vespere et mane, dies unus.

Dixit quoque Deus: Fiat firmamentum in medio aquarum, et dividat aquas ab aquis. Et fecit Deus firmamentum: divisitque aquas, quæ erant sub firmamento, ab his quæ erant super firmamentum. Et factum est ita. Vocavitque Deus firmamentum, Cœlum. Et factum est vespere et mane, dies secundus.

Dixit vero Deus: Congregentur aquæ, quæ sub cœlo sunt, in locum unum et appareat arida. Factumque est ita. Et vocavit Deus aridam Terram: congregationesque aquarum appellavit Maria. Et vidit Deus quod esset bonum, et ait: Germinet terra herbam virentem, et facientem semen: et lignum pomiferum faciens fructum juxta genus suum, cujus semen in semetipso sit super terram. Et factum est ita. Et protulit terra herbam virentem, et facientem semen juxta genus suum, lignumque faciens fructum: et habens unumquodque sementem secundum speciem suam. Et vidit Deus quod esset bonum: et factum est vespere et mane, dies tertius.

Dixit autem Deus: Fiant luminaria in firmamento cœli, et dividant diem ac noctem: et sint in signa et tempora, et dies, et annos: et luceant in firmamento cœli, et illuminent terram. Et factum est ita. Fecitque Deus duo luminaria magna, luminare majus, ut præesset diei: et luminare minus, ut præesset nocti: et stellas. Et posuit eas in firmamento cœli, ut lucerent super terram: et præessent diei ac nocti, et dividerent lucem ac tenebras. Et vidit Deus quod esset bonum. Et factum est vespere et mane, dies quartus.

Dixit etiam Deus: Producant aquæ reptile animæ viventis, et volatile super terram, sub firmamento cœli. Creavitque Deus cete grandia, et omnem animam viventem atque motabilem, quam produxerant aquæ in species suas: et omne volatile, secundum genus suum. Et vidit Deus quod esset bonum: benedixitque eis, dicens: Crescite, et multiplicamini, et replete aquas maris: avesque multiplicentur super terram. Et factum est vespere et mane, dies quintus.

Dixit quoque Deus: Producat terra animam viventem in genere suo: jumenta, et reptilia, et bestias terræ, secundum species suas. Factumque est ita. Et fecit Deus bestias terræ juxta species suas: et jumenta, et omne reptile terræ in genere suo. Et vidit Deus quod

be for signs, and for seasons, and for days and years; to shine in the firmament of heaven, and to give light upon the earth. And it was so done. And God made two great lights; a greater light to rule the day, and a lesser light to rule the night; and stars. And he set them in the firmament of heaven, to shine upon the earth. And to rule the day and the night, and to divide the light and the darkness. And God saw that it was good. And the evening and morning were the fourth day.

God also said: Let the waters bring forth the creeping creature having life, and the fowl that may fly over the earth under the firmament of heaven. And God created the great whales, and every living and moving creature, which the waters brought forth, according to their kinds, and every winged fowl according to its kind. And God saw that it was good. And he blessed them, saying: Increase and multiply, and fill the waters of the sea; and let the birds be multiplied upon the earth. And the evening and morning were the fifth day.

And God said: Let the earth bring forth the living creature in its kind, cattle, and creeping things, and beasts of the earth according to their kinds; and it was so done. And God made the beasts of the earth according to their kinds, and cattle, and everything that creepeth on the earth after its kind. And God saw that it was good. And he said : Let us make man to our image and likeness, and let him have dominion over the fishes of the sea, and the fowls of the air, and the beasts, and the whole earth, and every creeping creature that moveth upon the earth.

And God created man to his own image : to the image of God he created him: male and female he created them. And God blessed them, saying : Increase and multiply, and fill the earth, and subdue it, and rule over the fishes of the sea, and the fowls of the air, and all living creatures that move upon the earth. And God said : Behold I have given you every herb bearing seed upon the earth, and all trees that have in themselves seed of their own kind, to be your meat : and to all beasts of the earth, and to every fowl of the air, and to all that move upon the earth, and wherein there is life, that you may have to feed upon. And it was so done. And God saw all the things that he had made, and they were very good. And the evening and morning were the sixth day.

So the heavens and earth were finished, and all the furniture of them. And on the seventh day God ended his work which he had made : and he rested on the seventh day from all his work which he had done.

esset bonum : et ait : Faciamus hominem ad imaginem et similitudinem nostram : et præsit piscibus maris, et volatilibus cœli, et bestiis, universæque terræ, omnique reptili quod movetur in terra.

Et creavit Deus hominem ad imaginem suam : ad imaginem Dei creavit illum : masculum et feminam creavit eos. Benedixitque illis Deus, et ait : Crescite, et multiplicamini, et replete terram, et subjicite eam : et dominamini piscibus maris, et volatilibus cœli, et universis animantibus, quæ moventur super terram. Dixitque Deus : Ecce dedi vobis omnem herbam afferentem semen super terram : et universa ligna, quæ habent in semetipsis sementem generis sui : ut sint vobis in escam, et cunctis animantibus terræ, omnique volucri cœli, et universis quæ moventur in terra, et in quibus est anima vivens, ut habeant ad vescendum. Et factum est ita. Viditque Deus cuncta quæ fecerat : et erant valde bona. Et factum est vespere et mane, dies sextus.

Igitur perfecti sunt cœli et terra, et omnis ornatus eorum. Complevitque Deus die septimo opus suum, quod fecerat : et requievit die septimo ab universo opere quod patrarat.

After the Lesson, the Bishop says:

Oremus. Let us pray.

The Deacon, addressing the Faithful:

Flectamus genua. Let us kneel down

The Subdeacon:

Levate. Stand up again.

The Bishop then says this Prayer:

Deus, qui mirabiliter creasti hominem, et mirabilius redemisti: da nobis, quæsumus, contra oblectamenta peccati, mentis ratione, persistere: ut mereamur ad æterna gaudia pervenire. Per Dominum.	O God, who didst wonderfully create man, and redeem him by a still greater wonder: grant us, we beseech thee, such strength of mind and reason against all the allurements of sin, that we may deserve to obtain eternal joys. Through, &c.
℞. Amen.	℞. Amen.

SECOND PROPHECY.

(Genesis, CHAP. V.)

The second Lesson gives us the history of the *Deluge*. God makes the *Waters* serve as the minister of his justice, those very *Waters* which were, afterwards, by Jesus, to become the instrument of his mercy; the *Ark*, which is a type of the Church, is the shelter for those who would be saved from the flood; the human race is preserved by one family, which represents the Disciples of Christ, who, at first, were few in number, but afterwards peopled the whole earth.

Noe vero cum quingentorum esset annorum, genuit Sem, Cham et Japhet. Cumque cœpissent homines	And Noe, when he was five hundred years old, begot Sem, Cham, and Japheth. And after that men began to be

multiplied upon the earth, and daughters were born unto them, the sons of God seeing the daughters of men, that they were fair, took to themselves wives of all which they chose. And God said: My spirit shall not remain in man for ever, because he is flesh: and his days shall be one hundred and twenty years.

Now giants were upon the earth in those days. For after the sons of God went in to the daughters of men, and they brought forth children, these are the mighty men of old, men of renown. And God seeing that the wickedness of men was great on the earth, and that all the thought of their heart was bent upon evil at all times, it repented him that he had made man on the earth. And being touched inwardly with sorrow of heart, he said: I will destroy man, whom I have created, from the face of the earth, from man even to beasts, from the creeping thing even to the fowls of the air, for it repenteth me that I have made them.

But Noe found grace before the Lord. These are the generations of Noe: Noe was a just and perfect man in his generation, he walked with God. And he begot three sons, Sem, Cham, and Japheth. And the earth was corrupted before God, and was filled with iniquity. And when God had seen that the earth was corrupted, (for all flesh had

multiplicari super terram, et filias procreassent: videntes filii Dei filias hominum quod essent pulchræ, acceperunt sibi uxores ex omnibus, quas elegerant. Dixitque Deus: Non permanebit spiritus meus in homine in æternum, quia caro est: eruntque dies illius centum viginti annorum.

Gigantes autem erant super terram in diebus illis. Postquam enim ingressi sunt filii Dei ad filias hominum, illæque genuerunt: isti sunt potentes a sœculo viri famosi. Videns autem Deus, quod multa malitia hominum esset in terra, et cuncta cogitatio cordis intenta esset ad malum omni tempore, pœnituit eum, quod hominem fecisset in terra. Et tactus dolore cordis intrinsecus: Delebo (inquit) hominem quem creavi, a facie terræ, ab homine usque ad animantia, a reptili usque ad volucres cœli: pœnitet enim me fecisse eos.

Noe vero invenit gratiam coram Domino. Hæ sunt generationes Noe. Noe vir justus atque perfectus fuit in generationibus suis, cum Deo ambulavit, et genuit tres filios, Sem, Cham et Japhet. Corrupta est autem terra coram Deo, et repleta est iniquitate. Cumque vidisset Deus terram esse corruptam (omnis quippe caro corruperat viam suam super terram) dixit ad Noe: Finis universæ carnis venit coram me: repleta est terra iniquitate a facie eorum: et ego disperdam eos cum terra. Fac tibi arcam de lignis lævigatis. Mansiunculas in arca facies: et bitumine linies intrinsecus et extrinsecus. Et sic facies eam. Trecentorum cubitorum erit longitudo arcæ: quinquaginta cubitorum latitudo: et triginta cubitorum altitudo illius. Fenestram in arca facies: et in cubito consummabis summitatem ejus. Ostium autem arcæ pones ex latere deorsum. Cœnacula et tristega facies in ea. Ecce ego adducam aquas diluvii super terram: ut interficiam omnem carnem, in qua spiritus vitæ est subter cœlum, et universa, quæ in terra sunt, consumentur. Ponamque fœdus meum tecum: et ingredieris arcam tu, filii tui, uxor tua, et uxores filiorum tuorum tecum. Et ex cunctis animantibus universæ carnis bina induces in arcam, ut vivant tecum, masculini sexus et feminini. De volucribus juxta genus suum, et de jumentis in genere suo, et ex omni reptili terræ secundum genus suum: bina de omnibus ingredientur tecum, ut possint vivere. Tolles igitur tecum ex omnibus escis, quæ mandi possunt, et comportabis apud te: et erunt tam tibi, quam illis in cibum. Fecit igitur Noe

corrupted its way upon the earth,) he said to Noe: The end of all flesh is come before me, and the earth is filled with iniquity through them, and I will destroy them with the earth. Make thee an ark of timber planks: thou shalt make little rooms in the ark, and thou shalt pitch it within and without. And thus shalt thou make it. The length of the ark shall be three hundred cubits: the breadth of it fifty cubits, and the height of it thirty cubits. Thou shalt make a window in the ark, and in a cubit shalt thou finish the top of it: and the door of the ark shalt thou set in the side: with lower, middle chambers, and third stories shalt thou make it. Behold I will bring the waters of a great flood upon the earth, to destroy all flesh, wherein is the breath of life, under heaven. All things that are in the earth shall be consumed. And I will establish my covenant with thee: and thou shalt enter into the ark, thou and thy sons, and thy wife, and the wives of thy sons with thee. And of every living creature of all flesh, thou shalt bring two of a sort into the ark, that they may live with thee; of the male sex, and the female. Of fowls according to their kind, and of beasts in their kind, and of every thing that creepeth upon the earth according to its kind; two of every sort shall go in with thee, that they may live. Thou shalt take unto thee of all food that may be eaten, and thou shalt lay it up with thee : and it shall be food for thee and them. And Noe did all things which God commanded him.

And he was six hundred years old, when the waters of the flood overflowed the earth. All the fountains of the great deep were broken up, and the flood-gates of heaven were opened. And the rain fell upon the earth forty days and forty nights. In the self-same day Noe, and Sem, and Cham, and Japheth, his sons : his wife, and the three wives of his sons with them, went into the ark: they and every beast according to its kind, and all the cattle in their kind, and every thing that moveth upon the earth according to its kind, and every fowl according to its kind, all birds, and all that fly. And the ark was carried upon the waters. And the waters prevailed beyond measure upon the earth : and all the high mountains under the whole heaven were covered. The water was fifteen cubits higher than the mountains, which it covered. And all flesh was destroyed that moved upon the earth, both of fowl, and of cattle, and of beasts, and of all creeping things that creep upon the earth : and Noe only remained, and they that were with him in the ark. And the waters prevailed upon the earth a hundred and fifty days.

And God remembered Noe, and all the living creatures,

omnia, quæ præceperat illi Deus.

Eratque sexcentorum annorum, quando diluvii aquæ inundaverunt super terram. Rupti sunt omnes fontes abyssi magnæ, et cataractæ cœli apertæ sunt : et facta est pluvia super terram quadraginta diebus et quadraginta noctibus. In articulo diei illius ingressus est Noe, et Sem, et Cham, et Japhet, filii ejus, uxor illius, et tres uxores filiorum ejus, cum eis in arcam : ipsi et omne animal, secundum genus suum, universaque jumenta in genere suo, et omne quod movetur super terram in genere suo, cunctumque volatile secundum genus suum. Porro arca ferebatur super aquas. Et aquæ prævaluerunt nimis super terram : opertique sunt omnes montes excelsi sub universo cœlo. Quindecim cubitis altior fuit aqua super montes, quos operuerat. Consumptaque est omnis caro, quæ movebatur super terram, volucrum, animantium, bestiarum, omniumque reptilium quæ reptant super terram. Remansit autem solus Noe, et qui cum eo erant, in arca. Obtinueruntque aquæ terram centum quinquaginta diebus.

Recordatus autem Deus Noe, cunctorumque animantium, et omnium jumentorum, quæ erant cum eo in arca: adduxit spiritum super terram, et imminutæ sunt aquæ. Et clausi sunt fontes abyssi, et cataractæ cœli: et prohibitæ sunt pluviæ de cœlo. Reversæque sunt aquæ de terra euntes et redeuntes: et cæperunt minui post centum quinquaginta dies. Cumque transissent quadraginta dies, aperiens Noe fenestram arcæ quam fecerat, dimisit corvum. Qui egrediebatur, et non revertebatur, donec siccarentur aquæ super terram. Emisit quoque columbam post eum, ut videret si jam cessassent aquæ super faciem terræ. Quæ cum non invenisset ubi requiesceret pes ejus, reversa est ad eum in arcam. Aquæ enim erant super universam terram. Extenditque manum, et apprehensam intulit in arcam. Exspectatis autem ultra septem diebus aliis, rursum dimisit columbam ex arca. At illa venit ad eum ad vesperam, portans ramum olivæ virentibus foliis in ore suo. Intellexit ergo Noe, quod cessassent aquæ super terram. Exspectavitque nihilominus septem alios dies, et emisit columbam quæ non est reversa ultra ad eum. Locutus est autem Dominus ad Noe, dicens: Egredere de arca tu, et uxor tua: filii tui, et uxores filiorum tuorum tecum. Cuncta ani-

and all the cattle which were with him in the ark, and brought a wind upon the earth, and the waters were abated. The fountains also of the deep, and the floodgates of heaven were shut up, and the rain from heaven was restrained. And the waters returned from off the earth, going and coming: and they began to be abated after a hundred and fifty days. And after that forty days were passed, Noe opening the window of the ark which he had made, sent forth a raven; which went forth, and did not return till the waters were dried upon the earth. He sent forth also a dove after him, to see if the waters had now ceased upon the face of the earth. But she not finding where her foot might rest, returned to him into the ark: for the waters were upon the whole earth: and he put forth his hand, and caught her, and brought her into the ark. And having waited yet seven other days, he again sent forth the dove out of the ark. And she came to him in the evening, carrying a bough of an olive tree, with green leaves, in her mouth. Noe therefore understood that the waters were ceased upon the earth. And he stayed yet other seven days; and he sent forth the dove, which returned not any more unto him. And God spoke to Noe, saying: Go out of the ark, thou and thy wife, thy sons, and the wives of thy sons with thee. All living

HOLY SATURDAY: MORNING SERVICE.

things that are with thee of all flesh, as well in fowls, as in beasts, and all creeping things, that creep upon the earth, bring out with thee, and go ye upon the earth: increase and multiply upon it.

So Noe went out, he and his sons, his wife, and the wives of his sons with him: and all living things, and cattle, and creeping things that creep upon the earth, according to their kinds, went out of the ark. And Noe built an altar unto the Lord: and taking of all cattle and fowls that were clean, offered holocausts upon the altar. And the Lord smelled a sweet savour.

The Bishop: Let us pray.
The Deacon: Let us kneel down.
The Subdeacon: Stand up again.

O God, whose power is unchangeable, and whose light never faileth, mercifully regard the wonderful sacrament of thy whole Church, and by an effect of thy perpetual providence, accomplish in peace the work of human salvation: and let the whole world experience and see, that what was fallen, is raised up again: what was old, is become new; and that all things are again settled by him who gave them their first being, our Lord Jesus Christ thy Son. Who liveth, &c.
℟. Amen.

mantia, quæ sunt apud te, ex omni carne, tam in volatilibus, quam in bestiis, et universis reptilibus quæ reptant super terram, educ tecum, et ingredimini super terram. Crescite, et multiplicamini super eam.

Egressus est ergo Noe et filii ejus, uxor illius, et uxores filiorum ejus cum eo. Sed et omnia animantia, jumenta et reptilia quæ reptant super terram secundum genus suum, egressa sunt de arca. Ædificavit autem Noe altare Domino : et tollens de cunctis pecoribus et volucribus mundis, obtulit holocausta super altare. Odoratusque est Dominus odorem suavitatis.

The Bishop: Oremus.
The Deacon: Flectamus genua.
The Subdeacon: Levate.

Deus incommutabilis virtus et lumen æternum, respice propitius ad totius Ecclesiæ tuæ mirabile sacramentum, et opus salutis humanæ perpetuæ dispositionis effectu tranquillius operare : totusque mundus experiatur et videat, dejecta erigi, inveterata renovari, et per ipsum redire omnia in integrum, a quo sumpsere principium : Dominum nostrum Jesum Christum Filium tuum. Qui tecum.
℟. Amen.

THIRD PROPHECY.

(*Genesis*, Chap. XXII.)

Abraham, the Father of Believers, is here offered to our Catechumens as a model of Faith. They are taught how man should ever depend upon his God, and faithfully serve him. The obedience shown by *Isaac* to his father's orders is a figure of that which our Saviour has shown on Calvary. The *wood for the holocaust*, carried up the mountain by Abraham's son, brings to our minds the Son of God carrying his Cross.

In diebus illis : Tentavit Deus Abraham, et dixit ad eum : Abraham, Abraham. At ille respondit : Adsum. Ait illi : Tolle filium tuum unigenitum, quem diligis Isaac, et vade in terram visionis : atque ibi offeres eum in holocaustum super unum montium, quem monstravero tibi. Igitur Abraham de nocte consurgens, stravit asinum suum, ducens secum duos juvenes, et Isaac filium suum. Cumque concidisset ligna in holocaustum, abiit ad locum, quem præceperat ei Deus. Die autem tertio, elevatis oculis, vidit locum procul : dixitque ad pueros suos : Exspectate hic cum asino : ego et puer illuc usque properantes, postquam adoraverimus, revertemur ad vos. Tulit quoque ligna holocausti, et imposuit super Isaac filium suum : ipse vero portabat in manibus ignem

In those days : God tempted Abraham, and said to him : Abraham, Abraham. And he answered : Here I am. He said to him : Take thy only begotten son Isaac, whom thou lovest, and go into the land of vision : and there thou shalt offer him for an holocaust upon one of the mountains which I will shew thee. So Abraham rising up in the night, saddled his ass ; and took with him two young men, and Isaac his son ; and when he had cut wood for the holocaust, he went his way to the place which God had commanded him. And on the third day, lifting up his eyes, he saw the place afar off. And he said to his young men : Stay you here with the ass : I and the boy will go with speed as far as yonder, and after we have worshipped, will return to you. And he took the wood for the holocaust, and laid it upon Isaac his son: and he himself carried in his hands fire and a sword. And as they two went on together, Isaac said to his father: My father. And he answered: What wilt thou, son? Behold, saith he, fire and wood: where is the victim for the holocaust? And Abraham said: God will provide himself a victim for a holocaust, my son.

So they went on together: and they came to the place which God had shewed him, where he built an altar, and laid the wood in order upon it: and when he had bound Isaac his son, he laid him on the altar, upon the pile of wood. And he put forth his hand, and took the sword to sacrifice his son. And behold an Angel of the Lord from heaven called to him, saying: Abraham, Abraham. And he answered: Here I am. And he said to him: Lay not thy hand upon the boy, neither do thou any thing to him: now I know that thou fearest God, and hast not spared thy only begotten son for my sake. Abraham lifted up his eyes, and saw behind his back a ram amongst the briers, sticking fast by the horns, which he took and offered for a holocaust instead of his son. And he called the name of that place, The Lord seeth. Whereupon, even to this day, it is said: In the mountain the Lord will see.

And the Angel of the Lord called to Abraham a second time from heaven, saying: By

et gladium. Cumque duo pergerent simul, dixit Isaac patri suo: Pater mi. At ille respondit: Quid vis, fili? Ecce, inquit, ignis et ligna, ubi est victima holocausti? Dixit autem Abraham: Deus providebit sibi victimam holocausti, fili mi.

Pergebant ergo pariter: et venerunt ad locum, quem ostenderat ei Deus: in quo ædificavit altare, et desuper ligna composuit. Cumque alligasset Isaac filium suum, posuit eum in altare super struem lignorum. Extenditque manum, et arripuit gladium, ut immolaret filium suum. Et ecce Angelus Domini de cœlo clamavit, dicens: Abraham, Abraham. Qui respondit: Adsum. Dixitque ei: Non extendas manum tuam super puerum: neque facias illi quidquam. Nunc cognovi, quod times Deum: et non pepercisti unigenito filio tuo propter me. Levavit Abraham oculos suos, viditque post tergum arietem inter vepres, hærentem cornibus: quem adsumens, obtulit holocaustum pro filio. Appellavitque nomen loci illius: Dominus videt. Unde usque hodie dicitur: In monte Dominus videbit.

Vocavit autem Angelus Domini Abraham secundo de cœlo, dicens: Per memetipsum juravi, dicit Dominus: quia fecisti hanc rem, et non pepercisti filio tuo unigenito propter me: benedicam tibi, et multiplicabo semen tuum sicut stellas cœli, et velut arenam, quæ est in littore maris. Possidebit semen tuum portas inimicorum suorum: et benedicentur in semine tuo omnes gentes terræ, quia obedisti voci meæ. Reversus est Abraham ad pueros suos: abieruntque Bersabee simul, et habitavit ibi.

The Bishop: Oremus.
The Deacon: Flectamus genua.
The Subdeacon: Levate.

Deus, fidelium pater summe, qui in toto orbe terrarum, promissionis tuæ filios diffusa adoptionis gratia multiplicas: et per Paschale sacramentum, Abraham puerum tuum universarum, sicut jurasti, gentium efficis patrem: da populis tuis digne ad gratiam tuæ vocationis introire. Per Dominum.
℞. Amen.

my own self have I sworn, saith the Lord; because thou hast done this thing, and hast not spared thy only begotten son for my sake: I will bless thee, and I will multiply thy seed as the stars of heaven, and as the sand that is by the seashore: thy seed shall possess the gates of their enemies. And in thy seed shall all the nations of the earth be blessed, because thou hast obeyed my voice. Abraham returned to his young men, and they went to Bersabee together, and he dwelt there.

The Bishop: Let us pray.
The Deacon: Let us kneel down.
The Subdeacon: Stand up again.

O God, the sovereign Father of the faithful, who throughout the whole world multipliest the children of the promise by the grace of thy adoption, and makest thy servant Abraham, according to thy oath, the father of all nations by this Paschal sacrament; grant that thy people may worthily receive the grace of thy vocation. Through, &c.
℞. Amen.

FOURTH PROPHECY.

(*Exodus*, CHAP. XIV.)

Here we have the great type of Baptism. The People of God, delivered from Pharao's tyranny, are saved by the very water that destroys the Egyptian. The Catechumens will come forth from the Baptis-

HOLY SATURDAY: MORNING SERVICE. 581

mal Font freed from Satan's sway; their sins will perish for ever in its saving waters.

In those days: it came to pass in the morning watch, and behold the Lord looking upon the Egyptian army through the pillar of fire, and of the cloud, slew their host: and overthrew the wheels of the chariots, and they were carried into the deep. And the Egyptians said: Let us flee from Israel: for the Lord fighteth for them against us. And the Lord said to Moses: Stretch forth thine hand over the sea, that the waters may come again upon the Egyptians, upon their chariots and horsemen. And when Moses had stretched forth his hand towards the sea, it returned at the first break of day to the former place: and as the Egyptians were fleeing away, the waters came upon them, and the Lord shut them up in the middle of the waves. And the waves returned, and covered the chariots and the horsemen of all the army of Pharao, who had come into the sea after them, neither did there so much as one of them remain. But the children of Israel marched through the midst of the sea upon dry land, and the waters were to them as a wall on the right hand and on the left: and the Lord delivered Israel in that day out of the hands of the Egyptians. And they saw the Egyptians dead upon the seashore, and the mighty hand

In diebus illis: Factum est in vigilia matutina, et ecce respiciens Dominus super castra Ægyptiorum per columnam ignis et nubis, interfecit exercitum eorum: et subvertit rotas curruum, ferebanturque in profundum. Dixerunt ergo Ægyptii: Fugiamus Israelem: Dominus enim pugnat pro eis contra nos. Et ait Dominus ad Moysen: Extende manum tuam super mare: ut revertantur aquæ ad Ægyptios super currus et equites eorum. Cumque extendisset Moyses manum contra mare, reversum est primo diluculo ad priorem locum; fugientibusque Ægyptiis occurrerunt aquæ: et involvit eos Dominus in mediis fluctibus. Reversæque sunt aquæ, et operuerunt currus et equites cuncti exercitus Pharaonis, qui sequentes ingressi fuerant mare; nec unus quidem superfuit ex eis. Filii autem Israël perrexerunt per medium sicci maris: et aquæ eis erant quasi pro muro a dextris et a sinistris. Liberavitque Dominus in die illa Israël de manu Egyptiorum. Et viderunt Ægyptios mortuos super littus maris: et manum magnam, quam exercuerat Dominus contra eos. Timuitque populus Dominum: et crediderunt Domino, et Moysi servo ejus. Tunc cecinit Moyses, et filii Israël, carmen hoc Domino, et dixerunt:

that the Lord had used against them: and the people feared the Lord, and they believed the Lord, and Moses his servant. Then Moses and the children of Israel sang this canticle to the Lord, and said:

Here the Church sings the Canticle of Moses His sister Mary, and the daughters of Israel, sang it on the shore of the Red Sea, as they looked upon the dead bodies of the Egyptians.

TRACT.

Cantemus Domino: gloriose enim honorificatus est: equum et ascensorem projecit in mare: adjutor et protector factus est mihi in salutem.

℣. Hic Deus meus, et honorificabo eum: Deus patris mei, et exaltabo eum.

℣. Dominus conterens bella: Dominus nomen est illi.

The Bishop: Oremus.
The Deacon: Flectamus genua.
The Subdeacon: Levate.

Deus, cujus antiqua miracula etiam nostris sæculis coruscare sentimus: dum quod uni populo a persecutione Ægyptiaca liberando, dexteræ tuæ potentia contulisti, id in salutem gentium per aquam regenerationis operaris: præsta, ut in Abrahæ filios, et in Israeliticam dignitatem, totius

Let us sing to the Lord, for he is gloriously magnified: the horse and the rider he hath thrown into the sea: he is become my helper and protector unto salvation.

℣. He is my God, and I will glorify him: the God of my father, and I will exalt him.

℣. The Lord is he that destroyeth war: Almighty is his name.

The Bishop: Let us pray.
The Deacon: Let us kneel down.
The Subdeacon: Stand up again.

O God, whose ancient miracles we see renewed in our days: whilst, by the water of regeneration thou performest, for the salvation of the Gentiles, that which by the power of thy right hand thou didst for the deliverance of one people from the Egyptian persecution; grant that all the nations of the world may be-

come the children of Abraham, and partake of the dignity of the people of Israel. Through, &c.
℞. Amen.

mundi transeat plenitudo. Per Dominum.

℞. Amen.

FIFTH PROPHECY.

(*Isaias*, Chap. LIV.)

The sublimest of the Prophets, Isaias, here invites our Catechumens to *come to the waters*, that their thirst may be quenched: he bids them satiate their hunger with the sweetest food: he tells them of the *inheritance* which God has in store for them: they need not fear their poverty, for the infinitely rich God will overwhelm them with good things.

This is the inheritance of the servants of the Lord, and their justice with me, saith the Lord. All you that thirst, come to the water: and you that have no money, make haste, buy, and eat: come ye, buy wine and milk without money, and without any price. Why do you spend money for that which is not bread, and your labour for that which doth not satisfy you? Hearken diligently to me, and eat that which is good, and your soul shall be delighted in fatness. Incline your ear, and come to me: hear, and your soul shall live, and I will make an everlasting covenant with you, the faithful mercies of David. Behold I have given him for a witness to the people, for a leader and a master to the Gentiles. Behold thou shalt call a nation which thou knewest not: and the nations

Hæc est hæreditas servorum Domini, et justitia eorum apud me, dicit Dominus. Omnes sitientes venite ad aquas: et qui non habetis argentum, properate, emite et comedite. Venite, emite absque argento, et absque ulla commutatione vinum et lac. Quare appenditis argentum non in panibus, et laborem vestrum non in saturitate? Audite audientes me, et comedite bonum: et delectabitur in crassitudine anima vestra. Inclinate aurem vestram, et venite ad me: audite: et vivet anima vestra: et feriam vobiscum pactum sempiternum, misericordias David fideles. Ecce testem populis dedi eum, ducem ac præceptorem gentibus. Ecce gentem quam nesciebas, vocabis: et gentes, quæ te non cognoverunt, ad te current, propter Dominum Deum tuum, et Sanctum Israël, quia glorificavit te. Quærite Dominum, dum inveniri potest, invocate eum, dum prope est. Derelinquat impius viam suam, et vir iniquus cogitationes suas: et revertatur ad Dominum, et miserebitur ejus: et ad Deum nostrum, quoniam multus est ad ignoscendum. Non enim cogitationes meæ, cogitationes vestræ, neque viæ vestræ, viæ meæ, dicit Dominus. Quia sicut exaltantur cœli a terra: sic exaltatæ sunt viæ meæ a viis vestris, et cogitationes meæ a cogitationibus vestris. Et quomodo descendit imber, et nix de cœlo, et illuc ultra non revertitur, sed inebriat terram, et infundit eam, et germinare eam facit, et dat semen serenti, et panem comedenti: sic erit verbum meum quod egredietur de ore meo. Non revertetur ad me vacuum, sed faciet quæcumque volui, et prosperabitur in his, ad quæ misi illud: dicit Dominus omnipotens.

The Bishop: Oremus.

The Deacon: Flectamus genua.

The Subdeacon: Levate.

Omnipotens sempiterne Deus, multiplica in honorem nominis tui quod patrum fidei spopondisti: et promissionis filios sacra adoptione dilata: ut quod priores sancti non dubita-

that knew not thee shall run to thee, because of the Lord thy God, and for the Holy One of Israel, for he hath glorified thee. Seek ye the Lord while he may be found: call upon him while he is near. Let the wicked forsake his way, and the unjust man his thoughts, and let him return to the Lord, and he will have mercy on him; and to our God, for he is bountiful to forgive. For my thoughts are not your thoughts, nor your ways my ways, saith the Lord. For as the heavens are exalted above the earth, so are my ways exalted above your ways, and my thoughts above your thoughts. And as the rain and the snow come down from heaven and return no more thither, but soak the earth and water it, and make it to spring and give seed to the sower, and bread to the eater: so shall my word be, which shall go forth from my mouth: it shall not return to me void, but it shall do whatever I please, and shall prosper in the things for which I sent it, saith the Lord Almighty.

The Bishop: Let us pray.

The Deacon: Let us kneel down.

The Subdeacon: Stand up again.

O Almighty and Eternal God, multiply for the honour of thy name, what thou didst promise to the faith of our forefathers: and increase, by thy sacred adoption, the children of that promise: and

what the ancient saints doubted not would come to pass, thy church may now find in great part accomplished. Through, &c.
℟. Amen.

verunt futurum, Ecclesia tua magna jam ex parte cognoscat impletum. Per Dominum.
℟. Amen.

SIXTH PROPHECY.

(*Baruch*, Chap. III.)

In this admirable passage from the Prophet Baruch, God reminds the Catechumens, who are about to receive holy Baptism, of their past sins, which made them unworthy of pardon : but, by his gratuitous mercy, he has vouchsafed to pour out his *Wisdom* upon them, and they came unto him. He then speaks to them of those men of the Gentile world, who were wealthy, and powerful, and enterprising, and have left a name behind them. But they *perished*, and their earthly wisdom with them. The New People, whom the Lord this day forms to himself, shall not go astray: *Wisdom* is to be their portion. Heretofore, God spoke his mysteries to *Jacob ;* but this his word did not reach all men : now, he is come, in person, *upon earth ;* he *conversed with men,* and dwelt among them ; therefore, the people he now raises up for himself, shall be for ever faithful.

Hear, O Israel, the commandments of life : give ear, that thou mayest learn wisdom. How happeneth it, O Israel, that thou art in thy enemies' land ? Thou art grown old in a strange country, thou art defiled with the dead : thou art counted with them that go down into hell. Thou hast forsaken the fountain of wisdom : for if thou hadst

Audi Israël mandata vitæ : auribus percipe, ut scias prudentiam. Quid est Israël quod in terra inimicorum es ? Inveterasti in terra aliena, coinquinatus es cum mortuis : deputatus es cum descendentibus in infernum? Dereliquisti fontem sapientiæ. Nam si in via Dei ambulasses, habitasses utique in pace sempiterna. Disce ubi sit prudentia, ubi sit virtus, ubi sit intellectus: ut scias simul ubi sit longiturnitas vitæ et victus, ubi sit lumen oculorum, et pax.

Quis invenit locum ejus? Et quis introivit in thesauros ejus? Ubi sunt principes gentium, et qui dominantur super bestias, quæ sunt super terram? Qui in avibus cœli ludunt, qui argentum thesaurizant, et aurum, in quo confidunt homines: et non est finis acquisitionis eorum: qui argentum fabricant, et solliciti sunt: nec est inventio operum illorum. Exterminati sunt, et ad inferos descenderunt: et alii loco eorum surrexerunt. Juvenes viderunt lumen: et habitaverunt super terram. Viam autem disciplinæ ignoraverunt, neque intellexerunt semitas ejus, neque filii eorum susceperunt eam. A facie eorum longe facta est. Non est audita in terra Chanaan: neque visa est in Theman. Filii quoque Agar, qui exquirunt prudentiam quæ de terra est, negotiatores Merrhæ et Theman, et fabulatores, et exquisitores prudentiæ et intelligentiæ; viam autem sapientiæ nescierunt, neque commemorati sunt semitas ejus.

O Israël, quam magna est domus Dei, et ingens locus

walked in the way of God, thou surely hadst dwelt in peace for ever. Learn where is wisdom, where is strength, where is understanding: that thou mayest know also where is length of days and life, where is the light of the eyes, and peace.

Who hath found out her place? and who hath gone in to her treasures? Where are the princes of the nations, and they that rule over the beasts that are upon the earth? That take their pastime with the birds of the air, that hoard up silver and gold, wherein men trust, and there is no end of their getting? who work in silver and are solicitous, and their works are unsearchable? They are cut off, and are gone down to hell, and others are risen up in their place. Young men have seen the light, and dwelt upon the earth: but the way of knowledge they have not known, nor have they understood the paths thereof, neither have their children received it: it is far from their face. It hath not been heard of in the land of Chanaan, neither had it been seen in Theman. The children of Agar also, that search after wisdom that is of the earth, the merchants of Merrha, and of Theman, and the tellers of fables, and searchers of prudence and understanding: but the way of wisdom they have not known, neither have they remembered her paths.

O Israel, how great is the house of God, and how vast

is the place of his possession! It is great and hath no end: it is high and immense. There were the giants, those renowned men that were from the beginning, of great stature, expert in war. The Lord chose not them, neither did they find the way of knowledge: therefore did they perish. And because they had not wisdom, they perished through their folly. Who hath gone up into heaven, and taken her, and brought her down from the clouds? Who hath passed over the sea, and found her, and brought her preferably to chosen gold? There is none that is able to know her ways, nor that can search out her paths: But he that knoweth all things, knoweth her, and hath found her out with his understanding: he that prepared the earth for evermore, and filled it with cattle, and four-footed beasts: he that sendeth forth light, and it goeth; and hath called it, and it obeyed him with trembling. And the stars have given light in their watches, and rejoiced: they were called, and they said: Here we are. And with cheerfulness they have shined forth to him that made them. This is our God, and there shall no other be accounted of in comparison of him. He found out all the ways of knowledge, and gave it to Jacob his servant, and to Israel his beloved. Afterwards he was seen upon earth, and conversed with men.

possessionis ejus! Magnus est, et non habet finem, excelsus et immensus. Ibi fuerunt gigantes nominati illi, qui ab initio fuerunt, statura magna, scientes bellum. Non hos elegit Dominus: neque viam disciplinæ invenerunt: propterea perierunt. Et quoniam non habuerunt sapientiam, interierunt propter suam insipientiam. Quis ascendit in cœlum, et accepit eam, et eduxit eam de nubibus? Quis transfretavit mare, et invenit illam, et attulit illam super aurum electum? Non est qui possit scire vias ejus: neque qui exquirat semitas ejus. Sed qui scit universa, novit eam: et adinvenit eam prudentia sua. Qui præparavit terram in æterno tempore: et replevit eam pecudibus et quadrupedibus. Qui emittit lumen, et vadit: et vocavit illud, et obedit illi in tremore. Stellæ autem dederunt lumen in custodiis suis, et lætatæ sunt. Vocatæ sunt, et dixerunt: Adsumus. Et luxerunt ei cum jucunditate, qui fecit illas. Hic est Deus noster et non æstimabitur alius adversus eum. Hic adinvenit omnem viam disciplinæ, et tradidit illam Jacob puero suo, et Israël dilecto suo. Post hæc in terris visus est, et cum hominibus conversatus est.

The Bishop: Oremus.
The Deacon: Flectamus genua.
The Subdeacon: Levate.

Deus, qui Ecclesiam tuam semper gentium vocatione multiplicas : concede propitius : ut quos aqua baptismatis abluis, continua protectione tuearis. Per Dominum.
℞. Amen.

The Bishop: Let us pray.
The Deacon: Let us kneel down.
The Subdeacon: Stand up again.

O God, who continually multipliest thy church by the vocation of the Gentiles: mercifully grant thy perpetual protection to those whom thou washest with the water of baptism. Through, &c.
℞. Amen.

SEVENTH PROPHECY.

(*Ezechiel*, CHAP. XXXVII.)

This Lesson brings before our Catechumens the resurrection of the body,—a dogma which met with great opposition from the proud and sensual Gentiles. What a fitting occasion is this for remembering the promised resurrection, which God has mercifully made to us! for lo! Christ is about to rise from his grave, showing us hereby what *our* resurrection is to be, and giving us a pledge of its having to be.—Our Catechumens, also, are signified by these *dry bones*, which are to return to life, by the *Spirit of God* coming upon them: they are to form a numerous *people* to God.

In diebus illis : Facta est super me manus Domini; et eduxit me in Spiritu Domini, et dimisit me in medio campi, qui erat plenus ossibus : et circumduxit me per ea in gyro. Erant autem multa valde super faciem campi, siccaque vehementer. Et dixit ad me : Fili hominis, putasne vivent ossa ista? Et dixi : Domine Deus, tu

In those days : The hand of the Lord was upon me, and brought me forth in the spirit of the Lord : and set me down in the midst of a plain that was full of bones. And he led me about through them on every side : now they were very many upon the face of the plain, and they were exceeding dry. And he said to me : Son of man, dost thou think these bones shall live? And I answered: O Lord God, thou knowest. And he said to me: Prophesy concerning these bones: and say to them: Ye dry bones, hear the word of the Lord. Thus saith the Lord God to these bones: Behold, I will send spirit into you, and you shall live; and I will lay sinews upon you, and will cause flesh to grow over you, and will cover you with skin: and I will give you spirit, and you shall live, and you shall know that I am the Lord. And I prophesied as he had commanded me: and as I prophesied, there was a noise, and behold a commotion: and the bones came together, each one to its joint. And I saw, and behold the sinews and the flesh came up upon them: and the skin was stretched out over them, but there was no spirit in them. And he said to me: Prophesy to the spirit, prophesy, O son of man, and say to the spirit: Thus saith the Lord God: Come, spirit, from the four winds, and blow upon these slain, and let them live again. And I prophesied as he had commanded me: and the spirit came into them, and they lived; and they stood upon their feet, an exceeding great army. And he said to me: Son of man, all these bones are the house of Israel. They say: Our bones are dried up, and our hope is lost, and we are cut off. Therefore prophesy, and say to them: Thus saith the Lord God: Behold, I will open your graves, and

nosti. Et dixit ad me: Vaticinare de ossibus istis: et dices eis: Ossa arida, audite verbum Domini. Hæc dicit Dominus Deus ossibus his: Ecce ego intromittam in vos spiritum, et vivetis: et dabo super vos nervos, et succrescere faciam super vos carnes, et superextendam in vobis cutem: et dabo vobis spiritum, et vivetis: et scietis, quia ego Dominus. Et prophetavi sicut præceperat mihi. Factus est autem sonitus, prophetante me, et ecce commotio. Et accesserunt ossa ad ossa: unumquodque ad juncturam suam. Et vidi: et ecce super ea nervi et carnes ascenderunt, et extenta est in eis cutis desuper: et spiritum non habebant. Et dixit ad me: Vaticinare ad spiritum, vaticinare, fili hominis, et dices ad spiritum: Hæc dicit Dominus Deus: A quatuor ventis veni, Spiritus; et insuffla super interfectos istos, et reviviscant. Et prophetavi sicut præceperat mihi. Et ingressus est in ea Spiritus, et vixerunt; steteruntque super pedes suos exercitus grandis nimis valde. Et dixit ad me: Fili hominis, ossa hæc universa domus Israël est. Ipsi dicunt: Aruerunt ossa nostra, et periit spes nostra, et abscissi sumus. Propterea vaticinare, et dices ad eos: Hæc dicit Dominus Deus: Ecce, ego aperiam tumulos vestros, et educam vos de sepulcris vestris, popule meus, et inducam vos in terram Israël. Et scietis quia ego Dominus, cum aperuero sepulcra vestra, et eduxero vos de tumulis vestris, popule meus: et dedero Spiritum meum in vobis, et vixeritis : et requiescere vos faciam super humum vestram: dicit Dominus omnipotens.

will bring you out of your sepulchres, O my people : and will bring you into the land of Israel. And you shall know that I am the Lord, when I shall have opened your sepulchres, and shall have brought you out of your graves, O my people, and shall have put my spirit in you, and you shall live, and I shall make you rest upon your own land, saith the Lord Almighty.

The Bishop: Oremus.
The Deacon: Flectamus genua.
The Subdeacon: Levate.

The Bishop: Let us pray.
The Deacon: Let us kneel down.
The Subdeacon: Stand up again.

Deus, qui nos ad celebrandum Paschale Sacramentum, utriusque Testamenti paginis instruis : da nobis intelligere misericordiam tuam : ut ex perceptione præsentium munerum, firma sit exspectatio futurorum. Per Dominum.
℟. Amen.

O God, who by the scriptures of both testaments teachest us to celebrate the Paschal sacrament : give us such a sense of thy mercy, that, by receiving thy present favours, we may have a firm hope of thy future blessings. Through, &c.
℟. Amen.

EIGHTH PROPHECY.

(*Isaias,* CHAP. IV.)

The seven women here mentioned, as having been set free from ignominy and cleansed from defilement, represent the souls of our Catechumens, on whom God is about to pour his mercy. They desire to be called after the name of their Deliverer : their desire shall be granted, for, as they come from the Font, they shall be called *Christians,* that is, children of *Christ.* Henceforth, they shall abide on *Mount Sion,* sheltered *from whirlwind and rain.* The abode of light and rest here promised them, is the

Church; there shall they dwell in company with her divine Spouse.

In that day seven women shall take hold of one man, saying: We will eat our own bread, and wear our own apparel: only let us be called by thy name, take away our reproach. In that day the bud of the Lord shall be in magnificence and glory, and the fruit of the earth shall be high, and a great joy to them that have escaped of Israel. And it shall come to pass, that every one that shall be left in Sion, and that shall remain in Jerusalem, shall be called holy, every one that is written in life in Jerusalem. If the Lord shall wash away the filth of the daughters of Sion, and shall wash away the blood of Jerusalem out of the midst thereof, by the spirit of judgment, and by the spirit of burning. And the Lord will create upon every place of mount Sion, and where he is called upon, a cloud by day, and a smoke and the brightness of a flaming fire in the night: for over all the glory shall be a protection. And there shall be a tabernacle for a shade in the day time from the heat, and for a security and covert from the whirlwind, and from rain.	Apprehendent septem mulieres virum unum in die illa, dicentes: Panem nostrum comedemus, et vestimentis nostris operiemur: tantummodo invocetur nomen tuum super nos: aufer opprobrium nostrum. In die illa erit germen Domini in magnificentia, et gloria: et fructus terræ sublimis: et exsultatio his qui salvati fuerint de Israël. Et erit: omnis qui relictus fuerit in Sion, et residuus in Jerusalem, sanctus vocabitur: omnis qui scriptus est in vita in Jerusalem. Si abluerit Dominus sordes filiarum Sion: et sanguinem Jerusalem laverit de medio ejus in spiritu judicii, et spiritu ardoris. Et creabit Dominus super omnem locum montis Sion, et ubi invocatus est, nubem per diem, et fumum et splendorem ignis flammantis in nocte: super omnem enim gloriam protectio. Et tabernaculum erit in umbraculum diei ab æstu, et in securitatem et absconsionem a turbine et a pluvia.

This Lesson is followed by a Tract, taken from the same Prophet Isaias, wherein he foretells the favours to be lavished by Christ on his Church, his *Vineyard*, the object of his loving and ceaseless care.

TRACT.

Vinea facta est dilecto in cornu, in loco uberi.	My Beloved had a Vineyard on a Hill, in a fruitful place.
℣. Et maceriam circumdedit, et circumfodit: et plantavit vineam Sorec, et ædificavit turrim in medio ejus.	℣. He fenced it in, and digged it about: and planted it with Sorec, *the choicest of vines*, and built a Tower in the midst thereof.
℣. Et torcular fodit in ea: vinea enim Domini Sabaoth, domus Israël est.	℣. And he set up a winepress therein: for the Vineyard of the Lord of Hosts is the House of Israel.
The Bishop: Oremus.	*The Bishop:* Let us pray.
The Deacon: Flectamus genua.	*The Deacon:* Let us kneel down.
The Subdeacon: Levate.	*The Subdeacon:* Stand up again.
Deus, qui in omnibus Ecclesiæ tuæ filiis, sanctorum Prophetarum voce manifestasti, in omni loco dominationis tuæ satorem te bonorum seminum, et electorum palmitum esse cultorem: tribue populis tuis, qui et vinearum apud te nomine censentur et segetum: ut, spinarum et tribulorum squalore resecato, digna efficiantur fruge fœcundi. Per Dominum.	O God, who by the mouths of the holy prophets hast declared, that through the whole extent of thy empire it is thou that sowest the good seed, and improvest the choicest branches that are found in all the children of thy church: grant to thy people, who are called by the names of vineyards and corn, that they may root out all thorns and briers, and bring forth good fruit in plenty. Through, &c.
℟. Amen.	℟. Amen.

NINTH PROPHECY.

(*Exodus*, CHAP. XII.)

It was by the *blood* of the figurative *Lamb*, that Israel was protected against the sword of the destroying Angel, was delivered from Egypt, and began his journey towards the Promised Land:—it is by the Blood of the true Lamb, wherewith they are to be marked, that our Catechumens shall be delivered from eternal death, and from the slavery in which Satan has heretofore held them. They shall be guests of that Banquet, where the Flesh of this Divine Lamb is eaten, for the *Pasch* is close upon us, and they are to join us in its celebration.

In those days: The Lord said to Moses and Aaron in the land of Egypt: this month shall be to you the beginning of months: it shall be the first in the months of the year. Speak ye to the whole assembly of the children of Israel, and say to them: on the tenth day of this month let every man take a lamb by their families and houses. But if the number be less than may suffice to eat the lamb, he shall take unto him his neighbour that joineth to his house, according to the number of souls which may be enough to eat the lamb. And it shall be a lamb without blemish, a male of one year: according to which rite also you shall take a kid. And you shall keep it until the fourteenth day of this month: and the whole multitude of the children of Israel shall sacrifice it in the evening. And they shall take of the blood thereof, and put it upon both the side-posts, and upon the upper door-posts of the houses, wherein they shall eat it. And they shall eat the flesh that night roasted at the fire, and unleavened bread, with wild lettuce. You shall not eat thereof any thing raw, nor boiled in water, but only roasted at the fire. You shall

In diebus illis: Dixit Dominus ad Moysen et Aaron in terra Egypti: Mensis iste vobis principium mensium: primus erit in mensibus anni. Loquimini ad universum cœtum filiorum Israël, et dicite eis: Decima die mensis hujus tollat unusquisque agnum per familias et domos suas. Sin autem minor est numerus, ut sufficere possit ad vescendum agnum, assumet vicinum suum, qui junctus est domui suæ: juxta numerum animarum, quæ sufficere possunt ad esum agni. Erit autem agnus absque macula, masculus anniculus: juxta quem ritum tolletis et hœdum. Et servabitis eum usque ad quartamdecimam diem mensis hujus. Immolabitque eum universa multitudo filiorum Israël ad vesperam. Et sument de sanguine ejus: ac ponent super utrumque postem, et in superliminaribus domorum, in quibus comedent illum. Et edent carnes nocte illa assas igni, et azymos panes, cum lactucis agrestibus. Non comedetis ex eo crudum quid, nec coctum aqua, sed tantum assum igni. Caput cum pedibus ejus et intestinis vorabitis: nec remanebit quidquam ex eo usque mane. Si quid residuum fuerit, igne comburetis. Sic autem comedetis illum. Renes vestros accingetis: et calceamenta habebitis in pedibus, tenentes baculos in manibus, et comedetis festinanter. Est enim Phase, id est Transitus Domini.

The Bishop: Oremus.
The Deacon: Flectamus genua.
The Subdeacon: Levate.

Omnipotens sempiterne Deus, qui in omnium operum tuorum dispensatione mirabilis es: intelligant redempti tui non fuisse excellentius quod initio factus est mundus, quam quod in fine sæculorum Pascha nostrum immolatus est Christus. Qui tecum.

℞. Amen.

eat the head with the feet and the entrails thereof: neither shall there remain any thing of it until morning. If there shall be any thing left, you shall burn it with fire. And thus you shall eat it: you shall gird your reins, and you shall have shoes on your feet, holding staves in your hands, and you shall eat in haste. For it is the Phase (that is the Passage) of the Lord.

The Bishop: Let us pray.
The Deacon: Let us kneel down.
The Subdeacon: Stand up again.

O Almighty and Eternal God, who art wonderful in the performance of all thy works; let thy servants whom thou hast redeemed understand, that the creation of the world, in the beginning, was not a more excellent work, than the sacrificing of Christ our Passover at the end of the world. Who liveth, &c.

℞. Amen.

TENTH PROPHECY.
(*Jonas*, CHAP. III.)

Ninive is the Gentile world, debased by every crime, and a prey to false doctrines. God took compassion upon her and sent her his Apostles, in the name of his own Son. She heard their preaching, abjured her errors and vices, and *did penance:* and God made her the City of his elect. Our Catechumens were once children of Ninive: they are soon to be numbered among the children of Jerusalem. The grace of God, and their works of penance, have brought about this wondrous adoption.

In those days: The word of the Lord came to Jonas the second time, saying: Arise and go to Ninive the great city: and preach in it the preaching that I bid thee. And Jonas arose, and went to Ninive according to the word of the Lord: now Ninive was a great city of three days' journey. And Jonas began to enter into the city one day's journey: and he cried and said: Yet forty days and Ninive shall be destroyed. And the men of Ninive believed in God: and they proclaimed a fast, and put on sackcloth, from the greatest to the least. And the word came to the King of Ninive: and he rose up out of his throne, and cast away his robe from him, and was clothed with sackcloth, and sat in ashes. And he caused it to be proclaimed and published in Ninive from the mouth of the king and of his princes, saying: Let neither men nor beasts, oxen nor sheep, taste any thing: let them not feed, nor drink water. And let men and beasts be covered with sackcloth, and cry to the Lord, with all their strength, and let them turn every one from his evil way, and from the iniquity that is in their hands. Who can tell if God will turn, and forgive: and will turn away from his fierce anger, and we shall not perish? And God saw their works, that they were turned from their evil way: and the Lord our God had mercy on his people.

In diebus illis: Factum est verbum Domini ad Jonas prophetam secundo, dicens: Surge et vade in Niniven civitatem magnam, et prædica in ea prædicationem quam ego loquor ad te. Et surrexit Jonas, et abiit in Niniven, juxta verbum Domini. Et Ninive erat civitas magna, itinere dierum trium. Et cœpit Jonas introire in civitatem, itinere diei unius: et clamavit, et dixit: Adhuc quadraginta dies, et Ninive subvertetur. Et crediderunt viri Ninivitæ in Deum, et prædicaverunt jejunium, et vestiti sunt saccis a majore usque ad minorem. Et pervenit verbum ad regem Ninive. Et surrexit de solio suo, et abjecit vestimentum suum a se: et indutus est sacco, et sedit in cinere. Et clamavit, et dixit in Ninive ex ore regis, et principum ejus, dicens: Homines, et jumenta, et boves, et pecora non gustent quidquam: nec pascantur, et aquam non bibant. Et operiantur saccis homines, et jumenta: et clament ad Dominum in fortitudine. Et convertatur vir a via sua mala, et ab iniquitate, quæ est in manibus eorum. Quis scit, si convertatur, et ignoscat Deus: et revertatur a furore iræ suæ, et non peribimus? Et vidit Deus opera eorum, quia conversi sunt de via sua mala: et misertus est populo suo Dominus Deus noster.

596 HOLY WEEK.

The Bishop: Oremus.
The Deacon: Flectamus genua.
The Subdeacon: Levate.

Deus, qui diversitatem gentium in confessione tui nominis adunasti : da nobis et velle et posse quæ præcipis : ut populo ad æternitatem vocato una sit fides mentium, et pietas actionum. Per Dominum.

℞. Amen.

The Bishop: Let us pray.
The Deacon: Let us kneel down.
The Subdeacon: Stand up again.

O God, who hast united the several nations of the Gentiles in the profession of thy name ; give us both a will and a power to obey thy commands : that all thy people, who are called to eternity, may have the same faith in their minds, and piety in their actions. Through, &c.

℞. Amen.

ELEVENTH PROPHECY.

(*Deuteronomy*, CHAP. XXXI.)

The holy Church instructs the Catechumens, by this Lesson, upon the obligations they are about to contract with God. The grace of Regeneration is not to be conferred upon them, until they have made a solemn promise that they renounce Satan, the enemy of their God. Let them be faithful to their promise, and remember that God is the avenger of every infringement of so solemn a vow.

In diebus illis : Scripsit Moyses Canticum et docuit filios Israël. Præcepitque Dominus Josue filio Nun, et ait : Confortare, et esto robustus. Tu enim introduces filios Israël in terram, quam pollicitus sum eis : et ego ero tecum. Postquam ergo scripsit Moyses verba legis hujus in volumine, atque complevit ; præcepit Levitis, qui portabant arcum fœderis Do-

In those days : Moses wrote a canticle, and taught it the children of Israel. And the Lord commanded Josue, the son of Nun, and said : Take courage, and be valiant : for thou shalt bring the children of Israel into the land which I have promised, and I will be with thee. Therefore after Moses had wrote the words of this law in a volume, and finished it, he commanded the Levites, who carried the ark of the covenant of the Lord, saying: Take this book and put it in the side of the ark of the covenant of the Lord your God: that it may be there for a testimony against thee. For I know thy obstinacy, and thy most stiff neck. While I am yet living, and going in with you, you have always been rebellious against the Lord: how much more when I shall be dead? Gather unto me all the ancients of your tribes, and your doctors, and I will speak these words in their hearing, and will call heaven and earth to witness against them. For I know that, after my death, you will do wickedly, and will quickly turn aside from the way that I have commanded you: and evils shall come upon you in the latter times, when you shall do evil in the sight of the Lord, to provoke him by the works of your hands. Moses therefore spoke, in the hearing of the whole assembly of Israel, the words of this canticle, and finished it even to the end.

mini, dicens: Tollite librum istum, et ponite eum in latere arcæ fœderis Domini Dei vestri: ut sit tibi contra te in testimonium. Ego enim scio contentionem tuam, et cervicem tuam durissimam. Adhuc vivente me, et ingrediente vobiscum, semper contentiose egistis contra Dominum: quanto magis cum mortuus fuero? Congregate ad me omnes majores natu per tribus vestras, atque doctores: et loquar audientibus eis sermones istos, et invocabo contra eos cœlum et terram. Novi enim quod post mortem meam inique agetis: et declinabitis cito de via, quam præcepi vobis. Et occurrent vobis mala in extremo tempore, quando feceritis malum in conspectu Domini: ut irritetis eum per opera manuum vestrarum. Locutus est ergo Moyses, audiente universo cœtu Israël, verba carminis hujus: et ad finem usque complevit.

This Lesson is followed by a Tract, which is taken from the sublime Canticle sung by Moses, before quitting this earth. *The whole assembly of Israel* was present, and he put before them, in words of earnest zeal, the chastisements which God exercises against them that break the Covenant he vouchsafes to make with them.

TRACT.

Hear, O ye heavens, and I

Attende cœlum, et loquar: et audiat terra ex ore meo.

℣. Exspectetur sicut pluvia eloquium meum: et descendant sicut ros verba mea.

℣. Sicut imber super gramen, et sicut nix super fœnum: quia Nomen Domini invocabo.

℣. Date magnitudinem Deo nostro; Deus, vera opera ejus, et omnes viæ ejus judicia.

℣. Deus fidelis, in quo non est iniquitas: justus et sanctus Dominus.

The Bishop: Oremus.
The Deacon: Flectamus genua.
The Subdeacon: Levate.

Deus celsitudo humilium, et fortitudo rectorum: qui per sanctum Moysen puerum tuum, ita erudire populum tuum sacri carminis tui decantatione voluisti, ut illa legis iteratio fieret etiam nostra directio: excita in omnem justificatarum gentium plenitudinem potentiam tuam, et da lætitiam, mitigando terrorem: ut omnium peccatis tua remissione deletis, quod denuntiatum est in ultionem, transeat in salutem. Per Dominum.
℞. Amen.

will speak: and let the earth give ear to the words of my mouth.

℣. Let what I say be looked for like rain: and let my words drop down like dew.

℣. Like the shower upon the grass, and the snow upon the dry herb: for I will call upon the Name of the Lord.

℣. Publish the greatness of our God; he is God; his works are true, and all his ways are justice.

℣. God is faithful, in whom there is no iniquity: the Lord is just and holy.

The Bishop: Let us pray.
The Deacon: Let us kneel down.
The Subdeacon: Stand up again.

O God, who raisest the humble, and givest strength to the righteous: and who by thy holy servant Moses, wast pleased so to instruct thy people by the singing of the sacred canticle, that the repetition of the law might be also our direction: show thy power to all the multitude of Gentiles justified by thee, and, by mitigating thy terrors, grant them joy: that all their sins being pardoned by thee, the threatened vengeance may contribute to their salvation. Through, &c.
℞. Amen.

TWELFTH PROPHECY.

(Daniel, Chap. III.)

Here is the last instruction given to our Catechumens, before they descend into the Font of salvation. It is requisite that they should have a clear knowledge, of what the Christian warfare will demand of them. Perhaps, they will one day have to confess their God before the potentates of earth. Are they resolved to suffer every torture, even death itself, rather than deny his holy Name? Have there not been Apostates among those, whose Baptism was once a source of joy to the Church? It is of the utmost importance, therefore, that they should know the trials that await them. Our holy Mother the Church tells them the history of the three young Jews, who refused to adore the statue of the king of Babylon, though their refusal was to be punished by their being cast into a fiery furnace. Since the promulgation of the Christian law, millions of Martyrs have followed their example. The representation of these Three heroes of the true God is a favourite subject among the paintings of the Catacombs. It is true,—peace has been given to the Church; but the World is ever the enemy of Christ, and who knows but what Julian the Apostate may succeed Constantine?

In those days: King Nabuchodonosor made a statue of gold, of sixty cubits high, and six cubits broad, and he set it up in the plain of Dura, in the province of Babylon. Then Nabuchodonosor the king, sent to call together the nobles, the magistrates, and the judges, the captains, the rulers, and governors, and all the chief men of the provinces,	In diebus illis: Nabuchodonosor rex fecit statuam auream, altitudine cubitorum sexaginta, latitudine cubitorum sex: et statuit eam in campo Dura provinciæ Babyloniæ. Itaque Nabuchodonosor rex misit ad congregandos satrapas, magistratus et judices, duces et tyrannos, et præfectos, omnesque principes regio-

num: ut convenirent ad dedicationem statuæ, quam erexerat Nabuchodonosor rex. Tunc congregati sunt satrapæ, magistratus, et judices, duces et tyranni, et optimates, qui erant in potestatibus constituti, et universi principes regionum: ut convenirent ad dedicationem statuæ, quam erexerat Nabuchodonosor rex. Stabant autem in conspectu statuæ, quam posuerat Nabuchodonosor rex, et præco clamabat valenter: Vobis dicitur populis, tribubus et linguis: In hora, qua audieritis sonitum tubæ et fistulæ, et citharæ, sambucæ, et psalterii, et symphoniæ, et universi generis musicorum, cadentes adorate statuam auream, quam constituit Nabuchodonosor rex. Si quis autem non prostratus adoraverit, eadem hora mittetur in fornacem ignis ardentis.

Post hæc igitur statim ut audierunt omnes populi sonitum tubæ, fistulæ, et citharæ, sambucæ, et psalterii, et symphoniæ, et omnis generis musicorum, cadentes omnes populi, tribus, et linguæ adoraverunt statuam auream, quam constituerat Nabuchodonosor rex. Statimque in ipso tempore accedentes viri Chaldæi accusaverunt Judæos, dixeruntque Nabuchodonosor regi: Rex in

to come to the dedication of the statue which king Nabuchodonosor had set up. Then the nobles, the magistrates, and the judges, the captains, and rulers, and the great men that were placed in authority, and all the princes of the provinces were gathered together to come to the dedication of the statue which king Nabuchodonosor had set up. And they stood before the statue which king Nabuchodonosor had set up. Then a herald cried with a strong voice: To you it is commanded, O nations, tribes, and languages: that in the hour that you shall hear the sound of the trumpet, and of the flute, and of the harp, of the sackbut, and of the psaltery, and of the symphony, and of all kind of music; ye fall down and adore the golden statue which king Nabuchodonosor hath set up. But if any man should not fall down and adore, he shall the same hour be cast into a furnace of burning fire.

Upon this, therefore, at the time when all the people heard the sound of the trumpet, the flute, and the harp, of the sackbut, and the psaltery, of the symphony, and of all kind of music; all the nations, tribes, and languages, fell down and adored the golden statue, which king Nabuchodonosor had set up. And presently, at that very time, some Chaldeans came and accused the Jews: and said to king Nabuchodonosor: O king,

HOLY SATURDAY: MORNING SERVICE. 601

live for ever! Thou, O king, hast made a decree, that every man that shall hear the sound of the trumpet, the flute, and the harp, of the sackbut, and the psaltery, of the symphony, and of all kind of music, shall prostrate himself, and adore the golden statue: and that if any man shall not fall down and adore, he should be cast into a furnace of burning fire. Now there are certain Jews, whom thou hast set over the works of the province of Babylon, Sidrach, Misach, and Abdenago: these men, O king, have slighted thy decree: they worship not thy gods, nor do they adore the golden statue which thou hast set up.

Then Nabuchodonosor, in fury and in wrath, commanded that Sidrach, Misach, and Abdenago, should be brought: who immediately were brought before the king. And Nabuchodonosor the king spoke to them, and said: Is it true, O Sidrach, Misach, and Abdenago, that you do not worship my gods, nor adore the golden statue that I have set up? Now therefore if you be ready, at what hour soever you shall hear the sound of the trumpet, flute, harp, sackbut, and psaltery, and symphony, and of all kind of music, prostrate yourselves, and adore the statue which I have made: but if you do not adore, you shall be cast in the same hour into the furnace of burning fire: and who is the God that shall deliver you out of my hand?

æternum vive. Tu rex posuisti decretum: ut omnis homo, qui audierit sonitum tubæ, fistulæ, et citharæ, sambucæ, et psalterii, et symphoniæ, et universi generis musicorum, prosternat se, et adoret statuam auream. Si quis autem non procidens adoraverit, mittatur in fornacem ignis ardentis. Sunt ergo viri Judæi, quos constituisti super opera regionis Babylonis, Sidrach, Misach, et Abdenago: viri isti contempserunt, rex, decretum tuum: deos tuos non colunt, et statuam auream quam erexisti, non adorant.

Tunc Nabuchodonosor in furore et in ira, præcepit ut adducerentur Sidrach, Misach, et Abdenago. Qui confestim adducti sunt in conspectu regis. Pronuntiansque Nabuchodonosor rex, ait eis: Verene Sidrach, Misach, et Abdenago, deos meos non colitis, et statuam auream quam constitui, non adoratis? Nunc ergo, si estis parati, quacumque hora audieritis sonitum tubæ, fistulæ, citharæ, sambucæ, et psalterii, et symphoniæ, omnisque generis musicorum, prosternite vos, et adorate statuam quam feci. Quod si non adoraveritis, eadem hora mittemini in fornacem ignis ardentis: et quis est Deus, qui eripiet vos de manu mea?

Respondentes Sidrach, Misach, et Abdenago, dixerunt regi Nabuchodonosor: Non oportet nos de hac re respondere tibi. Ecce enim Deus noster quem colimus, potest eripere nos de camino ignis ardentis, et de manibus tuis, o rex, liberare. Quod si noluerit, notum sit tibi rex: quia Deos tuos non colimus, et statuam auream quam erexisti, non adoramus. Tunc Nabuchodonosor repletus est furore; et aspectus faciei illius immutatus est super Sidrach, Misach, et Abdenago. Et præcepit, ut succenderetur fornax septuplum, quam succendi consueverat. Et viris fortissimis de exercitu suo jussit, ut ligatis pedibus Sidrach, Misach, et Abdenago, mitterent eos in fornacem ignis ardentis. Et confestim viri illi vincti, cum braccis suis, et tiaris, et calceamentis, et vestibus, missi sunt in medium fornacis ignis ardentis; nam jussio regis urgebat. Fornax autem succensa erat nimis. Porro viros illos, qui miserant Sidrach, Misach, et Abdenago, interfecit flamma ignis. Viri autem hi tres, id est Sidrach, Misach, et Abdenago, ceciderunt in medio camino ignis ardentis, colligati. Et ambulabant in medio flammæ laudantes Deum, et benedicentes Domino.

Sidrach, Misach, and Abdenago, answered and said to king Nabuchodonosor: We have no occasion to answer thee concerning this matter. For behold our God, whom we worship, is able to save us from the furnace of burning fire, and to deliver us out of thy hands, O king. But if he will not, be it known to thee, O king, that we will not worship thy gods, nor adore the golden statue which thou hast set up. Then was Nabuchodonosor filled with fury: and the countenance of his face was changed against Sidrach, Misach, and Abdenago, and he commanded that the furnace should be heated seven times more than it had been accustomed to be heated. And he commanded the strongest men that were in his army, to bind the feet of Sidrach, Misach, and Abdenago, and to cast them into the furnace of burning fire. And immediately these men were bound, and were cast into the furnace of burning fire, with their coats and their caps, and their shoes, and their garments. For the king's commandment was urgent, and the furnace was heated exceedingly. And the flame of the fire slew those men that had cast in Sidrach, Misach, and Abdenago. But these three men, that is, Sidrach, Misach, and Abdenago, fell down bound in the midst of the furnace of burning fire. And they walked in the midst of the flame, praising God, and blessing the Lord.

HOLY SATURDAY: MORNING SERVICE.

The Bishop says a Prayer after this, as well as after the other Prophecies; but the Deacon gives not his invitation to kneel. The Church omits the genuflexion, in order to inspire the Catechumens with a horror for the idolatry of the Babylonians, who *bent their knee* before the statue of Nabuchodonosor.

LET US PRAY.

O Almighty and Eternal God, the only hope of the world, who by the voice of the prophets, hast manifested the mysteries of this present time: graciously increase the desires of thy people: since none of the faithful can advance in any virtue, without thy inspiration. Through, &c.

℟. Amen.

OREMUS.

Omnipotens sempiterne Deus, spes unica mundi, qui Prophetarum tuorum præconio, præsentium temporum declarasti mysteria: auge populi tui vota placatus: quia in nullo fidelium, nisi ex tua inspiratione, proveniunt quarumlibet incrementa virtutum. Per Dominum.

℟. Amen.

THE BLESSING OF THE FONT.

These Lessons, and Prayers, and Chants, have taken up a considerable portion of time: the sun has long since set, and the night is far advanced. All the preparatory exercises are over, and it is time to repair to the Baptistery. During the Prophecies, seven Subdeacons went thither, and there they have thrice recited the Litany; in the first recitation, they repeated each invocation seven times; in the second, five times; and in the third, three times. A Procession is formed towards this building, which is detached from the Church, and is either circular, or octagonal, in form. In the centre is a large Font, with several steps leading down to it. A stream of clear water flows into it from the mouth of a metal stag. Over the Font is suspended a canopy or cupola, in the centre of which is a dove with extended wings, which represents the Holy Ghost giving virtue to the Water beneath. Round the Font is a railing, within which none may enter but they who are to be baptised, the Sponsors, the Bishop and the Priests. Two Pavilions,—one for the men, the other for the women,—have been put up; they are for the Baptised, wherein, after they come from the Font, they may change their garments.

The Procession moves from the Church to the Baptistery in the following order. The Paschal Candle, (which represents the pillar of fire that guided the Israelites, by night, to the Red Sea, in whose waters they found salvation,) goes first, leading on the Catechumens. These follow, having their Sponsors on their right hand, for each candidate for Baptism is to be presented by a Christian. Then come two Acolytes; one carries the holy Chrism, the other the Oil of Catechumens. Next, the Clergy; and lastly, the Bishop and his assistant Ministers. The Procession is by torch-light. The stars are brightly shining in the canopy of heaven, and the air resounds with the melodious chanting. They are singing those verses of the Psalm, in which David compares his soul's pining after her God to the panting of a stag that thirsts for a fount of water. The Stag, an image of which is in the Font, is a figure of the Catechumen who longs for Baptism.

TRACT.

Sicut cervus desiderat ad fontes aquarum : ita desiderat anima mea ad te Deus.	As the Stag panteth after the fountains of water : so my soul panteth after thee, O God!
℣. Sitivit anima mea ad Deum vivum : quando veniam, et apparebo ante faciem Dei?	℣. My soul hath thirsted after the living God : when shall I come, and appear before the face of God?

℣. My tears have been my bread day and night, whilst it is said to me daily: Where is thy God?

℣. Fuerunt mihi lacrymæ meæ panes die ac nocte, dum dicitur mihi per singulos dies: Ubi est Deus tuus?

They soon reach the Baptistery. The Bishop, having come within sight of the Font, prefaces his blessing by a Prayer, in which he again uses the comparison of a *panting Stag*, to express to God the longing of this people after the *new life*, of which Christ is the source.

℣. The Lord be with you.
℞. And with thy spirit.

℣. Dominus vobiscum.
℞. Et cum spiritu tuo.

LET US PRAY.

Almighty and Everlasting God, look mercifully on the devotion of the people desiring a new birth, that as the hart pants after the fountain of thy waters: so mercifully grant that the thirst of their faith may, by the sacrament of Baptism, sanctify their souls and bodies. Through, &c.
℞. Amen.

OREMUS.

Omnipotens sempiterne Deus, respice propitius ad devotionem populi renascentis, qui, sicut cervus, aquarum tuarum expetit fontem: et concede propitius ut fidei ipsius sitis, Baptismatis mysterio animam corpusque sanctificet. Per Dominum.
℞. Amen.

The blessing of water for Baptism is of Apostolic institution, as we learn from many of the Holy Fathers, among whom we may mention St. Cyprian, St. Ambrose, St. Cyril of Jerusalem, and St. Basil. It is just, that the instrument of so divine a work should receive every mark of honour, that could secure to it the respect of mankind: and, after all, does not this honour and respect redound to that God, who chose this creature to be, as it were, the co-operator of his mercies to us? It was from water that we came forth Christians. The early Fathers allude to this, when they call Christians *the Fish* of Christ. We cannot be surprised, after this, that the sight of the element, that gave us our spiritual life, should excite us to joy, or that we should pay to this element an honour, which is referred to the Author of all the graces about to be bestowed.

The prayer used by the Bishop for blessing the Water, is so full of elevation of thought, energy of diction, and authority of doctrine, that we may, without hesitation, attribute it to the earliest ages of the Church. The ceremonies which accompany it bespeak its venerable antiquity. It is sung to the solemn tone of the Preface, which imparts such a lyric effect. The Pontiff first recites a preliminary prayer, and then begins his magnificent Blessing. He is filled with the holy enthusiasm of the Church. He turns to the Faithful, and they respond. He is going to lead them to such grand mysteries:—*Sursum corda!*

℣. Dominus vobiscum.
℟. Et cum spiritu tuo.

℣. The Lord be with you.
℟. And with thy spirit.

OREMUS.

Omnipotens sempiterne Deus, adesto magnæ pietatis tuæ mysteriis, adesto sacramentis; et ad recreandos novos populos, quos tibi fons Baptismatis parturit, Spiritum adoptionis emitte: ut quod nostræ humilitatis gerendum est ministerio, virtutis tuæ impleatur effectu. Per Dominum nostrum Jesum Christum Filium tuum, qui tecum vivit et regnat in unitate Spiritus Sancti, Deus,

Per omnia sæcula sæculorum.
℟. Amen.

LET US PRAY.

Almighty and Everlasting God, be present at these mysteries, be present at these sacraments of thy great goodness: and send forth the spirit of adoption to regenerate the new people, whom the font of Baptism brings forth: that what is to be done by our weak ministry, may be accomplished by the effect of thy power. Through our Lord Jesus Christ thy Son, who liveth and reigneth with thee, in the unity of the Holy Ghost, God,

For ever and ever!

℟. Amen.

HOLY SATURDAY: MORNING SERVICE.

℣. The Lord be with you.
℟. And with thy spirit.
℣. Lift up your hearts!
℟. We have them fixed on God.
℣. Let us give thanks to the Lord our God.
℟. It is meet and just.

It is truly meet and just, right and available to salvation, that we should always, and in all places, give thanks to thee, O Holy Lord, Almighty Father, Eternal God, who by thy invisible power dost wonderfully produce the effect of thy sacraments: and though we are unworthy to administer so great mysteries: yet as thou dost not forsake the gifts of thy grace, so thou inclinest the ears of thy goodness, even to our prayers. O God, whose Spirit, in the very beginning of the world, moved over the waters, that even then the nature of water might receive the virtue of sanctification. O God, who by water didst wash away the crimes of the guilty world, and by the overflowing of the deluge didst give a figure of regeneration, that one and the same element might, in a mystery, be the end of vice and the origin of virtue. Look, O Lord, on the face of thy church, and multiply in her thy regenerations, who by the streams of thy abundant grace fillest thy City with joy: and openest the font of Baptism all over the world, for the renovation of the Gentiles: that by the command of thy Majesty she may receive the grace of thy only Son from the Holy Ghost.

℣. Dominus vobiscum.
℟. Et cum spiritu tuo.
℣. Sursum corda.
℟. Habemus ad Dominum.
℣. Gratias agamus Domino Deo nostro.
℟. Dignum et justum est.

Vere dignum et justum est, æquum et salutare; nos tibi semper, et ubique gratias agere, Domine sancte, Pater omnipotens, æterne Deus, qui invisibili potentia, sacramentorum tuorum mirabiliter operaris effectum; et licet nos tantis mysteriis exsequendis simus indigni: tu tamen gratiæ tuæ dona non deserens, etiam ad nostras preces, aures tuæ pietatis inclinas. Deus, cujus Spiritus super aquas, inter ipsa mundi primordia ferebatur: ut jam tunc virtutem sanctificationis, aquarum natura conciperet. Deus, qui nocentis mundi crimina per aquas abluens, regenerationis speciem in ipsa diluvii effusione signasti; ut unius ejusdemque elementi mysterio, et finis esset vitiis, et origo virtutibus; respice, Domine, in faciem Ecclesiæ tuæ; et multiplica in ea regenerationes tuas, qui gratiæ tuæ affluentis impetu lætificas Civitatem tuam, fontemque Baptismatis aperis toto orbe terrarum gentibus innovandis: ut tuæ majestatis imperio, sumat Unigeniti tui gratiam de Spiritu Sancto.

Here the Pontiff pauses a moment, and putting his hand into the Water, divides it in the form of a cross, to signify, that it is by the Cross that this element receives the power of regenerating the souls of men. This wonderful power had been promised to Water; but the promise was not fulfilled until Christ had shed his Blood upon the Cross. It is this Blood which operates by the Water, on the souls of men; and with the action of this precious Blood, is joined that of the Holy Ghost, as the Pontiff tells us in his Prayer, which he thus continues:

Qui hanc aquam regenerandis hominibus præparatam, arcana sui numinis admixtione fœcundet: ut sanctificatione concepta, ab immaculato divini fontis utero, in novam renata creaturam, progenies cœlestis emergat: et quos aut sexus in corpore, aut ætas discernit in tempore, omnes in unam pariat gratia mater infantiam. Procul ergo hinc, jubente te Domine, omnis spiritus immundus abscedat: procul tota nequitia diabolicæ fraudis absistat. Nihil hic loci habeat contrariæ virtutis admixtio: non insidiando circumvolet, non latendo subrepat, non inficiendo corrumpat.	Who, by a secret mixture of his divine virtue, may render this water fruitful for the regeneration of men, to the end that those who have been sanctified in the immaculate womb of this divine font, being born again a new creature, may come forth a heavenly offspring: and that all that are distinguished either by sex in body, or by age in time, may be brought forth to the same infancy by grace, their spiritual mother. Therefore may all unclean spirits, by thy command, O Lord, depart far from hence: may the whole malice of diabolical deceit be entirely banished: may no power of the enemy prevail here: may he not fly about to lay his snares: may he not creep in by his secret artifice: may he not corrupt with his infection.

After having thus besought God to protect the Water of the Font from the influence which Satan seeks to exercise over every creature, the Bishop puts

HOLY SATURDAY: MORNING SERVICE. 609

his hand upon it. The august character of a Pontiff or Priest is a source of sanctification: the mere contact of their consecrated hand produces a salutary effect, as often as they act in virtue of the Priesthood of Christ, which dwells within them.

May this holy and innocent creature be free from all the assaults of the enemy, and purified by the destruction of all his malice. May it be a living fountain, a regenerating water, a purifying stream: that all those that are to be washed in this saving bath, may obtain, by the operation of the Holy Ghost, the grace of a perfect purification.	Sit hæc sancta et innocens creatura libera ab omni impugnatoris incursu, et totius nequitiæ purgata discessu. Sit fons vivus, aqua regenerans, unda purificans: ut omnes hoc lavacro salutifero diluendi, operante in eis Spiritu Sancto, perfectæ purgationis indulgentiam consequantur.

Whilst pronouncing the following words, the Bishop blesses the Water, thrice making over it the sign of the cross.

Therefore I bless thee, O creature of water, by the living God, by the true God, by the holy God: by that God who in the beginning separated thee by his word from the dry land, whose Spirit moved over thee.	Unde benedico te, creatura aquæ, per Deum vivum, per Deum verum, per Deum sanctum: per Deum, qui te; in principio, verbo separavit ab arida: cujus Spiritus super te ferebatur.

The Bishop next makes an allusion to the four rivers which watered the earthly Paradise. He again divides the Water with his hand, and sprinkles it towards the North, South, East and West, for the four parts of the World received the preaching of Baptism. Whilst performing this expressive ceremony, he continues his prayer as follows:

Who made thee flow from the fountain of Paradise, and	Qui te de Paradisi fonte manare fecit, et in quatuor

fluminibus totam terram rigare præcepit; qui te in deserto amaram, suavitate indita fecit esse potabilem, et sitienti populo de petra produxit. Benedico te, et per Jesum Christum Filium ejus unicum, Dominum nostrum: qui te in Cana Galilææ, signo admirabili, sua potentia convertit in vinum. Qui pedibus super te ambulavit: et a Joanne in Jordane in te baptizatus est. Qui te una cum sanguine de latere suo produxit: et discipulis suis jussit, ut credentes baptizarentur in te, dicens: Ite, docete omnes gentes, baptizantes eos in nomine Patris, et Filii, et Spiritus Sancti.

commanded thee to water the whole earth with thy four rivers. Who changing thy bitterness in the desert into sweetness, made thee fit to drink, and produced thee out of a rock to quench the thirst of the people. I bless thee also by our Lord Jesus Christ, his only Son: who in Cana of Galilee changed thee into wine, by a wonderful miracle of his power. Who walked upon thee dry foot, and was baptised in thee by John in the Jordan. Who made thee flow out of his side together with his blood, and commanded his disciples, that such as believed should be baptised in thee, saying: Go, teach all nations, baptising them in the name of the Father, and of the Son, and of the Holy Ghost.

Here the Bishop interrupts the solemn and triumphant tone of the Preface, and simply reads the following words. He has signed the Water with the sign of the Cross; he now invokes upon it the vivifying action of the Holy Ghost.

Hæc nobis præcepta servantibus, tu Deus omnipotens, clemens adesto: tu benignus adspira.

Do thou, Almighty God, mercifully assist us that observe this command: do thou graciously inspire us.

The Holy Ghost is called *Spirit*, which means a *Breath*: he is the Divine Breathing, that mighty Wind, which was heard in the Cenacle. The Pontiff, to express this character of the Third Person of the Blessed Trinity, thrice breathes, in the form of a cross, over the Water of the Font, and then continues in the same reading tone:

HOLY SATURDAY: MORNING SERVICE. 611

Do thou with thy mouth bless these clear waters: that besides their natural virtue of cleansing the body, they may also be effectual for the purifying of the soul.	Tu has simplices aquas tuo ore benedicito : ut præter naturalem emundationem, quam lavandis possunt adhibere corporibus, sint etiam purificandis mentibus efficaces.

Then taking the Paschal Candle, he dips the lower end of it into the Font. This rite signifies the mystery of Christ's Baptism in the Jordan, whereby the element of Water received the pledge of its future sanctifying power. The Son of God went down into the stream, and the Holy Ghost came upon him in the form of a Dove. But now, it is something more than a promise: the Water receives the reality, the virtue; and it receives it by the action of these two Divine Persons. The Bishop, therefore, resuming the tone of the Preface, chants these words, whilst plunging into the Font the Paschal Candle, the symbol of Christ, over whom hovers the celestial Dove:

May the virtue of the Holy Ghost descend into all the water of this font.	Descendat in hanc plenitudinem fontis virtus Spiritus Sancti.

After these words, the Pontiff takes the Candle out of the Water, and then plunges it in again still deeper, singing the same words, but on a higher note:

May the virtue of the Holy Ghost descend into all the water of this font.	Descendat in hanc plenitudinem fontis virtus Spiritus Sancti.

Having again withdrawn the Candle, he plunges it a third time into the Water, even to the bottom of the Font: he sings the same words to a still higher note:

Descendat in hanc plenitudinem fontis virtus Spiritus Sancti.	May the virtue of the Holy Ghost descend into all the water of this font.

Before taking the Candle from the water the third time, the Bishop leans forward over the Font: and that he may signify the union of the power of the Holy Ghost with that of Christ, he breathes again upon the Water, not, this time, in the form of a cross, but in that of the Greek letter Ψ, which is the initial of the Greek word for *Spirit*. This done, he resumes his Prayer by the following words:

Totamque hujus aquæ substantiam, regenerandi fœcundet effectu.	And make the whole substance of this water fruitful and capable of regenerating.

The Paschal Candle is then raised out of the Font, and the Bishop thus continues:

Hic omnium peccatorum maculæ deleantur: hic natura ad imaginem tuam condita, et ad honorem sui reformata principii, cunctis vetustatis squaloribus emundetur: ut omnis homo sacramentum hoc regenerationis ingressus, in veræ innocentiæ novam infantiam renascatur.	Here may the stains of all sins be washed out: here may human nature, created to thy image, and reformed to the honour of its author, be cleansed from all the filth of the old man: that all who receive this sacrament of regeneration, may be born again new children of true innocence.

The Bishop recites the rest in the simple reading tone:

Per Dominum nostrum Jesum Christum Filium tuum: qui venturus est judicare vivos et mortuos, et sæculum per ignem. ℟. Amen.	Through our Lord Jesus Christ thy Son: who shall come to judge the living and the dead, and the world by fire. ℟. Amen.

As soon as the people have answered *Amen*, one of the Priests sprinkles them with the Water, that has thus been blessed; and an Acolyte fills a large vessel with it, that it may be used in the service of the Church, and in sprinkling the houses of the Faithful.

But the Church is not satisfied with having given her blessing to the Water. On Thursday, she was put in possession of the graces of the Holy Ghost by receiving the Holy Oils: with these she would now honour the Font, by mingling a portion of them with the Water. The Faithful,—seeing how every symbol expressive of divine adoption is made to bear upon the Water, whence men receive salvation,—will learn what should be the reverence they should have for the Font. The Bishop, taking the Oil of Catechumens, pours it into the Water, saying:

May this font be sanctified and made fruitful by the Oil of salvation, for such as are regenerated therein unto life everlasting.	Sanctificetur, et fœcundetur fons iste Oleo salutis renascentibus ex eo, in vitam æternam.
℟. Amen.	℟. Amen.

Then taking the Holy Chrism, he pours it into the Font, saying:

May this infusion of the Chrism of our Lord Jesus Christ, and of the Holy Ghost the Comforter, be made in the name of the Holy Trinity.	Infusio Chrismatis Domini nostri Jesu Christi, et Spiritus Sancti Paracliti, fiat in nomine sanctæ Trinitatis.
℟. Amen.	℟. Amen.

Finally, taking the Chrism in his right hand, and the Oil of Catechumens in his left, he pours from the two phials, at one and the same time. This sacred rite signifies the superabundant grace of Baptism. Whilst pouring in the two Oils together, the Bishop says:

May this mixture of the Chrism of sanctification, and	Commixtio Chrismatis sanctificationis, et Olei unc-

tionis, et aquæ baptismatis, pariter fiat, in nomine Patris, et Filii, et Spiritus Sancti.	of the Oil of unction, and of the water of Baptism, be made in the name of the Father, and of the Son, and of the Holy Ghost.
℞. Amen.	℞. Amen.

After these words, the Bishop puts his hand into the Font, and mixes the holy Oils with the Water, that thus every portion of it may come into contact with this additional source of sanctification. Having wiped his hand, he takes off such of his Vestments as would inconvenience him in the administration of Baptism.

BAPTISM.

The Pontiff returns to the Font, and the Catechumens are called in turns. They come one by one, led by their Sponsors. The Bishop stands upon a platform, that reaches over the Font. The Catechumen takes off all garments as far as the waist, descends the steps, and goes into the Water, within reach of the Bishop's hand. The Bishop then asks the Catechumen: "Dost thou believe in "God, the Father Almighty, Creator of heaven and "earth?" The Catechumen answers: "I do believe."— "Dost thou believe in Jesus Christ, his only Son, "our Lord, who was born and suffered for us?"—"I "do believe."—"Dost thou believe in the Holy "Ghost, the holy Catholic Church, the communion "of Saints, the forgiveness of sins, the resurrection "of the body, and life everlasting?"—"I do believe." And having thus received the confession of the Catechumen's Faith, the Bishop asks him, or her: "Wilt thou be baptised?"—"I will," answers the Catechumen. Then the Bishop places his hand upon the Catechumen's head, and thrice immerges him, or her, under the Water, saying: "I baptise thee, in the

"name of the Father,—and of the Son,—and of the
"Holy Ghost."

Thrice, then, has the Catechumen entirely disappeared under the Water: they have closed over and shrouded him. We have the explanation of this given us by the great Apostle:—the Water of Baptism is the tomb, in which we are buried together with Christ; and, together with him, we rise again to life: the death we had suffered, was the death of sin; the life we are henceforth to live, is the life of grace.[1] Thus is the mystery of Jesus' Resurrection repeated, with all its fulness, in them that are baptised. But before the Baptised comes from the Font, a sacred rite is performed over him, which completes his resemblance with Christ. Whilst Jesus was yet standing in the waters of the Jordan, the Holy Ghost descended upon him in the form of a Dove: and before the Neophyte comes forth from the Font, a Priest anoints his head with the Chrism, which is a gift received from the Holy Spirit. This anointing expresses the kingly and priestly character that resides in the Christian, for, by his union with Jesus Christ, his Head, he partakes, in some degree, of the Royalty and the Priesthood of this Divine Mediator. Thus loaded with honours by the Divine Word and the Holy Ghost, and adopted by the Eternal Father, who sees in him a member of his own Son,—the Neophyte comes up from the Font by the steps of the side opposite to that by which he descended, beautiful in grace and spotless as the flocks of which the Canticle speaks such praises.[2] The Sponsor is ready to receive him from the Font; he stretches out his hand to help him to mount the steps, and covers his shoulders with a cloth.

Thus goes on the divine work of the holy Font: each Baptism is a resurrection from sin to justifica-

---

[1] Rom. vi. 4.   [2] Cant. iv. 2.

tion. But the Pontiff has to administer to the Neophytes another Sacrament, which is the *confirming* them by the gift of the Holy Ghost, and which he alone can confer. Were he to wait till all are Baptised, Easter-day would dawn upon them, before the whole of to-night's service is over. He therefore baptises a few himself,—men, women, and children,—and leaves his Priests to administer baptism to all the rest. In the Baptistery, there is a part which is called the *Chrismarium*, because the Sacrament of Chrism, or Confirmation, is given there. Thither does the Pontiff now repair, and sits upon the throne prepared for him. He resumes the Vestments he had laid aside, when descending to the Font; and immediately, they bring to him the Neophytes he has baptised, and, after them, those baptised by the Priests. He gives to each a white robe, which they must wear till the following Saturday; and as he gives it, he says: "Receive this "white garment, which is holy and unspotted: and "see thou carry it before the judgment-seat of our "Lord Jesus Christ, that thou mayest have eternal "life!" As soon as the Neophytes have received it, they retire to the Pavilions prepared in the Baptistery. There they change their wet clothes for others, and, aided by their Sponsors, they vest themselves with the White Robe. They then return to the Chrismarium, where they are to receive the Sacrament of Confirmation,

CONFIRMATION.

On Thursday last, when consecrating the Chrism, the Pontiff told us how, when the Waters of the deluge had fulfilled their office of purifying the earth, the Dove appeared, bearing an olive-branch in her beak ;—it was the symbol of peace, and of the reign of Him, whose sacred Name signifies *the Anointed:* his name is *Christ.* Our Neophytes have been purified from their sins by the Water of Baptism: they are now kneeling before the Pontiff, awaiting the gift of the Dove, and longing for that pledge of peace whereof the Olive is the symbol. The holy Chrism has been already marked upon their heads; but, then, it was only a sign of the dignity to which they had been raised. Now, it does more than *signify* grace,—it works it in the soul. Neither is it in the power of a Priest to give this anointing, which *confirms* the Christian; it requires the hand of a Bishop, for he alone can consecrate the Chrism.

The Neophytes are arranged before him:—on one side, the men; on the other, the women; the infants are in their Sponsors' arms. The Adults place their right foot on the right foot of their godfather or godmother, showing, by this sign of union, their spiritual filiation in the Church.

The sight of this innocent flock gladdens the heart of the Pontiff. He rises from his throne, and thus addresses them: "May the Holy Ghost come down "upon you, and may the power of the Most High keep "you from sin!" Then stretching forth his hands, he invokes upon them the seven gifts of the Holy Spirit, whose action is to *confirm,* in our Neophytes, the graces they have received in the Font of Baptism.

Led by their Sponsors, they come, one by one, before the Bishop. Their faces express the eagerness, wherewith they long to receive what will make them perfect Christians. The Pontiff signs the forehead of each of them with the holy Chrism; and, by this he imprints an indelible character on the soul. The words he uses are these: "I sign thee with the sign "of the Cross, and I confirm thee with the Chrism of "salvation, in the name of the Father, and of the "Son, and of the Holy Ghost." Then giving a slight blow on the cheek, (which, with the ancients, was the sign of a slave's being made a freedman,) he signifies that the Neophyte is admitted into the liberty of the Children of God; and he says: "Peace be with thee!" The assistant Ministers tie a bandlet round the forehead, so that nothing may touch the part which has been anointed with holy Chrism. The Neophytes have to wear this bandlet until the Saturday following, when they will lay aside the white garments received at their Baptism.

The night has passed away during the solemnisation of these sublime mysteries: the hour has come for the glad celebration of the Holy Sacrifice in honor of our Lord's Resurrection from the Tomb. It is time for the Pastor to lead back to the Temple his happy flock, that has received such a glorious addition. It is time for him to give to his dear Sheep the Divine Nourishment, to which they have henceforth a claim. The gates of the Baptistery are thrown open, and all return in procession to the Church. The Paschal Candle, the Pillar of Fire, goes before the troop of Neophytes, whose white robes glitter in the day-dawn of Easter. The faithful people follow after the Bishop and Clergy, and all enter, with an air of triumph, into the Church. During the Procession, they again chant the Canticle that was sung by Moses and the children of Israel after the Passage through the Red Sea. The Bishop repairs to the Secretarium, where he is robed in the richest Vestments of the Treasury. During this interval, the Chanters recommence the Litany, repeating each invocation thrice over. According to the present arrangement of the Liturgy, it is sung but once during the whole of to-day's Service,—that is, as soon as the Clergy return to the Choir, after the Blessing of the Font,—and each invocation is sung twice. In Churches where there is no Font, the Litany is sung after the Prayer which follows the Twelfth Prophecy; and as far as the words, *Peccatores, te rogamus audi nos*, the Celebrant and Ministers lie prostrate on the Altar steps, praying for the Neophytes who are this day added to the Church, throughout the world. We here give the Litany as it is now sung, with the additions that have been made to it at various periods.

THE LITANY.

Lord, have mercy on us.	Kyrie, eleïson.
Christ, have mercy on us.	Christe, eleïson.
Lord, have mercy on us.	Kyrie, eleïson.
Christ, hear us.	Christe, audi nos.
Christ, graciously hear us.	Christe, exaudi nos.
God the Father, of heaven, have mercy on us.	Pater de cœlis, Deus, miserere nobis.
God the Son, Redeemer of the world, have mercy on us.	Fili, Redemptor mundi Deus, miserere nobis.
God the Holy Ghost, have mercy on us.	Spiritus Sancte, Deus, miserere nobis.
Holy Trinity, one God, have mercy on us.	Sancta Trinitas, unus Deus, miserere nobis.
Holy Mary, pray for us.	Sancta Maria, ora pro nobis.
Holy Mother of God, pray for us.	Sancta Dei Genitrix, ora pro nobis.
Holy Virgin of Virgins, pray for us.	Sancta Virgo Virginum, ora pro nobis.
Saint Michael, pray for us.	Sancte Michael, ora pro nobis.
Saint Gabriel,	Sancte Gabriel,
Saint Raphael,	Sancte Raphael,
All ye holy Angels and Archangels,	Omnes sancti Angeli et Archangeli, orate pro nobis.
All ye holy orders of blessed Spirits,	Omnes sancti beatorum Spirituum ordines, orate pro nobis.
Saint John Baptist,	Sancte Joannes Baptista, ora pro nobis.
Saint Joseph,	Sancte Joseph,
All ye holy Patriarchs and Prophets,	Omnes sancti Patriarchæ et Prophetæ, orate pro nobis.

Sancte Petre, ora pro nobis.	Saint Peter,
Sancte Paule,	Saint Paul,
Sancte Andrea,	Saint Andrew,
Sancte Joannes,	Saint John,
Omnes sancti Apostoli et Evangelistæ, orate pro nobis.	All ye holy Apostles and Evangelists,
Omnes sancti Discipuli Domini, orate pro nobis.	All ye holy Disciples of our Lord,
Sancte Stephane, ora pro nobis.	Saint Stephen,
Sancte Laurenti,	Saint Laurence,
Sancte Vincenti,	Saint Vincent,
Omnes sancti Martyres, orate pro nobis.	All ye holy Martyrs,
Sancte Sylvester, ora pro nobis.	Saint Sylvester,
Sancte Gregori,	Saint Gregory,
Sancte Augustine,	Saint Augustine,
Omnes sancti Pontifices et Confessores, orate.	All ye holy Bishops and Confessors,
Omnes sancti Doctores, orate pro nobis.	All ye holy Doctors,
Sancte Antoni, ora pro nobis.	Saint Antony,
Sancte Benedicte,	Saint Benedict,
Sancte Dominice,	Saint Dominic,
Sancte Francisce,	Saint Francis,
Omnes sancti Sacerdotes et Levitæ, orate pro nobis.	All ye holy Priests and Levites,
Omnes sancti Monachi et Eremitæ, orate pro nobis.	All ye holy Monks and Hermits,
Sancta Maria Magdalena, ora pro nobis.	Saint Mary Magdalene,
Sancta Agnes,	Saint Agnes,
Sancta Cæcilia,	Saint Cecily,
Sancta Catharina,	Saint Catharine,
Sancta Agatha,	Saint Agatha,
Sancta Anastasia,	Saint Anastasia,
Omnes Sanctæ Virgines et Viduæ, orate pro nobis.	All ye holy Virgins and Widows,
Omnes Sancti et Sanctæ Dei, intercedite pro nobis.	All ye men and women, Saints of God, make intercession for us.
Propitius esto, parce nobis Domine.	Be merciful to us, spare us, O Lord.

HOLY SATURDAY: MORNING SERVICE.

Be merciful to us, graciously hear us, O Lord.	Propitius esto, exaudi nos Domine.
From all evil, deliver us, O Lord.	Ab omni malo, libera nos Domine.
From all sin, deliver us, O Lord.	Ab omni peccato, libera nos Domine.
From everlasting death,	A morte perpetua, libera nos Domine.
Through the mystery of thy holy Incarnation,	Per mysterium sanctæ Incarnationis tuæ, libera nos Domine.
Through thy Coming,	Per Adventum tuum, libera nos Domine.
Through thy Nativity,	Per Nativitatem tuam, libera nos Domine.
Through thy Baptism and holy Fasting,	Per Baptismum et sanctum Jejunium tuum, libera nos Domine.
Through thy Cross and Passion,	Per Crucem et Passionem tuam, libera nos Domine.
Through thy Death and Burial,	Per Mortem et Sepulturam tuam, libera nos Domine.
Through thy holy Resurrection,	Per sanctam Resurrectionem tuam, libera nos Domine.
Through thy admirable Ascension,	Per admirabilem Ascensionem tuam, libera nos Domine.
Through the coming of the Holy Ghost the Comforter,	Per adventum Spiritus Sancti Paracliti, libera nos Domine.
In the day of Judgment,	In die Judicii, libera nos Domine.
We sinners, we beseech thee, hear us.	Peccatores, te rogamus audi nos.
That thou spare us, we beseech thee, hear us.	Ut nobis parcas, te rogamus audi nos.
That thou vouchsafe to govern and preserve thy holy Church,	Ut Ecclesiam tuam sanctam regere et conservare digneris, te rogamus audi nos.
That thou vouchsafe to preserve our Apostolic Prelate, and all Ecclesiastical Orders, in holy religion,	Ut domnum Apostolicum, et omnes Ecclesiasticos Ordines, in sancta religione conservare digneris, te rogamus audi nos.

Ut inimicos sanctæ Ecclesiæ humiliare digneris, te rogamus audi nos.	That thou vouchsafe to humble the enemies of thy holy Church,
Ut regibus et principibus christianis pacem et veram concordiam donare digneris, te rogamus audi nos.	That thou vouchsafe to give peace and true concord to Christian Kings and Princes,
Ut nosmetipsos in tuo sancto servitio confortare et conservare digneris, te rogamus audi nos.	That thou vouchsafe to strengthen and preserve us in thy holy service,
Ut omnibus benefactoribus nostris sempiterna bona retribuas, te rogamus audi nos.	That thou render eternal good things to all our benefactors,
Ut fructus terræ dare et conservare digneris, te rogamus audi nos.	That thou vouchsafe to give and preserve the fruits of the earth,
Ut omnibus fidelibus defunctis requiem æternam donare digneris, te rogamus audi nos.	That thou vouchsafe to give eternal rest to all the Faithful departed,
Ut nos exaudire digneris, te rogamus audi nos.	That thou vouchsafe graciously to hear us,
Agnus Dei, qui tollis peccata mundi, parce nobis Domine.	O Lamb of God, who takest away the sins of the world, spare us, O Lord.
Agnus Dei, qui tollis peccata mundi, exaudi nos Domine.	O Lamb of God, who takest away the sins of the world, graciously hear us, O Lord.
Agnus Dei, qui tollis peccata mundi, miserere nobis.	O Lamb of God, who takest away the sins of the world, have mercy on us.
Christe audi nos.	Christ, hear us.
Christe exaudi nos.	Christ, graciously hear us.

MASS.

The solemn Litany is drawing to its end, and the Choir has already begun its closing invocation, the *Kyrie eleison!* The Pontiff comes forth from the Secretarium, with all the pomp that marks the principal Feasts of the Church. The chant becomes more majestic, and lingers on the brief words of supplication. *Kyrie eleison!*—thrice to the Father: *Christe eleison!*—thrice to the Son: *Kyrie eleison!*—thrice to the Holy Ghost. During this time, the Bishop is reciting, at the foot of the Altar, the usual Psalm and Prayers; and then, ascending to the Altar, he offers the homage of Incense to the Most High. Hence, an Introit, which, on other occasions, is sung by the Choir during the Procession from the Secretarium to the Altar, is not needed.

The Morning-star has blended its rays with those of our Paschal Candle, as the Deacon prayed might be; but now, the Morning-star itself begins to pale, for the Star of Day,—the figure of our Jesus, the Sun of Justice,—is soon to rise. The assembly of the Faithful people,—the men on the right, the women on the left,—is now greater than it was at first. The space near the doors, for Catechumens, is vacant. In a prominent part of the aisles, we see the Neophytes, with their White Robe, and Bandlet, and lighted taper in their hands.

The censing of the Altar is finished: and then,— O glorious triumph of our Risen Jesus!—the Pontiff sings forth, in a transport of joy: *Gloria in excelsis Deo!* The hitherto silent Bells peal to the glad Angelic Hymn. The enthusiasm of our holy Faith has mastered every heart, making it beat with emotion. The people take up the heavenly Canticle, and continue it to the end; and then the Bishop sings the following Prayer for the newly Baptised:

COLLECT.

O God, who enlightenest this most sacred night, by the glory of the Resurrection of the Lord; preserve in the new offspring of thy family the spirit of adoption thou hast

Deus, qui hanc sacratissimam noctem gloria Dominicæ Resurrectionis illustras: conserva in nova familiæ tuæ progenie adoptionis Spiritum quem dedisti: ut corpore et mente renovati, puram tibi exhibeant servitutem. Per eumdem Dominum.

given them; that being renewed in body and soul, they may serve thee with purity of heart. Through the same, &c.

After the Collect, the Subdeacon ascends the Epistle Ambo, and chants these impressive words, that are addressed by the great Apostle to the Neophytes, who have just risen, by Baptism, with Christ.

EPISTLE.

Lectio Epistolæ beati Pauli Apostoli ad Colossenses.

Lesson of the Epistle of Saint Paul the Apostle to the Colossians.

Cap. III.

Ch. III.

Fratres, si consurrexistis cum Christo, quæ sursum sunt quærite, ubi Christus est in dextera Dei sedens; quæ sursum sunt sapite, non quæ super terram. Mortui enim estis: et vita vestra est abscondita cum Christo in Deo. Cum autem Christus apparuerit vita vestra: tunc et vos apparebitis cum ipso in gloria.

Brethren: if you be risen with Christ, seek the things that are above, where Christ is sitting at the right hand of God: mind the things that are above, not the things that are upon the earth. For you are dead; and your life is hid with Christ in God. When Christ shall appear, who is your life; then you also shall appear with him in glory.

Having chanted these few, but telling, words, the Subdeacon comes down from the Ambo, and goes to the Bishop's throne. He bows before the Pontiff, and thus addresses him; and as he speaks, the souls of the Faithful, yea, the very walls of the Church, echo with the joyful tidings: "Venerable Father! I bring "you tidings of great joy: it is the *Alleluia!*" The Bishop rises, and, filled with holy ardour, intones the *Alleluia* to the well known melody. The Choir repeats it after him. Thrice, (and, each time, with an increase of joy,) is the heavenly word interchanged between the Pontiff and the Choir. At

HOLY SATURDAY: MORNING SERVICE. 625

this moment, all mournfulness is at an end. One feels that God has accepted the expiatory works of our Lent; and that, by the merits of his Son now Risen from the Grave, he pardons our earth, since he permits us to hear once more the Song of Heaven. The Choir subjoins this verse of the Psalm, which celebrates the mercy of Jehovah.

| Praise the Lord, for he is good : for his mercy endureth for ever. | Confitemini Domino quoniam bonus : quoniam in sæculum misericordia ejus. |

But there is still wanting something to the joy of our Easter. Jesus has risen from the Tomb; but, so far, he has not shown himself to all. His Blessed Mother, Magdalene, and the other holy women, are the only ones who have as yet seen him : it is not till the evening, that he will appear to his Apostles. We have but just begun the Day. Therefore it is, that the Church once more offers her praise to her God, under the Lenten formula of the *Tract*.

TRACT.

| Praise the Lord all ye nations ; join in his praise, all ye people.
℣. For his mercy is confirmed upon us ; and the truth of the Lord remaineth for ever. | Laudate Dominum omnes gentes : et collaudate eum omnes populi.
℣. Quoniam confirmata est super nos misericordia ejus : et veritas Domini manet in æternum. |

Whilst the Choir is singing this Psalm to a melody, which has something of mournfulness about it, the Deacon goes to the Ambo, from which he is to chant the Gospel. The Acolytes do not accompany him with their torches, but the Thurifer goes with him, as usual, with the Incense. Here again we have an allusion to the events which took place on this great morning :—the Women went to the Sepulchre, carrying *sweet spices* with them, but the light of faith in the Resurrection was not as yet in their hearts. The Incense signifies their spices; the absence of light signifies their want of faith.

GOSPEL.

| Sequentia sancti Evangelii secundum Matthæum. | Sequel of the holy Gospel according to Matthew. |

Cap. XXVIII. — *Ch. XXVIII.*

Vespere autem Sabbati quæ lucescit in prima Sabbati: venit Maria Magdalene, et altera Maria videre sepulcrum. Et ecce terræ motus factus est magnus. Angelus enim Domini descendit de cœlo, et accedens revolvit lapidem, et sedebat super eum. Erat autem aspectus ejus, sicut fulgur: et vestimentum ejus, sicut nix. Præ timore autem ejus, exterriti sunt custodes: et facti sunt velut mortui. Respondens autem Angelus, dixit mulieribus: Nolite timere vos. Scio enim, quod Jesum, qui crucifixus est, quæritis. Non est hic. Surrexit enim, sicut dixit: venite, et videte locum, ubi positus erat Dominus. Et cito euntes, dicite discipulis ejus, quia surrexit. Et ecce præcedit vos in Galilæam. Ibi eum videbitis: ecce prædixi vobis.

In the end of the Sabbath, when it began to dawn towards the first day of the week, came Mary Magdalene and the other Mary to the sepulchre. And behold there was a great earthquake. For an Angel of the Lord descended from heaven; and coming, rolled back the stone, and sat upon it; and his countenance was as lightning, and his raiment as snow. And for fear of him, the guards were struck with terror, and became as dead men. And the Angel answering, said to the women: Fear not you; for I know that you seek Jesus who was crucified. He is not here, for he is risen, as he said. Come, and see the place where the Lord was laid. And going quickly, tell ye his disciples that he is risen: and behold he will go before you into Galilee: there you shall see him. Lo, I have foretold it to you.

The Bishop does not intone the glorious Symbol of Faith: it is reserved for the second Mass, which is to be sung at a later hour in the morning. By this omission of the *Creed*, the Church would re-

HOLY SATURDAY: MORNING SERVICE. 627

mind us of the hours which elapsed, before the Apostles, who were to preach to the world the Mystery of the Resurrection, had themselves honoured it by their faith.

After having saluted the people with the usual *Dominus vobiscum*, the Pontiff at once proceeds to offer to the Divine Majesty the bread and wine, which are to be used in the Sacrifice; and the Choir omits the Antiphon, which is called the *Offertory*, and is sung or recited in every other Mass. The *Offertory* is intended as a chant to be sung whilst the people go up to the Sanctuary when offering the bread and wine for the Holy Sacrifice, and which they are to receive, at the Communion, changed into the Body and Blood of Christ. But the Service of Holy Saturday is so long, that this ceremony of the offering is omitted. The spirit is as prompt and fervent as ever, but the body begins to feel exhausted; and the little children, who are kept fasting, on account of having to go to holy Communion, show by their cries that they, too, are suffering from want of food. To save time, therefore, the bread and wine, the matter of the Sacrifice, are provided this morning by the Church. The Neophytes will, nevertheless, approach to holy Communion, although they themselves have not brought bread and wine to the Sanctuary.

After having made the offering, and censed, first the Bread and Wine, then the Altar, the Pontiff recites the Secret, which is followed by the Easter Preface.

SECRET.

Receive, O Lord, we beseech thee, the prayers of thy people, together with the offering of these hosts, that what is consecrated by these Paschal

Suscipe quæsumus, Domine, preces populi tui cum oblationibus hostiarum: ut Paschalibus initiata mysteriis, ad æternitatis nobis medelam, te operante, proficiant. Per Dominum.

℣. Per omnia sæcula sæculorum.
℟. Amen.
℣. Dominus vobiscum.
℟. Et cum spiritu tuo.
℣. Sursum corda.
℟. Habemus ad Dominum.
℣. Gratias agamus Domino Deo nostro.
℟. Dignum et justum est.

mysteries, may, by the help of thy grace, avail us to eternal life. Through, &c.
℣. For ever and ever.
℟. Amen.
℣. The Lord be with you.
℟. And with thy Spirit.
℣. Lift up your hearts.
℟. We have them fixed on God.
℣. Let us give thanks to the Lord our God.
℟. It is meet and just.

PREFACE.

Vere dignum et justum est, æquum et salutare, te quidem Domine, omni tempore, sed in hac potissimum Nocte gloriosius prædicare, cum Pascha nostrum immolatus est Christus. Ipse enim verus est Agnus, qui abstulit peccata mundi: qui mortem nostram moriendo destruxit, et vitam resurgendo reparavit. Et ideo cum Angelis et Archangelis, cum Thronis et Dominationibus, cumque omni militia cœlestis exercitus, hymnum gloriæ tuæ canimus, sine fine dicentes: *Sanctus! Sanctus! Sanctus!*

It is truly meet and just, right and available to salvation, to publish thy praise, O Lord, at all times; but chiefly and more gloriously on this Night, when Christ our Paschal Lamb is sacrificed. For he is the true Lamb, that has taken away the sins of the world. Who by dying destroyed our death, and by rising again, restored us to life. And therefore with the Angels and Archangels, with the Thrones and Dominations, and with all the heavenly host, we sing a hymn to thy glory, saying, unceasingly: *Holy! Holy! Holy!*

The Canon commences, and the divine mystery is effected. Nothing in the sacred rites is changed, until close upon the Communion. It is a custom, which has come down from the times of the Apostles, that, before receiving the Body and Blood of our Lord in Communion, the Faithful should give to each other the Kiss of Peace, saying: "Peace be with thee!" This ceremony is omitted in this first

HOLY SATURDAY: MORNING SERVICE.   629

Mass. It was not till the evening of the day of his Resurrection, that Jesus spoke these words to his Disciples. Holy Church, reverencing, as she does, every detail of her Jesus' life, loves to imitate them in her own practice. For the same reason, she omits the *Agnus Dei*,[1] which, in its third repetition, has these words: "Give us Peace."

And now the moment has come, when our Neophytes are to receive, for the first time, the Bread of Life and the Heavenly Chalice, which were instituted by Jesus at the Last Supper. Baptised in Water and the Holy Ghost, they have a right to approach the holy Table; and their White Robes are the outward expression of their souls' possessing the Wedding Garment, which all must have on, who would partake of the Banquet of the Lamb. They go up to the Altar with joy and reverence. The Deacon gives them the Body of our Lord, and then the Chalice of his precious Blood. The infants are also admitted to Communion: the Deacon dips his finger into the Chalice, and then puts it into their innocent mouths. Lastly, to signify that all are now, by their Baptism, those *new-born babes*, of whom St. Peter speaks,[2]—they receive, after holy Communion, a little milk and honey; it is a symbol of infancy, and, at the same time, an allusion to the Promised Land.

The Communion over, the Bishop ends the Holy Sacrifice with a Prayer, in which he beseeches God to unite us all to each other in a spirit of fraternal charity, seeing that we all participate in the celebration of the Pasch. We have all the same Mother,— the Church; the same Font of Baptism has given to us all the same life of grace; we are all members of Jesus, our Head; the same Holy Spirit has signed

---

[1] This formula does not date beyond the 7th century.
[2] I. St. Pet. ii. 2.

us all with his seal, and the Father has made us all one family by adopting us as his Children. The signal for departure being given by the Deacon, in the Bishop's name, the Faithful leave the Church, and return to their homes, there to remain till they re-assemble for the Holy Sacrifice, which is again to be offered up in a still more solemn celebration of this the Feast of Feasts,—the Pasch of the Resurrection.

VESPERS.

During the centuries, when the Church celebrated the Vigil of Easter in the manner we have been describing, Holy Saturday had no Vespers. The Vigil began towards the hour of None, and continued, as we have seen, till the early morning of the Sunday. It was not till later,—when custom had authorised the anticipating the Easter midnight Mass, and saying it on the morning of Holy Saturday,—that this last day of Holy Week was provided with the Office of Vespers. In consequence of the service being so long, the Church made these Vespers as short as possible, and gave them a joyous character, in keeping with the return of the "Alleluia." They are drawn up so as to form part of the Mass. They begin immediately after the Communion, and the Postcommunion serves as a conclusion both to them and the Mass itself. This Postcommunion Prayer is the one of which we have just been speaking, as terminating the ancient celebration of the Easter Vigil.

After the Communion, then, the Choir sings the following Antiphon and Psalm:

ANT. Alleluia, alleluia, alleluia.

ANT. Alleluia, alleluia, alleluia.

PSALM 116.

Praise the Lord, all ye nations; praise him all ye people.	Laudate Dominum omnes gentes : * laudate eum omnes populi.
For his mercy is confirmed upon us; and the truth of the Lord remaineth for ever.	Quoniam confirmata est super nos misericordia ejus: * et veritas Domini manet in æternum.
Glory, &c.	Gloria Patri, &c.
ANT. Alleluia, alleluia, alleluia.	ANT. Alleluia, alleluia, alleluia.

No other Psalm is sung at these Vespers. There is no Capitulum, Hymn, or Versicle; but the *Magnificat* follows at once, with this as its Antiphon:

ANTIPHON OF THE *Magnificat*.

In the evening of the Sabbath which dawns on the first day of the week, came Mary Magdalene, and another Mary, to see the sepulchre, alleluia.	Vespere autem Sabbati, quæ lucescit in prima Sabbati, venit Maria Magdalene, et altera Maria videre sepulcrum, alleluia.

During the *Magnificat*, (see *page* 88,) the Celebrant censes the Altar; and as soon as the Antiphon has been repeated, he sings, at the Altar, the following Prayer:

POSTCOMMUNION.

Pour forth on us, O Lord, the spirit of thy love; that those whom thou hast filled with the Paschal sacrament, may, by thy goodness, live in perfect concord. Through, &c.	Spiritum nobis, Domine, tuæ charitatis infunde: ut quos sacramentis Paschalibus satiasti, tua facias pietate concordes. Per Dominum.

When the Deacon turns to the people, to give them the signal for departure, he adds two *Alleluias* to the usual formula. The same is observed in every Mass till the following Saturday inclusively.

℣. Ite Missa est, alleluia, alleluia.
℟. Deo gratias, alleluia, alleluia.

℣. Go, the Mass is finished, alleluia, alleluia.
℟. Thanks be to God, alleluia, alleluia.

The Mass concludes, as usual, with the Blessing of the Celebrant, and the Gospel of St. John.

Such is the Service of this great Saturday. The Prayers and Ceremonies are precisely the same as in former times: but its being celebrated so early in the day, and the Baptism of Catechumens having ceased to be a part of the function, rendered it almost a necessity that we should have embodied in our explanation the ancient ceremonial, otherwise the Faithful would lose much of the meaning and grandeur of to-day's Service.

During the day, the Priest visits the houses of his parishioners, and sprinkles them with the Baptismal Water, taken from the Font before the Holy Oils were put into it. This pious practice is an allusion to the Command given by God to his people, on occasion of the first Passover,—that they should mark their houses with the blood of the Lamb, as a protection against the destroying Angel. In a country like our own, it may be difficult to observe this holy custom; but where it can be done, the Faithful should eagerly avail themselves of it, as it brings a special blessing upon our houses.

THE EVENING.

The description we have been giving of the magnificent ceremonies of Baptism, has made us forget the Sepulchre wherein reposes the Body of our Crucified Jesus. Let us return thither in thought, for the hour of his Resurrection is not yet come. Let us devote a few moments in meditating on the mystery of the three days, during which the Soul of our Redeemer was separated from his Body. We went, this morning, to visit the Tomb, where lies our buried Jesus; we adored that sacred Body, which Magdalene and her companions are preparing to honour, by anointing it early on the morrow. Now let us offer the tribute of our profound adoration to the Soul of our Divine Master. It is not in the Tomb, where his Body is:—let us follow it to the place where it lives during these hours of separation.

In the centre of the earth, there are four immense regions, into which no one living can ever enter: it is only by divine revelation that we know of their existence. The farthest from us is the Hell of the damned, the frightful abode where Satan and his angels and the reprobate are suffering eternal torments. It is here that the Prince of darkness is ever forming his plots against God and his creatures. Nearer to us, is the Limbo wherein are detained the souls of children, who departed this world before being regenerated. The opinion which has met most favour from the Church, is that these souls suffer no torment; and that although they can never enjoy the beatific vision, yet are they enjoying a natural happiness, and one that is proportionate to their desires. Above the abode of these children, is the place of expiation, where souls, that have departed this life in the state of grace, cleanse themselves from any stains of lesser sins, or satisfy for the debt of temporal punishment still due to divine justice. And lastly, still nearer to us, is the Limbo where are kept from heaven the saints who died under the Old Law. Here are our First Parents, Abel, Noe, Abraham, Moses, David, and the Prophets; the just Gentiles, such as that great Saint of Arabia, Job; and those holy personages who were closely connected with our Lord, such as Joachim and Anne, the parents of his Blessed Mother,—Joseph, her Spouse and his own foster-father,—and John, his Precursor, together with his holy parents, Zachary and Elizabeth.

Until such time as the gate of heaven shall have been opened by the Blood of the Redeemer, none of the Just can ascend thither. How holy soever they might have been during this life, they must descend into Limbo after death. We meet with innumerable passages of the Old Testament, where mention is made of *hell*, (that is, that portion of the regions in the centre of the earth, which we call *Limbo*,) as being the abode of even the holiest of God's Servants: it is only in the New Testament that *Heaven* is spoken of as being the abode of men. The Limbo of the Just is not one of torment, beyond that of expectation and captivity. The souls that dwell there are confirmed in grace, and are sure of enjoying, at some future period, an infinite happiness; they resignedly bear this long banishment, which is a consequence of Adam's Sin; and, as they saw the time drawing nigh for their deliverance, their joy was beyond all we can imagine.

The Son of God has subjected himself to every thing, (save sin,) that our human nature has to suffer or undergo: it is by his Resurrection that he is to triumph, it is by his Ascension alone that he is to open the gates of heaven:—hence, his Soul, having been separated from his Body by Death, was to descend into the depths of the earth, and become a companion with the holy exiles there. He had said of himself: *The Son of Man shall be in the heart of the earth three days and three nights.*[1] What must have been the joy of these countless Saints! and how majestic must not have been the entrance of our Emmanuel into their abode! No sooner did our Jesus breathe his last upon the Cross, than the Limbo of the Saints was illumined with heavenly splendour. The Soul of the Redeemer, united to the Divinity of the Word, descended thither, and changed it, from a

---

[1] St. Matth. xii. 40.

place of banishment, into a very Paradise. Thus did he fulfil the promise he had made to the Good Thief: *This day shalt thou be with me in Paradise.*

The happy hour, so long expected by these Saints, is come! What tongue could tell their joy, their admiration, and their love, as they beheld the Soul of Jesus, who thus comes among them, to share and close their exile! He looks complacently on this countless number of his Elect,—this fruit of four thousand years of his grace,—this portion of his Church purchased by his Blood, and to which the merits of his Blood were applied by the mercy of his Eternal Father, even before it was shed on Calvary! Let us who hope, on our departure from this world, to ascend to Him, who has *gone to prepare a place* for us in Heaven,[1]—let us joyfully congratulate these our holy ancestors. Let us also adore the condescension of our Emmanuel, who deigns to spend these three days in the *heart of the earth,* that so he might sanctify every condition of our Nature, and take upon himself even what was but a transient state of our existence.

But, the Son of God would have this his visit to the regions beneath our earth to be a manifestation of his sovereign power. His Soul does not, it is true, descend into the Hell of Satan, but he makes his power be felt there. The Prince of this world is now forced to *bend his knee* and humble himself.[2] In this Jesus, whom he has instigated the Jews to crucify, he now recognises the Son of God. Man is saved, Death is conquered, Sin is effaced. Henceforth, it is not to the *Bosom of Abraham,* but to Heaven itself, that the souls of the Just made perfect shall ascend, there to reign, together with the faithful Angels, with Christ their Divine Head. The reign of Idolatry is to be at an end: the altars,

---

[1] St. John, xiv. 2. [2] Philipp. ii. 10.

whereon men have offered incense to Satan, are to be destroyed. *The house of the strong one is to be entered* by his Divine Adversary, *and his goods are to be rifled.*[1] The *Hand-writing* of our condemnation is snatched from the Serpent.[2] The Cross, which he had exultingly prepared for the Just One, has been his overthrow, or, as St. Antony so forcibly expresses it, the bait thrown out to the Leviathan, which he took, and, taking it, was conquered.

The Soul of our Jesus makes its presence felt also by the just who dwell in the abode of expiation. It mercifully alleviates their sufferings, and shortens their Purgatory. Many of them are delivered altogether, and numbered with the Saints in Limbo, where they spend the Forty Days, between this and the Ascension, in the happy expectation of ascending to Heaven with their Deliverer. It is not contrary to the principles of Faith, to suppose, as several learned Theologians have taught, that the visit of the Man-God to Limbo was a source of blessing and consolation to the abode of unregenerated Children, and that they then received a promise, that the time would come when they should be re-united to their bodies, and, after the Day of Judgment, be placed in a happier land than that in which Divine Justice now holds them captives.

We adore thee, O holy Soul of our Redeemer! for thy having deigned to pass these hours with thy Saints, our fathers, *in the heart of the earth.* We extol thy goodness and love shown towards these thy Elect, whom thou hast made to be thine own Brethren. We give thee thanks for that thou didst humble our enemy: oh, give us grace to conquer him! But now, dearest Jesus! it is time for thee to rise from thy Tomb, and re-unite thy Soul to thy Body! Heaven and Earth await thy Resurrection! The Church, thy

[1] St. Matth. xii. 29. [2] Coloss. ii. 14.

Spouse, has already sung the *Alleluia* of her glad expectation! Rise, then, from thy Grave, O Jesus, our Life! Triumph over Death, and reign our King for ever!

Let us close our day and our volume with the following Preface, taken from the Ambrosian Missal. It is one of the finest pieces of this venerable Liturgy, and is the blessing of the Paschal Candle. The mystery of this great Night is here treated with an eloquence and poetry truly worthy of the subject.

PREFACE.

Truly it is meet and just, right and available to salvation, that we should here and in all places give thanks to thee, O Holy Lord, Almighty Father, Eternal God! Thou hast consecrated the Pasch, unto which thou invitest all mankind, not by the gore and fat of sheep, but by the Blood and Flesh of thine Only Begotten Son, Jesus Christ our Lord: that thus the rite of an ungrateful people being abolished, grace should succeed the law, and the sins of the whole world be expiated by one Victim, once, and by himself, offered up to thy Majesty.

This is the Lamb that was pre-figured on tablets of stone. He was not taken from the flock, but was brought from heaven. He needed not a shepherd, but was himself the one Good Shepherd, who laid down his life for his sheep, and again assumed it, that his divine condescension might show us how to be humble,

Vere, quia dignum et justum est, æquum et salutare nos tibi semper hic, et ubique gratias agere, Domine sancte, Pater omnipotens, æterne Deus. Qui populorum Pascha cunctorum, non pecudum cruore, nec adipe, sed Unigeniti tui Domini nostri Jesu Christi sanguine, corporeque dedicasti; ut supploso ritu gentis ingratæ, legi gratia succederet, et una victima, per semetipsam tuæ Majestati semel oblata, mundi totius expiaret offensam.

Hic est Agnus lapideis præfiguratus in tabulis: non abductus e gregibus, sed evectus e cœlo: non pastore indigens, sed Pastor bonus, ipse tantummodo: qui animam suam pro suis posuit ovibus, et rursus assumpsit; ut nobis et humilitatem divina dignatio, et spem resurrectio corporalis ostenderet.

Qui coram tondente se non vocem queruli balatus emisit, sed evangelico proclamavit oraculo, dicens: Amodo videbitis Filium hominis sedentem ad dexteram Majestatis. Ipse nobis et te reconciliet, Pater omnipotens, et pari tecum Majestate fultus indulgeat.

Nam quæ patribus in figura contingebant, nobis in veritate proveniunt. Ecce jam ignis columna resplendet, quæ plebem Domini beatæ noctis tempore ad salutaria fluenta præibat: in quibus persecutor mergitur, et Christi populus liberatus emergit. Nam Sancti Spiritus unda conceptus, per Adam natus ad mortem, per Christum regignitur ad vitam. Solvamus igitur voluntarie celebrata jejunia, quia Pascha nostrum immolatus est Christus: nec solum corpore epulemur Agni, sed etiam inebriemur et sanguine. Hujus enim tantummodo cruor non creat piaculum bibentibus, sed salutem. Ipso quoque vescamur et Azymo, quoniam non de solo pane vivit homo, sed de omni verbo Dei. Siquidem hic est Panis, qui descendit e cœlo, longe præstantior illo quondam mannæ imbre frugifluo, quo tunc Israël epulatus interiit. Hoc vero qui vescitur corpore, vitæ perennis possessor existit.

and his body's Resurrection teach us to hope. No plaintive voice came from him when under his shearer, but thus spake he the prophecy of his Gospel: *Hereafter, ye shall see the Son of man sitting on the right hand of Majesty.* May he, O Almighty Father! reconcile us with thee, and, by the Majesty wherewith he is co-equal with thee, may he be merciful unto us.

For those things which happened in figure to our fathers, have become realities to us. Lo! now shineth that pillar of fire, which, on that blessed night, went before the people of God, leading to waters that saved them: for in them was the persecutor drowned, and from the same came liberated the people of Christ. Conceived in the stream made fruitful by the Holy Ghost, man, that was born of Adam unto death, is regenerated by Christ unto life. Let us, therefore, bid farewell to the fast we have been voluntarily keeping, for Christ, our Pasch, is slain: let us not only feast on the Flesh of the Lamb, but let us also be inebriated with his Blood. Yea, let us also eat the Unleavened, for not by bread alone doth man live, but by every word of God, for Christ is the Bread that came down from heaven, more excellent far than that manna of old which fell in abundant showers, and of which the Israelites, who then were, ate, yet died. Whereas he that eats of this Body, is made a possessor of everlasting life

HOLY SATURDAY: EVENING. 639

Lo! the old things have passed away: all things are made new. The knife of the Mosaic Circumcision has become blunted, and the cruel sharp stone of Josue has gone out of use: but the people of Christ is signed on the forehead, and not invisibly; by a baptism, not by a wound; by Chrism, not by blood.

Rightly, therefore, during this Night,—when we are awaiting the Resurrection of the Lord our Saviour,—do we burn a rich waxen torch, whose properties are fair whiteness, sweet fragrance, and bright light: which flows not down as it melts, nor sends forth an offensive smell as it burns. For what could be more appropriate, what more festive, than that we should keep watch for the Flower of Jesse, with torches that are the juice of flowers? The more so, as Wisdom thus sang in her own praise: "*I am the flower of the field, and the lily of the valley.*" Wax is not the sweat that oozes from a burnt pine, nor the tear that trickles from the cedar when wounded with many blows of the axe: it is a mysterious virginal production; and one that is transfigured into the whiteness of snow. Its fount-like melted stream feeds the (wick of) papyrus, which, as a guileless soul, stands, with its unbent, unjointed oneness, surrounded by the virginal substance, and becomes, by the flame, the stream's much cherished guest.

Ecce vetera transierunt: facta sunt omnia nova. Nam Circumcisionis Mosaicæ mucro jam scabruit, et Jesu Nave acuta lapidum obsolevit asperitas: Christi vero populus insignitur in fronte, non inguine: lavacro, non vulnere: Chrismate, non cruore.

Decet ergo in hoc Domini Salvatoris nostri vespertinæ Resurrectionis adventu ceream nos adolere pinguedinem, cui suppetit candor in specie, suavitas in odore, splendor in lumine: quæ nec marcescenti liquore defluit, nec offensum tetri nidoris exhalat. Quid enim magis accommodum, magis festivum, quam ut Jesseïco flori floreis excubemus et tædis? Præsertim cum et Sapientia de semetipsa cecinerit: Ego sum flos agri, et lilium convallium. Ceras igitur nec pinus exusta desudat, nec crebris sauciata bipennibus cedrus illacrymat; sed est illis arcana de virginitate creatio; et ipsæ transfiguratione nivei candoris albescunt. Eamdem vero papyrum liquida fontis unda producit: quæ instar insontis animæ nullis articulatur sinuata compagibus; sed virginali circumsepta materie fit hospitalis ignibus alumna rivorum.

Decet ergo adventum Sponsi dulcatis Ecclesiam luminaribus opperiri: et largitatem sanctitatis acceptam quanta valet devotionis dote, pensare: nec sanctas interpolare tenebris excubias; sed tædam sapienter perpetuis præparare luminibus: ne, dum oleum candelis adjungitur, adventum Domini tardo prosequamur obsequio; qui certe in ictu oculi, ut coruscus, adveniet.

Igitur in hujus diei vespere cuncta venerabilis sacramenti plenitudo colligitur: et, quæ diversis sunt præfigurata, vel gesta temporibus, hujus noctis curriculo devoluta supplentur. Nam primum hoc vespertinum lumen, sicut illa dux Magorum stella, præcedit. Deinde mysticæ regenerationis unda subsequitur, velut, dignante Domino, fluenta Jordanis. Tertio resurrectionem Christi vox apostolica Sacerdotis annuntiat. Tum ad totius mysterii supplementum, Christo vescitur turba fidelium. Quæ summi Sacerdotis, et Antistitis tui Ambrosii oratione sanctificata et meritis, resurrectionis Dominicæ diem, Christo in omnibus prosperante, suscipiat.

Therefore doth it behove the Church to await, with sweet lights, the coming of the Spouse, and with all possible devotion, to weigh the holy gift she has received. Holy vigils, such as this, should have no fellowship with darkness. We should be wise, and make the light of our lamp be unceasing; lest, whilst preparing to trim it with oil, our Lord should come, and we be too late to do him homage, for we are assured that he will come in the twinkling of the eye, as a flash of light.

Therefore, this day's evening is rich in the fulness of the most august mysteries, which, though prefigured or accomplished at various times, are all brought before us during the course of this night. For firstly, we have this Evening Torch, which leads the way, as did the Star that guided the Magi. Then follows the Font of spiritual regeneration, as it were the river of Jordan, in which our Lord vouchsafed to be baptised. Thirdly, we have the Priest's apostolic words announcing the Resurrection of Christ. Then, to complete the mysteries, the faithful flock feeds on the flesh of Christ. Being sanctified by the prayer and merits of thy high Priest and Pontiff Ambrose, and being prospered in all things by Christ, may this flock enjoy the day of our Lord's Resurrection.

END OF PASSIONTIDE AND HOLY WEEK.

Made in the USA
San Bernardino, CA
27 June 2020